The EU as a Global Actor – Bridging Legal Theory and Practice

Studies in EU External Relations

Edited by

Marc Maresceau (*Ghent University*)

VOLUME 13

The titles published in this series are listed at *brill.com/seur*

The EU as a Global Actor – Bridging Legal Theory and Practice

Liber Amicorum in Honour of Ricardo Gosalbo Bono

Edited by

Jenő Czuczai
Frederik Naert

BRILL
NIJHOFF

LEIDEN | BOSTON

The Library of Congress Cataloging-in-Publication Data is available online at http://catalog.loc.gov
LC record available at http://lccn.loc.gov/

Typeface for the Latin, Greek, and Cyrillic scripts: "Brill". See and download: brill.com/brill-typeface.

ISSN 1875-0451
ISBN 978-90-04-33569-1 (hardback)
ISBN 978-90-04-34717-5 (e-book)

This book is printed on acid-free paper and produced in a sustainable manner.

Contents

PART 2
Principles of Union Law and Legal Theory

PART 3
International Law Aspects

PART 4
Specific EU External Policies

The Common Foreign and Security Policy

The Common Commercial Policy

Justice and Home Affairs

PART 5
EU International Agreements

Epilogue

Preface*

This collection of contributions dealing with *The EU as a Global Actor – Bridging Legal Theory and Practice at the Turn of the 21st Century* is a tribute to our distinguished former colleague and dear friend Ricardo Gosalbo Bono. It is a mark of sincere respect for a remarkable European civil servant, a great EU lawyer and at the same time a successful legal scholar whose activities over the last almost 40 years inspired and influenced the legal thinking of generations of legal practitioners in the legal services of the different EU institutions and beyond, but also of students, academics and diplomats all over the world.

Choosing a topic for this Liber Amicorum was rather easy. This was so because during his whole professional career Ricardo Gosalbo Bono has also always combined legal theory with legal practice. It has been possible for him since one of his main qualities is his very wide interest in different areas of law, not only EU law generally (beyond EU external relations law, from transport law to EU institutional law) but also international law and comparative law, and even legal theory/philosophy (see his impressive writings, for example, on sovereignty,[1] on general principles of law[2] or on the rule of law[3]). He could thus always – as those who wrote the *témoignages* about him also underlined – reach back to fundamental principles of law and draw inspiration from solutions found in other legal systems or areas of law. This personal legal conviction of Ricardo is certainly what drove his academic activities, which he managed to maintain always as something very important for himself, despite a very demanding job as a senior EU official and a former Director of the Council Legal Service.

Yet at the same time, Ricardo Gosalbo Bono had an excellent understanding of the politics of EU decision-making and his profound academic spirit did not

* The views of the editors in this book are purely personal and do not constitute an official position of the Council or of its Legal Service.

1 See his contribution 'Sur la théorie de la souveraineté et son application à (et dans) L'Union européenne' in Marta Arpio Santacruz et al. (eds), *A Man for All Treaties: liber amicorum en l'honneur de Jean-Claude Piris* (Bruylant 2012) 195.

2 See his contribution on 'The Development of General Principles of Law at National and Community Level: Achieving a Balance' in Reiner Schulze and Ulrike Seif (eds) *Richterrecht und Rechtsfortbildung in der Europaischen Rechtsgemeinschaft* (Mohr Siebeck 2003) 99.

3 See his article 'The Significance of the Rule of Law and its Implications for the European Union and the United States' (2010) 72 University of Pittsburg Law Review 229 and the three part article 'État de droit et droit de l'Union européenne' in (2011) Nos. 544, 545 and 546 Revue du Marché commun et de l'Union européenne respectively 13, 96 and 156.

prevent him from being very pragmatic and creative in finding solutions that corresponded to the political wishes in a legally correct way. There are indeed many phrases in international agreements, Council decisions or conclusions, and other texts adopted by or within the Council, that sprung from Ricardo's interventions. He was also a brilliant litigator before the European Court of Justice, which is demonstrated by the long list of cases, in which he acted as agent either on behalf of the Commission or of the Council. He pleaded in important cases relating to competence or legal basis questions (such as the proceedings of Opinion 2/94), etc. These practical legal aspects of his fascinating career will also be further reflected, of course, in a post-Lisbon context in many contributions in this book.

While trying to serve both the law and his political masters, Ricardo Gosalbo Bono has always been a real gentleman and a great European, who strove to limit conflicts as much as possible and to maintain good relations with all actors involved. Differences of legal opinions between the institutions are frequent and probably an inevitable part of the functioning of the Union, especially after Lisbon. They inevitably lead to conflicting positions but it makes a huge difference whether one revels in conflict and takes issues personally, or attempts to find mutually acceptable solutions and understands that counterparts may be friends despite defending different views and interests.

The friendship and respect which Ricardo had for so many colleagues was broadly reciprocated by them. This was demonstrated very clearly by the presence of so many of them at his farewell reception in the Council. It was also shown by the many positive responses we received from those who have been invited to contribute to this Liber Amicorum. While a few regretted not being able to contribute because of time or other constraints, the vast majority accepted immediately our invitation and contributed substantially to this book. We know that there are many others who also would have liked to express their appreciation to Ricardo, but with regret and apologies we have been limited by time and space constraints. We are convinced that Ricardo will be pleased to see the many distinguished authors from the different EU institutions and bodies, in particular the Council, Commission, Parliament, the Court of Justice and the European External Action Service, as well as from Member States' diplomatic services and, of course, from European academia.

Moreover, the combination of the topics addressed in this book, together with the diverse affiliations of the authors, has resulted in an exceptional insight into current challenges and legal practice in most key areas of EU external relations law, as well as in some broader areas of EU law, in particular institutional law and principles of EU law.

We will not repeat the table of contents here. However, we do wish to highlight the broad range of topics reflected in the titles of the five parts of the book. They were chosen in order to respect Ricardo's broad range of academic and practical legal interests as described above in the context of the development of his professional career. Thus it is important to note that most of the contributions relate in one way or another to EU external relations law, including the effect of international law in the EU legal order, or institutional dimensions and general principles in the field of, or relevant to, EU external relations (including sectoral legal aspects, fundamental rights questions or judicial autonomy debates in the trade policy field) as well as the current legal issues of the EU treaty-making process.

In this Liber Amicorum a lot of concrete cases have been analysed by the different authors (including even still pending ones before the European Court of Justice) as well as many topical and on-going legislative or treaty-making processes. It is very much up to date and the manuscript was closed on 1 October 2016.

Finally, the publication of the present volume of essays would not have been possible without our authors, to whom we are very grateful for their time and energy to contribute. Also, we wholeheartedly thank Emmanuel Robberecht, Tim Middleton, Emer Finnegan, Jed Odermatt and Kathleen Gutman for the editorial and linguistic assistance. A special word of thanks goes to Marjolein Schaake, Wilma de Weert and Anna Schmitt Nagelbach from Brill Academic Publishers, for their advice as well as for having ensured the timely publication of this book.

The Editors
Brussels, December 2016

List of Abbreviations and Acronyms

ACTA	Anti-Counterfeiting Trade Agreement
AETR	Accord européen sur les transports routiers
AFSJ	Area of Freedom, Security and Justice
AG	Advocate General
ATALANTA	European Union military operation to contribute to the deterrence, prevention and repression of acts of piracy and armed robbery off the Somali coast
BBNJ	(marine) biodiversity (of areas) beyond national jurisdiction
BGB	Bürgerliches Gesetzbuch ((German) Civil Code)
BGBL	Bundesgesetzblatt
BIT	bilateral investment treaty
BVerfGE	Entscheidungen des Bundesverfassungsgerichts
CAAS	Convention d'application de Schengen
Cah. Dr. Eur.	Cahier de Droit européen
Cambridge Y Eur Legal Studies	Cambridge Yearbook of European Legal Studies
CCP	Common Commercial Policy
CDDH	Steering Committee for Human Rights (of the Council of Europe)
CECA	Communauté européenne du charbon et de l'acier
CEDH	Convention européenne des droits de l'homme
CEE	Communauté économique européenne
CEEP	European Centre of Enterprises with Public Participation
CEPOL	European Union Agency for Law Enforcement Training (previously European Police College)
CETA	(EU – Canada) Comprehensive Economic and Trade Agreement
CETS	Council of Europe Treaties Series
CFSP	Common Foreign and Security Policy
CJEU	Court of Justice of the European Union
CJUE	Cour de justice de l'Union européenne
CLS	Council Legal Service
CML Rev	Common Market Law Review
COJUR	Public International Law Working Party (of the Council of the EU)
Columbia J Eur L	Columbia Journal of European Law

COMAR	Law of the Sea Working Party (of the Council of the EU)
COREPER	Committee of Permanent Representatives
Cour EDH	Cour européenne des droits de l'homme
CSDP	Common Security and Defence Policy
DCFTA	Deep and Comprehensive Free Trade Agreement
DG	Directorate General
DSU	Dispute Settlement Understanding (of the World Trade Organisation)
EASO	European Asylum Support Office
EC	European Community
ECHR	European Convention on Human Rights
ECJ	European Court of Justice
ECOWAS	Economic Community Of West African States
ECRE	European Council on Refugees and Exiles
EDA	European Defence Agency
EEA	European Economic Area
EEAS	European External Action Service
EEC	European Economic Community
EEZ	Exclusive Economic Zone
EFTA	European Free Trade Association
EGF	European Globalisation Adjustment Fund
EJIL	European Journal of International Law
EP	European Parliament
ERPL	European Review of Public Law
ERTA	European Road Transport Agreement
ESDC	European Security and Defence College
ESdF	European Solidarity Fund
ESIFS	European Structural and Investment Funds
ESM	European Stability Mechanism
ETS	Emissions Trading System
ETUC	European Trade Union Confederation
EU	European Union
EuConst	European Constitutional Law Review
EUFOR RCA	European Union military operation in the Central African Republic
EUNAVFOR MED	European Union military operation in the Southern Central Mediterranean
EUNAVFOR Somalia	European Union military operation to contribute to the deterrence, prevention and repression of acts of piracy and armed robbery off the Somali coast (ATALANTA)

EUPM	European Union Police Mission (in Bosnia and Herzegovina)
EuR	Europarecht (Zeitschrift)
Euratom	European Atomic Energy Community
Eur Foreign Affairs Rev	European Foreign Affairs Review
Eurojust	European Union Judicial Cooperation Unit
Europol	European Union Agency for Law Enforcement Cooperation (previously European Police Office)
Eur Public L	European Public Law
EUSR	European Union Special Representative
EUTM	EU Training Mission
EYIEL	European Yearbook of International Economic Law
FAC	Foreign Affairs Council
FAO	Food and Agriculture Organisation
FLC	(German) Federal Labour Court
FMOP Agreement	(EU-Switzerland) Free Movement of Persons Agreement
Fordham Int LJ	Fordham International Law Journal
FRONTEX	European Border and Coast Guard Agency (previously European Agency for the Management of Operational Cooperation at the External Borders of the Member States of the European Union)
FTA	Free Trade Agreement
GATS	General Agreement on Trade in Services
GATT	General Agreement on Tariffs and Trade
GDP	Gross Domestic Product
GFCC	German Federal Constitutional Court
GNSS	(European) Global Navigation Satellite System
GSC	General Secretariat (of the Council of the EU)
GSP	Generalised System of Preferences
HR	High Representative (of the Union for Foreign and Security Policy)
HR/VP	High Representative (of the Union for Foreign Affairs and Security Policy) / Vice-President (of the European Commission)
ICAO	International Civil Aviation Organisation
ICJ	International Court of Justice
IFLOS	International Foundation of the Law of the Sea
ICLQ	International and Comparative Law Quarterly
IGC	Intergovernmental Conference
ILC	International Law Commission

ILO	International Labour Organisation
INTA	International Trade Committee of the European Parliament
IPR	intellectual property rights
ISDS	investor-to-state dispute settlement
ITLOS	International Tribunal for the Law of the Sea
IUU (fishing)	Illegal, Unreported and Unregulated (Fishing)
JAI	justice et affaires intérieures
JCPOA	Joint Comprehensive Plan of Action (with Iran)
JHA	Justice and Home Affairs
JHA Protocol	Protocol No. 21 on the position of the United Kingdom and Ireland in respect of the Area of Freedom, Security and Justice
KNK	Kurdistan National Congress
Maastricht J Eur & Comp L	Maastricht Journal of European & Comparative Law
MAE	mandat d'arrêt européen
MFA	macro-financial assistance
MINURSO	United Nations Mission for the Referendum in Western Sahara (Mission des Nations Unies pour l'organisation d'un référendum au Sahara occidental)
MONEYVAL	Groupe d'experts sur l'évaluation des mesures de lutte contre le blanchiment des capitaux
NATO	North Atlantic Treaty Organisation
NJECL	New Journal of European Criminal Law
NYIL	Netherlands Yearbook of International Law
OIV	Organisation internationale de la vigne et du vin / International Organisation of Vine and Wine
ONU	Organisation des Nations Unies
OUP	Oxford University Press
PCA	Partnership and Cooperation Agreement
PFOS	perfluoroctane sulfonate
PKK	Kurdistan Workers' Party (Partiya Karkerên Kurdistanê)
PLO	Palestine Liberation Organisation
(Frente) Polisario	(Frente) Popular de Liberación de Saguía el-Hamra y Río de Oro
PSC	Political and Security Committee
QMV	qualified majority voting
REIO	Regional Economic Integration Organisation
RFMO	Regional Fisheries Management Organisation(s)
RTD Eur	Revue Trimestrielle de Droit européen

SGEI	services of general economic interest
SOFA / SOMA	Status of Forces / Mission Agreement
TAC	Total Allowable Catch
TAC	Treaty of Amity and Cooperation in Southeast Asia
TEC	Treaty establishing the European Community
TEU	Treaty on European Union
TFEU	Treaty on the Functioning of the European Union
TFUE	Traité sur le fonctionnement de l'Union européenne
ToL	Treaty of Lisbon
TPC	Trade Policy Committee (of the Council of the EU)
TRIPS	(Agreement on) Trade Related Aspects of Intellectual Property Rights
TRNC	Turkish Republic of Northern Cyprus
TTIP	(EU – US) Transatlantic Trade and Investment Partnership
TUE	Traité sur l'Union européenne
TzBfG	Teilzeit- und Befristungsgesetz
UIMP	University Internacional Menéndez Pelayo
UK	United Kingdom
ULB	Université libre de Bruxelles
UNCLOS	United Nations Convention on the Law of the Sea
UNGA	United Nations General Assembly
UNICE	Union of Industrial and Employers' Confederations of Europe
UNSC	United Nations Security Council
UNSCR	United Nations Security Council Resolution
UNTS	United Nations Treaty Series
US(A)	United States (of America)
WTO	World Trade Organisation
YEL	Yearbook of European Law

List of the Contributors

Paul Berman

Paul Berman succeeded Ricardo Gosalbo Bono as Director for External Relations in the Legal Service of the Council of the European Union. He studied at the Universities of Oxford and Geneva and after being called to the Bar of England and Wales joined the legal cadre of the British Diplomatic Service in 1991. As well as working at the Foreign and Commonwealth Office in London, he has served as legal adviser in the Legal Division of the International Committee of the Red Cross in Geneva, as international law adviser to the UK Attorney General, as Legal Counsellor at the UK Permanent Representation to the European Union in Brussels and as Director of the UK Cabinet Office European Law Division. He joined the Council Legal Service in 2012.

Michael Bishop

Michael Bishop graduated in English literature at Oxford University before qualifying as a lawyer. He worked for several years at law firms in London and Brussels before joining the Council Legal Service in 1991. He has spent most of his career in the Legal Service's external relations directorate where he is now senior legal advisor.

Thérèse Blanchet

Thérèse Blanchet is Director of the Justice and Home Affairs' Directorate in the Legal Service of the Council of the European Union. Graduated in law from the University of Geneva and the College of Europe in Bruges, practising lawyer at the Geneva bar, she then became legal advisor at the Legal Affairs' Department in EFTA for five years, before joining the Legal Service of the Council in 1995, where she was head of the Director General's office from 2000 to 2011.

Sonja Boelaert

Sonja Boelaert holds law degrees from the Katholieke Universiteit Leuven, Belgium (Licenciate in Law), from Harvard Law School (LL.M.) and from the London School of Economics and Political Science (Ph.D.). Her past professional experience includes academic teaching and working as an attorney at the Brussels Bar. Mrs Boelaert has served as legal adviser with the High Commissioner for Refugees in Rwanda and with IFAD and FAO in Rome, and from 1989 to 2003 she was a legal adviser and prosecutor with the International Criminal Tribunals for the former Yugoslavia and Rwanda. In 2004 Mrs Boelaert joined the EU institutions. She is now a senior legal adviser working for the Council of the EU and the European Council. Mrs Boelaert regularly appears before the Court of Justice of the EU in Luxemburg . She has also been in charge of litigation outside EU courts and has appeared before the International Tribunal for the Law of the Sea in Hamburg. Mrs Boelaert has a keen interest in issues and cases that straddle public international law and various branches of EU law. She regularly publishes academic articles in relation to various aspects of her work.

Marise Cremona

Marise Cremona has been a Professor in the Law Department of the European University Institute since 2006. She is a co-Director of the Academy of European Law and general editor (with Profs Nehal Bhuta and Claire Kilpatrick) of The Collected Courses of the Academy of European Law, Oxford University Press. Between November 2009 and June 2012 she was Head of the Department of Law at the EUI and between June 2012 and August 2013 she was President *ad interim* of the EUI. Before joining the EUI she held the Chair of European Commercial Law at the Centre for Commercial Law Studies, Queen Mary University of London. She is a member of the International Advisory Board of the Centre for European Research, University of Göteborg; member of the Scientific Advisory Board of the Lichtenberg-Kolleg Institute for Advanced Study in Humanities and Social Sciences, University of Göttingen; member of the Editorial Board of the Common Market Law Review; member of the Advisory Board of the European Foreign Affairs Review; member of the Editorial Board, Studies in EU External Relations, Martinus Nijhoff Publishers.

Jenő Czuczai

Jenő Czuczai is a Legal Adviser at the Legal Service of the Council of the EU since April 2006. He is also a Professor of the College of Europe, Brugge and Natolin (Warsaw) since the 1997/1998 academic year. He was Chief Legal Adviser to the Hungarian Presidency of the Council of the EU during the first half of 2011. He was also first (founding) President of the Hungarian FIDE Association (2003–2006), national rapporteur at the FIDE Congress in 2004 (Dublin) and chaired sessions at FIDE Congresses in 2008 (Linz), 2010 (Madrid) and 2016 (Budapest). He obtained a Doctorate degree, with summa cum laude, in Legal and Political Sciences from the ELTE University, Budapest (1991) and was Head of Unit in the Prime Minister Office of Hungary (1991–1992), Director at different Hungarian Privatisation Institutions (1992–1995), Legal Adviser at the Delegation of the European Commission in Budapest (1995–2001), as well as co-founder and Vice-President of the European Law Academy in Budapest (1999–2006). He taught EU law, Roman Law and Comparative legal transitology at several Hungarian Universities (1991–2006) and has been a member of the Budapest Bar Association since 2001. He was successful in an EU open (EPSO) *concours* for Head of Unit posts (AD 12) in 2005. He is a specialist of the law of EU Funds, EU external action law, the Law of EU enlargement and European Neighbourhood Policy, and of EU institutional law. He is member of ASIL, ESIL, SIPE, CLEER and FIDE (CD) and author, co-author, editor, co-editor of 14 books, and author of more than 100 academic articles.

Álvaro de Elera

Álvaro de Elera, LLM, MPhil, has been a Legal Advisor in the Legal Service of the Council since 2008, in its Directorates 1 (internal market), 2 (economic and financial issues) and 3 (external relations).

Bart Driessen

For the last fifteen years Dr Bart Driessen has been a member of the Legal Service of the Council of the European Union. Previously he has worked inter alia as an assistant to a Member of the European Parliament, in private practice and in the European Commission. He was an agent in numerous cases before the European courts, including in the case discussed in his contribution to this book.

Frank Hoffmeister

Prof. Dr Frank Hoffmeister studied law in Frankfurt, Geneva and Heidelberg (1989–1994) and received a PhD. at the Max-Planck-Institute for Foreign Public Law and International Law (1998). Between 1998 and 2001 he researched and taught as University Assistant at the Walter Hallstein-Institute for European Constitutional Law at the Humboldt-University in Berlin. He then entered the European Commission, first as Cyprus desk at DG Enlargement and afterwards as a member of the Legal Service, where he specialised on international law and WTO issues. From 2010–2014, he served as the Deputy Head of Cabinet of EU Trade Commissioner De Gucht, and as of 2015 he is Head of Unit dealing with anti-dumping at DG Trade. Besides, Frank teaches international economic law at the Free University University of Brussels and has published numerous articles on European and international law topics. Most recently he co-authored 'The Law of EU External Relations – Cases, Materials and Commentary on the EU as an International Legal Actor' (OUP 2013) together with PJ Kuijper, J Wouters, G de Baere and T Ramopoulos.

Pieter Jan Kuijper

Pieter Jan Kuijper has been Professor of the Law of International (Economic) Organisations at the Faculty of Law of the University of Amsterdam (UvA), the Netherlands, between 2007 and 2014. Presently he holds professorial rank without a chair. Prior to his appointment at the UvA, he was principal Legal Advisor and Director of the 'External Relations and International Trade' team of the Legal Service of the European Commission (2002–2007) and Director of the Legal Affairs Division of the WTO Secretariat (1999–2002). He is currently editor-in-chief of LEGAL ISSUES OF ECONOMIC INTEGRATION and has been awarded the Maastricht Prize for International Law 2016.

Hubert Legal

Hubert Legal is Legal Counsel of the European Council and of the Council of the EU and Director General of the Legal Service of the Council since February 2011. Before that, he was Director in the Legal Service of the Council (2008–2011); Rapporteur at the Litigation Section of the Conseil d'Etat (France, 2007–2008); Judge of the Court of First Instance of the European Communities (2001–2007) and President of its Fourth Chamber (2003–2007); Référendaire at the Court of Justice (1997–2001); Legal Counsellor of the French Permanent Representation to the United Nations (1993–1997); Chargé de mission with the Legal Service of the French Ministry of Foreign Affairs (1989–1993); and Member of the Conseil d'Etat (France) as Auditor, Maître des Requêtes and Commissaire du Gouvernement with the Litigation Section (1988–1993) and as Conseiller d'Etat (since 2005). He is a Member of the Société française de droit international and studied at the Ecole Normale Supérieure (1974–1979) and at the Ecole Nationale d'Administration (1986–1988).

Gilles Marhic

Gilles Marhic was previously a member of the Council Legal Service, and then became Head of the Legal Section at the EU Delegation to the United Nations in New York. He is currently a member of the Legal Affairs Division in the European External Action Service

Stephan Marquardt

Mr Marquardt is currently Deputy Head of the Legal Affairs Division of the European External Action Service (EEAS). Before taking up his duties at EEAS Headquarters, he was the legal adviser of the Delegation of the European Union to the United Nations in New York. From 1993 to 2007, Mr Marquardt was legal adviser in the Legal Service of the Council of the European Union, with a focus on the EU's external relations and the common foreign and security policy, in particular in the areas of sanctions, counter-terrorism and EU crisis management operations. Mr Marquardt also acted as agent of the Council in many proceedings before the European Courts. Before joining the

Council Legal Service, Mr Marquardt worked for the law firm Baker & McKenzie in Frankfurt, Germany. He is the author of several publications on EU institutional and external relations law.

Frederik Naert

Dr Frederik Naert is a member of the external relations Directorate of the Legal Service of the Council of the EU. As such, he has inter alia acted as an agent for the Council in several cases before the EU Court of Justice. He is also an affiliated senior researcher at Leuven University. He was previously a legal advisor at the Belgian Ministry of Defence (2004–2007) and an assistant at the Law Faculty of Leuven University (1998–2004). He is the author of *International Law Aspects of the EU's Security and Defence Policy, with a Particular Focus on the Law of Armed Conflict and Human Rights* (Intersentia, 2010) and co-editor of *Legal Instruments in the Fight Against International Terrorism. A Transatlantic Dialogue* (Brill, 2004). He has *inter alia* published and lectured on counter-terrorism, international humanitarian and human rights law, peace operations, international organisations and EU external relations law.

Esa Paasivirta

Esa Paasivirta is a Legal Adviser in the European Commission in Brussels. He studied law at the University of Turku (LL.M) and the University of Helsinki (LL.Lic), Finland, and obtained his Ph.D. in international law from the University of Cambridge, UK. He joined the European Commission in 1997 where he has worked especially in the areas of international law and external relations, including in 2004–2008 as First Counsellor and Legal Advisor in the Delegation of the European Commission to the United Nations in New York. Before joining the Commission, he worked as the Legal Adviser of the Energy Charter Secretariat (Brussels), at the Finnish Ministry for Foreign Affairs (Helsinki) and the International Trade Centre UNCTAD/WTO (Geneva). He has published in the areas of international law and EU law. He has been visiting professor College of Europe, Bruges (2008–2012) and is an adjunct professor in the Faculty of Law at the University of Helsinki.

Ricardo Passos

Ricardo Passos is a Judge at the General Court of the European Union since 2016. Previously, he worked at the European Parliament from 1988 until 2016, where he was Head of the Secretariat of the Legal Affairs Committee, Head of Division and Director for Institutional Affairs and External Relations in the Legal Service and Member of the Secretariat of the European Convention. He was an agent for the European Parliament before the European Court of

Justice in several cases, including the *PNR*, *ECOWAS*, *Mauritius Pirate Transfer Agreement* and *ECHR accession* cases. Before that, he was a *référendaire* at the European Court of Justice (from 1986 until 1988) and worked for the Council of Europe's European Commission on Human Rights (from 1978 until 1986). He studied at the University of Lisbon, University of Strasbourg (DEA) and Harvard Law School (LLM).

Ingolf Pernice

Ingolf Pernice is the former director of the Walter Hallenstein-Institute for European Constitutional Law. He studied in Marburg, Geneva, Freiburg and at the College of Europe in Bruges. After his legal clerkship at the Higher Regional Court in Munich and his doctorate on European Fundamental Rights, he became an official of the European Commission in Brussels in 1980, first on the topic of competition and later in the legal service. In 1987 he did his state doctorate about 'equity and hardship clause in public law' in Bayreuth. In 1993 he joined the Johann Wolfgang Goethe-Universität Frankfurt. From 1996 he was a professor of public law, public international law and European law at the Humboldt-Universität zu Berlin. From 1997 to 2001 he was a member of the 'European Forum for Environment and Sustainable Development' of the European Commission. In 1997 he founded the Walter Hallstein-Institute for European Constitutional Law and in 1998 the European Constitutional Law Network. From 2006 he led the DFG – Graduate School 'Verfassung jenseits des Staates' (Constitution Beyond the State) and from 2006 to 2008 he was the dean of his faculty. He was a senior research fellow and guest lecturer at the Law And Public Affairs (LAPA)-Programme in Princeton in 2008–2009.

Allan Rosas

Allan Rosas, Dr Jur., Dr Jur. h.c., Dr Pol.Sc. h.c. is a judge at the European Court of Justice since 2002; a Senior Fellow of the University of Turku; Fellow of the Robert Schuman Institute of European Affairs of the University of Luxembourg; Visiting Professor at the College of Europe and University of Helsinki; Chairman of the Advisory Board of the Faculty of Law of the University of Turku; Chairman of the Advisory Board of the Baltic Area Legal Studies (BALEX) programme of the University of Turku and the Åbo Akademi University and a member of the Advisory Scientific Board of the Finnish Institute of International Affairs. He is a former Professor of Public Law, University of Turku (1977–1981); Armfelt Professor of Law, Åbo Akademi University (1981–1995); former Principal Legal Adviser and Director at the Legal Service of the European Commission (1995–2001) and Deputy Director-General of the said Legal Service (2001–2002).

Ivan Smyth

Ivan Smyth is the Legal Counsellor at the United Kingdom Permanent Representation to the European Union. Prior to joining UK Permanent Representation in 2013 he worked as a Legal Counsellor in the Foreign and Commonwealth Office and as a Legal Adviser in the then Department of Trade and Industry in London. He also previously worked as the Legal Assistant to the House of Lords' Select Committee on the European Union.

Christiaan Timmermans

Christiaan Timmermans (Ph.D. University of Leiden 1973) was a judge of the Court of Justice of the European Union from 2000 to 2010, Deputy Director-General of the Legal Service of the European Commission (1989–2000), Professor of European law at the University of Groningen (1977–1989). He held a chair in European Judicial Protection law at the University of Amsterdam (1997–2004) and was visiting professor at the University of Cambridge and Fordham Law School (New York). From 1966 to 1969 he worked as a legal secretary at the Court of Justice, subsequently as an official of the European Commission (1969–1977). From 2010 to 2012 he held the Pieter Sanders chair at the Law Faculty of the University of Rotterdam, in 2011 he stayed at the European University Institute (Florence) as a Fernand Braudel Fellow.

Dirk Wouters

Dirk Wouters obtained in 1979 a Master of Science in Economics at the London School of Economics, after studies in Law and Economics at the Universities of Antwerp and Leuven. In 1980 he joined the Belgian Ministry of Foreign Affairs, where his career has included bilateral and multilateral assignments, inter alia as Deputy Permanent Representative at the UN, Chief of Staff to the Minister of Foreign Affairs and diplomatic advisor and Sherpa to the Prime Minister. At present he is the Belgian Ambassador to the USA. His functions relating to EU affairs have included involvement in negotiations for the Maastricht, Amsterdam, Nice and Lisbon Treaties; a role in Belgium's Presidencies of the Council in 2001 and 2010; assisting Jean-Luc Dehaene as Vice President of the Convention on the future of the EU, six years as Permanent Representative to the Political and Security Committee and five years as Permanent Representative of Belgium to the EU.

List of Publications of Ricardo Gosalbo Bono (1973–2016)

En español

1. 'Personalidad y competencias internationales de los Estados miembros de las federaciones en el federalismo contemporáneo' (1975) II *Anuario de Derecho Internacional* 379–400;
2. 'El Derecho del medio ambiente a la luz del Derecho Comparado y del Derecho Comuntario' (1988) Nº IV *Poder Judicial* 127–164;
3. 'La Competencia legislativa y el control judicial de la CEE en materia de medio ambiente' in *Universidad Internacional Menendez y Pelayo T.I.* (1991) 1–22;
4. 'La libertad de establecimiento' in *Consejo General del Poder Judicial* (Vitoria 1994) 485–523;
5. 'Reflexiones en torno al futuro de la protección de los Derechos humanos en el marco del Derecho Comunitario y del Derecho de la Unión: insuficiencias y soluciones' (1997) *Revista de Derecho Comunitario Europeo* 29–68;
6. 'Las disposiciones del Tratado de Amsterdam relativas a la cooperación policial y judicial en materia penal' (1998) Nº 644 *Revista General del Derecho* 5863–5901;
7. 'La ampliación: el estado de la cuestión' in *Cursos de la Universidad Internacional Menéndez y Pelayo Mayo* (2003) 1–19;
8. 'Legal and institutional inadequacies in the external action of the European Union' (2015) Nº 50 *Revista de Derecho Comunitario Europeo* 231–320;
9. 'The Polisario Front, the norms of International Law and the Law of the European Union' (2016) No 53 *Revista de Derecho Comunitario Europeo* 21–77;
10. 'Brexit or Bremaim?' (2016) No 39 *Revista General de Derecho Europeo* 1–23;

En francais

11. 'L'élaboration du Droit communautaire dérivé, avant et après le Traité de Maastricht' (1993) *Gazette du Palais. Doctrine* 4–26;

12. 'Maastricht et les citoyens: le Médiateur européen' (1992) n° 64 *Revue française d'administration publique* 639–649;
13. 'Médiateur' *Répertoire Dalloz. Répertoire du Droit communautaire* 1–9;
14. 'Les politiques et actions communautaires' (1997) 33 *Revue trimestrielle de droit européen* 769–800;
15. 'L'arrêt tabac ou l'apport de la Cour de justice au débat sur la délimitation des compétences' (2001) n°4 *Revue trimestrielle de droit européen* 785–809;
16. 'Etat de droit et droit de l'Union Européenne' (2011) n° 544-545-546 *Revue du Marché commun et de l'Union européenne* 13–35 (première partie); 96–116 (deuxième partie); 156–173 (troisième partie);
17. 'Sur la théorie de la souveraineté et son application à (et dans) l'Union européenne' in Marta Arpio Santacruz et al. (eds), *A Man for All Treaties: Liber Amicorum en l'honneur de Jean-Claude Piris* (Bruylant 2012) 195- 318;
18. 'Médiateur européen' (2014) *Recueil Dalloz* 1–14;

In English

19. 'Road safety in road transport legislation: an international comparison', in *Welkongress für Sicherheitswissenschaft* (Verlag TÜV Rheinland GmbH 1990, Part I) 132–176;
20. 'The International Powers of the European Parliament, the Democratic Deficit and the Treaty on the European Union' (1993) *Yearbook of European Law* 85–138;
21. 'Co-decision: an Appraisal of the Experience of the European Parliament as Co-legislator' (1994) *Yearbook of European Law* 21–71;
22. 'The Commission after Amsterdam: its Future in an Enlarged Union' in Ton Heukels et al. (eds), *The European Union after Amsterdam: a Legal Analysis* (Kluwer Law International 1998) 69–115;
23. 'The development of general principles of law at national and Community level: achieving a balance' in Reiner Schulze and Ulrike Seif (eds), *Richterrecht und Rechtsfortbildung in der Europäischen Rechtsgemeinschaft* (Mohr Siebeck 2003) 99–142;
24. 'Some reflexions on the CFSP Legal Order' (2006) 43 *Common Market Law Review* 337–394;
25. 'The significance of the Rule of Law and its implications for the European Union and the United States' (2010) 72 *University of Pittsburgh Law Review* 229–360;

26. 'The organisation of the external relations of the European Union in the Treaty of Lisbon', in Panos Koutrakos (ed), *The European Union's External Relations: A Year After Lisbon*, CLEER Working Paper 2011/3, http://www.asser.nl/upload/documents/772011_51358CLEER%20WP%20 2011-3%20-%20KOUTRAKOS.pdf, 13–47;
27. (With Sonja Boelaert) 'The European Union's Comprehensive Approach to Combating Piracy at Sea: Legal Aspects', in Panos Koutrakos and Achilles Skordas (eds), *Law and Practice of Piracy at Sea: European and International Perspectives* (Hart Publishing 2014) 81–166;
28. (With Frederik Naert) 'The Reluctant (Lisbon) Treaty and Its Implementation in the Practice of the Council', in Piet Eeckhout and Manuel Lopez-Escudero (eds), *The European Union's External Action in Times of Crisis* (Hart Publishing 2016) 13–81;

En portugués

29. 'A elaboração do direito comunitário derivado antes e depois de Maastricht', in (1992) *Cadernos de Ciencia de legislaçao* 7–67.

List of Cases before the CJEU in Which Ricardo Gosalbo Bono Acted as Agent Either on Behalf of the Council or of the Commission

Agent for the Council

C-13/07 *Commission v Council*
C-91/05 *Commission v Council* (ECOWAS)
C-313/00 P *Zino Davidoff and Davidoff & Cie v Parliament and Council*
C-281/00 P *Una Film 'City Revue' v Parliament and Council*
Opinion 2/00 (*Cartagena Protocol*)
Opinion 1/00 (*Agreement on the establishment of a European Common Aviation Area*)
T-196/99 *Area Cova and Others v Council and Commission*
C-74/99 *Imperial Tobacco and Others*
C-377/98 *Netherlands v Parliament and Council*
C-376/98 *Germany v Parliament and Council*
Joined Cases T-172/98 and T-175/98 to T-177/98 *Salamander AG and Others v Parliament and Council*

Agent for the Commission

C-36/98 *Spain v Council*
Opinion 2/94 (*Accession by the Community to the European Convention for the Protection of Human Rights and Fundamental Freedoms*)
C-350/92 *Spain v Council*
C-355/90 *Commission v Spain*
C-195/90 *Commission v Germany*
C-192/90 *Commission v Spain*
C-69/90 *Commission v Italy*
C-56/90 *Commission v United Kingdom*
C-17/90 *Pinaud Wieger*
C-354/89 *Schiocchet v Commission*
C-300/89 *Commission v Council* (*titanium dioxide*)
C-70/89 *Commission v Italy*
C-326/88 *Hansen*
C-108/88 *Jaenicke Cendoya v Commission*

This information is based on the CJEU's website.

Témoignages

Ricardo Gosalbo Bono: Some Reminiscences of a Friend and Colleague

Allan Rosas

Legal orders have become increasingly complex, dynamic and fluid. They are marked by pluralism rather than dualism or monism. The EU constitutional and legal order is no exception. On the contrary, it is an example *par excellence*. Where are the borderlines between international law, European law and national law? These distinctions can still be made, but the border lines are like lines in the water. What about the distinction between public and private law? It does not play a prominent role, if any role at all, in the context of EU law.

In view of these challenges, EU lawyers with demanding responsibilities should feel at home in a number of different contexts and areas of law. The European Commission and the EU Council have been lucky to be able to draw upon the expertise and wisdom of some high-ranking lawyers who met these requirements. Ricardo Gosalbo Bono definitely belongs to this category. The areas of law which he has covered, also through his many publications, include public international law, various aspects of EU law and comparative law. But knowledge of the law is not enough. You also have to understand it, to have a vision, and to pursue your responsibilities with devotion and perseverance. On this count, too, Ricardo scores high.

I had the pleasure of meeting him for the first time in October 1995. A professor from the deep Finnish forests and somewhat lost in the heart of Europe encountered Ricardo and some other outstanding personalities of the Commission Legal Service, such as the then Director-General Jean-Louis Dewost and the then Deputy Director-General Christiaan Timmermans (whom I succeeded in 2001, only to join him a year later at the European Court of Justice). Perhaps somewhat to my surprise, I encountered much support and encouragement, friendliness and collegiality. Ricardo was particularly helpful in introducing me to the inner and outer workings of the Legal Service.

Soon after my arrival at the Commission, I had the pleasure of accompanying Ricardo and the late Jörn Pipkorn, the agents of the Commission, for the oral hearing in Luxembourg on Opinion 2/94, an opinion requested from the Court on the competence of the then European Community to accede to the European Convention on Human Rights. That the Opinion, delivered in April 1996,[1]

1 EU:C:1996:140.

went against the position argued by the Commission and thus concluded that as Community law stood at the time, there was no competence, can certainly not be attributed to Jörn and Ricardo, who pleaded the Commission's case skilfully. This saga, of course, is still with us, as the Court, in its Opinion 2/13,[2] this time held that whilst there is now competence, in view of Article 6(2) TFEU, the draft accession agreement does not comply with the requirement notably of preserving 'the specific characteristics of the Union and Union law', as laid down in Protocol No 8 on the accession of the Union to the European Convention. I do not know how Ricardo feels about this latest development but I can imagine that he, as one of the architects behind the Commission's action in the 1990s, may feel somewhat frustrated by this never-ending story.[3]

As this example shows, things sometimes take a long time in the EU (and some things never get done…). But other projects may proceed surprisingly fast and Ricardo was often involved when that happened. In the Commission Legal Service, he was particularly involved in external relations (my own field) and institutional affairs, thus areas of a primordial importance for the EU constitutional order. It was a big loss for the Commission and its Legal Service when the Council, in 1998, managed to lure him over to its ranks. His decision to move to the Council Legal Service was perfectly understandable, though, as he was offered the post of Director and, alas, in an area where his expertise and experience was particularly sought-after.

Since 1998, our paths crossed somewhat less often, as Ricardo worked in the Council and its Legal Service (the 'cousins', as they were called in the Commission Legal Service), while I stayed at the Commission until the beginning of 2002. That said, we did meet both professionally (in COREPER or Council working parties) or socially. Unfortunately, the encounters became even less frequent after I had moved to the Court, although I had the pleasure of seeing him 'in Court' for instance when he pleaded the 'Small Arms' case dealt with in the Grand Chamber (C-91/05 *Commission v Council*)[4] and we did continue to stay in touch, at least by e-mail. I was very sad of not being able to participate in his farewell reception in 2015, due to an insurmountable duty at the Court.

It is to be strongly hoped that Ricardo, despite his retirement from the Council, will be willing to continue his involvement in European affairs, both in

2 EU:C:2014:2454. See also the chapter by Christiaan Timmermans in this book.

3 For an indication of Ricardo's views on this Opinion, see Ricardo Gosalbo Bono and Frederik Naert, 'The Reluctant (Lisbon) Treaty and Its Implementation in the Practice of the Council' in Piet Eeckhout and Manuel Lopez-Escudero (eds), *The European Union's External Action in Times of Crisis* (Hart Publishing 2016) 13, 76–78.

4 EU:C:2008:288.

terms of teaching, research and counselling, while at the same time being able to devote more time to family, friends and his beloved home region in Spain. I am in fact looking forward to being able to touch base with him a bit more often now than in recent years. Enjoy your new career, Ricardo, and thank you for your friendship!

Fantasía para un gentilhombre

Paul Berman

Lawyer, scholar, teacher, international civil servant, and *haut fonctionnaire* of the European Union, Professor Ricardo Gosalbo Bono has served, and serves, with distinction in many roles. Even to describe Ricardo as a lawyer fails to do justice to the breadth of his interests and experience. His work, teachings and publications have encompassed the worlds of international, EU, comparative, constitutional and public law. He has straddled many different perspectives and legal and political cultures – of the civil and common law traditions, of Europe and the United States, of the United Nations and European Union and within the latter (and some hard-bitten Brussels functionaries might say this demonstrates the greatest breadth of perspective of all) of the Commission and the Council.

In all his posts – first as a legal adviser in 1980's in the Office of Legal Affairs at the United Nations in New York, then as a lawyer for ten years in the Legal Service of the European Commission and from 1998 as a Director of the Legal Service of the Council of the European Union – Ricardo's legal skills and expertise have been fundamental. But it is perhaps the intellectual qualities underpinning those skills and expertise, and the personal qualities and values which he has brought to bear, which have so distinguished Ricardo's contribution.

This has been particularly evident during his service of some fifteen years as Director of the External Relations team – covering everything from enlargement to trade to military operations. Ricardo's tenure has seen a time of exceptional expansion in, and changes to, the European Union's external relations. It has coincided with a series of significant challenges: the largest set of accession negotiations in the history of the Union, significant restructuring of the Union's legal and institutional framework in the Convention and Lisbon Treaty negotiations,[1] increasing inter-institutional tensions and legal challenges on external matters, and an exponential increase in sanctions legislation and litigation.

Ricardo has in particular played a key role in shaping the legal framework of the Common Foreign and Security Policy (CFSP)[2] including the consolidation

---

1 See Ricardo Gosalbo Bono and Frederik Naert, 'The Reluctant (Lisbon) Treaty and Its Implementation in the Practice of the Council' in Piet Eeckhout and Manuel Lopez-Escudero (eds), *The European Union's External Action in Times of Crisis* (Hart Publishing 2016) 13.

2 Ricardo Gosalbo Bono, 'Some Reflections of the CFSP Legal Order' (2006) 43 CML Rev 377.

of the European Union's role as an international legal actor, the expansion of its overseas civilian and military operations[3] and the development of institutional structures unique to CFSP such as the High Representative, the European External Action Service and the Political and Security Committee (PSC).[4] As the PSC's legal adviser over many years he has made an essential contribution to reinforcing its role and ensuring that its work took full account of legal considerations. The collective heart-felt farewell given to him by PSC Ambassadors at his final meeting was testimony to the esteem with which he is held by the diplomatic community.

Like many others, I have been fortunate to work with Ricardo throughout his time as the Council Legal Service's External Relations Director – both from the perspective of a national administration and as a colleague in the Council Legal Service. Member States have valued him greatly as a trusted interlocutor, understanding of their concerns, and always ready to offer advice and to seek to find a constructive solution. I have seen him pour oil on the troubled waters of disagreements and calm an agitated ambassador with a few well-chosen words. In COREPER (Committee of Permanent Representatives) discussions, treaty negotiations, and at successive European Councils, to see Ricardo coming along the corridors in the Justus Lipsius building, with a large, unwieldy bundle of files under his arm[5] and a patient – and if things were getting tricky perhaps a rather pained – expression on his face, was an indicator that wise counsel was likely to prevail.

Within the Legal Service, I have joined Ricardo both in lively debates with colleagues on legal questions – where in the role of elder statesman he always strived to find common accord – and in-depth one-to-one discussions on difficult points of law or political handling. Legal Service colleagues could always count on being made welcome in his office where he would work late into evening, catching up with e-mails after long sessions in COREPER or the PSC, behind a desk invariably stacked high with books and papers and atop which

---

3 See e.g. Ricardo Gosalbo Bono and Sonja Boelaert, 'The European Union's Comprehensive Approach to Tackling Piracy at Sea – Legal Aspects' in Panos Koutrakos and Achilles Skordas (eds), *The Law and Practice of Piracy at Sea* (Hart Publishing 2014) 81.

4 Ricardo Gosalbo Bono, 'The Organization of the External Relations of the European Union in the Treaty of Union' in Panos Koutrakos (ed), *The European Union's External Relations: A Year After Lisbon* (2011) CLEER Working Paper 2011/3, 13 <http://www.asser.nl/upload/documents/772011_51358CLEER%20WP%202011-3%20-%20KOUTRAKOS.pdf> accessed 15 November 2016.

5 A common practice among Council Legal Service Directors and Directors General – rather like the plumage display of tropical birds, the more numerous and unwieldy the files, the greater the prestige.

was always precariously perched a small European flag. Perhaps rather like the changing fortunes of the Union, the flag would sometimes lean this way and that, often seemed close to falling over, and yet – as if buoyed by the commitment of its owner – always managed somehow to stay upright.

Alongside his work in the EU Institutions, Ricardo has pursued an academic career which in itself demonstrates his intellectual breath and range of vision. With doctorates from both the University of Valencia and the University of Cambridge, he is steeped in a culture of pan-European legal scholarship. He has spoken to me with affection of his Cambridge days studying with teachers such as the Frankfurt-born comparative and Roman law scholar Kurt Lipstein, his doctoral supervisor, and the Whewell Professor of International Law, and later British judge at the International Court of Justice, Sir Robert Jennings. His own academic posts equally extend across Europe including positions as Professor of International and Comparative Law at the Vrije Universiteit in Brussels, Honorary Professor of International Trade Law at the University of Barcelona, Professor of European Union Law at the International University Menéndez Pelayo (UIMP) as well as periods as Visiting Professor at both Geneva and Cambridge Universities.

One only needs to dip into Ricardo's numerous publications to see this same broad appreciation of legal cultures and legal disciplines as well as the combined perspectives of the legal practitioner and the legal scholar. His range of studies on the European Union's external relations and the Common Foreign and Security Policy are informed not just by a keen appreciation of the practical application of the legal rules but by a concern to place these within a wider conceptual framework. In doing so Ricardo, drawing on comparative and international as well as EU law, brings an original and innovative perspective to bear on some fundamental issues. It is sufficient here to mention two examples of his work which amply illustrate his intellectual breadth.

The title of his 2006 article, 'Some Reflections on the CFSP Legal Order',[6] modestly belies its scope. Ricardo provides, as one would expect, a comprehensive and authoritative account of the development of the legal framework for the Common Foreign and Security Policy. But he goes further. He seeks to understand the nature of the CFSP legal order in relation to EU law and of the EU legal order in relation to international law. On the former, he determines that 'one can only conclude that the CFSP legal order, although it is a distinct field of activity in comparison with the rest of the Union's activities, remains part of the unified EU legal system' but only after a rigorous assessment of whether the CFSP system is indeed a legal order at all and a careful

6 Gosalbo Bono (n 2).

examination of its specific characteristics – notably that 'the requirements of the principle of the rule of law as regards democratic and judicial control are primarily exercised (...) at the level of the Member States'.[7]

As regards EU law itself, his assessment of the nature of the Community (as it then was) legal order, again supported by painstaking analysis, is trenchant:

> Despite its unique features and the degree of integration and supranationalism which has no equivalent to any other system known to modern international law, the Community legal order owes a great deal (in fact, its very existence) to international law and forms part of the international legal order: Community law is nothing more than treaty law at its most integrated degree.[8]

It is an important conclusion given the extent to which relations between the practitioners of international and of EU law are often marked by mutual, and sometimes wilful, incomprehension – to the detriment both of each other and of the international effectiveness of the Union. It is also indicative of Ricardo's vocation for breaking down barriers – intellectual and professional – and finding common ground.

Perhaps most striking is Ricardo's attempt to identify the emergence of a 'European Union conception of international law'. He points in particular to the 'subtle but persistent differences between traditional concepts of international law in Germany, France and the United Kingdom, the three major international players of the European Union'[9] and how developments in CFSP 'have resulted in the assimilation and mutual approximation of the apparently different national conceptions'.[10] One can debate the extent to which differing national conceptions of international law have a practical impact at the international level and the extent to which those differences have been reduced within the framework of the CFSP. While it is true that the positions of EU Member States have converged on a number of international law issues, it is perhaps easier to see this as part of the wider process of foreign policy coordination rather than the more subtle emergence of a new conception of international law. Nevertheless the exercise is an engaging one and the combination of international, comparative and EU law which it involves is ideally suited to Ricardo's wider-ranging expertise.

---

7 Ibid 378.
8 Ibid 375.
9 Ibid 380.
10 Ibid 384.

One sees a similar breadth of expertise and perspective, and an even more wide-ranging scope, in Ricardo's substantial study, 'The Significance of the Rule of Law and its Implications for the European Union and the United States',[11] published four years later. It is a *tour de force,* going far beyond discussion of the EU itself, and drawing on analyses of Greek philosophy and Roman law, studies of the concepts of *Rechtsstaat, État de Droit* and Rule of Law in German, French and English law, and comparative studies of the rule of law in legal systems around the globe. In doing so, Ricardo postulates a 'universal definition of the rule of law' based on three principles – (i) that law must be not exercised arbitrarily; (ii) the supremacy of law; and (iii) that the law must apply to all persons equally – a definition which has itself attracted academic attention and discussion.[12] Always ready to address difficult questions, Ricardo then goes on to examine the application of the rule of law as a distinct concept in international law arguing that there is a need for the rule of law 'as a moral virtue' at the international level and concluding that 'important progress has been achieved in the development of an international rule of law and that remaining shortcomings should not constitute a roadblock for international lawyers that prevents continued work on the rule of law as a fundamental goal'.[13]

Ricardo focuses in particular on a detailed comparison of the development of the concept of the rule of law in both the United States and Europe, with an emphasis on US foreign policy and EU external action. Again with his usual intellectual breadth, this is examined through the prism of political philosophy and political developments as well as law. Without seeking to minimise legal and political differences, Ricardo argues for a shared trans-Atlantic heritage enshrined in the rule of law: 'there are no conceptual difficulties from a legal point of view because there is no legal difference between European and American laws with respect to the meaning of the rule of law. What needs to be improved is the mutual understanding of how the rule of law is to be promoted'. In order to succeed, the promotion of the rule of law in the world:

> will require elements of both the US 'bottom-up emphasis' on civil society and the EU 'top-down appreciation' on the role of the State. Without

11 (2010) 72 University of Pittsburg Law Review 229.

12 Ricardo's analysis is discussed in comparison with that of other scholars in Imogen Saunders, 'Principles of Law and a Source-Based Approach' (in Hitoshi Nasu and Kim Rubinstein (eds), *Legal Perspectives on Security Institutions* (Cambridge University Press 2015)) and in Christopher May, *The Rule of Law – the Common Sense of Global Politics* (Edward Elgar 2014) 174ff.

13 Gosalbo Bono (n 11) 299.

> the US enthusiasm and optimism, the promotion of democracy will not become more than a timid attempt, yet without the European attention to the rule of law and institution-building, the triumph of democracy will only be a short-lived parenthesis.[14]

There is much to discuss in the wealth of analysis in Ricardo's treatment of the rule of law. One might also debate the characterisation of the US and European positions and the promotion of the rule of law at the international level. But Ricardo's combination of detailed legal scholarship, political comment and strong sense of moral engagement is compelling and he concludes with a continuing hope that these shared values, particularly through the prism of human rights, will indeed become global:

> The international community has opted for the basic inventory of individual and social rights, of human dignity, personal freedom, protection against arbitrariness, active political rights, freedom of voting, equality before the law, and the responsibility of society for the social and economic conditions of its members. As we have seen, the realization of these postulates cannot succeed unless these rights are safeguarded by means of predictable legality and procedures enforced by independent courts. There are good reasons for hoping that the fundamental decision of these nations is more than lip service before international organizations by whatever politicians happen to be in power.[15]

In this analysis one sees much of Ricardo's own values – his commitment to building bridges across legal and political cultures and his aspirations for the global respect for the rule of law and human rights.

As a legal scholar, it is tempting to place Ricardo in a line of intellectual descent from the Spanish jurist Francesco de Vitoria, one of the fathers of modern international law, adviser to both the King of Spain and Holy Roman Emperor Charles V, advocate of the notion of freedom of international trade and of the High Seas, and proponent of the revived Roman law concept of *ius gentium*, the law of nations. But one might equally refer to the pan-European perspective and career of another father of international law, the Italian jurist Alberico Gentili who was active as a legal scholar, teacher and practitioner, served as Regius Professor of Civil Law in the University of Oxford and was legal adviser to the Spanish Embassy in London.

---

14 Ibid 356.

15 Ibid 360.

A breadth of intellectual approach, an innate sense of tolerance, a deep commitment to the rule of law and a concern to find common ground have been fundamental both to Ricardo's academic work and to his work in the Institutions. As someone equally at home in public international law and European Union law, he has been well-suited to tackling the difficult and delicate issues that have arisen in relation to issues such as those relating to State recognition, the responsibility of the Union in its international engagements and the treatment of international law in issues before the Court of Justice of the European Union. As someone alert to the range of national perspectives and traditions, he has promoted mutual understanding and respect in meetings and negotiations. And as someone committed to building bridges, he has sought to take a consensual approach in response to the institutional upheavals and differences of recent years while being ever-vigilant to uphold respect for the Treaties and for the role of the Council.

I, like many others, have benefited from Ricardo's generosity with his time, his careful advice and his kindness. I have equally, on occasion, heard him express justified concern where respect for the rule of law, legal rigour in opinions or rulings, and probity and courtesy in personal dealings fell short of the standards he expected. In his farewell speech on the occasion of his retirement from the Council Legal Service, Ricardo underlined the importance of honesty in professional as well as personal life – both as an innate principle and because of his observation of the corrosive effect that the lack of trust and straight dealing have all too often had on political discussions and negotiations. In all this there is again a fundamental correlation between his personal qualities, his professional probity and his academic preoccupations with respect for the rule of law and respect for the individual.

Whence comes the title of this piece. The great Spanish composer Joaquín Rodrigo – incidentally one of the first to lecture at the University of Menéndez Pelayo where Ricardo is now Professor – chose it in 1954 as the title of one of his most famous compositions in tribute to the virtuoso guitarist Andrés Segovia. It serves equally well as a tribute to Ricardo. For in his personal qualities – his integrity, calm, courtesy and generosity of spirit – he is indeed a modern example of the *gentilhombre*.

PART 1

Institutional Dimensions

CHAPTER 1

Still New Kids on the EU's Institutional Block? The High Representative and the European External Action Service Seven Years after the Entry into Force of the Treaty of Lisbon

*Stephan Marquardt**

1 Introduction

The Treaty of Lisbon, which entered into force on 1 December 2009, introduced significant changes in the institutional architecture of the EU, in particular in the field of external relations and the external representation of the EU. This article will provide an overview of the main institutional modifications, focussing on the role of the High Representative of the Union for Foreign Affairs and Security Policy (High Representative or HR) and of the entity supporting the HR in the implementation of his mandate, the European External Action Service (EEAS). It will also seek to analyse, seven years after the entry into force of the Treaty of Lisbon, how the HR and the EEAS have positioned themselves in the institutional system of the EU, and what challenges remain.

2 The Institutional and Structural Changes Introduced by the Treaty of Lisbon in the Domain of the European Union's External Action and External Representation

The Treaty of Lisbon brought a number of fundamental changes to the EU's institutional architecture, placed the EU's Common Foreign and Security Policy (CFSP) on a new footing as part of the EU's external action, and created new institutional actors responsible inter alia for the EU's external representation, in particular the function of 'High Representative of the Union for Foreign Affairs and Security Policy', responsible for conducting the CFSP and for the external

* The views expressed in this article are the personal opinion of the author and do not represent any official position of the High Representative or of the European External Action Service.

 | DOI 10.1163/9789004347175_002

representation of the EU in that domain. These changes are briefly outlined hereafter.

2.1 *The TEU and the TFEU – The 'Replacement and Succession' of the EC by the EU*

Through the Treaty of Lisbon, the former European Community (EC) has been 'replaced and succeeded' by the EU (Article 1, third paragraph, TEU), thereby creating a more coherent and unified single entity (the European Union). The Treaty of Lisbon also restructured the existing treaties accordingly.

The basic principles and institutional provisions, as well as the specific provisions relating to the CFSP, are set out in the TEU; the substantive provisions on the EU's domains of competence and more detailed institutional provisions, as well as the decision-making and legislative procedures, are contained in the TFEU (ex-Treaty establishing the European Community (TEC)).

Under the TEU as modified by the Treaty of Lisbon, the EU has now also expressly been endowed with legal personality.[1]

2.2 *The CFSP (and the CSDP) as an Integral Part of the EU's External Action and as a Competence of the EU*

The Treaty of Lisbon has introduced the following important modifications as regards the CFSP, which was previously 'self-contained' in the TEU, a treaty separate from the TEC.

The CFSP now forms an integral part of the EU's 'external action' (a new terminology introduced by the Treaty of Lisbon), even though it is still subject to specific rules. The EU's 'external action' thus now comprises both the CFSP and the 'ex-Community' domains of external relations (trade policy, development cooperation, technical and financial assistance, humanitarian aid, restrictive measures).[2]

The general principles and objectives of the EU's external action, including those relevant for the CFSP, are now set out in a common provision, Article 21 TEU. The CFSP is also (for the first time) expressly qualified as a 'competence'

1 Art 47 TEU. Already before the Treaty of Lisbon the EU had arguably already acquired legal personality, although this question was disputed in the legal doctrine. One element indicative of the EU's legal personality was its capacity to conclude international agreements, in accordance with the procedure set out in ex-art 24 TEU.

2 See generally Ricardo Gosalbo Bono, 'The Organization of the External Relations of the EU in the Treaty of Lisbon' in Panos Koutrakos (ed), *The EU's External Relations a Year after Lisbon* (2011) CLEER Working Papers 2011/3 <http://www.asser.nl/cleer/publications/cleer-papers/cleer-wp-20113-koutrakos-ed/>.

of the EU (Article 24(1) TEU and Article 4(4) TFEU), the exact nature of which however remains disputed.

Despite its formal integration into the domain of the EU's external competences, the CFSP however still remains subject to 'specific rules and procedures',[3] and its substantive provisions have not been transferred to the TFEU, but were maintained in the TEU, contrary to all other domains of EU competence.[4]

2.2.1 Specificities of the CFSP (Article 24(1) TEU)

The CFSP covers 'all areas of foreign policy and all questions relating to the Union's security'. Its scope is therefore potentially very wide, and the concrete actions are determined on a case-by-case basis in the light of international developments. In accordance with Article 26 TEU, the CFSP is defined by the European Council and the Council.

The basic voting rule is unanimity. In certain cases, decisions by qualified majority are however possible, e.g. for implementing decisions and decisions appointing EU Special Representatives pursuant to Article 33 TEU.[5] This demonstrates that the CFSP cannot be considered (at least from a legal point of view) as a form of intergovernmental cooperation, a view that is still held in legal doctrine even after the entry into force of the Treaty of Lisbon, sometimes based on the – incorrect – assumption that the European Council and the Council are intergovernmental bodies.[6] Even before the entry into force of the Treaty of Lisbon (where the possibility of qualified majority voting in the CFSP already existed), there were strong arguments pleading against an intergovernmental character of the EU's CFSP.[7]

The adoption of legislative acts (in the meaning of the TFEU) is excluded in the CFSP; however, the European Council and the Council can adopt legal acts in the CFSP, which are binding on the Member States. The form of legal acts

3 Art 24(1), subpara 2, TEU.

4 See also Declarations no 13 and 14 concerning the CFSP annexed to the Final Act of the Treaty of Lisbon ([2008] OJ C115/335).

5 Art 31(2) TEU.

6 See e.g. Uwe Puetter, 'The Latest Attempt at Institutional Engineering: The Treaty of Lisbon and Deliberative Intergovernmentalism in EU Foreign and Security Policy Coordination' in Paul James Cardwell (ed) *EU External Relations Law and Policy in the post-Lisbon Era* (Asser Press 2012) 17, 19–23; Aurel Sari, 'Between Legalisation and Organisational Development: Explaining the Evolution of EU Competence in the Field of Foreign Policy', in Cardwell (ibid) 80.

7 See e.g. Ricardo Gosalbo Bono, 'Some Reflections on the CFSP Legal Order' (2006) 43 CML Rev 364, 393.

in the CFSP has been unified (the basic form is that of a decision).[8] Decisions adopted in the framework of the CFSP are legal acts in the meaning of Article 288 TFEU and therefore are subject to the same formal requirements as legal acts adopted under the TFEU, in particular the statement of reasons and the reference to any proposals required under the Treaties (Article 296 TFEU). This is relevant in practice in the CFSP as legal acts in that domain are normally adopted on a proposal of the High Representative.

Lastly, the Court of Justice of the European Union (CJEU) in principle has no jurisdiction to review the legality of decisions and legal acts adopted on the basis of the CFSP provisions in the Treaties, with the exception of certain decisions affecting the rights of individuals in the area of restrictive measures (sanctions),[9] and to review the delimitation between the CFSP and other domains of the EU's external action (e.g. development cooperation) or the external dimension of other EU policies (Article 40 TEU). An emerging case-law of the CJEU however indicates that it is taking a narrow reading of this exemption, considering that certain decisions of an administrative nature, albeit taken in the framework of the CFSP, are subject to judicial review by the EU courts.[10]

2.2.2 The CSDP

The Treaty of Lisbon has introduced a new section in the TEU dedicated to the Common Security and Defence Policy (CSDP) (Articles 42 to 46), which however continues to form an integral part of the CFSP.

The core part of the CSDP consists of the operational missions that the EU may decide to undertake with the objective of peace-keeping, conflict prevention and the strengthening of international peace and security, with military and civilian means. The specific tasks to be undertaken by the EU for this purpose are further specified in Article 43 TEU.

---

8 Whereas before the Treaty of Lisbon, the TEU provided for the adoption of different instruments, in particular joint actions and common positions.

9 Art 24(1), subpara 2, TEU.

10 Case C-455/14 P *H v Council, Commission and European Union Police Mission* (EUPM) *in Bosnia and Herzegovina* EU:C:2016:569. At issue in that case was a decision by the Head of the EUPM mission to reassign a staff member (seconded by a Member State) to another location and function. The Council, as one of the defendants, had argued that such decisions had an operational character linked to the mandate of the mission (a view supported by the Advocate General) and were therefore covered by the exemption to the CJEU's jurisdiction. See also Case C-439/13 P *Elitaliana v Eulex Kosovo* EU:C:2015:753. This concerned a procurement decision in a civilian CSDP mission; the CJEU held that it was competent to verify compliance with horizontal EU financial regulations also in the CFSP context.

EU CSDP missions are undertaken using means and capabilities put at the disposal of the EU by the Member States, which have an obligation to put such means at the disposal of the Union.[11]

Furthermore, the CSDP includes the progressive framing of a common EU defence policy.[12]

Finally, through the Treaty of Lisbon, the European Defence Agency (EDA) is now expressly integrated in the CSDP framework.[13] The EDA inter alia has the mandate to support the development of Member States' military capabilities for the purposes of the CSDP.

2.2.3 The CFSP as a Union Competence

The Treaty of Lisbon confirms the autonomous character of the Union's CFSP vis-à-vis the individual foreign policies pursued by Member States, notably by integrating the CFSP into the system of competences of the Treaties: 'The Union's competence in matters of common foreign and security policy shall cover (...)';[14] 'The Union shall have competence (...) to define and implement a common foreign and security policy (...)'.[15]

The Union's competence in CFSP matters is of a special nature: it 'belongs' to the EU but it is not an exclusive competence in the meaning of the Treaties.[16] The Member States do not lose their sovereign competence to act in foreign policy matters even if the EU exercises its competence in the CFSP and adopts specific measures in this domain (subject only to their duty of loyal cooperation). The CFSP is therefore not a 'shared competence' between the EU and its Member States in the meaning of EU law.[17] Rather, it may be qualified as a 'parallel competence', ie exercised in parallel to that of the Member States.[18] The Member States, however, remain bound by the duty of loyal cooperation, they must support the EU's CFSP 'unreservedly in a spirit of loyalty and mutual solidarity' and must refrain from any acts contrary to the interests

11 Art 42(3) TEU.

12 Art 42(2) TEU.

13 Art 45 TEU.

14 Art 24(1) TEU.

15 Art 2(4) TFEU.

16 The areas of EU exclusive competence are set out in art 3(1) TFEU.

17 The CFSP is not referred to in the areas of shared EU/Member State competence as set out in art 4 TFEU.

18 See Stephan Marquardt and Jens-Christian Gaedtke, 'Vor Art 23–46 EUV' in Hans von der Groeben, Armin Hatje and Jürgen Schwarze (eds), *Europäisches Unionsrecht* (Commentary of the TEU, TFEU and Charter) (Nomos 2015) para 10.

of the Union.[19] The TEU not only delimits the CFSP vis-à-vis the foreign policy of the Member States, but also vis-à-vis other domains of EU competence: Article 40 TEU provides that measures under the CFSP must not affect the exercise of other EU competences and respective institutional powers; conversely, the exercise of other EU competences must not affect the exercise of the CFSP and the powers of the institutions competent for its implementation. This is also a new element introduced by the Treaty of Lisbon: whereas ex-Article 47 TEU previously contained an 'asymmetrical' clause protecting the EC from encroachment by CFSP measures, Article 40 TEU now also protects the CFSP from any measures adopted under the TFEU that may affect the CFSP. In accordance with Article 24(1) TEU, the CJEU would thus now also have jurisdiction to verify whether a measure adopted by the Council under the TFEU, e.g. in the domain of development cooperation, infringes the competences of the EU in the CFSP.[20]

2.2.4 Scope of the CFSP

The CFSP is also sui generis in nature (compared to other domains of EU competence) because its material scope is defined in very wide terms: it potentially covers 'all areas of foreign policy and all questions relating to the Union's security (…)'.[21] Some guidance as to the contents of possible CFSP measures is provided by the general objectives of the EU's external action as set out in Article 21(2)(a), (b) and (c) TEU. Even though the objectives of the EU's external action set out in Article 21(2) TEU now cover the entire range of the EU's external policies and not only the CFSP, a comparison with the objectives of the CFSP as they were set out in ex-Article 11(1) TEU before the Treaty of Lisbon suggests that the objectives set out in these specific provisions are most relevant for the CFSP. More specific illustrations of the potential scope of CFSP measures are

---

19 Art 24(3) TEU. On this aspect see Christophe Hillion, 'Cohérence et action extérieure de l'Union' in Eleftheria Neframi (ed) *Objectifs et compétences de l'Union européenne* (Bruylant 2012) 229.

20 It may be recalled in this context that prior to the Treaty of Lisbon, the Commission successfully challenged a measure adopted by the Council under the CFSP, on the ground that it infringed European Community competences in the field of development cooperation and was therefore contrary to ex-art 47 TEU. The Court confirmed, based on an analysis of the decision's objectives and contents, that it did not only pursue CFSP but also development cooperation objectives and could therefore have been adopted on the basis of the treaty provisions relating to the latter policy, therefore excluding a CFSP legal basis (Case C-91/05 *Commission v Council* EU:C:2008:288 (*ECOWAS*)).

21 Art 24(1), subpara 1, TEU.

provided by the different tasks for which the Council may decide to set up missions in the frame of the CSDP.[22]

The practice of the CFSP, ie the strategic documents, political guidelines and positions adopted by the European Council and the Council and the numerous legal acts adopted by the Council allow to identify the following broad categories of thematic and geographic CFSP areas: (a) operational missions (using civilian or military means) for peace-keeping, conflict prevention, strengthening international security (Article 42(1) TEU), potentially covering all the specific tasks referred to in Article 43(1) TEU; (b) non-proliferation and disarmament;[23] (c) human rights, democracy, rule of law, including support for international courts and tribunals; (d) country-specific restrictive measures (sanctions); (e) counter-terrorism (including related sanctions); (f) EU Special Representatives for specific policy issues.

It follows from this wide definition of the CFSP's scope that in principle no subject-matter is a priori excluded from the scope of the CFSP, provided (a) that it relates to 'foreign policy' as generally understood and (b) it does not fall under any other specific EU competence as set out in the TFEU (in accordance with Article 40 TEU).

2.2.5. Exercise of the CFSP Competence

The exercise of this competence of the Union by the competent EU institutions (European Council and Council) takes place on an ad hoc basis, in the light of international developments. While certain CFSP policies can be pre-established in a general manner (e.g. the 'EU Strategies' or 'Guidelines' adopted by the European Council or Council in specific areas such as Weapons of Mass Destruction, Small Arms and Light Weapons, counter-terrorism, restrictive measures), concrete implementing measures are generally adopted to address specific situations where action by the EU is deemed necessary: 'Where the international situation requires operational action by the Union, the Council shall adopt the necessary decisions',[24] or to 'define the approach of the Union to a particular matter of a geographical or thematic nature'.[25]

---

22 See arts 42(1) and 43(1) TEU.

23 Non-proliferation and disarmament have been CFSP domains from the very beginning: see e.g. Council Decision 94/509/CFSP of 25 July 1994 regarding the preparation for the 1995 Conference of the States parties to the Treaty on the Non-Proliferation of Nuclear Weapons [1994] OJ L205/1. This is also confirmed by the corresponding article in the CFSP chapter of the EU budget (see e.g. Chapter 19.03.02 on 'support to non-proliferation and disarmament' in the 2016 budget ([2016] OJ L48/1, 1273)).

24 Art 28(1), subpara 1, TEU.

25 Art 29 TEU.

Once the Council has agreed or decided a specific position or measure in the CFSP, this constitutes an ad hoc exercise of CFSP competence by the EU, which by definition cannot be 'shared' with the Member States because the latter have decided (as members of the Council) to define a CFSP position.

The claim in general terms that the CFSP is by definition always a matter of 'shared' competence between the EU and its Member States negates the specificity of the CFSP and the nature of its decision-making process; it would reduce the CFSP to the mere expression of the collective political position of 28 Member States and the type of intergovernmental process that existed before the TEU in the framework of the European Political Cooperation. The mere possibility of a 'constructive abstention'[26] and of qualified majority voting in the CFSP however demonstrates that the CFSP cannot be considered as an intergovernmental process.

2.2.6 National Positions of Member States

The Member States may always adopt national positions on an individual basis in relation to the same subject-matter and position adopted by the EU in a specific situation, provided they do not act in a manner contrary to the EU position and to the EU's interests. However, once the national positions converge to the extent that a common position under the CFSP can be defined and agreed in the Council, this ipso facto becomes a CFSP position of the EU and no longer represents a (collective) position of the Member States. This is the essence of the CFSP process.[27] This process may also happen when only a few Member States have a specific – shared – position on a given subject-matter, but choose to put their position forward in the Council in order to achieve an EU position.[28]

---

26 This possibility was used by one Member State when the Council adopted the Joint Action establishing EULEX Kosovo (Council Joint Action 2008/124/cfsp of 4 February 2008 on the European Union Rule of Law Mission in Kosovo, EULEX KOSOVO [2008] OJ L42/92, as amended).

27 See art 24(2) TEU: 'the Union shall conduct, define and implement a common foreign and security policy, based on (...) the achievement of an ever-increasing degree of convergence of Member State's actions'; art 32(1), 3rd sentence, TEU: 'Member States shall ensure, through the convergence of their actions, that the Union is able to assert its interests and values on the international scene'.

28 In accordance with art 30(1) TEU, any Member State may submit an initiative or proposal to the Council.

2.3 *External Representation – The Institutional Actors*

2.3.1 The President of the European Council

The Treaty of Lisbon has also introduced significant changes as regards the European Council. The latter is now for the first time fully integrated in the Unions' institutional framework and ranked among its institutions.[29] Furthermore, the European Council now has an express decision-making power, including the power to decide on amendments of the Treaties in specific cases.[30] The European Council may thus in principle adopt legally binding decisions. It has also adopted its own Rules of Procedure.[31]

The main innovation is that the European Council is no longer chaired by the Head of State or Government of the Member State holding the rotating Presidency of the Council, but by a President elected by the European Council (by qualified majority, whereas the general rule for decision-making in the European Council is consensus)[32] for a term of two and a half years, renewable once.[33] This development is to be seen in the same context as the creation of a permanent chair of the Foreign Affairs Council, with the objective of ensuring more continuity in the external action of the EU.[34] In matters of external representation, Article 15(6), last subparagraph, TEU provides that the President of the European Council, 'at his level and in that capacity', shall ensure the external representation of the Union on matters falling within the CFSP. The limitation to the CFSP can be explained by the fact that pursuant to Article 17(1) TEU, the Commission is responsible for the external representation of the EU in all other domains. It is noteworthy that Article 17 TEU does not confer any express representational capacity on the President of the Commission. In practice, the President of the Commission however often assumes the role of representing the EU at the level of Heads of State or Government outside CFSP matters.

---

29 Art 13(1) TEU.

30 E.g. art 48(6) and (7) TEU. The European Council has made use of this possibility in 2011 to amend art 136(3) TFEU in order to allow for the creation of the European Stability Mechanism (European Council Decision 2011/199/EU of 25 March 2011 amending Article 136 of the Treaty on the Functioning of the European Union with regard to a stability mechanism for Member States whose currency is the euro [2011] OJ L91/1).

31 European Council Decision 2009/882/EU of 1 December 2009 adopting its Rules of Procedure [2009] OJ L315/52.

32 Art 15(4) TEU.

33 Art. 15(5) TEU.

34 See Jean-Claude Piris, *The Lisbon Treaty – A Legal and Political Analysis* (Cambridge University Press 2010) 209.

2.3.2 The High Representative

The creation of the function of High Representative of the Union for Foreign Affairs and Security Policy is arguably the most important innovation in the EU's institutional framework. It can be seen as a reinforced continuation of the role previously exercised by the Secretary-General/High Representative of the Council, whose role was to assist the Presidency in the external representation of the EU.[35] The latter's role of ensuring the external representation of the EU in the area of the CFSP had been one of the specificities of the CFSP since its creation by the TEU in 1993. Even though the former Treaty establishing the European Community did not contain any provision to this effect, it was accepted and recognised in practice that the Commission was entitled to exercise the EC's external representation, even if in practice this was often done together with the Member State holding the Presidency of the Council.[36] By contrast, in the domains covered by the TEU, and in particular in the CFSP (as well as under the former 'Third Pillar'), the responsibility of acting as external representative of the EU was incumbent on the Member State holding the rotating Presidency of the Council.[37] The function of 'High Representative for the common foreign and security policy' was subsequently created by the Treaty of Amsterdam in 1999. This function was 'double-hatted' with that of Secretary-General of the Council. Under the impetus of Javier Solana, who was appointed to that double function for two consecutive mandates, the creation of this function laid the groundwork for the further development of the CFSP and CSDP and the creation of dedicated structures within the Council and its Secretariat, in particular for the planning and conduct of EU crisis management operations.

It was nonetheless another significant step for the Member States to relinquish the role of the Council Presidency as external representative of the EU in the CFSP to an institutional actor. Pursuant to Article 27(2) TEU, the High Representative is now responsible for this task, including the conduct of the 'political dialogue' with third parties on behalf of the Union and the task of expressing positions of the Union in international organisations and at international conferences.

---

35 See ex-arts 18(3) and 26 TEU.

36 On this basis the Commission also had set up a comprehensive network of Commission delegations in third countries and at international organisations.

37 Ex-art 18(1) TEU.

2.3.3 The European Commission

Pursuant to Article 17(1) TEU, the Commission has now expressly been endowed with the responsibility of representing the Union in matters not falling under the EU's CFSP (and except where the Treaties provide otherwise). Depending on the specific subject-matter, the role of external representation of the Union will in practice be exercised by the competent member of the Commission. As the case may be, this role can potentially also be exercised by the HR in his/her capacity as Vice-President (VP) of the Commission responsible for external relations, in which case he/she may cover both CFSP and non-CFSP subject-matters.

2.3.4 Union Delegations

Another institutional reinforcement in the external representation of the EU by the Treaty of Lisbon was the creation of Union delegations mandated to represent the Union (on all subject-matters falling under its competences) in third countries and at international organisations.[38] These delegations are placed under the authority of the HR[39] and form an integral part of the EEAS.[40] In practice, following the entry into force of the Treaty of Lisbon, the existing Commission delegations in third countries and at international organisations have henceforth been transformed into Union delegations under the authority of the HR and forming part of the EEAS. A number of new EU delegations have in the meantime been created (e.g. in Myanmar and South-Sudan).

3 The High Representative of the Union for Foreign Affairs and Security Policy – Responsibilities and Mandate

The function of 'High Representative of the Union for Foreign Affairs and Security Policy' introduced by the Treaty of Lisbon is a rather complex innovation in the institutional structure of the Treaties, besides being a major political step taken by the Member States towards an integration of the CFSP into other aspects of the EU's external action and a more unified external representation of the EU.

38 Art 221(1) TFEU.

39 Art 221(2) TFEU.

40 Council Decision 2010/427/EU of 26 July 2010 establishing the organisation and functioning of the European External Action Service [2010] OJ L201/30 (EEAS Decision), art 1(4).

3.1 *General Mandate of the HR*

The HR's general mandate is to 'conduct the CFSP', including the CSDP, and to contribute to its development through proposals.[41] The HR therefore has a general right of initiative in the CFSP, including the right to submit formal proposals for legal acts to the Council, as specified in Article 30(1) TEU. The HR further has the general mandate to ensure the implementation of the decisions of the European Council and the Council.[42]

3.2 *Main Functions of the HR – The Three 'Hats'*

The HR has a number of specific functions and responsibilities, the most important of which are: (a) to represent the EU in matters of the CFSP;[43] (b) to chair ('preside over') the Foreign Affairs Council (FAC);[44] (c) to exercise the responsibilities of one of the Vice-Presidents of the Commission, in charge of external relations and of coordinating the other aspects of the EU's external action.[45]

These three functions and 'hats' in themselves represent a significant complexity of roles and burden for one single person and raise the permanent question of how to properly delineate these functions vis-à-vis each other, in particular since two of these functions (president of the FAC and VP of the Commission) are tied to the institutional responsibilities of the Council and the Commission, both being bodies comprising individual members and functioning in a collective manner in accordance with their respective decision-making procedures. It may be noted in this regard that Article 18(4) TEU provides that when exercising the responsibilities as VP of the Commission, the HR 'shall be bound by Commission procedures' however only 'to the extent that this is consistent with paragraphs 2 and 3' (ie with the functions of the HR as HR and as chair of the FAC). It is interesting to note that Article 18 has no corresponding provision as regards the role of the HR as chair of the FAC. It follows from the Council's Rules of Procedure,[46] however, that the latter also applies to the HR when chairing the FAC.[47]

---

41 Art 18(2) TEU.

42 Arts 18(2) and 27(1) TEU.

43 Art 27(2) TEU.

44 Art 18(3) TEU.

45 Art 18(4) TEU.

46 Annexed to Council decision 2009/937/EU of 1 December 2009 adopting the Council's Rules of Procedure [2009] OJ L325/35.

47 It was however agreed that when the FAC discusses trade related questions, the HR would ask a representative of the Member States holding the rotating Presidency to chair (ibid, footnote to art 2(5)).

The function of HR, for its part, perhaps raises less complexities as this function is exercised by the person holding that position, and thus does not require a complex internal decision-making process. Indeed the HR has until now not adopted any formal rules of procedure setting out the working methods and decision-making processes within the EEAS.

To add to the complexity of the three main functions of the HR, his/her mandate under Article 18(4) TEU is itself threefold: it provides that as a VP of the Commission, the HR (a) 'should ensure the consistency of the Union's external action'; (b) is responsible within the Commission for the EU's external relations; and (c) is also responsible for 'coordinating the other aspects of the Union's external action'.

It follows from this provision that the HR, in his/her capacity of VP, should be considered as a *primus inter pares* among the members of the Commission having a portfolio in external relations. Hence, he/she chairs the corresponding group of Commissioners, and the group should serve as the principal forum for the coordination of the EU's external action. This has been implemented in practice by the current HR, Federica Mogherini.

It should be recalled in this context that in accordance with the Treaties, the EU's 'external action' covers both the CFSP and the domains of the Common Commercial Policy, development cooperation, technical and financial assistance to third countries, and humanitarian assistance. It also covers the specific domain of restrictive measures (sanctions) (Article 215 TFEU).[48]

However, even though the CFSP forms an integral part of the EU's external action, it is still subject to 'specific rules and procedures' (Article 24(1), second subparagraph, TEU), and Article 40 TEU still provides for a delimitation between the CFSP and the other domains of EU external action. As a consequence, part of the coordinating role of the HR will have to be devoted to ensuring consistency between the CFSP and the other domains of external action, besides ensuring consistency between the different areas of non-CFSP external action.

It may further be noted that while Article 18(4) TEU only refers to the coordination of the EU's 'external action' (as set out in Title V of the TEU – CFSP – and Part 5 of the TFEU – trade, development cooperation, technical assistance), Article 21(3) TEU also calls for consistency between the EU's external action and the 'external aspects of its other policies'. Hence, the participation

48 The fact that the solidarity clause (art 222 TFEU) is also placed in the part on external action, even though it mainly concerns actions to be undertaken within the Union, may be explained by the fact that it may also entail an external dimension, e.g. in the event of a terrorist attack.

of other members of the Commission not having an 'external' portfolio but where an external dimension exists (e.g. energy, environment) in the External Relations (RELEX) group of Commissioners may also prove necessary.

3.3 *The HR's Responsibilities as Regards the EEAS and Union Delegations*

3.3.1 Authority over the EEAS

Article 27 TEU, which describes the main responsibilities of the HR in the area of the CFSP and the external representation of the EU in this area, provides the legal basis for the establishment of the EEAS as the entity mandated to support the HR in the exercise of his/her mandate.[49] As a consequence, the EEAS Decision[50] provides in its Article 1(3) that the EEAS is placed under the authority of the HR. Furthermore, Article 6(5) of the EEAS Decision provides that the HR shall be vested with the powers conferred on the appointing authority by the EU Staff Regulations and the powers conferred on the authority authorised to conclude contracts under the Conditions of Employment of Other Servants of the EU, in respect of the staff of the EEAS.

As a consequence of the 'authority' of the HR over the EEAS, the EEAS Decision further provides that the HR is responsible for the adoption of internal rules for the EEAS in a number of domains, including security, data protection and access to documents.[51]

3.3.2 Authority over Union Delegations

Article 221(2) TFEU provides that Union delegations, mandated to represent the Union vis-à-vis third States and international organisations pursuant to paragraph 1 of that Article, are placed under the authority of the HR. It is probably for this reason that Article 1(4) of the EEAS Decision provides that Union delegations form part of the EEAS; it is further provided therein that Heads of Union Delegations are accountable to the HR for the overall management of the delegation (Article 5(2)) and that they have to implement the instructions received from the HR and the EEAS (Article 5(3)). Article 5(1) of the EEAS Decision confers on the HR the power to decide on the opening or closing of

---

49 Art 27(3) TEU.

50 Council Decision 2010/427/EU of 26 July 2010 establishing the organisation and functioning of the European External Action Service [2010] OJ L201/30 (EEAS Decision).

51 Ibid, arts 10–11. The HR has adopted the required rules by way of internal decisions (see e.g. Decision of the High Representative of the Union for Foreign Affairs and Security Policy of 19 April 2013 on the security rules for the European External Action Service [2013] OJ C190/1).

a delegation (subject to the agreement of the Commission and the Council). The HR is also responsible for concluding the necessary arrangements with the host State (Article 5(6)).

3.4 *Other Political Responsibilities of the HR*

3.4.1. Responsibilities regarding the CFSP Agencies

The Council has set up four EU entities within the framework of the CFSP (CFSP Agencies): the European Defence Agency,[52] the European Union Satellite Centre,[53] the European Union Institute for Security Studies,[54] and the European Security and Defence College (ESDC).[55]

Recital 7 of the EEAS Decision provides:

> The High Representative, or his/her representative, should exercise the responsibilities provided for by the respective acts founding the European Defence Agency, the European Union Satellite Centre, the European Institute for Security Studies, and the European Security and Defence College.

The initial legal acts establishing the CFSP Agencies (which predate the Treaty of Lisbon) provided for a number of responsibilities to be exercised by the (former) Secretary General/High Representative. As a consequence of the Treaty of Lisbon and in accordance with the above provision, these responsibilities are now incumbent on the HR. The Council has in the meantime adopted new decisions regarding the CFSP Agencies, based on their initial mandates, which consequently all provide for a number of responsibilities to be exercised by the HR. The main responsibilities of the HR are briefly described hereafter.

---

52 Council Decision 2011/411/CFSP of 12 July 2011 defining the statute, seat and operational rules of the European Defence Agency and repealing Joint Action 2004/551/CFSP [2011] OJ L 183/16.

53 Council Decision 2014/401/CFSP of 26 June 2014 on the European Union Satellite Centre and repealing Joint Action 2001/555/CFSP on the establishment of a European Union Satellite Centre [2014] OJ L188/73.

54 Council Decision 2014/75/CFSP of 10 February 2014 on the European Union Institute for Security Studies [2014] OJ L41/13.

55 Council Decision 2013/189/CFSP of 22 April 2013 establishing a European Security and Defence College (ESDC) and repealing Joint Action 2008/550/CFSP [2013] OJ L112/22. Strictly speaking the ESDC is not an 'agency' comparable to the three other entities, as it essentially consists of seconded staff embedded within EEAS structures, but is was nonetheless provided with the legal capacity necessary to perform its functions. It is therefore referred to as 'agency' for the purpose of this article.

The HR plays a leading role in the *European Defence Agency*'s structure and provides the essential link between the Agency and the Council (European Defence Agency's basic act, Recital 9).[56] As Head of the Agency the HR is responsible for the Agency's overall organisation and functioning and for ensuring that the guidelines issued by the Council and the decisions of the Agency's Steering Board are implemented by its Chief Executive (ibid, Article 7). The HR's other responsibilities include convening and chairing the Steering Board's meetings (ibid, Article 8) and appointing the staff of the Agency at senior management level (ibid, Article 11).

The HR provides operational direction to the *European Union Satellite Centre* and reports to the Political and Security Committee (PSC) and the Council (European Union Satellite Centre's basic act, Article 3).[57] The HR also chairs the Board of the Centre, either in person or through his/her representative, and reports to the Council on the work of the Board (ibid, Article 6).

The HR gives operational direction to the *European Union Institute for Security Studies* (European Union Institute for Security Studies' basic act, Article 3)[58] and chairs its Board, either in person or through his/her representative (ibid, Article 5).

The HR has the overall responsibility over the work of the European Security and Defence College (ESDC's basic act, Article 5(3))[59] and chairs its Steering Committee through a representative (ibid, Article 8).[60]

3.4.2 EU Crisis Management Operations

The decisions adopted by the Council setting up EU crisis management operations (military or civilian) all provide in the relevant Article on the 'chain of command' (for civilian missions) or on the 'political control and operational direction' that 'under the responsibility of the Council and the High Representative', the PSC shall exercise political control and strategic direction of the respective mission (consistent with Article 38 TEU). It is furthermore provided that the Civilian Operations Commander exercises his functions under the 'overall authority of the HR'.[61] This does not mean, however, that the HR is part

56 Council Decision (CFSP) 2015/1835 of 12 October 2015 defining the statute, seat and operational rules of the European Defence Agency (recast) [2015] OJ L266/55.

57 See supra n 53.

58 See supra n 54.

59 See supra n 55.

60 In addition, the EEAS provides significant support to the ESDC (see ibid, art 14).

61 See e.g. Council Joint Action 2008/124/CFSP of 4 February 2008 on the European Union Rule of Law Mission in Kosovo, EULEX KOSOVO [2008] OJ L42/92 (consolidated version), art 11(2); Council Decision (CFSP) 2015/778 of 18 May 2015 on a European Union military

of the operational chain of command. For civilian missions, the chain of command comprises the Civilian Operations Commander and the respective Head of Mission. For military operations, the chain of command comprises the EU Operation Commander,[62] who regularly reports to the EU Military Committee and the PSC, through the Chairman of the EU Military Committee as primary point of contact with the Operations Commander. For all CSDP missions, the PSC exercises the political control and strategic direction of the operation under the political responsibility of the Council and the HR, as well as a delegated decision-making power pursuant to Article 38(3) TEU for specific operational aspects of the respective mission.

This political supervisory role of the HR in respect of CSDP missions can be explained by his/her responsibilities in 'conducting' the CFSP, implementing Council decisions in the CFSP and by the HR's participation in the decision-making process, as Council decisions setting up EU crisis management operations are normally adopted on proposal by the HR, in accordance with Article 42(4) TEU.[63]

3.4.3 GNSS

Council Decision 2014/496/CFSP concerning the security aspects of the use of the European Global Navigation Satellite System (GNSS)[64] sets out the responsibilities to be exercised by the Council and the HR to avert a threat to the security of the Union or its Member States arising from the use of the GNSS. It provides in its Article 3 that the Council, acting on a proposal from the HR, may issue the necessary instructions to the Agency responsible for operating the system. Article 4(1) foresees the possibility, in situations of urgency requiring immediate action, that the HR may directly issue the necessary provisional instructions to the Agency. The Council must be immediately informed by the HR, and may confirm, modify or revoke the HR's provisional instructions (Article 4(2)).

---

operation in the Southern Central Mediterranean (EUNAVFOR MED) [2015] OJ L122/31, art 6(1).

62 Sometimes called Mission Commander (in cases where there is no Force Commander below the Operation Commander and where the Mission Commander exercises the functions normally exercised by the Operation and Force Commanders).

63 Even where the political initiative to undertake an operation comes from a Member State, formal proposals for legal acts have been presented by the HR.

64 Council Decision 2014/496/CFSP of 22 July 2014 on aspects of the deployment, operation and use of the European Global Navigation Satellite System affecting the security of the European Union and repealing Joint Action 2004/552/CFSP [2014] OJ L219/53.

3.4.4 Solidarity Clause

Article 222 of the TFEU (the 'solidarity clause') is one of the concrete expressions of the solidarity principle underlying the EU Treaties. Its general principle (obligation of Member States to assist each other in situations of a terrorist attack or a disaster) is also reflected in Article 42(7) TEU ('mutual assistance clause'). However, there are significant differences as regards the context and scope of application of these two provisions; in particular, Article 222 TFEU foresees specific implementation mechanisms at EU level, which also involve the HR both in terms of procedure and in operational terms, whereas Article 42(7) does not.

It may be noted that Article 222 is placed among the provisions of the TFEU concerning the EU's external action, even though some of the actions envisaged are targeted at assisting Member States in their territory (see Article 222(1)(a), third indent and (b)). This can easily be explained by the fact that terrorist attacks may obviously also have an external dimension; action by the EU to assist an affected Member State (e.g. with the objective to 'prevent the terrorist threat in the territory of the Member States' – Article 222(1)(a), first indent) may therefore also include external action instruments including CFSP/CSDP actions, where the HR would assume an institutional role.

Article 222(3) TFEU provides for the adoption by a Council decision of implementing arrangements, on a joint proposal from the High Representative and the Commission. Such implementing arrangements – which only apply to action by the Union under Article 222(1) TFEU – have been adopted on 24 June 2014.[65] They contain relatively detailed provisions concerning the objectives and scope of application of the clause, the relevant institutional actors (including the HR), definitions (notably of the term 'terrorist attack'), the procedure to be followed for the invocation of the clause and the possible elements of the EU response.

3.4.5. Relations with the UN and Other International Organisations

Article 220 TFEU provides:

> 1. The Union shall establish all appropriate forms of cooperation with the organs of the United Nations and its specialised agencies, the Council of

65 Council Decision 2014/415/EU of 24 June 2014 on the arrangements for the implementation by the Union of the solidarity clause [2014] OJ L 192/53. On the solidarity clause, see Steven Blockmans, 'L'Union fait la Force: Making the Most of the Solidarity Clause (Article 222 TFEU)' in Inge Govaere and Sara Poli (eds) *EU Management of Global Emergencies – Legal Frameworks for Combating Threats and Crises* (Brill Nijhoff 2014) 111.

> Europe, the Organisation for Security and Cooperation in Europe and the Organisation for Economic Cooperation and Development.
> The Union shall maintain such relations as are appropriate with other international organisations.
> 2. The High Representative of the Union for Foreign Affairs and Security Policy and the Commission shall implement this Article.

Article 220 TFEU takes over the provisions of ex-Articles 302, 303 and 304 TEC[66] and adds the Organisation for Security and Cooperation in Europe (OSCE) to the list of international organisations and entities that the EU can establish cooperation with. As compared with former Articles 302, 303 and 304 TEC, Article 220 TFEU stipulates that the High Representative and the Commission shall 'implement' this Article. Furthermore, while the previous version of this Article mandated the Commission to maintain relations with the United Nations (UN), Article 220 TFEU now refers to the Union.

On account of its wide scope (it covers not only the organisations listed, but potentially all other international organisations as well, see Article 220(1), second subparagraph), Article 220 TFEU must be considered as a provision of a general nature establishing the principle of the Union's relations with other international organisations, in line with the general objective of the Union to develop relations with international organisations as set out in Article 21(1) TEU. Its purpose is thus to lay down the general foundation for 'all appropriate forms of cooperation' with the UN and other international organisations.

The tasking to the HR and the Commission to 'implement' this Article cannot, on account of the general and programmatic nature of this Article, be taken to mean that the HR (or the Commission) could enter into agreements or arrangements on cooperation with a particular international organisation in a specific policy area on their own initiative without some form of approval by the Council (except for arrangements of a purely administrative or technical nature). The terms 'shall implement' would rather suggest that this provision should be interpreted in the sense that the Council must first decide on the principle of establishing relations between the EU and a particular international organisation before the HR (or the Commission) would enter into the necessary arrangements with the organisation concerned. This would also be consistent with the role of the Council as the policy-making organ

66 To note that arts 302, 303 and 304 were placed at that time in Part six ('General and Final Provisions') of the TEC.

of the EU.[67] If a formal international agreement is envisaged, the relevant substantive legal basis for its conclusion has to be determined according to the contents and purpose of the action to be undertaken and with regard to the relevant domain of EU competence, such as environment (Article 191(4) TFEU), development cooperation (Article 211 TFEU) or the CFSP (Article 37 TEU).[68] The substantive legal basis determines the procedure to be followed under Article 218 TFEU, notably the voting rule in the Council and the degree of participation of the European Parliament.

3.5 *Institutional Position of the HR: The Right of Initiative*

The HR and the Commission have a right of initiative in the domain of the EU's external action (the HR for the CFSP domain, the Commission for the non-CFSP domains), and pursuant to Article 22(2) TEU may also jointly submit 'proposals' to the Council. Article 22 being part of the general provisions of the TEU, the term 'proposal' should be given a wide interpretation, both as regards form and contents. It may thus be construed as covering any political initiative on any topic related to the EU's external action to the Council. In principle this provision also covers proposals in the stricter sense, ie proposals for legal acts; however, this possibility may already be foreseen in the specific legal basis allowing the Council to act (e.g. decision by the Council to establish a CSDP mission on the basis of Article 42(4) TEU, this provision expressly referring to a proposal from the HR – or from a Member State).

While Article 22(2) TEU foresees a joint right of initiative of the HR and the Commission, the HR also has a right of initiative of his/her own in the domain of the CFSP. This follows from Article 27(1) TEU in a general manner ('The High

67 Art 16(1) TEU. On the requirement of prior Council approval before the signature (by the Commission) of legally non-binding, political arrangements on behalf of the EU with third parties, see Case C- 660/13 *Council v Commission* EU:C:2016:616, paras 37–40, where the CJEU confirmed that such arrangements ('Memoranda of Understanding') cannot be concluded by the Commission alone on account of its powers of external representation under art 17 TEU, but that the conclusion of such arrangement on behalf of the EU represents a policy choice that must be made by the Council.

68 The only notable reference to art 220 TFEU in an agreement with an international organisation is to be found in the preambular paragraphs of the Memorandum of Cooperation between the EU and the International Civil Aviation Organization (ICAO). The Council decision approving its signature was however based on art 110(2) TFEU, in conjunction with art 218(5) TFEU (Council Decision 2011/530/EU of 31 March 2011 on the signing, on behalf of the Union, and provisional application of a Memorandum of Cooperation between the European Union and the International Civil Aviation Organization providing a framework for enhanced cooperation [2011] OJ L232/1).

Representative (…) shall contribute through his proposals to the development of the common foreign and security policy (…)'), and is laid down specifically in relation to the Council in Article 30(1) TEU ('[T]he High Representative (…) may refer any question relating to the common foreign and security policy to the Council and may submit to it (…) proposals'). It should be underlined that this right of initiative of the HR in the CFSP is not exclusive: in accordance with that provision, any Member State may also submit initiatives to the Council.[69]

Besides Article 30(1) TEU, some specific legal bases in the CFSP expressly provide that the Council acts upon a proposal from the HR (Article 33 TEU – appointment of EU Special Representatives)[70] or from the HR or a Member State (e.g. Article 42(4) TEU). It is noteworthy that even in the absence of any reference to a proposal by the HR in the legal basis, in practice the Council normally acts on a proposal from the HR, e.g. on the basis of Article 29 TEU when adopting decisions imposing restrictive measures.

As regards international agreements of the EU relating to the CFSP (e.g. status of forces or status of mission agreements for CSDP missions), the HR also has the right to submit recommendations to the Council regarding the opening of negotiations, pursuant to Article 218(3) TFEU; as a consequence, the Council authorises the HR to negotiate such agreements. Subsequently, it will be for the HR to submit a proposal for the signature and conclusion of the agreement to the Council (Article 218(6) TFEU).

In some cases, notably in the area of restrictive measures (sanctions), the Treaties expressly provide for joint proposals from the HR and the Commission (see Article 215 TFEU).[71] This is also the case for the implementing arrangements adopted by the Council for the solidarity clause (Article 222(3) TFEU).

---

69 Art 30(1) refers to 'initiatives or proposals'; the term 'respectively' appears to indicate that the Member States submit initiatives whereas the HR submits proposals; in practice, there should be no difference between the two. This provision also provides that HR proposals may be submitted 'with the Commission's support'; the practical implication of this possibility remains unclear.

70 This is one of the cases of an exclusive (ie not shared with the Member States or the Commission) right of initiative of the HR; see also art art 41(3), subpara 3, TEU.

71 See in this context case C-130/10 *European Parliament v Council* EU:C:2012:472, paras 104–105.

4 The European External Action Service

4.1 *Legal Basis*

The EEAS was created by a Council Decision adopted on 26 July 2010 on the basis of Article 27(3) TEU (EEAS Decision)[72] and officially started functioning on 1 January 2011. This decision also sets out the basic mandate of the EEAS to support the HR in the fulfilment of his/her mandate and the initial 'tripartite' composition of its staff, made up at the beginning from former Council and Commission officials, as well as diplomats from the Member States.[73]

The EEAS Decision defines its status, mains tasks and its organisational structure.

4.2 *Legal and Institutional Nature*

The EEAS Decision defines the EEAS as 'a functionally autonomous body of the European Union, separate from the General Secretariat of the Council and from the Commission', and endowed with 'the legal capacity necessary to perform its tasks and attain its objectives' (Article 1(2)).

4.3 *Tasks of the EEAS*

Article 2(1) of the EEAS Decision describes the main tasks of the EEAS:

- to support the HR in fulfilling his/her mandates in the framework of the CFSP (first indent); in practice, this involves for example the drafting of proposals for Council decisions;
- to support the HR in his/her capacity as President of the Foreign Affairs Council (second indent);
- to support the HR in his/her capacity as VP of the Commission (third indent).

Article 2(2) further provides that the EEAS also assists the President of the European Council, the President of the European Commission and the Commission in the exercise of their functions in the area of external relations. Article 3(4) also provides that the EEAS shall extend 'appropriate support and

---

72 Council Decision 2010/427/EU of 26 July 2010 establishing the organisation and functioning of the European External Action Service [2010] OJ L201/30.

73 On the EEAS and the EEAS Decision, see Steven Blockmans and Christophe Hillion (eds), *EEAS 2.0: A Legal Commentary on Council Decision 2010/427/EU Establishing the Organisation and Functioning of the European External Action Service* (Center for European Policy Studies 2013) <https://www.ceps.eu/publications/eeas-20-legal-commentary-council-decision-2010427eu-establishing-organisation-and>.

cooperation' to the other institutions and bodies of the Union, in particular the European Parliament.

Besides these core tasks, the Council Decision provides that one important role of the EEAS is to contribute to the programming of external assistance instruments (Article 9).

4.4 *Organisation and Structure*

The EEAS at Headquarters is organised in a 'central administration' composed of thematic and geographical departments, as well as departments for administration and budget and horizontal issues such as interinstitutional relations and legal affairs.[74]

An important part of the EEAS, in particular for the purposes of the external representation of the EU, are EU delegations in third countries and at international organisations (totalling around 140), which form and integral part of the EEAS[75] and are under the direct authority of the HR (see also above 2.3.4.).[76]

5 The Practice: Some Institutional and Legal Issues

5.1 *The EEAS: Its Position between the Council and the Commission*

The status and position of the EEAS vis-à-vis the other institutions, in particular the Commission and the Council, remain legally and institutionally somewhat unclear.[77]

First of all, the EEAS is not an 'institution' as it is not listed among the EU's institutions in Article 13 TEU.[78] Rather, the EEAS Decision qualifies the EEAS as a 'functionally autonomous body of the Union'.[79]

---

74 EEAS Decision, art 4.

75 Ibid, art 1(4).

76 Art 221(2) TFEU; EEAS Decision, arts 1(3) and 5(2).

77 On the legal status and capacity of the EEAS, see Bart van Vooren, 'A Legal-Institutional Perspective on the European External Action Service' (2011) 48 CML Rev 475.

78 It may however be noted that the EEAS is qualified as an institution for the purposes of the EU Staff Regulations (art 1b(a) of the Staff Regulations (latest version: Regulation (EU, Euratom) 1023/2013 of the European Parliament and of the Council of 22 October 2013 amending the Staff Regulations of Officials of the European Union and the Conditions of Employment of Other Servants of the European Union [2013] OJ L287/15)) as well as the EU Financial Regulation (Regulation (EU, Euratom) 966/2012 of the European Parliament and the Council of 25 October 2012 on the financial rules applicable to the general budget of the Union and repealing Council Regulation (EC, Euratom) 1605/2002 [2012] OJ L298/1, art 2(b)).

79 EEAS Decision, art 1(2).

The terms 'functionally autonomous body' are by themselves somewhat ambiguous. Paradoxically, this ambiguity is reinforced by the indication that the EEAS is 'separate from the General Secretariat of the Council and from the Commission', which gives the impression that absent this indication, the EEAS might otherwise in fact exercise tasks belonging to the Council Secretariat or the Commission. Indeed, if the EEAS is 'functionally autonomous', it seems redundant to add that it is 'separate' from the General Secretariat of the Council (GSC) and the Commission.[80]

The ambiguity is also reinforced by Article 2(1), second and third indent, respectively, of the EEAS Decision, which provide that the EEAS' role in supporting the HR as chair of the FAC and as VP of the Commission is 'without prejudice to the normal tasks of the General Secretariat of the Council' and 'without prejudice to the normal tasks of the Commission services'. This wording also seems to suggest that there might be some overlap between the tasks of the EEAS, the GSC and the Commission services (What are their 'normal' tasks? Is the EEAS fulfilling 'special' tasks in this respect?).[81]

From a legal and institutional perspective, it is however clear that the EEAS exercises functions that are different from those of the GSC and the Commission services.

The fact that the HR chairs the FAC and that representatives of the EEAS chair certain preparatory bodies of the Council in the field of external relations[82] does not affect GSC functions. The Council Secretariat assists the Council and the Presidency of the Council in their tasks (Article 23 of the Council's Rules of Procedure).[83] The same applies to the Council configuration and preparatory bodies chaired respectively by the HR and representatives of the HR who are staff of the EEAS. The role of the EEAS is not to assist the Council, but to assist the HR in his/her capacity as chair of the FAC, ie to assist the HR in formulating initiatives and proposals in the CFSP, including by chairing the relevant preparatory bodies of the Council, in particular the PSC. The role of the EEAS representative in the relevant Council Working Party must therefore

80 It also seems odd to place the GSC on the same plane as the Commission (rather than its services).

81 On this aspect, see Blockmans and Hillion (n 73) 17–19.

82 European Council Decision 2009/881/EU of 1 December 2009 on the exercise of the Presidency of the Council [2009] OJ L315/50, arts 2 and 4; Council Decision 2009/908/EU of 1 December 2009 laying down measures for the implementation of the European Council Decision on the exercise of the Presidency of the Council, and on the chairmanship of preparatory bodies of the Council [2009] OJ L322/28, art 2 and annex II.

83 Annexed to Council Decision 2009/937/EU of 1 December 2009 adopting the Council's Rules of Procedure ([2009] OJ L325/35 (as amended)).

be distinguished from the role of the EEAS staff member appointed as permanent chair of the same Working Party. The task of the former is to present the EEAS position as required (e.g. to defend a proposal for a Council decision of the HR). The role of the chair (even if also coming from the EEAS) is to conduct the deliberations of the Working Party and to achieve agreement on a given proposal under consideration with a view to its adoption by the Council. In practice, these roles are not always easy to distinguish, as both representatives normally belong to the same EEAS department.

Likewise, the fact that the EEAS supports the HR in his/her capacity of VP of the Commission does not transform the EEAS into a Directorate General (DG) of the Commission. In other words, the 'double-hatting' of the HR, being also one of the VPs of the Commission, is limited to the HR in person and does not mean that the EEAS itself is also 'double-hatted' as Commission Directorate General.[84] If that was a consequence of the 'VP hat' of the HR, then the EEAS should also be considered as being part of the General Secretariat of the Council, in order to support the HR in her capacity of chair of the FAC. This would obviously run counter to the whole concept of the EEAS as an autonomous entity.

It should also be noted in this context that Article 18(4) TEU provides that the HR is bound by Commission procedures only when he/she exercises the responsibilities incumbent on him/her as VP within the Commission, and only to the extent that this does not conflict with his/her roles as HR and chair of the FAC. This is a further indication that the EEAS cannot be considered as a Directorate General of the Commission, even when acting in support of the HR in his/her capacity of VP of the Commission.[85]

A further element of ambiguity lies in Article 2(2) of the EEAS Decision, which provides that the EEAS shall assist the President of the European Council, the President of the Commission, and the Commission in the exercise of their functions in the domain of external relations. The EEAS Decision thus endows the EEAS with 'autonomy' on the one hand, but on the other hand tasks the latter with 'assisting' the above-mentioned actors, which could be interpreted as creating a hierarchical link between them and the EEAS. As regards

84 Under the Rules of Procedure of the Commission, the Commission establishes Directorates-General and equivalent departments to *assist* it (the Commission) in the preparation and performance of its tasks ((C(2000) 3614) [2000] OJ L308/26 (consolidated version), art 21). The EEAS, however, was established by a Council decision pursuant to Article 27(3) TEU in order to assist the HR in the fulfilment of her mandate.

85 In practice, however, when Commission services initiate an inter-service consultation, the EEAS is listed as if it was a DG of the Commission.

the Commission, the question may also be raised in this regard to what extent the 'assistance' by the EEAS is not already covered by Article 2(1), third indent of the EEAS Decision (support of the HR in his/her capacity as VP).

Finally, it may be noted that the EEAS Decision provides that the EEAS has the necessary legal capacity, but is silent on the question of who can act as its legal representative. It can be derived from Article 4(1) of the EEAS Decision that the legal representation of the EEAS should be ensured by the Executive Secretary-General. This may be relevant notably for any judicial proceedings before local jurisdictions where the EEAS may be involved, or for official contacts with local authorities.

5.2 *The Three 'Hats' of the HR – The 'HR/VP' Acronym*

From a legal and institutional point of view, the systematic use of the 'HR/VP' acronym (standing for 'High Representative/Vice-President') in the practice of the EEAS and relevant Commission services (it is also systematically used by the European Parliament, even inverted as 'VP/HR') creates some confusion and renders a clear demarcation between their respective roles and those of the EEAS and Commission services unnecessarily difficult.

The Treaty of Lisbon has not created a 'double-hatted' 'HR/VP' function, but only one new single function in the field of the EU's CFSP, namely that of 'High Representative of the Union for Foreign and Security Policy', for which the acronym 'HR' is appropriate.[86] The function of Vice-President and member of the Commission existed before and is not new. Likewise, the role of President of the Council existed before. The specificity of the new role of the HR is that the latter, besides having the specific mandate to conduct the CFSP and to represent the EU externally in this domain, also exercises two other functions, namely that of presiding over the Foreign Affairs Council, and that of being 'one of the Vice-Presidents of the Commission', responsible for external relations and the coordination of the other aspects of the EU's external action.

Accordingly, the EEAS Decision provides that 'This Decision and, in particular, the reference to the term "High Representative", will be interpreted in accordance with his/her different functions under Article 18 TEU'. (Recital 1, last sentence).

The 'HR/VP' acronym thus creates the impression that the HR is only and principally 'double-hatted', whereas the HR has three main functions under the TEU, besides several other specific responsibilities in the domain of the CFSP.

---

86 In comparison, the TEU in its pre-Lisbon version provided for the function of 'Secretary-General of the Council, High Representative for the common foreign and security policy' (ex-art 26 TEU), for which the acronym 'SG/HR' was therefore appropriate.

If at all, the correct acronym should be 'HR/PRESFAC/VP', in the order of the HR's functions as described in Article 18 TEU.

It further suggests that the HR and the VP operate on the same institutional level. This is not the case under the Treaties. The HR has to be considered as being on the same institutional level as the Commission as a whole. The HR has the power to submit proposals for legal acts in the CFSP to the Council, to the same extent that the Commission may submit legislative proposals to the Council in other domains. In some cases (e.g. adoption of sanctions regulations) the Treaties foresee joint HR/Commission proposals. A VP of the Commission, by contrast, does not have any such power. As a member of the Commission, the HR as VP participates in the Commission's decision-making process on the same footing as the other Commissioners, notwithstanding the fact that the HR has the additional responsibility as VP to coordinate the EU's external action. Finally, while the President of the European Commission is part of the European Council, the HR also participates in its work in his/her own right.[87]

Finally, it seems to imply that the HR, as a general rule, always acts with his/her 'double-hat' on, which does not correspond to institutional and legal reality. It thereby also makes his/her autonomous role as HR, in charge of conducting the CFSP, contributing to its development, ensuring implementation of the Council's decisions in this area of competence, and representing the Union (Articles 18(2), 27(1) and (2) TEU), less visible. Conversely, it also makes the identification of his/her role as VP and his/her responsibility of 'coordinating the other aspects of the Union's external action' (Article 18(4) TEU) more difficult.

5.3 *Negotiation of International Agreements by the EEAS*

The Treaties provide for the possibility for the EU to negotiate comprehensive international agreements with third countries,[88] whether called framework, partnership and cooperation, cooperation or association agreements, or otherwise. They are legally binding and negotiated and concluded pursuant to the procedure foreseen in Article 218 TFEU. Such agreements usually cover a wide range of issues, encompassing both non-CFSP and CFSP matters.

Under Article 218(3) TFEU, the Commission and/or the High Representative recommend(s) to the Council to authorise the negotiations. Depending on the subject-matter of the agreement, the Council nominates the Union negotiator or the head of the Union's negotiating team. It follows from Article 218(3)

87 Art 15(2) TEU.

88 Arts 216(1) and 217 TFEU.

TFEU that only the Commission and/or the HR can in principle be nominated as negotiators.[89]

According to its Rules of Procedure, and for reasons of consistency in view of this kind of negotiation, the Commission can take the decision to empower its Vice-President responsible for external relations and for coordinating other aspects of the Union's external action (ie the HR, in accordance with Article 18(4) TEU) to negotiate, on behalf of the Commission, non-CFSP subject-matters falling under Union competences. In practice, this is one of the situations where the EEAS truly acts in support of the HR in both his/her capacities: for the purpose of the negotiation, the EEAS acts on behalf of the HR for the CFSP part of these agreements, and on behalf of the Commission for the non-CFSP parts (on account of the responsibility of the HR as VP of the Commission). Practical arrangements to this effect have been agreed between the EEAS and the competent Commission services.

A difficulty however arises for the EEAS when following the negotiations such agreements reach the competent Council Working Parties at the stage of the proposals for signature, provisional application and conclusion.

The Commission has given itself the political directive that it should endeavour to negotiate comprehensive agreements as 'EU-only' agreements. The negotiating directives normally state that the legal nature of these agreements, EU-only or mixed (EU and Member States), will be determined at the end of negotiations on the basis of an analysis of the precise scope of the provisions contained therein. In line with the instructions from the Commission, the agreements are normally negotiated by the EEAS on the assumption that they would be initialed and signed, or at least proposed for signature, as 'EU only', ie not as mixed agreements.

This approach has run into resistance from both Member States and the third parties concerned.

Member States perceive EU only agreements as an encroachment upon their prerogatives in the areas of CFSP, with regard to non-exercised shared and parallel competences as well as with regard to the external representation of the EU (lack of visibility and of control over the running of the joint bodies established under these agreements). Except for those cases where EU only

89 This can be seen as an emanation of the responsibilities of the Commission and the HR in the external representation of the EU (art 17(1) and 27(2) TEU). In certain cases, the HR or the Commission may be prevented from exercising their functions as EU negotiators due to the specificities of the negotiating framework. In such cases, the Council may decide to empower the Member States to negotiate in the interest of the EU. One example of such a situation was the negotiation leading to the signature of the Arms Trade Treaty.

agreements are used as a political go-between (e.g. Kosovo due to the non-recognition policy of some Member States),[90] Member States are not yet ready to accept EU only agreements on matters other than those falling under EU exclusive competence.[91]

Against this backdrop, the EEAS may find itself in a delicate position, being faced with the dilemma of reconciling instructions from the Commission services to exclusively negotiate EU only agreements with the standpoint of the Member States in the competent Council Working Parties, as well as the position of the third party concerned. This dilemma is in particular affecting the EEAS chairs of the competent Council Working Parties, where they act on behalf of the HR in his/her capacity as president of the FAC.

5.4 *Joint HR/Commission Recommendations for Negotiating Mandates*

One institutional question that has arisen in the context of the negotiation of international agreements, at the stage of submitting a recommendation to the Council for an authorisation to start negotiations in accordance with Article 218(3) TFEU, is whether this provision allows the HR and the Commission to submit joint recommendations to the Council in cases where the envisaged agreement would cover both a CFSP and a non-CFSP part.

It is argued by Commission services in that regard that Article 218(3) TFEU envisages a single negotiator and that two negotiators would be against the principle of 'unity of the negotiator' which is at the heart of Article 218(3) TFEU, and that negotiations for framework agreements should therefore be based on a Commission recommendation, while the HR could be part of the negotiating team led by the Commission, but that the HR cannot be authorised by the Council to open negotiations and negotiate alongside the Commission.

While Article 218(3) TFEU is not explicit on the question of a joint recommendation by the HR and the Commission, a reading of this provision in the context of other Treaty provisions and taking into account the respective prerogatives of the HR and the Commission does not support this view.

If Article 218(3) TFEU required a single negotiator in cases of agreements covering both CFSP and non-CFSP matters, the Commission and the HR would

90 The Stabilisation and Association Agreement between the EU and Kosovo has been signed on 27 October 2015 and was concluded by Council Decision (EU) 2016/342 of 12 February 2016 on the conclusion, on behalf of the Union, of the Stabilisation and Association Agreement between the European Union and the European Atomic Energy Community, of the one part, and Kosovo, of the other part [2016] OJ L71/1. It entered into force on 1 April 2016.

91 See also the chapter by Frederik Naert in this book.

in theory be authorised to exercise powers in a field in which the Treaties prevented them from doing so – ie the HR exercising powers in non-CFSP and the Commission exercising powers in CFSP matters. Supposing that the Treaties established the principle of 'unity of the negotiator', such 'unity' should not necessarily translate into a single negotiator. 'Unity' can actually be ensured by appointing the head of the negotiating team, as provided by Article 218(3) TFEU.

According to Article 218(3) TFEU, either a 'Union negotiator' or a 'negotiating team' could conduct the negotiations. The latter possibility implies at least two team members empowered with genuine negotiating authority. The term 'negotiating team' can only be understood as including the Commission and the HR 'depending on the subject matter of the agreement envisaged'. This reading is in line with the spirit of this Article as well as with the distribution of powers between the Commission and the HR. Another reading would actually lead to the conclusion that the term would refer to the administrative organisation of negotiations by services (ie the officials participating in negotiations). In practice this would translate into a situation whereby the Commission would always be the head of the negotiating team for itself – which is at odds with the language and spirit of this Article.

Article 218(3) TFEU uses the conjunction 'or' when referring to the initiators of the recommendation ('The Commission, or the High Representative of the Union for Foreign Affairs and Security Policy (…) shall submit (…)'). However, the conjunction 'or' should not be interpreted as meaning that only one actor or another can make the recommendation. In the context of Article 218(3) TFEU the conjunction 'or' cannot be read in a disjunctive way, but must be attributed an alternative and cumulative sense.[92] Therefore the literal interpretation of Article 218(3) TFEU cannot exclude the possibility of joint recommendations. The fact that Article 22(2) TEU foresees joint proposals by the HR and the Commission further supports this interpretation (see also above Part 3.5).

92 Cf Case C-304/02 *Commission v France* EU:C:2005:444, para 83: 'This interpretation cannot be countered by reference to the use in Article 228(2) EC of the conjunction "or" to link the financial penalties capable of being imposed. As the Commission and the Danish, Netherlands, Finnish and United Kingdom Governments have submitted, that conjunction may, linguistically, have an alternative or a cumulative sense and must therefore be read in the context in which it is used. In light of the objective pursued by Article 228 EC, the conjunction "or" in Article 228(2) EC must be understood as being used in a cumulative sense'.

5.5 *The High Representative as Chair of Joint Bodies under Agreements between the EU and Third States*

Another issue that has remained disputed between the concerned institutional actors has arisen in the context of joint bodies established under agreements between the EU (and it Member States) and third States, e.g. Association Councils bringing together representatives of the parties at Ministerial level and having decision-making powers. On the EU side, the question has arisen in the context of the elaboration and adoption of the Rules of Procedure of such joint bodies, who could replace the HR as chair of such meetings in case he/she should not be able to attend. As the TEU does not provide for a 'deputy HR', this issue is directly linked to the different functions to be exercised by the HR pursuant to Articles 18 and 27 TEU and their respective scopes.

It has been suggested by members of the Council that in the absence of the HR, the latter should be replaced by the member of the Council holding the Council Presidency, by analogy to the Council's Rules of Procedure,[93] taking into account the fact that Association Councils have decision-making powers and can therefore be compared to the Council as the policy-making body of the EU. Following that view, the rules applicable to the replacement of the HR as chair of the FAC should apply.

Other actors, including the EEAS, have taken the position that chairing an Association Council also constitutes an exercise of external representation of the EU, and that the Association Council also constitutes a forum for the political dialogue with the third country concerned. As a consequence, the HR should have the possibility to also be replaced, as appropriate, by a member of the Commission, on account of the fact that the he/she is also a VP of the Commission and that the Commission is also responsible – together with the HR – for the external representation of the EU. This should however as a consequence only apply to the extent that non-CFSP matters are discussed in the Association Council.

The practice of the Council has not been entirely consistent: on two occasions, the Council approved draft Rules of Procedure for adoption by joint bodies providing that they would, on the EU side, be chaired by the 'High Representative' without further specification, thus leaving some flexibility on the question of the HR's replacement.[94] In other cases, it was specified that they

93 Annexed to Council Decision 2009/937/EU of 1 December 2009 adopting the Council's Rules of Procedure ([2009] OJ L325/35 (as amended)), art. 2(5), subpara 2.

94 The chair of the Association Council EU-Central America was assigned to the HR (Decision 1/2014 of the EU-Central America Association Council of 7 November 2014 adopting

would be chaired by the 'High Representative in his or her capacity as President of the Foreign Affairs Council', thereby implying that the HR could only be replaced by the member of the Council holding the Presidency.[95]

5.6. *The Responsibilities of the HR and the Role of the Commission in the CFSP*

As indicated above (Part 3.4.), the HR has an autonomous right of initiative in the CFSP, including the right to submit formal proposals for Council decisions in that domain. Following the entry into force of the Treaty of Lisbon, the Commission no longer has any formal role in the CFSP, whereas the latter was, prior to the Treaty of Lisbon, 'fully associated' with the external representation tasks assumed by the Presidency and, more generally, 'with the work carried out in the common foreign and security policy field'.[96] Moreover, the Commission had a right of initiative in the CFSP, together with the Member States.[97]

The Commission, pursuant to Article 317 TFEU, however remains responsible for the implementation of the EU's budget, including the CFSP budget. Article 9(6) of the EEAS Decision provides in this regard, somewhat ambiguously, that actions undertaken under the CFSP budget 'shall be under the responsibility of the HR/EEAS', but that the Commission remains responsible for their financial implementation 'under the authority of the High Representative in his/her capacity as Vice-President of the Commission'. It further specifies that the 'Commission department responsible for this implementation shall be co-located with the EEAS'.[98]

---

its Rules of Procedure and those of the Association Committee [2015/1215] OJ L196/28, annex A, art 2); to note as well that in the case of the EU-Indonesia Joint Committee established by the Partnership and Cooperation Agreement, the chairing was also assigned to the HR, without any qualifications (art 1(3) of the Rules of Procedure annexed to Council Decision (EU) 2016/1170 [2016] OJ L193/32).

95 See the relevant Council and Commission Decisions regarding the EU-Georgia (Decision (EU, Euratom) 2015/55 [2015] OJ L9/31) and EU-Moldova (Decision (EU, Euratom) 2015/55 [2015] OJ L9/46) Association Councils; in the case of the EU-Iraq Cooperation Council, the Rules of Procedure provide that on the EU side the chair is the President of the Foreign Affairs Council of the European Union, without any reference to the HR (Decision 1/2013 of the EU-Iraq Cooperation Council of 8 October 2013 adopting its rules of procedure and those of the Cooperation Committee [2013] OJ L352/68, annex I, art 1).

96 Ex-arts 18(4) and 27 TEU.

97 Ex-art 22(1) TEU. The Commission never made use of this prerogative in practice.

98 In practice, this task is assumed by the so-called 'Foreign Policy Instruments Service' (FPI) of the Commission.

The above provisions illustrate that the combination of these two functions in one single person can have an added value: on the basis of the exercise of the HR's right of initiative in the CFSP, it brings together the latter's responsibility 'to ensure the implementation of the decisions adopted by the Council'[99] with the financial responsibility of the Commission, in particular as they provide the HR with the power to ensure the financial implementation of Council decisions in the CFSP by the relevant Commission service, being placed under his/her authority acting as VP on behalf of the Commission.

In practice, however, the effective application of these provisions, which certainly reflect the 'spirit' of the 'HR/VP double hat' as probably intended by the drafters of the Treaty of Lisbon, has encountered some difficulties: a number of CFSP initiatives prepared by EEAS services on behalf of the HR (notably relating to CSDP missions), which could have led to formal proposals for Council decisions in the CFSP, have run into resistance by competent Commission services following informal consultations and have not been pursued further.[100] It is interesting to note that the 'double-hatted' nature of the HR's functions ('HR/VP'), as well as the Commission's responsibility to implement the (CFSP) budget, have been used as arguments to suggest that initiatives of the HR in the CFSP should receive prior Commission approval before being submitted to the Council. This would however run counter to the prerogatives of the HR under the TEU, and be contrary to the principle of institutional balance set out in Article 13(2) TEU.[101] While it is obviously a matter of political choice on the part of the HR to use his/her right of initiative or not, its exercise cannot be subject to any formal scrutiny on the part of the Commission. The abovementioned provisions provide the HR with the necessary powers to ensure the implementation of any decision adopted by the Council in the CFSP (normally on proposal of the HR), including on the financial aspects.

It may be noted in this context that Article 30(1) TEU provides that the HR may also submit proposals to the Council 'with the Commission's support'. This provision, which has not been used in practice until now, could perhaps provide a basis to allow the Commission to formally associate itself with a

99 Art 27(1) TEU.

100 It should be noted in this context that to date no formal consultation procedures have been put in place which would allow the EEAS to consult relevant Commission services on draft HR proposals in the CFSP, unlike the inter-service consultations regularly launched by Commission services on non-CFSP initiatives, to which the EEAS is formally associated.

101 It is to be recalled in this context that according to Article 18(4) TEU the HR is only subject to Commission procedures as far as her role as VP is concerned.

proposal by the HR, without calling into question the latter's autonomous right of initiative as such.

6 Conclusion

Seven years after the entry into force of the Treaty of Lisbon, the function and role of the High Representative, despite the support provided by the European External Action Service, remains a difficult one. As one of the legal crafters of the Treaty of Lisbon remarked at the time, 'the "triple hat" of the High Representative means that his/her tasks are very heavy, while he/she has to travel a lot and also exercise his/her mandates both as member of the Commission (weekly meetings) and as President of the Foreign Affairs Council (monthly meetings). The Treaty does not provide for deputies having the same extraordinary "triple-hatted" responsibilities'.[102] Other commentators were even more sceptical: 'mission impossible'.[103]

Taking into account the many other, often overlooked responsibilities of the HR besides his/her three main 'hats', one may indeed wonder whether the authors of the Treaty of Lisbon were not too ambitious or unrealistic in assuming that one single person, even assisted by an autonomous service, would manage to fulfil all of them in an efficient manner and be able to ensure unity and continuity of the EU's external action and representation. Even if only looking at the three main functions of the HR, the potential risk always is that one of the functions is given more weight to the detriment of others.

This being said, the roles of the HR and of the EEAS, being the first 'diplomatic service' of the EU, nonetheless continue to be a central one in the EU's external action. Under the HR's impetus the European Union has undoubtedly continued to make its mark on the international scene, be it by having successfully obtained an enhanced observer status at the UN General Assembly following the entry into force of the Treaty of Lisbon,[104] by conducting international civilian and military crisis management operations (in several cases in close cooperation with the UN) under the HR's political responsibility, by the prominent role played by the HR in the facilitation of the on-going dialogue between Kosovo and Serbia, and by the arduous negotiations coordinated by

102 Piris (n 34) 248–249.

103 Steven Blockmans and Marja-Liisa Laatsit, 'The European External Action Service: Enhancing Coherence in EU External Action?' in Cardwell (ed) (n 6) 140.

104 UN General Assembly Res 65/276 (3 May 2011) UN doc A/RES/65/276.

the HR on behalf of the EU that led to the successful agreement on the 'Joint Comprehensive Plan of Action' (JCPOA) between the so-called 'E3/EU + 3' (USA, Russia, China, France, the United Kingdom, Germany and the High Representative of the EU) and Iran, in Vienna on 14 July 2015.[105]

105 The JCPOA has been endorsed by the UN Security Council and is annexed to UNSC Res 2231 (20 July 2015) UN doc S/RES/2231.

CHAPTER 2

The Two-way Flexibility Clause in Article 48(2) TEU and Declaration 18 of the Intergovernmental Conference

*Gilles Marhic**

1 Introduction

Article 48(2) TEU provides that:

> The Government of any Member State, the European Parliament or the Commission may submit to the Council proposals for the amendment of the Treaties. These proposals may, *inter alia*, serve either *to increase or to reduce* the competences conferred on the Union in the Treaties. These proposals shall be submitted to the European Council by the Council and the national Parliaments shall be notified.[1]

This provision is mirrored in paragraph 3 of Declaration 18 annexed to the Final Act of the Intergovernmental Conference (IGC) which adopted the Treaty of Lisbon (Declaration 18).[2]

At first sight, the 'increase or reduce' aspect in those provisions does not seem to deserve particular attention, since it merely reflects the well-known rule under public international law that 'A treaty may be amended by agreement between the parties', as provided for in Article 39 of the Vienna Convention on the Law of Treaties of 23 May 1969, leaving open the possibility for the concerned parties to agree on a broad array of different amendments, which could have the effect either to increase or reduce the scope of the said treaty.[3]

---

* The views expressed are personal to the author. Many thanks to Mr Moritz Thorner and to Ms Hanna Brux for their kind support.

1 Emphasis added.

2 [2008] OJ C115/335.

3 See e.g. Jean-Claude Piris, *The Lisbon Treaty: A Legal and Political Analysis* (Cambridge University Press, 2010) 83: 'Declaration 18 shows the degree of distrust (or misunderstanding) of the political authorities of one or several Member State(s) regarding the EU legal system as it had been established in the 1950s and as it has been working since then. From a legal point of view, these texts only confirm or clarify the pre-existing situation. They do not bring anything which would be legally new. The EU institutions have always had the power to amend or

 | DOI 10.1163/9789004347175_003

It is however interesting to see how the political circumstances[4] surrounding the adoption of the Treaty of Lisbon, and the recent discussions about the integrating nature of the EU, notably when it comes to provisions in the TEU on 'an ever closer union among the peoples of Europe', have put this language into the light, and to see how those discussions also relate to the *acquis* of the EU.

2 Two-way Flexibility and Primacy of EU Law

No provision containing an 'increase or reduce' language had been introduced, or even proposed during the negotiation of the Constitutional Treaty.[5] The so-called two-way flexibility clause, as it appears in Article 48(2) of the TEU and in Declaration 18, was proposed by the Czech Republic during the Intergovernmental Conference of 2007 which led to the adoption of the Lisbon Treaty.[6]

The Czech Republic had even tried to introduce a more compulsory language in paragraph 2 of Declaration 18, which eventually provided that with regard to possible Council requests to the Commission to submit proposals for repealing a legislative act, 'The Conference welcomes that the Commission declares that it shall devote particular attention to these requests'. Reportedly, the Czech Republic asked to transform this language into an obligation, in cases where a qualified majority or unanimity in favor of the proposal would exist.[7]

---

repeal an act they had previously adopted. The possibility has always been available to Member States to amend the Treaties in order to reduce the competences they conferred upon the Union'.

4 Ibid 84: 'the fact that these legal possibilities are now expressly included in EU texts has a political significance not to be underestimated. This was probably the purpose aimed at'.

5 Art IV-443(1) of the Treaty establishing a Constitution for Europe ([2004] OJ C310/1) provides for an ordinary revision procedure. It contains no sentence specifying that proposals for amendment may inter alia serve either to increase or to reduce the competences conferred on the Union in this Treaty.

6 See David Phinnemore, *The Treaty of Lisbon – Origins and Negotiation* (Palgrave Macmillan 2013) 250, n 10: 'There were indications that the Czech Republic was also seeking formal clarification on the delimitation of EU competences and formal confirmation that legislation might be repealed at the request of a member state and that treaty revision could be used to reduce the competences conferred on the EU. The Czech position was often stated late and generally lacked clarity. In part this was due, according to one leading IGC participant, to a lack of coordination domestically'.

7 See Robert Zbiral, 'Restoring Tasks from the European Union to Member States: A Bumpy Road to an Unclear Destination?' (2015) 52 CML Rev 51, 81: 'This was in fact demanded by the Czech delegation at the Lisbon Intergovernmental Conference as part of a two-way flexibility concept. Ultimately, the proposal was rejected due to the opposition from the Commission's Legal Service'.

Many commentaries of the Lisbon Treaty, relating to the circumstances of its negotiation and eventual adoption, highlight the fact that the 'increase or reduce' language in Article 48(2) of the TEU and Declaration 18 constituted one element amongst others demonstrating how keen some of the EU Member States were at that time to set clear limits to the competences of the EU,[8] and to avoid a creeping effect of the jurisprudence of the Court of Justice of the European Union (CJEU) on the scope of those competences.[9]

Of interest in this regard is the fact that during the negotiation of the Treaty of Lisbon, some Member States did not agree to incorporate in the Treaties (for the first time) a provision on the primacy of the EU Treaties and law over the law of the Member States. While Article I-6 of the Treaty establishing a Constitution for Europe stated that 'The Constitution and law adopted by the institutions of the Union in exercising competences conferred on it shall have primacy over the law of the Member States', no such provision can be found in the TEU. Only Declaration 17 annexed to the Final Act of the IGC contains language to this effect.[10]

---

8 See e.g. Loïc Azoulai (ed), *The Question of Competence in the European Union* (Oxford 2014) 10: 'The overabundance of provisions limiting the Union's competences is one of the most obvious marks left by the Lisbon Treaty. The new Treaty on European Union (...) states that proposals for the amendment of the Treaties may serve either to increase or to reduce the competences conferred on the Union (Article 48(2) TEU)'.

9 See Valérie Michel, 'Union européenne (Traité de Lisbonne)' *Répertoire de Droit Européen Dalloz* (2010) 21: 'Il ne fait donc aucun doute que la rédaction du Traité de Lisbonne est sous-tendue par cette crainte d'élargissements furtifs des compétences de l'Union (...) Pour preuve encore, cette conséquence logique du principe des compétences d'attribution est encore mentionnée dans la déclaration 18 annexée au traité (...) les raisons incitant les rédacteurs du traité à marteler ainsi l'interdiction faite à l'Union d'intervenir dans des domaines qui ne lui sont pas dévolus se comprennent aisément au regard des développements passés des actions de la Communauté. En effet, un regard rétrospectif démontre que la portée de chaque base juridique, et donc du partage de compétence, dépend de l'interprétation du traité'.

10 Declaration 17 reads as follows: 'The Conference recalls that, in accordance with well settled case law of the Court of Justice of the European Union, the Treaties and the law adopted by the Union on the basis of the Treaties have primacy over the law of Member States, under the conditions laid down by the said case law. The Conference has also decided to attach as an Annex to this Final Act the Opinion of the Council Legal Service on the primacy of EC law as set out in 11197/07 (JUR 260): "Opinion of the Council Legal Service of 22 June 2007: It results from the case-law of the Court of Justice that primacy of EC law is a cornerstone principle of Community law. According to the Court, this principle is inherent to the specific nature of the European Community. At the time of the first judgment of this established case law (Costa/ENEL, 15 July 1964, Case 6/641 [1]) there was

Interestingly enough, the CJEU judged in *Costa v Enel* that 'The transfer by the states from their domestic legal system to the Community legal system of rights and obligations arising under the Treaty carries with it a *permanent* limitation of their sovereign rights against which a subsequent unilateral act incompatible with the concept of the Community cannot prevail'.[11]

The CJEU then judged in *Commission v France* that 'powers thus conferred could not, therefore, be withdrawn from the Community, nor could the objectives with which such powers are concerned be restored to the field of authority of the Member States alone, except by virtue of an express provision of the Treaty'.[12]

3 The 'Ever Closer Union' and Related Principles

In relation to this discussion there necessarily comes to one's mind Recital 13 of the preamble of the TEU, which reads: 'Resolved to continue the process of creating an ever closer union among the peoples of Europe (…)',[13] as well as Article 1, second paragraph, of the TEU reading 'This Treaty marks a new stage in the process of creating an ever closer union among the peoples of Europe (…)'. It is a fact that, so far, all revisions of the EU Treaties have been aiming at a stronger integration of the EU Member States.[14] Actually, the CJEU has rarely mentioned this provision in its decisions (around fifty cases contain an explicit reference to the 'ever closer union' language). It appears for instance in

no mention of primacy in the treaty. It is still the case today. The fact that the principle of primacy will not be included in the future treaty shall not in any way change the existence of the principle and the existing case-law of the Court of Justice. [1] 'It follows (…) that the law stemming from the treaty, an independent source of law, could not, because of its special and original nature, be overridden by domestic legal provisions, however framed, without being deprived of its character as Community law and without the legal basis of the Community itself being called into question'".

11 Case 6/64 *Flaminio Costa v ENEL* EU:C:1964:66, p 594 (emphasis added).

12 Case 7/71 *Commission v French Republic* EU:C:1971:121, para 20.

13 Recital 1 of the preamble of the Treaty of Rome of 25 March 1957 (nowadays recital 1 of the preamble of the Treaty on the Functioning of the European Union) reads: 'Determined to lay the foundations of an ever-closer union among the peoples of Europe'.

14 See Alina Kaczorowska, *European Union Law* (Routledge 2013) 165: 'Although it has always been possible for the Member States to reduce competences of the EU, until the Treaty of Lisbon this had never been specified so clearly. In fact, any revision of the Treaties had been in favour of the development of the EU acquis and thus in favour of the extension of competences of the EC and the EU'.

the Opinion of Advocate General Bot of 6 March 2012 in Case C-364/10, stating that:

> [A]s in the case of any competence reserved for them, the Member States should not exercise their diplomatic competence in a manner that might lead to a lasting break in diplomatic relations between two Member States. Such a break would, in fact, be incompatible with the integration process aimed at creating, in the words of the preamble of the EU Treaty, 'an ever closer union among the peoples of Europe' and would constitute a barrier to the attainment of the essential objectives of the Union, including the aim of promoting peace.[15]

However, the integration principle is not only reflected in the 'ever closer union' language provided for in the Treaties, but more fundamentally in the very principles and objectives underpinning the Treaties.[16] As recalled by the CJEU in its Opinion 2/13 of 18 December 2014:

> [The] essential characteristics of EU law have given rise to a structured network of principles, rules and mutually interdependent legal relations linking the EU and its Member States, and its Member States with each other, which are now engaged, as is recalled in the second paragraph of Article 1 TEU, in a 'process of creating an ever closer union among the peoples of Europe'.
>
> This legal structure is based on the fundamental premiss that each Member State shares with all the other Member States, and recognizes that they share with it, a set of common values on which the EU is founded, as stated in Article 2 TEU. That premiss implies and justifies the existence of mutual trust between the Member States that those values will be recognized and, therefore, that the law of the EU that implements them will be respected.[17]

---

15 Opinion of AG Bot in Case C-364/10 *Hungary v Slovakia* EU:C:2012:124, para 58. On that case, see the chapter by Sonja Boelaert in this book.

16 See Gunnar Beck, *The Legal Reasoning of the Court of Justice of the EU* (Hart Publishing 2012) 320–321: 'The integrationist principles reinforce the broadly defined aspirational "closer union" objective in the context of the central policy areas and in its application to certain types of interpretative problems (…) By invoking one or more of the integrationist principles the Court is usually able to justify a *communautaire* solution to problems of legal uncertainty, and it usually does so without express reference to the unequivocally explicitly integrationist "closer union" objective'.

17 Opinion 2/13 (*Accession of the European Union to the European Convention for the Protection of Human Rights and Fundamental Freedoms*) EU:C:2014:2454, paras 167–68.

In its judgment on the Lisbon Treaty, the German Constitutional Court also provided interesting considerations on the EU integration process and its very nature. In particular:

> An Act that grants powers of integration, like the Act Approving the Treaty of Lisbon, can therefore, despite the principle of conferral, only outline a programme in whose boundaries a political development occurs which cannot be determined in advance in every respect. When striving for integration one must expect the institutions of the Union to form independent opinions. Therefore a tendency towards maintaining the *acquis communautaire* and to effectively interpreting powers along the lines of the doctrine of implied powers (…) or the principle of *effet utile* under the law of international treaties (…) must be tolerated.[18]

It is equally true that the German Constitutional Court also recognized that it would be incorrect to pretend that the approval of the Treaty of Lisbon would de facto include an 'unrestricted primacy' of the EU law over the law of the EU Member States and that it would result in a 'federal-state primacy of validity'.[19]

4 Reversibility and the Union *Acquis*

The phrase *acquis communautaire* no longer appears in the consolidated version of the TEU following the entry into force of the Lisbon Treaty: the *acquis* after the entry into force of Lisbon is known as the 'Union *acquis*'.[20]

---

18 German Constitutional Court, Judgment of 30 June 2009 – 2 BvE 2/08 (English version) <http://www.bundesverfassungsgericht.de/SharedDocs/Entscheidungen/EN/2009/06/es20090630_2bve000208en.html> accessed 1 December 2016, para 237.

19 Astéris Pliakos, 'Le contrôle de constitutionnalité et le droit de l'Union européenne: la réaffirmation du principe de primauté' [2010] Cah. dr. eur. 487, 501 : 'D'après ce jugement, le fait que l'ordre juridique de l'Union est un ordre dérivé, un ordre procédant des Constitutions nationales, ne peut que relativiser la primauté du droit de l'Union. Celle-ci n'a pas la même valeur juridique que celle d'un Etat fédéral (…) Par conséquent, il ne s'agit pas d'une "primauté sans réserve", qui en fin de compte instaurera une primauté de validité fédérale inadmissible pour la Cour constitutionnelle'.

20 Article 20(4) TEU refers to 'the acquis' and since the Community no longer exists, this necessarily means the Union *acquis*. Furthermore, even before the Treaty of Lisbon, the *acquis* which new Member States had to accept already included Union instruments adopted under the former Second and Third Pillars: see Jenö Czuczai, 'Accession to the EU, but to which EU?: the Legal Impact of the Constantly Evolving EMU "acquis" on the EU

The concept of *acquis communautaire* has been broadly interpreted.[21] The Acts of Accession of new Member States provide that they are bound from the date of accession by the original Treaties and by the acts adopted by the EU institutions before their accession. In addition, the new Member States are in the same situation as the current Member States in respect of declarations or resolutions of, or other positions taken up by, the European Council or the Council and in respect of those concerning the Communities or the Union adopted by common agreement of the Member States.[22]

Many commentaries on the *acquis communautaire* have highlighted the definitive and irreversible engagement taken by the EU Member States in this regard.[23] Even after the entry into force of the Lisbon Treaty, Blanke and Mangiameli consider that:

> [T]he dynamicity inherent in the notion of 'European integration process', stated in the Preamble does not substantiate, at least theoretically, the hypothesis of 'withdrawing' from this process (…) Ultimately, according to the logic of the EU Treaty, even though there is no express reference to the protection of the levels of integration achieved thus so far, it

---

Enlargement Process', in Inge Govaere et al. (eds), *The European Union in the World: Essays in Honour of Professor Marc Maresceau* (Martinus Nijhoff 2014) 589.

21 See Roman Petrov, 'The Dynamic Nature of the *Aquis Communautaire* in European Union External Relations' (2006) 18 ERPL 741, 746: 'The dynamism of the legal order is based on acquired common rules, practices and values, which are embraced by the complex notion of *acquis communautaire*. In other words, the *acquis communautaire* ensures the continuity of the EU legal order through the fact that it encompasses everything that has been achieved within the EU, even beyond legal practices'.

22 See Olivier Audéoud, 'L'acquis communautaire, du mythe à la pratique' (2002) 33(3) Revue d'études comparatives Est-Ouest 67, 77: 'L'acquis communautaire est surtout, pourrait-on dire, une méthode ou un principe de congruence qui impose aux Etats membres le respect du droit partagé et qui exige des Etats candidats qu'ils en intègrent pratiquement tous les aspects avant d'adhérer. L'acquis n'est pas un mythe de l'Europe mais l'ébauche de l'Etat de droit européen'.

23 See in particular Pierre Pescatore, 'Aspects judiciaires de l'acquis communautaire' [1981] RTDEur 617: 'On désigne par là tout ce qui, parmi les choses réalisées, apparaît comme une conquête définitive, qui ne saurait être remise en question. *L'acquis*, en d'autres termes, est plus qu'un simple *actif*. Car un actif peut être dilapidé: l'acquis doit être, à tout prix, préservé et défendu (…)' (p. 618); 'Juridiquement, il n'y a donc pas, dans la Communauté, de retour en arrière. Il n'est pas permis de remettre en question les engagements une fois assumés […]' (p. 622); 'Le système communautaire est un système évolutif, étant entendu cependant que le mouvement est à "sens unique": il y a transition dans le sens d'une progression ; le retour en arrière est inconcevable' (p. 623).

can be inferred that the integration process has an incremental logic, for which there is no going back, but there can only be 'further steps to be taken in order to advance European integration'.[24]

In this regard, the fact that the Treaties, as modified after the entry into force of the Lisbon Treaty, do not refer anymore to the notion of *acquis communautaire*, is irrelevant and the EU institutional framework still has to ensure consistency and continuity while respecting and building upon the *acquis communautaire*.[25] Gosalbo-Bono considers in this regard that 'there is an EU supranational concept of the rule of law that appears to be the most important principle promoting unity both of the law of the European Union and of the political integration of the European Union. This EU rule of law has been described as a "constitutional principle" of the European Union'.[26]

Because of its permanence, and of the continuing duty for the EU Member States to implement it, the Union *acquis* constitutes a factor of integration which should be considered when addressing the question of the reversibility of EU law, since the two notions may be seen as conflicting.

5 Tensions: Reversibility and Integration

Blanke and Mangiameli recognize the existence of a 'tension' between the principle of integration, and Article 48(2) TEU as well as Declaration 18, in relation to the possibility to transfer competences back to the domestic level by way of a Treaty revision,[27] and further consider that this tension 'must be resolved by reconciling the two conflicting principles, i.e. the principle of integration

24 Hermann-Josef Blanke and Stelio Mangiameli, *The Treaty on European Union (TEU) – A Commentary* (Springer 2013) 18–19.

25 See ibid 18: 'In this connection, the disappearance from the text of the TEU of any reference to the acquis communautaire, which was present instead in the Preamble to the Constitutional Treaty, is not significant. The fact that the acquis communautaire was expressly stated, before the Treaty of Lisbon, in Articles 2 and 3 (…) was a consequence of the EU/EC dualism. The absence of any reference to this in the TEU text that came out of Lisbon can be explained therefore as being the result of the unification brought about by this Treaty'.

26 Ricardo Gosalbo Bono, 'The Significance of the Rule of Law and Its Implications for the European Union and the United States' (2010) 72 University of Pittsburgh Law Review 229, 260–261.

27 Blanke and Mangiameli (n 24) 59.

on the one hand and the principle of subsidiarity on the other, in the light of practical concordance'.[28]

The notion of practical concordance indeed reflects an attempt to conciliate two diverging orientations, and may therefore constitute a relevant tool for addressing the above-mentioned tension between the 'ever closer union' notion and the idea of transferring competences back to the EU Member States.[29]

The interest of the practical concordance in this context is also acknowledged by Calliess and Ruffert who consider, when addressing the tension between Articles 1, second paragraph, and 48(2) TEU, that since the EU Member States are the 'masters of the Treaties', they have in principle the possibility to get back the competences conferred on the EU by the Treaties, and that this possibility is an expression of the principle of subsidiarity. They also consider that Declaration 18 echoes this view, since it refers to the possible repealing of a legislative act 'in particular better to ensure constant respect for the principles of subsidiarity and proportionality'. The possibility of transferring some EU competences back to the EU Member States would therefore have to be implemented in the light of the integration principle, to give the best possible useful effect to both principles.[30]

---

28 Ibid 60.

29 See Olivier De Schutter, *International Human Rights Law: Cases, Materials, Commentary* (Cambridge University Press 2014) 518: 'In situations of conflicting rights, the doctrine of "practical concordance" seeks to avoid, to the fullest extent possible, sacrificing one right against the other. Instead, it posits, a compromise should be sought between the rights in conflict which will respect their respective claims, by "optimizing" each of the rights against the other. This idea already represents a significant progress from the metaphor of "balancing": whereas the "balancing" of one right against another should lead to preferring the right with the highest "value" (or the most important "weight"), above the other, the principle of "practical concordance" instead rejects the very idea that this may be a desirable outcome: in substance, it acknowledges that it is inappropriate to set aside one claim simply because a competing claim appears, in the particular circumstances of a case, to deserve to be accorded more weight'. See also French Constitutional Court, décision no 94–352 DC du 18 janvier 1995 relative à la loi d'orientation et de programmation relative à la sécurité (Official Journal of the French Republic of 21 January 1995, p 1154), para 23: 'Considérant qu'il est loisible au législateur de prévoir de nouvelles infractions en déterminant les peines qui leur sont applicables ; que toutefois il lui incombe d'assurer ce faisant la conciliation des exigences de l'ordre public et de la garantie de libertés constitutionnellement protégées'.

30 Christian Calliess and Matthias Ruffert *EUV/AEUV* (TEU and TFEU commentary) (4th edn, CH Beck 2011) available at <https://beck-online.beck.de> accessed 15 November 2016, art 1, para 16 (not translated).

6 Conclusion

It therefore appears that the two-way flexibility clause in Article 48(2) TEU should not be read in isolation, as it clearly interacts with other notions fundamental to EU law, in particular the principles of integration and subsidiarity, as well as the Union *acquis*. In addition, attention should be paid to the practical conditions under which this provision may be implemented. As observed by Piris, 'These possibilities will be difficult to exploit in practice, as they would need a proposal from the Commission and the necessary majority in the European Parliament and in the Council, in accordance with the applicable legal base (or common accord in the case of Article 48(2) TEU)'.[31]

31 Piris (n 3) 84.

CHAPTER 3

The Court and the New EU Foreign Relations Law: Institutional Balance?

*Pieter Jan Kuijper**

1 Post-Lisbon International Relations Law

One of the objectives of the Constitution for Europe[1] was to forge a clearer and more coherent international relations law so that the EU would be capable to project a forceful, single identity on the international scene. This objective survived the Lisbon Treaty adjustment of the Convention nearly unscathed. A symbolic name such as the 'Minister of Foreign Affairs of the Union' and some other overly ambitious details were removed in the Lisbon Treaty, but the core of the new 'external action' and trade policy provisions remained.[2] On the other hand it was pointed out that some of the vaunted improvements and qualifications were awkwardly drafted or contained broad terms that would need further clarification. This was the case in particular for Article 3(2) of the TFEU on implied exclusive external relations powers, which attempted to summarize the so-called *ERTA* case law of the Court of Justice of the European Union (CJEU),[3] and a term like foreign direct investment in Article 207 TFEU on the Common Commercial Policy, which remained undefined.[4]

---

* The author is grateful for the editors' remarks and suggestions. A different and somewhat shorter version of the initial draft of this contribution appeared as editorial in (2016) 43 Legal Issues of Economic Integration 1.

1 Treaty establishing a Constitution for Europe [2004] OJ C310/1 (not entered into force).

2 Marise Cremona, 'Defining Competence in EU External Relations: Lessons from the Treaty Reform Process' in Alan Dashwood and Marc Maresceau (eds) *Law and Practice of EU External Relations – Salient Features of a Changing Landscape* (Cambridge University Press 2008) 34. See also Ricardo Gosalbo Bono, 'The Organization of the External Relations of the European Union in the Treaty of Lisbon' in Panos Koutrakos (ed), *The European Union's External Relations – A Year After Lisbon* (2011) CLEER Working Papers 2011/3, 13 <http://www.asser.nl/upload/documents/772011_51358CLEER%20WP%202011-3%20-%20KOUTRAKOS.pdf> accessed 20 November 2016.

3 Case 22/70 *Commission v Council* EU:C:1971:32 (European Road Transport Agreement).

4 Pieter Jan Kuijper, 'Super-Power Frustrated? The Costs of Non-Lisbon in the Field of External Relations' (2008) 51 German Yearbook of International Law 9.

 | DOI 10.1163/9789004347175_004

It was only a matter of time before the CJEU had to rule on these controversial points. And indeed, some two years after the entry into force of the Lisbon Treaty, the first of what would become a series of over a dozen 'foreign relations cases' started to come in from the CJEU. Roughly these cases can be divided into four categories.

1.1 *Exclusive External Powers of the EU*

The first category of cases consists of those cases that have to do with the exclusive external powers of the EU. Traditionally exclusive external relations powers had been derived by the CJEU, before Lisbon, directly from certain Treaty provisions interpreted in their context: the exclusivity of the Common Commercial Policy from the articles on that policy and on the customs union,[5] whereas the exclusive nature of the common external fisheries policy linked to the conservation of the natural resource of the seas was said to be rooted in the Accession Treaty of the UK and Ireland.[6] The codification of these two domains of exclusive external powers of the EU in Article 3(1)(d) and (e) TFEU was simple and uncontroversial. However the codification of the *ERTA* doctrine[7] in Article 3(2) TFEU raised the question whether the CJEU would seek new meaning in the words of this provision or simply shrug its shoulders and proceed with further developing the *ERTA* doctrine and applying it in individual cases that would come before it. In the two cases of which this category is composed[8] the latter approach has been taken by the CJEU, precisely on the basis that the Treaty drafters intended to give expression to the main points of its *ERTA* case law and that hence one must have recourse to that case law for interpretation of Article 3(2).[9] This was to be expected and hence these cases do not deserve to be analyzed in depth here. What does deserve our attention is the fact that a large number of Member States intervened against the position of the Commission and strained to push the CJEU in the direction of a narrow interpretation of the exclusive implied powers in the field of external relations, seemingly in opposition to their express objectives, when

---

5 Opinion 1/75 (*Common Commercial Policy*) EU:C:1975:145.

6 Joint Cases 3, 4 and 6/76 *Kramer* EU:C:1976:114.

7 The doctrine says that exclusive external power for the EU derives from internal legislation, where such legislation rests on power shared between the Union and its Member States. The main sources for the *ERTA* doctrine are Case 22/70 (*ERTA* case) (n 3) and Opinion 1/03 (*new Lugano Convention*) EU:C:2006:81. The latter case attempts to give a synthesis of the development of the case law since the initial *ERTA* case.

8 Case C-114/12 *Commission v Council* EU:C:2014:2051 and Opinion 1/13 (*Convention on the civil aspects of international child abduction*) EU:C:2014:2303.

9 Case C-114/12 (n 8), paras 65–67.

negotiating the Constitution for Europe with help of the Convention method and later when adjusting that draft in the Lisbon Treaty.[10]

1.2 *Scope of Common Commercial Policy*

The second category of cases that can usefully be distinguished are the cases concerning the scope of the Common Commercial Policy. They suffered from the same unwillingness of the Member States, and consequently of the Council, to assume fully the Treaty modifications they had consented to. Since the exclusive nature of the commercial policy powers of the EU has generally been accepted on the grounds of economic and legal logic, it is common knowledge that fights about competence in this field have always been about limiting or expanding the scope of that policy. Article 207 TFEU after Lisbon simply declares that 'the conclusion of tariff and trade agreements relating to trade in goods and services, and the commercial aspects of intellectual property' is part of the Common Commercial Policy, without any exception or reservation (whereas exceptions were still present in the Nice version of the Treaty establishing the European Community (TEC)). It was generally admitted at the time of drafting that this would serve to make all trade matters covered by the World Trade Organisation (WTO) Agreement and its Annexes part of the Common Commercial Policy. Hence it was odd that in the case of Trade-Related Aspects of Intellectual Property Rights (TRIPS)[11] still eight Member States and in the case of broadcasting services under conditional access systems[12] still five Member States attempted to argue that Article 207 TFEU did not say what it evidently said. Especially in the *Daiichi Sankyo* case the CJEU emphasizes the difference in drafting between the relevant passages of Article 133(1) TEC and of Article 207(1), (5) and (7) TFEU. It states that this is a 'significant development in primary law' and that its inquiry must be based 'on the basis of the Treaty now in force'. After this gentle rebuke to the Member States, the Court goes on to perform a painstaking analysis in both cases in order to show that both agreements fell truly in the Common Commercial Policy and were not an external manifestation of the internal market. Again, this category of cases does not deserve further analysis here and, as hinted above, is mainly

---

10 In spite of the objective so clearly underlying art 3(2) TEU, it was easy for Member States to argue that its text limited *ERTA*, as it was in the nature of the codification to leave out the details of the later development of that case. Otherwise the article would have run for at least a page.

11 Case C-414/11 *Daiichi Sankyo Co. Ltd and Sanofi-Aventis Deutschland GmbH v DEMO Anonimos Viomikhaniki kai Emporiki Etairia Farmakon* EU:C:2013:520.

12 Case C-137/12 *Commission v Council* EU:C:2013:675.

interesting because of the resistance of the Member States against their own new Treaty provisions. In the past Member States had found the CJEU to be responsive to a strict interpretation of the scope of the Common Commercial Policy and this may still apply to the undefined scope of the notion 'foreign direct investment' that was added to the other components of the Common Commercial Policy in the new Article 207 TFEU.[13]

1.3 *New Decision-making Techniques in Dispute*

The third category of cases contain those which are linked to more technical details of external relations. One example is the adoption of hybrid acts in relation to mixed agreements,[14] ie an act that is in part a Council decision and in part a decision of the representatives of the (Governments of the) Member States meeting within the Council. The CJEU did not approve this technique, as the unanimity required for an intergovernmental decision of the Member States would distort the decision-making procedure under the TFEU.[15] Another instance is the conclusion of a broad development agreement, including a cooperation provision on the re-admission of third country nationals, on the basis of Articles 208 and 209 TFEU alone. This case gave the CJEU an opportunity to reconfirm its long-standing pre-Lisbon case law on this question.[16] Finally there are two cases that fall in this third category since they deal with questions of treaty technique in a situation of 'treaty arrears' of the Union, ie the situation in which all Member States are parties to an international agreement, the domain of which over the years has been covered by exclusive external powers, but the Union nevertheless is not a party. One case related to

13 The answer to this question will be given in the CJEU's forthcoming Opinion 2/15 requested by the Commission with a view to obtaining clarity about the legal basis for the conclusion of a trade agreement with Singapore that also includes investment rules and investor-State dispute settlement. See also generally the chapter by Frank Hoffmeister in this book.

14 Case C-28/12 *Commission v Council* EU:C:2015:282 (hybrid Council decision on the signing and provisional application of a mixed agreement).

15 Ibid, paras 52–53.

16 Case C-377/12 *Commission v Council* EU:C:2014:1903 (Framework Agreement with the Philippines on Partnership and Cooperation); cf Case C-268/94 *Portuguese Republic v Council* EU:C:1996:461. In spite of this obvious and long-standing precedent six Member States intervened on the side of the Council. Some believe, however, that the CJEU has introduced new elements or at least new nuances in its interpretation of the provisions on development and cooperation policy (see Morten Broberg and Rass Holdgaard, 'Demarcating the Union's Development Cooperation Policy after Lisbon: *Commission v Council* (*Philippines PCFA*)' (2015) 52 CML Rev 547, 563 ff).

the notification of acceptance of the ratification of other new parties to multilateral agreements, insofar as the Treaty powers in that domain had become exclusive under the *ERTA* doctrine.[17] The other was concerned with a position concerning standards of behavior for Member States that were Members of international organisations of which the activities had come to fall in the course of the years under exclusive Union powers, but which had not adapted their founding treaties so as to make full participation of the EU in their activities possible, as a Member or otherwise.[18]

Another way of looking at the above-mentioned three categories of controversial issues is to define them all as cases concerning the vertical distribution of power in EU foreign relations law, ie they treat the question whether the powers in question are EU powers or within the realm of Member States' powers.

1.4 *Institutional Balance*

The fourth category of cases, however, is different, insofar as it is concerned with the balance between the main EU institutions and thus with the horizontal division of competences between the different institutions. This is a very important principle of the foreign relations law of the EU. As the CJEU already mentioned in 1991, the provision on treaty-making by the EC constituted an autonomous general provision of constitutional import in that it confers specific powers on the EU institutions with a view to establishing a balance between those institutions.[19] This is the main reason to concentrate our attention on this last category of cases.

---

17 This is the other side of Opinion 1/13 (n 8), which also fell into the first category as far as the aspect of continuation of the *ERTA* doctrine was concerned. Of the 21 Member States that submitted observations in the case none took the position that was defended by the Commission and ultimately adopted by the Court to the effect that the acceptance of such ratification notifications should be handled by the EU and not by the Member States.

18 Case C-399/12 *Federal Republic of Germany v Council* EU:C:2014:2258 (International Organisation of Vine and Wine). See Inge Govaere, 'Novel Issues Pertaining to EU Member States Membership of other International Organisations: The OIV Case' in Inge Govaere and others (eds) *The EU in the World – Essays in Honour of Marc Maresceau* (Martinus Nijhoff Publishers 2013) 225.

19 See in this vein Opinion of AG Wathelet in Case C-425/13 *Commission v Council* EU:C:2015:174, para 84.

2 Post-Lisbon Cases on the Balance between the Institutions

There are four important cases of this kind, two almost identical ones relating to the powers of the European Parliament, Case C-658/11 and Case C-263/14 and two relating to the powers of the Commission, Cases C-425/13 and C-73/14.[20]

2.1 *The Powers of the European Parliament*

At issue in the first two cases (Cases C-658/11 and C-263/14[21]) were the decisions on the conclusion of an agreement between the EU and Mauritius and between the EU and Tanzania respectively about the transfer of Somali pirates, captured in the course of Operation *Atalanta*, the Common Foreign and Security Policy (CFSP) naval anti-piracy operation, to the Mauritian and Tanzanian authorities in order to be put on trial in those countries.[22] There are some subtle differences between the two cases, how they were construed and how they were pleaded, but the gist of both cases can be summarized as follows.[23]

20 There are two further cases which one might classify as cases relating to the balance of power between the institutions. The first one is the very important case concerning the power of the Commission to withdraw its proposals, if they threaten to be totally perverted by the legislative power (Case C-409/13 *Council v Commission* EU:C:2015:217), but it arose in external relations only by happenstance and hence has no place in this overview (for the viewpoint of the author on this case see Pieter Jan Kuijper, 'Commission's Right of Withdrawal of Proposals: Curtailment of the Commission's Right or Acceptance by the Court of the Commission's Longstanding Position?' (*ACELG BlogActiv*, 1 June 2015) <https://acelg.blogactiv.eu/2015/06/01/commissions-right-of-withdrawal-of-proposals-curtailment-of-the-commissions-right-or-acceptance-by-the-court-of-the-commissions-long-standing-position/> accessed 20 November 2016). The other case is C-363/14 *European Parliament v Council* EU:C:2015:579, which concerns the interpretation of the secondary law provisions by which the treaty-making power of Europol is restrained – which does not make it a case on the balance between the institutions in the strict sense of the words.

21 Case C-658/11 *European Parliament v Council* EU:C:2014:2025 and Case C-263/14 *European Parliament v Council* EU:C:2016:000. In both cases, the Commission intervened on the side of the Parliament and five, respectively three Member States (Czech Republic, (France, Italy), Sweden and the UK) intervened on the side of the Council.

22 E.g. Council Decision 2011/640/CFSP of 12 July 2011 on the signing and conclusion of the Agreement between the European Union and the Republic of Mauritius on the conditions of transfer of suspected pirates and associated seized property from the European Union-led naval force to the Republic of Mauritius and on the conditions of suspected pirates after transfer [2011] OJ L254/1 (for the Agreement itself, see [2011] OJ L254/3).

23 See Case C-263/14 (n 21), paras 26ff under the heading 'error in the choice of legal basis'.

The crucial question was whether these agreements, which were foreseen in general terms in the CFSP decision establishing *Atalanta*,[24] could be concluded as pure CFSP agreements on the basis of Article 37 TEU alone or needed additional legal bases in the TFEU, notably in the EU policy on police and judicial cooperation and protection of transfer of personal data. In the latter case a decision approving an international agreement could become 'mixed' across the treaty frontier between TEU and TFEU and might thus be exposed to incompatible procedures of approval. Even if it were admitted for the sake of argument that the principal aim of the agreement was part and parcel of the CFSP, the ancillary aspects that fell under the TFEU, would trigger the Parliament's right to give its consent to the agreement as not 'falling exclusively within the CFSP' within the meaning of Article 218(6) TFEU, without the ancillary legal bases necessarily having to be included in the decision approving the agreement.[25]

As was to be expected on the basis of the *ECOWAS* case,[26] the Court did not want any of this. Preferably, a definitive, single substantive legal basis has to be found in cases that are potentially on the boundary line between the two Treaties. This is to be decided on the basis of the usual criteria for the choice of a legal basis, according to which, next to the text of the act, also its objective and context play an important role. In the present case the Court let itself be largely led by the preponderance of the objective, which was clearly CFSP, as the Parliament itself admitted in the *Mauritius* case. Equipoise between TEU and TFEU objectives, as in *ECOWAS*, is no longer an option, as the precedence of the TFEU over the TEU (and thus over the CFSP) does no longer exist in the Lisbon Treaty.[27]

The Court attaches great importance to the link between the substantive legal basis – that can be justified or criticized on the basis of objective criteria, in the last instance by the Court itself – and the procedural legal basis. As appears from the three different procedures for the approval of international agreements contained in Article 218 TFEU, this link is of the utmost importance, as it determines the degree of parliamentary power over the conclusion of EU international agreements: approval, consultation or none. And, as Advocate General (AG) Bot pointed out, it embodies the parallelism between the

---

24 Council Joint Action 2008/851/CFSP of 10 November 2008 on a European Union military operation to contribute to the deterrence, prevention and repression of acts of piracy and armed robbery off the Somali coast [2008] OJ L 301/33 (as amended), art 12.

25 See e.g. Case C-658/11 (n 21), paras 44–46.

26 Case C-459/03 *Commission v Council* EU:C:2006:345, paras 90–97.

27 cf ex-art 47 TEU (Treaty of Nice version) and art. 40 TEU (Treaty of Lisbon version).

division of powers in the internal field and in the domain of external action.[28] The Court can finally agree to this, since the anomaly of the difference between the internal and external power divisions in the Common Commercial Policy has been rectified by the Lisbon Treaty.[29]

The final conclusion that the Court drew from this, is that the Parliament has no powers of consent or consultation in respect of the agreement with Mauritius and that with Tanzania. On the other hand, the Court is not willing to draw the consequence that the right of information granted to the Parliament by Article 218(10) TFEU does not apply either, because the subject-matter of the agreement is primarily CFSP. On the strength of its own assertion that Article 218 TFEU contains a single (but differentiated) procedure for the negotiation and conclusion of international agreements, it arrives at the conclusion that Article 218(10) TFEU applies equally to the three possibilities of parliamentary involvement in treaty-making, including the one where the Parliament has no power whatsoever.[30] This is further bolstered by the Court's invoking of the fundamental democratic principle, which in this case takes the form of a right of scrutiny. That scrutiny is a serious possibility only if the right to information of the Parliament in all stages of the procedure is promptly respected by the other institutions involved in treaty-making, in this case the Council[31] (but on other occasions the Commission).

This part of the judgment inevitably begins with the Court ruling itself competent to decide the question whether there is a duty of full information in conformity with Article 218(10) TFEU in respect of the conclusion of an agreement falling within the domain of the CFSP. The Court deduced this from the unitary character of the procedure mentioned before and the consequent application of the duty of information to all three procedures of treaty conclusion foreseen in Article 218 TFEU.

The Court thus comes to a well-balanced conclusion, given the text of the Lisbon Treaty: no powers for the Parliament as to the conclusion of CFSP agreements, but full information in view of an effective exercise of the Parliament's general right of scrutiny. In doing so it confirms that it has at least some

---

28 Opinion of AG Bot in Case C-658/11 *European Parliament v Council* EU:C:2014:41, paras 30–32.

29 Case C-658/11 (n 21), paras 53–57.

30 ibid, paras 72–73.

31 It is interesting to note that in Case C-263/14 (n 21), para 73 the CJEU rejects the idea that keeping the Parliament informed of the evolving negotiations in the CFSP domain would be rather the duty of the High Representative/Vice-President (HR/VP) than of the Council, while the HR/VP is much more directly involved in the actual progress of negotiations than the Council.

jurisdiction on the scope of the CFSP.[32] We will return to the question of delimitation of the CFSP from other aspects of external action at the end of this contribution. A further implication of these cases is that, if and when Union acts for the conclusion of Union agreements need to be based on both CFSP and TFEU legal bases, the procedures for the adoption of such acts should not be incompatible. It is not impossible that this will lead to a proliferation of association agreements that include important CFSP and CSDP aspects. Unanimity in the Council and consent of Parliament are a rare combination in the TFEU, but in respect of association agreements they co-exist (Articles 217 and 218(6)(a)(i) and 218(8) second sentence).[33]

2.2 *The Powers of the European Commission*

The Commission's powers that are at issue in the two cases to be briefly discussed here, are its power as negotiator and its power as external representative of the EU, more particularly before foreign and international courts and tribunals. After Lisbon the Commission obviously has lost its virtually exclusive right to be the Union's negotiator in the TFEU domain, but it would seem from the text of Article 218(3) and (5) TFEU that, once the negotiator is appointed, its position is not in any way different from the one in force before Lisbon and would seem to afford the negotiator, whether the High Representative or the Commission, the usual flexibility under the 'directives' or 'guidelines' issued by the Council.

The same would seem to be true in respect of the position of the Commission as external legal representative of the Union before foreign and international courts, if the subject matter of litigation does not fall under the CFSP or under some exclusionary clause of the TFEU.[34] If anything, on this point the

32 On the power of the CJEU over CFSP more generally, see Christophe Hillion, 'A Powerless Court? The European Court of Justice and the EU Common Foreign and Security Policy' (30 January 2014) <https://ssrn.com/abstract=2388165> accessed 20 November 2016. See also the chapter by Christiaan Timmermans in this book.

33 An early example is the accession of the European Union to one of the basic treaties of the ASEAN, which contains both development and political aspects (Council Decision 2012/308/CFSP of 26 April 2012 on the accession of the European Union to the Treaty of Amity and Cooperation in Southeast Asia [2012] OJ L154/1). For further details see the chapter by Frederik Naert in this book.

34 An example that comes to mind immediately is the security exception of art 346 TFEU, where Member States that had invoked this clause both in respect of Member States and third States might at least be co-defendants in cases initiated by third States.

position of the Commission, recognized by the CJEU in the *Reynolds* case[35] seems to have been strengthened by Article 17(1) TEU, which explicitly mentions that 'It shall ensure the [Union's] external representation' – a provision that was not included in this way in the Treaty before.

In the light of this apparent continuity after the entry into force of the Lisbon Treaty, it is all the more remarkable that the Council sought to disturb the balance of power with the Commission, which at least on paper had not been changed at all. When the Commission asked for an authorisation to open negotiations with Australia with a view to linking their greenhouse gas trading systems to each other, the Council imposed such an extremely detailed set of negotiating directives on the Commission as had hardly been seen in the past.[36] And when the Commission ventured to exercise its power of external representation by intervening in a request for an advisory opinion brought before the International Tribunal for the Law of the Sea (ITLOS), the Council decided to bring a case asking for the annulment of the Commission decision authorising this intervention.[37] The advisory opinion was of direct relevance to international agreements concluded by the EU and Union law relating to illegal, unreported and unregulated fishing (IUU fishing), as well as to bilateral fishing agreements concluded by the EU with third States.[38]

However, the Commission on its part is also tempted from time to time to stretch the limits of its powers as negotiator, as in the case of the discussions it was carrying on with Switzerland about the latter's increase in its contribution to the EU's budget for the running of the internal market after its extension with Croatia. It would seem that the Commission was well instructed by the Council in these discussions and went so far as to assume that, once the desired increase in the contribution was broadly agreed, it could also sign the agreement. Even if it was justified to regard the 'agreement' rather as a political and voluntary commitment from the Swiss side and not as a binding agreement under international law, the Commission's signature without having

35 Case C-131/03 P *R.J. Reynolds Tobacco Holdings, Inc. and Others v Commission* EU:C:2006:541, para 94.

36 This resulted in an action for annulment of this authorisation and the directives attached (Case C-425/13, *Commission v Council* EU:C:2015:483). The Commission received support from the European Parliament, while eight Member States intervened in support of the defense of the Council. It should also be noted that the agreement in question was to be an EU only agreement.

37 Case C-73/14 *Council v Commission* EU:C:2015:663. The Council was supported in its claim by ten Member States; the Commission had to fend for itself.

38 ITLOS, Case no 21, *Request for an advisory opinion submitted by the Sub-Regional Fisheries Commission* (*SFRC*) (Advisory Opinion, 2 April 2015) ITLOS Reports 2015, 4.

assured itself that the Council agreed seemed an act of great temerity. It was no surprise then, that Council took umbrage and instituted proceedings before the CJEU.[39]

2.2.1 The Powers of the Commission as Negotiator

One of the first lessons on the relative powers of the Commission and of the Council in the phase of negotiation of international agreements, which the present writer received when he started work at the European Commission Legal Service in 1979, concerned the question of negotiation directives. One day in 1979 or early 1980, I ran into my countryman, the venerable Mr Wellenstein,[40] who had only recently stepped down as Director-General of the External Relations Directorate-General and whom I happened to know rather well, in the lift of the old Berlaymont. I told him that I was involved in some international negotiations and blithely mentioned that we had just obtained a *mandate* for negotiations from the Council. He eyed me sternly and said:

> You should never call it a *mandate* again. The Commission is not a mandatory that cannot deviate one bit from the instructions of its principal, the Council. The Commission receives *directives for negotiation* from the Council and has a certain margin of manoeuver during the negotiations. Don't forget that.

Obviously I never did and later repeated this cogent formulation *ad nauseam* to my colleagues in the Commission services.[41]

It is fair to say that in the practice of the institutions, there has always been a certain tension between the 'mandate' approach, advanced from time to time by the Council and individual Member States, and the 'directives' orthodoxy

39 Case C-660/13 *Council v Commission* EU:C:2016:616. Ten Member States intervened on the side of the Council.

40 Edmund Wellenstein, who was until very late in life a much appreciated counselor on matters of EU policy for people from all walks of life, sadly passed away in February 2016 at the age of 96.

41 This anecdote is recounted here not just for the pithy formulation of the essential difference between the Commission as mandatory and as recipient of directives for negotiation, but also because I surmise that the career of Ricardo Gosalbo Bono also must have been punctuated by similar moments that colour one's views on certain aspects of the founding Treaties of the EC and the EU forever. On the 'wrong' use of the word 'mandate', see also Opinion of AG Wathelet (n 19), paras 156 ff. He rightly points out that the use of this word would only be justified if the Commission negotiates in the name of the Member States.

defended by the Commission and, as Advocate General Wathelet clearly demonstrated in his Opinion, fully shared by the doctrine.[42] Another aspect that plays an important role in this discussion is the proper role of the 'Special Committee' that follows the negotiations in consultation with the Commission, according to Article 218(4) TFEU. Is it compatible with the consultative role of this Committee for the Council to give it the power to further define and circumscribe the directives for negotiations, whenever the Committee believes this is necessary, so that the Special Committee in reality becomes an instrument of the Council and lays down negotiation positions rather than negotiation directives?

The CJEU was guided in this case by the extensive and remarkable Opinion by AG Wathelet, who opted for the orthodox position, based on the fact that the Commission indeed had the right of external representation under Article 17(1) TEU and was supposed to be, in TFEU matters, the negotiator for the EU as a whole, and not for the Council.[43] However, he also pointed out that there was nothing wrong with the Council laying down fairly stringent quarterly reporting requirements (in written form) for the Commission, which in no way hindered the Commission's substantive work as negotiator.[44]

On this point the Court fully agreed with AG Wathelet and this was an important point for the Council to win. The Court, however, also agreed with AG Wathelet that the negotiating directives went too far and actually made the Council or the Special Committee into (co-)negotiators by imposing on the Commission certain negotiating positions that left the Commission no margin of manoeuver except in the way of presenting these positions. These were the points, contained in the Annex to the authorisation to open negotiations with Australia, according to which the Special Committee or the Council could lay down detailed negotiating positions and the Special Committee was authorised to establish negotiating positions before each negotiation session.[45] Such provisions, in the Court's view, sought to bind the negotiator and went beyond the consultative nature of the Special Committee. Moreover, neither that committee nor the Council itself had the power to impose 'detailed negotiating positions' on the Commission. Thus the Council had exceeded its powers and in so doing had also infringed the principle of institutional balance.[46]

42 See his view on the nature of negotiating directives (Opinion of AG Wathelet (n 19), para 71), and his many references to the literature (paras 91ff).

43 Ibid, para 173.

44 Ibid, para 133.

45 Case C-425/13 (n 36), paras 85 ff.

46 Ibid, paras 89–92.

Thus nothing much changed in the balance between the Council and the Commission in the matter of international negotiations; matters stayed largely as they had been before the Lisbon Treaty which, indeed, had not touched this part of the institutional balance at all.

2.2.2 The Powers of the Commission as External Legal Representative of the EU

These powers were at issue in Case 73/14 and concerned the question of which institution was to be in charge of the defense of the EU's legal interests before international courts and tribunals (in this case ITLOS) and, in relevant cases, before the courts of third States. In many ways, this question is comparable to the one broached in the case discussed above in that the Council wanted to have the last word about the position to be taken before ITLOS, after which the Commission could deliver it exactly as prescribed by the Council, leaving the Commission no autonomous margin of manoeuver in its task as external representative of the Union. The Commission would thus be reduced to the function of a mere Secretariat, a notion that is rejected in any basic manual of EU law.[47]

There was still another old controversy underlying this dispute, namely to what extent the 'policy of international law' of the Union is inherently a matter of 'foreign policy' and thus part and parcel of the CFSP. The Council Legal Service was a defender of this view. However, its counterpart of the Commission took the view that international law relevant to TFEU issues ought to be handled by the Commission as external arm of the EU and that the Council could take care only of international law as applied to the CFSP. This did not imply, in the view of the Commission, that the Council should not be *consulted* by the Commission (and *vice versa*). A good example of this was the way in which contributions from the EU to the debate about the draft articles on the responsibility of international organizations were prepared. Drafts by the Commission were discussed in the Council Working Group on Public International Law (COJUR group, consisting of the legal advisers of the Ministries of Foreign Affairs of the Member States), after which the Commission would take this discussion into account in the final version that was sent to the International Law Commission (ILC) or to the United Nations General Assembly Sixth Committee. The Commission's interventions in cases affecting the interests of the Union before the United States Supreme Court were handled in the same

47 In the same way AG Sharpston rejected the idea that the position of the Commission was comparable to that of a lawyer representing his client, namely the Council (Opinion of AG Sharpston in Case C-73/14 *Council v Commission* EU:C:2015:490, para 107).

manner: a Commission decision to intervene followed by circulation of rough drafts to the Council and/or all Member States and, if necessary, discussion in the competent Council group.[48]

In the case at hand, the Commission had its draft of a written statement in intervention discussed in the FISH and COMAR working groups of the Council (dealing with fisheries and law of the sea issues respectively) during October/November of 2013 before sending it off to ITLOS. This was sufficient for the Court to decide that in any case there was no lack of sincere cooperation on the part of the Commission. A further argument by the Council was that a decision under Article 218(9) TFEU was necessary, since filing a document before a court was equivalent to taking a position on behalf of the EU in a body set up by an international organization that had been bestowed with decision-making powers by which the Members could be bound. For the Court there was little doubt that this was a mis-characterization of taking a position before an international judicial body and that hence invoking Article 218(9) TFEU was beside the point. The Court simply stuck with its view, as advanced in the *Reynolds* case, to the effect that Article 335 TFEU (on representation of the EU before judicial bodies of the Member States), although restricted by its wording, is the expression of a general principle, namely that the EU has legal capacity and is to be represented, to that end, by the Commission, also at the international level.[49]

The old idea that the 'policy of international law' was the prerogative of the Council under the CFSP and should be handled by the Commission merely as an instrument of transmission in the hands of the Council also came to the fore again. The Council argued before the Court that the Commission in transmitting its written statement to ITLOS had indulged in 'policy making' which was not its task and competence, as this was allocated to the Council under the second sentence of Article 16(1) TEU. The Court rejected this approach by noting that the Commission's written statement, filed with ITLOS on behalf of the EU, ventured to reply to the four specific questions of the request for an advisory opinion and did in no way formulate a policy on IUU fishing. In the same way the Commission's remarks on the jurisdiction of ITLOS to entertain a request for an advisory opinion are merely characteristic of participation in

48 Based on the writer's personal experience.

49 Case C-73/14 (n 37), paras 58–59. For the *Reynolds* case see n 35. AG Sharpston had also reminded the CJEU that it had already accepted this view in that case, leaving no room for the CJEU to turn back (Opinion of AG Sharpston (n 47), para 106). More generally the AG's Opinion seems to have heavily influenced the Court's judgment.

proceedings before a court or tribunal and not of policy making, according to the CJEU.[50]

In sum, in this case, as in the case concerning the Commission's power as negotiator, the Lisbon Treaty had not basically changed the provisions on the basis of which the CJEU had concluded earlier in *Reynolds* that the Commission was the natural (legal) representative of the EU as an international person, not only in respect of the Member States, but also in respect of third States. Moreover, this position of the Commission had, if anything, been strengthened by the one but last sentence of Article 17(1) TEU on the Commission being the external representative of the Union, except in the CFSP. Hence, there was no need for the Court to change its position on this issue; it merely needed to police the duty of loyal cooperation, which it found to have been respected.

In the case concerning the additional Swiss contribution to the costs of making the internal market function after the accession of Croatia, the Commission ventured to argue that, since the agreement with Switzerland on this extra contribution was not binding under international law, a general authorisation by the Council for the Commission to carry on these negotiations included the power to sign them. In the Commission's view such signature was simply part and parcel of its power of external representation under Article 17(1) TEU in the case of non-binding agreements.[51] However in an older case on non-binding agreements the CJEU had already hinted that, given the strict attribution of powers in the Treaties, the institutions should respect the existing decision-making procedures and balance between the institutions in respect of treaty making.[52] The Court extrapolated this reasoning to the new provisions on trade policy and external relations of the TFEU, combined with Article 17(1) TEU after Lisbon and the conclusion was the same: the Commission

50 Case C-73/14 (n 37), paras 70–73. This jurisdiction was controversial, as the possibility to entertain requests for an advisory opinion had been introduced by the Tribunal itself in its Rules of Procedure and did not figure in Part XV of the United Nations Convention on the Law of the Sea (UNCLOS) on dispute settlement or in the Tribunal's Statute (annex VI to UNCLOS). However, none of the Parties to UNCLOS had protested against this provision in the Rules of Procedure in the fifteen years after its adoption before Case no 21 (n 38) was brought before the Tribunal.

51 Case C-660/13 (n 39), paras 36–38.

52 Case C-233/02 *French Republic v Commission* EU:C:2004:173. In this case the CJEU accepted that the Commission could approve a non-binding text negotiated with the US on regulatory cooperation, but only because it concerned trade policy and the Commission had broadly followed the usual decision-making steps for concluding a binding trade agreement.

could not, under its own steam, sign the agreement on the increase of the Swiss contribution.[53]

3 Final Conclusions

There is little doubt that much energy has been invested in and commotion has surrounded the cases that have been merely briefly mentioned in Section 1 above, as well as those that have been analysed in somewhat greater detail in Section 2. The number of cases that the Commission (and in two instances the Parliament) has felt constrained to bring and the number of interventions by Member States (all against the Commission) in these cases is testimony to that. Given these numbers it is equally striking that the Council and the Member States have merely won two of these cases (Case C-660/13, discussed above, and Case C-399/12, brought by Germany against the Council, which was supported by the Commission) and, if one is generous, scored three draws, ie the two Pirates cases[54] and Case C-425/13 on the Council's directives for negotiation, if one takes the view in the latter case that the right of the Council to impose periodic reporting about the negotiations is of equal weight to the confirmation of the Commission's margin for manoeuver. The large majority of these cases (eight) were won by the Commission.

What does all this mean: is the Commission exceptionally trigger-happy; have the Member States gone reactionary; has the CJEU become unhinged and lost its sense of fairness and balance between the parties? The answer is: probably none of these. Although some Member States' authorities may be tempted to agree with the last characterization, such a conclusion is certainly not warranted.[55]

Where the three cases relating to the balance between the institutions are concerned, it is possible to distinguish Cases C-658/11 and C-263/14 on the right of Parliament to be fully informed of the developments of the progress of the negotiation and approval of international agreements from the other two, concerning the relationship between the Council and the Commission in situations of negotiation for and representation of the EU in various international

53 Case C-660/13 (n 39), paras 40–48.

54 Cases C-658/11 and C-263/14 (n 21).

55 There is little doubt that Opinion 2/13 on the accession of the EU to the European Convention on Human Rights (EU:C:2014:2454) has traumatized many scholars and practitioners in the field of EU external relations, but the cases discussed here should not be interpreted in that light.

settings (Cases C-425/13 and C-73/14 respectively). As we have seen, in the latter two cases the legal provisions had not fundamentally changed after Lisbon. In the first case, however, the legal situation had changed, as the right of Parliament to be informed was placed in an article on treaty-making, which now also covered CFSP agreements. The reaction of the CJEU was as one would expect. In the case where the Lisbon Treaty had created a new situation, the CJEU was forced to break new ground. In the two cases where the Lisbon Treaty simply maintained the existing balance between the Council and the Commission, the CJEU also maintained the existing balance and let the party that had wanted to use the Lisbon Treaty as a pretext for changing that balance fail.

Although the cases briefly mentioned in Section 1 have not been analysed in any detail, it can be argued that the pattern is remarkably similar. In the cases concerning Article 3(2) TFEU, which was basically a codification, though imperfect, of the string of cases based on the *ERTA* doctrine, the CJEU felt no need to change its line on *ERTA* and its progeny. Where the Treaty of Lisbon did bring change, however, by including trade in services and trade-related intellectual property rights without reservation in the Common Commercial Policy, the CJEU acknowledged that change and adapted its approach to the new provisions.

Again, as one would expect, the CJEU is thus the defender of treaty orthodoxy, old and new. The Commission that probably has created the impression by bringing so many cases of being aggressive, simply turns out to be the guardian of the Treaties, old and new. In contrast, the Member States did not want the new Treaty provisions to be implemented and at the same time strove to upset the balance between the institutions where it had been maintained unchanged by… the Member States as constitutional legislators. In short the Member States did not want their own creation any longer, whether old or new. Looked at with a cold eye, this may be the reality, but it is certain that the Member States and their representatives in the Council machinery do not see it that way and it is unfortunately this *falsches Bewusstsein* that will determine their reaction.[56]

56 At the moment of finalisation of the first draft of this contribution a new article by Inge Govaere is published that discusses the same cases more or less in the same vein: Inge Govaere, '"Setting the International Scene": EU External Competence and Procedures Post-Lisbon Revisited in the Light of ECJ Opinion 1/13' (2015) 52 CML Rev 1277.

CHAPTER 4

The External Relations of the European Union Since Lisbon: A Practitioner's Perspective

Dirk Wouters

1 Introduction

Having shared with my distinguished friend Ricardo Gosalbo Bono many Council, Committee of Permanent Representatives (COREPER) and Political and Security Committee (PSC) meetings, I will attempt to formulate an answer – coming from the other side of the table[1] – to the question of what a Permanent Representative of a Member State to the European Union should broadly know, when he enters the new complex post-Lisbon world of EU external relations and has to act on behalf of his country. This new world is clearly a world of law and politics. It is also a world of permanent tensions. There are tensions following the inclination of Member States to re-create their proper zone of external action, rather than use the full potential of the Treaties for moving towards more common action. Tensions also exist between the different principles that constitute the legal foundations of EU external action. I refer to the tension between the constitutional and existential requirement of conferred powers to the EU and the laudable aspiration for overall vertical/horizontal consistency and effectiveness in the framing and implementation of EU external action.

My answer to the question will therefore be a mix of law and politics, a mix of provisions of the Treaties and implementation of those provisions in practice. This answer therefore captures two dimensions: the legal dimension and the political or diplomatic dimension. The focus on or the confrontation between these two dimensions can hopefully add value to this contribution to the Liber Amicorum.

It seems appropriate in this context, to recall that Ricardo Gosalbo Bono has always tried to find a balanced way through those tensions. Rare were the occasions in the Council, in COREPER or in the PSC, when he was not able to

1 The Legal Service seat in meetings of the Council and Council preparatory bodies is at the table where the Presidency is seated, whereas (other) Member States are seated at the tables in front and on both sides thereof.

 | DOI 10.1163/9789004347175_005

find a practical solution that could be supported by the Member States and the institutions.

My answer and this contribution are structured around ten general and very personal propositions. Each proposition, each thesis or postulate if one prefers these terms, will be briefly developed. It will only focus on some aspects, without being exhaustive. Several EU policy areas, for example, will not be covered or developed for lack of space. This will be the case for the common commercial policy, the external environment policy, humanitarian aid, migration, the enlargement and neighborhood policy, security and defence and the European External Action Service (EEAS).

2 Ten Propositions

2.1 *A Reinforced Distinct International Community of Law with Legal Personality and Principles*

The European Union remains an important international community of law, with a legal personality, with its own general principles of law that apply to the whole of the activities of the Union and with its own general provisions that apply for the whole of its external action. These general provisions cover both the Common Foreign and Security Policy (CFSP) of the EU and the broader field of EU external relations. The Lisbon Treaty has introduced major innovations in this field.

Only two aspects of this proposition are developed: legal personality and major innovations.

2.1.1 Legal Personality of the Union

Legal personality or, better, 'international' legal personality is an important requirement for any international organisation that operates and wants to act on the international scene. For the European Union, the question has often been asked whether this legal personality or international legal personality did or did not exist before the Lisbon Treaty. And if it did exist, what was its scope? Was it limited to the treaty-making powers of the Union or did it cover all domains that fall under the Treaties? What happens if the Union has exercised competence internally but not externally? In other words, what is the legal situation when the Union finds itself in a position where, for formal reasons, it cannot act on the international scene, in a field where it has already enacted internal legislation? Unfortunately, this situation occurs frequently for the EU. This is particularly the case when international agreements do not accept international organisations, like the EU, as parties to those agreements, and when membership of international organisations is restricted to States only.

On these questions, important case law has been developed by the Court of Justice of the European Union (CJEU). It started with the *ERTA* case (1971),[2] followed by Opinion 1/76 (1977)[3] and Opinion 1/03 (2006).[4] The Lisbon Treaty has tried to introduce new provisions that are directly linked to this case law as it has developed over the years. Articles 1 and 47 TEU, as amended by the Lisbon Treaty, and Articles 3 and 216 TFEU are the relevant articles and have to be read together.

Practitioners in the Council assumed that legal personality existed *before* Lisbon and that the Union fulfilled the criteria set by the International Court of Justice for international organisations to enjoy international legal personality anyway.[5] Today, practitioners accept it is *still* there. It was even reinforced, as legal personality has resurfaced as *one* legal personality for the whole Union. We are conscious of the fact that there was, and probably still is, an issue with the scope of this one legal personality. If there are critical scholarly comments today on the way the Lisbon codification of earlier case law has been operated, these comments are mainly related to the question of the scope of the legal personality. But Permanent Representatives[6] integrate in their daily work in the Council, without too much reluctance, the fact that the European Union, although not a State, is a subject of international law, which may act in international fora, which can conclude international agreements, which can be held responsible in legal terms and which possesses a right of legation.

2.1.2 Major Innovations of the Lisbon Treaty

Introducing and achieving greater consistency and coherence in the field of external relations was one of the *key objectives* of the Lisbon Treaty, after the failure of the planned constitutional Treaty.[7] This remains a commendable objective that proves to be difficult to implement in practice however. Permanent Representatives and Representatives to the PSC will look at consistency and coherence mostly at intra-institutional and agency level. Rarely will they address vertical coherence and consistency. This is unfortunate in an area where the

2 Case 22/70 *Commission v Council (European Road Transport Agreement)* EU:C:1971:32.

3 Opinion 1/76 (*Draft Agreement establishing a European laying-up fund for inland waterway vessels*) EU:C:1977:63.

4 Opinion 1/03 (*Convention on jurisdiction and the recognition and enforcement of judgments in civil and commercial matters*) EU:C:2006:81.

5 See especially *Reparation for Injuries Suffered in the Service of the United Nations* (Advisory Opinion) [1949] ICJ Rep 174.

6 This term as used in this chapter refers to Permanent Representatives of the Member States to the EU.

7 Treaty establishing a Constitution for Europe [2004] OJ C310/1.

available instruments of action are to be found both at European and national level. The beauty would be to bring existing instruments at all levels together all the time for all EU policies and EU actions. Searching for the reasons why this does not happen more often in practice, one cannot escape mentioning the sometimes widely differing starting points among Member States when looking at a certain international situation. Some Member States will ask what the EU can do or should do in a given situation, whereas others will start with the question, 'Is the EU empowered to do something?' These differing starting points may lead to serious tensions as we have seen in the case of the Iraq war. They also translate into a different state of mind when it comes to acting and may result in national action instead of common European action.

But this is also one of the lessons that a Permanent Representative involved in European and multilateral diplomacy must learn: the issues never arrive on the negotiation table in the way and form he or she wishes. But he or she always needs to take a position in relation to the issue in the way it has arrived on the table.

The major *structural* changes in the Lisbon Treaty concern the merger of pre-existing pillars but with the maintenance of specific arrangements for CFSP, the introduction of a new chapter entitled 'General Provisions on the Union's External Action', a new Article 21 TEU setting out the principles underpinning the external action of the EU, and finally the incorporation in the TFEU of a Part 5 which brings together the main external policy areas except CFSP.[8]

The most important *specific* changes are:

- The introduction of horizontal overall objectives for all EU external relations in Articles 3(5) and 21 TEU, and Article 205 TFEU;
- The attribution of multiple roles to the High Representative of the Union for Foreign and Security Policy (HR), who is also a Vice-President of the Commission and chair of the Foreign Affairs Council, assisted by the EEAS (Articles 18 and 27 TEU);
- The increased participation of the European Parliament in decision making, notably in relation to international agreements (Article 218(6) TFEU) and as regards the Common Commercial Policy (Article 207 TFEU);

8 See also Ricardo Gosalbo Bono, 'The Organization of the External Relations of the European Union in the Treaty of Union' in Panos Koutrakos (ed), *The European Union's External Relations: A Year After Lisbon* (2011) CLEER Working Paper 2011/3, 13 <http://www.asser.nl/upload/documents/772011_51358CLEER%20WP%202011-3%20-%20KOUTRAKOS.pdf> accessed 11 December 2016.

- A unified procedure for negotiating and concluding international agreements, including in the area of the CFSP,[9] albeit with partially different modalities (Article 218 TFEU and Article 207 TFEU);
- A permanent chair for the Foreign Affairs Council, namely the HR, and for the European Council, namely its President;
- Amendments to the specific provisions for CFSP, including the introduction of new provisions;
- Amendments to the provisions regarding the Common Security and Defence Policy (CSDP), including the introduction of new provisions: the role of the HR, increased cases of decision-making by qualified majority voting (which have not yet been used in practice), a mutual assistance clause in case of an armed aggression against a Member State (invoked for the first time by France after the terrorist attacks in Paris on 13 November 2015[10]), the Permanent Structured Cooperation (not yet established), and the authorisation to create a startup fund for expenditure for CSDP tasks which are not charged to the Union budget (not yet established either);
- A revised provision on the relationship between CFSP and other Union policies (Article 40 TEU), which amounts to a pact of mutual non- interference;
- A solidarity clause imposing assistance by the Union and the Member States if a Member State is the object of a terrorist attack or the victim of a natural or man-made disaster (Article 222 TFEU).[11]

With the benefit of hindsight, and having been involved in the Convention on the future of the European Union and the Intergovernmental Conference leading to the Lisbon Treaty, I cannot escape the observation that the coherence objective, as well as the abovementioned structural and specific changes, were and still are more ambitious, compared to the actual state of mind and willingness of Member States in the Council, to respect that level of ambition. Room for improvement in implementing existing provisions of the Treaties is therefore still available.

---

9 For CFSP agreements art 37 TEU is the substantive legal basis, while the procedural legal basis is art 218 TFEU.

10 See the Outcome of the meeting of the Foreign Affairs Council on 17 November 2015 (Council doc 14120/15) 6.

11 See also Council Decision 2014/415/EU of 24 June 2014 on the arrangements for the implementation by the Union of the solidarity clause [2014] OJ L192/53.

2.2 *The Treaties Do Not Fully Capture EU External Relations*

The Treaties[12] *do not capture the totality of the CFSP Policy or external action*[13] *of the European Union.*

This second proposition is to a certain extent the consequence of the first proposition. The Treaties approach the CFSP and EU external relations more broadly mainly, if not exclusively, from a legal point of view. Foreign Policy and diplomacy can of course do more than implementing legal provisions. The Lisbon Treaty therefore does not cover 100 percent of what foreign policy does or can do. One illustration in the field of position taking: practitioners and diplomats prepare, for their Heads of State and Government and for their Ministers of Foreign Affairs, conclusions of the European Council and of the Foreign Affairs Council. The EU expresses itself collectively, politically and frequently through these instruments. But this form of collective expression of positions in EU Foreign Policy is not even foreseen in the Treaties. It is however clear that some Member States attach significant importance to these instruments. The importance they attach may seem exaggerated. Sometimes the impression is created that the main objective of a drafting exercise is to limit the role of the EU rather than advance it, or to give prominence to agreed Council conclusions over and above the Treaties.

The more routine instruments which are foreseen in the Treaties are *Council decisions* (replacing the 'common positions' and 'joint actions' as the new instrument and terminology for CFSP decisions since Lisbon), *financial instruments, international agreements, operations in the framework of the CSDP, Special Representatives of the European Union* (EUSRs), etc.

My second proposition is also the logical consequence of the fact that the Member States have constructed the Foreign Policy of the Union as a *Common* Policy but *not as a Single* or unique policy. The Foreign Policy construction in the Treaties is a construction of two floors or two layers: a European one and a national one. National positions on Foreign Policy are coordinated in the Council until a common position on Foreign Policy is obtained at EU level. This coordination effort within the EU is huge. It sometimes fails. It often succeeds. But it is a continuous and energy-consuming process, involving many people in institutions and national capitals. Not only EU capitals! Coordination has different meanings for smaller and bigger countries. They handle it differently around the Council table. A practitioner around the Council table

12 The term 'the Treaties' is used to cover both the TEU and TFEU.

13 The term 'external action' is used to cover other areas of EU external relations than the CFSP, whereas 'external relations' is used to cover all EU external policies, including the CFSP.

learns quickly that smaller Member States need this coordination of national positions in order to survive internationally. Bigger Member States sometimes resist it and often resent this coordination effort as a concession, especially when big international political issues are at stake. Two Member States are permanent members of the Security Council and bear special responsibility that other Member States do not. Five Member States are members of the G20 and four of the G7. Within the Bretton Woods Institutions Member States have different weights. The principle of equality between Member States, enshrined in the Treaties, gets a different meaning in the daily reality of initiating and conducting Foreign Policy at EU level. On the other hand, all Member States recognise the added value of a common or central system, especially the increased availability of information on a very wide range of international issues. A huge amount of information is provided to national capitals by this European central system, mainly through the EEAS and the High Representative.

2.3 *The CFSP and the Union's (Other) External Action: Distinct Rules and Procedures*

The Common Foreign and Security Policy of the European Union and the External Action of the European Union are two specific worlds with their own specific rules and procedures.

Under the Lisbon Treaty, the CFSP has remained 'subject to specific rules and procedures' (Article 24 TEU), which differentiates it from other external policy areas.

What are these specificities?

In the first place they concern the decision making procedures. In principle, EU foreign policy decisions are taken by unanimity. There are some exceptions. Member States have the possibility to abstain constructively (Article 31 TEU). In certain cases, Council decisions can be taken by qualified majority. (Article 31(2) TEU). There is also a bridging clause in the Treaties (Article 31(3) TEU) allowing the European Council to decide unanimously to pass to qualified majority in the Council. Apart from one case of constructive abstention (the constructive abstention by Cyprus in 2008 when setting up an important Rule of Law Mission in Kosovo without an explicit UN Security Council authorisation[14]), I note that in practice it is very difficult to abandon the

---

14 Nevertheless, this operation is based on United Nations Security Council Resolution 1244(1999) (UN Doc S/RES/1244). See Jean Paul Jacqué, 'Review of the EULEX Kosovo Mission's implementation of the mandate with a particular focus on the handling of the recent allegations' (Report to the attention of High Representative/Vice President of the European Commission Ms Federica Mogherini, 31 March 2015) available through <http://

consensus rule in Foreign Policy. I do not have the impression that the new High Representative is going to change this practice. From a practitioner's perspective one can only note that the Council systematically favours unanimity in its decision-making on Foreign Policy, irrespective of qualified majority rules laid down in the Treaties.

A second specificity refers to the nature of the decisions adopted in the framework of the CFSP. These decisions are of a non-legislative nature, meaning that they are not adopted in accordance with the legislative procedure. But they are binding and committing for Member States (Articles 28(2) and 29 TEU).

A third specificity concerns the role of the other EU Institutions than the Council in the field of the CFSP. In this field their role is more limited, compared to their role in other fields of external action. The CJEU lacks jurisdiction over CFSP provisions, save for its role in ensuring mutual respect between the CFSP and other EU policies (Article 40 TEU) and – very important – the review by the Court of the legality of certain restrictive measures against natural or legal persons (Article 275 TFEU).[15] The European Commission has lost all power with regard to the CFSP save for the management of the EU budget, while the right of initiative is shared between the High Representative (which may be supported by the Commission) and the Member States and is, in some cases, reserved to the High Representative alone (e.g. for EUSRs and CFSP agreements). The European Parliament is regularly consulted by the High Representative (Article 36 TEU) and fully informed at all stages of the procedures relating to the negotiation, signature, conclusion and implementation of CFSP international agreements (Article 218(10) TFEU).[16]

The case law of the CJEU in this field is especially interesting when it comes to the delimitation between the CFSP and other Union competences. I refer in particular to the 2008 *ECOWAS* judgment.[17] The court annulled a Council decision dealing with the fight against small arms and light weapons in relation to the Economic Community of West African States, on the basis that it

---

eeas.europa.eu/statements-eeas/2015/150414_01_en.htm> accessed 20 November 2016, annex I, especially 65–66. Cyprus does not appear to have maintained this abstention in relation to subsequent decisions on this mission.

15 However, the CJEU has interpreted the exclusion of its jurisdiction in the CFSP very narrowly in a number of recent cases, thus expanding its role in relation to the CFSP. See especially Cases C-658/11 *Parliament v Council* EU:C:2014:2025; C-439/13 P *Elitaliana SpA v Eulex Kosovo* EU:C:2015:753; and C-455/14 P *H v Council and Commission* EU:C:2016:569.

16 See also Cases C-658/11 *Parliament v Council* EU:C:2014:2025 and C-263/14 *Parliament v Council* EU:C:2016:435.

17 Case C-91/05 *Commission v Council* EU:C:2008:288 (*ECOWAS*).

pursued not only security but also (and not merely incidentally) development policies and therefore could not be adopted solely under the CFSP ('first pillar always wins!'). Since then, a new Article 40 TEU has been introduced in the Lisbon Treaty, which moves the delimitation approach in the Treaties from a unilateral protection of Community policies to the principle of mutual non-interference. The Court seems to have adjusted its case law since then in order to respect the proper scope and proper specificity of the CFSP. In the Mauritius and Tanzania pirate transfer agreements cases for example, the Court ruled that the agreements at issue providing for the transfer of suspected pirates arrested by an EU military operation to Mauritius and Tanzania fell within the CFSP.[18] Another example: in its judgment on Regulations (EC) No 881/2002 and (EU) No 1286/2009 about restrictive measures directed against certain persons and entities associated with Osama bin Laden, the Al-Qaeda network and the Taliban, the CJEU accepted that these measures fell within the CFSP and were correctly adopted under Article 215 TFEU rather than Article 75 TFEU.[19]

But what has been separated by treaties, legislators or case law, must sometimes come together in the real world. Member States may want this when they deal with real situations on the ground. This includes Member States that until recently preferred to build an iron wall between the two worlds. Sometimes they let the wall come down. The use of financial instruments for foreign policy and diplomatic actions[20] is a positive case in point.

18 Cases C-658/11 *Parliament v Council* EU:C:2014:2025 and C-263/14 *Parliament v Council* EU:C:2016:435. In para 55 of the latter judgment, the Court ruled that 'Since the Agreement falls predominantly within the scope of the CFSP, and not within the scope of judicial cooperation in criminal matters or police cooperation, the contested decision could legitimately be based on Article 37 TEU alone. Consequently, its adoption in accordance with the procedure laid down in the first clause of the second subparagraph of Article 218(6) TFEU was correct'. In the former judgment, the Court ruled that an agreement relates exclusively to the CFSP within the meaning of art 218(6) TFEU when its substantive legal basis is solely a CFSP one, even where such an agreement has incidental components or aims relating to other legal bases (paras 43–62).

19 Case C-130/10 *Parliament v Council* EU:C:2012:472 (note that art 215 TFEU is not itself a CFSP provision but it is used to implement CFSP decisions under the TFEU).

20 Member States and the Council have been rather open to funding measures which come very close to the CFSP under the EU development cooperation policy and under economic, financial and technical cooperation with third countries other than developing ones. This is reflected in particular in Regulation (EU) 230/2014 of the European Parliament and of the Council of 11 March 2014 establishing an instrument contributing to stability and peace [2014] OJ L77/1 (adopted under arts 209(1) and 212(1) TFEU).

2.4 Competences, Legal Bases, Decision-making Rules and External Representation

For a practitioner, competences, legal bases, decision-making rules and representation of the Union abroad, constitute primary issues, but above all, they are often interrelated and have to be handled together.

Whatever initiative one wants to undertake in order to act with or on behalf of the Union, the first question is often about competence: is the Union competent or not? If so, can one find, as a practitioner, the appropriate legal basis in the Treaties? Which rule of decision-making applies? Who can represent the Union to promote the action? Who can speak on behalf of the Union? These questions of who represents the Union and who can speak on behalf of the Union often come down to the question 'Who is competent: the Union or the Member States?'

Let us look at one particular issue, the external representation of the Union. One of the reasons for the multiple functions conferred on the High Representative was to end the external representation of the EU by the former Troika, the so called Solana/Patten/Rotating Presidency combination.[21] This Troika did not prove effective enough in transmitting a single voice to the outside world. In practice, the new arrangements for external representation in the Lisbon Treaty have not necessarily simplified or unified things, but rendered them more complex, by assigning the function of external representation to multiple actors.

First of all, in the field of CFSP, the role has been given to the High Representative and to the President of the European Council. The Council may also appoint European Union Special Representatives (Article 33 TEU). Secondly, the Commission represents the Union for non-CFSP matters, except where the Treaties provide otherwise (Article 17(1) TEU). Thirdly, the Council can decide on a proposal by the Commission to ensure unified representation within the international financial institutions (Article 138 TFEU). Fourthly, Union delegations in third countries and at international organisations represent the Union there (Article 221 TFEU). Fifthly, a number of EU agencies have distinct rules for their external representation (e.g. Europol and Eurojust). Sixthly, the specific rules mentioned above apply to the representation of the Union, within its competences, but they do not apply to the representation of the Member States. Seventhly, there is the specific case of EU representation in bilateral

---

21 I.e. the (pre-Lisbon) Secretary-General (of the Council)/High Representative, the external relations Commissioner and the Foreign Minister of the rotating Presidency of the Council.

joint bodies established on the basis of agreements between the EU and a third country or organisation (which are not further discussed here).

The Lisbon Treaty has failed to simplify or unify the Union's external representation, since the Union itself as well as the Union and its Member States may be represented by more than one institution or person. Therefore cooperation among all those involved is necessary.

There are other difficulties in practice beyond the question of who represents whom. There is also the question of the content of that representation, which is closely related to the question of who defines or determines the Union's position. Finally there is the question of the organisation of the coordination among the multiple actors, a question on which the Treaties are largely silent (except for Article 34(1) TEU on CFSP matters). A lot of coordination takes place locally. However this cannot replace the determination of the content of the position taken by the EU, which remains the responsibility of the EU institutions (see especially Articles 29 TEU and 218(9) TFEU).

2.5 *The Broad Jurisdiction of the CJEU in EU External Relations*

When operating in the area of EU external relations, a practitioner has to realise that most of his acts are subject to the jurisdiction of the CJEU.

This is a very important proposition. A diplomat operating at national level has probably not the same legal reflex that a Permanent Representative to the EU inevitably needs to develop when dealing with external action at the EU. Even when taking into account the limitations imposed by the Treaties on the role of the CJEU in CFSP,[22] the overall control of the Court in the area of external relations remains impressive. A very significant volume of case law has developed in the field of EU external relations. A practitioner must be conscious that there are judges in Luxembourg who have a significant say in this field. He must know that individuals and companies can challenge many of the decisions taken by the Council. There is serious judicial oversight and control.

Therefore, a Permanent Representative, when considering and discussing a decision, must very often make a balanced risk assessment between diplomacy and politics, on the one hand, and legal certainty, on the other. In order to preserve the credibility of decisions taken in the field of foreign policy and external action, a practitioner would naturally prefer to limit the number of cases that are lost before the CJEU. If the legal construct of a decision is inadequate or lacks proper reasons, the foreign policy choice of the Council loses all credibility, once it is successfully attacked before the CJEU.

22 But see n 15.

But there is also the broader role of the CJEU. Its role is not just about upholding the legal soundness and credibility of a given policy choice in external relations. The CJEU also arbitrates often in the overall inter-institutional balance, the respect of competences, as well as the respect of the fundamental objectives of the European Union in external relations, among which is the objective of respect for international law.

For these reasons it is important for a Permanent Representative to have some knowledge of the case law of the CJEU, in particular on the relationship between international law and the law of the European Union.

Describing the different aspects of this fascinating world of case law of the CJEU would go beyond the scope of this contribution.

I will therefore limit myself to mentioning ten relatively recent interesting cases:[23]

- Joined Cases C-584/10 P, C-593/10 P and C-595/10 P, *Commission and Others v Yassin Abdullah Kadi*, 18 July 2013, EU:C:2013:518 (*Kadi II*) – sanctions, fundamental rights, United Nations.
- Opinion 2/13 of 18 December 2014, EU:C:2014:2454 – draft agreement of the accession of the European Union to the European Convention on Human Rights (ECHR).
- Case C-377/12, *Commission v Council*, 11 June 2014, EU:C:2014:1903 (*Philippines agreement*) – choice of a legal basis for an international agreement between the EU, its Member States, and the Philippines; no addition of legal bases regarding third country nationals, transport and environment to those on trade and development.
- Case C-399/12, *Germany v Council*, 7 October 2014, EU:C:2014:2258 – position to be taken by the EU in an international organisation of which it is not a member but on an issue for which competence has been conferred on the Union.

23 During the editing phase of this contribution, some further cases were decided by the CJEU which might have merited inclusion in this list. See e.g. Case C-73/14, *Council v Commission* EU:C:2015:663 (on the submission of a written statement on behalf of the EU to the International Tribunal for the Law of the Sea); Case C-660/13 *Council v Commission* EU:C:2016:616 (on the signature of an Addendum to a Memorandum of Understanding on a Swiss financial contribution); Case C-455/14 P *H v. Council and Commission* EU:C:2016:569 (on the jurisdiction of the CJEU over staff seconded by Member States to EU civilian crisis management operations). Furthermore, the case law on restrictive measures includes some additional important cases (beyond *Kadi*) but these cannot be included here either. See also the chapters by Pieter-Jan Kuijper and by Allan Rosas in this book.

- Case C-658/11, *Parliament v Council*, 24 June 2014, EU:C:2014:2025 – information to the European Parliament in the context of an international agreement that is exclusively based on the CFSP as well as the European Parliament's role in relation to such agreements.
- Case C-130/10, *Parliament v Council*, 19 July 2012, EU:C:2012:472 – delimitation between the CFSP and the area for freedom, security and justice as regards counter-terrorism measures.
- Case C-246/07, *Commission v Sweden*, 20 April 2010, EU:C:2010:203 (*PFOS*) – limitations on the possibilities for individual Member States to undertake action in international conferences or organisations; general principle of sincere cooperation.
- Case C-366/10, *Air Transport Association of America and Others v Secretary of State for Energy and Climate Change*, 21 December 2011, EU:C:2011:864 – preliminary ruling on the validity of the inclusion of air transport activities in the trade system of emission rights under international law.
- Case C-114/12, *Commission v Council*, 4 September 2014, EU:C:2014:2151 (international convention for the protection of neighbouring rights of broadcasting organisations) – extent of the exclusive external competence of the Union in an area that is subject to EU regulation.
- Case C-81/13, *United Kingdom v Council*, 18 December 2014, EU:C:2014:2449 – coordination of social security systems in the context of Turkey-EU Association agreement; choice of legal basis, qualified majority voting.

2.6 *Knowing Who May Do What under the Treaties*

A practitioner must know exactly what the persons in the Treaty are authorised to do and what the institutions may, can or want to do in the field of the CFSP and External Action.

The important office holders in the Treaties are clearly the High Representative for Foreign Affairs and Security Policy, the President of the Commission and the (now Permanent) President of the European Council.

A Permanent Representative must not only know exactly which tasks and duties the Treaties have entrusted upon these office holders, but also what happens in practice and how this practice develops. With the entry into force of the Lisbon Treaty, the High Representative of the Union for Foreign Affairs and Security Policy, first Baroness Ashton and today Federica Mogherini, replaced both the former High Representative for CFSP (who was also the Secretary-General of the Council) and the Commissioner for External Relations. The intention therefore was clearly set out: closing the distance between traditional foreign policy and the other external policies of the Union. The core objective to ensure consistency within the Union's external relations was therefore present from the start. However, the High Representative has to share the international scene with the President of the European Council. The latter ensures 'at his level and in that capacity' the external representation of the Union on issues concerning its CFSP, without prejudice to the powers of the High Representative (Article 15(6) TEU).

Everybody would agree that this arrangement allows for the President of the European Council to represent the Union at the level of Heads of State or Government in the area of the CFSP, whereas the High Representative would do the same at Ministerial level. In practice this distinction according to the level of contacts is widely respected. But also in practice, Permanent Representatives have witnessed during the Van Rompuy years, that this first President of the European Council went beyond the subject matter of the CFSP in his international contacts. He always integrated in his conversations the so called ex-first pillar matters. Integrating national and international issues in diplomatic contacts and conversations is a normal practice at national level for heads of state and government. But at European level, the President of the European Commission could have contested the fact that the President of the European Council went beyond the CFSP. Every subject other than the CFSP that falls within Union competence is in principle reserved to the Commission when it comes to external representation. But President Barroso never complained. Moreover, he and Herman Van Rompuy very wisely agreed on a division of labour for interventions on behalf of the EU in the G20 and the then G8. On the other hand, Permanent Representatives have witnessed in the first post-Lisbon years certain actions in the Commission, including by President Barroso, to break into the Treaty remit of the High Representative or at least to hamper the execution of some of her multiple tasks under the Treaties.

Today's practice has evolved with the new personalities in the institutions. Two of the more striking illustrations are the following. First one can witness a more pro-active and political role of the Commission, of its President and its first Vice-President, including on the international scene. The recent negotiation by Vice-President Timmermans of a Turkey-EU action plan and draft Summit declaration, without Council mandate, was an interesting case from the institutional point of view. Secondly, the High Representative has taken her role as Vice-President of the Commission very seriously and is engaged in much appreciated coordinating efforts on external relations within the European Commission.

2.7 *The Frequent Recourse to Restrictive Measures*

EU sanctions or restrictive measures constitute an increasingly used and sometimes exclusive instrument to achieve the objectives of the EU's CFSP.

Within the framework of the CFSP, the Council can impose restrictive measures against third countries and against natural or legal persons and groups or non-State entities (under Articles 29 TEU and 215 TFEU). These sanctions, as they are often called, may implement UN Security Council resolutions adopted under Chapter 7 of the UN Charter or they can be autonomous measures of the Union.

One of the first political questions a practitioner must ask himself is therefore: UN and/or EU sanctions? What is the best approach or option? The UN and the EU are different international organisations. They represent different legal orders each with their legal/diplomatic advantages and disadvantages. In some situations, like for example today's situation in Libya, the UN route may be more appropriate, because it mobilises a wider or even universal political coverage, compared to the coverage and the effects of a regional sanctions regime. On the other hand, a practitioner must take into account the provisions of the Charter. Legally he has to deal with the primacy question of the international legal order.[24] Politically, he has to assess whether a majority in the Security Council can be mobilised without encountering a veto by one of the five Permanent Members of the Security Council.

A second obvious question for the practitioner is to make an evaluation of the precise objective he wants the EU to achieve. In general terms, the EU imposes sanctions to bring about a change in policy, activity, and behaviour by the target country, by part of a country, the government, selected entities, individuals or groups etc. Sanctions are generally presented as a preventive, non-punitive instrument that allows the EU to react swiftly to political challenges and developments. The political objectives and criteria of sanctions have to be defined in the legal acts. They are supposedly part of a wider policy approach, involving diplomacy, dialogue, or other efforts and instruments.

It is worth highlighting the increased recourse by the EU over the last few years to this instrument. It is difficult to imagine today a meeting of EU Foreign Ministers, without there being a suggestion or discussion on sanctions.

Today more than 30 different EU sanctions regimes are in existence and more than 2300 persons and entities have been designated under these measures.[25] This is enormous. It is difficult to assess the effectiveness of this arsenal of sanctions. The oil embargo against Iran and the sanctions against Myanmar come to mind as some of the more effective ones.

---

24 See from the international law perspective in particular art 103 UN Charter.

25 For an overview, including a consolidated list of sanctions in force, see EEAS website <https://eeas.europa.eu/topics/sanctions-policy/423/sanctions-policy_en> accessed 20 November 2016.

But today the Ukraine sanctions are very topical. There are four different regimes with different dates of expiry and specific implementing and amending rules. The first regime concerns the misappropriation of funds. The second deals with the respect for the territorial sovereignty and integrity of Ukraine. The third separate regime concerns the illegal annexation of Crimea. The fourth consists of economic measures against the Russian State.

A lot of investment went into these sanction regimes. Until recently much more than the investment that went into diplomatic effort.

Each listing of (additional) persons and entities implies a restriction of individual liberties and an obligation on Member States to freeze funds.

That is precisely the reason why the question of the legality of restrictive measures has become so important. For each specific case, the EU lays down clear criteria for the purpose of determining who should be listed and de-listed. For each person or entity on the list, a file has to be available at the Council. Other strict legal conditions related to the introduction and implementation of sanctions concern the respect for human rights and fundamental freedoms, in particular the right of defence and the right to an effective remedy.

It remains to be seen if this recent trend to develop its own regional system of sanctions in an EU-context will continue in the longer term.

2.8 *The Resources Available for EU External Relations: Potential versus Reality*

The resources potentially available to the European Union to conduct the CFSP and to undertake External Action are huge in theory but not necessarily in practice.

The resources available to the Union and the Member States are potentially huge. And they can and should be taken together as foreseen in Articles 21 and 26(3) of the TEU: 'The Common Foreign and Security policy shall be put into effect by the High Representative and by the Member States, *using national and Union resources*' (emphasis added).

The Union may not be a power in the Pentagon meaning of the word and it may not be a geopolitical power in the real world of today, but it can claim this status by way of potential.

Despite the rise of strong new partners in the world, the EU remains at the top of world rankings regarding its foreign trade, its diplomatic cooperation with third countries, its development cooperation, its financial centres (London, Frankfurt, Paris, Amsterdam, ...), its participation in scientific, technological and academic progress, its rich history and experience in the world of business, and its cultural and economic wealth.

There are two downsides today to this rosy picture of huge potential: the first is the reduction of the means that Member States spend on defence, and the huge differences in the level of expenditure among Member States. Today only four EU Member States respect the North Atlantic Treaty Organisation (NATO) commitment to spend 2 percent of GDP on defence. A second downside is the inadequate use of resources put at the disposal of the Union budget to undertake actions in the field of external relations: 6,35 billion euro in the 2014 budget and 7,42 billion euro in the 2015 budget. Although this last amount represents an increase, which will be further increased in 2016, the overall sum remains modest. But a real challenge is the lack of coordination and complementarities between the resources available at European level and at national level. Those resources are therefore only potentially and statistically at the disposal of the European Union. The huge discrepancy between the resources made available for development cooperation and the resources available for action in other fields of EU external relations is also striking.

2.9 *An Unsatisfactory Participation in International Organisations*

The participation of the European Union in international organisations is not satisfactory today.

The EU is a full member of the World Trade Organisation and the Food and Agricultural Organisation. In most other international organisations it has fewer rights of participation.

In theory, the EU could become a member of a vast number of international organisations, as it has received a wide scope of competences in the Treaties. But it is difficult to detect today what the policy of the Commission and the High Representative is in this regard. One does not see a plan or a strategy indicating for which organisations the EU would need to seek membership. One could imagine a minimalistic scenario like joining only organisations dealing with issues that fall under exclusive competence, including competences that have become exclusive through being internally exercised in accordance with the *ERTA* case law. But other approaches are possible. The point however is that neither a deliberate approach nor any coherent plan seems to be promoted.

This does not mean that it would be an easy task to devise and agree upon such a plan. Indeed the possibility for the EU to become a member of international organisations depends mainly on the following question: does the original or amended constitution of the international organisation concerned, allow for an organisation like the EU to become a member or not?

If this is not the case, the greatest challenge for the EU lies in overcoming the objections of the other members of the organisation to the accession of the

EU. This challenge is particularly difficult when these other members are in a position to prevent the Union from joining that organisation or seek to obtain a hefty price for the Union's membership. There is one example in the framework of the UN that illustrates the difficulties the EU has sometimes faced in attempting to obtain an appropriate status. I refer to the difficulties experienced in order to obtain enhanced observer status for the EU at the UN General Assembly. It proved more difficult than expected to have Resolution 65/276 adopted by the United Nations General Assembly (UNGA) on 3 May 2011. Long and laborious negotiations had to be undertaken with a number of UN Member States, in particular those belonging to the Caribbean Community which were mindful of the status quo in the UNGA.[26] The conditions under which the new enhanced observer status of the EU has to be exercised were set out in the annex to the Resolution. These so-called modalities have been further clarified by the UN Secretary-General in his Note of 1 June 2011 to the UNGA.[27]

If some commentators have criticised these restrictions on the actual participation rights of the Union in the work of the UNGA, thereby limiting the EU's capacity to influence decisions in the organisation,[28] one can understand this against the background of the Lisbon objective in favour of a stronger external representation of the EU. It is probably true that the resistance to enhanced EU participation in the UNGA had been underestimated at the time, including by Permanent Representatives in Brussels and in New York. This not entirely successful experience may also have tempered further appetite by the Commission and the HR to seek EU accession to more international organisations.

2.10 *Continued Challenges Relating to International Agreements*

The negotiation, signing and conclusion of international agreements by the European Union still give rise to difficulties in the application of the streamlined procedure after Lisbon.

In the different stages of the Treaties (Rome, Maastricht, Amsterdam, Nice), various provisions have governed the internal procedure for the negotiation, signing and conclusion of international agreements by the EU. The Rome

26 For an insider's view, see Pedro A Serrano de Haro, *Participation of the EU in the work of the UN: General Assembly Resolution 65/276* (2012) CLEER Working Paper 2012/4 <http://www.asser.nl/media/1633/cleer2012-4web.pdf> accessed 15 November 2016.

27 'Participation of the European Union in the work of the United Nations – Note by the Secretary-General' UN doc A/65/856.

28 See e.g. Jan Wouters, Jed Odermatt and Thomas Ramopoulos, 'The Status of the European Union at the United Nations after the General Assembly Resolution of 3 May 2011' (Global Governance Opinions, Katholieke Universiteit Leuven, July 2011).

Treaty, for example, endowed the European Economic Community (EEC) with the power to conclude trade agreements (the well known Article 113 EEC, which subsequently became Article 133 TEC!) or Association Agreements, but also contained a general treaty-making clause (Article 228 EEC). Subsequent Treaty reforms introduced new provisions. These were not always easy to apply. I still remember that, in the period 2000–2009, practitioners struggled with different legal bases for the different pillars (then Articles 24 and 38 TEU and 300 TEC). The Treaty of Lisbon did away with this distinction. Nowadays, in principle, Article 218 TFEU is the sole provision on treaty-making of the Union.

However, the subject matter of the envisaged agreement will still play a role, in order to ascertain the substantive legal basis for the Union to conclude it and to identify the respective powers of the institutions in this process, including the voting rules in the Council and the respective roles of the HR and the Commission. Moreover, Article 207 TFEU on the common commercial policy introduces special provisions to the single negotiation procedure under the Lisbon Treaty. Furthermore, Article 219 TFEU expressly maintains the derogation from the single procedure when it comes to agreements on monetary policy.

It would go beyond the scope of this contribution to address the so-called *non-legal* agreements (such as memoranda of understanding) which are frequently used instruments in external relations and diplomacy.[29] Nor will the other provisions of the Treaties be covered, allowing the Union to conclude international agreements in various fields: agreements with neighbouring countries, readmission agreements, and agreements in the field of research, space, technological development or environment, agreements for economic and financial cooperation with third countries or providing humanitarian aid.

What are the different steps that a Permanent Representative has to keep in mind in the single procedure for the negotiation, signature and conclusion of a legally binding international agreement?

The first step under Article 218(3) TFEU is a recommendation from the Commission (or the High Representative when the envisaged agreement relates exclusively or principally to the CFSP) to the Council. It is therefore the Commission that takes the first step and makes the first assessment of the question whether a negotiation is useful, desirable etc. The Council gives the authorisation to the Commission (or the HR for CFSP agreements)[30] to open the

29 See on this Case C-660/13 *Council v Commission* EU:C:2016:616.

30 In practice, the Commission and HR have sometimes presented a joint recommendation for agreements covering CFSP and non-CFSP matters, and the Council has appointed a negotiating team comprising both with one of them in the lead (see the chapters by Frederik Naert and by Stephan Marquardt in this book).

necessarynegotiations. The Permanent Representative has to realise that there is always a negotiator. This person negotiates on behalf of the Union, on the basis of negotiating directives which are in principle contained in a document of a classified nature, and are therefore, at least in principle, not published. The negotiation normally ends when the chief negotiators on both sides initial a common text. The initialing by an EU negotiator is normally covered by the negotiating directives. The signature and conclusion of the agreement constitute the next steps. Here it becomes more complicated because of the increased role given to the European Parliament. On CFSP agreements there is no such problem. Sometimes, authorisation of signature and conclusion is one step. In other cases, there are two steps in the procedure. The Council will first take a decision on signature thereby empowering the signature on behalf of the EU of the authentic text. This act triggers the good faith requirement under Article 18 of the Vienna Convention on the Law of Treaties. The Union's consent to be bound, however, is only expressed in a second step through an act of approval. In five cases, the Council takes decisions on 'conclusion' after obtaining the consent of the European Parliament: association agreements, the accession agreement to the ECHR, agreements having budgetary implications, agreements covering fields to which either the ordinary legislative procedure applies, or the special legislative procedure where consent by the European Parliament is required, and agreements establishing a special institutional framework by organising cooperation procedures. In practice, especially given the wide use of the ordinary legislative procedure, this covers most agreements. In other cases, and with the further exception of the CFSP, the Council must only consult the European Parliament.

One drawback of the two-step procedure is that considerable time may pass between signature and conclusion. In order to bridge this time gap, it is possible to provide for provisional application of the Agreement in line with Article 25 of the Vienna Convention on the Law of Treaties. The Council can take this decision on provisional application when deciding on signature. It did so recently on an Agreement with Ukraine[31] and the European Parliament was informed afterwards.

The possibility *to suspend* an agreement existed before Lisbon and the procedure remains the same (Article 218(9) TFEU). Suspension or partial suspension

31 See Council Decision 2014/295/EU of 17 March 2014 on the signing, on behalf of the European Union, and provisional application of the Association Agreement between the European Union and the European Atomic Energy Community and their Member States, of the one part, and Ukraine, of the other part, as regards the Preamble, Article 1, and Titles I, II and VII thereof [2014] OJ L161/1.

decisions have been taken by the Council in relation to agreements between the EU and Syria for example.[32]

While Article 218 TFEU contains detailed provisions on treaty-making, it is silent on *termination of agreements*. To identify the applicable procedure, recourse can be had to constitutional principles common to Member States, EU practice and institutional balance considerations. An important question in this regard is to know the role of the European Parliament when terminating an international agreement to which the EU is a party.

What are the difficulties and problems in practice?

Many of the difficulties have to do with the whole issue of competences and the mixed character of agreements.

One of the intellectually and legally more stimulating exercises in the work of the Convention on the future of the European Union was the successful attempt to codify the division of competences in the Union. The safeguarding of the competences of Member States was part of this exercise.

What were the implications of this exercise in the field of external relations? On the one hand, there was an expansion of the scope of competences (e.g. foreign direct investments, intellectual property, humanitarian aid, solidarity clause) and on the other hand, the Treaty of Lisbon attempted to safeguard the external competences of Member States.

Applied to the abovementioned question of treaty-making powers of the EU, it implies that it will continue to be possible to negotiate and conclude agreements with a 'mixed character'. Such mixed agreements contain provisions relating to matters within the competence of the EU and also provisions relating to matters within the competence of Member States. In those situations dual decisions by the EU and the Member States are needed, with ratification/conclusion at both levels.

The Commission has in several cases proposed negotiating directives for EU-only agreements, ie non-mixed agreements to which only the EU and not the Member States would be party. The Council has a tendency to reject this.[33] The Association Agreement with Kosovo can be mentioned as a recent interesting exception to this trend in the Council. This agreement became an

32 See Council Decision 2011/523/EU of 2 September 2011 partially suspending the application of the Cooperation Agreement between the European Economic Community and the Syrian Arab Republic [2011] OJ L 228/19.

33 See also the chapter by Frederik Naert in this book and Ricardo Gosalbo Bono and Frederik Naert, 'The Reluctant (Lisbon) Treaty and is Implementation in the Practice of the Council' in Piet Eeckhout and Manuel Lopez-Escudero (eds), *The European Union's External Action in Times of Crisis* (Hart Publishing 2016) 13.

EU-only agreement, because of a question that still divides the EU Member States, ie the recognition of Kosovo.[34] The CJEU has a tendency to continue or even reinforce its traditional views on the scope of EU competences in the field of external relations. At the same time, it accepts, as far as I understand, that mixed agreements are an integral part of the EU legal order.

3 Conclusion

There are of course other aspects and difficulties related to the tenth and last proposition of this contribution. But the fact itself that the Treaties recognise explicitly the competences of Member States was worth mentioning at the end. In the field covered by this contribution, it symbolises an open door for EU Member States to avail themselves of certain possibilities. During my most recent years in COREPER, I have been witness to significant attempts of some Member States to carve out for themselves a more prominent role in the whole area of EU external relations, including in the CFSP. This last remark should not be read as an encouragement for future members of COREPER or the PSC to go in the same direction, but rather as a remark to pause on, and to integrate in the broader knowledge that is needed when entering the new post-Lisbon world of external action and foreign policy. I hope that a brief pause will also help in resisting those temptations. May it also help eventually to use the full potential of the Lisbon Treaty, instead of preventing it. I think this is what our friend Ricardo also would have wished for.

34 See the Chapter by Frederik Naert in this book.

CHAPTER 5

The Role of the Council Legal Service in Ensuring Respect for the Law

*Michael Bishop and Frederik Naert**

1 Introduction

Among the EU institutions, the Council is probably not the one best known to the public or to lawyers. The way in which the Council works in practice is even less known, as is the role of its Legal Service. Not much has been written about the latter.[1]

We therefore thought it would be fitting to offer a glimpse into the work of the Council Legal Service (CLS), the service in which Ricardo Gosalbo Bono spent the latter part of his career in the EU institutions.

As the work of the CLS is an intrinsic part of the work of the Council, it cannot be understood without some knowledge of the main functions of the Council and the way it operates in practice. We will therefore first explain what the Council does and how it operates,[2] before addressing how the CLS participates in this work of the Council.

The work of the Council is linked to that of the European Council, which is now also an institution of the Union in the formal sense, ie within the meaning of Article 13(1) TEU.[3] Moreover, the European Council does not have its own secretariat but is assisted by the General Secretariat of the Council. This also

* The views expressed are those of the authors and do not bind the Council, its General Secretariat, or its Legal Service.

1 For two exceptions, see Antonio Tizzano, 'Quelques brèves réflexions sur le rôle du jurisconsulte du Conseil' in Marta Arpio Santacruz and others (eds), *A Man for All Treaties: Liber amicorum en l'honneur de Jean-Claude Piris* (Bruylant 2012) 531 and Michael Bishop, 'The Council's Legal Service' in Martin Westlake and David Galloway (eds) with Toon Digneffe, *The Council of the European Union* (3rd edn, John Harper Publishing 2006) 357–364. The present contribution builds on the latter text.

2 See generally Westlake and Galloway (eds) with Digneffe (n 1).

3 In addition to these institutions, the Union also comprises a broader range of entities, such as agencies, bodies and offices. These inter alia include the European External Action Service (EEAS).

 | DOI 10.1163/9789004347175_006

means that the Council Legal Service provides legal advice to the European Council as well as to the Council. We will therefore also briefly discuss the European Council.

2 The Council of the EU and Its Main Functions, Organisation and Operation

The Council of the European Union is one of the institutions of the Union within the meaning of Article 13(1) TEU. Its composition, main functions and key features are set out in Article 16 TEU, which is complemented by Articles 237 to 243 TFEU, and by the Council's Rules of Procedure.[4]

These legal provisions form the basis for the four components of the Council in the broad sense: (i) the Council in the formal sense, ie a meeting composed of representatives of the (currently 28) Governments of the Member States at ministerial level as Council of the EU; (ii) the Presidency (or rather, since the Treaty of Lisbon, Presidencies); (iii) the various Council preparatory bodies; and (iv) the General Secretariat of the Council (GSC), of which the CLS is a part.

We will briefly address each of these four components, as well as the functions of the Council, its decision-making and voting rules, and the issue of transparency of the work of the Council.

2.1 *Composition – A Meeting of Ministers*

The Council consists of a representative of each Member State 'at ministerial level, who may commit the government of the Member State in question and cast its vote' (Article 16(2) TEU). Representatives at ministerial level normally means ministers or State secretaries, but this depends on national constitutional arrangements of each Member State.

The quorum required for the Council to be able to take decisions and to vote is achieved when the majority of its members who are entitled to vote[5] are present.[6] This is linked to the rule that when a member of the Council

4 The Council's Rules of Procedure are annexed to Council Decision 2009/937/EU of 1 December 2009 adopting the Council's Rules of Procedure [2009] OJ L325/35 (last amended by Council Decision (EU, Euratom) 2015/2393 of 8 December 2015 [2015] OJ L332/133). They are adopted under art 240(3) TEU.

5 See Council's Rules of Procedure, art 16 on cases where a member of the Council may not participate in a vote under the Treaties.

6 Ibid, art 11(4).

is absent, it can delegate its vote to another member of the Council, but a member of the Council may only act on behalf of one other member.[7] While a member of the Council who is not present may arrange to be represented,[8] typically by the Permanent Representative of that Member State, who may participate in the discussions, it can only delegate a vote to another member of the Council.

The Council meets in different configurations, 'the list of which shall be adopted in accordance with Article 236 [TFEU]'.[9] Article 16(6) TEU names and specifies the role of two of these configurations:

> The *General Affairs Council* shall ensure consistency in the work of the different Council configurations. It shall prepare and ensure the follow-up to meetings of the European Council, in liaison with the President of the European Council and the Commission.
>
> The *Foreign Affairs Council* shall elaborate the Union's external action on the basis of strategic guidelines laid down by the European Council and ensure that the Union's action is consistent.[10]

There are currently ten Council configurations and they are listed in Annex I to the Council's Rules of Procedure:

- General affairs;
- Foreign affairs;
- Economic and financial affairs, including budget;
- Justice and home affairs, including civil protection;
- Employment, social policy, health and consumer affairs;
- Competitiveness (internal market, industry, research and space), including tourism;
- Transport, telecommunications and energy;
- Agriculture and fisheries;
- Environment;
- Education, youth, culture and sport, including audiovisual affairs.

---

7 Art 239 TFEU; Council's Rules of Procedure, art 11(3).

8 Council's Rules of Procedure, art 4.

9 Art 16(6) TEU. Art 236(a) TFEU provides that the European Council shall adopt by a qualified majority 'a decision establishing the list of Council configurations, other than those of the General Affairs Council and of the Foreign Affairs Council, in accordance with Article 16(6) [TEU]'.

10 Emphasis added.

While the General Affairs Council and Foreign Affairs Council have a specific role, there is no hierarchy among the different Council configurations and the Council is a single body. As a consequence, a configuration can adopt acts falling within the remit of another configuration – this is typically the case for non-discussion points (the items on the agenda of the Council are divided into A items and B items, A items being points for which approval by the Council is possible without discussion[11]).

2.2 *The Presidency*

The Presidency of the Council configurations, other than that of Foreign Affairs, is held by a Member State representative in the Council 'on the basis of equal rotation, in accordance with the conditions established in accordance with Article 236 [TFEU[12]]'.[13] This Presidency is often referred to as 'the rotating Presidency'. The High Representative of the Union for Foreign Affairs and Security Policy (High Representative) presides over the Foreign Affairs Council.[14] Where necessary, the High Representative is replaced in this capacity by the relevant Minister of the rotating Presidency.[15]

The order in which the Member States hold the Presidency of the Council from 1 January 2007 is set out in the Annex to Council Decision of 1 January 2007 determining the order in which the office of President of the Council shall be held.[16] It is also the order in which members of the Council are seated in Council meetings.

---

11 See Council's Rules of Procedure, art 3(6).

12 Art 236(b) TFEU provides that the European Council shall adopt by a qualified majority 'a decision on the Presidency of Council configurations, other than that of Foreign Affairs, in accordance with Article 16(9) [TEU]'.

13 Art 16(9) TEU.

14 Art 18(3) TEU.

15 Council's Rules of Procedure, art 2(5).

16 Decision 2007/5/EC, Euratom [2007] OJ L1/11. This order was confirmed in art 1 of Council Decision 2009/908/EU of 1 December 2009 laying down measures for the implementation of the European Council Decision on the exercise of the Presidency of the Council, and on the chairmanship of preparatory bodies of the Council [2009] OJ L322/28. Pursuant to art 3 of the latter decision 'The order in which the Member States will hold the Presidency as from 1 July 2020 shall be decided by the Council before 1 July 2017'. Following the outcome of the UK referendum, this decision was amended by Council Decision (EU) 2016/1316 of 26 July 2016 amending Decision 2009/908/EU, laying down measures for the implementation of the European Council Decision on the exercise of the Presidency of the Council, and on the chairmanship of preparatory bodies of the Council [2016] OJ L 208/42, which also takes into account the accession of Croatia to the EU.

Furthermore, on 1 December 2009, the European Council adopted a decision[17] which inter alia provides that:

- 'The Presidency of the Council, with the exception of the Foreign Affairs configuration, shall be held by pre-established groups of three Member States for a period of 18 months. The groups shall be made up on a basis of equal rotation among the Member States, taking into account their diversity and geographical balance within the Union' (Article 1(1)). This group of three Member States is referred to as the Presidency 'Trio'. The groups were fixed by the Council late 2009[18] and the current Trio is formed by the Netherlands, Slovakia and Malta. Each Trio establishes an 18 month programme.[19] Within this framework, each Presidency also establishes a six month planning.[20]
- 'Each member of the group shall in turn chair for a six-month period all configurations of the Council, with the exception of the Foreign Affairs configuration. (...) Members of the team may decide alternative arrangements among themselves' (Article 1(2)).
- 'The Committee of Permanent Representatives of the Governments of the Member States shall be chaired by a representative of the Member State chairing the General Affairs Council' (Article 2, first paragraph).
- 'The Chair of the Political and Security Committee shall be held by a representative of the High Representative (...)' (Article 2, second paragraph).
- 'The chair of the preparatory bodies of the various Council configurations, with the exception of the Foreign Affairs configuration, shall fall to the member of the group chairing the relevant configuration, unless decided otherwise [by the Council in an implementing decision]' (Article 2, third paragraph).

The latter cases are set out in Articles 4 and 5 of Council Decision 2009/908/EU of 1 December 2009 laying down measures for the implementation of the European Council Decision on the exercise of the Presidency of the Council, and on the chairmanship of preparatory bodies of the Council and in Annexes II and III thereto.[21] Under these rules, most external relations working parties

17 European Council Decision 2009/881/EU of 1 December 2009 on the exercise of the Presidency of the Council [2009] OJ L315/50.

18 Council Decision 2009/908/EU (n 16), art 1 and annex I.

19 Council's Rules of Procedure, art 2(6). For the programme of the current Trio, see Council doc 12396/15 of 3 December 2015.

20 Council's Rules of Procedure, art 2(7).

21 [2009] OJ L322/28.

are chaired by representatives of the High Representative,[22] with the exception of those working parties in the field of trade and development, six 'horizontal' preparatory bodies, and the EU Military Committee and its Working Group.[23] Furthermore, eight preparatory bodies have elected chairs and seven are chaired by the General Secretariat of the Council, including some by the Legal Service (see below).

The Presidency has an important role in advancing the Council's work and is responsible for the smooth conduct of the discussion in the Council. As chair of Council meetings and of the meetings of preparatory bodies,[24] it proposes the agenda for these meetings and is responsible for the proper conduct of the discussions.[25] This includes ensuring that the Council's Rules of Procedure and working methods are correctly applied.[26] It is also the Presidency's task to try and find common ground and suggest compromises that enable the Council to adopt its positions and decisions. To do so, it must act as an honest broker.

In principle, the Presidency also represents the Council in relations with the other EU institutions, especially in the legislative process, including in the so-called 'trilogues' and in Conciliation Committee meetings.[27]

2.3 *Preparatory Bodies*

Pursuant to the seventh paragraph of Article 16 TEU, 'A Committee of Permanent Representatives of the Governments of the Member States shall be

22 The decision adds that 'Where (...) a preparatory body (PSC and relevant working parties) shall be chaired by a representative of the High Representative, the responsibility for appointing the chair shall belong to the High Representative. (...) The High Representative shall ensure that the person he or she intends to appoint as chairperson will enjoy the confidence of Member States. If that person is not yet a member of the EEAS, he or she shall become one in accordance with the EEAS recruitment procedures, at least for the time of the appointment' (ibid, annex II). Such chairs are often referred to as 'EEAS chairs'.

23 These two groups have chairs elected by the EU Military Committee and appointed respectively by Council and COREPER. They are included among the eight preparatory bodies with elected chairs.

24 Pursuant to art 1(5) of the Council's Rules of Procedure 'Unless otherwise specified, references in these Rules of Procedure to the Presidency or the President shall apply to any person chairing one of the Council configurations or, as appropriate, one of its preparatory bodies'.

25 See Council's Rules of Procedure, arts 3 (in particular para 1) and 20. See also generally Westlake and Galloway (eds) with Digneffe (n 1) 325–339.

26 Art 20 of the Council's Rules of Procedure sets out in some detail the prerogatives of the Presidency in this respect, as do the Working Methods in Annex V thereto.

27 See in relation to the European Parliament Council's Rules of Procedure, art 26.

responsible for preparing the work of the Council' (COREPER). This is repeated and further developed in Article 240(1) TFEU, which provides that:

> A committee consisting of the Permanent Representatives of the Governments of the Member States shall be responsible for preparing the work of the Council and for carrying out the tasks assigned to it by the latter. The Committee may adopt procedural decisions in cases provided for in the Council's Rules of Procedure.

In fact, there are two COREPER configurations: COREPER II, comprised of the Permanent Representatives, which prepares the General Affairs and Foreign Affairs Council, as well as the Justice and Home Affairs and Economic and Financial Affairs Council configurations, whereas COREPER I, comprised of the deputy Permanent Representatives, prepares the work of the other Council configurations.[28]

Article 19 of the Council's Rules of Procedure further specifies the role of COREPER. It inter alia provides that 'All items on the agenda for a Council meeting shall be examined in advance by Coreper unless the latter decides otherwise'; that 'Coreper shall endeavour to reach agreement at its level to be submitted to the Council for adoption'; and that:

> It shall (…) ensure consistency of the European Union's policies and actions and see to it that the following principles and rules are observed: (a) the principles of legality, subsidiarity, proportionality and providing reasons for acts; (b) rules establishing the powers of Union institutions, bodies, offices and agencies; (c) budgetary provisions; (d) rules on procedure, transparency and the quality of drafting.

Furthermore, in paragraph 7, it identifies eleven kinds of procedural decisions which COREPER may adopt.[29] These include authorisation to produce a copy of or an extract from a Council document for use in legal proceedings; decision

---

28 For a brief description, including of the genesis of COREPER, see General Secretariat of the Council, 'The Council of the European Union – 1952–2012: Sixty Years of Law- and Decision-making' (Publications Office of the European Union 2013) <http://www.consilium.europa.eu/en/documents-publications/publications/2013/council-european-union-1952-2012-sixty-years-law-decision-making/> accessed 15 November 2016, 17–20. See also Westlake and Galloway (eds) with Digneffe (n 1) 201–216.

29 As provided for in art 240(1) TFEU.

to use the written procedure; and approval of the wording of a letter to be sent to an institution or body.

Moreover, Article 19(3) of the Council's Rules of Procedure provides that 'Committees or working parties may be set up by, or with the approval of, Coreper with a view to carrying out certain preparatory work or studies defined in advance'. On this basis, COREPER or the Council[30] have established some 160 working parties and committees to help prepare the work of the Council. These working parties and committees are comprised of officials from all the Member States. These officials may work within the Permanent Representation of the Member States or may be based in the Member State capitals and only come to Brussels for working party meetings (the frequency of which can vary from multiple meetings a week to a few meetings per year). Every six months a list of Council preparatory bodies is published.[31]

Thus in practice the vast majority of the Council's work is done at the level of working parties (with on average some 15 to 20 working party meetings taking place on working days), under the coordination of COREPER.

2.4 *The General Secretariat*

The Council is assisted by a General Secretariat, under the responsibility of a Secretary-General appointed by the Council, and the Council decides on the organisation of the General Secretariat by a simple majority (Article 240(2) TFEU).

The role of the General Secretariat of the Council (GSC) is inter alia laid down in various provisions of the Council's Rules of Procedure, and especially Article 23. That Article states inter alia that, under the authority of the Council, 'the Secretary-General shall take all the measures necessary to ensure the smooth running of the General Secretariat' (Article 23(2)) and that 'The General Secretariat shall be closely and continually involved in organising, coordinating and ensuring the coherence of the Council's work and implementation of its 18-month programme. Under the responsibility and guidance of the Presidency, it shall assist the latter in seeking solutions' (Article 23(3)).

In essence, the role of the GSC includes an administrative aspect, namely ensuring that the Council and its preparatory bodies can meet and do their work (including availability of meeting rooms, translation, production of

30 It should be noted that some committees are provided for in the Treaties. See e.g. art 38 TEU on the Political and Security Committee. On Council preparatory bodies see also generally Westlake and Galloway (eds) with Digneffe (n 1) 217–222.

31 For the most recent version, see Council doc 11502/16 of 27 July 2016. Some working parties have different formations.

documents, security, etc.), and a policy supporting aspect, namely assisting the Presidency and ultimately the Council and its preparatory bodies in reaching agreement (e.g. suggesting compromise proposals and providing legal advice).[32]

The GSC also supports Intergovernmental Conferences both on amendment of the Treaties and on accession negotiations.

When the European External Action Service was established in 2010, it was stipulated that the EEAS is to support the High Representative, including 'in his/her capacity as President of the Foreign Affairs Council' but 'without prejudice to the normal tasks of the General Secretariat of the Council'.[33]

The GSC is organised into seven Directorates-General as well as a number of specific services/departments.[34] The Legal Service is part of the GSC (see below).

The GSC's mission statement reads as follows:

> As an open, efficient, independent and permanent European public service, the General Secretariat of the Council ensures that the European Council and the Council operate smoothly and lends them every assistance necessary so they can perform the missions conferred on them by the treaties to further the development of the Union. The General Secretariat provides advice and support to members of the European Council and the Council and to their Presidents in all areas of activity, as well as in the context of ministerial meetings and intergovernmental conferences.
>
> The core values that guide the General Secretariat – as an organisation as well as its individual employee – in carrying out its mission are:
>
> Professionalism
>
> In our work, we demonstrate integrity, professional competence, efficiency and commitment. We are active and open-minded in seeking solutions. We are responsible and accountable for our work.
>
> Esprit de corps

32 For a brief description, including of the evolution of the GSC, see GSC, 'The Council of the European Union – 1952–2012' (n 28) 21–23. See also generally Westlake and Galloway (eds) with Digneffe (n 1) 340–356.

33 Council Decision 2010/427/EU of 26 July 2010 establishing the organisation and functioning of the European External Action Service [2010] OJ L201/30, art 2(1). See also the chapter by Stephan Marquardt in this book.

34 See generally <http://www.consilium.europa.eu/en/general-secretariat/> accessed 15 November 2016.

We cooperate and communicate clearly so that the General Secretariat can carry out its mission effectively and consistently.

Impartiality

We are objective in carrying out our duties and treat all members of the European Council and the Council impartially in keeping with our duty of loyalty to the European Union. In our multicultural environment, we treat everybody with equal respect.[35]

2.5 *Functions*

The first paragraph of Article 16 TEU summarizes the Council's functions as follows: 'The Council shall, jointly with the European Parliament, exercise legislative and budgetary functions. It shall carry out policy-making and coordinating functions as laid down in the Treaties'.

The most important function among these is that of (co-)legislature. The Council has always been the Union's legislative body but over time it has increasingly shared this role with the European Parliament. Since the Treaty of Lisbon, in most cases EU legislation is adopted by the Council and the European Parliament together (on a proposal from the Commission), through the ordinary legislative procedure (commonly referred to as 'co-decision'). In some cases, a special legislative procedure applies and the Parliament has a more limited role. The Council may also reserve for itself implementing powers when adopting a legal act (Article 291(2) TFEU).

The EU budget is also adopted jointly by the Council and the Parliament.

In addition, the Council exercises policy-making and coordinating functions. One area where the Council's policy-making role is crucial is the Common Foreign and Security Policy (CFSP). In this field, the Council decides on specific legal acts and other actions without involving the European Parliament, although the European Parliament must be informed about all stages in the procedure for concluding international agreements under the CFSP.[36] By contrast, the Parliament must be regularly consulted on the main aspects and the basic choices of the CFSP and it may address questions and recommendations to the Council (Article 36 TEU).

---

35 CSG, 'Mission statement', available through <http://www.consilium.europa.eu/en/general-secretariat/> accessed 15 November 2016.

36 Furthermore, exceptionally, art 28(3) TEU requires consultation of the Parliament when the Council would adopt a decision establishing the specific procedures for guaranteeing rapid access to appropriations in the Union budget for urgent financing of initiatives in the framework of the CFSP.

The Council exercises a coordinating role inter alia by adopting guidelines and/or recommendations on economic and employment policies.

The Council also plays a key role in the process leading to the conclusion of international agreements by the Union (Article 218 TFEU). In particular, it adopts decisions authorising the opening of negotiations, it may issue negotiating directives to the Union negotiator (ie the Commission and/or High Representative), it may designate a special committee which has to be consulted by the negotiator (usually a Council working party), and it adopts decisions on the signing, provisional application (where applicable) and conclusion of agreements. In some cases the GSC performs depositary functions in respect of international agreements concluded by the Union.[37]

2.6 *Decision-making and Voting Rules*

Article 16(3), (4) and (5) TEU provide that 'The Council shall act by a qualified majority except where the Treaties provide otherwise' and specify what constitutes a qualified majority, including transitional provisions, including by reference to Article 238(2) TFEU and the Protocol on transitional provisions.[38]

We will not go into further detail on this, except to indicate that:

- as from 1 November 2014, a qualified majority is defined as at least 55 per cent of the members of the Council, comprising at least fifteen of them and representing Member States comprising at least 65 per cent of the population of the Union;
- however, where the Council does not act on a proposal from the Commission or from the High Representative, the qualified majority is defined as at least 72 per cent of the members of the Council representing the participating Member States, comprising at least 65 per cent of the population of these States;
- where the Council acts on a proposal from the Commission, it may amend that proposal only by acting unanimously, except in a few specific cases (Article 293(1) TFEU).

---

37 Art 25 of the Council's Rules of Procedure provides that 'In the event of the Secretary-General of the Council being designated as depositary of an agreement concluded by the Union or the European Atomic Energy Community and one or more States or international organisations, the acts of ratification, acceptance or approval of those agreements shall be deposited at the address of the Council. In such instances the Secretary-General shall perform the duties of a depositary and shall also ensure that the dates of entry into force of such agreements are published in the Official Journal'.

38 See also Council's Rules of Procedure, art 11.

Cases where the Treaties provide otherwise include cases where the Council acts by unanimity (e.g. this is the rule in the CFSP and applies for the conclusion of some international agreements; see respectively Articles 31 TEU and 218(8) TFEU) or by simple majority (e.g. regarding procedural matters and for the adoption of its Rules of Procedure; see Article 240(3) TFEU).

The Council adopts most decisions during a Council meeting, but in cases of urgency it may also adopt decisions by written procedure.[39] Legal acts can be adopted through the 'normal' written procedure, whereas some other decisions may be adopted through a 'simplified' written procedure. The latter is especially used in the field of the CFSP, through the 'COREU' network (which allows for the transmission of classified documents).

2.7 *Transparency*

Pursuant to Article 16(8) TEU, 'The Council shall meet in public when it deliberates and votes on a draft legislative act. To this end, each Council meeting shall be divided into two parts, dealing respectively with deliberations on Union legislative acts and non-legislative activities'.

The work of the Council has become increasingly transparent, but important parts of it remain outside the public domain. Thus while Articles 7, 8 and 9 of the Council's Rules of Procedure set out those cases in which the work of the Council takes place in public (including its legislative work) or may become public, Article 6 of these Rules of Procedure provides that 'Without prejudice to Articles 7, 8 and 9 and to provisions on public access to documents, the deliberations of the Council shall be covered by the obligation of professional secrecy, except in so far as the Council decides otherwise' (Article 6(1)) and adds that 'The Council or Coreper may authorise the production for use in legal proceedings of a copy of or an extract from Council documents which have not already been released to the public in accordance with the provisions on public access to documents' (Article 6(2)).

The Council is furthermore subject to the 'transparency' rules (access to documents) laid down in Regulation (EC) No 1049/2001[40] and in Article 10 *juncto* Annex II of the Council's Rules of Procedure.

39 Ibid, art 12.

40 Regulation (EC) 1049/2001 of the European Parliament and of the Council of 30 May 2001 regarding public access to European Parliament, Council and Commission documents [2001] OJ L145/43.

3 The European Council

The composition, functions and main features of the European Council are set out in Article 15 TEU. It may suffice to mention the following elements here:

- 'The European Council shall consist of the Heads of State or Government of the Member States, together with its President and the President of the Commission. The High Representative (…) shall take part in its work' (Article 15(2));
- 'The European Council shall provide the Union with the necessary impetus for its development and shall define the general political directions and priorities thereof. It shall not exercise legislative functions' (Article 15(1));
- 'Except where the Treaties provide otherwise, decisions of the European Council shall be taken by consensus' (Article 15(4)). Where qualified majority applies, the voting rules are the same as those applicable to the Council (Article 235(1) (TFEU));
- 'The European Council shall elect its President, by a qualified majority, for a term of two and a half years, renewable once' (Article 15(5) TEU). 'The President of the European Council: (a) shall chair it and drive forward its work; (b) shall ensure the preparation and continuity of the work of the European Council in cooperation with the President of the Commission, and on the basis of the work of the General Affairs Council; (…) The President of the European Council shall, at his level and in that capacity, ensure the external representation of the Union on issues concerning its common foreign and security policy, without prejudice to the powers of the High Representative (…)' (Article 15(6)).

Furthermore, Article 235 TFEU adds that 'The European Council shall act by a simple majority for procedural questions and for the adoption of its Rules of Procedure' (Article 235(3)) and that 'The European Council shall be assisted by the General Secretariat of the Council' (Article 235(4)). As indicated above, the European Council shall also adopt decisions on the Council configurations and their Presidency.

The European Council's Rules of Procedure[41] furthermore stipulate that 'Meetings of the European Council shall not be public' (Article 4(3)), while setting out rules on publicity and access to documents (Article 10); that 'The President shall be responsible for the application of these Rules of Procedure

41 The European Council's Rules of Procedure are annexed to European Council Decision 2009/882/EU of 1 December 2009 adopting its Rules of Procedure [2009] OJ L315/51.

and for ensuring that discussions are conducted smoothly' (Article 4(4)); that the quorum for voting is the presence of two thirds of its members (Article 6(3)); and they allow for the use of a written procedure (Article 7). They also provide that 'The European Council and its President shall be assisted by the General Secretariat of the Council, under the authority of its Secretary-General' (Article 13(1)) and that 'The Secretary-General of the Council shall attend the meetings of the European Council. He or she shall take all the measures necessary for the organisation of proceedings' (Article 13(2)).

The European Council now meets much more frequently than in the past, not least to deal with various crises and serious challenges for the Union. Also, its general political directions have on occasion become more specific. This has brought to the fore the importance of ensuring close coordination between the work of the Council and that of the European Council. The General Affairs Council plays a key role in this respect. This development also enhances the importance of legal advice to the European Council.

4 The Council Legal Service

It is not surprising that the Union's institutions have a legal service at their disposal. Indeed, most international organisations have legal advisors and offices. However, it is less common for different organs of an international organisation to each have their own legal office.[42] However, since the Court of Justice of the European Union (CJEU) can adjudicate disputes between the institutions, it would have been difficult for the Union to operate with a single legal service. This reason alone may explain why the Council, the European Parliament and the Commission, amongst others, have their own legal services. Similarly, when the EEAS was established, its central administration was to include a legal department.[43]

4.1 *Organisation of the CLS*

As indicated above, the CLS is part of the GSC. It is headed by a Director-General, currently Mr Hubert Legal, who is the legal advisor ('jurisconsulte') to

42 For example, the United Nations (UN) has a single Office of Legal Affairs, with the mission inter alia 'To provide a *unified central legal service* for the Secretariat and *the principal and other organs* of the United Nations', including 'By providing substantive secretariat functions *to United Nations bodies*' (Office of Legal Affairs' mission statement, <http://legal.un.org/ola/mission.aspx> accessed 15 November 2016, emphasis added).

43 See Council Decision 2010/427/EU (n 33), art 4(3)(b).

the Council and the European Council. In administrative terms, as regards staff and budget issues, the CLS operates like other parts of the GSC and is subject to the authority of the Secretary-General of the Council. However, it is autonomous as regards its legal advice and its Director-General ultimately determines the positions of the CLS.

The CLS currently consists of two principal components.[44] On the one hand, it comprises some 50 legal advisors and their assistants, spread over six Directorates, each headed by a Director. These lawyers perform the tasks of giving legal advice to the Council and its preparatory bodies, and of representing the Council in litigation before the Union courts. They include nationals of almost all Member States. On the other hand, it includes the 'Legislative Quality' Directorate in which some 100 'lawyer-linguists' and their assistants ensure the quality of legal acts adopted by the Council, including their identical meaning in all EU official languages. The consistency of the work of the CLS is facilitated by a coordination unit. An information unit provides horizontal support, including through the CLS library and research support. The CLS also has a number of interns.

The six Directorates and their areas of responsibility are the following:

- Directorate I: Competitiveness, Environment, Transport, Telecom, Energy;
- Directorate II: Employment, Social Affairs, Education, Agriculture, Fisheries;
- Directorate III: External Relations (including Trade Policy and Enlargement);
- Directorate IV: Institutional Questions / Staff Regulations / Litigation;[45]
- Directorate V: Justice and Home Affairs;
- Directorate VI: Economic and Financial Affairs, Budget, Structural Funds.

The 'Legislative Quality' Directorate is organised into three units as well as an office for coordination and the Official Journal. It comprises teams of in principle four lawyer/linguists covering each of the EU's 24 official languages.

The CLS holds a weekly meeting for all its members, in which the main current issues are addressed. This helps to ensure consistency in the work of the service. In addition, there is a weekly meeting of Directors with the Director-General and the Head of the Coordination Unit, and each Directorate usually holds its own weekly meeting as well.

44 The CLS no longer includes a Directorate responsible for inter-institutional relations, nor the unit for managing the 'co-decision procedure' with the European Parliament. These were transferred to other parts of the GSC.

45 This Directorate includes the CLS registry for Court cases. However, the cases are assigned to legal advisors depending on the subject-matter and language (see below).

4.2 *The Role of the* CLS

The best starting point to describe the CLS's main functions and approach is its mission statement. This mission statement reads as follows:

1. The Legal Service is the legal adviser to the Council and the European Council.
2. It assists the European Council, the Council and its preparatory bodies, the Presidency, and the General Secretariat, in order to ensure the legality and the drafting quality of legal acts. It contributes, by taking a creative approach where appropriate, to identifying legally correct and politically acceptable solutions, in cooperation with other Council departments. To that end, it gives opinions in complete impartiality – orally or in writing, at the request of the Council or on its own initiative – on any question of a legal nature.
3. The Legal Service also represents the European Council and the Council in proceedings before the courts of the European Union.
4. The Legal Service is responsible for checking the drafting quality of legal acts of the European Council and the Council and ensuring that they are legally and linguistically consistent in all of the Union's official languages.
5. The constant objective of the Legal Service is to provide timely contributions which are distinguished by their full respect for the law, their impartiality and their clarity.[46]

4.2.1 Advisory Role

The advisory role of the Legal Service consists of giving legal opinions, either orally or in writing, to the Council (and European Council) or its preparatory bodies, on any legal or institutional questions which may be raised in the course of the Council's work. The Legal Service may be asked for an opinion but even where this is not the case, it is still entitled and expected to draw the Council's attention to legal problems which would not have been noticed otherwise.

In order to be able to perform this role, the Legal Service has a seat at the table in meetings of the Council and of its preparatory bodies.[47] It also has a seat in meetings of the European Council.[48] The Legal Service ensures a systematic presence at meetings of the Council and COREPER (in principle at the level of its Director-General and/or a Director). By contrast, in most preparatory bodies the CLS occupies its seat on a more selective basis, depending on

46 CLS, 'Mission statement' (on file with the authors).

47 This seat is normally to the left of the Presidency, with the GSC usually seated in between.

48 The Legal Service seat is among those behind the President of the European Council.

when legal issues arise or are expected to arise (as most members of the CLS are responsible for following the work of multiple working parties, many of which meet frequently, a constant presence is not feasible, nor would it be an effective use of time). Despite this selective presence, the legal advisors spend much of their time in working party meetings.

As an overall approach, the CLS prefers to intervene at an early stage at working party level to steer the work in a legally correct direction. It would not be much appreciated if legal issues are raised after a political agreement on a given solution has been reached. Nevertheless, legal issues regularly arise at the level of COREPER, whose responsibilities include legal aspects (see above). Usually this is because they have been raised but not resolved at working party level. Legal issues may also be dealt with at the level of the Council.

As the work of the European Council is largely prepared through the General Affairs Council and COREPER, legal advice can be provided in those fora. It can also be provided through the cabinet of the President of the European Council or directly to the European Council – in the latter cases usually orally. For a visible example of the contribution of the Legal Service to the work of the European Council, see an opinion of the Legal Service in the early stages of the development of the Union's Security and Defence Policy, which was reflected in the Presidency Report to the Feira European Council on Strengthening the Common European Security and Defence Policy.[49]

As indicated in its mission statement, the CLS aims to 'tak[e] a creative approach where appropriate, to identifying legally correct and politically acceptable solutions'. Therefore it is often not sufficient merely to state whether a given proposal is legally correct or not. Rather, whenever possible the CLS will identify alternative ways to achieve the politically desired outcome in a legally correct manner and it may make concrete drafting suggestions. Very often, this will involve active engagement with the Presidency, the GSC, the Commission and/or EEAS and Member State delegations in between Council and working party meetings to come up with such solutions. Legal advisors also regularly take part in the 'trilogue' meetings between the Council Presidency (assisted by the GSC) and representatives of the European Parliament and the Commission, with a view to obtaining an agreement in co-decision files.

Advice of the Legal Service may be given on questions such as whether the Commission has proposed the correct legal basis in the Treaty for a draft legislative act or decisions relating to an international agreement, whether a

49 See Council doc 9149/00 of 15 June 2000, pt II.E, 9–10, citing the conclusion reached by the Legal Service. The opinion itself is contained in Council doc 8332/00 of 8 May 2000, which is not in the public domain.

proposed Union act falls within the competence of the Union and/or that of Member States,[50] or whether certain provisions of the draft act comply with general rules and principles of Union law, including fundamental rights. The Legal Service also has to check that a proper statement of reasons is provided in the recitals to a measure. Furthermore, the Legal Service is often called to advise on whether certain matters should be the subject of delegated acts or implementing acts, or be included in a legislative act itself. It may also have to interpret the scope of a provision in the Treaties or in secondary law, or clarify the procedures set out in such provisions. In the field of international relations, and occasionally in other areas too, the Legal Service may have to advise on questions of international law, including the compatibility of proposed secondary law with international agreements concluded by the Union.

One area within the field of external relations which deserves specific mention is restrictive measures (often referred to as 'sanctions') against third States and/or specific persons, legal entities or groups, adopted on the basis of Article 29 TEU and Article 215 TFEU. The Legal Service not only defends Council acts in this field before the EU Courts (see below) but also spends much time and effort advising the Council when the restrictive measures are established, amended or extended, and when the Council decides to include specific persons or entities on a list of designated persons and entities subjected to these restrictive measures. This includes a thorough review of the reasons proposed for such designations and the elements adduced to support those reasons. It also involves advice on requests for public or 'privileged' access to the file[51] and on replies to delisting requests.

In addition, the Legal Service often has to advise on the application of the Council's Rules of Procedure, for example whether a quorum is present, whether the items on the provisional agenda have been included in good time, the possibility of adopting Council acts by written procedure, rules on languages, publications in the Official Journal, etc.

The Legal Service's views are rarely ignored. Nevertheless, they are not always followed. Indeed, they remain advice and it is ultimately up to the Council to decide whether or not to follow the opinion of the Legal Service in any given case. When the Council does not follow that view, it may be because it disagrees with the legal analysis or it may be that the Council decides for pressing political reasons to adopt a decision which it understands may be open to legal challenge.

50 E.g. whether a proposed international agreement can be concluded by the Union alone or must or may also be concluded by Member States.

51 Privileged access refers to access to the file by listed persons or entities as part of their rights of the defence.

The Legal Service also acts as Secretariat for a few Council preparatory bodies (in particular the working parties on public international law, the law of the sea, the Court of Justice, Codification of Legislation, and Legal-Linguistic Experts). It also acts as Secretariat for the panel established pursuant to Article 255 TFEU, which gives an opinion on candidates' suitability to perform the duties of Judge and Advocate-General of the Court of Justice and the General Court before the Governments of the Member States appoint them as judges.[52] Moreover, a member of the Legal Service chairs the Council working party on Codification of Legislation.

Furthermore, the Legal Service provides advice internally within the Council Secretariat, on administrative and budgetary questions such as the application of the Staff Regulations, public procurement, building projects, security rules, etc.

Last but not least, the Council's Legal Advisor has acted as advisor to the intergovernmental conferences from 1991 (Maastricht) onwards.[53] For a visible example of this role, see the opinion of the Legal Service included in Declaration (17) concerning Primacy, which the intergovernmental conference that adopted the Lisbon Treaty attached to the Final Act of that conference.

Written opinions and contributions of the Legal Service are produced as distinct Council documents. Previously, they were rarely made public as it was considered that making legal advice public would risk affecting the ability of the Legal Service to provide independent and frank legal advice. In particular, it was thought that if negative advice became public this might call into question the legality of acts adopted contrary to such advice. Furthermore, negative advice could be used against the Council. Both these considerations could lead to a degree of reluctance to provide negative advice, or even to seek legal advice at all.

This concern was recognised in early case law[54] and was reflected in Article 4(2) of Regulation (EC) No 1049/2001.[55] This provision states that 'The

52 See pt 4 of the annex to Council Decision 2010/124/EU of 25 February 2010 relating to the operating rules of the panel provided for in Article 255 of the Treaty on the Functioning of the European Union [2010] OJ L50/18.

53 For a flavour of this role, see Giorgio Maganza, 'Jean-Claude Piris, un seul homme pour cinq traités' in Arpio Santacruz and others (eds) (n 1).

54 See e.g. Case T-610/97 R *Hanne Norup Carlsen and Others v Council* (Order) EU:T:1998:48, paras 46–47. See also Case T-44/97 *Piera Ghignone and Others v Council* EU:T:2000:258, paras 47–48, as regards the use of legal advice in court proceedings.

55 Regulation (EC) 1049/2001 of the European Parliament and of the Council of 30 May 2001 regarding public access to European Parliament, Council and Commission documents [2001] OJ L145/43.

institutions shall refuse access to a document where disclosure would undermine the protection of: (…) – court proceedings and legal advice, (…) unless there is an overriding public interest in disclosure'.

However, in its judgment of 1 July 2008 in *Turco v Council*,[56] the CJEU gave a restrictive interpretation of this exception to public access to documents. While it recognized that 'the exception relating to legal advice laid down in the second indent of Article 4(2) of Regulation No 1049/2001 must be construed as aiming to protect an institution's interest in seeking legal advice and receiving frank, objective and comprehensive advice',[57] it held that the risk of interest being undermined 'must be reasonably foreseeable and not purely hypothetical'[58] and that the Council has 'to ascertain whether there is any overriding public interest justifying disclosure'.[59] The latter interest includes enhanced legitimacy and democracy resulting from greater openness, which is especially important as regards a legislative process.[60] The Court concluded that 'Regulation No 1049/2001 imposes, in principle, an obligation to disclose the opinions of the Council's legal service relating to a legislative process'.[61] It added that:

> That finding does not preclude a refusal, on account of the protection of legal advice, to disclose a specific legal opinion, given in the context of a legislative process, but being of a particularly sensitive nature or having a particularly wide scope that goes beyond the context of the legislative process in question. In such a case, it is incumbent on the institution concerned to give a detailed statement of reasons for such a refusal.[62]

This line of reasoning was confirmed in subsequent cases, which has partially extended these criteria to legal advice on non-legislative acts.[63]

Following these judgments, the Legal Service assesses any requests for access to its opinions in the light of the criteria set out in these judgment as

56 Joined Cases C-39/05 P and C-52/05 P *Kingdom of Sweden and Maurizio Turco v Council* EU:C:2008:374.

57 Ibid, para 42.

58 Ibid, para 43.

59 Ibid, para 44.

60 Ibid, paras 45–47.

61 Ibid, para 68.

62 Ibid, para 69.

63 See Case C-506/08 P *Kingdom of Sweden v Commission and MyTravel Group plc.* EU:C:2011:496, paras 109–19 and Case C-350/12 P, *Council v Sophie in 't Veld* EU:C:2014:2039, paras 95–113.

well the case law on other exceptions to public access under Regulation No 1049/2001, including those on the protection of the Council's decision-making process[64] and of international relations[65] and provides more specific reasons for any refusal to grant public access.

4.2.2 Defending the Council and European Council before the Union Courts

In principle, the task of representing the Council before the Court of Justice, the General Court and until recently the Civil Service Tribunal is/was assigned to members of the Legal Service. In some cases, the Council has recourse to external lawyers, under the supervision of a member of the Legal Service (e.g. in anti-dumping cases).

In most cases, the Council is the defendant in direct actions – actions for the annulment of a Council act, actions for failure to act, or actions seeking compensation for damages. It is also possible that preliminary questions call into question the validity of a Council act. In all these cases, the Legal Service does not require any authorisation by the Council to defend the validity and legality of the Council's acts.

There are also cases in which the Council brings an action against another institution, notably against the Commission or the European Parliament. These cases are far less numerous, although their number has increased in the post-Lisbon era. The Council may also lodge an appeal against a judgment in which it was defendant and which it lost before the General Court, e.g. a case on restrictive measures. In both these cases, the Legal Service needs a decision by Council authorising it to bring the case or the appeal. Such a decision can be recommended by the Legal Service but it may also be taken where the Legal Service has not recommended it.

Litigation accounts for an important part of the work-load of the legal advisors, although the proportion varies from one sector to another. The Directorates dealing with external relations and with staff issues have most of the cases. In the field of external relations, it is the number of restrictive measures cases which has seen a huge increase – at the end of 2015, there were more than one hundred such cases pending.

Two or sometimes three members of the Legal Service are appointed to represent the Council in each case; they will usually be the lawyer(s) responsible

64 On this exception, see e.g. Case C-280/11 P *Council v Access Info Europe* EU:C:2013:671 and *My Travel* (n 63), paras 72–103.

65 On this exception, see e.g. *In't Veld* (n 63).

for the subject-area in question and if necessary a lawyer who is fluent in the language of the case. It may happen that the Legal Service has to defend an act of the Council on which it had advised the Council to adopt a different approach. Yet even in such cases, the lawyers concerned will naturally defend the Council to the best of their abilities. The agents normally circulate a draft of the main initial written submissions (statement of defence, application, appeal or observations) to designated points of contact in the Member States' delegations so that they can provide comments. It is then for the agents to consider to what extent any observations received can be taken into account.[66] Where appropriate, the agents hold coordination meetings with the agents of other institutions and/or of Member States represented in a case.

If the Council loses a case, then it will have to take the necessary measures to comply with the CJEU's judgment, e.g. by readopting an annulled act on another legal basis, or by amending provisions which have been found contrary to the Treaties.

Recently, the Council Legal Service has also ensured the representation of the European Council before the EU Courts. This first happened when the European Council intervened in the *Pringle* case[67] and subsequently, a number of cases have been brought against the European Council.[68]

4.2.3 Legislative Quality

The Legal Service has a vital role to play in improving the drafting quality of EU legislation and other legal acts, which should be as clear, simple and precise as possible for its users, whether they be national authorities, businesses or citizens generally.

Article 22 of the Council's Rules of Procedure stipulates that:

> In order to assist the Council in its task of ensuring the drafting quality of the legislative acts which it adopts, the Legal Service shall be responsible for checking the drafting quality of proposals and draft acts at the appropriate stage, as well as for bringing drafting suggestions to the attention of the Council and its bodies, pursuant to the Interinstitutional

---

66 Bearing in mind that written submissions are subject to approval by the Director concerned.

67 Case C-370/12 *Thomas Pringle v Government of Ireland, Ireland and The Attorney General* EU:C:2012:756.

68 Cases T-834/16 *QC v European Council*; T-257/16 *NM v European Council*; T-193/16 *NG v European Council* and T-192/16 *NF v European Council* (the latter three cases are actions for annulment of the 'EU-Turkey statement' of 18 March 2016).

Agreement of 22 December 1998 on common guidelines for the quality of drafting of Community legislation.

According to the latter Interinstitutional Agreement,[69] 'the role played by the institutions' legal services [ie those of the European Parliament, Council and Commission], including their legal/linguistic experts, in improving the quality of drafting of Community legislative acts should be strengthened' (Recital 5) and the institutions 'shall organise their respective internal procedures in such a way that their legal services, including their legal/linguistic experts, may, each for their own institution, make drafting suggestions in good time, with a view to applying these guidelines' (Implementing measure (b)).

Improving the drafting quality of Council legal acts is performed in the first place by the lawyers in the Legal Service who follow proposals through the Council and its preparatory bodies, and secondly by the 'Legislative Quality' Directorate. This Directorate is responsible for the final editing of draft acts to be adopted by the Council. That involves laying the text out properly, using the right terminology and ensuring the act says exactly the same in all the language versions, each of which is equally authentic. It also manages the procedures for making corrections before or after an act is adopted, e.g. where differences between language versions are identified. Assistance of a jurist/linguist often is already provided earlier on in the process, including at meetings of the Council working parties.

5 Final Remarks

The Legal Service plays a prominent role in all aspects of the Council's and the European Council's work, including questions dealt with at the highest level. Thanks to its independence and the quality of its work, as well as its pro-active and constructive approach, even in times where the increased workload poses serious challenges to covering all of the Council's activities properly, the Legal Service is highly valued by the Council.[70] Ricardo Gosalbo Bono certainly

69 [1999] OJ C73/1.

70 See e.g. the following citation from a letter of reply to the Chairman of a European Parliament Committee by the President of the Council in the first half of 2015: 'the Council Legal Service acts in full independence from the Institution it is called to assist. The Council respects such independence, as the condition for the high quality work which the Legal Service provides for it'. Also, when the reform of the staff regulations led to Court cases between the Council and the Commission, the Council knew that the agents from the

played a significant part in earning that appreciation. However, all this cannot be taken for granted and it is up to all the members of the Legal Service to continue to live up to the Service's mission statement by providing independent, high quality, timely and constructive advice to the Council and the European Council.

Legal Service would loyally defend the Council's acts even where these had negative consequences for the staff, including the agents themselves.

PART 2

Principles of Union Law and Legal Theory

CHAPTER 6

CJEU Jurisprudence and the Audience: Making Law in a Public Discourse – Ten Years after CJEU Case C-144/04 *Mangold v Helm*

*Ingolf Pernice**

1 Introduction: Case Law, Critique and the Legitimacy of the EU Courts

Criticizing others is often easier than giving satisfactory reasons for what we are doing or deciding ourselves. This is particularly true for lawyers and legal academics among each other but especially in their relationship with the courts. Ricardo Gosalbo Bono and I were colleagues and have been friends since the 1980's, working together at the European Commission's Legal Service, preparing cases, defending the Commission in Luxembourg, advising the Commission on legislative proposals and international negotiations and commenting on or even criticizing the judgments that the Court of Justice of the European Union (CJEU) gave in 'our cases' by notes prepared for the Commission. It was a productive legal dialogue not only between us, but also within our team of lawyers responsible for environmental law, transport and culture at the Commission's Legal Service. The members of this team represented the legal cultures of five or more Member States. We experienced how productive and enriching such an intercultural legal dialogue can be. Discussing with Ricardo questions such as those concerning competences and legal bases for EU action in the *Titanium Dioxide*, *Waste Directive* and other cases,[1] was always a challenge, and I learned enormously from his Spanish and – thanks to his PhD in Cambridge – Anglo-Saxon law perspectives on EU law, as much as from his experience in international law and at the United Nations legal office.

---

* This is a revised an updated version of a paper prepared to the 9th ECLN Conference held at the European University Institute Florence on 18–19 November 2013. I am most grateful to my research assistant Jonas Hein for collecting materials for this contribution, and to Lars Otto and Maria Decheva for their assistance in the review and updating process.

1 Case C-300/89 *Commission v Council* EU:C:1991:244 (*Titanium Dioxide*); Case C-155/91 *Commission v Council* EU:C:1993:98 (*Waste Directive*).

 | DOI 10.1163/9789004347175_007

Law, and in particular European Union law, as we experienced, is a product of intercultural dialogues at all levels. It is more than a result of a judicial dialogue, the cooperation among judges and their networks in the European constitutional compound.[2] A multiplicity of actors participate in the process of developing the European Union as a Community or Union of Law (*Rechtsgemeinschaft*).[3] Primary law is negotiated, whether on the basis of a draft worked out by a convention, as in the case of the draft Constitutional Treaty, which eventually led to the Treaty of Lisbon, or directly among the governments of the Member States, whereby the diverse national traditions, values and concepts are integrated into one common text. Secondary EU law is generally based on proposals of the Commission and its services that are composed of nationals from all the Member States, and it is mostly negotiated and adopted by the European Parliament and the Council where, again, the involvement of people from the diverse legal and political cultures in the Member States ensures that the outcome of the legislative process results, in the form of common provisions of Union law, in a unity arising from diversity. To some extent, similar processes can be observed regarding the implementation of Union law. While it is true that the implementation of Union law is basically left to the national administrations and courts, we can observe that, apart from uniform conditions laid down by implementing acts under Article 291 TFEU, horizontal dialogue, networks and other forms of cooperation among

2 See Koen Lenaerts, 'Kooperation und Spannung im Verhältnis von EuGH und nationalen Verfassungsgerichten' (2015) 50 EuR 3, stressing the system of sharing and assigning responsibilities in a complex multilevel system, an expression coined by Andreas Voßkuhle in his article 'Multilevel Cooperation of the European Constitutional Courts. Der Europäische Verfassungsgerichtsverbund' (2010) 6 EuConst 175, 189. With regard to the protection of fundamental rights see also Ferdinand Kirchhof, 'Kooperation zwischen nationalen und europäischen Gerichten' (2014) 49 EuR 267, 272–276, pleading for restraint and dialogue. See still in this respect Ingolf Pernice, 'Einheit und Kooperation: Das Gemeinschaftsrecht im Lichte der Rechtsprechung von EuGH und nationalen Gerichten. Randbemerkungen zu einem ungeklärten Verhältnis' in Albrecht Randelzhofer, Rupert Scholz and Dieter Willke (eds), *Gedächtnisschrift für Eberhard Grabitz* (CH Beck 1995) 523. For a more critical approach see Aida Torres Pérez, 'Melloni in Three Acts: From Dialogue to Monologue' (2014) 10 EuConst 308, while Lenaerts ((n 2) 21–25) takes the same case as an example for a successful dialogue.

3 See Andreas Voßkuhle, 'Integration durch Recht. Der Beitrag des Bundesverfassungsgerichts' (Humboldt-Speech on Europe, Berlin, 22 October 2015) <https://plone.rewi.hu-berlin.de/de/lf/oe/whi/humboldt-reden-zu-europa/archiv-humboldt-reden/rede-vosskuhle> accessed 10 December 2016, 3.

the competent executives and administrative bodies of the Member States and with the Commission are established to ensure the uniform application of EU law. This allows for talking about the 'European Administrative Compound' (*Verwaltungsverbund*).[4]

In the area of Common Foreign and Security Policy (CFSP), which is exempt from the supranational method, Ricardo demonstrates in a fascinating way how at least three 'traditionally distinct conceptions of international law' – from Germany, France and the United Kingdom – converge, at the EU level, into 'the emergence of an incipient EU conception of international law'.[5] This process arises from EU secondary legislation, as he finds, and CFSP practice in particular.[6] It is characterized by the 2003 EU Security Strategy,[7] which is based upon the principles of the Treaties and especially the conception of effective multilateralism.[8]

Specifically with regard to the judiciary, the preliminary ruling procedure under Article 267 TFEU institutes the judicial dialogue between the national courts and the CJEU in order to ensure the uniform application of Union law. It is the composition of the CJEU with judges from all the Member States,[9] but it is also the procedure providing for the inclusion of the views not only of the parties in each case, but also of the Commission and the national governments, where they chose to intervene, which ensures that the judgments given by the Court are the result of an inclusive deliberation merging the diverse concepts and cultures into one decision. Apart from the constitutional foundation of the institutions and processes for the choice of their members and their subjection to the law, it is this inclusive deliberative process that gives the

4 See Eberhard Schmidt-Aßmann, 'Einleitung: Der Europäische Verwaltungsverbund und die Rolle des Europäischen Verwaltungsrechts', in Eberhard Schmidt-Aßmann and Bettina Schöndorf-Haubold (eds), *Der Europäische Verwaltungsverbund. Formen und Verfahren der Verwaltungszusammenarbeit in der EU* (Mohr Siebeck 2005) 2–15 and 22.

5 Ricardo Gosalbo Bono, 'Some Reflections on the CFSP Legal Order' (2006) 43 CML Rev 337, 379–392 and 394.

6 Ibid 384–385.

7 European Council, 'A Secure Europe in a Better World' (European Security Strategy adopted on 12–13 December 2003). See para 84 of the Presidency conclusions of this meeting <https://www.consilium.europa.eu/uedocs/cmsupload/78367.pdf> accessed 10 December 2016.

8 Gosalbo Bono (n 5) 385–391.

9 For the difficulties arising from the diversity of legal systems and cultures see Ulrich Everling, 'Zur Begründung der Urteile des Gerichtshofs der Europäischen Gemeinschaften' (1994) 29 EuR 127, 140–141.

CJEU like the other European courts, not only power and authority, but also a specific procedural legitimacy.[10]

Yet this internal institutional discourse is not sufficient for ensuring the legitimacy of the jurisprudence of the CJEU. Another important element is the responsiveness of the EU courts to the general public, openness for critique and dialogue. Courts are not acting in isolation, and jurisprudence itself is a dynamic process over time. It is a process of trial and error, and the courts are part of intensive legal debates not only among each other, but also across a broad public. In this discourse, political leaders, commentators from the legal academia, from the media and more and more from the 'digital public', from blogs and comments in the internet in addition to EU institutions or national governments, as well as from national judges and courts also have a voice and cannot be ignored if they are not happy with judgments of the CJEU.[11] For good or bad reasons, one can be dissatisfied politically or with regard to the economic consequences that follow from the judgment. For legal scholarship and courts, and thus for the present analysis, legal grounds are more important.

Instead of Fritz Scharpf's distinction between input and output legitimacy or empirical studies of the 'level of popular support for the Court's judgments',[12] it seems to be primarily the constitutional role, composition and procedures of the CJEU that provide for a fundamental institutional legitimacy of the Court, as well as, increasingly, its functioning as one of many participants in an inclusive discursive law making system that allows the Court to gain authority and supports the legitimacy of the case law over time. This approach includes the 'internal and external legitimacy', as discussed by Koen Lenaerts,[13] but extends beyond defining the function of the EU courts in order to say what the law is by 'interpreting and applying the law' and not making politics, on the one hand, and 'the quality of the legal process', ie mutual respect and deference among

10 See Ingolf Pernice, 'Die Dritte Gewalt im Europäischen Verfassungsverbund' (1996) 31 EuR 27, 38–42. The question of legitimacy has been deeply explored in the contributions in Maurice Adams and others (eds), *Judging Europe's Judges: The Legitimacy of the Case Law of the European Court of Justice* (Hart Publishing 2013); for the notion of legitimacy and procedural legitimacy see Maurice Adams and others, 'Introduction: Judging Europe's Judges' in ibid, 4–6.

11 For a short overview also on the debates among academics see Adams and others (n 10) 2–3.

12 So discussed by Adams and others (ibid) 4–6, 17, 40 and 59.

13 'The Court's Outer and Inner Selves: Exploring the External and Internal Legitimacy of the European Court of Justice' in Adams and others (n 10) 13.

the European and national courts, on the other.[14] In particular, legitimacy depends on more than 'whether or not national courts are satisfied with the Court's decisions'.[15] The relevant audience is broader; it also includes private persons and governments involved in proceedings before the Court and, above all, the general and learned public. Judging the judges is a relevant factor. Legitimacy of judge-made law, thus, is the result of a functioning open public dialogue among judges and with the public in a broad sense. If Michal Bobek rightly states that 'every decision needs to secure its legitimacy by giving substantive reasons',[16] this regards not only the parties involved in the proceedings and the national courts having made the reference to the CJEU, but also critical legal scholarship, the media and the public at large. While in the relevant discourse legal arguments and critiques play a crucial role, they are by no means reserved to lawyers or legal academics but include all interested people being subject to the European legal system.

Reasoning in this legal discourse means a rational presentation and exchange of arguments related to individual cases and to the development of case law over time. In this process, rational critical legal analysis of a judgment or a jurisprudence established in a series of cases may be oriented by, or founded upon, diverse criteria: for example: one may not share the reasons given or does not find certain reasons convincing at all. One may detect a violation of generally accepted higher principles of law or of methodology; there might be a lack of coherence with earlier case law, or one may expect that new approaches or concepts developed in a case have adverse legal or even political consequences in the future.[17] The allegation of judicial activism[18] may be

14 Ibid 13–14.

15 This is what Michal Bobek writes about in 'Of Feasibility and Silent Elephants: The Legitimacy of the Court of Justice through the Eyes of National Courts' in Adams and others (n 10) 200 and 204–205. Bobek focuses on the national judges in the preliminary ruling procedure under Article 267 TFEU, but there are other procedures including private persons and states as applicants which seem to be relevant too.

16 Ibid 207.

17 Some of these aspects have been submitted for discussion by Joseph Weiler during the 9th ECLN Conference held at the European University Institute Florence on 18–19 November 2013.

18 See the outcry of the former president of the German Constitutional Court (and later president of the Convention established for drafting the Charter of Fundamental Rights) Roman Herzog and Lüder Gerken, 'Stoppt den EuGH' *Frankfurter Allgemeine Zeitung* (Frankfurt, 8 September 2008); see already Haltje Rasmussen, *On Law and Public Policy in the European Court of Justice: A Comparative Study in Judicial Policymaking* (Martinus Nijhoff Publishers 1986); Haltje Rasmussen, 'On Legal Normative Dynamics and

put forward where a judgment is deemed to exceed what we consider to be the constitutional limits of the Court's competences with regard to other EU institutions and, in particular, the legislature, or even with regard to the limits of the powers conferred on the European Union at large. A methodology for a meaningful review of the CJEU case law has yet to be developed. The same can be said as regards a typology of arguments that could be put forward concerning a judgment with a view to engaging in a dialogue or provoking a change of jurisprudence. All of these aspects are also related to the legitimacy of the Court and the case law, and neither the Court nor the criticising community have the last word; it can only be the result of a dynamic interactive process.

Consequently, specific cases, or the case law of the CJEU in general, have to be studied in this context. As explained, the openness of the courts to public feedback is a fundamental condition for the proper functioning of the judiciary in a democratic society and, thus, of the democratic system – understood as an overall system of openness, deliberation and dialogue. Whatever arguments a critique might put forward, the acceptance or criticism of the jurisprudence of the EU courts and their responsiveness to the 'critical audience'[19] add to their authority and legitimacy.[20] The more judges act in a permanent dialogue

---

Jurisdictional Dialogue in the field of Community General Principles of Law' in Ulf Bernitz and Joakim Nergelius (eds), *General Principles of European Community Law: Reports from a Conference in Malmö* (Kluwer Law International 2000) 39–46; Anthony Arnull, 'Judicial Activism and the ECJ: How Should Academics Respond?' in Mark Dawson, Bruno de Witte and Elise Muir (eds), *Judicial Activism at the European Court of Justice* (Edward Elgar Publishing 2013) 217 and 230–32 (arguing that the term 'judicial activism' is inadequate as a benchmark for evaluating the Court's jurisprudence on account of the plurality of doctrinal perspectives of its international interlocutors). On this question see also Ditlev Tamm, 'The history of the Court of Justice of the European Union Since its Origin' in Allan Rosas, Egils Levits and Yves Bot (eds), *The Court of Justice and the Construction of Europe: Analyses and Perspectives on Sixty Years of Case-law* (Springer 2013) 29–30. A substantial recapitulation of the issue is provided by Henri de Waele, 'The Role of the European Court of Justice in the Integration Process: A Contemporary and Normative Assessment' (2010) 6 Hanse Law Review 3.

19 For examples of a change or further development of jurisprudence by the CJEU as a consequence of the critiques, see Everling 'Zur Begründung der Urteile des Gerichtshofs der Europäischen Gemeinschaften' (n 9) 138 and 141–142.

20 For an account of the specific legitimacy problems the CJEU is faced with, see Ulrich Haltern and Andreas Bergmann 'Einleitung: Der EuGH in der Kritik' in Ulrich Haltern and Andreas Bergmann (eds), *Der EuGH in der Kritik* (Mohr Siebeck 2012) paras 14–9 and 15–7.

with the public and, therefore, are responsible to the citizens at large, striving to make clear that their decisions are based upon a shared understanding of the law, the greater their contribution to the functioning of the legal system, particularly in a multilevel context. Although, as the former judge at the CJEU, Ulrich Everling, wrote already in 1994, mere shaming or threatening the Court, as he understands the Maastricht judgment of the German Federal Constitutional Court (GFCC),[21] is counterproductive,[22] well-argued critiques can – and should – have the beneficial effect of encouraging the Court to provide better reasoning or even to revise its views.[23]

Mangold v Helm[24] seems to present a particularly telling example to study how the EU system of cooperative 'discursive jurisprudence' functions. This judgment of the CJEU was considered, at least in Germany, as a leading example for of the Court 'getting it wrong', or at least 'approaching the limits of legitimate judicial adjudication'.[25] There were broad expectations that, in a subsequent attempt to challenge the judgment, the GFCC would hold it inapplicable in Germany – which the GFCC did not do, while instead taking the opportunity to develop more precise limits of its own powers for the constitutional review of CJEU judgments. The critiques nevertheless led the CJEU, if not to revise, to better reason – and confirm – the concepts established by *Mangold* in subsequent case law.

In order to assess the strengths and weaknesses of the *Mangold* judgment and its critique, as well as their impact on the subsequent jurisprudence, as an example for what may be called a 'discursive jurisprudence' it seems appropriate not to neglect the special background of the matter. It is, thus, upon the basis of a brief presentation of the facts and the debate on this case in Germany (Section 2) that not only the judgment, but also the critique and further developments will be analysed (Section 3) in this chapter with a view to draw some lessons from this ex post evaluation of this judgment (Section 4).

---

21 GFCC, Judgment of 12 October 1993, BVerfGE 89, 155 – *Maastricht* (for an English translation, see (1994) 1 CML Rev 57, also available at <http://www.unizar.es/euroconstitucion/library/Brunner_Sentence.pdf> accessed 10 December 2016).

22 Ulrich Everling, 'Bundesverfassungsgericht und Gerichtshof der Europäischen Gemeinschaft nach dem Maastricht-Urteil' in Randelzhofer and others (n 2) 74–75.

23 With examples, see Everling, 'Zur Begründung der Urteile des Gerichtshofs der Europäischen Gemeinschaften' (n 9) 128–129 and 135. In more general terms see also Lenaerts (n 2) 25: Courts and, above all, constitutional courts always also reflect changes in opinion and mind regarding European integration in the Member States.

24 Case C-144/04 *Werner Mangold v Rüdiger Helm* EU:C:2005:709.

25 See Ján Mazák and Martin Moser, 'Adjudication by Reference to General Principles of EU Law; A Second Look at the Mangold Case Law' in Adams and others (n 10) 85.

2 *Mangold v Helm*: Facts and Background

The proceedings in the Case C-144/04, *Mangold v Helm* dealt with a case of age discrimination in the context of provisions of German labour law concerning contract termination requirements. As an integral element of the storied German 'Hartz' law of 2002,[26] these provisions permitted the unrestricted conclusion of fixed-term contracts with unemployed workers aged 52 years and older. With this threshold, the provisions deviated from the general rule according to which fixed term contracts could only be concluded upon a sufficient showing of objective grounds. The German legislator had adopted this partial abrogation of worker protection law in order to facilitate and encourage the employment of older workers who, under general labour law, allegedly had little chance to find work at all.

However, an idiosyncratic and, perhaps for the German legislator, unfortunate twist of EU law loomed: the German provisions had been enacted after the entry into force of Directive 2000/78,[27] which established a general framework for equal treatment in employment and occupation, but before the expiration of its extended period of transposition.

Mr Mangold, at the age of 56 years, was employed at the law firm of Mr Helm on the basis of a fixed-term contract in which specific reference was made to the 'Hartz' law. In fact, the terms of the contract clearly stated that the use of its fixed-term clause could not be based on any other justification. In a case brought before the Munich Labor Court, Mr Mangold argued that the clause fixing the term of the contract was invalid on the grounds that the provision of German law referred to, in order to justify the fixed term, was contrary to Directive 2000/78. Mr Helm, in contrast, argued that this provision was justified as the 'Hartz' law was made to facilitate the employment of people who otherwise would not find a job because of their age.

The Labour Court referred, in relevant part, the following questions to the CJEU for a preliminary ruling:

> (…) 2. Is Article 6 of … Directive 2000/78 … to be interpreted as precluding a provision of national law which, like the provision at issue in this

---

26 § 14(3) Teilzeit- und Befristungsgesetz (TzBfG), as amended by the 'Erstes Gesetz für moderne Dienstleistungen am Arbeitsmarkt' of 23 December 2002, BGBl I p 4607, introducing a 4th sentence in para 3 by which the relevant age was reduced from 58 to 52 years for the period ending 31 December 2006.

27 Council Directive 2000/78/EC of 27 November 2000 establishing a general framework for equal treatment in employment and occupation, [2000] OJ L 303/16 (the Directive).

> case, authorises the conclusion of fixed-term employment contracts, without any objective reason, with workers aged 52 and over, contrary to the principle requiring justification on objective grounds?
>
> 3. (...) must the national court refuse to apply the provision of domestic law which is contrary to Community law and apply the general principle of internal law, under which fixed terms of employment are permissible only if they are justified on objective grounds?[28]

The Court said yes, broadly speaking, to both questions. Its ruling, however, was strongly criticized[29] because:

- the Directive referred to was not yet applicable as the period prescribed for the transposition of the Directive into national law had not yet expired;
- the Directive, according to the established case law of the CJEU, in any event could not produce horizontal effects among private persons;[30]
- in light of the diversity of national constitutional laws regarding age discrimination, there was insufficient ground for extracting a general principle of EU law prohibiting age discrimination;[31]
- such a principle, even if it were generally recognised, would not apply to a case where national legislation is not within the scope of EU law and, thus, not intended to implement EU law;
- in any event, a fundamental right prohibiting age discrimination could not be invoked between private persons in a situation involving an exclusively private law contract;

28 *Mangold* (n 24), para 31.

29 See in particular the summary of the allegations put forward by the complainant in GFCC, Judgment of 6 July 2010, BVerfGE 126, 286 – *Honeywell*, para 40. Another summary is given in the Opinion of Advocate General Sharpston in Case C-427/06 *Birgit Bartsch v Bosch und Siemens Hausgeräte (BSH) Altersfürsorge GmbH* EU:C:2008:297, paras 31ff; see also 'Editorial Comments: Horizontal Direct Effect – A Law of Diminishing Coherence?'(2006) 43 CML Rev 1. In defence of the ruling, at a later stage, see Ulrich Haltern, 'Eine Lanze für Mangold. Bemerkungen zum Mangold-Urteil, zur Folgenrechtsprechung und zur Kritik an beiden' in Haltern and Bergmann (n 20) in particular 49–51.

30 See also the Opinion of Advocate General Tizzano in Case 144 /04 *Werner Mangold v Rüdiger Helm* EU:C:2005:420, paras 96–111.

31 E.g. Axel Metzger, 'Allgemeine Rechtsgrundsätze in Europa' (2011) 75 The Rabel Journal of Comparative and International Private Law 845, 855–56; Andrea Eriksson, 'European Court of Justice: Broadening the Scope of European Non- Discrimination Law' (2009) 7 International Journal of Constitutional Law 731, 735–40.

– for all these reasons, the preliminary ruling constitutes a manifest transgression of competences on the part of the CJEU.[32]

In a subsequent case,[33] the Federal Labour Court (FLC) handed down a judgment expressly referring to and applying the *Mangold* ruling. It accepted the argument of the applicant that the fixed-term in his employment contract was invalid on the grounds that it violated the principle of non-discrimination on grounds of age under EU primary law.

The defendant in this case, the applicant's employer, filed a constitutional complaint against this judgment with the GFCC, putting forward the arguments listed above. This became the famous '*Honeywell*' case. In anticipation of the judgment, many observers[34] expected that the GFCC would give effect to its self-declared ultra vires jurisdiction[35] and declare Union law inapplicable in Germany for a first time. Yet, the GFCC did not do so, although it clearly did not concur with the CJEU's judgment in *Mangold*. Nevertheless, with a view to complying with the 'supranational integration principle' and driven by the principles of cooperation, mutual respect and tolerance, as enshrined in Article 4 (3) TEU, the GFCC found the *Mangold* judgment to be within the limits of the competences conferred on the European Union and, in particular, on the CJEU. It stated, as a general rule, that:

> [T]he task and status of the independent suprastate case-law must be safeguarded. This means, on the one hand, respect for the Union's own methods of justice to which the Court of Justice considers itself to be bound and which do justice to the 'uniqueness' of the Treaties and goals that are inherent to them (see ECJ Opinion 1/91 EEA Treaty [1991] ECR I-6079 para. 51). Secondly, the Court of Justice has a right to tolerance of error. It is hence not a matter for the Federal Constitutional Court in questions of the interpretation of Union law, which with a methodical interpretation of the statute can lead to different outcomes in the usual

32 See Lüder Gerken and others, *„Mangold" als ausbrechender Rechtsakt* (Sellier european law publishers 2009) available at <http://www.zaar.uni-muenchen.de/pub/vr2009-12.pdf> accessed 10 December 2016. On this line see also the dissenting opinion of judge Landau in GFCC, *Honeywell* (n 29), paras 105ff.

33 FLC, Judgment of 26 April 2006, BAGE 118, 76 – *Honeywell Bremsbelag GmbH.*

34 See e.g. Frank Schorkopf, 'Die Europäische Union im Lot – Karlsruhes Rechtsspruch zum Vertrag von Lissabon' (2009) 20 Europäische Zeitschrift für Wirtschaftsrecht 718, 722.

35 See GFCC, Judgment of 12 October 1993, BVerfGE 89, 155, 188 – *Maastricht*; Judgment of 30 June 2009, BVerfGE 123, 267 – *Lisbon*, paras 238ff.

> legal science discussion framework, to supplant the interpretation of the Court of Justice with an interpretation of its own. Interpretations of the bases of the Treaties are also to be tolerated which, without a considerable shift in the structure of competences, constitute a restriction to individual cases and either do not permit impacts on fundamental rights to arise which constitute a burden or do not oppose domestic compensation for such burdens.[36]

This is not the place to discuss the general approach that the GFCC has chosen regarding its own relationship with the CJEU and European law.[37] What is more important in the present context is a basic insight of the GFCC confirmed by the *Honeywell* judgment: even judges may err, and it is not for the national courts, in principle, to play the role of watchdogs of the CJEU's jurisprudence. This clear expression of mutual respect and trust shows, nonetheless, how seriously the matter was taken in Germany and that the GFCC abstains from supervising the CJEU.[38]

Several questions seem to be worth examining further. Did the CJEU err and, if so, what did it get wrong? Did it listen to the critical comments, both from academia and the GFCC? What can we learn from the *Mangold* proceedings?

3 The *Mangold* Judgment and Its Critique

The list of critical issues mentioned above needs a closer look. They cover fundamental questions regarding the duties of the Member States and their courts under Union law as well as the fundamental rights which the Member States and their courts are required to safeguard under EU law in a field that is not within the scope of Union law. The judgment seems to conflict with general assumptions concerning the established EU law and jurisprudence. Quite possibly it is this circumstance that has created considerable confusion in legal doctrine.

---

36 GFCC, *Honeywell* (n 29), para 66.

37 For some remarks on this, see Ingolf Pernice, 'Autonomy of the European Legal Order – Fifty Years after Van Gend & Loos' in Antonio Tizzano, Juliane Kokott and Sacha Prechal (eds) *50th Anniversary of the Judgment in Van Gend en Loos, 1963–2013* (Conference proceedings, Luxembourg 13 May 2013, Office des publications de l'Union européenne 2013) 63–70.

38 For the opposite, see the 'Lantova saga' (n 111).

3.1 *'Advance Effect' of Directives during the Period of Transposition*

A first assumption regarding EU directives in general is that they lack legally binding effect before the expiration of the prescribed period of transposition.

Yet, the Court found that the German 'Hartz' law was contrary to Article 6(1) of Directive 2000/78. It also emphasized 'the fact that, when the contract was concluded, the period prescribed for the transposition into domestic law of Directive 2000/78 had not yet expired cannot call that finding into question'.[39] It based this claim on its earlier judgment in *Inter-Environnement Wallonie*. There it stated that 'during the period prescribed for transposition of a directive, the Member States must refrain from taking any measures liable seriously to compromise the attainment of the result prescribed by that directive'.[40]

In reaction to the *Mangold* ruling, some critical commentators argued inter alia that there was no evidence in the specific facts of the case that the disputed provision of German law could not have been made to comply with the directive before the expiration of its transposition period.[41] Moreover, given that the validity of the provisions of German law was to expire before the end of the period of transposition, there was no violation of EU secondary law. Thus, it was said, the CJEU had adopted an 'advance effect' of directives contrary to its established case law.[42]

However, the Treaties can be read to lay down a duty of the Member States to use the period of transposition positively to adopt the measures necessary to achieve the objectives of the directive, rather than measures which run the risk of jeopardizing them. The concept of a directive's entry into force is itself not dependent on any period of transposition. Article 288(3) TFEU states that 'the directive shall be binding', and Article 297(2), second subparagraph, TFEU defines the 'entry into force' of regulations or directives – as a rule – 'on the twentieth day following that of their publication'. A directive, therefore, produces legal obligations from that day forward. Also, in light of the general principle of 'sincere cooperation' under Article 4(3) TEU, Member States are obliged to undertake all action necessary in order to ensure compliance until the date that the period of transposition expires, rather than implementing conflicting measures.

---

39 *Mangold* (n 24), para 66.

40 Case C-129/96 *Inter-Environnement Wallonie* ASBL *v Région wallonne* EU:C:1997:628, paras 40–45.

41 Gerken and others (n 32) 25.

42 Ibid.

It has been noted that this construction is beyond what the Court had decided in *Inter-Environnement Wallonie*.[43] There, it stated that 'measures liable seriously to compromise the attainment of the result prescribed by that directive' are prohibited. In *Mangold*, the fact that the national measure was limited in time, so to expire shortly after the end of the period of transposition, can certainly be seen as sufficient to ensure compliance with this rule.[44] Hence, the reference to this judgment does not justify the rule established in *Mangold*. However, the Court also took note of the special situation that Germany had made use of the additional period of three years allowed 'if necessary' under the second subparagraph of Article 18 of the Directive, 'in order to take account of particular conditions'. According to the clear wording of this provision, Germany was obliged to report annually on the measures taken 'to tackle age discrimination' and 'on the progress it is making towards implementation'. The Court ruled that this provision would be 'redundant' if the Member State were permitted to act incompatibly during the period of transposition.[45] It seems reasonable to consider that such behaviour is in the violation of the obligation to proceed towards the implementation of the Directive and to report upon this during the special grace period allowed in the Directive.

The question, thus, is not whether or not the violation of a seemingly negative duty not to act contrary to the objectives of the Directive is equivalent to a violation of the positive duty to comply with the Directive after the period of transposition has expired. The Court does not go so far. Contrary to what is suggested by Karl Riesenhuber,[46] the provisions of Article 18 of the Directive specifically underline the obligations of the Member States to positively proceed towards implementation. It follows that any action which goes against this may legitimately be declared contrary to the Treaties and, in particular, to violate the duties under Article 4(3) TEU and 288(3) TFEU.

The reasons given by the Court leave open the question what the duties of the Member States are more generally, if provisions like Article 18 of the

43 See Karl Riesenhuber, 'Case: ECJ – Mangold' (2007) 3 European Review of Contract Law 63, 70. Similarly Michael Dougan, 'In Defence of Mangold?' in Anthony Arnull and others (eds), *A Constitutional Order of States? Essays in EU Law in Honour of Alan Dashwood* (Hart Publishing 2011) 234–235.

44 See also the argument made in the Editorial Comments (n 29) 6–7. The Court rightly stated that this element of exceeding the period of transposition is 'not decisive' (*Mangold* (n 24), para 70).

45 *Mangold* (n 24), para 72.

46 Riesenhuber (n 43) 70–71 stresses that the Court failed to distinguish between this 'duty of loyalty which is essentially negative' and the positive duty to transpose the directive.

Directive did not exist or were not applicable. Would the mere fact that the period of transposition of the Directive had not expired at the relevant time and that the measures in question expired shortly after the end of the period of transposition be sufficient to consider them as contrary to the Treaties? This was understood as the 'advance effect' (*Vorwirkung*) of directives in the literature as well as in the *Honeywell* judgment of the GFCC[47] – meaning some sort of a new normative barrier to the freedom of national legislators anticipating what would normally apply after the period of transposition has expired. Yet, assuming that a Directive enters into force, as already said, on the twentieth day after its publication, the obligation to work towards the achievement of its objectives can also be understood as a simple expression of the duties of the Member States from the date of entry into force of the Directive which they have agreed upon.

It was criticised that the Court had accepted a direct effect of the substantive provisions of the Directive, as if the period of transposition had already expired.[48] Already in his conclusions on the case, Advocate General Tizzano had stated that setting aside the German law in order to render it compliant with the substantive obligations arising from the Directive would amount to acknowledging its 'horizontal effect' and thus be contrary to earlier case law. This doctrine, he added, applied with even greater force in cases where the period of transposition had not yet expired.[49]

More convincing, however, could be a reference to the general obligations of a more procedural character. In the light of the principle of primacy, it is at least arguable that national provisions adopted during the period of transposition of a Directive but contrary to its clear objectives and, thus, in violation of general Treaty obligations, as they can be derived from Article 4(3) TEU and Article 288(3) TFEU, read together with Article 18 of the Directive, cannot be applied by a national court. The question whether these obligations of sincere cooperation can be read to exclude the application of any national measure contrary to what the Directive expressly requires the Member States to do, and to have an effect such as in *Mangold*, has never been asked. It should be answered in the affirmative.

---

47 E.g. Gerken and others (n 32) 25.

48 See the critique on this line of Arnold Bauer, 'Auf "Junk" folgt "Mangold" – Europarecht verdrängt deutsches Arbeitsrecht' [2006] Neue Juristische Wochenschrift 6, 9. See also Gerken and others (n 32) 24 and 25ff with more references.

49 Opinion of Advocate General Tizzano (n 30), paras 106–110, referring to a clear statement to this effect in Case C-157/02 *Rieser Internationale Transporte GmbH v Autobahnen- und Schnellstraßen-Finanzierungs- AG (Asfinag)* EU:C:2004:76, para 69.

The Court, therefore, could have answered the preliminary question by stating that the German law in question was inapplicable in the given case because of the objective obligation under the principle of sincere cooperation that is binding for any institution of the Member States. But the CJEU did not take this position[50] and referred, 'in a second place and above all' to the prohibition of discrimination on grounds of age as a general principle of EU law.[51]

3.2 *Horizontal Effects of the Directive*

There is an established jurisprudence that directives may have direct effect after the period of transposition has expired only in so far as they contain provisions that are clear, unconditional and conferring rights upon the individual.[52] However, in order to maintain the difference drawn between regulations and directives in Article 288 TFEU, there is a similarly established case law of the CJEU excluding such direct effect where private parties are involved on both sides, the so-called horizontal effect.[53]

Nonetheless, in *Mangold*, the Court does not distinguish between direct and horizontal effects of the Directive. It was strongly criticized for this position in an editorial of the Common Market Law Review.[54] Interestingly, it is the GFCC that refers to the cases *CIA Security* and *Unilever* in an attempt to construe a duty of the courts to set aside a provision of national law in a dispute between private individuals even before expiration of the directive's transposition period. It eventually rejects the claim that the *Mangold* ruling was ultra vires in this point, by placing the said duty within the doctrine of 'negative effect' of directives:

> With the advance effect of directives that was presumed in the Mangold ruling, the Court of Justice creates a further case group for the so-called

50 Interestingly, however, it referred to the principle of primacy at a later stage in order to confirm the duty of the national judge to set aside the German law in question (*Mangold* (n 24), para 77).

51 Ibid, paras 74ff. For this see Section 3.3 below.

52 Case 8/81 *Ursula Becker v Finanzamt Münster-Innenstadt* EU:C:1982:7, paras 19–25.

53 Case 152/84 *M.H. Marshall v Southampton and South-West Hampshire Area Health Authority (Teaching)* EU:C:1986:84, para 48; Case C-91/92 *Paola Faccini Dori v Recreb Srl* EU:C:1994:292, para 20. For a critical assessment with the proposal of a fundamental change of the *Marshall* approach of the CJEU see Sebastian Graf von Kielmansegg, 'Tücken im Dreieck – Die individualbelastende Richtlinienwirkung im Unionsrecht' (2014) 49 EuR 30.

54 Editorial Comments (n 29).

> 'negative' effect of directives. Like the case-law on the 'negative' effect of directives, this serves all in all only to carry out existing legal obligations of the Member States, but does not create any new obligations of the Member States violating the principle of conferral.[55]

In so concluding, did the GFCC take account of the specific conditions given in the cases referred to and the express distinction drawn by the CJEU to the direct effect of directives providing for rights or obligations of individuals in cases of non-transposition?

The cases referred to regarded technical regulations adopted by a Member State in breach of procedural requirements under Article 8 and 9 of Directive 83/189 laying down a procedure for the provision of information in the field of technical standards and regulations.[56] The CJEU ruled that such technical regulations, if the Commission had not been notified in advance, would not be applicable by national courts in civil proceedings between private individuals concerning contractual rights and obligations. To underline the difference the Court stated in the *Unilever* case:

> Whilst it is true, as observed by the Italian and Danish Governments, that a directive cannot of itself impose obligations on an individual and cannot therefore be relied on as such against an individual (see Case C-91/92 *Faccini Dori* [1994] ECR I-3325, paragraph 20), that case-law does not apply where non-compliance with Article 8 or Article 9 of Directive 83/189, which constitutes a substantial procedural defect, renders a technical regulation adopted in breach of either of those articles inapplicable.
>
> In such circumstances, and unlike the case of non-transposition of directives with which the case-law cited by those two Governments is concerned, Directive 83/189 does not in any way define the substantive scope of the legal rule on the basis of which the national court must decide the case before it. It creates neither rights nor obligations for individuals.[57]

---

55 GFCC, *Honeywell* (n 29), para 77.

56 Council Directive 83/189/EEC of 28 March 1983 laying down a procedure for the provision of information in the field of technical standards and regulations [1983] OJ L 109/8. See for a brief discussion of negative direct effect of directives in horizontal constellations, Christoph Hermann, 'Die negative unmittelbare Wirkung von Richtlinien in horizontalen Rechtsverhältnissen' (2006) 17 Europäische Zeitschrift für Wirtschaftsrecht 69.

57 Case C-443/98 *Unilever Italia SpA v Central Food SpA* EU:C:2000:496, paras 50–51.

Without saying so, the GFCC, in assimilating the reasoning in *Mangold* with this jurisprudence, to some extent comes to the conclusions which would better resonate with the *Mangold* judgment if the CJEU had reasoned the way suggested above, namely if it had based its decision on the violation of the more procedural obligations of Member States regarding the transposition of directives. Considering how the GFCC understood the *Mangold* judgment, it is not clear, though, if this approach to reconcile *Mangold* with *Faccini Dori* and not to understand the former as contrary to the established case law excluding the horizontal effect of directives would be shared by the CJEU. Unfortunately, there is no answer to this question in the *Mangold* decision nor in any later judgment of the CJEU so far.

When the Court took a position in *Kücükdeveci* in recalling the *Faccini-Dori* jurisprudence, this was prior to *Honeywell* and, thus, could not be a reply to the GFCC. The CJEU, however, was clearly aware of the critique of *Mangold*, but confirmed the duties of national courts faced with the problem by referring to the general principle of non-discrimination on grounds of age, as confirmed by Article 21(1) of the Charter of Fundamental Rights of the European Union (the Charter), which in the meantime had been given binding effect under Article 6(1) TEU.[58] The Court confirmed this approach very clearly in recent case law, stating that:

> [T]he principle prohibiting discrimination on grounds of age confers on private persons an individual right which they may invoke as such and which, *even in disputes between private persons*, requires the national courts to disapply national provisions that do not comply with that principle.[59]

This does not mean that the Court had not heard the critique of the *Mangold* ruling. In 2012, in *Dominguez*, it confirmed without any reservation that:

> [I]t should be borne in mind that even a clear, precise and unconditional provision of a directive seeking to confer rights or impose obligations on individuals cannot of itself apply in proceedings exclusively between private parties.[60]

58 Case C-555/07 *Seda Kücükdeveci v Swedex GmbH & Co. KG* EU:C:2010:21, paras 21–25 and 46–56.

59 Case C-441/14 *Dansk Industri (DI), acting on behalf of Ajos A/S v Estate of Karsten Eigil Rasmussen* EU:C:2016:278, para 36 (emphasis added).

60 Case C-282/10 *Maribel Dominguez v Centre informatique du Centre Ouest Atlantique and Préfet de la région Centre* EU:C:2012:33, para 42. See also Case C-176/12 *Association*

What remained open at this stage, however, was the effect of the combined application, among private parties, of a provision of a directive and a general principle of Union law or of the EU Charter of Fundamental Rights with the result that conflicting provisions of the national law had to be set aside. Yet, at the time of writing, it seems to be confirmed as established case law of the CJEU without any further discussion.

3.3 *A General Principle of Law Excluding Age Discrimination*

When *Mangold* was decided in November 2005, the EU Charter of Fundamental Rights had not yet been given legally binding force. The Court accepted the principle of non-discrimination on grounds of age to be a general principle of Community, now Union, law. The judgment gives no further justification other than the simple reference to the third and fourth recitals in the preamble of the Directive stating that the source of the actual principle is to be found 'in various international instruments and in the constitutional traditions common to the Member States'.[61] The Court refers to this principle 'in the second place and above all',[62] and emphasizes that the Directive does not do more than, as set out in its Article 1, 'lay[ing] down a general framework for combating discrimination on the grounds of religion or belief, disability, age or sexual orientation'. The Court even goes on to underline that the observance of this principle 'cannot as such be conditional upon the expiry of the period allowed the Member States for the transposition' of the Directive.[63] It seems, thus, to be the general principle of non-discrimination that, finally, underpins the *Mangold* ruling.

Accordingly, the GFCC quotes the President of the CJEU in *Honeywell* with the statement that in fact the *Mangold* ruling was based on this general principle of Union law.[64] As the GFCC notes, it is puzzling nonetheless why – in apparent contrast to this clear priority expressed in paragraphs 74 and 78 of the judgment, as well as in the final answer – the Court stresses that:

---

de médiation sociale v Union locale des syndicats CGT and Others EU:C:2014:2 (AMS), para 37.

61 *Mangold* (n 24), paras 74–75.

62 Ibid, para 74. Note that the 'above all' (implying a certain hierarchy of arguments) does not appear in the German translation of the *Mangold* judgment.

63 Ibid, para 76.

64 GFCC, *Honeywell* (n 29), para 70, referring to Vassilios Skouris, 'Methoden der Grundrechtsgewinnung in der EU' in Detlef Merten and Hans-Jürgen Papier (eds), *Handbuch der Grundrechte in Deutschland und Europa* (vol VI/1, CF Müller 2010), § 157, para 24.

> Community law and, more particularly, Article 6(1) of Directive 2000/78, must be interpreted as precluding a provision of domestic law such as that at issue in the main proceedings which authorizes, without restriction, unless there is a close connection with an earlier contract of employment of indefinite duration concluded with the same employer, the conclusion of fixed-term contracts of employment once the worker has reached the age of 52.[65]

This does not sound as if the judgment were based 'above all' on the general principle of Union law. It was also criticised for insufficient motivation regarding the existence of this principle.[66] Only two of the constitutions of the Member States seem to contain a fundamental right of non-discrimination on grounds of age, and international agreements do not more than prohibit discrimination generally. Critics of the judgment therefore argue that there was no basis for accepting such a principle.[67] As a result, the Court was accused to have acted as a legislator and in so doing, exceeded the powers conferred on it by the Treaties.[68]

Yet, the GFCC did not find that the Court had acted ultra vires in the judgment because it neither created new competences of the Union nor encroached on fundamental rights.[69] Nonetheless, nothing in the judgment methodologically speaking explains how the Court reached the conclusion that such a general principle of law could be recognised.[70] This might be a lack of reasoning only, and the question is whether there is a convincing justification for recognising

65 *Mangold* (n 24), para 78.

66 See e.g. Metzger (n 31) 851 and 855.

67 See also the summary of the critique by national governments in the Opinion of Advocate General Sharpston (n 29), para 29; her own analysis comes to a negative result (see paras 42–65). In contrast, the Court defends the principle – together with the provisions of Directive 2000/78 – against the claim of exceptions with a very precise examination of their invoked justification, see e.g. Case C-286/12, *Commission v Hungary* EU:C:2012:687, paras 60–80.

68 Gerken and others (n 32) 18ff; at least indirectly critical also the Opinion of Advocate General Mazák in Case C-411/05 *Félix Palacios de la Villa v Cortefiel Servicios SA* EU:C:2007:106, paras 88–89; Metzger (n 31).

69 GFCC, *Honeywell* (n 29), para 78.

70 See already Metzger (n 31) 851ff. On the rather minimalist reasoning of the CJEU in its human rights jurisprudence also after the Charter was given legally binding force, see Gráinne de Búrca, 'After the EU Charter of Fundamental Rights: The Court of Justice as a Human Rights Adjudicator?' (2013) 20 Maastricht Journal of European and Comparative Law 168, 174ff.

the prohibition of discrimination on grounds of age as a general principle of EU law at all.

It seems to be possible to argue that the EU Charter of Fundamental Rights provides for this right in its Article 21(1) since 2000. This recognition by the Convention and, finally, by the Governments of the Member States when they solemnly proclaimed the Charter in Nice, cannot be deprived of any value whatsoever, even before it was given legally binding force. This seems to be particularly relevant since the Preamble of the Charter expressly stresses that the Charter 'reaffirms (…) the rights as they result, in particular, from the constitutional traditions and international obligations common to the Member States (…)'.[71] The German text even more clearly states that it renders these rights more visible. Advocate General Bot, in his opinion on the case *Kücükdeveci*, pointed out that the argument – together with a reference to Article 13(1) EC (now Article 19(1) TFEU) – would indeed have strengthened the reasoning of the Court. The recognition of the prohibition of age discrimination as a general principle of EU law, he states, 'is in accord with the wish expressed by the Member States and the Community institutions to counteract age discrimination effectively'.[72] Concluding from a 'wish' to the existence of a general principle of law, is questionable methodologically nevertheless. Given the limited powers of the Union under Article 19 TFEU to take action on the implementation of this principle, a more profound reasoning would be required in order to avoid any accusation of having exceeded the limits of the Court's competence.[73]

3.4 *Binding Effect of Fundamental Rights on Member States*

Fundamental rights, found among the general principles of EU law, have been recognized by the Court to protect the individual against acts of the

71 Koen Lenaerts and José A Gutiérrez-Fons, 'The Constitutional Allocation of Powers and General Principles of EU Law' (2010) 47 CML Rev 1629, state that indeed the Charter was 'the internal source of inspiration supporting the findings of the ECJ in *Mangold*'.

72 Opinion of Advocate General Bot in Case C-555/07 *Seda Kücükdeveci v Swedex GmbH & Co. KG* EU:C:2009:429, para 77. For the legitimacy of a reference to the Charter see also Felipe Temming, 'Freie Rechtsschöpfung oder nicht: Der Streit um die EuGH-Entscheidung Mangold spitzt sich zu' [2008] Neue Juristische Wochenschrift 3404, 3405.

73 Eriksson (n 31) 737ff. See also Dougan (n 43) 221–224, who states that a reference to the Charter, at that period of time, would 'have come at the expense of a different accusation: that the Court was conferring constitutionally problematic legal effects upon the unincorporated Charter'. Yet, he concedes also that after the Charter was given binding effect 'this entire critique of the *Mangold* ruling should now be considered of largely historical interest'.

institutions of the Union.[74] Whereas Member States' authorities are bound to fundamental rights under their respective constitutions and the European Convention on Human Rights (ECHR), similar boundaries for the public authority exercised at the EU level initially remained to be developed. The GFCC encouraged the CJEU in its *Solange* jurisprudence to develop a system of protection of fundamental rights at EU level.[75] Doctrinally, these rights were derived from the common constitutional traditions of the Member States as well as their obligations under international agreements, namely the ECHR. Their focus was not the action of the Member States' institutions. The question may be asked on what basis the CJEU finds in its *Mangold* ruling the prohibition of age-discrimination to be applicable to national legislation with the effect that the 'Hartz' law had to be set aside by the Munich Labour Court having filed the reference.

Yet, the Court refers to its earlier jurisprudence, namely the *Rodriguez Caballero* case, in which it confirmed a binding effect of Union fundamental rights for Member States' institutions both when implementing Union law and when acting within its scope. It stresses that:

> [A]ccording to settled case-law fundamental rights form an integral part of the general principles of law whose observance the Court ensures and, second, that the requirements flowing from the protection of fundamental rights in the Community legal order are also binding on Member States when they implement Community rules. Consequently, Member States must, as far as possible, apply those rules in accordance with those requirements (see Case C-2/92 *Bostock* [1994] ECR I-955, paragraph 16, and Case C-292/97 *Karlsson and Others* [2000] ECR I-2737, paragraph 37).

---

74 Initially Case 29/69 *Erich Stauder v City of Ulm – Sozialamt* EU:C:1969:57, paras 2–7; For the period until 1979 see in more detail Ingolf Pernice, *Grundrechtsgehalte im Europäischen Gemeinschaftsrecht – Ein Beitrag zum gemeinschaftsimmanenten Grundrechtsschutz durch den EuGH* (Nomos 1979). For later developments see Vassilios Skouris (n 64) 864–872. For an overview of the system of fundamental rights protection see Ingolf Pernice, 'The Treaty of Lisbon and Fundamental Rights' in Stefan Griller and Jaques Ziller (eds), *The Lisbon Treaty. EU Constitutionalism without a Constitutional Treaty?* (Springer 2008) 235.

75 GFCC, Judgment of 29 May 1974, BVerfGE 37, 271 – *Solange I*; Judgment of 22 October 1986, BVerfGE 73, 339 – *Solange II*; a description of the resurgent conflict between the GFCC and the CJEU as to the increasingly conflicting spheres of the scope of applicability of EU and national fundamental rights norms is offered by Daniel Thym, 'Die Reichweite der EU-Grundrechtecharte-Charta – Zu viel Grundrechtsschutz' (2013) 32 Neue Zeitschrift für Verwaltungsrecht 889–896.

> Where national rules fall within the scope of Community law, and reference is made to the Court for a preliminary ruling, the Court must provide all the criteria of interpretation needed by the national court to determine whether those rules are compatible with the fundamental rights the observance of which the Court ensures (Case C-260/89 *ERT* [1991] ECR I-2925, paragraph 42, and Case C-85/97 *SFI* [1998] ECR I-7447, paragraph 29).[76]

In *Mangold*, the CJEU found that the EU principle of non-discrimination on grounds of age is binding for the German legislator regarding the 'Hartz' law, since the latter falls 'within the scope of Community law (...) as (...) a measure implementing Directive 1999/70'.[77] The latter Directive gives effect to the framework agreement on fixed-term work which was concluded by the Union of Industrial and Employers' Confederations of Europe (UNICE), the European Centre of Enterprises with Public Participation (CEEP) and the European Trade Union Confederation (ETUC).[78] Although it does not deal with age specifically, the Court refers to clause 8(3) of the Framework Agreement in the Directive, under which the 'implementation of this agreement shall not constitute valid grounds for reducing the general level of protection afforded to workers in the field of the agreement'. This is meant to cover age discrimination and serves as a basis for concluding that the German provisions are within the scope of Union law and that the prohibition of age discrimination is binding on the German authorities.[79]

---

76 Case C-442/00 *Ángel Rodríguez Caballero v Fondo de Garantía Salarial (Fogasa)* EU:C:2002:752, paras 30–31.

77 *Mangold* (n 24), para. 75.

78 Council Directive 1999/70/EC of 28 June 1999 concerning the framework agreement on fixed-term work concluded by ETUC, UNICE and CEEP [1999] OJ L175/ 43.

79 *Mangold* (n 24), para 75 in conjunction with para 51, where it states: 'The term "implementation", used without any further precision in Clause 8(3) of the Framework Agreement, does not refer only to the original transposition of Directive 1999/70 and especially of the Annex thereto containing the Framework Agreement, but must also cover all domestic measures intended to ensure that the objective pursued by the directive may be attained, including those which, after transposition in the strict sense, add to or amend domestic rules previously adopted'. Consenting in this point with no reserve: Opinion of Advocate General Sharpston in *Bartsch* (n 29), para 70. This approach was confirmed in Case C-427/06 *Birgit Bartsch v Bosch und Siemens Hausgeräte (BSH) Altersfürsorge GmbH* EU:C:2008:517, para 24, stressing that these conditions did not apply in the given case.

How general may obligations under EU law be in order to entail the applicability of EU general principles and fundamental rights at the national level? This very sensitive question of delimiting the reach of EU fundamental rights has not yet been fully clarified with respect to Article 51(1) of the EU Charter of Fundamental Rights.[80] It received great attention with the *Åkerberg Fransson* judgment of 23 February 2013.[81] A subsequent judgment of the GFCC on the German anti-terrorrism legislation underlines that the GFCC would only accept that German laws implementing EU legislation to be subject to the fundamental rights of the EU.[82] It expressly referred to the judgment in *Åkerberg Fransson* and admonished restraint in the application of EU fundamental rights to national measures. With a view to the original reasons for developing the protection of fundamental rights at the EU level, their application must stop where the institutional legal action lacks a substantial relationship to, or does not fall within, the scope of EU law in more than an abstract manner.[83]

Such a substantial relationship to EU law was available with the Directive 2000/78, which was adopted precisely to give effect to the principle of non-discrimination based upon age. As explained above, this Directive was binding upon the Member States to some extent already during the period of transposition. During that period Member States are bound to transpose and, therefore, work towards implementing the Directive. How is it possible to argue that measures taken within the scope of this Directive are not within the scope of Union law? Yet, as the final point of the period of transposition was not reached, the Court decided to rely upon Directive 1999/70, thus implying that this would suffice to establish that the situation is within the scope of Union law.

---

80 For a recent critical analysis made by an acting judge of the GFCC, see Gabriele Britz, 'Grundrechtsschutz durch das Bundesverfassungsgericht und den Europäischen Gerichtshof' (2015) 42 Europäische Grundrechte-Zeitschrift 275. With an emphasis on the 'method of cooperation' see also Kirchhof (n 2) 272–295.

81 Case C-617/2010 *Åklagaren v Hans Åkerberg Fransson* EU:C:2013:105, paras 17–31. For critical comments see Hannes Radtke, 'Mangold Reloaded?' (*Verfassungsblog*, 8 March 2013) <http://verfassungsblog.de/mandold-reloaded/> accessed 10 December 2016; Nikos Lavranos, 'The ECJ Judgments in Melloni and Åkerberg Fransson: Une ménage à trois difficulté' [2013] European Law Reporter 4/2013 133; Andreas Voßkuhle, 'European Integration and the Bundesverfassungsgericht' (Sir Thomas More Lecture, London, 31 October 2013) <http://www.lincolnsinn.org.uk/images/word/education/euro/Thomas%20More%20Lecture%20Oct%202013.pdf> accessed 10 December 2016, 15ff.

82 GFCC, Judgment of 24 April 2013, BVerfGE 133, 277 – *Antiterrordatei*, paras 88–90.

83 Ibid, para 91.

In the *Kücükdeveci* case, the Court could easily consider the related German provision (§ 622(2) of the German Civil Code (BGB)) to fall within the scope of EU law, since the transposition period of Directive 2000/78 had effectively expired and the 'directive had the effect of bringing within the scope of European Union law the national legislation at issue in the main proceedings, which concerns a matter governed by that directive'.[84] This was not possible, though, in *Bartsch*, in which the transposition period had not expired by the date on which the discrimination occurred.[85] Was it in reaction to the criticism of *Mangold* that the CJEU held in the *Bartsch* judgment that the Directive could not be relied upon for this reason?[86] In her Opinion to this case, Advocate General Sharpston summarises the arguments put forward by some national governments as follows:

> [T]he transposition period, and indeed the very nature of a directive, mean that it cannot provide a link to Community law prior to the end of that period. The effects of a directive during its transposition period are limited to preventing a Member State from adopting incompatible measures. The directive does not, however, widen the scope of application of Community law during that period. Such an effect would undermine the legislator's decision.[87]

Yet, must not the legislator's decision here be understood as obliging the Member States to transpose the objectives laid down in the Directive within the period defined in the Directive into binding law, as required under Articles 10(3) TEU and 288(3) TFEU, like it could have been argued in the *Mangold* case? Once such a Directive is in force – as set out in Article 297(2) TFEU – and throughout the period of transposition, is it possible to deny the applicability of Union law to an action contrary to the objectives of the Directive as being outside its scope? The answer must be negative at least in a situation as presented in *Mangold*, where under Article 18(2) of the Directive a Member State having been accorded an additional period of transposition is also required to 'report annually to the Commission on the steps it is taking to tackle age and disability discrimination and on the progress it is making towards implementation'.[88]

---

84 *Kücükdeveci* (n 58), para 25.

85 Ibid, para 24.

86 *Bartsch* (n 79), paras 15–18.

87 Opinion of Advocate General Sharpston (n 79), para. 67.

88 See already *supra* (Section 3.1). The Court specifically refers to this provision in *Mangold* (n 24), para 72.

3.5 *Horizontal Effects of General Principles or EU Fundamental Rights*

Traditionally, fundamental rights are constitutional rights, which protect the individual against acts of public authorities and act as a barrier against the State by limiting its power. They may not be invoked horizontally among private persons. Article 51(1) of the EU Charter of Fundamental Rights clearly confirms this limit:

> The provisions of this Charter are addressed to the institutions, bodies, offices and agencies of the Union with due regard for the principle of subsidiarity and to the Member States only when they are implementing Union law.

Nothing is said about private persons. It follows that in a case like *Mangold*, the employee in the dispute with his employer could not rely simply on the general principle of non-discrimination based on age in order to argue that the fixed-term clause in his contract must be declared invalid. General principles of Union law, like fundamental rights, bind public authorities only. The question is how to reconcile the approach taken by the CJEU in *Mangold* and the subsequent case law with this principle.

The Court does not address the issue in the *Mangold* ruling. With respect to national provisions that fall within the scope of Union law relevant in a given case, it simply regards it as its duty to 'provide all the criteria of interpretation needed by the national court to determine whether those rules are compatible with such a principle'.[89] The result is similar to that of a horizontal application of a directive. The Court concludes:

> In those circumstances it is the responsibility of the national court, hearing a dispute involving the principle of non-discrimination in respect of age, to provide, in a case within its jurisdiction, the legal protection which individuals derive from the rules of Community law and to ensure that those rules are fully effective, setting aside any provision of national law which may conflict with that law.[90]

The Court does not even raise the question of horizontal application of the principle. The focus is on the objective task of the national court to provide 'the legal protection which individuals derive from the rules of Community law

89 Ibid, para 75.

90 Ibid, para 77.

(…) setting aside any provision of national law which may conflict with that law'. Here, it seems generally to rely on the primacy of Union law and the obligation to ensure that 'those rules are fully effective'. Similarly, in *Kücükdeveci*, the Court stresses the limits of the direct effect of the Directive with respect to the relations between individuals; it only stresses the obligation of interpretation of national law in conformity with the Directive.[91] Yet, where no room is given for such an interpretation, the Court introduces a reference to the general principle of non-discrimination, recalling that 'Directive 2000/78 merely gives expression to, but does not lay down, the principle of equal treatment in employment and occupation' and that 'the principle of non-discrimination on grounds of age is a general principle of European Union law in that it constitutes a specific application of the general principle of equal treatment (see, to that effect, *Mangold*, paragraphs 74 to 76)'.[92] There is no mention of limits to the application of this principle to relations between private parties; thus, the question of the horizontal effects of the general principle of law – or a fundamental right – is not addressed.

An explanation could be that, in *Mangold*, the 'Hartz' law abolished a protective rule from which workers aged 52 years and older would benefit under the previous legislation with regard to fixed-term contracts. Similarly, in *Kücükdeveci*, the age of 25 years was taken as a criterion for denying some advantages to employees regarding the applicable notice period required in case of termination of the employment relationship. If such provisions of national law had to be considered by the national courts in both cases, the principle of non-discrimination on grounds of age in fact was directed at the national legislator. The latter is bound thus by European law, and it is for the judges to give effect to it. In terms of constitutional law, this result amounts to what the Court generally rules in cases where provisions of national law are in conflict with EU primary law: national courts would not be allowed to apply such provisions, whether the case is of a horizontal nature or not.[93]

Given the 'objective' obligations of national courts under Union law, the question of 'horizontal effect' of fundamental rights, therefore, was rightly not addressed in the judgment. The real problem, as Eleanor Spaventa sees it, is the 'dissonance between trigger and general principle' in this case, which she says 'is both novel and problematic'.[94] Only because of a directive that

91 *Kücükdeveci* (n 58), paras 46–48.

92 Ibid, para 50.

93 See on this Eleanor Spaventa, 'The Horizontal Application of Fundamental Rights as General Principles of Law' in Arnull and others (eds) (n 43) 209–210.

94 Ibid 210 and 214.

does not reach as far as the general principle is this principle held to be applicable at all. But is it new? The mechanism of 'trigger' is taken up in Article 51(1) of the EU Charter of Fundament Rights, at least in the way the CJEU understands it. Fundamental rights are applicable to cases that are within the scope of Union law, be it primary or secondary law. Nothing is said about a requirement that the scope or reach of the provisions that trigger the applicability of a Union fundamental right have to be similar to that of the fundamental right. In cases where a Member State is implementing Union law, the opposite seems to be true: the fundamental right of the Union is limiting the discretion of the Member States regarding the conditions and modalities of national implementation. Implementing acts violating a Union fundamental right would, thus, not be applicable by national courts even in situations where they decide upon cases between individuals. The same is true for general principles of Union law made visible by the EU Charter of Fundamental Rights.[95]

The more recent case law of the CJEU seems to confirm this approach, while setting out clear limits. As the Court develops in its 2014 *AMS* judgment, only general principles of law or fundamental rights that are 'sufficient in itself to confer on individuals an individual right which they may invoke as such' can produce these binding effects for the national courts. This is accepted for the prohibition of discrimination on grounds of age; it was not for the more general provision of Article 27 of the EU Charter of Fundamental Rights. As the Court explains, this latter Article 'provides that workers must, at various levels, be guaranteed information and consultation in the cases and under the conditions provided for by European Union law and national laws and practices', and for it 'to be fully effective, it must be given more specific expression in European Union or national law'.[96]

What is more important than this limitation, however, seems to be the distinction drawn by the Court between the present case and its earlier judgments in *Mangold* and *Kücükdeveci*:

95 This conclusion does not imply, contrary to Spaventa (ibid 215–218), that the general principle is horizontally applicable in all cases, even 'in the absence of national rules'. The rule of *Mangold* is not more than giving effect to the binding effect of the principle – or fundamental right – for the Member States (including legislators and judges required to apply their acts), the mere fact that it may apply also in horizontal situations does not mean that individuals are directly bound by the fundamental rights. For this see also Dougan (n 43) 224–25.

96 *AMS* (n 60), paras 44–49; see, however, as further development *Dansk Industri* (n 59).

> In this connection, the facts of the case may be distinguished from those which gave rise to *Kücükdeveci* in so far as the principle of non-discrimination on grounds of age at issue in that case, laid down in Article 21(1) of the Charter, is sufficient in itself to confer on individuals an individual right which they may invoke as such.[97]

This statement was made within the context of the question discussed by the Court of a horizontal effect of the directive at stake, when the Court confirmed once again that:

> [A]ccording to settled case-law, even a clear, precise and unconditional provision of a directive seeking to confer rights or impose obligations on individuals cannot of itself apply in proceedings exclusively between private parties (see *Pfeiffer and Others*, paragraph 109, and Case C-555/07 *Kücükdeveci* [2010] ECR I-365, paragraph 46).[98]

As a result, directives would not create rights or obligations directly among private parties, unless they are giving expression to a general principle of law conferring rights clearly on the individual, such as Article 21 of the EU Charter of Fundamental Rights. In this case, however, the horizontal effect that such provisions seem to produce are no more than indirect and 'collateral' effects of the binding character of the Union fundamental right all national public authorities, including the courts, have to respect under the conditions set out in Article 51(1) of the EU Charter of Fundamental Rights.[99]

By making this distinction, the CJEU takes a more restrictive approach to the effects between private parties of general provisions of the Charter such as Article 27 of the EU Charter of Fundamental Rights, even if combined with a precise provision of a directive. The Court does not follow the conclusions of Advocate General Pedro Cruz-Villalón that 'Article 27 of the Charter, given specific substantive and direct expression in Article 3(1) of Directive 2002/14,

97 *AMS* (n 60), para 47.

98 Ibid, para 36.

99 With an interpretation of this ruling as widening the horizontal application of fundamental rights under the Charter, see the contribution of Christopher Unseld, 'Mangold hat Grenzen: Zur Horizontalwirkung von EU-Grundrechten' (*Verfassungsblog*, 17 January 2014) <http://verfassungsblog.de/mangold-hat-grenzen-zur-horizontalwirkung-von-eu-grundrechten/> accessed 10 December 2016.

may be relied on in a dispute between individuals, with the potential consequences which this may have concerning non-application of the national legislation'.[100]

This conclusion was based upon an elaborate comparative study including elements of the doctrinal debate in some Member States. In addition, the Advocate General pointed out in particular that his position was:

> consistent with the development of the case-law of the Court of Justice, which has allowed, also in a very specific way, objective review of national acts in the light of directives in disputes inter privatos. Without the need for me to elaborate further on this point, the solution I propose here, far from being a turning point in the Court's case-law, is, on the contrary, in keeping with an approach which began in *CIA Security*, *Mangold* and *Kücükdeveci*.[101]

An explanation for why the Court did not follow the Advocate General in this case could be the strong criticism in the literature against the case law referred to. The Court's view also seems to take account of the concerns of the UK, in particular, regarding the Charter and the effects namely of the social rights enshrined in Title IV on solidarity, as found expression in the Protocol (no. 30) on the application of the Charter of Fundamental Rights of the European Union to Poland and the United Kingdom.

Accordingly, what remains is that individuals may invoke an EU fundamental right contained in the Charter in proceedings against other private persons or bodies before national courts in all cases where that right is clear and precise, and where the provision of national law within 'the scope' of Union law, relevant for the decision in that case, has been adopted in violation of that fundamental right. Even if indirectly or 'as a collateral effect', the fundamental right of the Charter, thus, produces a horizontal effect. National courts are given competence and power of a rights-based 'constitutional' oversight upon their respective national legislative – power that they may not enjoy under national constitutional law.[102]

---

100 Opinion of Advocate General Pedro Cruz-Villalón in Case C-176/12 *Association de médiation sociale v Union locale des syndicats CGT and Others* (*AMS*) EU:C:2013:491, para 80.

101 Ibid, para 77.

102 See for Germany the mandatory reference to the GFCC under art 100 § 1 of the Basic Law.

4 Conclusions: Discursive Jurisprudence – A Source of Legitimacy

Much of the criticism brought against the *Mangold* ruling was not unjustified and the CJEU has not been immune against it. Some ambiguities,[103] such as the legal basis of the decision – Article 6(1) of Directive 2000/78 or a general principle of non-discrimination on grounds of age – have been clarified, most recently in the *Dansk Industri* case.[104] It is the general principle 'as given concrete expression by Directive 2000/78' and 'now enshrined in Article 21 of the Charter of Fundamental Rights of the European Union'. So, the debate about the 'advance effects' of a directive remains academic so far; any solution will be relevant, however, for other cases. The Court made clear that there should no longer be any concerns about the question whether a directive can produce horizontal effects: the Court confirms the negative answer, as already stated in *Faccini-Dori*. Methodological questions regarding the establishment of the prohibition of age-discrimination as a general principle of Union law are settled in the specific instance with the entry into force of the EU Charter of Fundamental Rights and, in particular, its Article 21. The general question, however, may arise henceforth in cases where a new general principle of law might be contemplated in accordance with Article 6(3) TEU.

With regard to the further question how the Court establishes the binding effect of a general principle of Union law on the Member States, the criterion of the 'scope of Union law' remains vague, even after the entry into force of Article 51(1) of the EU Charter of Fundamental Rights. The dialogue between the CJEU, with the ruling in *Åkerberg-Fransson*, and the GFCC, with the warnings in the judgment on the anti-terrorism legislation, continues,[105] and there are signals in the subsequent jurisprudence of the Court indicating a more restrictive approach.[106] The entry into force of Directive 2000/78, which covers age discrimination, entails the solution of the problem in the given case, so that any alternative line of argument, based upon the legally binding effects of the

---

103 Haltern (n 29) 46, talks about 'verheerende Argumentationskultur'; see also p 50: 'sehr schlecht argumentiert'.

104 *Dansk Industri* (n 59), para 22.

105 See the contributions of the Vice President of the GFCC Kirchhof (n 2) and of the judge of the same senate of the GFCC, Britz (n 80); see also the remarks of the President of the GFCC, Voßkuhle 'Integration durch Recht' (n 3) 9–19.

106 Case C-112/13 *A v B and Others* EU:C:2014:2195, paras 41–44; Case C-206/13 *Cruciano Siragusa v Regione Sicilia – Soprintendenza Beni Culturali e Ambientali di Palermo* EU:C:2014:126, paras 19–33, with references to other rulings; for a recent summary see Matthias Bäcker, 'Das Grundgesetz als Implementationsgarant der Unionsgrundrechte' (2015) 50 EuR 389, 391–395, with more references.

Directive even before the transposition period has expired, such as developed above, might become relevant in future cases. Finally, the question of the horizontal effect of general principles of law and, in particular, of EU fundamental rights invoked before the national judge in disputes between private persons has received a differentiated but, perhaps, not final answer.[107]

After all, notwithstanding its possible deficiencies, the *Mangold* ruling of the CJEU has triggered important and instructive judicial developments, e.g. clarity as regards the exclusion of direct effect of directives among private persons. In turn, the GFCC has been given the opportunity to clarify further its position on the relationship between EU law and national constitutional courts. It seems to be clear that the Union is based upon the principles of sincere cooperation and mutual respect, as Article 4(3) TEU requires, in a complex system of checks and balances. This includes the 'right to err' on both sides,[108] and learning by doing.[109] The very restrictive conditions set by the GFCC for an ultra vires control of EU legal acts in the *Honeywell* ruling seem to be a reaction to the very harsh criticisms of the preceding *Lisbon* judgment.[110]

Not only the CJEU but also other constitutional courts, like the GFCC or, with the first case where a national constitutional court refused to give effect to a ruling of the CJEU, the Czech Constitutional Court,[111] are subject to a lively public media and doctrinal review, and are responsive to it. Judges, at all levels, have to understand their role, after all, as participants in a general European legal discourse that is constitutive of the European legal system. Judgments

107 It is among the remaining questions raised by Mazák and Moser (n 25) 84.

108 See also Matthias Mahlmann, 'The Politics of Constitutional Identity and its Legal Frame – the *Ultra Vires* Decision of the German Federal Constitutional Court' (2011) 11 German Law Journal 1408, 1419.

109 Voßkuhle ('Multilevel Cooperation of the European Constitutional Courts' (n 2) 198), rightly talks about 'a discursive struggle for the "best solution", which makes the multilevel cooperation between the European constitutional courts ultimately a multilevel instance for learning (Lernverbund)'.

110 GFCC, *Lisbon* (n 35). For the assumption that the criticisms against the *Lisbon* judgment had an impact on the *Honeywell* judgment see also Haltern (n 29) 69–70.

111 Czech Constitutional Court, Judgment of 31 January 2012, Pl. ÚS 5/12 – *Holubek*, with regard to Case C-399/09 *Marie Landtová v Česká správa socialního zabezpečení* EU:C:2011:415. See the comments of Michal Bobek, '*Landtová, Holubec*, and the Problem of an Uncooperative Court: Implications for the Preliminary Rulings Procedure' (2014) 10 EuConst 54, suggesting that '*Holubek* was a revolt that in fact did not take place' (pp 55 and 71–73) and that 'to generate any theory of "judicial disobedience" on the basis of *Holubek* would be unwise' (p 87). Lenaerts (n 2) 17–19, regards the judgment as 'intolerable' and calls for the establishment of a cooperative relationship among the courts through dialogue (p 19). See also Bobek, 'Of Feasibility and Silent Elephants' (n 15) 225–226: 'comedy of errors'.

are not a monologue of some judges;[112] they have to be read as contributions to a continued dialogue. The vertical and horizontal constitutional dialogues within the 'multilevel cooperation of the European Constitutional Courts', as Andreas Voßkuhle put it,[113] together with the more general European-wide public discourse on their case law, old and new legal concepts and solutions to upcoming problems are key for a constructive and balanced development of European constitutional law across the Union. Similarly, openness to well-argued criticism is just as much a condition for the continued authority and legitimacy of the courts altogether and for the functioning of the European Union as a Union of law – or, as the CJEU puts it, a 'union based on the rule of law' (*Rechtsunion*).[114] In accordance with Article 19(1) TEU, and as implied in Article 267 TFEU, thus, the EU courts and the national courts in the European Union ultimately share co-responsibility and have to cooperate and to listen openly to the broader public in ensuring that the law is observed in a Union that is constructed according to the principles of multilevel constitutionalism.[115]

---

112 See also Haltern and Bergmann (n 20) 19, stressing the 'dialogische Dimension' of the CJEU rulings, though this dialogue is depicted as one with other institutions while the dialogue with the public as an important audience is not addressed. For this see Pernice, 'Die Dritte Gewalt im Europäischen Verfassungsverbund' (n 10) 38 and 40.

113 Voßkuhle 'Multilevel Cooperation of the European Constitutional Courts' (n 2); see also Ingolf Pernice, 'La Rete Europea di Costituzionalità, Der Europäische Verfassungsverbund und die Netzwerktheorie' (2010) 70 Zeitschrift für ausländisches öffentliches Recht und Völkerrecht 51.

114 Case C-583/11 *Inuit Tapiriit Kanatami and Others v Parliament and Council* EU:C:2013:625, para 91.

115 In defense of the concept: Ingolf Pernice, 'Multilevel Constitutionalism and the Crisis of Democracy in Europe' (2015) 11 EuConst 541; for the co-responsibility see Ingolf Pernice, 'Autonomy of the European Legal Order' (n 37) 63–65.

CHAPTER 7

The Principle of Solidarity in the EU Legal Order – Some Practical Examples after Lisbon

*Jenő Czuczai**

1 Introduction

The principle of solidarity undoubtedly has a very broad scope within EU law and has been identified by the Court of Justice of the European Union (CJEU) already very early as a 'general principle, inferred from the nature of the Communities'.[1] Nevertheless, the concept of solidarity, as generally believed, is not necessarily a legal principle in EU law, although this contribution has the aim to prove that it is getting to become more and more important also in legal terms in the EU, especially after Lisbon.

The principle (or the value) of solidarity has, however, clearly – as demonstrated by its historical dimension[2] – a strong political aspect as well, which is rather about a functional and operational principle of EU decision-making, when there is an obvious need to demonstrate solidarity among Member States, even if such a legal obligation cannot be derived obviously from applicable EU

---

* The Views and opinions expressed in this contribution are exclusively personal and those of the author, they do not constitute under no way a formal and official position neither of the Council of the EU nor of its Legal Service.

1 See Joined Cases C-63/90 and C-67/90 *Portuguese Republic and Kingdom of Spain v Council* EU:C:1992:381, para 51; Case C-335/09 P *Republic of Poland v Commission* EU:C:2012:385, paras 30ff and the case law referred to therein; or in more details Koen Lenaerts and Piet Van Nuffel, *Europees Recht* (1st edn, Intersentia 2011) 103–109. The most recent and very comprehensive and detailed elaboration on the principle of solidarity under EU law can be found in Kris Pollet, 'Enhancing Intra-EU Solidarity Tools To Improve Quality and Fundamental Rights Protection in the Common European Asylum System' (ECRE policy paper, January 2013) <http://www.emnbelgium.be/sites/default/files/publications/intra-eu_solidarity_-_full_paper1.pdf> accessed 20 November 2016. As a good overview article see still Peter Hilpold, 'Understanding Solidarity Within EU Law: An Analysis of the "Islands of Solidarity" With Particular Regard to Monetary Union' (2015) 34 YEL 257, in particular 257–275.

2 See e.g. Robert Schuman, *Pour l'Europe* (Nagel Paris 1963) 33 and 129; Peter G Xuereb, 'The Future of Europe: Solidarity and Constitutionalism. Towards a Solidarity Model' (2002) 27 EL Rev 643.

 | DOI 10.1163/9789004347175_008

law. This contribution will start to give first of all a general overview about the legal sources of this principle in EU law, including a deep analysis of the relevant case law of the CJEU. In the second part, it will address the horizontal and vertical nature of the principle of solidarity as well as the internal and external dimension of it. Thirdly, it will go through some practical examples, following further the legal sources-matrix, where this principle has been applied over the last decades in legal practice, while in the fourth part some tendencies will be drawn up as regards the most recent EU primary and secondary laws' developments in this context. Finally, I would like to draw up some concluding remarks, of course, first and foremost from a legal point of view concerning, for example, the current migration crisis or in terms of some other topical 'solidarity'-related challenges in the EU legal order.

2 The Legal Context in General

2.1 *Primary Law and General Case Law*

In order to prove the presumption that the EU has a legal order, which is based also on the principle (or on the fundamental value) of solidarity and shared responsibility the starting point should be that the solidarity principle is one of the founding values of the EU. Article 2 TEU (on the values of the EU) specifically stipulates that 'The EU is founded on [certain values]. These values are common to the Member States in a society, *in which* (…) *solidarity* (…) *prevail*[*s*]' (emphasis added). This means, according to the relevant scientific literature,[3] that at national level the principle of solidarity is one of the driving forces in the EU Member States concerning their society-building processes.

Article 3 TEU (about the aims and tasks of the EU) goes even further when it provides clearly that '[*the Union*] *shall promote* economic, social and territorial cohesion and *solidarity among the Member States*' (Article 3(3) TEU, emphasis added). This is legally an obvious obligation, imposed on the EU. The concrete implementation of this obligation at EU level is carried out, for example, under

3 See e.g. Irina Domurath, 'The Three Dimensions of Solidarity in the EU Legal Order: Limits of the Judicial and Legal Approach' (2013) 35 Journal of European Integration 459; Andrea Ott, 'Unity in Diversity? Differentiation in EU Law and Policy in an Enlarged EU' (Working paper, European Center Natolin, 2004) <http://www.natolin.edu.pl/pdf/zeszyty/NatolinZeszyt15_Ott.pdf> accessed 1 December 2016. It is still worth noting that the Preamble of the TEU reads as follows: 'Desiring to deepen the solidarity between their peoples [ie of the EU Member States] while respecting their history, their culture and their traditions' ([2012] OJ C326/15).

the EU cohesion policy (see Articles 174–179 TFEU and Protocol No. 28 attached to the Lisbon Treaty on EU economic, social and territorial cohesion etc.).

One must, however, add that *the principle of solidarity appears* expressis verbis *in the Treaties still in more than fifteen places,*[4] from the EU policies of energy and climate change, through the EU common policy on asylum, immigration and refugees, until the EU humanitarian policy and civil protection (or in broader sense EU external actions), not speaking about the new Article 222 TFEU, specifically titled in the Lisbon Treaty as 'Solidarity Clause'.[5] These sector-specific appearances of the principle of solidarity will be addressed later on in more detail.

It should be, of course, noted that the EU Charter of Fundamental Rights[6] (which has the same legal value as the Treaties – Article 6(1) TEU) gives also special attention to the principle of solidarity at least in two senses:

- first of all in the Preamble of the Charter (second sentence) it is stressed that 'Conscious of its spiritual and moral heritage, *the Union is founded on the indivisible, universal values of* human dignity, freedom, equality and *solidarity* (…)' (emphasis added), which wording even upgrades the principle of solidarity, since this language of the Charter, as opposed, for example, to Article 2 TEU, makes it even one of the universal fundamental values, based on which the Union is founded;
- the above upgraded significance of the solidarity principle in the Charter can also be seen in Title IV of the Charter, the title of which interestingly enough is 'Solidarity', covering Articles 27 to 38 (from the social and economic rights, over the services of general economic interest (SGEI) until the protection of consumers' rights etc.).

According to the relevant legal doctrine another concrete expression in the Treaties in more general terms of the principle of solidarity is *the principle of sincere cooperation as laid down in Article 4(3) TEU*. This principle among other obligations requires the Union and the Member States, in full mutual respect

4 See as relevant Articles in the Treaties: art 2. TEU; art 3(3) and (5) TEU; art 21(1) TEU; art 24(2) and (3) TEU; art 31(1) TEU; art 32 TEU; art 67(2) TFEU; art 78(1) and (3) TFEU; art 80 TFEU; art 107(2)(b), (3)(a) and (3)(b) TFEU; art 122(1) TFEU; art 194(1) TFEU; art 222 TFEU; Protocol No 28; Declaration No 27 on Article 222 TFEU.

5 See in more detail Steven Blockmans, 'L'Union fait la Force: Making the Most of the Solidarity Clause (Article 222 TFEU)' in Inge Govaere and Sara Poli (eds) *EU Management of Global Emergencies: Legal Framework for Combating Threats and Crises* (Brill-Nijhoff 2014) 111.

6 [2007] OJ C303/1 (the Charter).

and based on solidarity, to 'assist each other in carrying out tasks which flow from the Treaties'. The CJEU has developed the principle of sincere cooperation in its jurisprudence and has interpreted this notion as encompassing first a duty for Member States to cooperate with the Commission as well as with all the institutions and administrative organs in the other Member States, responsible for the implementation of Union law, in addition to a general duty of diligence in implementing EU law, and secondly a duty to respect the general interests of the Union and the institutional balance principle of the Union.[7] The principle of sincere cooperation, which applies to all policy areas of the EU, exists as a duty also between the Member States, in particular where this is necessary to achieve the objectives of the Union. That is exactly why in the EU legal doctrine *a distinction is to be made between the horizontal and the vertical aspects of the principle of solidarity*, namely when it applies horizontally between the institutions of the EU and the Member States, but also this principle has clear-cut practical relevance between the EU institutions and the Member States when they cooperate with each other vertically.[8]

It is to be noted that in the field of EU Common Foreign and Security Policy (CFSP) and EU external action a similar provision (like Article 4(3) TEU) can be found, namely Article 24(3) TEU, which specifically underlines that Member States shall support the EU CFSP actively and unreservedly *in a spirit of loyalty and mutual solidarity* and shall comply with the Union's action in this area (and by working together *to enhance and develop their mutual political solidarity* etc.). Member States *shall show mutual solidarity* in international relations towards the Union as well as other Member States and *shall act 'in a spirit of mutual solidarity'* (emphasis added) *in order* to preserve the effectiveness as a cohesive force of the Union actions in international context.[9]

A good example for solidarity in the EU international relation' context – though under very specific circumstances – can be found in the CJEU post-Lisbon jurisprudence, when the Court spelled out in October 2014 that:

> Lorsque le domaine concerné relève d'une compétence de l'Union telle que celle décrite au point précédent, l'absence de participation de l'Union à l'accord international en cause ne l'empêche pas d'exercer cette

7 See further Jenő Czuczai, 'The Respect for the Principle of "Institutional Balance" and its Developing Inter-Institutional Practice After Lisbon' in Nagy Csongor Istvàn (ed), *Liber Amicorum in honour of J. Martonyi*' (HVG Orac 2014) 145.

8 See all these issues in more detail in Rupert Scholz, 'Solidarität – ein Rechtsprinzip?' (2014) VII Beihefte zum Archiv des öffentlichen Rechts 1.

9 See still art 31(1) TEU about the constructive abstention as well as art 32 TEU in this regard.

> compétence en établissant, dans le cadre de ses institutions, une position à prendre en son nom dans l'instance, créée par cet accord, notamment par l'intermédiaire des Etats membres parties audit accord agissant *solidairement* dans son intérêt (…).[10]

2.2 *Typology of Solidarity – Internal and External Dimensions*

I have already mentioned above the horizontal and vertical context of the implementation of the principle of solidarity. A more important typology of the different practical appearances of the concept of solidarity can be observed when one is distinguishing between *its internal and external dimensions.*

The most obvious example for the internal dimension of the *EU solidarity principle* is the greatest novelty of the Lisbon Treaty, namely the introduction into the Treaties of Article 222 TFEU on the solidarity clause.[11] This clause clearly shows that if a Member State falls in a serious emergency problem (e.g. a terrorist attack or a natural disaster occurs in its territory etc.), then the other Member States, at its request, must help to it '*in a spirit of solidarity*' (emphasis added) as Article 222(1) TFEU requires it. How this help should be carried out, based on which modalities and decision-making mechanism, that is regularly monitored and followed in practice in the Council.[12]

Yet, the internal dimension of the EU *solidarity principle* can be touched upon, for example, in the context of Article 42(7) TEU (about the mutual assistance obligation within the EU's *Common Security and Defence Policy* (*CSDP*), which practically corresponds to the Article 5 clause of the North Atlantic Treaty) or what concerns Article 43 TEU (in relation to the humanitarian and rescue tasks in the same field involving close cooperation among Member

---

10 Case C-399/12 *Federal Republic of Germany v Council* EU:C:2014:2258 (*OIV* case), para 52 and the further case law referred to therein (emphasis added). In addition, as literature see Inge Govaere, 'Novel Issues Pertaining to EU Member States Membership of Other International Organisations: The OIV Case' in Inge Govaere and others (eds), *The EU in the World – Essays in Honour of Marc Maresceau* (Martinus Nijhoff Publishers 2013) 225.

11 In this respect, it should be noted that the Council adopted also practical arrangements on how the solidarity clause should be implemented when its application becomes unavoidable in practice. This Council Decision has further strengthened the practical modalities of the principle of solidarity (see in more detail Council Decision 2014/415/EU of 24 June 2014 on the arrangements for the implementation by the Union of the Solidarity Clause [2014] OJ L192/53, especially recitals 1, 2, 3, 5, 6, 15, 18 and 20 as well as arts 1(1) and (2), 4(1) and (2), 5 and 7).

12 See in more detail the mandate of the relevant Friends of Presidency Council working group on the Solidarity clause implementation (Council doc 16757/14).

States and in principle even possible support to third countries in combating terrorism in their territories).[13]

As a final example for the *EU internal policy-making relevance of the solidarity principle*, one should still refer to some regulatory principles of the EU, like e.g. as regards the consumer protection area in Article 12 TFEU (e.g. the protection principle of the consumers being always in the weaker position); or concerning social affairs (including the social inclusion issues) in Article 9 TFEU (e.g. the helping obligation to those who are endangered or to the children or to the elderly people, to the handicapped people[14] or to those having serious health risks (e.g. epidemics etc.) etc.). Here, as one could say, there is always a kind of 'solidarity' dimension as well in the EU law-making practice.

Now turning to the *external dimension of the solidarity principle*, just to mention some examples, one could immediately refer to Article 3(5) TEU (aims and tasks of the EU), which provides that the Union 'shall contribute to (…) solidarity and mutual respect among peoples (…)'. This notion is further detailed later on already in the EU CFSP Part of the TEU under Article 21(1), where, as I already quoted earlier, it is written that 'The Union's action on the international scene *shall be guided by the principle* (…) [*of*] *solidarity* (…)' (emphasis added)![15] What this means in concrete practical terms is still amplified, for example, in Article 21(2)(g) (natural catastrophes etc.); or in the field of

13 See as concrete example for the relevance of art 42(7) TEU: 'Activation of Article 42(7) TEU – France's request for assistance and Member States' responses' (European Council Briefing, April 2016) doc PE 581.402, as well as the European Parliament resolution of 21 January 2016 on the mutual defence clause (Article 42(7) TEU) (EP doc P8_TA-PROV(2016)0019). In addition, with regard to art 42(7) TEU, see still art 3 of the so-called Irish Protocol to the Lisbon Treaty, which specifically underlines: 'It will be for Member States – including Ireland, acting *in a spirit of solidarity* and without prejudice to its traditional policy of military neutrality – *to determine the nature of aid or assistance to be provided to a Member State*, which is the object of a terrorist attack or the victim of armed aggression on its territory' (Protocol on the concerns of the Irish people on the Treaty of Lisbon [2013] OJ L60/131, emphasis added).

14 From the relevant case law of the CJEU, it is interesting to note that the Court declared that the Treaty on the Functioning of the EU allows a national legislation, which envisages that health (in fact medical urgency services)-related transport services could be made directly available with priority to organisations (local non-profit associations) of charitative purposes and without full transparency, based on obvious social reasons *and also on implementing effectively the principle of solidarity within the EU* (see in more details Case C-113/13 *Azienda sanitaria locale n. 5 «Spezzino» and Others v San Lorenzo Soc. coop. sociale and Croce Verde Cogema cooperativa sociale Onlus* EU:C:2014:2440).

15 See in more detail Markus T Kotzur and Kirsten Schmalenbach, 'Solidarity Among Nations' (2014) 52 Archiv des Völkerrechts 68.

development cooperation and other financial and technical assistance to third countries (Articles 208 to 212 TFEU e.g. concerning poverty reduction programmes etc.); or in the already mentioned humanitarian aids-related provisions of the Treaties etc., but with an external dimension (see Article 214 TFEU).

3 Some Concrete Examples for the Principle of Solidarity in the Legal Frameworks of the Different EU Sectorial Policy-fields

As a starting point, one could say that practically there should be always an *EU legal framework in place, expressing the Union solidarity for certain emergency situations* (e.g. terrorist attacks, or huge refugees and immigration inflows in the EU, or floods, forests fires and other natural catastrophes/disasters, unexpected serious financial instabilities etc.), or other events justifying the application – exceptionally – of derogations or temporary special rules as compared to the general EU laws. This is even so after the global economic and financial crisis or the EU sovereign debt crisis has broken out in 2008 or the EU banking crisis in 2012. The Lisbon Treaty has specifically addressed some of these notions by introducing a lot of legal novelties in the EU primary law as well as in EU secondary legislation, but could not offer legal solutions for all these emergencies etc.[16] This section tries to give a short, but certainly not exhaustive inventory of the main examples.

3.1 *Concerning EU Primary Law*

First of all, especially after the tragedy in Lampedusa in 2012 or the migration crisis in the Western Balkan from September 2015, one should make reference to the EU internal policies on *border checks, asylum and immigration within the Union area of freedom, security and justice* (Part III, Title V, Chapter 2 TFEU), which policies should be guided by the principle of solidarity as a whole. Article 80 TFEU in an eloquent manner makes this clear when it provides that:

> The policies of the Union set out in this Chapter and their implementation *shall be governed by the principle of solidarity* and fair sharing of responsibility, including its financial implications, *between the Member States.*

16 See further 'From Eurocrisis to Asylum and Migration Crisis: Some Legal and Institutional Considerations About the EU's Current Struggles' (editorial comments) (2015) 52 CML Rev.1437; Hilpold (n 1) 275ff.

> Whenever necessary, the Union acts adopted pursuant to this Chapter shall contain appropriate measures to give effect to this principle.[17]

Some 'solidarity' element can also be found in the EU *State aid policy*, when, for instance, Article 107 TFEU ex lege declares certain aids, granted by a Member State 'compatible with the internal market' in case when the subject aid aims 'to make good the damage caused by *natural disasters or exceptional occurrences*' (Article 107(2)(b) TFEU, emphasis added); or aid may also be considered to be compatible with the internal market, when aiming 'to promote the economic development of areas where the *standard of living is abnormally low* (...)'; or 'to *remedy a serious disturbance in the economy of a Member State*' (Article 107(3)(a) and (b) TFEU, emphasis added).

As concerns *the Economic and Monetary Union* (EMU) it should be recalled that under Article 122(1) TFEU, 'the Council, on a proposal from the Commission, may decide, *in a spirit of solidarity between Member States*, upon measures appropriate to the economic situation, in particular if severe difficulties arise in the supply of certain products, notably in the area of energy' (emphasis added).[18] Article 122(2) TFEU still adds that:

17 Emphasis added. See further Jürgen Bast, 'Deepening Supranational Integration: Interstate Solidarity in EU Migration Law' (2016) 22 Eur Public L 289. It is still to be noted that practically and to some extent the whole title V of Part III TFEU is 'governed' by the principle of solidarity since art 67(2) TFEU also provides that '[the EU] shall ensure the absence of internal border controls for persons and *shall frame a common policy* on asylum, immigration and external border control, *based on solidarity between Member States*, which *is fair towards third country nationals*. For the purpose of this Title, stateless persons shall be treated as third country nationals' (emphasis added). Of course, it is an open question, that what is to be meant by 'fairness' in the given context and how should it be understood that '*and fair sharing of responsibility, including its financial implications, between Member States*' in art 80 TFEU (emphasis added)? We will know more about the interpretation of art 80 TFEU when two pending cases will be decided by the CJEU in 2017, namely Case C-643/15 *Slovakia v Council* ([2016] OJ C38/41) and Case C-647/15 *Hungary v Council* ([2016] OJ C38/43).

18 It is interesting to note that the CJEU specifically referred to this important legal basis, expressing solidarity when a Member State falls in real and serious economic situation in the well-known *Thomas Pringle* case, which was heard by the full Court taking into account that, for the first time in the history of the European integration process, the European Council was also a party (as an intervenant) to the case (see in more detail Case C-370/12 *Thomas Pringle v Government of Ireland and the Attorney General* EU:C:2012:756, in particular para 115).

> *Where a Member State* is in difficulties or *is seriously threatened with severe difficulties caused by natural disasters or exceptional occurrences beyond its control, the Council,* on a proposal from the Commission, may grant, under certain conditions, *Union financial assistance to the Member State concerned.* The President of the Council shall inform the European Parliament of the decision taken.[19]

Similarly, concerning the so-called *euro-crisis or sovereign debt-crisis within the EU* in 2011 a new legal basis was created in the Treaties,[20] namely Article 136(3) TFEU, in order that Member States, whose currency is the euro, could, under certain conditions, create a financial stability mechanism among themselves, that is to say outside the EU legal framework, for example, by virtue of an intergovernmental agreement, based to some extent also on the principle of solidarity. This resulted in the creation of the so-called *European Stability Mechanism* (ESM), which can help those euro-area Member States, which fall in serious financial instability.[21]

A further clear-cut solidarity element can be touched upon among Member States as regards the concept of *Union's citizenship*. Article 46 of the EU Charter of Fundamental Rights provides that Union citizens have the right to *diplomatic and consular protection* even in a third country, in which the Member State that he or she is a national of, has neither diplomatic nor consular representation (see further: Article 35 TEU, Article 20 TFEU, Article 23 TFEU).

Finally, a very strong solidarity value-orientation should be noted in relation to the *EU Energy policy*, which is though a new, but undoubtedly a very rapidly

---

19 Emphasis added. In relation to the possible application of this legal basis for any Union financial assistance it should be stressed, however, that the concerned Member State's responsibility for the occurance of the prevailing situation should be also carefully examined etc. See further this 'responsibility' aspect in the context of arts 121–126 TFEU etc. in Hilpold (n 1) 275ff.

20 European Council Decision 2011/199/EU of 25 March 2011 amending Article 136 of the Treaty on the Functioning of the EU with regard to a stability mechanism for Member States, whose currency is the euro [2011] OJ L91/1. Art 136(3) TFEU provides that 'The Member States whose currency is the euro may establish a stability mechanism to be activated if indispensable to safeguard the stability of the euro area as a whole. The granting of any required financial assistance under the mechanism will be made subject to strict conditionality'.

21 See in more detail Roland Bieber and Francesco Maiani, 'Sans solidarité point d'Union européenne – Regards croisés sur les crises de l'Union économique et monétaire et du Système européen commun d'asile' (2012) 48 RTDEur 295.

and steadily developing policy area of the EU. In this respect, Article 194 TFEU provides that:

> In the context of the establishment and functioning of the internal market and with regard for the need to preserve and improve the environment, Union policy on energy shall aim, *in a spirit of solidarity between Member States*, to: (a) ensure the functioning of the energy market; (b) ensure security of energy supply in the Union; (c) promote energy efficiency and energy saving and the development of new and renewable forms of energy; and (d) promote the interconnection of energy networks.[22]

3.2 *Under EU Secondary Law*

Concerning the impact of the global economic and financial crisis on the EU, and in particular on the economies of the Member States in the context of *the EU cohesion and regional development policies* a clear-cut solidarity element can be demonstrated[23] in relation to the series of the so-called 'top up Regulations'. The specificity of these Regulations[24] is that in practice only

---

22 Emphasis added.

23 See in more detail Hilpold (n 1) 268ff.

24 See e.g. Regulation (EU) 1310/2011 of the European Parliament and of the Council of 13 December 2011 amending Council Regulation (EC) 1083/2006 as regards certain provisions relating to financial management for certain Member States experiencing or threatened with serious difficulties with respect to their financial stability [2011] OJ L337/5; Regulation (EU) 1312/2011 of the European Parliament and of the Council of 19 December 2011 amending Council Regulation (EC) 1698/2005 as regards certain provisions relating to financial management for certain Member States experiencing or threatened with serious difficulties with respect to their financial stability [2011] OJ L339/1; Regulation (EU) 387/2012 of the European Parliament and of the Council of 19 April 2012 amending Council Regulation (EC) 1198/2006 on the European Fisheries Fund, as regards certain provisions relating to financial management for certain Member States experiencing or threatened with serious difficulties with respect to their financial stability [2012] OJ L129/7; Regulation (EU) 423/2012 of the European Parliament and of the Council of 22 May 2012 amending Council Regulation (EC) 1083/2006 as regards certain provisions relating to risk-sharing instruments for Member States experiencing or threatened with serious difficulties with respect to their financial stability [2012] OJ L133/1; Regulation (EU) 1297/2013 of the European Parliament and of the Council of 11 December 2013 amending Council Regulation (EC) 1083/2006 as regards certain provisions relating to financial management for certain Member States experiencing or threatened with serious difficulties with respect to their financial stability, to the de-commitment rules for certain Member States, and to the rules on payments of the final balance [2013] OJ L347/1, especially recital 3.

Later on, this 'top up' beneficial mechanism was still extended *into other policy areas*, see in this regard Decision 258/2013/EU of the European Parliament and of the Council

some Member States can/could become their beneficiaries (not all!), namely those which are in serious financial difficulties due to the crisis, and which thus – because of their verified exceptional circumstances – needed immediate help, especially in order that they could properly absorb the allocated EU funds, and this way no EU financial support could be lost for them just because they could not provide the required national co-financing (owning to their financial difficulties, caused by the crisis etc.). Therefore, practically the aim and the content of these legislative acts to a certain extent have always been *linked somehow to the concrete implementation of the EU solidarity principle* even if in the legal drafting, for political reasons, this has not always been made clear in each and every legal act. The legislative derogation for the concerned Member States has been that they could top up their EU contribution in principle even to 99 percent, while under normal situations the national co-financing should have been for each investment between 20 and 50 percent of the total funding.

The relevance of the principle of solidarity is more specifically underlined in the EU legal order, when it is directly, that is to say *expressis verbis*, addressed in EU secondary legislation, for example, when a legislative act is even referring to this principle in its title or in its concrete legal wording. This is clearly the case with two Regulations, namely with the so-called *European Solidarity Fund Regulation*[25] (ESdF) as well as the *European Globalisation Adjustment Fund Regulation*[26] (EGF).

The first regulation (in the title of which solidarity is specifically referred to) has a two-fold main objective, namely that 'It is important for the Union

of 13 March 2013 amending Decisions 573/2007/EC and 575/2007/EC of the European Parliament and of the Council and Council Decision 2007/435/EC with a view to increasing the co-financing rate of the European Refugee Fund, the European Return Fund and the European Fund for the Integration of third country nationals as regards certain provisions relating to financial management for certain Member States experiencing or threatened with serious difficulties with respect to their financial stability [2013] OJ L82/1 (for the reasoning, see especially recitals 11–13); Decision 259/2013/EU of the European Parliament and of the Council of 13 March 2013 amending Decision 574/2007/EC with a view to increasing the co-financing rate of the External Borders Fund for certain Member States experiencing or threatened with serious difficulties with respect to their financial stability [2013] OJ L82/6; etc.

25 Regulation (EU) 661/2014 of the European Parliament and of the Council of 15 May 2014 amending Council Regulation (EC) 2012/2002 establishing the European Union Solidarity Fund [2014] OJ L189/143 (ESdF Regulation).

26 Regulation (EU) 1309/2013 of the European Parliament and of the Council of 17 December 2013 on the European Globalisation Adjustment Fund (2014–2020) and repealing Regulation (EC) 1927/2006 [2013] OJ L347/855 (EGF Regulation) (see especially recitals 2 and 17 and arts 1 and 9(3)). It should be noted that the EGF is used very frequently in practice (see e.g. [2014] OJ L 350 in which it was used four times; see at pp 7, 9, 11 and 15).

to have at its disposal a sound and flexible instrument to allow it *to show solidarity*, send a clear political signal and provide genuine assistance *to citizens affected by major natural disasters that have serious repercussions on economic and social development*', while at the same time 'The Union should continue to *show solidarity with the third countries that are involved in accession negotiations* with it (…)' with the aim that 'a clear European perspective *should not be set back by the adverse effects of major natural disasters*', therefore the Union '*shall ensure Union-wide solidarity action to support natural disaster-stricken States* [including accession States as well] (…)'.[27]

The second Regulation on the EGF is worded in the spirit of solidarity, which can be proved in several places of the legislative act, when it is pointed out, for example, that:

> The EGF enables the Union to *show solidarity towards workers made redundant as a result of major structural changes in world trade patterns due to globalisation and global financial and economic crisis*, and can also support (…) in exceptional circumstances [the adverse consequences in the different national labour markets] (…).[28]

The principle of solidarity is very much the founding inspiration also of the European Agency for the Management of Operational Cooperation at the External Borders of the Member States of the EU (FRONTEX)[29] as it is clearly

27 ESdF Regulation, recitals 2, 3 and 26 (emphasis added).

28 EGF Regulation, recital 2 (emphasis added). In this context, it should be noted, however, that interestingly enough *the European Social Fund* is not based on the principle of solidarity as a regulatory concept, though one of the support objectives from the Fund can be 'promoting social entrepreneurship and vocational integration in social enterprises and the social and *solidarity economy* in order to facilitate access to employment' (Regulation (EU) 1304/2013 of the European Parliament and of the Council of 17 December 2013 on the European Social Fund and repealing Council Regulation (EC) 1081/2006 [2013] OJ L347/470, art 3(b)(v), emphasis added).

29 See Regulation (EU) 1168/2011 of the European Parliament and of the Council of 25 October 2011 amending Council Regulation (EC) 2007/2004 establishing a European Agency for the Management of Operational Cooperation at the External Borders of the Member States of the EU [2011] OJ L304/1, as well as Case C-77/05 *United Kingdom of Great Britain and Northern Ireland v Council* EU:C:2007:803, paras 22–23. *Mutatis mutandis* the same can be said about Regulation (EU) 2016/1624 of the European Parliament and of the Council of 14 September 2016 on the European Border and Coast Guard and amending Regulation (EU) 2016/399 of the European Parliament and of the Council and repealing Regulation (EC) No 863/2007 of the European Parliament and of the Council, Council Regulation (EC) No 2007/2004 and Council Decision 2005/267/EC [2016] OJ L251/1.

addressed, for example, in Article 1(3) of that Regulation, when it provides that 'The Agency shall also provide the Commission and the Member States with the necessary technical support and expertise in the management of the external borders and *promote solidarity between Member States, especially those facing specific and disproportionate pressures*' (emphasis added). It is still to be stressed that in the context of EU common visa policy the special relevance of solidarity is similarly embodied in that:

> [A] reciprocity mechanism (…) needs to be adapted in the light of the entry into force of the Treaty of Lisbon and of the case-law of the Court of Justice of the European Union on secondary legal bases (…) that *mechanism needs to be adapted to provide for a Union response as an act of solidarity, if a third country listed* in Annex II to Regulation (EC) No 539/2001 applies a visa requirement for nationals of at least one Member State.[30]

Another policy field, where the principle of solidarity has a great importance, especially after Lisbon, and it is laid down primarily in EU secondary legislations, is the *EU civil protection and crisis management actions* (*including humanitarian aid operations*). Clear proof for this can be found in many acts, like e.g. when in the Decision on a Union Civil Protection Mechanism it is written that 'The *European Union should promote solidarity* and should support, complement, and facilitate the coordination of the Member States' actions in the field of civil protection with a view to improving the effectiveness of systems for preventing, preparing for and responding to natural and man-disasters'.[31]

Or another example as far as the humanitarian aid operations are concerned is stemming from the new Regulation on the European Voluntary Humanitarian Aid Corps when, for instance, it reads as follows:

30 Council Regulation (EC) 539/2001 of 15 March 2001 listing the third countries whose nationals must be in possession of visas when crossing the external borders and those whose nationals are exempt from that requirement [2001] OJ L81/1, as amended by Regulation (EU) 1289/2013 ([2013] L347/74), recital 1 (emphasis added) (see also recital 3). Similarly relevant is Case C-606/10 *Association nationale d'assistance aux frontière pour les étrangers* (ANAFE) *v Ministre de l'Interieur, de l'Outre-mer, des Collectivités territoriales et de l'immigration* EU:C:2012:348, in particular paras 2 and 25.

31 Decision 1313/2013/EU of the European Parliament and of the Council of 17 December 2013 on a Union Civil Protection Mechanism [2013] OJ L347/924, recital 1 (emphasis added) (see also recital 5 and art 1(3)). See still in more detail Theodore Konstadinides, 'Civil Protection Cooperation in EU Law: Is There Room for Solidarity to Wriggle Past?' (2013) 19 ELJ 267.

> *Solidarity is a fundamental value of the Union* and there is potential for further *developing means of expressing solidarity of Union citizens with people in third countries vulnerable to or affected by man-made crises or natural disasters.* (…)
>
> Volunteering is a concrete and visible *expression of solidarity* allowing individuals to dedicate their knowledge, skills and time to the service of fellow human beings, without pecuniary motivation.[32]

> The objective of the EU Aid Volunteers initiative (…) is to provide needs-based humanitarian aid aimed at *preserving* life, *preventing and alleviating human suffering and maintaining human dignity* (…). That objective shall be attained through the added value of joint contributions of EU Aid Volunteers, *expressing the Union values and solidarity with people in need and visibly promoting a sense of European citizenship.*[33]

This means that 'showing and/or expressing solidarity with those in needs' is one of the Union's fundamental values, but it is also an inherent element of the European identity.

The solidarity aspect can also be detected in actual EU reactions to a security crisis and humanitarian catastrophe and its broader consequences in the given region like, for example, what we can see in terms of the current situation in Ukraine. A good practical example for this is the decision of the EU Agriculture and Fishery Council as regards the Russian ban on a number of agricultural products, raw materials and foodstuffs (e.g. meat, fish and crustaceans, milk and dairy products, fruit and vegetables, sausages and food or finished products etc.), originating from the EU, introduced on 7 and 20 August 2014 in connection with the Ukraine crisis as a countermeasure to sanctions, imposed on the Russian Federation by the EU earlier in 2014 because of Russia's actions against Ukraine. Estonia, Latvia and Lithuania called for direct support measures for their dairy farmers, who faced drastic fall in milk prices following the subject Russian ban. As it was stressed in the Council press

32 Regulation (EU) 375/2014 of the European Parliament and of the Council of 3 April 2014 establishing the European Voluntary Humanitarian Aid Corps [2014] OJ L122/1 (EVHAC Regulation), recitals 1–2 (emphasis added) (see also recital 11). See still in this context Joint Statement by the Council and the Representatives of the Governments of the Member States meeting within the Council, the European Parliament and the Commission of 2008 ('The European Consensus on Humanitarian Aid') [2008] OJ C25/1, in particular paras 1 and 4.

33 EVHAC Regulation, art 4 (emphasis added).

release: 'Most ministers *acknowledged the need for EU solidarity towards the most affected member states* as regards the dairy sector and the Commission showed its readiness to consider such direct support'.[34] The Council and the Commission finally agreed at political level to provide financial support, exceptionally, and in order to encounter the liquidity problems of the dairy industry (notably milk producers) of the mentioned three Baltic Member States.[35]

Finally, as was already indicated above, the solidarity principle has become, especially in the last three-four years, a crucial driving force for regulating on the EU common migration and asylum policy. This was very eloquently amplified in the Commission staff working document in relation to the impact assessments for the related legislative proposals, when the Commission stressed:

> *Based on the principle of solidarity*, the EU needs to be able to provide support to Member States to compensate for [the differences of migratory pressures among Member States]. *The External Borders Fund and the Frontex Agency complements each other for this purpose with former being a tool for financial solidarity, not covering running costs, and the latter a tool for operational solidarity on a temporary and punctual basis, covering such costs.* Operational solidarity is implemented in practice through joint operations, channelling additional resources to sections of the external borders where Member States cannot act alone with the migratory pressures they are facing.[36]

In fact the given legislative acts in force, with other related legal measures,[37] create a *solidarity framework* to address and tackle exceptional situations and

34 Agriculture and Fisheries Council press release of 13 October 2014 (Council doc 14199/14) <http://www.consilium.europa.eu/uedocs/cms_data/docs/pressdata/en/agricult/145101.pdf> accessed 1 December 2016, 15.

35 See in more detail Commission, '€28 million package for Baltic Milk Produce' (Press release of 19 November 2014) IP/14/1960 <http://europa.eu/rapid/press-release_IP-14-1960_en.htm> accessed 1 December 2016.

36 Commission, 'Impact Assessment accompanying the Proposal for a Regulation of the European Parliament and of the Council amending Council Regulation (EC) 2007/2004 establishing a European Agency for the Management of Operational Cooperation at the External Borders of the Member States of the European Union (FRONTEX)' (Staff Working Paper) SEC (2010) 149, 11 (emphasis added).

37 See e.g. Council Decision (EU) 2015/1601 of 22 September 2015 establishing provisional measures in the area of international protection for the benefit of Italy and Greece [2015] OJ L248/80 or Council, 'Refugee crisis: Council shows solidarity with Greece by approving

difficulties in the given policy area, arising in the concerned Member States, based on Article 80 TFEU.[38]

3.3 *Concerning the Jurisprudence of the CJEU*

During the long history of the European integration process, the principle of solidarity (or the value of solidarity) had also been recalled several times by the Communities' courts in concrete rulings, in particular when there was a serious crisis in the European Communities. For example, in *the late 70s and early 80s*, there was a series of judgments, which related to the application of *the European Coal and Steel Community Treaty* (ECSC Treaty), since there had been a huge production crisis in the coal and steel industries in Europe, but also worldwide. The CJEU laid down thus in its very early jurisprudence practically the principle of solidarity and emphasized in essence that *based on the principle of solidarity* in case of seeking *to spread in an equitable manner among all undertakings in the Community the inevitable sacrifices*, entailed by

---

emergency support' (Press release of 9 March 2016) 113/16 <http://www.consilium.europa.eu/en/press/press-releases/2016/03/09-refugee-crisis/> accessed 1 December 2016.

38 See e.g. Council Directive 2001/55/EC of 20 July 2001 on minimum standards for giving temporary protection in the event of a mass influx of displaced persons and on measures promoting a balance of efforts between Member States in receiving such persons and bearing the consequences thereof [2001] OJ L212/12, especially recital 20; Regulation (EU) 439/2010 of the European Parliament and of the Council of 19 May 2010 establishing a European Asylum Support Office (EASO) [2010] OJ L132/11, especially recital 7 and arts 7 and 46; Regulation (EU) 516/2014 of the European Parliament and of the Council of 16 April 2014 establishing the Asylum, Migration and Integration Fund, amending Council Decision 2008/381/EC and repealing Decisions 573/2007/EC and 575/2007/EC of the European Parliament and of the Council and Council Decision 2007/435/EC [2014] OJ L150/168, especially recitals 1, 2, 7, 44, 46 and 53 and arts 3(2)(d) and 18(1)-(4).

It should be also recalled that the previous Decisions of the European Parliament and of the Council regarding the European Refugee Fund for the period 2008 to 2013 (Decision 573/2007/EC [2007] L144/1); or the External Borders Fund for the period 2007 to 2013 (Decision 574/2007/EC [2007] L144/22); or the European Return Fund (Decision 575/2007/EC [2007] L144/45) were all adopted as part of the Framework programme on '*Solidarity* and Management of Migration Flows' (emphasis added) (see COM (2005) 123 final), but by now they are all repealed.

As regards the relevant case law of the CJEU, see Case C-179/11 *Cimade and Groupe d'information et de soutien des immigrés (GISTI) v Ministre de l'Interieur, de l'Outre-mer, des Collectivités territoriales et de l'Immigration* EU:C:2012:594, paras 23 and 60; Joined Cases C-411/10 and C-493/10 *N.S. (C-411/10) v. Secretary of State for the Home Department and M.E. and Others (C-493/10) v Refugee Applications Commissioner and Minister for Justice, Equality and Law Reform* EU:C:2011:865, paras 10, 12 and 93.

the general crisis in the steel industry, a special system of production quotas could be established by the Commission.[39]

The solidarity element has also been noted, for example, in the jurisprudence of the CJEU as far as the *fighting against international terrorism*-related case law is concerned. In a concrete related case, the Commission, for example, specifically referred to the relevance of the principle of solidarity, when in its argumentation, it specifically quoted the preamble of the former EC Treaty, 'in which the Contracting Parties confirmed "*the solidarity, which binds Europe and the overseas countries* (…) *in accordance with the principles of the Charter of the United Nations*" and declared themselves resolved to "strengthen peace and liberty"'.[40]

Further relevance of the solidarity principle can be touched upon in relation to the CJEU case law dealing with the issues about how to help unemployed students within the EU. The Court in this respect, however, pointed out that:

> *Although EU law relating to the free movement of persons and, in particular, students, allows for a certain degree of financial solidarity as amongst the nationals of the host Member States and nationals of other Member States* (…), as stated in recital 10 in the preamble to Directive 2004/38, persons exercising their right of residence, including students, should not become un *unreasonable burden on the social assistance system* of the host Member State during an initial period of residence. Therefore, under Article 21 TFEU and the provisions of Directive 2004/38, the right of residence for Union citizens and their family members for periods in excess of three months is subject to conditions.[41]

The CJEU case law is also well-developed concerning the EU common asylum and immigration policies and the relevance of the solidarity principle in those policy fields. The CJEU established, however, a number of restrictions on the invocation of the principle of solidarity in this area, when it ruled, for example, that:

---

39 See in more detail Case 64/84 *Queenborough Rolling Mill Company Ltd v Commission of the European Communities* EU:C:1985:26, in particular para 11; see also Case 276/80 *Ferriera Padana SpA v Commission* EU:C:1982:57 and plenty of similar rulings.

40 Case T-306/01 *Ahmed Ali Yusuf and Al Barakaat International Foundation v Council and Commission* EU:T:2005:331, para 100 (emphasis added).

41 Case C-75/11 *Commission v Republic of Austria* EU:C:2012:605, para 60 (emphasis added); see also still in a broader context Case C-333/13 *Elisabeta Dano et Florin Dano v Jobcenter Leipzig* EU:C:2014:2358, especially paras 56ff.

> As is apparent from recital 20 in the preamble to [Council Directive 2001/55/EC], *one of its objectives is to provide for a solidarity mechanism intended to contribute to the attainment of a balance of effort between Member States* in receiving and bearing the consequences of receiving displaced persons in the event of a mass influx. (...)
>
> *Directive 2001/55 is an example of that solidarity* but, as was stated at the hearing, the solidarity mechanisms which it contains *apply only to wholly exceptional situations falling within the scope of the Directive*, that is to say, a mass influx of displaced persons.[42]

Certainly, the issue of *social security benefits* in the Member States is also an important topic in the jurisprudence of the CJEU as regards the implementation of the principle of solidarity within the EU. One group of cases relates to the different schemes in the Member States concerning the supplementary reimbursement of healthcare costs (e.g. in terms of accidents at the work-place or occupational diseases etc.). In this regard, the CJEU stressed in several rulings of the last two decades the importance of the principle of solidarity and that it is necessary to be examined in order to define whether the service-provider insurance body can be considered under EU law as an 'undertaking' in the given context (because if not, then in principle it can justify an exemption from the freedom to provide services under ex-Articles 49 and 50 TEC etc.).[43]

Another basket of litigations concern the main characteristics of national social security regimes in the Member States, in which field the Court underlined from the view-point of the solidarity principle at national level that 'the obligation to pay contributions because of the existence of a right to benefits, even if those benefits are not actually received, *is inherent in the principle of solidarity*, which is implemented by national social security schemes (...)',[44] or that 'the Member States retain their powers to organize their social security

---

42 *N.S.* (n 38), paras 12 and 93 (emphasis added); see also the CJEU case law referred to in n 38.

43 See Case C-437/09 AG2R *Prévoyance v Beaudout Père et Fils SARL* EU:C:2011:112, paras 41–42, 44–46, 64–65; see also Case C-218/00 *Cisal di Battistello Venanzio & C. Sas v Istituto nazionale per l'assicurazione contro gli infortuni sul lavoro (INAIL)* EU:C:2002:36, paras 44–46; Case C-350/07 *Kattner Stahlban Gmbh v. Machinenbau- und Metall-Berufsgenossenschaft* EU:C:2009:127, paras 44, 50–55, 61–62, 64–68; and plenty of similar rulings of the CJEU.

44 Case C-345/09 *J.A. van Delft and Others v College voor zorgverzekeringen* EU:C:2010:610, para 75 (emphasis added) (see also paras 52, 57, 61–65 and 72–75).

systems and thus to set up compulsory schemes [e.g. as regards non-life insurance] *based on the principle of solidarity* (...)'.[45]

As far as the EU *structural funds and the EU cohesion policy* is concerned, the Court almost 20 years ago already established that when *the Commission imposes penalties*, it must always take into account whether *the Community principle of solidarity is preserved* since 'action taken by it cannot have infringed either the principle of Community solidarity and its corollary, the principle of regional partnership, or the principle of proportionality'.[46]

In relation to the current economic and financial crisis, perhaps it is still worth recalling that the CJEU in its early case law already laid down the doctrine that '*Adoption of exceptional measures*, which derogate from the normal rules governing the working of the common market and which clearly entail non-compliance with [the Treaty]' is permissible, in case of an 'anti-crisis policy in the iron and steel sector, *based on the fundamental principle of solidarity between different undertakings* [(ECSC Treaty Articles 3, 49 et seq., 53, 55(2) and 56)] (...)'.[47]

4 Future Tendencies: What Legal Directions to Attribute in the Future to This Important Legal Principle?

One could argue that the principle of solidarity should be further developed and strengthened, especially vis-à-vis third countries (developed or less developed or just being in serious difficulties),[48] as well as in relation to foreign nationals, refugees, asylum-seekers and stateless people in a way expressing support and help from the Union side in case of needs and crises and thus showing that it is not just a fundamental value of the EU legal order and a consistent policy approach of the EU, but it is also an inherent element of the European identity in a much broader context.

In my view, the principle of (especially financial) solidarity will remain within the EU an important driving force (but based on shared responsibility

45 Case C-238/94 *José Garcia and Others v Mutuelle de Prévoyance Sociale d'Aquitaine and Others* EU:C:1996:132, summary of the judgment (emphasis added).

46 Case C-84/96 *Kingdom of the Netherlands v Commission* EU:C:1999:478, para 47. The case related to the automatic cancellation of payments from the European Regional Development Fund.

47 Joined Cases 154, 205, 206, 226 to 228, 263–264/78 and 39, 31, 83 and 85/79 *SpA Ferriera Valsabbia and others v Commission* EU:C:1980:81, paras 55 and 59 (emphasis added); and plenty of similar rulings.

48 See in more detail *Hilpold* (n 1) 266ff.

among Member States) and the leading regulatory pattern at horizontal level as regards future EU legislation and/or other contractual engagements/arrangements vis-à-vis those Member States suffering from or threatened by financial instability due to the prevailing EU sovereign debt crisis or in more general terms because of the global economic and financial crisis.

The principle of solidarity is (and will remain in the future too) also a subsidiary regulatory policy-reasoning/justification in order to show solidarity towards those, who are in real needs (either within the EU or outside the EU or either towards States in a more horizontal context or just to citizens or other entities in a rather vertical matrix) even if the available legal basis is not necessarily highlighting it (e.g. against terrorist attacks, natural disasters etc.). This is simply because solidarity is stemming from the very nature of the Union as a community, based on the principle of rule of law and the values of peace, security and prosperity since already its very foundation in the 50s.[49]

5 Conclusions

I think that after Lisbon the solidarity principle has been given again special emphasis in EU law partly due to the global economic and financial crisis, broken out in 2008, and the so-called EU banking crisis since 2012, but partly also because of the unprecedented so-called immigration crisis in the EU, which has caused a lot of difficulties in the last couple of years.[50]

Although the solidarity principle is not *strictu sensu* a classical EU law principle,[51] but rather a so-called operational and functional one and a value-orientation for the EU, nonetheless, as proved in this contribution, it plays a significant role in legal practice, and also in political terms it serves as a factual reality justifying exceptional EU measures, especially in the many current crisis situations. Thus its legal relevance in the daily functioning of the EU today is becoming more and more important.

As demonstrated above, it should be also concluded that, for example, in the field of EU cohesion policy, the principle of solidarity is not a main decisive

49 See ibid, in particular 257–265.

50 See Council, 'The European Council December 2014 to April 2016, Report by the President of the European Council, Donald Tusk' (Press release of 9 May 2016) 224/16 <http://www.consilium.europa.eu/en/press/press-releases/2016/05/09-tusk-report-european-council/> accessed 1 December 2016, in particular 7–15, 45–46., 48ff, 51–56, 60–61. and.77.

51 As a contrast, see, however, the very strong legal relevance of the principle of solidarity in an infringement case (Case 39/72 *Commission v Italian Republic* EU:C:1973:13).

factor anymore of EU policy-making after Lisbon. The use of the EU budget as regards the implementation of the policy objectives of the European Structural and Investment Funds (ESIFs) today is rather based on objective criteria and quality requirements of project designs and strategic programming, including (as a new element after the break-out of the global economic and financial crises in 2008) full compliance obligations with certain conditionalities (e.g. ex-ante conditionalities, or sector-specific policy conditionalities; or the so-called macro-economic conditionality concerning the compliance with the EU economic governance *acquis* etc.).

In other words, the EU cohesion policy nowadays is much more results-oriented and focusing clearly on the principle of partnership (and co-financing requirements by the Member States) as well as rather on the more and more effective use of EU funds in terms of financing only those investments, which are really capable to create more jobs and growth in Europe. Of course, as was highlighted above, certain EU Funds are still exemptions from the conception of the ESIFs, and are still very much based on the practical implementation of the EU principle of solidarity, namely: the European Solidarity Fund, or the European Global Adjustment Fund, or the European Asylum, Migration and Integration Fund etc. On the other hand, it is to be noted that this practice is becoming rather the exception than the main rule in the present EU financial framework (which is, indeed, a great change in legal practice, for instance, concerning the future of the EU cohesion policy etc.).[52]

Finally, it can also be concluded that, based on the concrete examples above, it is clear that in certain situations and/or conditions the principle of solidarity applies even if the specific Treaty provision or EU secondary law disposition doesn't refer to it *expressis verbis*. This horizontal EU law nature of the solidarity principle – which was demonstrated earlier via the relevant CJEU jurisprudence as well – stems clearly from Article 2 and Article 3(3) TEU as common fundamental value-orientations of the EU.

52 See Conclusions of the European Council meeting (20 and 21 October 2016) EUCO 31/16, 1–4, and the follow up discussions on the possible different interpretations of 'solidarity', e.g. in the context of the next Multiannual Financial Framework (2021–2027) (see further the relevant press releases at <www.consilium.europa.eu/press>).

CHAPTER 8

How Elastic is Article 263 TFEU? Some Comments from a Sore Winner

*Bart Driessen**

1 Introduction

In his capacity as the Director of the Council Legal Service's external relations directorate, Ricardo Gosalbo Bono spent considerable time on the development of the law of restrictive measures. This field of law has developed from humble beginnings fifteen years ago to the most litigatious part of EU law nowadays. The field has seen vast developments in recent years: only five years ago important cases such as *Bamba*,[1] *Kala Naft*,[2] *Gbagbo*[3] and *Kadi II*[4] had not yet been ruled. This makes it too early to write a definite analysis of the law in the field: despite ample case law, too many questions are still open at the time of writing. Instead I shall limit myself in this modest contribution to a little interesting procedural problem with potentially large consequences.

On 22 April 2015 the General Court rendered its judgment in *Tomana and Others v Council*.[5] The judgment is of considerable interest for lawyers dealing with restrictive measures but I will not focus on the bounty of points of interest relating to the substantive law on restrictive measures. Rather, I do want to spend some attention on an issue of (in)admissibility which may have the potential to broaden the scope of Article 263 TFEU, namely: does *Tomana* open the door to an *actio popularis*?

Before discussing the legal conundrum, it is perhaps best to first sketch the background of the case.

---

* No opinion in this contribution may be attributed to the Council or to its Legal Service.

1 Case C-417/11 P *Council v Nadiany Bamba* EU:C:2012:718.

2 Case C-348/12 P *Council v Manufacturing Support & Procurement Kala Naft Co. Tehran* EU:C:2013:776.

3 Joined Cases C-478/11 P to C-482/11 P *Laurent Gbagbo and Others v Council* EU:C:2013:258.

4 Joined cases C-584/10 P, C-593/10 P and C-595/10 P *Commission and Others v Yassin Abdullah Kadi* EU:C:2013:518.

5 Case T-190/12 *Johannes Tomana and Others v Council* EU:T:2015:222.

 | DOI 10.1163/9789004347175_009

Mr Tomana and a host of other persons and entities from Zimbabwe had been subjected to restrictive measures for years. From February 2011 onwards, these were based on Council Decision 2011/101/CFSP.[6]

On 1 September 2011 Mr Tomana – at the time the Attorney General of Zimbabwe – wrote to Mr Van Rompuy, president of the European Council, 'on behalf of all the natural and legal persons and legal entities'[7] subject to restrictive measures imposed on Zimbabwe, disputing that the grounds stated in the Council Decision justified the imposition of restrictive measures. Mr Van Rompuy's cabinet replied to him,[8] referring to the legislation in force and to the reasons why it had been adopted (ie the abysmal state of democracy, human rights and the rule of law in Zimbabwe).

In the Spring of 2012 Mr Tomana lodged the application leading to Case T-190/12 with the General Court, on behalf of himself and 120 others, in order to contest the February 2012 extension of the restrictive measures imposed on them. With his application a letter was included in which he informed his lawyers that he acted on behalf of all of the other applicants.[9]

The Council, which harboured strong doubts whether the 120 'Others' were actually aware that they were parties in the proceeding, pleaded inadmissibility on this point and asked the Court to verify that all the applicants who are natural persons 'indeed support the current court proceeding'.[10] It pointed out that, even if it was beyond doubt that Mr Tomana had instructed his lawyers to act, there was no evidence (and quite some circumstantial evidence to the contrary) that the other 120 were even in contact with Mr Tomana or with his lawyers. The lawyers could only assume that Mr Tomana was representing the other 120.

Following a most interesting hearing, the General Court requested from Mr Tomana's lawyers copies of all authorities to act. These were duly produced, even though most of them post-dated the lodging of the action.[11]

This now, leads to an interesting point of procedural law: is it possible for someone to bring an application to contest restrictive measures on behalf of a large number of people, without him having to prove that he has been mandated by them to do so?

---

6 Council Decision 2011/101/CFSP of 15 February 2011 concerning restrictive measures against Zimbabwe [2011] OJ L42/6.

7 *Tomana* (n 5), para 195.

8 Ibid, para 198.

9 Ibid, para 197.

10 Ibid, para 53.

11 Ibid, para 62.

2 The General Court's Findings

To its credit, the General Court took the trouble to consider the matter in some detail. It reasoned[12] that, under Article 19 of the Statute of the Court, parties must be represented by a lawyer. However, Article 44(5)(b) of the General Court's Rules of Procedure[13] required only for legal persons that a power of attorney be submitted.[14] There was no concomitant obligation for natural persons. The General Court explained that:

> [N]ormally, the Court regards the fact that a lawyer has signed and lodged an application in the name of a natural person as an implicit declaration on the part of that lawyer that he has been duly instructed by the natural person concerned, and the Court regards that form of declaration as being sufficient. However, if there are specific factors which are capable of casting doubt on the reality of that implicit declaration, the Court may justifiably request the lawyer concerned to prove that he is in fact instructed.[15]

The General Court then referred to the Court's *PKK* judgment[16] to conclude that 'if a member of the bar of one of the Member States, subject as such to a code of professional ethics, declares that he has been duly instructed by his client, that declaration is, as a general rule, deemed to be sufficiently reliable'.[17]

In *PKK* the question before the Court arose because, on the one hand, it was clear that the PKK's leader Mr Öcalan did not bring the action on his own behalf. On the other hand, it was not clear that the PKK had indeed authorised him to bring it on its behalf. The problem was compounded by the fact that the PKK had actually dissolved itself and had resolved that 'all activities under the name of "PKK" would [henceforth] be deemed illegitimate', leading the

12 Ibid, paras 55ff.

13 This remains the case under Article 51(3) of the current version of the Rules of Procedure of the General Court ([2015] OJ L105/1), which apply from 1 July 2015.

14 For a similar finding by the General Court see Case T-34/02 *EURL Le Levant 001 and Others v Commission* EU:T:2006:59.

15 *Tomana* (n 5), para 58.

16 Case C-229/05 P *Osman Ocalan, on behalf of the Kurdistan Workers' Party (PKK) and Serif Vanly, on behalf of the Kurdistan National Congress (KNK) v Council* EU:C:2007:32, para 119.

17 *Tomana* (n 5), para 57.

General Court in that proceeding to wonder if at all it was possible for the PKK to be represented in court.[18]

The Court did not share the General Court's doubts, taking into account a statement by PKK's (or Mr Öcalan's) lawyer. The Court considered that the lawyer was 'a member of the bar of one of the Member States, who is subject as such to a code of professional conduct'. Therefore, 'in the particular circumstances of the case' the lawyer's statements sufficed to establish that the lawyers had been appropriately mandated. Those 'particular circumstances' consisted precisely of the fact that the whole capacity of PKK to appoint a lawyer following its dissolution was in doubt.

As shown above, the General Court in *Tomana* quoted the Court without referring to the 'particular circumstances' which formed the basis of the *PKK* ruling.

As a last point, the Council had relied on *Barge v High Authority*, in which the Court had ruled that the lawyer is not required to produce a duly executed authority to act in the lodging of an application, 'subject to proof if challenged that he is so authorised'.[19] The General Court dismisses the argument, arguing that the fact pattern in *Barge* showed that the Court did not intend to allow the opposite party to challenge the existence of a power of attorney, but rather the Court itself.[20] With this it rejected the admissibility point.

3 A Critical Analysis

The General Court's reasoning seems superficially compatible with the Court's case law, but if one prods deeper, the position is not tenable.

To begin with, the circumstances in *Tomana* differed from those in *PKK*. The decision by PKK to decree, before dissolving itself, that 'all activities under the name of "PKK" would [henceforth] be deemed illegitimate' did, of course, raise a question whether it actually wanted to be represented. Even stronger, one could wonder whether there still existed a principal that was represented by Mr Öcalan. However, the Court's logic made sense since, first, the Council still listed PKK as a terrorist organisation irrespective of its 'dissolution'. Moreover, Mr Öcalan's position in the PKK was obvious and well-documented. It is

18 Case T-229/02 *Kurdistan Workers' Party (PKK) and Kurdistan National Congress (KNK) v Council* (Order) EU:T:2005:48, para 35.

19 Case 14/64 *Mrs Emilia Gualco (née Barge), widow of Mr Leone, v High Authority of the European Coal and Steel Community* EU:C:1965:13.

20 *Tomana* (n 5), para 61.

a matter of public knowledge that Mr Öcalan is the founder and figure head of the PKK and was himself very much involved with the PKK's decision.

Mr Tomana's role vis-à-vis the 120 alleged co-applicants in his case was very different. First, unlike the PKK, the existence of those co-applicants was not in doubt. Secondly, the history of the litigation was entirely different. Mr Tomana had originally written to the Council in his capacity as Attorney General of Zimbabwe. An action for annulment brought by the state or Government of Zimbabwe itself would, however, have shipwrecked on the cliffs of Article 263(4) TFEU: arguably, neither the Government nor the state of Zimbabwe are individually concerned by restrictive measures imposed on certain persons and entities (even if individual members of the Government are). Thus, since Mr Tomana wanted to contest the entire list[21] in order to show a national stand against the EU, he could only do so if he claimed to represent each and every applicant. However, there is no evidence that Mr Tomana knew or had any contact with each and every applicant.

Arguably, under such circumstances, the General Court could not have simply ignored the Court's 'particular circumstances' clause and it should have distinguished *Tomana* from *PKK*. Its failure to do so leads to two consequences. To begin with, the General Court opened the door for any applicant to claim that he acts on behalf of other unrelated persons or entities. In practical terms, this may be relevant if an applicant wants to (ab)use the legal challenge to make a political point. Since restrictive measures are a quintessentially political measure, this may lead to abuses in cases where targeted governments want to maximise the legal challenges against restrictive measures. If the General Court's reasoning were accepted as case law, it would make it very easy to circumvent Article 263(4) TFEU.

In addition, the General Court's reasoning leads to another result. In *Tomana* the applicants ultimately submitted powers of attorney but even these were dated months after the application was submitted.[22] That, however, leads to a legal difficulty. Even when assuming that the 120 applicants indeed mandated Mr Tomana to act on their behalf three months after the action in their name was lodged,[23] they endorsed that action well after the two months' deadline of Article 263(6) TFEU. That implies that, in the future, it suffices for applicant A to bring a court action on behalf of himself and of persons B, C and D

21 With the exception of president Mugabe and his wife, for reasons unknown to this author.

22 As the Court recognised in the *Tomana* judgment (n 5), para 62.

23 A point of fact on which the present author prefers to remain silent. For the sake of argument I will follow the General Court in assuming that this was the case.

within that deadline. B, C and D can later always decide to join the action at their leisure.

Such an interpretation seems difficult to defend in view of the Court's strict interpretation of Article 263 TFEU. For example, the Court has always adopted a strict view of the direct and individual concern restrictions: when the General Court attempted an interpretation that broadened the scope of the provision[24] the Court stopped the breach immediately.[25] It seems obvious that the measures imposed on the other 120 were not of direct and individual concern to Mr Tomana. Thus, whilst he clearly did have standing to contest his own listing, he was not individually concerned by the measures imposed on the 120 'Others'. It was therefore for them to bring their own court action.

The Court has similarly been strict with the interpretation of the two months' deadline in Article 263(6) TFEU. In *Gbagbo* it ruled that 'the strict application of procedural rules serves the requirements of legal certainty and the need to avoid any discrimination or arbitrary treatment in the administration of justice'.[26] The Court also stressed that 'it is important that the appellants should not be able to defer the starting point of the period for bringing proceedings by relying on the fact that there was no direct communication or that they actually became aware of the contested measures at a later date'. It emphasized that – barring the possibility of force majeure – any such deferment 'would jeopardise the very objective of a time-limit for bringing proceedings, which is to protect legal certainty by ensuring that European Union measures which produce legal effects may not indefinitely be called into question'.[27] In *Ipatau* it stressed that a 'the strict application' of the rules concerning procedural time limits does not undermine neither the right to effective judicial protection nor the right to be heard.[28] In the Court's philosophy the Article 263(6) TFEU deadline applies from the moment of notification (which, in the case of the 120 'Others', was effected through a notice in the Official Journal). The General Court added in *Fluorsid* that the deadline of Article 263(6) TFEU 'is fixed, absolute and may not be extended'.[29] Moreover:

> [T]he question of the admissibility of an action had to be assessed on the basis of the situation existing at the date on which the application was

24 Case T-177/01 *Jégo-Quéré & Cie SA v Commission* EU:T:2002:112.
25 Case C-50/00 P *Unión de Pequeños Agricultores v Council* EU:C:2002:462, para 44.
26 *Gbagbo and Others v Council* (n 3), para 71.
27 Ibid, para 62.
28 Case C-535/14 P *Vadzim Ipatau v Council* EU:C:2015:407, para 14.
29 Case T-404/08 *Fluorsid SpA and Minmet financing Co. v Commission* EU:T:2013:321, para 51.

> lodged. If at that time the conditions which must be satisfied to enable an action to be brought are not fulfilled, the action is therefore inadmissible. A defect can be rectified only before the expiry of the period for bringing proceedings.[30]

The question thus arises whether the construction in *Tomana* is compatible with the Court's case law. It was for each of the 120 to bring their own action, individually or collectively. The admissibility of that action had to be assessed on the date the Article 263(6) TFEU deadline expired. The documents in the file show that the 120 supported the action only several months later. Thus, the determination whether Article 263(6) has been complied with (a matter of public policy)[31] hinges on the assurance given by one of the lawyers that she was aware that the others actually supported the action at the time it commenced.

In the General Court's logic, respect for the public-order provisions of Article 263 thus hinges on the word of the applicant's lawyer (who, in turn, had to rely on her client's assurance). However, the General Court relied in this strongly on the Court's *PKK* judgment which, as was shown above, concerned quite a different situation. Moreover, the General Court's interpretation is the only exception in an otherwise strict interpretation of virtually all aspects of Article 263 TFEU.

4 Concluding Remarks

In its *PKK* Order cited above, the General Court observed that 'excessive formalism would amount to the denial, in certain cases, of any possibility of applying for annulment, even though those groups and entities were the object of restrictive Community measures'.[32] This is true, but *Tomana* shows that an excessive lack of formalism may be hard to combine with the stringent character of Article 263. In the *Tomana* logic, one applicant can bring a court case within the Article 263(6) deadline on behalf of other persons. The other persons can then decide at leisure whether they wish to bring the case without being bound by Article 263(6). It is this author's belief that this is incompatible with the strict interpretation of Article 263.

Article 263 is a provision of public order and thus it is for the General Court to check on its own initiative whether or not it has been complied with.

30 Ibid, para 53.

31 *Gbagbo and Others v Council* (n 3), para 53.

32 *PKK and KNK v Council* (Order) (n 18), para 28.

Certainly when the defendant argues that it has *not* been complied with, there should be an obligation on the General Court to verify the point. The present author submits that the Rules of Procedure of the General Court (and those of the Court) seem deficient in this respect, since respect of a public order provision in *Tomana* hinged not even on the legal representative's declaration to the General Court, but on Mr Tomana's declaration to his legal representatives.

To its credit, the General Court – notwithstanding its interpretation of the *Barge* judgment[33] – did, in fact, demand from Mr Tomana's lawyers that they submit a written authorisation from each of those individual applicants. Where, ultimately, the General Court erred beyond repair was in accepting those authorisations, even though all of them post-dated the lodging of the case (and the date of expiry of the Article 263(6) deadline) with several months. By not ruling that the case was inadmissible insofar the 120 'Others' were concerned, the General Court essentially waived the Article 263(6) deadline for them. Clearly, that cannot be correct.

In view of the General Court's findings on the substance (the designation of the applicants was upheld), the Council can hardly complain about the final outcome of the case. Moreover, the Court of Justice affirmed the findings on substance in ringing terms (the admissibility point was not appealed).[34] Still, the doctor buries his mistakes; those of the judge become the law of the land. Even if, in the end, Tomana (and the 120 'Others') lost on substance, the procedural point has an importance for the future.

One lesson the present author learned from Ricardo Gosalbo Bono is to be wary of merely looking at the obvious result in the present and to always look at the potential future implications. In the light of its implications for the future, the General Court's admissibility ruling in *Tomana* may be regretted.

33 See n 20.

34 Case C-330/15 P *Johannes Tomana and Others v Council* EU:C:2016:601.

CHAPTER 9

Aie confiance! – La confiance mutuelle peut-elle se décréter?

*Thérèse Blanchet**

1 Prologue

'Aie confiance, crois en moi', susurrait le serpent Kaa d'une voix mielleuse au pauvre Mowgly pour l'hypnotiser et le manger, dans une scène fameuse du dessin animé pour enfants, le Livre de la Jungle, d'après Kipling.

Mais non, l'Union européenne n'est pas une jungle où les enfants confiants risqueraient d'être mangés par des serpents hypnotiseurs.

Comme nous l'a dit la Cour de justice de l'Union européenne (CJUE) en décembre 2014, dans son désormais célèbre avis 2/13, l'Union européenne est un espace sans frontières intérieures pour la création et le maintien duquel le principe de confiance mutuelle entre les États membres a une importance fondamentale. Ce principe de confiance mutuelle:

> *impose*, notamment en ce qui concerne l'espace de liberté, de sécurité et de justice, *à chacun de ces États de considérer*, sauf dans des circonstances exceptionnelles, *que tous les autres* États membres *respectent le droit de l'Union et*, tout particulièrement, *les droits fondamentaux* reconnus par ce droit.[1]

Pourtant, écrire ces mots mi-2016, au cœur d'une tourmente sans précédent, alors que plusieurs tornades balayent impitoyablement depuis plusieurs mois notre 'espace sans frontière intérieures' et notre 'espace de liberté, de sécurité et de justice', qu'il s'agisse de la crise des migrants et des réfugiés ou de celle du terrorisme, venues s'ajouter à une crise bancaire, financière, budgétaire et économique ravageuse commencée il y a huit ans, sans compter un référendum (négatif) au Danemark le 3 décembre 2015 sur la modification de

---

* Les opinions exprimées ici sont purement personnelles.

1 Avis 2/13 (*Adhésion de l'Union européenne à la convention européenne de sauvegarde des droits de l'homme et des libertés fondamentales*) EU:C:2014:2454, para 191 (c'est nous qui soulignons).

 | DOI 10.1163/9789004347175_010

son protocole concernant la justice et les affaires intérieures, un référendum (négatif) aux Pays-Bas le 6 avril 2016 sur l'accord d'association entre l'Union européenne et l'Ukraine, un référendum (négatif) au Royaume-Uni le 23 juin 2016 sur son maintien ou non dans l'Union européenne et un référendum annoncé pour le 2 octobre 2016 en Hongrie au sujet de la répartition entre États membres des demandeurs d'asile,[2] provoque un malaise.

Force est de constater que les 'circonstances exceptionnelles' évoquées par la Cour nous guettent de toutes parts. La jungle n'est pas loin et les bêtes féroces rôdent.

2 Quelle confiance? Qu'en est-il dans les relations internationales?

La confiance renvoie à quelque chose d'humain, à un sentiment. C'est le 'sentiment qui fait qu'on se fie à quelqu'un ou à quelque chose' nous dit le Littré. Il y a deux sortes de confiance, une confiance d'aval ou ex-post et une confiance d'amont ou ex-ante. La première est un résultat, elle ne va pas de soi, c'est une confiance construite, dont le point de départ est, si ce n'est la méfiance, du moins l'expectative ou la circonspection dans laquelle on se trouve devant l'inconnu. Cette confiance-là sera le résultat d'un cheminement, d'une relation d'égal à égal qui aura permis de se tester, de se connaître, pour aboutir à se faire confiance. La seconde est un point de départ, une confiance déférente, la confiance innée, instinctive, qu'a le petit enfant en ses parents, celle un peu contrainte de l'ignorant vis-à-vis du sachant, du patient en son médecin, ou la confiance craintive du faible vis-à-vis du fort dont il attend la protection. Cette confiance-là relève davantage de la croyance ou de la foi, sans preuves

2 Voir article paru dans *La Libre Belgique* du 24 février 2016 selon lequel le premier ministre Orban a annoncé lors d'une conférence de presse que 'Le gouvernement [hongrois] a décidé la tenue d'un référendum sur la question des quotas obligatoires de répartition de réfugiés' ('Réfugiés: la Hongrie organisera un référendum sur le plan européen de relocalisation' <http://www.lalibre.be/actu/international/refugies-la-hongrie-organisera-un-referendum-sur-le-plan-europeen-de-relocalisation-56cdac543570ebb7a8b17952> dernier accès le 20 novembre 2016). Cette annonce a été confirmée officiellement le 5 juillet par le chef de l'État, Janos Ader ('En Hongrie, le référendum sur la relocalisation des réfugiés dans l'UE aura lieu le 2 octobre' *Le Monde* (Paris, 5 juillet 2016) <http://www.lemonde.fr/international/article/2016/07/05/en-hongrie-le-referendum-sur-la-relocalisation-des-refugies-dans-l-ue-aura-lieu-le-2-octobre_4964036_3210.html> dernier accès le 20 novembre 2016). La question posée aux électeurs hongrois sera la suivante: 'Voulez-vous que l'Union européenne décrète une relocation obligatoire de citoyens non-hongrois en Hongrie sans l'approbation du parlement hongrois?'.

ni questions. La langue anglaise utilise d'ailleurs deux mots qui illustrent cette différence: *confidence* et *trust*, la première construite sur l'expérience et la seconde déférente, voire religieuse (le *in God we trust* des billets verts).[3]

Transposée aux relations entre États, les 'monstres froids' de Nietzche,[4] la confiance est loin d'être une évidence et, en tout état de cause, elle ne pourra qu'être acquise et pas innée. Les théoriciens des relations internationales[5] la considèrent soit comme impossible ou difficile, s'ils appartiennent à l'école réaliste, soit comme possible pour peu que le contexte la favorise, s'ils sont plutôt de l'école libérale. Pour les réalistes, enfants de Machiavel et de Hobbes, le monde est une jungle, anarchique par nature, dans laquelle la méfiance entre États est une constante, plus qu'une variable, ceux-ci rivalisant constamment pour accroître leur puissance, leur richesse et leur sécurité et où seuls l'hégémonie d'un État très puissant sur d'autres ou l'équilibre des puissances sont susceptibles d'apporter un semblant de stabilité. Pour les libéraux, enfants des Lumières, de Locke, Rousseau et Kant, du contrat social[6] et de la paix démocratique,[7] bien que, contrairement à l'homme, les États ne puissent être

---

3 Dans leur article 'The Tale of Multilateral Trust and the European Law of Civil Procedure', Felix Blobel et Patrick Späth expliquent qu'étymologiquement, le mot *confidence* est de racine latine comme en français et renvoie plutôt à un sentiment construit, alors que le mot *trust*, de racine germanique, renvoie aux arbres, en particulier le chêne, vénéré par les tribus germaniques pour sa solidité ((2005) 30 EL Rev 528).

4 'L'Etat, c'est le plus froid de tous les monstres froids. Il ment froidement et voici le mensonge qui rampe de sa bouche: "Moi, l'Etat, je suis le Peuple"'. (Friedrich Nietzsche, *Ainsi parlait Zarathoustra* (Société du Mercure de France 1898) 61, disponible sur <gallica.bnf.fr> dernier accès le 20 novembre 2016).

5 Voir par exemple Jean-Louis Martres, 'De la nécessité d'une théorie des relations internationales, l'illusion paradigmatique' (2003) 4 Annuaire français de relations internationales 19; Andrew K Kydd, *Trust and Mistrust in International Relations* (Princeton University Press 2005); 'Classification des théories des relations internationales', <http://mapageweb.umontreal.ca/zaharm/Théories.pdf> (dernier accès le 12 décembre 2016).

6 En 1762, dans *Du contrat social ou principes du droit politique*, Jean-Jacques Rousseau, dans le chapitre intitulé 'Du pacte social', écrivait: 'Trouver une forme d'association qui défende et protège de toute la force commune la personne et les biens de chaque associé, et par laquelle chacun, s'unissant à tous, n'obéisse pourtant qu'à lui-même, et reste aussi libre qu'auparavant. Tel est le problème fondamental dont le Contrat social donne la solution'. ((Marc Michel Rey) 27, disponible sur <gallica.bnf.fr> dernier accès le 20 novembre 206).

7 En 1795, dans son *Essai philosophique sur la paix perpétuelle*, Emmanuel Kant, dans la deuxième section intitulée 'Contenant les articles définitifs pour la paix perpétuelle', écrivait que 'Pour les hommes, l'état de nature n'est pas un état de paix, mais de guerre sinon ouverte du moins toujours prête à s'allumer. Il faut donc que l'état de paix soit établi, car, pour que l'on soit à l'abri de tout acte d'hostilité il ne suffit pas qu'il ne se commette point de tels actes, il

considérés comme naturellement bons, ils sont néanmoins susceptibles de résoudre leurs différents et de coopérer pacifiquement, en particulier lorsqu'ils sont démocratiques, liés par des accords au sein d'institutions multilatérales et rendus interdépendants grâce au commerce.

L'Union européenne est fille des deux: elle est née des décombres et des millions de morts d'une Europe-jungle où les monstres froids s'étaient vautrés dans les abîmes d'une horreur sans fond. Au bout de cette guerre hobbesienne de tous contre tous, les réalistes étaient aphones. Les libéraux tentèrent alors le pari des Lumières: un traité entre les monstres, la mise en commun de l'acier de leur armes et du charbon pour le fondre, un contrat social, une paix entre démocrates, le tout avec une méthode de réalistes, celle des petits pas, celle des 'réalisations concrètes créant d'abord une solidarité de fait'. Le préambule du traité de 1951 est un bijou de brièveté; en cinq considérants, tout est dit:

> Considérant que la paix mondiale ne peut être sauvegardée que par des efforts créateurs à la mesure des dangers qui la menacent;
>
> Convaincus que la contribution qu'une Europe organisée et vivante peut apporter à la civilisation est indispensable au maintien des relations pacifiques;
>
> Conscients que l'Europe ne se construira que par des réalisations concrètes créant d'abord une solidarité de fait, et par l'établissement de bases communes de développement économique;

---

faut de plus qu'un voisin garantisse à l'autre sa sécurité personnelle ce qui ne saurait avoir lieu que dans un état légal'. ((G. Fischbacher 1880) 12, disponible sur <gallica.bnf.fr> dernier accès le 20 novembre 2016).

Pour Kant, seul un mode d'organisation républicain (ou démocratique) est à même de permettre d'aboutir à la paix: 'elle [une constitution républicaine ou démocratique] est la seule qui puisse nous faire espérer une pacification permanente', parce que les citoyens n'ont pas intérêt à décider de faire la guerre. 'Suivant cette constitution, il faut que chaque citoyen concoure, par son assentiment, à décider la question "Si l'on fera la guerre, ou non". Or, décréter la guerre, n'est-ce pas pour des citoyens décréter contre eux-mêmes toutes les calamités de la guerre'. (ibid 15).

Quant aux Etats, seule une fédération d'Etats peut les pacifier: 'Il en est des peuples, en tant qu'Etats, comme des individus s'ils vivent dans l'état de nature, c'est-à-dire sans lois extérieures, leur voisinage seul est déjà une lésion réciproque, et pour garantir sa sûreté, chacun d'eux peut exiger des autres qu'ils établissent d'accord avec lui une constitution garantissant les droits de tous. Ce serait là une Fédération de peuples, et non pas un seul et même Etat (…)' (ibid 18).

> Soucieux de concourir par l'expansion de leurs productions fondamentales au relèvement du niveau de vie et au progrès des œuvres de paix;
>
> Résolus à substituer aux rivalités séculaires une fusion de leurs intérêts essentiels, à fonder par l'instauration d'une communauté économique les premières assises d'une communauté plus large et plus profonde entre des peuples longtemps opposés par des divisions sanglantes, et à jeter les bases d'institutions capables d'orienter un destin désormais partagé.[8]

Certes, dehors, la jungle était encore là, mais on tentait de l'organiser en créant l'Organisation des Nations Unies (ONU), la guerre était devenue froide et les puissances plus ou moins à l'équilibre. Dans sa clairière au milieu de la jungle, l'Europe allait pouvoir expérimenter son pari du contrat social et de la paix démocratique.

3 'Tu ne te feras pas justice toi-même' ou l'interdiction du principe de réciprocité

Par la force des choses, confrontée aux réticences, voire à la franche hostilité des États membres qui lui expliquaient que le traité était, comme tout traité international, destiné à créer des droits et obligations pour les seuls États, et certainement pas pour les particuliers, et qu'il était impensable que la Cour s'aventura à dire les effets du droit communautaire sur le droit national, cette question étant à leurs yeux du ressort exclusif du droit national et des tribunaux nationaux, la CJUE pris soin, dans les années 60, de s'assurer des fondations de l'édifice en affirmant d'abord sa compétence propre pour interpréter le traité, puis l'étendue de cette compétence, que les États membres cherchaient à restreindre, mais aussi et surtout la spécificité et l'originalité de la Communauté européenne, nouvel ordre juridique autonome par rapport aux 'traités internationaux ordinaires' qui, eux, restaient confrontés aux affres de la jungle.

En 1963, la CJUE affirmait dans *van Gend en Loos* que la Communauté 'constitue un nouvel ordre juridique de droit international, au profit duquel les États ont limité, bien que dans des domaines restreints, leurs droits souverains, et dont les sujets sont non seulement les États membres mais également

---

8 Préambule du traité instituant la Communauté européenne du charbon et de l'acier (traité CECA), signé à Paris le 18 avril 1951 et entré en vigueur le 23 juillet 1952. Six ans après, le 25 mars 1957, était signé le traité instituant la Communauté économique européenne (traité CEE), qui entra en vigueur le 1er janvier 1958.

leurs ressortissants',[9] consacrant ainsi le principe de l'effet direct du droit communautaire en tant qu'il est invocable aussi par les particuliers, si la disposition en question est claire et inconditionnelle, et pas seulement par les États.

En 1964, dans *Costa c. ENEL*, la CJUE réaffirmait 'qu'à la différence des traités internationaux ordinaires, le traité [CEE] a institué un ordre juridique propre, intégré au système juridique des États membres (...) et qui s'impose à leurs juridictions', de sorte que, et ce fut un pas décisif, 'issu d'une source autonome, le droit né du traité ne pourrait donc, en raison de sa nature spécifique originale, se voir judiciairement opposer un texte interne quel qu'il soit, sans perdre son caractère communautaire et sans que soit mise en cause la base juridique de la Communauté elle-même'.[10] Consacrant ainsi le principe de la primauté du droit communautaire, la Cour en concluait que:

> [L]e transfert opéré par les États, de leur ordre juridique interne au profit de l'ordre juridique communautaire, des droits et obligations correspondant aux dispositions du traité, entraîne donc une limitation définitive de leurs droits souverains contre laquelle ne saurait prévaloir un acte unilatéral ultérieur incompatible avec la notion de Communauté.[11]

Poursuivant dans cette logique d'autonomie et d'élévation au-dessus des lois de la jungle, elle allait expliquer fin 1964 aux État membres, qui continuaient à plaider devant elle le droit international classique, que certes celui-ci permet, au titre de la réciprocité, à la partie lésée par l'inexécution des obligations incombant à une autre partie de se dispenser de l'exécution des siennes,[12] mais que:

---

9 Affaire 26/62 *NV Algemene Transport- en Expeditie Onderneming van Gend & Loos c. Administration fiscale néerlandaise* EU:C:1963:1, p. 23.

10 Affaire 6/64 *Flaminio Costa c. ENEL* EU:C:1964:66, pp. 1158 et 1160. La Cour appuyait son raisonnement sur les caractéristiques de l'édifice – durée illimitée, institutions, personnalité et capacité juridiques, représentation extérieure, compétences d'attribution, pouvoirs d'action et effet direct – qu'elle décrit comme suit: '[E]n instituant une Communauté de durée illimitée, dotée d'institutions propres, de la personnalité, de la capacité juridique, d'une capacité de représentation internationale et plus particulièrement de pouvoir réels issus d'une limitation de compétence ou d'un transfert d'attributions des États à la Communauté, ceux-ci ont limité, bien que dans des domaines restreints, leurs droits souverains et créé ainsi un corps de droit applicable à leurs ressortissants et à eux-mêmes'. (p. 1159).

11 Ibid, p. 1160.

12 Par exemple, l'art 55 de la Constitution française du 4 octobre 1958 prévoit que 'Les traités ou accords régulièrement ratifiés ou approuvés ont, dès leur publication, une autorité

> [C]e lien entre les obligations des sujets ne saurait être reconnu dans le cadre du droit communautaire. (…) le traité ne se borne pas à créer des obligations réciproques entre les différents sujets auxquels il s'applique, mais établit un ordre juridique nouveau qui règle les pouvoirs, droits et obligations desdits sujets, ainsi que les *procédures nécessaires pour faire constater et sanctionner toute violation* éventuelle. (…) partant, en dehors des cas expressément prévus, l'économie du traité comporte *interdiction pour les États membres de se faire justice eux-mêmes.*[13]

Lorsqu'il y a un contrat social, on ne se fait pas justice soi-même, ce sont les institutions communes qui s'en chargent.

En 1996, l'Avocat général Léger résumait ainsi cette interdiction:

> [*R*]*ien n'est plus étranger au droit communautaire que la notion de mesure de rétorsion ou de réciprocité* propre au droit international public classique. (…) *Le droit communautaire ne permet pas d'invoquer le principe de réciprocité* pour assurer le respect des obligations découlant du traité. Un État membre ne peut agir unilatéralement contre les manquements d'autres États membres. Le traité de Rome a créé un ordre juridique original dans lequel les procédures nécessaires pour faire constater et sanctionner une violation éventuelle de ses dispositions sont étroitement

supérieure à celle des lois, *sous réserve*, pour chaque accord ou traité, *de son application par l'autre partie*'. (c'est nous soulignons). L'art 60 de la Convention de Vienne sur le droit des traités de 1969 ((adoptée le 23 mai 1969, entrée en vigueur le 27 janvier 1980) 1155 UNTS 331) prévoit qu'une violation substantielle par l'une des parties autorise l'autre à invoquer la violation comme motif pour mettre fin ou suspendre son application en tout ou partie.

13 Affaires jointes 90/63 et 91/63 *Commission c. Luxembourg et Belgique* EU:C:1964:80, pp. 1231–1232 (c'est nous qui soulignons). La Cour réaffirmera cette ligne à plusieurs reprises: '[L]es retards éventuels pris par d'autres États membres dans l'exécution des obligations imposées par une directive ne sauraient être invoqués par un État membre pour justifier l'inexécution, même temporaire, des obligations qui lui incombent' (Affaire 52/75 *Commission c. Italie* EU:C:1976:29, para 11); '[E]n aucun cas, un État membre ne saurait s'autoriser à prendre, unilatéralement, des mesures correctives ou des mesures de défense, destinées à obvier à une méconnaissance éventuelle, par un autre État membre, des règles du traité' (Affaire 232/78 *Commission c. France* EU:C:1979:215, para 9); '[D]ans l'ordre juridique établi par le traité, la mise en œuvre du droit communautaire par les États membres ne peut être soumise à une condition de réciprocité. Les articles 169 et 170 du traité prévoient les voies de recours appropriées pour faire face aux manquements des États membres aux obligations qui découlent du traité'. (Affaire C-38/89 *Ministère public c. Guy Blanguernon* EU:C:1990:11, para 7).

> réglementées. C'est par le biais du recours en manquement, qu'il soit diligenté par un État membre ou par la Commission, qu'une infraction au droit communautaire peut être constatée.[14]

Ainsi, avant même qu'il soit question de confiance mutuelle entre États membres quant au respect par les uns et les autres de leurs obligations communautaires, c'est la confiance dans la force de la loi communautaire s'appuyant sur les procédures de contrôle du respect de ces obligations qui constituait le bouclier contre des actions unilatérales au potentiel délétère. Dans *van Gend en Loos*, la CJUE avait d'ailleurs enrôlé les particuliers comme autant de vigies supplémentaires pour assurer le respect du droit communautaire: '[L]a vigilance des particuliers intéressés à la sauvegarde de leurs droits entraîne un contrôle efficace qui s'ajoute à celui que les articles 169 et 170 confient à la diligence de la Commission et des États membres'.[15]

On peut voir dans l'interdiction du principe de réciprocité entre États membres dans l'Union, et entre les États membres et les institutions,[16] une expression du principe de coopération loyale énoncé à l'article 4, paragraphe 3, du traité sur l'Union européenne (TUE) en vertu duquel 'l'Union et les Etats membres se respectent et s'assistent mutuellement dans l'accomplissement des missions découlant des traités. (…) [Ils] prennent toute mesure générale ou particulière propre à assurer l'exécution [de leurs] obligations (…) [et] s'abstiennent de mettre en péril la réalisation des objectifs de l'Union', dont la confiance mutuelle est un sous-produit.[17] L'interdiction d'invoquer la réciprocité repose sur la nature de l'ordre juridique communautaire, la primauté et la nécessaire efficacité des contrôles du respect des règles par tous. Sans lois, sans institutions, sans contrôle du respect de ces lois par ces institutions, pas

---

14 Conclusions de l'Avocat général Léger dans l'affaire C-5/94 *The Queen c. Ministry of Agriculture, Fisheries and Food, ex parte: Hedley Lomas (Ireland) Ltd* EU:C:1995:193, para 27 (c'est nous qui soulignons).

15 *Van Gend en Loos* (n 9), p. 25. Les ex-arts 169 et 170 du traité CEE correspondent aux arts 258 et 259 du traité sur le fonctionnement de l'Union européenne (TFUE) relatifs à l'action en manquement.

16 Les Etats membres ne peuvent pas non plus, par exemple, tirer argument de l'inaction d'une institution pour ne pas respecter leurs obligations communautaires, la voie appropriée étant dans ce cas-là l'introduction d'une action en carence contre l'institution fautive sur le fondement de l'art 265 TFUE.

17 Pour Felix Blobel et Patrick Späth, 'it could be regarded as a sub- or by-category to the principle of loyalty and solidarity enshrined in Art. 10 EC' (Blobel et Späth (n 3) 528, 535). L'obligation de coopération loyale existe depuis l'origine (voir art 86 du traité CECA et art 5 du traité CEE).

de confiance possible, et risque d'invocation de la réciprocité et de détricotage général.

Dans un arrêt *Hedley Lomas* de 1996, la CJUE a jugé qu'un État membre ne peut pas invoquer l'article 36 TFUE, qui autorise les États membres à restreindre la libre circulation des marchandises pour divers motifs d'intérêt légitime, 'pour justifier une limitation des exportations de marchandises vers un autre État membre au seul motif que, selon le premier État, le second ne respecte pas les prescriptions d'une directive communautaire d'harmonisation poursuivant l'objectif que le recours à l'article 36 tendrait à protéger'.[18]

4 Les premiers pas de la confiance mutuelle dans le domaine du marché intérieur

La confiance que devraient se témoigner les États dans la Communauté est évoquée pour la première fois par la CJUE dans une jurisprudence *Bauhuis* de 1977 dans le domaine du marché intérieur, à l'occasion d'une affaire de contrôles sanitaires. Une directive avait harmonisé le système de contrôles sanitaires en instituant la responsabilité de l'État membre expéditeur, rendant ainsi superflus les contrôles frontaliers, notamment par l'État de destination, des animaux transportés. La CJUE a jugé que:

> [L]e système de contrôles sanitaires harmonisé, mis en place par la directive, est fondé sur l'équivalence des garanties sanitaires exigées dans l'ensemble des États membres, d'où résulte à la fois la garantie de la protection de la santé et l'égalité de traitement des produits; (…) *ce système est fondé sur la confiance que doivent se témoigner les États membres en ce qui concerne les garanties offertes par les contrôles effectués*, au départ, par les services sanitaires de l'État membre d'où les animaux sont expédiés; (…) *en vue de rendre ces garanties effectives, la directive a harmonisé les dispositions* des États membres en généralisant des méthodes de contrôle particulièrement sévères.[19]

18 Affaire C-5/94 *Hedley Lomas* EU:C:1996:205, para 21. Voir aussi l'affaire C-1/96 *The Queen c. Minister of Agriculture, Fisheries and Food, ex parte Compassion in World Farming Ltd* EU:C:1998:113, para 47.

19 Affaire 46/76 *W.J.G. Bauhuis c. État néerlandais* EU:C:1977:6, paras 20, 22 et 23 (c'est nous qui soulignons).

On voit ici que c'est par l'harmonisation communautaire des contrôles qu'est assurée l'effectivité des garanties offertes par les contrôles, et par là l'équivalence des contrôles, desquelles résulte la confiance que les États membres 'doivent se témoigner'. La confiance entre États est donc un résultat, elle résulte de l'harmonisation qui crée l'équivalence.

Cet arrêt – et son raisonnement – sera suivi dans d'autres affaires similaires, qu'il s'agisse de normes sanitaires, de santé et bien-être des animaux ou de reconnaissance mutuelle des diplômes. Dans l'affaire *Hedley Lomas*, après avoir précisé, comme expliqué plus haut, qu'un État membre ne pouvait pas utiliser l'article 36 TFUE pour punir le supposé non-respect du droit communautaire par d'autres États membres, la CJUE affirmait une nouvelle fois que 'les États membres doivent se témoigner une confiance mutuelle en ce qui concerne les contrôles effectués sur leur territoire respectif' et que conformément au traité les États membres sont obligés de prendre toutes mesures propres à garantir la portée et l'efficacité du droit communautaire (obligation de coopération loyale, voir plus haut).[20]

En 2003, dans l'affaire *Tennah-Durez* qui concernait une question de reconnaissance mutuelle des diplômes de médecins, la CJUE a jugé que du fait qu'une directive communautaire, dite sectorielle, 'harmonis[e] et coordonn[e] au niveau communautaire, d'une part, la formation médicale tant de base que de spécialiste (aspect harmonisation) et, d'autre part, les règles pour l'accès aux activités de médecin dans les États membres et l'exercice de celles-ci (aspect coordination)', elle oblige les États membres a une reconnaissance automatique et inconditionnelle des diplômes délivrés par les autres États membres dans les conditions édictées par la directive. Pour la Cour, cette reconnaissance '*repose sur la confiance mutuelle des États membres* dans le caractère suffisant des diplômes de médecin délivrés par les autres États membres, *cette confiance étant fondée sur un système de formation dont le niveau a été fixé d'un commun accord*'.[21]

Là encore, c'est sur l'harmonisation préalable que repose la confiance entre États, elle est le résultat de cette harmonisation, elle ne la précède pas, ni ne la supplée.

Deux ans après l'affaire *Bauhuis*, la CJUE rendait en 1979 son célèbre arrêt dans l'affaire *Cassis de Dijon* qui fut considéré comme ayant jeté les bases du principe de reconnaissance mutuelle sans harmonisation préalable. La Cour décida qu'en l'absence d'harmonisation (ici dans le domaine de la production

---

20 *Hedley Lomas* (n 18), paras 19–21; voir aussi *Compassion in World Farming* (n 18), para 47.

21 Affaire C-110/01 *Malika Tennah-Durez c. Conseil national de l'ordre des médecins* EU:C:2003:357, paras 30–31 (c'est nous qui soulignons).

et de la commercialisation de l'alcool et des boissons spiritueuses), il appartenait aux États membres de réglementer le secteur concerné, ce qui, du fait des disparités des législations nationales, était susceptible de créer des obstacles à la circulation intracommunautaire. Ces obstacles ne sont cependant justifiés que s'ils sont nécessaires pour satisfaire à des exigences impératives d'intérêt général tenant, notamment, à l'efficacité des contrôles fiscaux, à la protection de la santé publique, à la loyauté des transactions commerciales et à la défense des consommateurs. Dans le cas d'espèce, la Cour jugea qu'il n'y avait 'aucun motif valable d'empêcher que des boissons alcoolisées, à condition qu'elles soient *légalement produites et commercialisées dans l'un des États* membres, soient *introduites dans tout autre État membre* (...)'.[22]

Aucune mention d'une nécessaire confiance entre États membres dans leurs normes respectives. Simplement l'application de l'interdiction des restrictions quantitatives à l'importation et des mesures d'effet équivalent prévue par l'ex-article 30 du traité CE (l'actuel article 34 TFUE).

C'est en 1989, dans l'affaire *Bouchara* qui concernait, comme l'affaire *Cassis de Dijon,* l'application des articles 30 et 36 dans un secteur non-harmonisé, que la CJUE a pour la première fois mentionné la confiance mutuelle entre États sans harmonisation préalable. Tout en reconnaissant qu'un État membre pouvait, pour des raisons légitimes de protection des consommateurs, exiger d'un importateur d'obtenir un agrément préalable à la mise sur le marché de produits textiles, la Cour a toutefois jugé qu'il était disproportionné, et donc contraire au traité, d'exiger des analyses techniques dans l'État d'importation alors que l'importateur pouvait produire de telles analyses effectuées dans l'État membre d'exportation. Pour la Cour, 'cette règle constitue une expression spécifique d'un *principe plus général de la confiance mutuelle entre les autorités des États membres* (...)'.[23]

La confiance mutuelle dont il est question ici vient au soutien de l'application du principe de proportionnalité aux mesures de contrôle que les États membres peuvent appliquer dans un secteur non-harmonisé: ces mesures sont possibles, mais elles ne doivent pas aller au-delà de ce qui est nécessaire. En quelque sorte: les États ne doivent pas exagérer, ils doivent se faire un peu confiance quand même. La confiance mutuelle est, ici encore, un sous-produit du principe de coopération loyale.

---

22 Affaire 120/78 *Rewe-Zentral* AG *contre Bundesmonopolverwaltung für Branntwein* EU:C:1979:42 (*Cassis de Dijon*), paras 8 et 14 (c'est nous qui soulignons).

23 Affaire 25/88 *Procédure pénale c. Esther Renée Wurmser, veuve Bouchara et société Norlaine Bouchara* EU:C:1989:187, para 18 (c'est nous qui soulignons).

Il faut en effet se rappeler que le cœur du marché intérieur fonctionne directement sur le fondement des articles du traité qui instituent les quatre libertés de circulation (marchandises, personnes, services et capitaux),[24] sans qu'il soit a priori nécessaire d'harmoniser au préalable les législations nationales. Le traité prévoit certes les bases juridiques appropriées pour harmoniser afin de permettre un meilleur fonctionnement du marché intérieur, mais les articles

---

24 Pour mémoire, les dispositions pertinentes du TFUE concernant la libre circulation des marchandises se lisent comme suit:

- art 30: 'les droits de douane à l'importation et à l'exportation ou taxes d'effet équivalent sont interdits entre les États membres. Cette interdiction s'applique également aux droits de douane à caractère fiscal';
- art 34: 'les restrictions quantitatives à l'importation ainsi que toutes mesures d'effet équivalent, sont interdites entre les États membres';
- art 35: 'les restrictions quantitatives à l'exportation, ainsi que toutes mesures d'effet équivalent, sont interdites entre les États membres';
- art 36: 'les dispositions des articles 34 et 35 ne font pas obstacle aux interdictions ou restrictions d'importation, d'exportation ou de transit, justifiées par des raisons de moralité publique, d'ordre public, de sécurité publique, de protection de la santé et de la vie des personnes et des animaux ou de préservation des végétaux, de protection des trésors nationaux ayant une valeur artistique, historique ou archéologique ou de protection de la propriété industrielle et commerciale. Toutefois, ces interdictions ou restrictions ne doivent constituer ni un moyen de discrimination arbitraire ni une restriction déguisée dans le commerce entre les États membres'.

Celles concernant la libre circulation des personnes se lisent comme suit:

- art 45, paras 1 et 2: '1. La libre circulation des travailleurs est assurée à l'intérieur de l'Union. 2. Elle implique l'abolition de toute discrimination, fondée sur la nationalité, entre les travailleurs des États membres, en ce qui concerne l'emploi, la rémunération et les autres conditions de travail'. Les limitations ne peuvent être justifiées que par des raisons d'ordre public, de sécurité publique et de santé publique (para 3).
- art 49, première phrase: 'Dans le cadre des dispositions ci-après, les restrictions à la liberté d'établissement des ressortissants d'un État membre dans le territoire d'un autre État membre sont interdites'.

Celles concernant la libre prestation des services se lisent comme suit:

- art 56, premier alinéa: 'Dans le cadre des dispositions ci-après, les restrictions à la libre prestation des services à l'intérieur de l'Union sont interdites à l'égard des ressortissants des États membres établis dans un État membre autre que celui du destinataire de la prestation'.

Celles concernant la libre circulation des capitaux se lisent comme suit:

- art 63: '1. Dans le cadre des dispositions du présent chapitre, toutes les restrictions aux mouvements de capitaux entre les États membres et entre les États membres et les pays tiers sont interdites. 2. Dans le cadre des dispositions du présent chapitre, toutes les restrictions aux paiements entre les États membres et entre les États membres et les pays tiers sont interdites'.

de base qui instituent les quatre libertés sont tous d'effet direct, ils énoncent tous, pour reprendre les termes de l'arrêt *van Gend en Loos*, une interdiction suffisamment 'claire et inconditionnelle (...) assortie d'aucune réserve des Etats de subordonner sa mise en œuvre à un acte positif de droit interne (...) se [prêtant], pas sa nature même, à produire des effets directs dans les relations juridiques entres les Etats membres et leurs justiciables'.[25] Ainsi, par exemple, l'article 30 TFUE, sur l'interdiction entre États membres des droits de douane à l'importation ou à l'exportation ou l'article 34 TFUE sur l'interdiction entre États membres des restrictions quantitatives à l'importation sont d'effet direct et s'appliquent indépendamment d'une harmonisation européenne.

Comme l'illustre l'arrêt *Cassis de Dijon*, la conséquence de l'absence d'harmonisation est que les États membres restent libres de réglementer le secteur concerné. Ils ne peuvent cependant le faire qu'à condition de respecter les interdictions prévues par le traité qui, du fait de la primauté, obligent leurs autorités et juridictions à laisser inappliquées toutes dispositions nationales contraires et interdisent l'adoption de dispositions contraires. Les réglementations nationales en question ne peuvent aboutir à restreindre les quatre libertés que si elles sont nécessaires pour satisfaire à des exigences impératives d'intérêt général. L'arrêt *Bouchara* précise simplement que même justifiées, les mesures nationales doivent être proportionnées de sorte que des contrôles équivalents déjà faits dans l'État membre d'exportation devront être pris en compte au titre du 'principe plus général de la confiance mutuelle entre les autorités des États membres'. Ce n'est pas le principe de confiance mutuelle qui interdit, c'est l'article du traité lui-même qui interdit, article que les États membres doivent mettre en œuvre loyalement.

Lorsque des mesures d'harmonisation communautaires ont été adoptées et permettent de réaliser l'objectif d'intérêt général en question, les mesures nationales restrictives qui poursuivaient le même objectif ne sont plus possibles. Dans l'affaire *Hedley Lomas*, la CJUE a ainsi jugé que '[le] recours [à l'article 36] n'est plus possible lorsque des directives communautaires prévoient l'harmonisation des mesures nécessaires à la réalisation de l'objectif spécifique que poursuivrait le recours à l'article 36'.[26]

Dans le marché intérieur, la construction est donc suffisamment solide sans qu'il soit besoin de faire appel à un (relativement récent et flou) principe de confiance mutuelle pour cimenter l'édifice: le traité prévoit lui-même les règles et interdictions de base, que les États membres doivent appliquer et respecter parce que ces règles, ainsi que les éventuelles mesures d'harmonisation qui

---

25 *Van Gend en Loos* (n 9), p. 24.

26 *Hedley Lomas* (n 18), para 19.

viennent en soutien, ont primauté sur le droit national et que leur respect est assuré par une armée de vigies, qu'il s'agisse de la Commission et des autres États membres, par la voie de l'action en manquement, ou des particuliers eux-mêmes, par la voie des questions préjudicielles, le tout contrôlé par la CJUE. C'est l'état de paix de Kant établi par 'l'état légal', c'est-à-dire l'État de droit ou, comme la CJUE l'a baptisée, la 'communauté de droit'.[27]

5 De la reconnaissance mutuelle à la confiance mutuelle, ou *vice versa*, dans l'espace de liberté, de sécurité et de justice

La construction n'était pas aussi claire dans ce qu'on appelait modestement la JAI, pour justice et affaires intérieures, devenue depuis un plus ambitieux 'espace de liberté, de sécurité et de justice'.

Commencée dans les années 70 par une coopération intergouvernementale en dehors des traités, la coopération dans les domaines de souveraineté que sont la police, la justice, la gestion des frontières, la migration et l'asile fit son entrée dans les traités de manière progressive, d'abord par le traité de Maastricht en 1993 dans ce qu'on appelait le troisième pilier – le titre VI du traité sur l'Union européenne (ex-TUE) de l'époque – qui coexistait avec l'espace Schengen lancé à côté des traités en 1985, développé en 1990 par la Convention d'application et effectivement réalisé en 1995, puis par le traité d'Amsterdam en 1999. Celui-ci fit passer la migration, l'asile et la coopération judiciaire civile du troisième pilier dans le traité communautaire et intégra dans les traités l'acquis de Schengen. Enfin, le traité de Lisbonne en 2009 normalisa le tout, en y étendant la majorité qualifiée au Conseil, la codécision avec le Parlement européen et des pouvoirs complets de contrôle par la Commission et la CJUE.[28]

La sensibilité des États membres était telle que le troisième pilier fut pendant des années qualifié de coopération intergouvernementale quand bien même les institutions de l'Union y exerçaient des compétences d'adoption

---

27 Affaire C-294/83 *Parti écologiste 'Les Verts' c. Parlement européen* EU:C:1986:166, dans lequel la CJUE a dit pour droit que 'la Communauté économique européenne est une communauté de droit en ce que ni ses Etats membres ni ses institutions n'échappent au contrôle de la conformité de leurs actes à la charte constitutionnelle de base qu'est le traité' (para 23).

28 Pour un aperçu général, voir Thérèse Blanchet, 'Justice and Home Affairs: A Laboratory for Differentiation' (2013) LXVI(3) Studia Diplomatica 33. Les pouvoirs complets de contrôle ne sont entrés en vigueur que le 1er décembre 2014, à l'échéance de la période transitoire de cinq ans après l'entrée en vigueur du traité de Lisbonne prévue par l'art 10, paras 1 à 3, du protocole 36 sur les dispositions transitoires.

(le Conseil à l'unanimité) et, un peu, de contrôle (la CJUE, en annulation et interprétation), certes avec des limitations – la Commission et le Parlement européen étaient alors les parents pauvres de ce pilier et la CJUE n'avait pas tout l'éventail de ses compétences – mais des actes juridiques obligatoires pour les États membres y étaient adoptés par une institution de l'Union, le Conseil. Cependant, le défaut principal de la construction était la faiblesse du contrôle de la mise en œuvre. Les pouvoirs en manquement de la Commission et de la CJUE n'existaient pas et la compétence préjudicielle de la Cour en interprétation était limitée d'abord aux seuls cas où des protocoles aux conventions entre États membres la prévoyaient puis, avec le traité d'Amsterdam, aux seuls États membres qui l'avaient acceptée.[29] En outre, lorsqu'ils rédigèrent le traité d'Amsterdam, les États membres, auteurs du traité, avaient expressément exclu que les instruments juridiques du troisième pilier – les décisions-cadre et les décisions – soient dotés d'effet direct.[30]

Malgré la jurisprudence *Pupino*,[31] le bras armé au soutien de la force de la loi, l'outil principal du succès du marché intérieur, manquait dans l'espace de liberté, de sécurité et de justice. Or cela allait durer plus de 20 ans, de 1993 à 2014, de Maastricht à la fin de la période transitoire de Lisbonne, et, du fait de l'article 9 du protocole 36, même au-delà en ce qui concerne l'absence d'effet direct.[32]

---

29 Voir art K.3, para 2, point c), de l'ex-TUE (Maastricht); art 35 de l'ex-TUE (Amsterdam); art 68 du TCE (Amsterdam).

30 Voir art 34, para 2, points b) et c), de l'ex-TUE (Amsterdam) qui définit les effets juridiques des décisions-cadre comme ceux d'une directive et les effets d'une décision JAI comme ceux d'une décision communautaire, mais dans les deux cas en précisant que '[elles] ne peuvent entraîner d'effet direct'.

31 Affaire C-105/03 *Procédure pénale c. Maria Pupino* EU:C:2005:386. Dans cet arrêt, répondant aux Etats membres qui tiraient argument de l'absence d'effet direct des décisions-cadre, et de l'absence dans l'ex-TUE d'une disposition similaire à l'article 10 TCE sur la coopération loyale, pour restreindre la compétence de la CJUE et nier l'obligation d'interprétation conforme, la Cour a jugé que sa compétence d'interprétation préjudicielle 'serait privée de l'essentiel de son effet utile si les particuliers n'étaient pas en droit d'invoquer les décisions-cadres en vue d'obtenir une interprétation conforme du droit national devant les juridictions des États membres' (para 38) et que 'il serait difficile pour l'Union de remplir efficacement sa mission si le principe de coopération loyale (…) ne s'imposait pas également dans le cadre de la coopération policière et judiciaire en matière pénale, qui est d'ailleurs entièrement fondée sur la coopération entre les États membres et les institutions' (para 42).

32 L'art 9 du protocole 36 prévoit que les effets juridiques des actes de l'ancien troisième pilier, et donc notamment l'absence d'effet direct des décisions-cadre et des décisions, perdurera aussi longtemps que les actes en question n'auront pas été 'lisbonnisés',

De plus, contrairement au marché intérieur (voir plus haut), il n'y a pas dans le titre sur l'espace de liberté, de sécurité et de justice d'interdictions ou de règles inscrites dans le droit primaire susceptibles d'effet direct, si ce n'est peut-être la règle de base de Schengen sur l'absence de contrôles des personnes lorsqu'elles franchissent les frontières intérieures (article 67, paragraphe 1, point a), TFUE), bien qu'elle ne soit pas formulée de manière aussi directe que les interdictions du marché intérieur. Rien en tout cas de comparable aux règles du marché intérieur en ce qui concerne, par exemple, la reconnaissance mutuelle des décisions judiciaires et extrajudiciaires, pas de règle dans le traité qui prévoirait par exemple que 'toute décision rendue par une juridiction d'un État membre est reconnue dans les autres États membres sans qu'il soit nécessaire de recourir à aucune procédure'. La mise en place de la coopération dépend entièrement de l'adoption de mesures de droit secondaire par le législateur de l'Union. Par conséquent, impossible dans ce domaine de procéder comme dans l'affaire *Cassis de Dijon*: en l'absence de règles européennes obligeant à la reconnaissance de tels ou tels types de décisions nationales, impossible de se fonder directement sur le traité pour obliger un État membre à reconnaître un jugement légalement rendu dans un autre État membre. Ni l'affirmation par le traité du principe de reconnaissance mutuelle, ni l'affirmation par la CJUE du principe de confiance mutuelle ne sont susceptibles de combler ce vide.

Un grand nombre d'actes furent adoptés pendant les 16 ans de vie du troisième pilier entre 1993 et 2009, surtout à partir de 1999, année d'entrée en vigueur du traité d'Amsterdam, et l'adoption par le Conseil européen du programme dit de Tampere qui fut suivi d'une période d'intense production législative.[33] C'est dans ce programme que les tenants de la reconnaissance mutuelle, menés par le Royaume-Uni qui en avait déjà semé les graines sous sa présidence lors du Conseil européen de Cardiff en juin 1998,[34] réussirent à insérer

---

c'est-à-dire modifiés ou remplacés par un acte adopté après l'entrée en vigueur du traité de Lisbonne. Sur les arts 9 et 10 du protocole 36, voir Thérèse Blanchet, 'The Genesis of Protocol 36' (2015) 6 NJECL 434. A titre d'illustration, voir la liste des actes 'lisbonnisés' établie à l'occasion de l'exercice par le Royaume-Uni de son option de sortie en bloc le 1er décembre 2014 d'une centaine d'actes de l'ancien troisième pilier, et de sa re-participation dans 35 de ces mesures ([2014] JO C430/23).

33 Sur le tournant qu'a représenté le Conseil européen de Tampere, sous présidence finlandaise, voir notamment Pierre de Boissieu et autres (eds) *National Leaders and the Making of Europe – Key Episodes in the Life of the European Council* (John Harper Publishing 2015) Ch. 11.

34 Voir les Conclusions de la présidence, Conseil européen de Cardiff, 15 et 16 juin 1998 (doc SN 150/1/98 REV 1), para 39. A ce sujet, voir Hans G Nilsson, 'Mutual Trust or Mutual

la fameuse phrase selon laquelle le principe de reconnaissance mutuelle serait désormais la 'pierre angulaire de la coopération judiciaire' civile et pénale dans l'Union, les tenants de l'harmonisation comme préalable ou au moins accessoire à la reconnaissance mutuelle devant partiellement déclarer forfait et se contenter de mentions plus vagues.[35]

L'élévation de la reconnaissance mutuelle au rang de principe sera finalement consacrée par le traité de Lisbonne qui l'inséra dans l'article introductif du titre V sur l'espace de liberté, de sécurité et de justice (article 67 TFUE):

> 3. L'Union œuvre pour assurer un niveau élevé de sécurité (...) par la reconnaissance mutuelle des décisions judiciaires en matière pénale et, si nécessaire, par le rapprochement des législations pénales.

Mistrust?' dans Gilles de Kerchove et Anne Weyembergh (eds) *La confiance mutuelle dans l'espace pénal européen* (Editions de l'Université de Bruxelles 2005) 29.

35 Conclusions de la présidence, Conseil européen de Tampere, 15 et 16 octobre 1999, paras 5 et 33–37. Dans le Chapitre VI des conclusions, intitulé 'Reconnaissance mutuelle des décisions judiciaires', voir en particulier le para 33 où 'le Conseil européen approuve (...) *le principe de reconnaissance mutuelle, qui*, selon lui, *devrait devenir la pierre angulaire de la coopération judiciaire* en matière tant civile que pénale au sein de l'Union. Le principe devrait s'appliquer tant aux jugements qu'aux autres décisions émanant des autorités judiciaires'. (c'est nous qui soulignons).

Pour les tenants du rapprochement et de l'harmonisation, une phrase générale figurait au début parmi 'Les Jalons posés à Tampere' aux termes de laquelle 'il convient d'arriver à une meilleure compatibilité et à une convergence accrue entre les systèmes juridiques des Etats membres' (para 5). Le rapprochement des législations comme facilitateur était aussi évoqué au Chapitre VI: 'Le renforcement de la reconnaissance mutuelle des décisions judiciaires et des jugements et *le rapprochement nécessaire des législations* faciliteraient la coopération entre autorités et la protection judiciaire des droits de la personne'. (para 33, c'est nous qui soulignons); 'Ce dispositif pourrait s'accompagner de la *fixation de normes minimales pour certains aspects de procédure civile*'. (para 34, c'est nous qui soulignons); '[Le] programme de mesures destinées à mettre en œuvre le principe de reconnaissance mutuelle (...) [devrait comprendre] des travaux (...) sur les aspects du droit procédural pour lesquels la *fixation de normes minimales communes est considérée comme nécessaire pour faciliter l'application du principe de reconnaissance mutuelle*, dans le respect des principes fondamentaux du droit des Etats membres'. (para 37, c'est nous qui soulignons).

Un programme ambitieux de mise en œuvre du principe de reconnaissance mutuelle fut adopté par le Conseil fin 2000, tant dans le domaine civil que pénal (Projet de programme des mesures sur la mise en œuvre du principe de reconnaissance mutuelle des décisions en matière civile et commerciale [2001] JO C12/1).

> 4. L'Union facilite l'accès à la justice, notamment par *le principe de reconnaissance mutuelle des décisions judiciaires et extrajudiciaires* en matière civile.[36]

Le principe de reconnaissance mutuelle est ensuite mentionné:[37]

- à l'article 70 TFUE, base juridique pour l'adoption de mesures sur l'évaluation mutuelle par les États membres et la Commission de la mise en œuvre de l'acquis fondé sur le titre V 'en particulier afin de favoriser la pleine application du principe de reconnaissance mutuelle';
- à l'article 81, base juridique pour la coopération judiciaire civile, qui mentionne à la fois le principe de reconnaissance mutuelle sur laquelle la coopération est fondée, et le fait que la coopération 'peut inclure l'adoption de mesures de rapprochement des dispositions législatives et réglementaires des États membres';
- à l'article 82, paragraphe 1, premier alinéa, paragraphe introductif de la coopération judiciaire pénale, laquelle 'est fondée sur le principe de reconnaissance mutuelle des jugements et décisions judiciaires et inclut le rapprochement des dispositions législatives et réglementaires des États membres' dans les domaines de la procédure pénale (article 82, paragraphe 2) et de l'harmonisation minimale de la définition des infractions et sanctions pénales (article 83); et
- à l'article 82, paragraphe 2, base juridique pour l'adoption de mesures minimales d'harmonisation de la procédure pénale 'dans la mesure où cela est nécessaire pour faciliter la reconnaissance mutuelle des jugements et décisions judiciaires'.

On voit qu'à côté du principe de reconnaissance mutuelle, il est quand même question aussi de rapprochement des législations nationales, ne serait-ce que pour faciliter cette reconnaissance. Il est question aussi, pour favoriser la reconnaissance mutuelle, de s'assurer de la bonne mise en œuvre des obligations.

Bien qu'elles se rejoignent sur l'idée de faire en sorte que la libre circulation des personnes dans l'Union permette aux honnêtes citoyens d'avoir accès partout à la justice et n'offre pas aux criminels une échappatoire empêchant que

---

36 C'est nous qui soulignons.

37 La seule autre mention dans les traités de la reconnaissance mutuelle, non pas comme un principe, mais comme le résultat de mesures européennes de coordination des règles nationales afin de faciliter la libre circulation des indépendants, est à l'art 53, para 1, TFUE, sur les diplômes, dans le chapitre sur le droit d'établissement.

justice soit rendue, il y a toujours eu (au moins) deux écoles: ceux qui plaident pour un certain degré d'harmonisation, au moins minimal, de certaines règles de procédure civile ou pénale et de droit matériel, comme catalyseur de la nécessaire confiance préalable à une reconnaissance mutuelle heureuse, et ceux qui, plus soucieux de protéger les spécificités des 'différents systèmes et traditions juridiques des Etats membres' (article 67, paragraphe 1, TFUE), conçoivent la reconnaissance mutuelle comme une sorte de libre échange des jugements, sans qu'il soit nécessaire ou utile de perturber les traditions nationales par des mesures d'harmonisation intempestives.[38]

Interprétant les bases juridiques de l'ex-TUE en matière de coopération pénale et la convention d'application de Schengen (CAAS), la Cour avait constaté dans l'affaire *Gözütok*, que:

> [A]ucune disposition du titre VI [de l'ex-TUE] (…) ni de l'accord de Schengen (…) ne subordonne l'application de l'article 54 de la CAAS [sur le principe ne bis in idem] à l'harmonisation ou, à tout le moins, au rapprochement des législations pénales des États membres dans le domaine des procédures d'extinction de l'action publique.[39]

---

38 Sur ces problématiques, voir notamment Gilles de Kerchove et Anne Weyembergh (eds) *La reconnaissance mutuelle des décisions judiciaires pénales dans l'Union européenne* (éditions de l'Université de Bruxelles 2001); Lars B Larsen, 'Some Reflections on Mutual Recognition in the Area of Freedom, Security and Justice' dans Pascal Cardonnel et autres (eds) *Constitutionalising the EU Judicial System – Essays in Honour of Pernilla Lindh* (Hart Publishing 2012) 139; Valsamis Mitsilegas, 'The Limits of Mutual Trust in Europe's Area of Freedom, Security and Justice: From Automatic Inter-State Cooperation to the Slow Emergence of the Individual' (2012) 31 YEL 319; Christine Janssens, *The Principle of Mutual Recognition in EU Law* (OUP 2013); Ester Herlin-Karnell, 'From Mutual Trust to the Full Effectiveness of EU Law: 10 Years of the European Arrest Warrant' (2013) 38 EL Rev 79; Henry Labayle, 'Droit d'asile et confiance mutuelle: regard critique sur la jurisprudence européenne' [2014] Cah. dr. eur. 501; Koen Lenaerts, 'The Principle of Mutual Recognition in the Area of Freedom, Security and Justice' (Fourth Annual Sir Jeremy Lever Lecture, All Souls College, université d'Oxford, 30 janvier 2015); Gilles de Kerchove et Anne Weyembergh (eds) (n 34), notamment Daniel Flore 'La notion de confiance mutuelle: l'"alpha" ou l'"omega" d'une justice pénale européenne?' (p. 17); Emmanuelle Bribosia et Anne Weyembergh, 'Confiance mutuelle et droits fondamentaux: "Back to the future"' [2016] Cah. dr. eur. 469.

39 Affaires jointes C-187/01 et C-385/01 *Procédures pénales c. Hüseyin Gözütok (C-187/01) et Klaus Brügge (C-385/01)* EU:C:2003:87, para 32. Voir aussi l'affaire C-303/05 *Advocaten voor de Wereld VZW c. Leden van de Ministerraad* EU:C:2007:261, où la Cour dit la même chose: 'aucune disposition du titre VI [de l'ex-tue] (…) ne subordonne l'application du mandat

Cela reste vrai dans les traités actuels: la reconnaissance mutuelle n'est pas subordonnée à l'harmonisation. Cependant, les bases juridiques existent pour adopter des mesures d'harmonisation minimale, à la fois dans le domaine de la coopération judiciaire civile (article 81, paragraphe 2, point f), TFUE) et dans celui de la coopération judiciaire pénale, qui permet d'harmoniser la procédure pénale (article 82, paragraphe 2, TFUE) et le droit pénal matériel (définition des infractions et des sanctions, article 83, paragraphes 1 et 2, TFUE). Le traité reconnaît que ces mesures d'harmonisation sont susceptibles de faciliter la reconnaissance mutuelle.

Les mots 'confiance' ou 'confiance mutuelle' ne sont par contre mentionnés nulle part, ni dans les chapitres relatifs aux quatre libertés du marché intérieur, ni dans le titre V sur l'espace de liberté, de sécurité et de justice. Le mot 'confiance' n'apparaît qu'une seule fois dans les traités, tout à fait ailleurs, dans la section relative à la Cour des comptes, à l'article 287, paragraphe 3, TFUE qui concerne la coopération entre la Cour des comptes de l'Union et les cours des comptes nationales, une coopération qui doit être 'empreinte de confiance'.

Le (défunt) traité établissant une Constitution pour l'Europe contenait une mention de la confiance mutuelle dans sa partie I, la seule partie véritablement nouvelle du traité, sorte de *reader's digest* introductif qui visait à décrire en quelques articles l'essentiel de ce qu'est l'Union. A l'article I-42 sur l'espace de liberté, de sécurité et de justice, l'Union se voyait confier le soin de constituer cet espace 'en *favorisant la confiance mutuelle* entre les autorités compétences des Etats membres, en particulier *sur la base de la reconnaissance mutuelle* des décisions judiciaires et extra-judiciaires' (c'est nous qui soulignons). Cette formulation, non reprise par le traité de Lisbonne, est assez étrange en tant qu'elle paraît fonder la confiance mutuelle sur la reconnaissance mutuelle, alors que la logique voudrait que ce soit au contraire la confiance mutuelle qui permette ou qui fonde la reconnaissance mutuelle.

C'est d'ailleurs ainsi que le législateur de l'Union, lorsqu'il mentionne la confiance mutuelle dans les considérants de différents instruments de coopération judiciaire, présente la relation entre celle-ci et la reconnaissance mutuelle.

5.1 *La confiance mutuelle comme préalable à la reconnaissance mutuelle*

Dans le domaine de la coopération judiciaire civile, par exemple, le considérant 26 du règlement Bruxelles I explique que 'La confiance réciproque dans

d'arrêt européen à l'harmonisation des législations pénales des États membres dans le domaine des infractions concernées' (para 59).

l'administration de la justice au sein de l'Union justifie le principe selon lequel les décisions rendues dans un État membre devraient être reconnues dans tous les États membres sans qu'une procédure spéciale ne soit nécessaire'.[40] De même, le considérant 22 du règlement sur les procédures d'insolvabilité explique que 'La reconnaissance des décisions rendues par les juridictions des Etats membres devrait reposer sur le principe de la confiance mutuelle'[41] et le considérant 21 du règlement Bruxelles IIbis que 'La reconnaissance et l'exécution des décisions rendues dans un État membre devraient reposer sur le principe de la confiance mutuelle et les motifs de non-reconnaissance devraient être réduits au minimum nécessaire'.[42]

Dans le domaine de la coopération judiciaire pénale, la rédaction est moins systématique, peut-être en raison du fait que les textes émanaient souvent d'initiatives des États membres. Le considérant 10 de la décision-cadre sur le mandat d'arrêt européen est le plus direct lorsqu'il énonce que 'Le mécanisme du mandat d'arrêt européen repose sur un degré de confiance élevé entre les États membres'.[43] Le considérant 5 de la décision-cadre sur le transfèrement des prisonniers explique que 'Dans leurs relations, qui sont marquées par une confiance réciproque particulière envers leurs systèmes judiciaires respectifs, les États membres autorisent l'État d'exécution à reconnaitre les décisions rendues par les autorités de l'État d'émission'.[44] Par contre, dans le considérant 9 de la décision-cadre sur la reconnaissance mutuelle des décisions de confiscation, il est question de certitude plutôt que de confiance:

> La coopération entre les États membres, fondée sur le principe de la reconnaissance mutuelle et de l'exécution immédiate des décisions

---

40 Règlement (UE) 1215/2012 du Parlement européen et du Conseil du 12 décembre 2012 concernant la compétence judiciaire, la reconnaissance et l'exécution des décisions en matière civile et commerciale (Bruxelles I) [2012] JO L351/1.

41 Règlement (CE) 1346/2000 du Conseil du 29 mai 2000 relatif aux procédures d'insolvabilité [2000] JO L160/1.

42 Règlement (CE) 2201/2003 du Conseil du 27 novembre 2003 relatif à la compétence, la reconnaissance et l'exécution des décisions en matière matrimoniale et en matière de responsabilité parentale, abrogeant le règlement (CE) 1347/2000 (Bruxelles IIbis) [2003] JO L338/29.

43 Décision-cadre 2002/584/JAI du Conseil du 13 juin 2002 relative au mandat d'arrêt européen et aux procédures de remise entre États membres [2002] JO L190/1.

44 Décision-cadre 2008/909/JAI du Conseil du 27 novembre 2008 concernant l'application du principe de reconnaissance mutuelle aux jugements en matière pénale prononçant des peines ou des mesures privatives de liberté aux fins de leur exécution dans l'Union européenne [2008] JO L327/27.

> judiciaires, repose sur la certitude que les décisions à reconnaître et à exécuter sont toujours rendues dans le respect des principes de légalité, de subsidiarité et de proportionnalité.[45]

La CJUE présente aussi les choses dans cet ordre: la confiance mutuelle comme élément nécessaire à la coopération et à la reconnaissance mutuelle.

Dans le domaine de la coopération judiciaire civile, la CJUE a par exemple jugé dans l'affaire *Aguirre Zarraga* concernant une situation d'enlèvement d'enfant par la mère alors que la garde avait été attribuée au père par l'autorité compétente de l'État responsable conformément au règlement Bruxelles IIbis en matière de responsabilité parentale, que:

> [L]es systèmes de reconnaissance et d'exécution des décisions rendues dans un État membre établis par [le règlement Bruxelles IIbis] sont fondés sur le principe de confiance réciproque entre les États membres quant au fait que leurs ordres juridiques nationaux respectifs sont en mesure de fournir une protection équivalente et effective des droits fondamentaux, reconnus au niveau de l'Union, en particulier, dans la charte des droit fondamentaux.[46]

Dans le domaine de la coopération judiciaire pénale, la CJUE a par exemple jugé dans l'affaire *Gözütok*, qui concernait la question de savoir si, pour l'application du principe ne bis in idem, le fait que l'action publique ait été éteinte sans l'intervention d'une juridiction satisfaisait la condition d'avoir été définitivement jugée, que:

> [L]e principe ne bis in idem (…) qu'il soit appliqué à des procédures d'extinction de l'action publique comportant ou non l'intervention d'une juridiction ou à des jugements, implique nécessairement qu'il existe une confiance mutuelle des États membres dans leurs systèmes respectifs de justice pénale et que chacun de ceux-ci accepte l'application du droit pénal en vigueur dans les autres États membres, quand bien même la mise en œuvre de son propre droit national conduirait à une solution différente[47]

45 Décision-cadre 2006/783/JAI du Conseil du 6 octobre 2006 relative à l'application du principe de reconnaissance mutuelle aux décisions de confiscation [2006] JO L328/59.

46 Affaire C-491/10 PPU *Joseba Andoni Aguirre Zarraga c. Simone Pelz* EU:C:2010:828, para 70.

47 *Gözütok* (n 39), para 33.

la Cour précisant que:

> [C]ette interprétation (...) s'impose d'autant plus qu'elle est la seule à faire prévaloir l'objet et le but de [l'article 54 CAAS sur le principe ne bis in idem] sur des aspects de procédure ou de pure forme, au demeurant variables selon les États membres concernés, et à garantir une application utile dudit principe.[48]

Dans les affaires *Radu* et *Melloni*, la CJUE a rappelé que le système simplifié du mandat d'arrêt européen 'tend (...) à faciliter et à accélérer la coopération judiciaire en vue de contribuer à réaliser l'objectif assigné à l'Union de devenir un espace de liberté, de sécurité et de justice en se fondant sur le degré de confiance élevé qui doit exister entre les États membres'.[49]

Dans le domaine de l'asile, la Cour a jugé dans l'affaire *NS* que:

> [L]e système européen commun d'asile (...) a été conçu dans un contexte permettant de supposer que l'ensemble des États y participant (...) respectent les droits fondamentaux (...) et que les États membres peuvent s'accorder une confiance mutuelle à cet égard. C'est précisément en raison de ce principe de confiance mutuelle que le législateur de l'Union a adopté le règlement [Dublin II] (...) en vue de rationaliser le traitement des demandes d'asile. Dans ces conditions, il doit être présumé que le traitement réservé aux demandeurs d'asile dans chaque État membre est conforme aux exigences de la charte, à la convention de Genève ainsi qu'à la CEDH.[50]

Dans ce dernier arrêt il est question à la fois de confiance mutuelle et de présomption de respect par les États membres des droits fondamentaux.

5.2 *Les motifs de non-exécution*

Dans les trois domaines de la coopération judiciaire civile et pénale ou de l'asile évoqués plus haut, les instruments de droit secondaire qui organisent

---

48 Ibid, para 35.

49 Affaire C – 396/11 *Ciprian Vasile Radu* EU:C:2013:39, para 34; Affaire C-399/11 *Stefano Melloni contre Ministerio Fiscal* EU:C:2013:107, para 37. La Cour reprend le vocabulaire utilisé au considérant 10 de la décision-cadre.

50 Affaires jointes C-411/10 et C-493/10 *N.S. (C-411/10) c. Secretary of State for the Home Department et M.E. et autres (C-493/10) c. Refugee Applications Commissioner et Minister for Justice, Equality and Law Reform* EU:C:2011:865, paras 78–80.

la coopération prévoient eux-mêmes des normes de fonctionnement qui dans une certaine mesure rapprochent les normes nationales. Ils précisent comment l'autorité compétente pour adopter la décision dans l'État d'origine doit procéder et comment devra procéder celle qui devra l'exécuter dans l'État d'exécution, y compris la liste des motifs de non-exécution qu'elle pourra utiliser, l'autorité d'origine étant celle qui doit s'assurer du respect des droits fondamentaux et des grands principes de droit. Certains de ces instruments de coopération sont accompagnés de mesures d'harmonisation de la procédure ou du droit matériel, renforçant ainsi la confiance entre États et donc la coopération.

L'obligation de reconnaissance mutuelle n'est en réalité jamais absolue,[51] les instruments eux-mêmes prévoient des motifs de non-exécution et des soupapes de sécurité en cas de risque sérieux de violation grave des droits fondamentaux dans un État membre. C'est donc en premier lieu au législateur de l'Union qu'il appartient de réglementer ce type de situations, y compris en prévoyant que l'État membre confronté à un tel problème puisse s'adresser aux institutions de l'Union plutôt que de devoir assumer seul la situation, contraint de recourir à des mesures unilatérales. Comme dans le cas de l'interdiction d'appliquer le principe de réciprocité et de se faire justice soi-même, c'est en utilisant les outils de contrôle et de sanctions prévus par l'ordre juridique de l'Union qu'il convient avant tout de traiter les problèmes.

Dans le domaine de la coopération judiciaire civile, les instruments de reconnaissance mutuelle contiennent en général un motif de non-exécution tiré de l'ordre public de l'État d'exécution. Ainsi, l'article 45, paragraphe 1, point a), du règlement Bruxelles I prévoit que 'à la demande de toute partie intéressée, la reconnaissance d'une décision est refusée (…) si la reconnaissance est manifestement contraire à l'ordre public de l'État membre requis; (…)'.[52] De même, l'article 26 du règlement sur les procédures d'insolvabilité prévoit que:

> Tout Etat membre peut refuser de reconnaître une procédure d'insolvabilité ouverte dans un autre Etat membre ou d'exécuter une

51 Koen Lenaerts identifie trois limites au principe de reconnaissance mutuelle: l'application du principe de proportionnalité (par l'autorité d'émission, pas par celle d'exécution); l'utilisation par l'Etat membre de sa marge d'appréciation dans la transposition et l'application des motifs de non-exécution prévus par la législation de l'Union; et l'application de la clause d'ordre public (national ou européen) (Lenaerts (n 38)).

52 Règlement (UE) 1215/2012 du Parlement européen et du Conseil du 12 décembre 2012 concernant la compétence judiciaire, la reconnaissance et l'exécution des décisions en matière civile et commerciale (Bruxelles I) [2012] JO L351/1.

> décision prise dans le cadre d'une telle procédure, lorsque cette reconnaissance ou cette exécution produirait des effets manifestement contraires à son ordre public, en particulier à ses principes fondamentaux ou aux droits et aux libertés individuelles garantis par sa constitution.[53]

L'article 23, point a), du règlement Bruxelles IIbis prévoit que 'une décision rendue en matière de responsabilité parentale n'est pas reconnue (...) si la reconnaissance est manifestement contraire à l'ordre public de l'État membre requis eu égard aux intérêts supérieurs de l'enfant'.[54]

S'agissant d'un motif permettant de ne pas donner suite à une reconnaissance normalement obligatoire aux termes du droit secondaire, la CJUE a interprété strictement ce motif d'ordre public, le réservant à des cas exceptionnels. Ainsi, dans l'arrêt *Krombach* qui concernait une affaire où M. Krombach résidant en Allemagne avait été reconnu coupable par défaut en France, sans avoir pu se faire représenter, d'avoir tué une jeune fille et avait été condamné à verser des dommages et intérêts au père de la jeune fille, la Cour a jugé que:

> [S]i le but de [la convention de Bruxelles I] est d'assurer la simplification des formalités auxquelles sont subordonnées la reconnaissance et l'exécution réciproques des décisions judiciaires, cet objectif ne saurait toutefois être atteint en affaiblissant les droits de la défense (...). Il découle de cette évolution jurisprudentielle que le recours à la clause de l'ordre public doit être considéré comme étant possible dans les cas exceptionnels où les garanties inscrites dans la législation de l'État d'origine et dans la convention elle-même n'ont pas suffi à protéger le défendeur d'une violation manifeste de son droit de se défendre devant le juge d'origine, tel que reconnu par la CEDH.[55]

---

53 Règlement (CE) 1346/2000 du Conseil du 29 mai 2000 relatif aux procédures d'insolvabilité [2000] JO L160/1.

54 Règlement (CE) 2201/2003 du Conseil du 27 novembre 2003 relatif à la compétence, la reconnaissance et l'exécution des décisions en matière matrimoniale et en matière de responsabilité parentale, abrogeant le règlement (CE) 1347/2000 (Bruxelles IIbis) [2003] JO L338/29.

55 Affaire C-7/98 *Dieter Krombach c. André Bamberski* EU:C:2000:164, paras 43–44. Cette affaire a connu une suite dramatique, le père de la jeune fille allant jusqu'à faire enlever en 2009 M. Krombach, qui avait bénéficié d'un non-lieu en Allemagne, pour qu'il soit jugé en France, ce qui a été fait en 2012, la justice française l'ayant condamné à 15 ans de réclusion. Le père de la jeune fille a été condamné en 2014 pour enlèvement à un an avec sursis.

Plus récemment, dans l'affaire *Diageo Brands*, la Cour a précisé sa pensée en jugeant que:

> [U]n recours à la clause de l'ordre public (...) n'est concevable que dans l'hypothèse où la reconnaissance de la décision rendue dans un autre État membre heurterait de manière inacceptable l'ordre juridique de l'État requis, en tant qu'elle porterait atteinte à un principe fondamental. Afin de respecter la prohibition de la révision au fond de la décision rendue dans un autre État membre, l'atteinte devrait constituer une violation manifeste d'une règle de droit considérée comme essentielle dans l'ordre juridique de l'État requis ou d'un droit reconnu comme fondamental dans cet ordre juridique.[56]

Les instruments de coopération pénale ne contiennent pas de motifs de non-exécution tirés de l'ordre public. Ils contiennent le plus souvent une clause générale spécifiant que l'instrument 'ne saurait avoir pour effet de modifier l'obligation de respecter les droits fondamentaux et les principes juridiques fondamentaux tels qu'ils sont consacrés par l'article 6 du [TUE]'.[57] En outre, ils énumèrent en général des motifs de non-exécution classiques tels que le principe ne bis in idem,[58] cette énumération étant limitative. En outre, leurs considérants contiennent des indications sur les circonstances exceptionnelles qui pourraient donner lieu à un refus d'exécuter fondé sur le respect des droits fondamentaux. Par exemple, le considérant 10 de la décision-cadre sur le mandat d'arrêt européen explique, dans sa deuxième phrase, que la mise en œuvre du mécanisme du mandat d'arrêt européen ne pourrait être suspendue qu'en cas de constatation par le Conseil d'une situation au titre de l'article 7 TUE

56 Affaire C-681/13 *Diageo Brands BV contre Simiramida-04 EOOD* EU:C:2015:471, para 44.

57 Voir par exemple décision-cadre 2002/584/JAI du Conseil du 13 juin 2002 relative au mandat d'arrêt européen et aux procédures de remise entre États membres [2002] JO L190/1 (décision-cadre MAE), art 1, para 3. Voir aussi décision-cadre 2005/214/JAI du Conseil du 24 février 2005 concernant l'application du principe de reconnaissance mutuelle aux sanctions pécuniaires [2005] JO L76/16, art 3; décision-cadre 2006/783/JAI du Conseil du 6 octobre 2006 relative à l'application du principe de reconnaissance mutuelle aux décisions de confiscation [2006] JO L328/59, art 1, para 2; décision-cadre 2008/909/JAI du Conseil du 27 novembre 2008 concernant l'application du principe de reconnaissance mutuelle aux jugements en matière pénale prononçant des peines ou des mesures privatives de liberté aux fins de leur exécution dans l'Union européenne [2008] JO L327/27 (décision-cadre transfèrement des prisonniers), art 3, para 4.

58 Voir par exemple décision-cadre MAE, arts 3, 4 et 4bis.

(violation grave et persistante des valeurs de l'Union). Le considérant 12 explique en outre que la remise d'une personne peut être refusée:

> s'il y a des raisons de croire, sur la base d'éléments objectifs, que [le mandat d'arrêt] a été émis dans le but de poursuivre ou de punir une personne en raison de son sexe, de sa race, de sa religion, de son origine ethnique, de sa nationalité, de sa langue, de ses opinions politiques ou de son orientation sexuelle, ou qu'il peut être porté atteinte à la situation de cette personne pour l'une de ces raisons.
>
> La (…) décision-cadre n'empêche pas un État membre d'appliquer ses règles constitutionnelles relatives au respect du droit à un procès équitable, à la liberté d'association, à la liberté de la presse et à la liberté d'expression dans d'autres médias.[59]

Enfin, le considérant 13 rappelle que 'nul ne devrait être éloigné, expulsé ou extradé vers un État où il existe un risque sérieux qu'il soit soumis à la peine de mort, à la torture ou à d'autres peines ou traitements inhumains ou dégradants', reprenant ainsi le texte du paragraphe 2 de l'article 19 de la Charte des droits fondamentaux de l'Union européenne (la Charte).

Dans l'affaire *Melloni*, dans laquelle la Cour constitutionnelle espagnole demandait si, à titre de motif de non-exécution d'un jugement italien prononcé par défaut, elle pouvait appliquer le standard espagnol plus élevé que celui harmonisé par l'article 4bis de la décision-cadre sur le mandat d'arrêt européen, la CJUE a jugé que:

> [L'article 4bis] vise à *remédier aux difficultés de la reconnaissance mutuelle des décisions rendues en l'absence* de la personne concernée à son procès *résultant de l'existence, dans les États membres, de différences dans la protection des droits fondamentaux*. À cet effet, *cette décision-cadre procède à une harmonisation des conditions d'exécution d'un mandat d'arrêt européen en cas de condamnation par défaut*, qui reflète le consensus auquel

---

59 Un texte similaire est repris dans plusieurs instruments de coopération pénale. Voir par exemple décision-cadre transfèrement des prisonniers (n 57), considérants 13 et 14; décision-cadre 2008/947/JAI du Conseil du 27 novembre 2008 concernant l'application du principe de reconnaissance mutuelle aux jugements et aux décisions de probation aux fins de la surveillance des mesures de probation et des peines de substitution [2008] JO L337/102, considérants 5 et 6; décision-cadre 2009/829/JAI du Conseil du 23 octobre 2009 concernant l'application, entre les États membres de l'Union européenne, du principe de reconnaissance mutuelle aux décisions relatives à des mesures de contrôle en tant qu'alternative à la détention provisoire [2009] JO L294/20, considérants 16 et 17.

> sont parvenus les États membres dans leur ensemble au sujet de la portée qu'il convient de donner, au titre du droit de l'Union, aux droits procéduraux dont bénéficient les personnes condamnées par défaut qui font l'objet d'un mandat d'arrêt européen. (...) Par conséquent, permettre à un État membre de se prévaloir de l'article 53 de la Charte pour subordonner la remise d'une personne condamnée par défaut à la condition, non prévue par la décision-cadre (...), que la condamnation puisse être révisée dans l'État membre d'émission, afin d'éviter qu'une atteinte soit portée au droit à un procès équitable et aux droits de la défense garantis par la Constitution de l'État membre d'exécution, aboutirait, en *remettant en cause l'uniformité du standard de protection des droits fondamentaux défini par cette décision-cadre, à porter atteinte aux principes de confiance et de reconnaissance mutuelles que celle-ci tend à conforter et, partant, à compromettre l'effectivité de ladite décision-cadre.*[60]

Dans cet arrêt, la CJUE applique donc strictement le caractère limitatif de la liste des motifs de non-exécution, en refusant de donner suite à l'argumentation fondée sur l'article 53 de la Charte qui se référait aussi, indirectement, au considérant 12 de la décision-cadre relatif aux règles constitutionnelles des États membres sur le droit à un procès équitable. Cependant, il est intéressant de noter, en référence au débat sur l'harmonisation des règles de procédure pénale susceptible de faciliter la confiance et la reconnaissance mutuelle, que le refus de la Cour d'accepter l'application d'un standard national plus élevé se fonde surtout sur un raisonnement tout à fait classique tiré de la primauté du standard harmonisé européen établi par l'article 4bis de la décision-cadre, dans la droite ligne d'un raisonnement du type *Bauhuis* ou *Tennah-Durez* dans le domaine du marché intérieur (voir plus haut).[61]

D'ailleurs, dans l'optique 'de renforcer la confiance mutuelle au sein de l'Union européenne' et donc d'améliorer la reconnaissance mutuelle des décisions en matière pénale, le Conseil avait décidé en 2009 d'adopter une série de mesures d'harmonisation des droits procéduraux, en complément de la Convention européenne des droits de l'homme (CEDH), laquelle 'dans l'Union

---

60 *Melloni* (n 49), para 62 (c'est nous qui soulignons).

61 Cela est d'ailleurs conforme à l'art 53 de la Charte qui, lorsqu'il permet des différences de niveau de protection y compris par les constitutions nationales par rapport au droit de l'Union, le fait en spécifiant que cela s'applique 'dans leur champ d'application respectif', c'est-à-dire que si le droit de l'Union a fixé un standard de protection, les Etats membres sont tenus de le respecter et ne peuvent lui opposer leur standard national éventuellement plus élevé.

européenne (…) constitue la base commune de la protection des droits des suspects et des personnes poursuivies dans le cadre des procédures pénales' et qui 'telle qu'interprétée par la Cour européenne des droits de l'homme, constitue un fondement important permettant aux États membres de nourrir et de renforcer la confiance réciproque dans leurs systèmes judiciaires pénaux'.[62] Le Conseil adopta donc une résolution énumérant six mesures d'harmonisation à adopter rapidement.[63] Toutes ont été adoptées, la dernière en octobre 2016.

L'affaire *NS* en 2011,[64] comme l'arrêt de la Cour européenne des droits de l'homme (Cour EDH) dans l'affaire *MSS* quelques mois plus tôt,[65] a eu des conséquences importantes sur la rédaction des instruments de coopération qui sont intervenus par la suite, qu'il s'agisse bien entendu du règlement Dublin III adopté en 2013,[66] mais également de la directive sur la décision d'enquête européenne en matière pénale adoptée en 2014.[67] Dans l'affaire *NS*, la CJUE, constatant que le système d'asile pouvait 'rencontre[r], en pratique, des difficultés majeures de fonctionnement dans un État membre déterminé, de sorte qu'il existe un risque sérieux que des demandeurs d'asile soient, en cas de transfert vers cet État membre, traités d'une manière incompatible avec leurs droits fondamentaux',[68] a cependant exclu 'que la moindre violation des [trois directives d'harmonisation en matière d'asile] suffise à empêcher tout transfert

---

62 Résolution du Conseil du 30 novembre 2009 relative à la feuille de route visant à renforcer les droits procéduraux des suspects ou des personnes poursuivies dans le cadre des procédures pénales [2009] JO C295/1, considérants 1, 2 et 8.

63 Ibid. La liste des mesures concernait la traduction et l'interprétation (directive 2010/64 du 20 octobre 2010 [2010] JO L280/1); l'information sur les droits et les charges retenues (directive 2012/13 du 22 mai 2012 [2012] JO L142/1); l'accès à l'avocat et le droit de communiquer avec les tiers et les autorités consulaires (directive 2013/48 du 22 octobre 2013 [2013] JO L294/1); la présomption d'innocence (directive 2016/343 du 9 mars 2016 [2016] JO L65/1); les droits des mineurs (directive 2016/800 du 11 mai 2016 [2016] JO L132/1); et l'aide juridictionnelle (directive 2016/1919 du 26 octobre 2016 [2016] JO L297/1). La Commission a aussi adopté le 27 novembre 2013 une recommandation sur les droits des personnes vulnérables ([2013] JO C378/8).

64 *NS* (n 50), paras 81–100.

65 *M.S.S. c. Belgique et Grèce* Req n°30696/09 (Cour EDH, 21 janvier 2011).

66 Règlement (UE) 604/2013 du Parlement européen et du Conseil du 26 juin 2013 établissant les critères et mécanismes de détermination de l'État membre responsable de l'examen d'une demande de protection internationale introduite dans l'un des États membres par un ressortissant de pays tiers ou un apatride (règlement Dublin III) [2013] JO L180/31.

67 Directive 2014/41/UE du Parlement européen et du Conseil du 3 avril 2014 concernant la décision d'enquête européenne en matière pénale [2014] JO L130/1.

68 *NS* (n 50), para 81.

d'un demandeur d'asile vers l'État membre normalement compétent',[69] parce que cela reviendrait à ajouter au règlement Dublin II un critère supplémentaire d'exclusion et a permettre à l'État membre normalement compétent de s'exonérer de ses obligations au titre du règlement,[70] remettant ainsi en cause 'la raison d'être de l'Union et de la réalisation de l'espace de liberté, de sécurité et de justice'.[71]

La Cour a néanmoins admis que:

> [D]ans l'hypothèse où il y aurait lieu de craindre sérieusement qu'il existe des défaillances systémiques de la procédure d'asile et des conditions d'accueil des demandeurs d'asile dans l'État membre responsable, impliquant un traitement inhumain ou dégradant, au sens de l'article 4 de la charte, des demandeurs d'asile transférés vers le territoire de cet État membre, ce transfert serait incompatible avec ladite disposition.[72]

Dans une telle situation, lorsque les autres États membres

> ne peuvent ignorer que les défaillances systémiques de la procédure d'asile et des conditions d'accueil des demandeurs d'asile dans [l'État membre normalement responsable] constituent des motifs sérieux et avérés de croire que le demandeur courra un risque réel d'être soumis à des traitements inhumains ou dégradants au sens de l'article 4 de la charte[73]

ils sont obligés de ne pas transférer le demandeur d'asile vers cet État membre, et ce afin de permettre à l'Union et à ses États membres de respecter leurs obligations relatives à la protection des droits fondamentaux des demandeurs d'asile. La Cour en conclut que:

> [Une] application du règlement [Dublin II] sur la base d'une présomption irréfragable que les droits fondamentaux du demandeur d'asile seront respectés dans l'État membre normalement compétent pour connaître de sa demande est incompatible avec l'obligation des États membres d'interpréter et d'appliquer le règlement [Dublin II] d'une

---

69 Ibid, para 84.

70 Ibid, para 85.

71 Ibid, para 83.

72 Ibid, para 86.

73 Ibid, para 94.

manière conforme aux droits fondamentaux. (…) si le règlement [Dublin II] imposait une présomption irréfragable de respect des droits fondamentaux, il pourrait lui-même être considéré comme remettant en cause les garanties visant à la protection et au respect des droits fondamentaux par l'Union et par ses États membres.[74]

On rappellera que le régime commun d'asile de l'Union européenne est fondé sur trois directives qui harmonisent les législations des États membres sur la procédure d'asile,[75] les motifs d'octroi de l'asile[76] et les conditions d'accueil[77] ainsi que sur le système, dit de Dublin, de désignation de l'État membre responsable de l'examen des demandes d'asile,[78] accompagné de la base de donnée Eurodac où sont enregistrées les données des demandeurs d'asile et des personnes entrées illégalement.[79] Les directives ont donc fixé le standard de protection du droit d'asile dans l'Union. Le non-respect par un État membre de ce standard devrait être sanctionné par la voie ordinaire dans l'ordre juridique de l'Union qu'est l'action en manquement.[80]

74 Ibid, paras 99 et 100.

75 Directive 2013/32/UE du Parlement européen et du Conseil du 26 juin 2013 relative à des procédures communes pour l'octroi et le retrait de la protection internationale (directive procédures) [2013] JO L180/60.

76 Directive 2011/95/UE du Parlement européen et du Conseil du 13 décembre 2011 concernant les normes relatives aux conditions que doivent remplir les ressortissants des pays tiers ou les apatrides pour pouvoir bénéficier d'une protection internationale, à un statut uniforme pour les réfugiés ou les personnes pouvant bénéficier de la protection subsidiaire, et au contenu de cette protection (directive qualification) [2011] JO L337/9.

77 Directive 2013/33/UE du Parlement européen et du Conseil du 26 juin 2013 établissant des normes pour l'accueil des personnes demandant la protection internationale (directive accueil) [2013] JO L180/96.

78 Règlement Dublin III (n 66).

79 Règlement (UE) 603/2013 du Parlement européen et du Conseil du 26 juin 2013 (règlement Eurodac) [2013] JO L180/1.

80 En raison de la gravité de la crise des réfugiés en 2015 et 2016, reconnaissant que le régime commun d'asile 'présent[e] d'importantes faiblesses et lacunes structurelles, que la crise à mises en évidence' et que 'les règles de l'UE [en la matière] ont été de moins en moins respectées', la Commission a proposé de réformer, cette fois en profondeur, tant le système de Dublin – en y insérant un mécanisme de répartition automatique des demandeurs d'asile en cas d'afflux massif – que les trois directives d'harmonisation, pour en augmenter l'intensité (Commission, 'Vers une réforme du régime d'asile européen commun et une amélioration des voies d'entrée légale en Europe' (Communication) COM (2016) 197 final). La Commission a donc présenté deux séries de propositions: la première série le 4 mai 2016 concernant Dublin (IV), Eurodac et l'agence de l'UE pour l'asile et la seconde

Cependant, en cas de situation très grave, parce qu'il s'agit des droits fondamentaux des personnes, et en particulier de ceux relatifs à la dignité humaine, le règlement Dublin ne peut pas être interprété et appliqué d'une manière qui serait contraire à ces droits fondamentaux. Les États membres sont certes présumés respecter le standard fixé par les directives et la Charte, mais cette présomption ne peut pas être irréfragable, car si elle l'était, non seulement les États membres mais aussi l'Union, auteur du règlement Dublin, violeraient la Charte.[81]

Depuis l'arrêt *NS*, le règlement Dublin III prévoit à la fois une disposition qui modifie les critères de responsabilité pour l'examen de la demande d'asile en obligeant l'État membre qui s'apprêtait à renvoyer un demandeur d'asile vers un autre État membre à ne pas le faire lorsque 'il y a de sérieuses raisons de croire qu'il existe dans cet État membre des défaillances systémiques dans la procédure d'asile et les conditions d'accueil des demandeurs, qui entraînent un risque de traitement inhumain ou dégradant au sens de l'article 4 de la charte (…)' (article 3, paragraphe 2, deuxième alinéa) et un mécanisme d'alerte rapide, de préparation et de gestion de crise, lorsque 'l'application du [règlement Dublin III] peut être compromise soit en raison d'un risque sérieux de pression particulière exercée sur le régime d'asile d'un État membre et/ou en raison de problèmes de fonctionnement du régime d'asile d'un État membre', avec élaboration d'un plan d'action préventif ou d'un plan d'action de gestion de crise (article 33).[82]

Quant à la directive sur la décision d'enquête européenne, son considérant 19 explique que:

série le 13 juillet 2016 concernant le remplacement des deux directives sur la procédure et les conditions d'octroi par deux règlements, la refonte de la directive sur les conditions d'accueil et une proposition de cadre pour la réinstallation directe depuis les pays tiers.

81 Koen Lenaerts voit dans cette obligation de ne pas appliquer un instrument de coopération un (nouveau) motif de non-exécution tiré de l'ordre public non pas national mais européen, une 'European public-policy exception' (Lenaerts (n 38)).

82 Règlement Dublin III (n 66). Le considérant 21 se lit comme suit: 'Les défaillances ou l'effondrement des régimes d'asile, souvent aggravés ou favorisés par les pressions particulières dont ils font l'objet, peuvent compromettre le bon fonctionnement du régime mis en place au titre du présent règlement, ce qui pourrait entraîner un risque de violation des droits des demandeurs énoncés dans l'acquis de l'Union en matière d'asile et dans la charte (…), d'autres droits internationaux de l'homme et des réfugiés'. On pourra regretter l'erreur de plume dans l'utilisation des mots 'autres droits internationaux' qui donne l'impression que les droits tirés des directives sur l'asile et de la Charte sont du droit international!

> [L]a création d'un espace de liberté, de sécurité et de justice dans l'Union est fondée sur la confiance mutuelle et *la présomption que les autres États membres respectent le droit de l'Union* et, en particulier, les droits fondamentaux. *Cette présomption est toutefois réfragable.* Par conséquent, *s'il existe des motifs sérieux de croire que l'exécution d'une mesure* d'enquête indiquée dans la décision d'enquête européenne *porterait atteinte à un droit fondamental de la personne concernée* et que l'État d'exécution méconnaîtrait ses obligations concernant la protection des droits fondamentaux reconnus dans la charte, *l'exécution* de la décision d'enquête européenne *devrait être refusée.*[83]

Son (article 11, paragraphe 1, point f)), prévoit parmi les motifs de non-reconnaissance ou de non-exécution, le motif suivant: 'il existe des motifs sérieux de croire que l'exécution de la mesure d'enquête indiquée dans la décision d'enquête européenne serait incompatible avec les obligations de l'État d'exécution conformément à l'article 6 du traité sur l'Union européenne et à la charte'.[84]

Depuis l'arrêt *NS* et l'avis 2/13, la CJUE a systématisé son raisonnement, en avril 2016, dans une affaire *Aranyosi* qui concernait un mandat d'arrêt contre l'exécution duquel étaient invoquées les conditions gravement défaillantes de détention auxquelles la personne risquerait d'être soumise dans l'État membre d'émission.[85] Après avoir rappelé sa jurisprudence sur la reconnaissance

83 Directive 2014/41/UE du Parlement européen et du Conseil du 3 avril 2014 concernant la décision d'enquête européenne en matière pénale [2014] JO L130/1 (c'est nous qui soulignons).

84 Ce nouveau motif de non-exécution, qui ne figurait pas dans le texte de l'initiative soumise par les sept Etats membres, a été ajouté au cours des travaux, à la demande du Parlement européen. Une autre nouveauté, par rapport aux instruments précédents, tel le mandat d'arrêt européen, est que la directive prévoit parmi les conditions à respecter par l'État d'émission la vérification que 'l'émission de la décision d'enquête européenne est nécessaire et proportionnée aux finalités des procédures visées à l'article 4, compte tenu des droits du suspect ou de la personne poursuivie' (art 6, para 1, point a), condition de proportionnalité qui ne sera donc pas vérifiée par l'Etat d'exécution.

85 Affaires jointes C-404/15 et C-659/15 PPU *Pál Aranyosi et Robert Căldăraru* EU:C:2016:198. La juridiction allemande a posé le 12 septembre 2016 des questions préjudicielles supplémentaires dans une nouvelle affaire *Aranyosi* (C-496/16). Claus Dieter Classen, dans son article 'Confiance mutuelle et identité constitutionnelle nationale – Quel avenir dans l'espace juridique européen ? A propos de la décision de la Cour constitutionnelle allemande sur le mandat d'arrêt européen du 15 décembre 2015', explique l'arrêt Aranyosi de la CJUE comme une réaction à l'arrêt de la Cour constitutionnelle allemande ([2016] Cah. dr. eur. 667).

mutuelle qui fonde le système du mandat d'arrêt lequel repose sur la confiance mutuelle,[86] la Cour, interprétant l'article 1, paragraphe 3, de la décision-cadre selon lequel celle-ci ne modifie pas l'obligation de respecter les droits fondamentaux, souligne que l'interdiction des peines ou des traitements inhumains ou dégradants prévue à l'article 4 de la Charte – qui correspond à l'article 3 de la CEDH – 'revêt un caractère absolu', aucune dérogation à cette interdiction n'étant possible, conformément à l'article 15, paragraphe 2, de la CEDH.[87] Or:

> Les articles 1er et 4 de la Charte ainsi que l'article 3 de la CEDH consacrent l'une des valeurs fondamentales de l'Union et de ses États membres. C'est la raison pour laquelle, en toutes circonstances, y compris dans le cas de la lutte contre le terrorisme et le crime organisé, la CEDH interdit en termes absolus la torture et les peines et traitements inhumains ou dégradants, quel que soit le comportement de la personne concernée.[88]

Par conséquent:

> [L]orsque l'autorité judiciaire de l'Etat membre d'exécution dispose d'éléments attestant d'un risque réel de traitement inhumain ou dégradant des personnes détenues dans l'État membre d'émission, à l'aune du standard de protection des droits fondamentaux garanti par le droit de l'Union et, en particulier, de l'article 4 de la Charte (…), elle est tenue d'apprécier l'existence de ce risque lorsqu'elle doit décider de la remise aux autorités de l'État membre d'émission de la personne concernée par un mandat d'arrêt européen. En effet, l'exécution d'un tel mandat ne saurait conduire à un traitement inhumain ou dégradant de cette personne.[89]

La Cour explique ensuite que l'autorité compétence doit procéder en deux étapes:

- d'abord examiner s'il existe un risque réel de traitement inhumain et dégradant en raison des conditions générales de détention dans l'État membre d'émission, en 'se [fondant] sur des éléments objectifs, fiables, précis et dûment actualisés sur les conditions de détention qui prévalent dans

---

86 Affaires jointes C-404/15 et C-659/15 PPU (n 85), paras 76–79.

87 Ibid, paras 85–86.

88 Ibid, para 87.

89 Ibid, para 88.

l'État membre d'émission et démontrant la réalité de défaillances soit systémiques ou généralisées, soit touchant certains groupes de personnes, soit encore certains centres de détention';[90]

– puis, une fois constatée l'existence d'un tel risque, 'apprécie[r], de manière concrète et précise, s'il existe des motifs sérieux et avérés de croire que la personne concernée courra ce risque en raison des conditions de sa détention envisagées dans l'État membre d'émission', parce que la seule existence d'éléments témoignant de telles défaillances n'implique pas nécessairement que la personne dans le cas concret sera soumise à des traitements interdits.[91] Pour procéder à cette vérification, l'autorité compétente doit, conformément à la décision-cadre, demander à l'autorité judiciaire de l'État membre d'émission la fourniture urgente de toute information complémentaire, y compris sur l'existence d'éventuels mécanismes de contrôle des établissements pénitentiaires.[92]

Ce raisonnement est similaire à celui suivi par la Cour européenne des droits de l'homme dans l'arrêt *M.S.S.* puis dans l'arrêt *Tarakhel*[93] dans lesquels la Cour EDH avait aussi procédé en deux étapes (d'abord l'examen de la situation générale dans l'État concerné et ensuite l'examen du cas individuel): 'la Cour estime devoir suivre une approche similaire à celle qu'elle avait adoptée dans l'arrêt M.S.S. (…), où elle avait examiné la situation individuelle du requérant à la lumière de la situation générale existant en Grèce à l'époque des faits'.[94]

Dans l'arrêt *Tarakhel*, elle avait expliqué que le caractère systémique des défaillances n'était pas le seul motif de renversement de la présomption de respect des droits:

---

90 Ibid, para 89.

91 Ibid, paras 91–93.

92 Ibid, paras 94–96.

93 *Tarakhel c. Suisse* Req n°29217/12 (Cour EDH, 4 novembre 2014). Bien entendu, du fait de leurs rôles différents, la Cour EDH se prononçait elle-même sur le fond de l'affaire, à savoir si dans le cas d'espèce l'Etat concerné avait ou non violé la CEDH, alors que la CJUE, dans l'affaire *Aranyosi*, répondait à une question préjudicielle en interprétation posée par un juge national – appelé à se prononcer sur le fond – auquel elle a donné la marche à suivre pour respecter à la fois son obligation d'appliquer la décision-cadre en exécutant un mandat d'arrêt (primauté du droit de l'Union) et son obligation de respecter la Charte dans cette mise en œuvre du droit de l'Union (art 51, para 1, de la Charte; obligation de droit primaire).

94 *Tarakhel c. Suisse* Req n°29217/12 (Cour EDH, 4 novembre 2014), para 101.

> L'origine du risque encouru ne modifie en rien le niveau de protection garanti par la Convention et les obligations que celle-ci impose à l'État auteur de la mesure de renvoi. Elle ne dispense pas cet État d'examiner de manière approfondie et individualisée la situation de la personne objet de la mesure et de surseoir au renvoi au cas où le risque de traitements inhumains ou dégradants serait avéré. (…) la Cour doit donc rechercher si, au vu de la situation générale du dispositif d'accueil des demandeurs d'asile en Italie et de la situation particulière des requérants, il existe des motifs sérieux et avérés de croire qu'en cas de renvoi vers l'Italie les requérants risqueraient de subir des traitements contraires à l'article 3.[95]

Le mieux serait évidemment de prévenir de tels problèmes, par exemple en développant le rôle des réseaux de points de contact et de coopération directe entre autorités, ainsi que le rôle des agences qui permettent de créer des liens entre les autorités compétentes des États membres dans les domaines judiciaire (Eurojust), policier (Europol et Cepol), de l'asile (EASO) et de la gestion des frontières extérieures (Frontex) et en ciblant mieux les programmes de financement européens dans le domaine de la justice et des affaires intérieures.

Mais surtout, il conviendrait d'établir un système efficace d'évaluation mutuelle couvrant, comme le permet l'article 70 TFUE, la mise en œuvre de toutes les politiques et de l'acquis du titre V, et pas seulement de l'acquis de Schengen.[96] On ne peut en effet que regretter que la Commission n'ait pas (encore) proposé de remplacer le très ancien mécanisme d'évaluation mutuelle dans la coopération judiciaire pénale[97] par un nouveau système, ni proposé

95 Ibid, paras 104–105. La Cour européenne des droits de l'homme se réfère à l'approche suivie par la Cour suprême du Royaume-Uni qui avait 'considéré qu'indépendamment de l'existence ou non de "défaillances systémiques" dans le système d'accueil des demandeurs d'asile (…) [il faut] procéder à un examen au cas par cas du risque que les requérants fussent soumis à des traitements contraires à la Convention en cas de renvoi (…)' (para 54).

96 Voir règlement (UE) 1053/2013 du Conseil du 7 octobre 2013 portant création d'un mécanisme d'évaluation et de contrôle destiné à vérifier l'application de l'acquis de Schengen et abrogeant la décision du comité exécutif du 16 septembre 1998 concernant la création d'une commission permanente d'évaluation et d'application de Schengen [2013] JO L295/27, adopté sur la base de l'art 70 TFUE, qui a remplacé l'ancien système d'évaluation mutuelle qui datait de l'époque où Schengen existait en dehors des traités.

97 Voir action commune 97/827/JAI du 5 décembre 1997 instaurant un mécanisme d'évaluation de l'application et de la mise en œuvre au plan national des engagements internationaux en matière de lutte contre la criminalité organisée [1997] JO L344/7. La Commission n'a pas manifesté un grand intérêt à utiliser l'art 70 comme base juridique,

d'utiliser les potentialités de l'article 70 TFUE en instaurant un mécanisme d'évaluation dans les autres domaines du titre V tels que l'asile, l'immigration, la coopération judiciaire civile ou la coopération policière. En ces temps où la confiance mutuelle tant vantée est durement mise à l'épreuve, un instrument d'évaluation mutuelle par les pairs où les experts des États membres, praticiens du domaine en question, évaluent leurs voisins et partenaires et vice versa ne peut que contribuer à 'favoriser la pleine application du principe de reconnaissance mutuelle', comme le demande l'article 70 TFUE. On a vu plus haut que l'une des faiblesses de l'ancien troisième pilier était l'absence pendant 20 ans de mesures de contrôle sérieuses, il est temps de rattraper le temps perdu, avec intelligence.

6 Epilogue

La confusion de raisonnement dans laquelle semblaient être tombés les rédacteurs du traité constitutionnel, lorsqu'ils entendaient favoriser la confiance mutuelle sur la base de la reconnaissance mutuelle, illustre la difficulté qu'il y a à manier ce concept de confiance entre États, surtout lorsqu'on pousse le raisonnement jusqu'à en faire un principe et même une obligation de confiance mutuelle, au point de frôler l'oxymore, alors qu'on sent bien que c'est en grande partie un substitut, une sorte de placebo, un acte de foi pour tenter de combler un manque, manque à la fois d'harmonisation mais aussi, et peut

l'une des raisons étant, vraisemblablement, que cet article ne prévoit pas la codécision, ce qui le rend en quelque sorte illégitime aux yeux de certains au Parlement européen. De plus, pendant les négociations du traité constitutionnel, puis du traité de Lisbonne, la Commission considérait avec suspicion ce mécanisme d'évaluation mutuelle qu'elle percevait comme une scorie du temps intergouvernemental et un concurrent potentiel de ses pouvoirs en manquement. C'est pourtant une méthode qui a fait ses preuves au Conseil de l'Europe, précurseur de la coopération pénale plus étroite en Europe, dans un domaine de souveraineté où les contacts réguliers entre praticiens sont de nature à améliorer la coopération. Ainsi par exemple le groupe d'experts sur l'évaluation des mesures de lutte contre le blanchiment des capitaux (MONEYVAL) ou le Groupe d'Etats contre la Corruption (GRECO), mécanisme auquel la Commission, paradoxalement, envisage de faire adhérer l'Union, semblant préférer un contrôle externe, alors qu'elle a (jusqu'ici) négligé l'utilisation de l'art 70 TFUE, qui permettrait un contrôle interne. Sur l'utilité de l'évaluation mutuelle pour améliorer la confiance, voir Roland Genson, 'Une confiance mutuelle qui ne se limite pas au processus de la reconnaissance mutuelle' et Olivier De Schutter, 'La contribution du contrôle juridictionnel à la confiance mutuelle' dans Kerchove et Weyembergh (eds) *La confiance mutuelle dans l'espace pénal européen* (n 34) respectivement 69 et 79.

être surtout, manque de mise en œuvre, d'application correcte et de contrôle, manque d'Union de droit.

Dans son avis 2/13, la CJUE déduit du principe de confiance mutuelle, dont elle nous dit qu'il impose aux États membres de considérer que les autres respectent le droit de l'Union (voir plus haut), une obligation de présomption d'un tel respect. La Cour nous dit que:

> Ainsi, *lorsqu'ils mettent en œuvre le droit de l'Union, les États membres peuvent être tenus, en vertu de ce même droit, de présumer le respect des droits fondamentaux par les autres États membres*, de sorte qu'il ne leur est pas possible non seulement d'exiger d'un autre État membre un niveau de protection national des droits fondamentaux plus élevé que celui assuré par le droit de l'Union, mais également, *sauf dans des cas exceptionnels*, de vérifier si cet autre État membre a effectivement respecté, dans un cas concret, les droits fondamentaux garantis par l'Union.[98]

Un raisonnement par la présomption directement tirée du droit de l'Union, appuyée sur sa primauté, sans qu'il soit nécessaire de passer par la case 'confiance mutuelle', paraît plus solide, moins sujet à malaise. La présomption est un concept bien connu en droit. Réfragable, elle permet d'apporter la preuve contraire. C'est sur une telle présomption (de protection équivalente) qu'est bâti le raisonnement de la Cour européenne des droits de l'homme dans son célèbre arrêt *Bosphorus* dans lequel elle a accepté d'exonérer un État membre de l'Union pour une mesure prise en exécution de ses obligations de droit de l'Union:

> [D]ès lors qu'il est constant que l'organisation en question accorde aux droits fondamentaux (cette notion recouvrant à la fois les garanties substantielles offertes et les mécanismes censés en contrôler le respect) une protection à tout le moins équivalente à celle assurée par la Convention (…) *il y a lieu de présumer qu'un Etat respecte les exigences de la Convention* lorsqu'il ne fait qu'exécuter des obligations juridiques résultant de son adhésion à l'organisation. *Pareille présomption peut toutefois être renversée* dans le cadre d'une affaire donnée si l'on estime que la protection des droits garantis par la Convention était entachée d'une *insuffisance manifeste*.[99]

---

98 *Avis 2/13* (n 1), para 192 (c'est nous qui soulignons).

99 *Bosphorus c. Irlande* Req n°45036/98 (Cour EDH, 30 juin 2005), paras 155–156 (c'est nous qui soulignons).

Dans un arrêt *Avotiņš*[100] concernant une affaire d'application du règlement Bruxelles I, la Cour européenne des droits de l'homme a examiné la récente jurisprudence de la CJUE sur la confiance mutuelle et la reconnaissance mutuelle et a confirmé, à la lumière de cette jurisprudence, le principe et le fonctionnement de la présomption *Bosphorus*, ou présomption de protection équivalente. Elle résume dans cet arrêt sa jurisprudence *Bosphorus*, rappelant que l'application de la présomption de protection équivalente dans l'ordre juridique de l'Union européenne est soumise à deux conditions (absence de marge de manœuvre pour les autorités nationales et déploiement de l'intégralité des potentialités du mécanisme de contrôle), la présomption ne pouvant alors être renversée qu'en cas d'insuffisance manifeste dans la protection des droits fondamentaux.[101]

Alors que dans l'avis 2/13, la CJUE avait placé la barre de ce renversement de présomption au niveau des seuls 'cas exceptionnels', dans l'arrêt *Avotiņš*, la Cour européenne des droits de l'homme insiste pour que la barre du renversement de la présomption *Bosphorus* soit celle de l'insuffisance manifeste. Elle considère que:

> [L]imiter aux seuls cas exceptionnels le contrôle par l'Etat requis du respect des droits fondamentaux par l'Etat d'origine de la décision de justice à reconnaître pourrait, dans des situations concrètes, aller à l'encontre de l'obligation qu'impose la Convention de permettre au moins au juge de l'Etat requis de procéder à un contrôle adapté à la gravité des allégations sérieuses de violation des droits fondamentaux dans l'Etat d'origine afin d'éviter une insuffisance manifeste dans la protection de ces droits.[102]

La Cour européenne des droits de l'homme explique ensuite que, tout en tenant compte, dans un esprit de complémentarité, du mode de fonctionnement des dispositifs du droit de l'Union en matière de reconnaissance mutuelle, et notamment de leur objectif d'efficacité, 'elle doit vérifier que le principe de reconnaissance mutuelle n'est pas appliqué de manière automatique et mécanique (…) au détriment des droits fondamentaux'. Ainsi, lorsque les juridictions des États qui sont à la fois membre de l'Union et de la CEDH sont appelées à appliquer un mécanisme de reconnaissance mutuelle institué par le droit de l'Union, elles ne peuvent donner son plein effet à ce mécanisme qu'en l'absence de toute insuffisance manifeste. En revanche:

---

100 *Avotiņš c. Lettonie* Req n°17502/07 (Cour EDH, 23 mai 2016), paras 101–116.
101 Ibid, paras 101–112.
102 Ibid, para 114.

> [S]'il leur est soumis un grief sérieux et étayé dans le cadre duquel il est allégué que l'on se trouve en présence d'une insuffisance manifeste de protection d'un droit garanti par la Convention et que le droit de l'Union européenne ne permet pas de remédier à cette insuffisance, [les juridictions nationales] ne peuvent renoncer à examiner ce grief au seul motif qu'elles appliquent le droit de l'Union.[103]

Compte tenu de ces clarifications, la meilleure solution est que le législateur de l'Union organise ou encadre la présomption de respect des droits fondamentaux et du droit de l'Union qui devrait s'appliquer entre États membres. Il a d'ailleurs déjà commencé à le faire dans le règlement Dublin III ou la directive sur l'enquête européenne (voir plus haut), et lorsqu'il y a harmonisation sous-jacente, la barre du renversement peut être placée assez haut. La CJUE a placé cette barre de renversement au niveau des 'cas exceptionnels'. La Cour européenne des droits de l'homme a fixé, et confirmé, que la barre était celle d'une 'insuffisance manifeste'.

Dans le domaine des droits fondamentaux, l'harmonisation se fait de différentes manières.

Les standards minimums ont été fixés par la CEDH, qui lie tous les États membres, telle qu'interprétée par la Cour européenne des droits de l'homme, droits fondamentaux dont l'article 6, paragraphe 3, du TUE nous dit qu'ils 'font partie du droit de l'Union en tant que principes généraux'. Le Conseil a estimé dans sa résolution de 2009 (voir plus haut) que ce socle de droits 'constitue un fondement important permettant aux États membres de nourrir et de renforcer la confiance réciproque dans leurs systèmes judiciaires'. Dans son arrêt *Aranyosi*, la Cour a d'ailleurs utilisé comme standard celui institué par la jurisprudence de la Cour européenne des droits de l'homme:

> [I]l ressort de la jurisprudence de la Cour EDH que *l'article 3 de la CEDH fait peser sur les autorités de l'État sur le territoire duquel a lieu une détention, une obligation positive* qui consiste à s'assurer que tout prisonnier est détenu dans des conditions qui garantissent le respect de la dignité humaine, que les modalités d'exécution de la mesure ne soumettent pas l'intéressé à une détresse ou à une épreuve d'une intensité qui excède le niveau inévitable de souffrance inhérent à la détention et que, eu égard aux exigences pratiques de l'emprisonnement, la santé et le bien-être du prisonnier sont assurés de manière adéquate (…).[104]

---

103 Ibid, para 116.

104 Affaires jointes C-404/15 et C-659/15 PPU (n 85), para 90 (c'est nous qui soulignons).

La Charte vient s'ajouter à l'édifice, sachant que, en application de son article 52, paragraphe 3, lorsque les droits qu'elle contient correspondent à ceux garantis par la CEDH, 'leur sens et leur portée sont les mêmes que ceux que leur confère ladite convention', ce qui permet d'importer dans l'Union par une référence dynamique tout le corpus, en quelque sorte déjà harmonisé, des standards minimums développés dans le cadre de la CEDH, la dernière phrase du paragraphe 3 prévoyant que le droit de l'Union peut accorder une protection plus étendue que celui de la CEDH. Cependant, comme le précisent tant l'article 6, paragraphe 1, second alinéa, TUE, que l'article 51, paragraphe 2, de la Charte, celle-ci n'étend pas les compétences de l'Union. La Charte énonce les droits, elle les réaffirme, mais elle ne contient pas de bases juridiques qui permettraient l'adoption de normes définissant le standard de protection des droits fondamentaux.

Les traités, eux, contiennent une série de bases juridiques qui permettent au législateur de l'Union de fixer les standards concernant un certain nombre de droits fondamentaux, tels que par exemple l'accès aux documents (article 15 TFUE), la protection des données (article 16 TFUE), la non-discrimination (articles 18 et 19 TFUE), le droit d'asile (article 78 TFUE), les droits des personnes dans la procédure pénale (article 82 TFUE), un certain nombre de droits des travailleurs (article 153 TFUE) ou l'égalité des rémunérations entre les hommes et les femmes (article 157 TFUE). Les bases juridiques ordinaires d'harmonisation législative permettent aussi au législateur de l'Union d'insérer au cas par cas des règles de protection de tel ou tel droit fondamental, de manière limitée et à titre accessoire, lorsque c'est nécessaire pour permettre à l'Union de se conformer à la Charte lorsqu'elle légifère dans le secteur concerné.

Bien entendu, le tout est couronné par la jurisprudence de la CJUE qui interprète et contrôle le respect de tout cet édifice, et ce faisant contribue à son uniformité et à son développement.

Recourir au mécanisme de la présomption simplifie le raisonnement et, en évitant d'aller fouiller l'âme, évite le malaise. C'est plus froid, mais plus efficace. Il faut surtout l'appuyer, autant que le permettent les compétences conférées au législateur de l'Union dans les traités, de standards harmonisés – les 'garanties substantielles' évoquées dans l'arrêt *Bosphorus* – et d'une réelle application des 'mécanismes censés en contrôler le respect', parce que lorsqu'on en arrive à la situation où il faut renverser la présomption, c'est que le travail de prévention en amont n'a pas été fait, qu'il est peut-être trop tard et que la jungle n'est pas loin.

PART 3

International Law Aspects

CHAPTER 10

Minding the Gap: Reflections on the Relationship between EU law and Public International Law in the Light of the Judgment in Case C-364/10 *Hungary v Slovakia*

*Sonja Boelaert**

1 Introduction

Ricardo Gosalbo Bono dedicated his professional life to the interaction between Union law and public international law. A number of years ago, before I joined his service, I had the privilege of working on a case[1] following a diplomatic row between Hungary and Slovakia, that raised difficult questions of how to reconcile Union law and public international law, particularly on issues where both spheres of law appear to lead to dramatically different outcomes. I suspect that Ricardo would have relished the opportunity to give his erudite and well-researched views on this textbook case of the sometimes difficult interaction between Union law and public international law.

2 The Incident

On 21 August 2009 the motorcade of Mr László Sólyom, who was Hungary's president at the time, approached the Elisabeth bridge in Komárom on the Hungarian side of the Danube river with the intention of crossing and entering into Slovakian territory. Mr Sólyom had been invited by a civic association of the city of Komárno in Slovakia to attend a ceremony for the inauguration of the statue of St. Stephen. The Elisabeth bridge was once a border post between Hungary and Slovakia, but as a result of the application of the Schengen *acquis*, the border controls had been lifted.[2] It was when he was *en route* to the

* No opinion in this contribution may be attributed to the Council or to its Legal Service.

1 Case C-364/10 *Hungary v Slovak Republic* EU:C:2012:630. The author was involved in this case as an agent for the European Commission.

2 Insofar as land borders and sea borders were concerned the Schengen *acquis* was fully applicable to both Hungary and Slovakia as from 21 December 2007 (see Council Decision (EC)

 | DOI 10.1163/9789004347175_011

bridge that the Hungarian president was informed of a *note verbale* issued by the Slovakian authorities, stating that his entry into the territory of the Slovakia was refused for security reasons, on the basis of EU's free movement directive 38/2004 (EU free movement Directive)[3] and of provisions of domestic law on the stay of foreign nationals and on the national police.[4] Mr Sólyom acknowledged receipt of the note and decided against entering Slovakia. He walked to the middle of the bridge and gave a press conference in which he protested that Slovakia had unlawfully relied on the EU free movement Directive to block the free movement of a citizen of one EU Member State into another EU Member State.

The diplomatic spat eventually reached its judicial *dénouement* with the (Grand Chamber) judgment of the Court of Justice of the European Union (CJEU) in Case C-364/10 *Hungary v Slovakia* of 16 October 2012, which is the main subject of this contribution.

3 Brief Historical Background

The facts surrounding the dispute have been summarised in the Court's proceedings,[5] and were also reported on at length in Hungarian and Slovakian media. However, it may be difficult to understand the depth of the views held by both Member States in relation to the diplomatic row, without knowledge of some of the historical background.

The town of Komárno in Slovakia once formed part of the historical town of Komárom in Hungary, situated along both banks of the Danube river. Following World War I and the Treaty of Trianon, the border of the newly

801/2007 of 6 December 2007 on the full application of the provisions of the Schengen acquis in the Czech Republic, the Republic of Estonia, the Republic of Latvia, the Republic of Lithuania, the Republic of Hungary, the Republic of Malta, the Republic of Poland, the Republic of Slovenia and the Slovak Republic [2007] OJ L323/34, art 1).

3 European Parliament and Council Directive (EC) 38/2004 on the right of citizens of the Union and their family members to move and reside freely within the territory of the Member States, amending Regulation (EEC) 1612/68 and repealing Directives 64/221/EEC, 68/360/EEC, 72/194/EEC, 73/148/EEC, 75/34/EEC, 75/35/EEC, 90/364/EEC, 90/365/EEC and 93/96/EEC [2004] OJ L158/77.

4 *Hungary v Slovakia* (n 1), paras 6–7.

5 See in particular the details provided in the Opinion of Advocate General Bot delivered on 6 March 2012 (EU:C:2012:124, paras 1–22).

created Czechoslovakia cut the once unified town in two, creating two new towns: Komárno (in Slovakia) and Komárom (in Hungary).[6]

Prior to the dramatic scene on the bridge on 21 August 2009, both EU Member States had been at odds for some time over the plans of the Hungarian president, Mr Sólyom, to go to Komárno, Slovakia. He had been invited to take part in a ceremony in Komárno for the inauguration of a statue of Saint Stephen. The latter personality is regarded as the founder and first king of the Hungarian State. The inauguration ceremony was to take place on 21 August 2009, one day after Hungary's national holiday. The Hungarian president had been invited to the ceremony by a civic association ('St. Stephen Statue Committee') of the Slovakian town, Komárno (in Hungarian: Révkomárom).

However, 21 August is regarded as a sensitive date in Slovakia, since it was on that day in 1968 that the Warsaw Pact troops, which included Hungarian troops, had invaded Czechoslovakia.

After several diplomatic exchanges between the embassies of the two Member States regarding President Sólyom's planned visit, the three highest representatives of the Slovak Republic, namely, the President of the Republic, Mr Gašparovič, the Prime Minister, Mr Fico, and the President of the Parliament, Mr Paška, adopted a joint declaration, in which they indicated that President Sólyom's visit was considered inappropriate, having regard in particular to the fact that he had not expressed any desire to meet Slovak dignitaries and that the date of 21 August was particularly sensitive.[7]

Nonetheless, following further diplomatic contacts, President Sólyom stated that he wished the visit to go ahead.

As mentioned above, on the fateful day of 21 August 2009, President Sólyom was informed of the contents of the note when *en route* to Slovakia. He acknowledged receipt at the border and refrained from entering the territory of Slovakia.

The incident of 21 August 2009 was followed by further diplomatic exchanges between the two countries. At a meeting held on 10 September 2009 in Szécsény (Hungary) the Hungarian and Slovak Prime Ministers adopted a joint declaration maintaining their respective positions regarding the legal aspects of the contested decision, while regretting the circumstances of President Sólyom's trip. On that same occasion a memorandum was adopted to clarify

6 Treaty of Trianon between the Allied and Associated Powers and Hungary 6 League of Nations Treaties Series 187, 113 British Foreign and State Papers 486, Articles 27–30.

7 Opinion of AG Bot (n 5), para 5.

certain practical arrangements for future official and unofficial visits to the two countries.[8]

Following further diplomatic exchanges on the incident between the two Member States, representations were made to the European Commission in which both countries defended their views on whether EU law had been breached by either Member State. After some initial hesitation, the European Commission came to the view that EU law was not applicable to the incident. Hungary ultimately decided to bring the case before the CJEU, alleging a breach of European Union law by Slovakia.

4 The Legal Framework: Elements of EU and Public International Law

Mr Sólyom, being of Hungarian nationality, was undisputedly a citizen of the European Union pursuant to Article 20(1) TFEU. Hence he was an individual beneficiary of the primary law provision of the right to move freely into Slovakia pursuant to Article 3(2) TEU, Article 20(2)(a) and Article 21(1) TFEU, under the conditions and limits set out in the Treaties and in particular in the EU free movement Directive.[9]

If Mr Sólyom had been an ordinary citizen, there could have been little doubt that Slovakia would have been hard pressed to explain how the entry ban (set out in the *note verbale* of 21 August) and his treatment would be in compliance with the EU free movement Directive. The case law of the CJEU which is codified in this Directive would have required a demonstration by Slovakia that Mr Sólyom's proposed entry presented 'a genuine, present and sufficiently serious threat affecting one of the fundamental interests of society'; the ban would have needed to comply with the proportionality principle and be based exclusively on the personal conduct of the individual concerned.[10]

---

8 Ibid, para 10.

9 Under art 2 of the EU free movement Directive, a 'Union citizen' means any person having the nationality of a Member State. Under art 5 of the Directive, Union citizens have the right to entry 'with a valid identity card or passport', without prejudice to the provisions on travel documents applicable to national border controls.

10 Pursuant to art 27(1) of the EU free movement Directive, Member States may restrict the freedom of movement of Union citizens on grounds of public policy, public security or public health. In accordance with art 27(2) of the Directive, 'Measures taken on grounds of public policy or public security shall comply with the principle of proportionality and shall be based exclusively on the personal conduct of the individual concerned. Previous criminal convictions shall not in themselves constitute grounds for taking such measures.

Slovakia would also have been under an obligation to give Mr Sólyom a precise notification setting out the individual nature of these reasons, with a specification of the court or administrative authority with which the person concerned could lodge an appeal, as well as an indication of the time limit for the appeal as well as further procedural safeguards.[11]

But Mr Solyom was in addition to being a Union citizen, also a Head of State on 21 August 2009. Interestingly, there are almost no EU law provisions dealing with Heads of State.

For starters, Article 2(1) of the EU free movement Directive defines 'Union citizen' for the purpose of the Directive as 'any person having the nationality of a Member State'. But Article 2 does not mention – let alone provide for – an exception for Heads of State. Does this silence mean that Heads of State are covered by the EU free movement Directive? During the Court proceedings Hungary argued that this silence meant indeed that Heads of State were covered by the right of entry provisions set out in that Directive. In particular, Hungary put forward an a contrario argument, on the grounds that another directive of the EU in the free movement subject area contains an express provision exempting diplomatic and consular personnel from its scope of application.[12] However, as will be seen below, this argument appears far from

The personal conduct of the individual concerned must represent a genuine, present and sufficiently serious threat affecting one of the fundamental interests of society. Justifications that are isolated from the particulars of the case or that rely on considerations of general prevention shall not be accepted'.

11 Art 30 of the EU free movement Directive establishes a procedure for notification applicable, inter alia, to entry bans, and reads as follows: '1. The persons concerned shall be notified in writing of any decision taken under Article 27(1), in such a way that they are able to comprehend its content and the implications for them. 2. The persons concerned shall be informed, precisely and in full, of the public policy, public security or public health grounds on which the decision taken in their case is based, unless this is contrary to the interests of State security. 3. The notification shall specify the court or administrative authority with which the person concerned may lodge an appeal, the time limit for the appeal and, where applicable, the time allowed for the person to leave the territory of the Member State. Save in duly substantiated cases of urgency, the time allowed to leave the territory shall be not less than one month from the date of notification'.

12 See Council Directive 2003/109/EC concerning the status of third-country nationals who are long-term residents [2004] OJ L16/44, art 3(2)(g), which states explicitly that the Directive does not apply to those who enjoy 'a legal status governed by the Vienna Convention on Diplomatic Relations of 1961, the Vienna Convention on Consular Relations of 1963, the Convention of 1969 on Special Missions or the Vienna Convention on

compelling, as Heads of State cannot be equated with diplomatic or consular personnel.

One provision that was not raised by Hungary is the EU Schengen Borders Code, even though it contains an express provision dealing with Heads of State, which reads in relevant part as follows:

> Heads of State and the members of their delegation, whose arrival and departure have been officially announced through diplomatic channels to the border guards, may not be subject to border checks.[13]

In public international law the position of Heads of State is largely a question of *customary* international law, not treaty law. But there is precious little guidance to be found in international law on Heads of State. Relevant State practice appears sparse and the treatment of Heads of State appears to depend as much on considerations of protocol and the courtesy rules (comitas) as on rules of international law.[14] In public international law parlance, the position of the Head of State is 'sui generis'.

Most writers seem to agree that, unlike other high government officials,[15] Heads of State have a separate legal status because they are recognised as a personification of the State itself. Their position has been described as reflecting 'remnants of the majestic dignity that once attached to kings and princes as well as remnants of the idea of the incarnation of the state in its ruler'.[16]

---

the Representation of States in their Relations with International Organisations of a Universal Character of 1975'.

13 Regulation (EC) 562/2006 of the European Parliament and of the Council of 15 March 2006 establishing a Community Code on the rules governing the movement of persons across borders (Schengen Borders Code) [2006] OJ L105/1, annex VII, pt 1. The relevant provision explicitly derogates from art 5 and arts 7–13 of the Code. Art 5 applies to third country nationals whereas arts 7–13 contain provisions that apply to citizens of the EU and of third countries.

14 Arthur Watts, 'Heads of State' (October 2010), *Max Planck Encyclopedia of Public International Law* (online edition, OUP) <http://opil.ouplaw.com/view/10.1093/law:epil/9780199231690/law-9780199231690-e1418?prd=EPIL> accessed 15 November 2016, para 4.

15 See Robert Jennings and Arthur Watts (eds) *Oppenheim's International Law* (9th edn, OUP 1992) 1033, para 445: 'the head of government (…) does not represent the international persona of the state in the same way in which the Head of State does'.

16 Dapo Akande and Sangeeta Shah, 'Immunities of State Officials, International Crimes, and Foreign Domestic Courts' (2011) 21 EJIL 815, 824; See also Arthur Watts, 'The Legal Position in International Law of Heads of States, Heads of Governments and Foreign Ministers' (1994) 247 Collected Courses of The Hague Academy of International Law 10, 53,

There is jurisprudence on the question of the 'dignity' that needs to be accorded to a Head of State. For example, in a case brought by Djibouti against France the International Court of Justice held that an invitation to a foreign Head of State to testify as a witness in criminal proceedings did not violate his inviolability and was not in itself sufficient to constitute a breach of the obligation to prevent attacks on his dignity. It noted, however, that the invitation which was sent without prior consultation and which set a short deadline for response did constitute a failure 'to act in accordance with the courtesies due to a foreign Head of State'.[17]

It has been argued that a Head of State is accorded immunity ratione personae under customary international law, not only because of the functions he performs, but also because of what he symbolizes: the sovereign State, which means that the person and the position of the Head of State reflects the sovereign equality of the State. It is also recognised that even when travelling privately, the Head of State retains his special position.[18]

On the question of immunity that Heads of State enjoy under customary international law, most notably, the International Court of Justice held in the *Arrest Warrant Case* (*Congo v Belgium*) that 'In international law it is firmly established that (…) certain holders of high-ranking office in a State, such as the Head of State (…) enjoy immunities from jurisdiction in other States, both civil and criminal'.[19]

One of the foremost authorities on the subject writes on the question of immunity that:

> [T]he application of this general principle will often involve the interplay of various factors, such as whether the Head of State is in the territory of the foreign State in which the question of jurisdiction has arisen, whether if so he is there on official business or on a personal visit, whether the conduct in relation to which the question of jurisdiction arises was official conduct or private conduct, and whether the jurisdiction to be exercised is criminal or civil. If a senior official is granted immunity in

---

102–103; Rosanne van Alebeek, *The Immunity of States and Their Officials in International Human Rights Law* (OUP 2008) 179–180; Hazel Fox, *The Law of State Immunity* (2nd edn, OUP 2008) 673.

17 *Certain Questions of Mutual Assistance in Criminal Matters* (*Djibouti v France*) (Judgment of 4 June 2008) [2008] ICJ Rep 177, para 172.

18 Michael Wood, 'The Immunity of Official Visitors' in (2012) 16 *Max Planck Yearbook of United Nations Law* 35, 47, n 33.

19 *Arrest Warrant Case* (*Democratic Republic of the Congo v Belgium*) (Judgment of 11 April 2000) [2002] ICJ Rep 3, para 19.

given circumstances this suggests, a fortiori, a like conclusion for a Head of State in like circumstances.[20]

Whilst there is little doubt that a Head of State enjoys absolute immunity under international law insofar as criminal proceedings in foreign courts are concerned,[21] there is no uniform view in international law as to whether the same applies for civil and administrative jurisdiction of a foreign State.[22]

The above elements nevertheless provide some guidance for the Sólyom incident on 21 August 2009, from the perspective of public international law. Had Slovakia applied the terms of the EU free movement Directive literally and had Slovakia complied fully with all the substantive and procedural requirements under the Directive, in order block the entry, Hungary might have had a claim against Slovakia for breach of international law. For example, a request that Mr Sólyom present himself, in accordance with the terms of Article 30 of the EU free movement Directive, to a particular 'court or administrative authority' in Slovakia, should he wish to lodge an appeal against the entry ban, would have raised sovereignty immunity questions. But one could also wonder whether the *note verbale* of 21 August that Slovakia did send to Hungary could already be construed as a breach of the dignity of a Head of State under international law, in accordance with the jurisprudence of the International Court of Justice, referred to above.

Only a few aspects of the position of Heads of State are now regulated by treaty under public international law. What proved crucial for the Commission's ultimate view, described below, was that under international treaty law, States have an obligation to protect the person of a visiting Head of State, and to punish those who cause him injury. In particular, according to Article 2 of the Convention on the Prevention and Punishment of Crimes against Internationally Protected Persons, including Diplomatic Agents[23] (the Convention),

---

20 Watts, 'Head of State' (n 16), para 18.

21 This follows a fortiori from the *Arrest Warrant Case*, where the ICJ held, in relation to a Foreign Minister, that 'throughout the duration of his or her office, he or she when abroad enjoys full immunity from criminal jurisdiction and inviolability (…). In this respect, no distinction can be drawn between acts performed by a Minister for Foreign Affairs in an "official" capacity, and those claimed to have been performed in a "private capacity", or, for that matter, between acts performed before the person concerned assumed office (…) and acts committed during the period of office' (*Arrest Warrant Case* (n 21), paras 54–55).

22 Watts, 'Heads of State' (n 16), para 20. But see Wood (n 20) 44–45: 'Heads of State (…) enjoy immunity ratione personae while in office. This includes inviolability of the person, and complete immunity from criminal jurisdiction'.

23 (adopted 14 December 1973, entered into force 20 February 1977) 1035 UNTS 167.

the person of a foreign Head of State is protected against certain specific serious acts. In addition, according to Article 2(3) of the Convention these provisions do not 'derogate from the obligation of States Parties under international law to take all appropriate measures to prevent other attacks on the person, freedom or dignity of [a Head of State]'.[24]

What proved helpful is that this Convention, which is currently binding 178 United Nations (UN) Member States, meant that there was even no need to verify whether the provisions at issue reflect customary international law.[25] Both Hungary and Slovakia are a party to this Convention[26] and were at the time of the dispute bound by its provisions as a matter of public international law.

Whilst the Convention in question does not state so explicitly, arguably, it is not possible for a receiving State to ensure the protection of a visiting Head of State in case if it has not been appraised beforehand of the visit. Hence, a visiting Head of State who enters another country fully *incognito*, without advising the host country of the impending visit could not reasonably expect to be protected in the host country in accordance with the provisions of Article 2 of the Convention. Building on the foregoing one could also argue that a Head of State who needs, under international law, to be protected by the host country with 'all appropriate measures' to prevent any attack 'on the person, freedom or dignity' of the Head of State[27] cannot expect such protection when the host country takes the view that for certain reasons or circumstances the (date of the) proposed visit is 'inappropriate'. In other words, under international law,

24 Art 2(3) of the Convention reads as follows: '1. The intentional commission of: (a) A murder, kidnapping or other attack upon the person or liberty of an internationally protected person; (b) A violent attack upon the official premises, the private accommodation or the means of transport of an internationally protected person likely to endanger his person or liberty; (c) A threat to commit any such attack; (d) An attempt to commit any such attack; and (e) An act constituting participation as an accomplice in any such attack shall be made by each State Party a crime under its internal law. 2. Each State Party shall make these crimes punishable by appropriate penalties which take into account their grave nature. 3. Paragraphs 1 and 2 of this article in no way derogate from the obligations of States Parties under international law to take all appropriate measures to prevent other attacks on the person, freedom or dignity of an internationally protected person'.

25 Neither the Advocate General nor the CJEU mentioned this Convention without verifying whether both States were bound by it, either as a matter of treaty law or customary international law (Opinion of AG Bot (n 5), para 56; *Hungary v Slovakia* (n 1), paras 46–48).

26 See the status information from the United Nations Treaty Collection <https://treaties.un.org/Pages/Treaties.aspx?id=18&subid=A&clang=_en> accessed 1 December 2016.

27 Art 2(3) of the Convention (see n 24).

arguably, a visit of a Head of State appears to require *consent* of the host State. It is plausible that the main reason for the paucity of State practice on disputes involving visits by Heads of State is that such visits are, in practice, always arranged on a consensual basis.

And this is where we may have reached a crucial intersection, where EU law and international law appear to pull in totally different directions. Under EU law, Mr Sólyom had the individual right to enter Slovakian territory without any formalities, and without the need for consent. As explained above, under the EU free movement Directive Slovakia could only have prohibited his entry provided that it could demonstrate 'a genuine, present and sufficiently serious threat affecting one of the fundamental interests of society'; Slovakia would also have been under an obligation to give Mr Sólyom a precise notification setting out the individual nature of these reasons, and with a specification of the court or administrative authority with which the person concerned could lodge an appeal, as well as an indication of the time limit for the appeal as well as further procedural safeguards. Under international law, however, Slovakia was under an obligation to ensure all appropriate measures to protect the person, freedom or dignity of Mr Sólyom, as a visiting Head of State, but this requires in the first place that his visit must be arranged on a consensual basis with Hungary.

5 The Views Which Led the European Commission Not to Bring Infringement Proceedings

Initially, both Hungary and Slovakia took the view that EU law was applicable to the dispute, but disagreed as to whether EU law had been correctly relied on by Slovakia. The Hungarian authorities argued, in a note of 24 August 2009, that the EU free movement Directive could not form a valid legal basis justifying the refusal of the Slovak Republic to allow President Sólyom to enter its territory. They also found that insufficient reasons had been given for the decision by Slovakia to refuse access. For those reasons, they considered that Slovakia had adopted that measure in breach of EU law. In their response of 17 September 2009, the Slovak authorities stated that, in view of the circumstances of the incident, the application of the Directive was the 'last chance' to stop President Sólyom entering the territory of the Slovak Republic, and that they had not acted in any way contrary to EU law.[28]

---

28 See Opinion of AG Bot (n 5), paras 9–11.

The European Commission, for its part, gave at first a rather ambivalent response as to whether Union law was applicable, let alone breached. On 3 September 2009 the Hungarian Minister for Foreign Affairs sent a letter to Mr Barrot, Vice-President of the European Commission, seeking the Commission's opinion on the possible breach of EU law by the Slovak Republic. In his reply dated 10 September 2009, Mr Barrot acknowledged that, in accordance with the Directive, any restriction of freedom of movement must observe the principle of proportionality; that, under Article 27(2) of the Directive, it must be based on the personal conduct of the individual concerned, and that the person concerned must be notified, in the manner prescribed in Article 30 of the Directive, of that restriction and given a full, precise explanation of the reasons. He also considered that it was for the national courts in the first place to consider whether the rules of Directive 38/2004 had been properly applied. The Commission's Vice President emphasised that everything possible must be put in hand in order to avoid any repetition of such situations and stated that he was confident that a constructive bilateral dialogue between the two Member States could resolve the dispute. He further expressed the hope that both parties would be able to solve the matter bilaterally.[29] This equivocal response failed to satisfy Hungary.

On 12 October 2009 Hungary then sent a formal complaint to the Commission, requesting it to bring formal infringement proceedings, as a guardian of the EU Treaties, against the Slovak Republic under Article 258 TFEU for violation of EU law, in particular, Article 21 TFEU and the EU free movement Directive. Hungary's main stance in the request to the Commission was that the entry of its President into the Slovakian territory could not be refused on the basis of the Directive.

The Commission, though, took a different view and declined to commence infringement proceedings against Slovakia. In its letter of 11 December 2009 to Hungary, i.e. a mere eleven days after the entry into force of the Lisbon Treaty, the Commission set out its reasons for not commencing infringement proceedings against Slovakia. The Commission had come to the conclusion that Slovakia had actually been wrong to refer to EU law on free movement of citizens because, in the Commission's view, under international law, EU Member States reserve the right to control the access of a foreign Head of State to their territory, regardless of whether that Head of State is a Union citizen. In the Commission's opinion, the Member States of the European Union continue to

29 Ibid, para 13.

arrange such official visits through bilateral political channels, so this was not a sphere in which EU law applies.[30]

This response again failed to satisfy Hungary, which subsequently decided to introduce, of its own motion, infringement proceedings against Slovakia in accordance with Article 259 TFEU.[31] This article refers to an extremely rarely used 'inter-State' infringement proceeding[32] under the EU Treaties.

It allows one Member State to bring a claim against another Member State before the CJEU on the grounds of failure to fulfil an obligation under the Treaties. As a first step, the Member State which alleges breach of Union law must bring the matter before the European Commission. The Commission must then allow each of the Member States an opportunity to submit its own case and its observations on the other party's case both orally and in writing, following which it shall issue a reasoned opinion. If the Commission does not issue this opinion within three months of the date on which the matter was brought before it, or even when it has done so, the matter can be brought before the CJEU.

In accordance with the procedure laid down in Article 259 TFEU Hungary and Slovakia were given the formal opportunity to present their case in writing, as well as orally, to the Commission. Following the conclusion of this procedure, the Commission issued a reasoned opinion dated 24 June 2010, in which it again dismissed Hungary's complaint. The Commission explained in some detail why it took the view that Article 21(1) TFEU and the EU free movement

30 Ibid, para 15.

31 Art 259 TFEU (ex-art 227 TEC) reads as follows: 'A Member State which considers that another Member State has failed to fulfil an obligation under the Treaties may bring the matter before the Court of Justice of the European Union. Before a Member State brings an action against another Member State for an alleged infringement of an obligation under the Treaties, it shall bring the matter before the Commission. The Commission shall deliver a reasoned opinion after each of the States concerned has been given the opportunity to submit its own case and its observations on the other party's case both orally and in writing. If the Commission has not delivered an opinion within three months of the date on which the matter was brought before it, the absence of such opinion shall not prevent the matter from being brought before the Court'.

32 Such 'inter-State' infringement proceedings had been brought before the CJEU only on five previous occasions. Only three of them proceeded to judgment: Case 141/78 *France v UK* EU:C:1979:225, in which France successfully challenged the UK's unilateral fishery conservation measures; Case C-388/95 *Belgium v Spain* EU:C:2000:244, in which Belgium failed to convince the Court to let it use the Rioja designation for bulk transported wine and Case C – 145/04 *Spain v UK* EU:C:2006:543, which concerned the voting rights of citizens of Gibraltar (the Court found in favour of the UK).

Directive do not apply to visits made by the Head of one Member State to the territory of another Member State and that, in those circumstances, the alleged infringement was unfounded.[33]

Hungary then had three months to bring the case before the CJEU.

6 Procedure before the CJEU

On 8 July 2010 Hungary brought an infringement case against Slovakia before the CJEU under Article 259 TFEU. The Commission was given leave to intervene in support of the form of order sought by Slovakia.

At the oral hearing before the CJEU both parties and the European Commission were given the opportunity to develop their written arguments and to answer the many questions that the judges had with respect to various hypotheses involving visits of Heads of State of one Member State to another Member State.

A preliminary question that needed to be dealt with by the Court was whether it had jurisdiction at all over this dispute. According to Article 344 TFEU, 'Member States undertake not to submit a dispute concerning the interpretation or application of the Treaties to any method of settlement other than those provided for therein'.

Slovakia tried to argue that the Court had no jurisdiction on the basis of this article because in its view, EU law was not applicable to the dispute. This objection to admissibility was succinctly dismissed both by the Advocate General[34] and subsequently also by the CJEU. The Court held that the infringement proceeding related to the possible breach of EU law by a Member State and the question of whether EU law was applicable to the dispute at all meant that the matter was 'within the Court's jurisdiction'.[35]

Insofar as the substance of the dispute was concerned, and in particular the question of whether EU law was applicable at all, Hungary essentially stuck to its guns before the Court. Interestingly, Slovakia had, by the time it came to the proceedings before the Court, modified its initial legal stance. It was now in total agreement with the Commission that it had on 21 August 2009 mistakenly referred to the EU free movement law as a reason to block Mr Sólyom's entry. As the Commission rightly pointed out, in Slovakia's view too, EU law was not

33 Opinion of AG Bot (n 5), para 19.

34 Ibid, para 24.

35 *Hungary v Slovakia* (n 1), paras 24–26.

applicable to the incident at all. Hence, both Slovakia and the European Commission took the position before the Court that the only rules governing the matter in dispute were those of international diplomatic relations between Member States for which, as they submitted, the Union had no conferred competence under the Union's Treaties.

AG Bot, who advised the Court on this matter, was, as it became apparent, rather persuaded by this stance.

First, AG Bot dismissed the suggestions by Hungary that the planned visit had a private character:

> I would at the start point out that, having regard to the objective circumstances of Mr Sólyom's proposed visit, as indicated by the observations submitted to the Commission, that visit must be classed as being public in nature. It is common ground that Mr Sólyom intended to go to the town of Komárno in order to attend the inauguration of a symbolic monument linked to the history of the Hungarian State, and that he was to give a speech on that occasion. There is, therefore, no question here of a purely private visit, or even of a visit made incognito, since the Slovak authorities had been notified several times of this visit through diplomatic channels.
>
> Consequently, it was indeed in the performance of his duties as the President of Hungary, and not simply as a citizen of the Union, that Mr Sólyom wished to visit the town of Komárno.[36]

Secondly, AG Bot firmly dismissed Hungary's main legal stance, which was that EU law on free movement of citizens somehow 'trumps' international diplomatic convention. In his view, the subject matter of access to the territory of an EU Member State by the Head of State of another State was not a competence that had been conferred on the Union at all:

> While the movement of citizens of the Union between Member States is governed by EU law, and in particular by Article 21 TFEU and Directive 2004/38, the same does not apply to visits to Member States by Heads of State.
>
> As stated in Article 5(2) TEU, '[u]nder the principle of conferral, the Union shall act only within the limits of the competences conferred upon it by the Member States in the Treaties to attain the objectives set out

36 Opinion of AG Bot (n 5), paras 48–49.

> therein. Competences not conferred upon the Union in the Treaties remain with the Member States'. The Treaties being silent on the question of access for Heads of State to the territory of Member States, (...) this is a competence reserved for the Member States. (...)
>
> Consequently, the sphere of diplomatic relations remains within the purview of the Member States, in accordance with international law (...).
>
> [T]he idea put forward by Hungary that the status of citizen of the Union and the resulting rights and obligations should prevail over the status enjoyed by Heads of State of the Member States (...) would ultimately extend the competences of the Union in a manner incompatible with the principle of the conferral of competences.
>
> Moreover, that is a view that ignores the specific character of the position of Heads of State, which lies essentially in their capacity as the supreme organ of the State, representing, personifying and committing the State at international level. In other words, that special position implies that, when a Head of State travels on a public visit, he can never do so on an entirely personal basis in so far as it is primarily the community he represents that is welcomed by the State receiving him. (...)
>
> The special treatment afforded by international law to Heads of State is derived largely from international custom and, to a lesser extent, concerning certain particular aspects, from international conventions. That special treatment concerns the protection, facilities, privileges and immunity accorded them.
>
> [T]he status of the highest representative of the State, which is that of Head of State, and the principle of the sovereign equality of States militate in favour of the opposite proposition to that supported by Hungary, namely, that visits by Heads of State within the Member States of the Union depend on the consent of the host State and the detailed conditions defined by the latter within the framework of its competence, and cannot be understood in terms of freedom of movement.[37]

There was however, one dark – if not nightmarish – scenario that led AG Bot to express some final hesitation. When the above logic would be pushed to the extreme, could one not end up with a situation of a total breakdown of diplomatic relations between EU Member States, and would that not raise a question under the EU Treaties? AG Bot acknowledged that this might be a ground for breach of EU law. But this would, in his view, only be the case in extreme

37 Ibid, paras 50–57.

situations of 'persistent paralysis in diplomatic relations', and would then raise primary law questions, not of free movement, but of 'good-neighbourly relations' and the EU's 'integration process' towards 'an ever closer union among the peoples of Europe', all of which are linked with the obligation of sincere cooperation that EU Member States have under the TEU:

> That said, as in the case of any competence reserved for them, the Member States should not exercise their diplomatic competence in a manner that might lead to a lasting break in diplomatic relations between two Member States. Such a break would, in fact, be incompatible with the integration process aimed at creating, in the words of the preamble to the EU Treaty, 'an ever closer union among the peoples of Europe' and would constitute a barrier to the attainment of the essential objectives of the Union, including the aim of promoting peace.
>
> Only a situation of persistent paralysis in diplomatic relations between two Member States, contrary to their commitment to maintain good-neighbourly relations consubstantial with their decision to join the Union, would be covered by EU law, if only because, in accordance with the last paragraph of Article 4(3) TEU, Member States must refrain from any measure that could jeopardise the attainment of the Union's objectives.[38]

But (with a barely hidden sigh of relief) AG Bot dismissed this possible dark cloud on the legal horizon, by noting that this nightmare scenario had not materialised between Hungary and Slovakia.[39]

For starters, the Court expressed difficulties with the legal approach proposed by AG Bot. The Court was obviously reluctant to explicitly state that EU law could effectively be set aside by public international law. Instead, the Court came to the same conclusion as AG Bot, but on the basis of an alternative theory.

On the main question of whether or not EU law on free movement was applicable to the dispute at all, the Court started by recalling its earlier case law on the fundamental significance of the 'citizenship of the Union':

> [C]itizenship of the Union is intended to be the fundamental status of nationals of the Member States (see, inter alia, Case C-184/99 Grzelczyk

38 Ibid, paras 58–59.

39 Ibid, para 60.

> [2001] ECR I-6193, paragraph 31; Case C-135/08 Rottmann [2010] ECR I-1449, paragraph 43; and Case C-256/11 Dereci and Others [2011] ECR I-11315, paragraph 62).
>
> To that end, Article 20 TFEU confers the status of citizen of the Union on every person holding the nationality of a Member State (see, inter alia, Case C-224/98 D'Hoop [2002] ECR I-6191, paragraph 27; Case C-148/02 Garcia Avello [2003] ECR I-11613, paragraph 21; and Case C-34/09 Ruiz Zambrano [2011] ECR I-1177, paragraph 40).[40]

The Court then noted that 'since Mr Sólyom is of Hungarian nationality, he unquestionably enjoys that status'.[41]

Next, the Court noted that whilst EU citizens have the 'primary and individual' right to move freely within the territory of the Member States, this right is not unqualified:

> It is true, first, that, in accordance with Article 21 TFEU, citizenship of the Union confers on each Union citizen a primary and individual right to move and reside freely within the territory of the Member States, subject to the limitations and restrictions laid down by the Treaties and the measures adopted for their implementation (Case C-162/09 Lassal [2010] ECR I-9217, paragraph 29, and Case C-434/09 McCarthy [2011] ECR I-3375, paragraph 27).[42]

In a further crucial step in its argumentation the Court set out to explain the reasons why in this particular case, it considered that the primary and individual right under EU law on free movement must be held to incorporate a restriction based on international law, specifically for visits of Heads of State:

> EU law must be interpreted in the light of the relevant rules of international law, since international law is part of the European Union legal order and is binding on the institutions (see, to that effect, Racke, paragraphs 45 and 46, and Joined Cases C-402/05 P and C – 415/05 P Kadi and Al Barakaat International Foundation v Council and Commission [2008] ECR I-6351, paragraph 291).

40 *Hungary v Slovakia* EU:C:2012:630, paras 40–41.

41 Ibid, para 42.

42 Ibid, para 43.

[I]t is therefore necessary to establish whether, as the Slovak Republic claims, the fact that Mr Sólyom, while a Union citizen, was carrying out, at the material time, the duties of the Hungarian Head of State is liable to constitute a limitation, on the basis of international law, on the application of the right of free movement conferred on him by Article 21 TFEU.

To that end, it should be noted that, on the basis of customary rules of general international law and those of multilateral agreements, the Head of State enjoys a particular status in international relations which entails, inter alia, privileges and immunities.

In particular, Article 1 of the New York Convention of 14 December 1973 on the Prevention and Punishment of Crimes against Internationally Protected Persons, including Diplomatic Agents, states, inter alia, that every Head of State, while on the territory of a foreign State, enjoys that protection.

Thus, the presence of a Head of State on the territory of another State imposes on that latter State the obligation to guarantee the protection of the person who carries out that duty, irrespective of the capacity in which his stay is effected.

The status of Head of State therefore has a specific character, resulting from the fact that it is governed by international law, with the consequence that the conduct of such a person internationally, such as that person's presence in another State, comes under that law, in particular the law governing diplomatic relations.

Such a specific character is capable of distinguishing the person who enjoys that status from all other Union citizens, with the result that that person's access to the territory of another Member State is not governed by the same conditions as those applicable to other citizens.

Accordingly, the fact that a Union citizen performs the duties of a Head of State is such as to justify a limitation, based on international law, on the exercise of the right of free movement conferred on that person by Article 21 TFEU.

In the light of all of the foregoing, it must be held that, in the circumstances of the present case, neither Article 21 TFEU nor, a fortiori, Directive 2004/38 obliged the Slovak Republic to guarantee access to its territory to the President of Hungary and that, therefore, the first head of complaint must be rejected as unfounded.[43]

43 Ibid, paras 45–52.

As a result, in its final ruling on the serious diplomatic dispute that had arisen between two EU Member States, the CJEU agreed with the Commission that Slovakia had not breached EU law, but it did so following a different legal path from that adopted by the Commission and AG Bot.

7 A Departure from a Long Line of 'Dualist' Jurisprudence?

This CJEU judgement is, on reflection, quite remarkable.

Rather than stating, as AG Bot had opined, that EU law did not apply to the dispute, the Court held that EU law *did* apply. In particular, it took the view that EU law on free movement of EU citizens itself contains a restriction incorporating the international law exception of visits of Heads of State. Whilst this seems at first instance, a clever way to reconcile both legal orders, without subjecting one to the other, on reflection this happy coexistence is more apparent than real. The reason for this is that the restriction of EU law as a result of the application of international law, which the Court accepted, can hardly be described as a mere *nuance* or qualification of EU rules by public international law: the application of the restriction leads to core rights under EU law being set aside *tout court,* without a clear indication by the Court in its judgment of what could be the 'hook' for such a restriction in EU primary or secondary law.

One question that has been asked, quite rightfully in this author's view, is whether the Court's judgment in Case C-364/10 should be seen as 'monist' departure from a long line of established jurisprudence, in which the Court consistently emphasises the special nature of the European Union law, and where 'infiltration' of the latter system by public international law is permitted only in selected instances, in a 'dualist'-system fashion.[44]

A firm reminder of the predominantly 'dualist' line of reasoning came in the CJEU's Opinion 2/13 of 18 December 2014 on the draft accession agreement regarding the European Convention for the Protection of Human Rights and Fundamental Freedoms.[45] When reading through the latter opinion one

---

44 In monist thinking international law is directly incorporated into EU law, whereas in a dualist legal system, EU law and international law are distinct and public international law cannot be directly incorporated into the EU legal system; See 'Case C-364/10, Hungary v. Slovak Republic – European Court of Justice Holds that the Slovak Republic Did Not Violate EU Law in Banning the President of Hungary from Entering Its Territory', (2013) 126 Harvard Law Review 2425, 2429–2434.

45 Opinion 2/13 (*Accession of the European Union to the European Convention for the Protection of Human Rights and Fundamental Freedoms*) EU:C:2014:2454.

cannot help but question how to reconcile this with the legal reasoning deployed by the Court in its judgment in Case C-364/10. In particular, in Opinion 2/13, where the Court recalls the following:

> As the Court of Justice has repeatedly held, the founding treaties of the EU, unlike ordinary international treaties, established a new legal order, possessing its own institutions, for the benefit of which the Member States thereof have limited their sovereign rights, in ever wider fields, and the subjects of which comprise not only those States but also their nationals (see, in particular, judgments in van Gend & Loos, 26/62, EU:C:1963:1, p. 12, and Costa, 6/64, EU:C:1964:66, p. 593, and Opinion 1/09, EU:C:2011:123, paragraph 65).[46]

The specific characteristics of Union law, as the Court recalled further in Opinion 2/13, mean that:

> EU law is characterised by the fact that it stems from an independent source of law, the Treaties, by its primacy over the laws of the Member States (see, to that effect, judgments in Costa, EU:C:1964:66, p. 594, and Internationale Handelsgesellschaft, EU:C:1970:114, paragraph 3; Opinions 1/91, EU:C:1991:490, paragraph 21, and 1/09, EU:C:2011:123, paragraph 65; and judgment in Melloni, C-399/11, EU:C:2013:107, paragraph 59), and by the direct effect of a whole series of provisions which are applicable to their nationals and to the Member States themselves (judgment in van Gend & Loos, EU:C:1963:1, p. 12, and Opinion 1/09, EU:C:2011:123, paragraph 65).[47]

Furthermore, in Opinion 2/13 the Court still put special emphasis on the 'mutual trust' between Member States and the process of EU integration:

> These essential characteristics of EU law have given rise to a structured network of principles, rules and mutually interdependent legal relations linking the EU and its Member States, and its Member States with each other, which are now engaged, as is recalled in the second paragraph of Article 1 TEU, in a 'process of creating an ever closer union among the peoples of Europe'.

46 Ibid, para 157.

47 Ibid, para 166.

> This legal structure is based on the fundamental premiss that each Member State shares with all the other Member States, and recognises that they share with it, a set of common values on which the EU is founded, as stated in Article 2 TEU. That premiss implies and justifies the existence of mutual trust between the Member States that those values will be recognised and, therefore, that the law of the EU that implements them will be respected.[48]

In Opinion 2/13 the Court also recalled its most recent case law, including in particular on restrictive measures and UN sanctions, in which it refused to accept 'infiltration' of EU law by international law measures which it considered to be incompatible with EU fundamental rights:

> Also at the heart of that legal structure are the fundamental rights recognised by the Charter (which, under Article 6(1) TEU, has the same legal value as the Treaties), respect for those rights being a condition of the lawfulness of EU acts, so that measures incompatible with those rights are not acceptable in the EU (see judgments in ERT, C-260/89, EU:C:1991:254, paragraph 41; Kremzow, C-299/95, EU:C:1997:254, paragraph 14; Schmidberger, C-112/00, EU:C:2003:333, paragraph 73; and Kadi and Al Barakaat International Foundation v Council and Commission, EU:C:2008:461, paragraphs 283 and 284).[49]

The overall conclusion from this line of case law, as recalled by the Court in Opinion 2/13, is that EU law is 'autonomous' not only in relation to the laws of the Member States but also in relation to international law:

> The autonomy enjoyed by EU law in relation to the laws of the Member States and in relation to international law requires that the interpretation of those fundamental rights be ensured within the framework of the structure and objectives of the EU (see, to that effect, judgments in Internationale Handelsgesellschaft, EU:C:1970:114, paragraph 4, and Kadi and Al Barakaat International Foundation v Council and Commission, EU:C:2008:461, paragraphs 281 to 285).[50]

48 Ibid, paras 167–68.

49 Ibid, para 169.

50 Ibid, para 170.

It is particularly the latter paragraph that raises a doubt as to how the judgment in Case C-364/10 *Hungary v Slovakia* can possibly fit in the long line of 'dualist' case law of the Court.

8 A Dangerous Precedent?

The judgment in *Hungary v Slovakia* is noteworthy for other reasons as well. For example, the Court chose not to address the nightmare scenario of 'persistent paralysis in diplomatic relations' that had made AG Bot hesitate for a brief moment. In addition, the Court, whilst recalling earlier case law on the fundamental status and rights of EU citizens, did not specifically address the need for entry bans on Heads of State to comply with the principle of proportionality. Nor did the Court explicitly recall that in cases where Member States retain competence, EU citizens may not be deprived of the genuine enjoyment of the substance of the rights.

Some commentators have consequently expressed a fear that the derogation recognised to the EU's free movement principles in Case C-364/10 represents 'a dangerous precedent for the future of diplomatic relations between Member States'.[51]

This fear is probably unfounded. There is an intriguing reference to 'the circumstances of the present case' in paragraph 52 of the judgment which hints at considerations that were possibly decisive for the Court's view:

> In the light of all of the foregoing, it must be held that, in the circumstances of the present case, neither Article 21 TFEU nor, a fortiori, Directive 2004/38 obliged the Slovak Republic to guarantee access to its territory to the President of Hungary and that, therefore, the first head of complaint must be rejected as unfounded.[52]

---

51 Mattia Filippin, 'A Change for Future Intra-European Diplomatic Relations? Case C-364/10 Hungary v. Slovakia, Judgment of 16 October 2012, not yet reported' [2013] Maastricht J Eur & Comp L 120, 126. See for equally critical views on the approach taken by the Court: Lucia S Rossi, 'EU Citizenship and the Free Movement of Heads of State: Hungary v. Slovak Republic' (2013) 50 CML Rev 1451; Krisztian Kecsmár, 'Le Président de la République de Hongrie n'est pas un citoyen de l'Union comme les autres?' [2014] Revue de l'Union européenne 479; Marc Maresceau, 'Het arrest Hongarije t. Slovaakse Republiek van het hof van justitie met enkele kanttekeningen bij de huidige positie van Hongarije in de EU' in Maud Piers, Henri Storme and Jinske Verhellen (eds) *Liber Amicorum Johan Erauw* (Intersentia 2014) 121.

52 *Hungary v Slovakia* (n 1).

The latter paragraph demonstrates palpable discomfort on the part of the CJEU at having to take sides in what was in essence a deplorable diplomatic incident between two EU Member States. This impression is reinforced when one notes that the Court declined to answer Hungary's follow-up question as to which categories of senior government officials other than Heads of State would need to be considered as not benefiting from the right to move freely within the Union, as a rules of international law.[53]

9 Final Remarks

The relationship between EU law and general international law is the subject of much academic debate.[54] Unquestionably, the Union's origins lie in public international law. Its founding and amending treaties are multilateral international agreements between subjects of international law (States), creating rights and obligations for these States. However, early on the CJEU signalled that it regarded the European Community as constituting a new legal order, which is distinct from international law in general and which reaches far into the domestic sphere of its Member States.[55] It is true however, that the main focus of this early seminal case law has been mostly inward looking, as it concentrates mainly on the relationship between Union's primary and secondly law on the one hand, and the domestic law (including constitutional law) of its Member States on the other.

Nonetheless, the relationship between the Union and the 'outside world' has been the subject of a steady stream of case law as well. Throughout its case law the CJEU has consistently held that in the exercise of its powers, including in particular legislative powers, the EU needs to abide by the rules of international law that are binding on the EU, regardless of their source (customary law or treaty law). That obligation is now codified in Article 21(1) TEU.[56]

---

53 Ibid, paras 67–72.

54 E.g. Christiaan Timmermans, 'The EU and Public International Law' (1999) 4 European Foreign Affairs Review 181; Allan Rosas, 'The European Court of Justice and Public International Law' in Jan Wouters, André Nollkaemper and Erika de Wet (eds), *The Europeanisation of International Law* (TMC Asser Press, 2008) 71.

55 Case 6/64 *Flaminio Costa v E.N.E.L.* EU:C:1964:66, p. 594; see also Case 26/62 *NV Algemene Transport- en Expeditie Onderneming van Gend & Loos v Netherlands Inland Revenue Administration* EU:C:1963:1, paras 10–12.

56 For a more detailed discussion of the case law of the Court of Justice relating to (General) Customary Law and Treaty law see, see Sonja Boelaert, 'European Union Courts' in Chiara

The main question raised by the diplomatic dispute between Hungary and Slovakia and in the ensuing legal proceedings before the Court of Justice was, in reality, fairly simple: whether in certain circumstances, core norms of primary law such as in casu, EU law on free movement of Union citizens, can be set aside by principles of public international law, including in particular, diplomatic convention.

The fairest assessment of the Hungary-Slovakia dispute is probably that this was 'fact-specific' or as some might put it more plainly, a case of 'bad facts' making 'bad law'.

What is remarkable in the above saga, nonetheless, is the extent to which both Member States and the two EU institutions whose views were sought, lacked confidence as to how to handle a diplomatic incident between two EU Member States from the perspective of Union law.

Undeniably, the EU's search for a stable relationship with the sphere of public international law in general is still very much a work in progress.

Georgetti, *The Rules, Practice and Jurisprudence of International Courts and Tribunals* (Martinus Nijhoff Publishers 2012) 415, 433–454.

CHAPTER 11

Four Contributions of the European Union to the Law of the Sea

*Esa Paasivirta**

1 Introduction

At the Third Conference on the Law of the Sea (1973–1982) the then European Economic Community (EEC) was present in the negotiations, but only as an observer. During the long negotiations the interests of the EEC were brought to the attention of other participants by the rotating Presidencies of the Council of the EU. However, the Commission felt that it was necessary for the EEC to become party to the Convention in its own right. This was agreed amongst the EEC Member States, especially due to the Community's exclusive competence in fishery matters.[1] Consequently, in 1998 the United Nations Convention on the Law of the Sea (UNCLOS) was concluded, including by the European Community.[2]

Today, the European Union, alongside its Member States, is an active participant in the law of the sea process and has become a party to a whole series of other oceans-related agreements. The EU has become a major proponent of UNCLOS and it takes an active role in advancing the Union's interests in the relevant international fora. In 2014, marking the 20th anniversary of the entry into force of UNCLOS, the statement on behalf of the EU and its Member States at the United Nations (UN) General Assembly explained their general position as follows:

* This chapter is based on a guest lecture at the Summer Academy of the International Foundation of the Law of the Sea (IFLOS), Hamburg, in August 2015. The views expressed in this chapter are personal only.

1 See Esa Paasivirta, 'The European Union and the United Nations Convention on the Law of the Sea' (2015) 38 Fordham Int LJ 1045, 1061–1070.

2 Council Decision 98/392/EC of 23 March 1998 concerning the conclusion by the European Community of the United Nations Convention of 10 December 1982 on the Law of the Sea and the Agreement of 28 July 1994 relating to the implementation of Part XI thereof [1998] OJ L 179/1.

 | DOI 10.1163/9789004347175_012

> The EU and its Member States continue to believe that this framework convention represents the constitution of the oceans, reflects customary international law and establishes the overarching legal framework within which all activities in oceans and seas must be carried out and wish that the goal of universal participation in this Convention will soon be met.[3]

UNCLOS is indeed of critical importance for the peaceful use of the oceans and it is now an integral part of the EU's legal system and a cornerstone of its maritime policies. UNCLOS along with its nine annexes covers almost all aspects of international law relating to the oceans. It takes largely a zonal approach to the law of the sea, including zones such as the territorial sea, continental shelf, contiguous zone, exclusive economic zone (EEZ), and the high seas. Its comprehensive subject matter covers areas including freedom of navigation, utilisation of resources, the protection and preservation of the maritime environment and international dispute settlement. The Convention also establishes a compulsory dispute settlement system, including the International Tribunal for the Law of the Sea (ITLOS), which further highlights its importance in ocean affairs. Some issues, in particular fisheries, were addressed to a limited extent at the time of its negotiations, but have later been subject to subsequent agreements or soft law instruments which complement the general framework of UNCLOS, as noted below. Aspects not addressed in UNCLOS remain governed by customary international law.[4]

This chapter will outline the EU's contributions to the law of the sea in four main ways. First, it reviews the EU's participation in international agreements and soft law instruments and in particular how the EU legal framework can enhance the implementation of the law of the sea. Secondly, it addresses the practice of the EU judiciary by considering how the public interest aspect of oceans-related activities is reflected in its practice. Thirdly, the chapter outlines the EU's stand on international dispute settlement. Finally, it will comment on the potential of the EU to contribute to the formation of customary international law in the area of the law of the sea.

---

3 See <http://eu-un.europa.eu/eu-statement-united-nations-general-assembly-oceans-and-law-of-sea-including-sustainable-fisheries/> (accessed 23 October 2016).

4 The last preamble of UNCLOS reads as follows: 'Affirming that matters not regulated by this Convention continue to be governed by the rules and principles of general international law'.

2 The EU's Legal System Enhances Effective Implementation of Oceans Related International Agreements and Soft Law Instruments

The EU is today an active participant in the key law of the sea related agreements and other instruments. The key agreements concluded by the EU include:

- The United Nations Convention on the Law of the Sea (1982) and the Agreement relating to the implementation of Part XI thereof (1994), a mixed agreement to which the EU Member States are also parties;[5]
- The Agreement on Straddling and Highly Migratory Stocks (1995) (Fish Stocks Agreement), also a mixed agreement;[6]
- The Food and Agriculture Organisation (FAO) Compliance Agreement (1993), which is an 'EU-only' agreement, strengthening the Fish Stocks Agreement;[7]
- The FAO Port State Measures Agreement to prevent, deter, and eliminate Illegal, Unreported and Unregulated (IUU) Fishing (2009),[8] also an 'EU-only' agreement, which aims to strengthen the role of port States in relation to 'IUU fishing'.

The EU is also a member of most Regional Fisheries Management Organisations (RFMOs), where it has largely replaced its Member States.[9]

The EU has also been an important actor promoting a process towards developing a legally binding instrument under UNCLOS on the conservation and

5 Council Decision 98/392/EC of 23 March 1998 concerning the conclusion by the European Community of the United Nations Convention of 10 December 1982 on the Law of the Sea and the Agreement of 28 July 1994 relating to the implementation of Part XI thereof [1998] OJ L 179/1.

6 Council Decision 98/414/EC of 8 June 1998 on the ratification by the European Community of the Agreement for the implementing of the provisions of the United Nations Convention on the Law of the Sea of 10 December 1982 relating to the conservation and management of straddling stocks and highly migratory fish stocks [1998] OJ L 189/14.

7 The Agreement to Promote Compliance with international Conservation and Management Measures by fishing Vessels on the High Seas [1996] OJ L 177/24.

8 [2011] OJ L 191/1.

9 See Community participation in Regional Fisheries Organisations (RFMOs), COM(1999) 613 final of 8 December 1999 and Commission communication on the external dimension of the common fisheries policy, COM(2011) 424 final of 13 July 2011, Annex II with a list of the relevant RFMOs.

sustainable use of marine biodiversity of areas beyond national jurisdiction (BBNJ). As of April 2016, this instrument is being developed by a preparatory committee under the auspices of the UN.[10]

From the viewpoint of the implementation of treaties that the EU has concluded in the field, the legal system of the Union establishes an additional layer of ways and means to ensure their effective implementation. This covers the areas of its 28 Member States and thus these means apply on a region-wide basis. In essence, these legal and institutional means provide additional discipline for effective compliance and help to prevent or dissuade its institutions and the Member States from infringing the obligations binding the Union. This is embedded in the way that the Union's institutional and legal system functions. It can also serve the broader international interests and objectives aimed at by international treaties.

A central element of this legal system is the 'monist' approach to international law in EU law, according to which international obligations are automatically integrated as part of the EU's own legal system. This well-established principle is today reflected in Article 216(2) TEU, which provides that '[a]greements concluded by the Union are binding upon the institutions of the Union and on its Member States'. While the provision says nothing about the status of customary international law, it has been confirmed in the practice of the EU judiciary that customary law is also binding on the EU.[11] In line with these constitutional principles, EU secondary legislation is interpreted in conformity with its international obligations.[12] According to this approach, even when the Union itself is not a contracting party to an international agreement, but all of its Member States are, the provisions of Union secondary law are to be interpreted by 'taking into account' the international agreement concerned.[13] Furthermore, under EU law, in so far as the Union is bound by the international obligations concerned, these obligations prevail over secondary legislation and may result in the invalidity of conflicting provisions of secondary legislation.[14] It is also significant that according to Article 216(2) TFEU international

10 UN General Assembly Resolution 69/292 of 19 June 2015 (A/RES/69/292).

11 Case C-366/10 *Air Transport Association of America* EU:C:2011:864, para 101.

12 In Case C-61/94 *Commission v Germany* EU:C:1996:313, the Court confirmed that 'the primacy of international agreements concluded by the Community over provisions of secondary Community legislation means that such provisions must, so far as is possible, be interpreted in a manner that is consistent with those agreements' (para 52).

13 Recently confirmed in Case C-537/11 *Mattia Manzi, Compagnia Naviera Orchestra v Capitaneria di Porto di Genova* EU:C:2014:19, paras 45–47.

14 *Air Transport Association of America* (n 11), paras 49–51.

agreements concluded by the Union are binding, not only on its institutions, but also on the Member States. This means, for instance, that the EU law principle of sincere cooperation applies with regard to the EU's international obligations and thus the Member States are under a legal commitment under EU law to ensure the fulfilment of these obligations and to facilitate the achievement of the Union's tasks in that respect.[15]

The monist approach discussed above goes even further, in that the normal institutional mechanisms and legal disciplines that control the action of the institutions and the Member States regarding internal law also apply in principle to international obligations. This opens the way for a variety of actions and remedies to be used to ensure compliance with international law, including the role of the Commission and the EU courts. Thus, the Commission's role as 'the guardian of the Treaties' in the internal sphere is also applicable in the case of external commitments. As is well known, the Commission may initiate infringement procedures, involving an administrative and judicial phase, against a Member State in case of suspected infringements of EU law and this may ultimately result in a judgment of the CJEU if not settled before.[16] While such action is not used frequently to enforce international obligations, this is not exceptional. Thus, the Commission has brought Member States to the CJEU for non-compliance with certain international treaty obligations. The Commission has brought such cases against Member States in matters related to, for instance, an instrument related to the General Agreement on Trade in Tariffs (GATT),[17] association agreements,[18] other bilateral cooperation agreements,[19]

15 Article 4(3) TEU provides that: 'Pursuant to the principle of sincere cooperation, the Union and the Member States shall, in full mutual respect, assist each other in carrying out tasks which flow from the Treaties. The Member States shall take any appropriate measure, general or particular, to ensure fulfilment of the obligations arising out of the Treaties or resulting from the acts of the institutions of the Union. The Member States shall facilitate the achievement of the Union's tasks and refrain from any measure which could jeopardise the attainment of the Union's objectives'.

16 See generally Esa Paasivirta and Pieter Jan Kuijper, 'Does One Size Fit All? The European Community and the Responsibility of International Organizations' (2005) 36 NYIL 169, 198–199.

17 Case C-61/94 *Commission v Germany* EU:C:1996:313, where Germany was found to have failed to fulfil its obligations under the International Dairy Arrangement, which was concluded as part of the GATT Tokyo round agreements.

18 See e.g. Case C-92/07 *Commission v the Netherlands* EU:C:2010:228, relating to the EEC-Turkey Association Agreement.

19 See e.g. Case C-173/05 *Commission v Italy* EU:C:2007:362, relating to the EC-Algeria Cooperation Agreement.

the European Economic Area (EEA) Agreement,[20] in connection with compliance with fisheries agreements,[21] as well as in relation to maritime-related pollution.[22]

Case *C-239/03 Commission v France*, relating to pollution of the Mediterranean Sea, is a good illustration of how the institutional framework of the EU can be used to enhance the implementation of international obligations.[23] This case concerned the obligations based on the Barcelona Protocol for the protection of the Mediterranean Sea against pollution from land-based sources. The Court found that France had failed to fulfil its obligations under this agreement by not having a sufficient authorisation procedure for discharges of certain substances to the sea. An interesting aspect of this case was that it involved a mixed agreement, concluded by the Community and the Member States, given their shared competence in the area of the environment. While the discharges of the particular substances at stake (freshwater and alluvium inputs into a saltwater marsh at the '*Étang de Berre*') were covered by the obligations under the Protocol, they had not been subject to a particular harmonisation measure at the EU level. However, the Court did not accept the argument that the issue did not fall within the scope of Community law and it went on to assume jurisdiction, finding that France had infringed its obligations under the Protocol. Thus, the judicial control by the CJEU was extended to cover a situation of a mixed agreement, in the absence of an internal harmonising measure. As a reason for its approach, the Court noted that the 'field' (subject matter) of the Protocol was 'covered in large measure by Community legislation' and hence there was a 'Community interest' to ensure compliance 'both by the Community and its Member States' with their obligations, stemming from the Protocol.[24] It was explained further that the Community had

---

20 Case C-13/00 *Commission v Ireland* EU:C:2002:184; Case C-465/01 *Commission v Austria* EU:C:2004:530. The former case concerned Ireland's failure to adhere to the Berne Convention for the Protection of Literary and Artistic Works (1971), in contravention to its undertaking under Article 5 of Protocol 28 to the EEA Agreement, and the latter case related to Austria's failure to fulfil its obligations under Article 28 of the EEA Agreement, as well as other international agreements, by denying workers who are nationals of the EEA the right to stand for election to workers and employees' chambers.

21 Case C-62/89 *Commission v France* EU:C:1990:123, where France was found to have failed to establish sufficient control measures to ensure observance of the quotas allocated to it for catches of redfish and flatfish in the waters of Faroe Islands.

22 Case C-239/03 *Commission v France* EU:C:2004:598.

23 For a comment on the different facets of this case, see Pieter-Jan Kuijper's annotation in (2005) 42 CML Rev 1491.

24 Case C-239/03 *Commission v France* EU:C:2004:598, paras 26–29.

'assumed responsibility for the due performance of the agreement'. This seems to point in the direction of a kind of preventive approach in the face of risks related to potential international liabilities also with respect to the Community, and not only a particular Member State alone.[25] Such an approach, echoed also in other contexts, illustrates the dynamics and the broad availability of remedies under the EU legal system.[26] This extends to mixed agreements in certain situations and takes account of international perspectives and potential risks in addressing issues of internal implementation. For present purposes, it suffices to note that such a 'broad' approach in mixed agreement situations provides for further assurance and enhancement in respect of the proper internal implementation of international obligations.[27]

In addition to actions initiated by the Commission outlined above, international law related issues can also come before the CJEU in a number of other ways. These include requests for preliminary rulings from domestic courts[28] as well as actions for annulment and actions for damages for non-contractual liability against the EU institutions.[29] Action against the EU institutions can be brought before the CJEU (under certain time limits) by the Member States, other EU institutions and, subject to restrictive conditions, by individuals and companies.[30] In respect of the latter, whether an individual can file suit depends in particular on the general character of the agreement in question as well as on the precision and unconditional nature of the particular provision at stake. Certain provisions, for instance, of free trade agreements or association agreements have been invoked successfully by individuals, as these agreements were found to be capable of having direct effect.[31] However, this has not been the case for some other international agreements, such as the WTO obligations. This more restrictive approach has been followed with regard to

25 In terms of its own case law, the Court referred (at para 25) back to Case 12/86 *Demirel* EU:C:1987:400, and Case C-13/00 *Commission v Ireland* EU:C:2002:184.

26 In a mirror image, in the context of the conclusion of international agreements, the 'large measure' formula used in Case C-239/03 is also relevant for the assessment of the exclusive EU competence in connection with Article 3(2) TFEU. For an analysis of those aspects and the development of the Court's practice, see Allan Rosas, 'EU External Relations: Exclusive Competence Revisited' (2015) 38 Fordham Int LJ 1073, 1087–1094.

27 See also Andrés Delgado Casteleiro, *The International Responsibility of the European Union. From Competence to Normative Control* (Cambridge University Press 2016) 37–38.

28 Art 275 TFEU like in the Cases C-366/10 and C-537/11 mentioned in n 11 and 13.

29 Art 263 TFEU and 340, second paragraph, TFEU respectively.

30 Art 263 TFEU.

31 Case 104/81 *Kupferberg* EU:C:1982:362, paras 22–26. See also the Chapter by Álvaro de Elera in this book.

UNCLOS. Clearly, international law agreements do not constitute a homogenous scene for those purposes. This is connected with substance and public interest reasons in the law of the sea field, as will be suggested further below.

As regards internal remedies for non-contractual liability, such actions are in principle available also in the case of a violation of international obligations. The mere existence of that possibility can operate so as to dissuade parties from infringing these obligations. Again, as in the case of annulment, there are restrictions on individuals invoking international obligations, depending on whether a provision is intended to apply to individuals and on the seriousness of the breach.[32]

In general, these internal supervisory mechanisms and the possibility of legal actions available under the EU legal system add further institutional oversight concerning compliance with international obligations. A Member State which has been found to have failed to fulfil its obligations under EU law is under an obligation to take measures to comply with the Court's judgment and, furthermore, in case of non-compliance with the judgment, the Commission may bring a case before the Court with a view to impose a lump sum or a penalty.[33] This also applies in principle to international obligations. All these institutional and legal means potentially contribute to the strengthening of international law and advance its effective implementation on a region-wide basis in the European Union.

Apart from the above legally binding obligations, a brief note should be added on 'soft law' instruments. It may be noticed that, regarding commitments that are originally contained in instruments of a soft law nature, there is a certain tendency in EU policy-making, in particular in the area of fisheries, to turn such commitments into legally binding EU legislation. This way, the commitments gain further strength in the EU area, since in the case of regulations these norms would become directly applicable law in the EU Member States. One example of this relates to the practice of 'bottom trawling', which was in the past addressed in General Assembly Resolution No. 61/105 of 8 December 2006 on sustainable fisheries. By virtue of this resolution, the international community agreed to adopt measures to protect vulnerable marine ecosystems from the destructive effects of bottom fishing activities. In the EU, this has since been carried out by way of Council Regulation (EC) No 734/2008 of

32 Piet Eeckhout, *EU External Relations Law* (Oxford University Press 2012, 2nd edition) 299–300.

33 Art 260 (1) and (2) TFEU.

15 July 2009.[34] Similarly, when the FAO adopted in 2001 an international plan of action to prevent, deter and eliminate illegal, unreported and unregulated fishing, the EU adopted its own legally binding regulation covering all facets of the phenomenon, including blacklisting of vessels and uncooperative countries, in order to enhance its action against IUU fishing.[35] Since 2010 the Commission has also been engaged in different forms of dialogues with a large number of States in respect of IUU related practices, including States such as Fiji, Panama, Togo and Vanuatu, Korea and the Philippines. Where the EU did not receive the necessary commitments for reform, the products caught by vessels from the States concerned may be banned from being imported, as was the case with Sri Lanka (since October 2014), Guinea, and Cambodia (since November 2013).[36]

Such practice with regard to the implementation of soft law commitments adds to the strengthening of the law of the sea. Again, once integrated into EU law by means of EU legislation, they are subject to the normal institutional and judicial supervision mechanisms that apply to EU law in general.

3 The Practice of the EU Judiciary Advances Public Interest in Oceans Related Activities

Issues related to the law of the sea have been addressed on several occasions in the practice of the CJEU.[37] Many of these cases have been brought before the Court by way of preliminary rulings from national courts; others have been brought by the EU institutions. In general, the Court's jurisprudence seems to reflect particular public interest considerations pertaining to the use of the oceans, which seem important to highlight. This can be manifested by positions taken on matters concerning legal status, forms of arrangements or required institutional procedures. Though the matters brought to the Court's attention pose different legal or institutional issues, they do not appear to be wholly independent and isolated from one other. That is why they are here

34 Council Regulation (EC) No 734/2008 of 15 July 2008 on the protection of vulnerable marine ecosystems in the high seas from the adverse impacts of bottom fishing gears [2008] OJ L 201/8.

35 Council Regulation (EC) No 1005/2008 of 29 September 2008 establishing a Community system to prevent, deter and eliminate illegal, unreported and unregulated fishing (IUU Regulation)[2008] OJ L 286/1.

36 Commission's press release of 1 October 2015, <http://europa.eu/rapid/press-release_IP-15-5736_en.htm> (accessed 23 October 2016).

37 See Paasivirta (n 1) 1061–1070.

grouped together and considered through the lens of public interest. The emphasis on public interest guarantees is also something which is very characteristic of the European approach to the law of the sea. The following examples from the Court's practice may be approached along these lines.

Case C-308/06 Intertanko v Secretary of State for Transport, a preliminary ruling request from the UK High Court of Justice, addressed the issue of the status of private litigants.[38] In particular the issue was whether they could invoke the provisions of UNCLOS (and the Marpol Convention) to challenge the validity of the Ship-source Pollution Directive (2005/35/EC).[39] As regards UNCLOS, the Court rejected the proposition that its provisions could have 'direct effect' against the EC secondary law. It stated that 'UNCLOS seeks to strike a fair balance between the interests as coastal States and the interests as flag States'.[40] It went on to stress the importance of a 'genuine link' and that the individuals 'can enjoy the freedom of navigation only if they establish a close connection between their ship and a State which grants its nationality to the ship'.[41] In this respect, it was emphasised that the 'ship's international status is dependent on the flag State and not on the fact that it belongs to certain natural or legal persons'.[42] Considering the broader role of the flag State vis-à-vis other States, the Court said that '[l]ikewise, it is the flag State which, under the Convention, must take such measures as are necessary to ensure safety at sea and, therefore, protect the interests of other States'.[43] This was explained by pointing out that '[t]he flag State may thus be held liable, visa-vis other States, for harm caused by a ship flying its flag to marine areas place under those States' sovereignty, where that harm results from a failure of the flag State to fulfil its obligations'.[44] It was in this scenario that the Court, while confirming the principle that international obligations prevail over secondary legislation, then emphasised that the Convention 'does not establish rules intended to apply directly and immediately to individuals and to confer upon them rights or freedoms capable of being relied upon against States irrespective of the attitude of the ship's flag State'.[45]

38 Case C-308/06 *Intertanko v Secretary of State for Transport* EU:C:2008:312.

39 Directive 2005/35/EC of the European Parliament and of the Council of 7 September 2005 on ship-source pollution and on the introduction of penalties for infringements [2005] OJ L 255/ 11.

40 *Intertanko* (n 38), para 58.

41 Ibid, para 59.

42 Ibid, para 61.

43 Ibid, para 61.

44 Ibid, para 62.

45 Ibid, para 64.

Following the *Intertanko* case, the same restrictive approach to 'direct effect' is reflected in *Case C-366/10 Air Transport Association of America*, a request for a preliminary ruling also from the UK High Court.[46] It concerned the alleged invalidity of Directive 2003/87/EC establishing a scheme for greenhouse gas emission allowance trading.[47] The claimants argued that since the calculation of relevant landing charges took account of areas beyond EU territories/airspace, this directive had an extra-territorial effect, and therefore affected their rights to freedom of air transportation. This plea in law was, however, rejected by the Court because the Directive did not infringe any rule of international law that was binding on the Union and that could be invoked by the applicants. The international law aspects of the case pertained primarily to airspace and were only marginally connected with the law of the sea, namely by way of airspace over the oceans. Moreover, the latter aspects were addressed on the basis of customary international law, probably due to the fact that the litigants were US based companies (and the US not being a party to UNCLOS). The case left only limited scope for the claimants to invoke the law of the sea, subject to the high threshold of a 'manifest error' criterion related to assessment.[48] The only rule of customary international law that could be relied upon in this case was the principle prohibiting claims of sovereignty over high seas, but this was not accepted as the Court found that the directive had a close connection with EU territory. In any event, it is interesting to note that the principle prohibiting claims of sovereignty over high seas is in fact the only provision in UNCLOS where the Convention itself (Article 89) makes clear that a claim in violation of the freedoms established is actually 'invalid'.

Both of the above cases sustain the idea that the conduct of oceans-related activities requires reciprocal or multilateral ties between the flag States and coastal States. It is in this manner that the respective obligations can be ensured and public interest maintained in the oceans. Similar ideas are reflected in the other cases mentioned below.

In *Joined Cases C-103/12 and C-165/12 Commission and Parliament v Council* (*'Venezuelan fishers'*) the question of access to waters for fishing purposes was

46 EU:C:2011:864.

47 Directive 2003/87/EC of the European Parliament and of the Council of 13 October 2003 establishing a scheme for greenhouse gas emission allowance trading within the Community and amending Council Directive 96/61/EC [2003] OJ L 275/32.

48 EU:C:2011:864, paras 110–111 ('since a principle of customary international law does not have the same degree of precision as a provision of an international agreement, judicial review must necessarily be limited to the question whether, in adopting the act in question, the institutions of the European Union made manifest errors of assessment concerning the conditions for applying those principles').

approached from the viewpoint of the coastal State.[49] In this instance the 'coastal State' was the EU since the question related to fishing activities in the EEZ off the coast of the French Guiana, which is a part of EU waters. This was an internal inter-institutional case relating to the proper EU decision-making procedure concerning access for third country fishing vessels in the EU waters. In particular, the rights of the European Parliament were at stake, as the Council had opted for simple consultation, rather than seeking consent of the Parliament, but lost its case on that point. The Court concluded that 'ordinary' decision-making procedures applied, and the consent of the Parliament was required (Article 218(6)(a) TFEU). Thus, access to coastal waters by third country fishing vessels was seen to go beyond a mere 'technical' arrangement involving 'policy interests' of the European Union. Hence, the Parliament's consent was a central element for the issues at stake.[50] In other words, access to EU waters for conducting fishing activities by third country vessels was considered to be a matter of public interest to such a degree that all the political institutions of the EU should be fully involved.

The difficulties and indeed the peculiarity of the case were connected with the fact that the granting of fishing rights to third-country vessels had been done by way of a unilateral declaration of the EU instead of a fishing agreement, as would normally be the case.[51] It was this peculiar aspect that led the CJEU to look, beyond the pure EU law aspects, also into the law of the sea, including the role of the flag States and the coastal States in ensuring compliance. The Court's consideration of these aspects seems to have influenced the position it took on the nature of the instrument involved and the proper internal decision-making procedures.

Somewhat surprisingly the Court did not follow fully its Advocate General, who considered that the EU's full treaty-making procedure (Article 218(6)(a) TFEU) applied 'by analogy'.[52] Instead, the Court chose to construe the EU

49 EU:C:2014: 2400.

50 Specifically, the issue was whether the legal base of the EU approval should be TFEU art 42(2) (ordinary legislative procedure) or art 42(3) (the special procedure; for 'apportionment' of fishing opportunity), which made a big difference for Parliament's participatory rights. The Court opted for the former, as argued by the Commission and Parliament. Judgment, EU:C:2014:2400, paras 79–81.

51 This was due to the difficulties of concluding a normal fisheries agreement with Venezuela. As regards the form of a unilateral declaration, the Commission was inspired by the ICJ's judgment of 20 December 1974 in the *Nuclear Test case* (Australia v. France) [1974] ICJ Rep 253.

52 The Opinion of AG Sharpston, delivered in Joined Cases C-103/12 and C-165/12 *Commission and European Parliament v Council* EU:C:2014:334, para 123.

declaration as an offer, requiring an approval from the part of Venezuela, and the two expressing the 'concurrence of wills of the coastal State and the interested States', which established an agreement. It may be noted that the formula 'agreements and arrangements' is used in Article 62(2) of UNCLOS relating to access of resources of the coastal State.[53] The whole process was construed in a rather complex manner. The Court relied partly on the behaviour patterns and exchanges involving the Venezuelan authorities. In addition, it considered the role of the flag State and the role the coastal State in the process of utilisation of the living resources in the latter's EEZ. It stressed that 'it is for each interested State to take, as regards the vessels which fly its flag, all measures necessary to protect the interests of the coastal State'.[54] Furthermore, the Court stated that 'the interested State must undertake vis-à-vis the coastal State ... to ensure that the vessels that fly its flag comply with the measures that the coastal State has adopted in respect of that zone'.[55] These elements, taken together, led the Court to conclude that the declaration issued by the European Union and its acceptance by Venezuela must be regarded as an agreement concluded between those two parties concerning the authorisation to utilise the allowable catch in the EEZ of French Guiana.[56]

The emphasis on 'double control' by the coastal State and the flag State is also reflected in the Case *C – 565/13 Ove Ahlström and Others,*[57] a preliminary ruling from a Swedish court, *Hovrätten för Västra Sverige*. It related to criminal proceedings against representatives of Swedish companies which owned a Swedish registered vessel, carrying out fishing activities off the coast of Western Sahara. This was done under a charter arrangement with a Moroccan company, which had its own fishing rights in Moroccan waters, but a permit by the relevant Swedish authority, as the flag State, was missing, allegedly because the EC-Morocco Fisheries Agreement did not cover such 'bareboat' charter arrangements. The Court rejected this and stated that:

> dispensing with the intervention of the competent European Union authorities would run contrary to the objective of the Fisheries Agreement, which seeks, as is apparent from its preamble and from Articles 1 and 3, to introduce responsible fishing in those fishing zones in order to ensure the long-term conservation and sustainable exploitation of fisheries

---

53 Judgment, EU:C:2014:2400, para 61.

54 Ibid, para 63.

55 Ibid, para 64.

56 Ibid, para 73.

57 Case C-565/13 EU:C:2014:2273, para 31.

> resources [...] Such a possibility might be liable to increase access by Community vessels to those fishing zones and to intensify their exploitation of those resources there, and that without the control of the competent European Union authorities.[58]

The above cases suggest a readiness by the Court to approach questions concerning access to waters for fishing purposes in reciprocal terms, stressing the respective responsibilities of both the coastal State and the flag State. In the *Venezuelan Fishers* case, this emphasis is particularly striking given the laborious way that the Court construed the EU's unilateral declaration as a reciprocal engagement involving the flag State (Venezuela).

The above tendencies in the judicial practice indeed reflect a kind of 'European approach' to the law of the sea. The idea of a 'reciprocal guardianship' by the flag State and the coastal State to ensure public control and interest are central elements in respect of the exploitation of the oceans' living resources. Generally, this is in tune with post-UNCLOS developments in the law of the sea. In particular from the 1995 UN Fish Stocks Agreement onwards there has been an increasing emphasis on international cooperation between the flag States and coastal States. It is, of course, one thing to make certain requirements with regard to vessels and access in one's own jurisdiction and another thing to consider that it is obligatory for all others to take the same line. In any event, the emphasis on reciprocal public control mechanisms seems to be an emerging trend. Some of that trend can be seen reflected also in the 2014 FAO Voluntary Guidelines for Flag State Performance, which appears to move in the direction of favouring an agreement between a coastal State and the Flag State.[59]

---

58 Ibid, para 31.

59 The FAO Guidelines, on the negotiation of which the EU actively participated, in a section concerning cooperation between flag States and coastal State, address the matters as follows:

> "39. Where a coastal State decides to engage in a fisheries access agreement with a flag State, the flag State should cooperate with the coastal State to agree on how to implement their respective roles and responsibilities under that agreement in advance of any fishing and fishing related activities by flag State vessels while in the national jurisdiction of the coastal State pursuant to paragraph 3.
>
> 40. The flag State should only enter into fisheries access agreements with a coastal State when both are satisfied that such activities will not undermine the sustainability of living marine resources within the jurisdiction of the coastal State. The flag State should also be ready to cooperate with the coastal State in that regard."

For the Guidelines, see: <http://www.fao.org/3/a-mk052e.pdf> (accessed 24 October 2016). Proposals to introduce similar provisions clarifying the responsibilities at

4 The EU Promotes the Rule of Law and Compulsory Dispute Settlement in Ocean Affairs

Compulsory dispute settlement is the hallmark of the rule of law in international relations. This is also a key achievement of UNCLOS. In addition to its own standing tribunal, ITLOS, the Convention provides for alternative means, in particular the International Court of Justice (ICJ) and binding arbitration, depending on the choice of the parties.[60] While one can observe an increasing readiness to resort to the dispute settlement mechanisms under UNCLOS, it has also become evident that some parties refuse to participate in those procedures.

The importance of compulsory dispute settlement was highlighted by the EU at UNCLOS's 25th Meeting of the States Parties (2015) as follows:

> The EU and its Member States consider the establishment of this elaborate system of compulsory dispute settlement as one of the most important innovations of the Convention. However, we note with great concern that some States Parties have refused to take part in arbitral proceedings brought against them under the Convention. We would like to urge all States Parties to comply with the regime established under the Convention, to participate in such proceedings, and to accept and implement the decisions adopted on the basis of such proceedings.[61]

The dispute settlement under UNCLOS is compulsory in the sense that non-participation by one of the parties does not constitute an obstacle for the proceedings to continue and to result in a decision binding on the parties to

Union, national and operator level have since been included in the Commission Proposal for a Regulation on the sustainable management of external fishing fleets, repealing Council Regulation (EC) No 1006/2008, COM(2015) 636 final of 10 December 2015, <http://ec.europa.eu/transparency/regdoc/rep/1/2015/EN/1-2015-636-EN-F1-1.PDF> (accessed 24 October 2016).

60 Art 287 UNCLOS provides for a choice amongst four principal binding dispute settlement procedures, including ITLOS, International Court of Justice, Annex VII arbitration or the special arbitration tribunal under Annex VIII, by means of a declaration. Annex VII arbitration applies as fall-back in case of absence of a specific declaration or if the parties to a dispute have not chosen the same procedure.

61 Statement of the EU and its Member States, 25th Meeting of the States Parties to the United Nations Convention on the Law of the Sea (8–12 June 2015), <http://eu-un.europa.eu/eu-statement-united-nations-convention-on-the-law-of-the-sea-report-of-the-international-tribunal-for-law-of-the-sea/> (accessed 24 October 2016).

the dispute.[62] This has proven to be useful in recent years, as great powers such as China and Russia have abstained from participating in the proceedings, yet it has not prevented the tribunals from continuing their normal course of action.[63]

The EU as a party to UNCLOS is bound by the dispute settlement system as provided for by the Convention. Since it has not issued a specific declaration on the choice of the procedures (it has not – at least so far – opted for ITLOS), it is deemed to have accepted the arbitration under Annex VII of the Convention.[64]

The EU's commitment to international dispute settlement under UNCLOS has been put to test in two cases. The first one was the *Swordfish Case* (*Chile v European Community*[65]) where Chile initiated arbitration proceedings in 2000 pursuant to UNCLOS Annex VII, conducted by a Special Chamber of ITLOS. Chile invoked its unilaterally set conservation measures regarding highly migratory fish, challenging the EC's freedoms on the high seas in an area adjacent to Chile's exclusive economic zone. According to Article 116 of UNCLOS, all States have the right to ensure that their nationals can fish freely on the high seas, while Article 64 sets a duty of cooperation between the coastal States and other States whose nationals fish in the region. The proceedings under UNCLOS followed immediately after the EC had submitted a dispute to the WTO concerning Chile's unilateral measures, requesting the establishment of a WTO panel (Chile – Measures Affecting the Transit and Importation of Swordfish). The EC complained of a violation of the GATT (Articles V and XI) by Chile as its measures prevented EC fishing vessels from unloading their swordfish in Chilean ports either to land or to transfer them to other vessels.[66] However, there were no final decisions on the merits in these parallel cases since the parties remained in contact while the disputes were pending, and finally reached a compromise after nine years of negotiations. This resulted in a bilateral

62 Art 296 UNCLOS.

63 See respectively the *Philippines v China*, Permanent Court of Arbitration Case No 2013–19, Award on jurisdiction and admissibility, 29 October 2015, <http://www.pcacases.com/web/sendAttach/1506> (accessed 13 November 2016) and the Arctic Sunrise arbitration, the *Netherlands v Russia*, Award on the merits, 14 August 2015, <http://www.pcacases.com/web/sendAttach/1438> (accessed 13 November 2016).

64 Art 287(3) of UNCLOS.

65 Conservation and Sustainable Exploitation of Swordfish Stocks in the South-Eastern Pacific Ocean (*Chile v European Community*), ITLOS Case No. 7, <https://www.itlos.org/cases/list-of-cases/case-no-7/> (accessed 13 November 2016).

66 WT/DS193/1 of 26 April 2000, <http://trade.ec.europa.eu/doclib/docs/2004/january/tradoc_114329.pdf> (accessed 24 October 2016).

arrangement that permitted both parties' fishing activities of swordfish to continue within certain maximum limits and monitoring, and which provided for access to ports.[67] Consequently, the ITLOS case and the WTO case were discontinued respectively in 2009 and in 2010.[68]

More recently, in *Atlanto-Scandian Herring Arbitration*,[69] Denmark, in respect of the Faroe Islands, initiated arbitration proceedings against the EU in 2013 under Annex VII of UNCLOS, conducted under the auspices of the Permanent Court of Arbitration. The claimant alleged a violation by the EU of its cooperation obligations under UNCLOS (Article 63(1)). The dispute originated in a disagreement between the Faroe Islands (which are an integral part of Denmark, but outside the EU) and the EU over the sharing of fishing quotas concerning Atlanto-Scandian herring. The sharing arrangements agreed amongst the relevant coastal States in the past provided that the Faroe Islands would obtain 5.16% of the Total Allowable Catch (TAC). However, in the coastal state consultations for the arrangements for 2013, the Faroe Islands refused to continue the sharing and announced that a new catch limit of 105,230 tonnes had been set unilaterally for the Faroese fleet, which represented 17% of the recommended TAC. The EU considered that the Faroe Islands had failed to fulfil its cooperation obligations under UNCLOS (Article 61(2) and Article 63(1–2)) and notified the Faroe Islands of its intention to identify it as a country allowing unsustainable fishing. The EU then adopted measures banning the import into the EU of fish or fishery products caught by vessels flying the flag of the Faroe Islands and the vessels were subjected to restrictions on the use of EU ports.[70] In parallel to the UNCLOS arbitration, the claimant initiated proceedings under the WTO dispute settlement mechanism to contest the GATT compatibility of the EU trade measures.[71] Again, negotiations continued while the two proceedings were pending. In the settlement that was reached the Faroe Islands reduced its quota (from 105,230 tonnes for 2013 to 40,000 for 2014), to the effect that this was not considered to undermine the EU's conservation efforts,

67 Understanding concerning the conservation of swordfish stocks in the South Eastern Pacific Ocean [2010] OJ L 155/3.

68 Order 2009/1 of 16 December 2009, available at <http://www.itlos.org> (accessed 24 October 2016); Joint Communication WT/DS193/4, G/L/367/Add.1 June 2010.

69 *In re* Atlanto-Scandian Herring (*Denmark in respect of Faroe Islands v the European Union*) Permanent Court of Arbitration Case 2013–30, <https://pcacases.com/web/view/25> (accessed 6 December 2016).

70 Commission Implementing Regulation (EU) No. 793/2012 [2003] OJ L 223/1.

71 Request for Consultations by Denmark in Respect of the Faroe Islands, *European Union – Measures on Atlanto-Scandian Herring*, WTO Doc. WT/DS469/1 (7 November 2013).

and trade measures were repealed.[72] Both cases were terminated in September 2014.[73]

Thus, neither of these disputes resulted in a final award as the parties reached an amicable settlement. They were both negotiated 'under the shadow of law', which sends a message on how effective dispute resolution procedures often work in practice. They also demonstrate the EU's readiness to respect international dispute settlement engagements. This is in fact quite striking in relation to the *Faroe Islands v. EU* case. While the EU was ready to argue its case by all means, the EU never considered abstaining from the proceedings, even though the claimant was a tiny island community (50 000 inhabitants) in comparison to the EU (500 million inhabitants). That in itself speaks for the rule of law and stands in glaring contrast to the non-participation of great powers which have abstained from proceedings under UNCLOS.

The EU's attitude to international judicial bodies can also be seen in its readiness to participate in the ITLOS advisory opinion proceedings in *Case No 21*.[74] This was a case where a West-African fisheries organisation, involving seven member States, introduced a request for an ITLOS advisory opinion seeking replies to four questions related to flag State liability for IUU fishing. The issues addressed by ITLOS were of significant interest to the EU given its fishery activities and due to its well-settled policy to combat IUU fishing. As noted further below, the case also raised important questions concerning the international responsibility of the EU. Here it is merely noted that, while the ITLOS advisory jurisdiction as such proved to be a highly controversial issue, there was no principled objection to the EU's participation in the proceedings under certain terms.[75] The Commission, representing the EU, submitted its written observations and participated in the oral proceedings, alongside some

72 Commission Implementing Regulation (EU) 896/2014, Establishing Measures in Respect of the Faroe Islands to Ensure the Conservation of the Atlanto-Scandian Herring [2014] OJ L 244/10.

73 The Tribunal's termination order of 23 September 2014 is available at <https://pca-cpa.org> (accessed 6 December 2016).

74 *Request for an Advisory Opinion Submitted by the Sub-Regional Fisheries Commission* (2 April 2015), <https://www.itlos.org/en/cases/list-of-cases/case-no-21/> (accessed 24 October 2016).

75 It is a different matter that there were also disagreements concerning the EU representation, which were later addressed by the CJEU as the Council brought an action against the Commission. The Council lost its case as the Court confirmed that it is for the Commission to represent the EU before international courts, without that requiring formal approval or authorisation by the Council. See Case C-73/14 *Council v Commission* EU:C:2015:663. See still on this case Marise Cremona's, Pieter-Jan Kuijper's and Hubert Legal's chapters in this book.

Member States. It is however notable that the EU observations were made 'without prejudice' to the jurisdiction of ITLOS. This outcome was a practical compromise, reflecting the controversies over these aspects amongst the EU Member States, while at the same time relating to important EU interests that were at stake in the area of IUU fishing.

The above cases no doubt reflect the EU's attitude to international dispute resolution procedures. It would indeed be difficult to contemplate the EU adopting an approach where it would choose just to abstain from proceedings, without putting forward its own legal argument in due form. This basic attitude probably stems from three sources. The EU itself is a creation of international law and it has no powers except those established by law, and thus legal means play a central role in the Union. In its internal functioning, the EU is also an environment where quite a lot of litigation takes place, and legal action involving both the EU institutions and the Member States are regular and often result in cases before the EU judiciary. Yet this is normally conducted without particular political overtones. That same attitude is directed to its international relations. It can be traced back to its own founding treaties, which commit the EU to international law. This is echoed in the basic guidance that Article 21(1) TEU provides for Union action in the external field. It lays down that '[t]he Union's action on the international scene shall be guided by the principles which have inspired its own creation', amongst them 'the rule of law', 'which it seeks to advance in the wider world'. Furthermore, the same provision pledges the Union to 'respect for the principles of the United Nations Charter and international law'.

5 The EU Will Continue to Contribute to the Development of the Customary Law of the Sea

In international law doctrine, customary law, the second main source of international obligations alongside treaties, is closely linked with the concept of 'State practice'. In so far as there is evidence of consistent common practice of States, and provided that such practice also reflects a sense of obligation (*opinio juris*) on the part of States, it can give rise to rules of customary law. Subject to that, it is the practice of States which guides the formation of customary international law. As far as international organisations are concerned, their practice is, generally speaking, more related to serve as evidence of *opinio juris*, if at all relevant.[76]

76 International organisations have been given variable relevance in respect of the formation of customary international law, see the review of international law doctrine in the

In so far as that summary is a fair account of the general position of international law doctrine, it stands oddly in relation to an organisation such as the European Union. The EU's participation in international treaties such as UNCLOS, technically as a 'State Party',[77] is not a marginal or exceptional phenomenon. The EU's participation in international treaties is a large-scale international practice whereby the international community has embraced the EU's participation in multilateral and bilateral treaties, often alongside its own Member States.[78] In addition, in the area of oceans and fisheries there exists plenty of EU legislation as well as judicial practice of the CJEU. Such practice and exercise of public powers by the EU institutions is based on the competences conferred on them by the 28 Member States in the EU's founding Treaties. There is clearly a strong presumption that the exercise of such treaty-making, legislative and judicial powers is equally relevant for the formation of customary international law as the exercise of public powers by States.

In the light of its founding treaties, the EU aims to contribute to the development of international law by promoting its own practice. This commitment can be found in the provisions of the Treaty on European Union (TEU) that provide policy guidance in respect of external relations. Article 3(5) TEU provides that, in its relations with the wider world, the Union 'shall uphold and promote its values and interests' and that 'it shall contribute … [among other things]… to the strict observance and the development of international law'. Likewise, Article 21 TEU provides that Union action 'shall promote' multilateral solutions to common problems in particular in the framework of the United Nations.

In the light of those provisions, it seems that the EU expects that it is also able to contribute to the formation of customary international law. Indeed, it has become a part of the Union's regular practice to make statements at the UN fora in relation to international law issues, including matters concerning customary international law. Recently, the EU has made statements during the on-going work of the International Law Commission (ILC) concerning the

---

Third report on identification of customary international law by Michael Wood, Special Rapporteur, UN Doc. A/CN.4/682, 27 March 2015, paras 68–79.

77 UNCLOS art 1(2)(2) and art 305(1)(f).

78 This covers participation to 259 multilateral agreements and 865 bilateral agreements, as recorded by the Treaty Office of the European External Action Service (EEAS). See the EEAS Treaty Office Database, for multilateral agreements at <http://ec.europa.eu/world/agreements/searchByType.do?id=2> and for bilateral agreements at <http://ec.europa.eu/world/agreements/searchByType.do?id=2> (both accessed 24 October 2016).

identification of customary international law.[79] The Union's basic approach concerning the role of international organisations is reflected in a statement at the UN General Assembly's Sixth Committee (2015) stating as follows:[80]

> [T]he contribution of international organisations to the formation of rules of customary international law depends on the competences that States have conferred on them and on the powers that the States have provided the international organisation with in order to attain the objectives set out in the constituent Treaty. Indeed, in so far as the exercise of the competences and the powers used produce a practice where the international organisation supplants in whole or in part that of its Member States, such practice may be equated with the practice of States for the purpose of the Report. This makes both practical and legal sense as otherwise, as the Special Rapporteur points out, it would mean that not only would the organization's practice not be taken into account, but its Member States would themselves [be] deprived or reduced of their ability to contribute to State practice, an incongruous conclusion to be drawn.

It is important, of course, not just how the EU may see its role, but also how this is seen by others. The gist of the matter is perhaps best evidenced in the Union's evolving multilateral treaty practice. As noted above the increasing participation of the EU, alongside other treaty partners, has become part of the regular international scene. This evolving treaty practice has even generated new notions such as 'REIO' (Regional Economic integration Organisation), which are by now widely used to enable such participation, even though the scope of EU activities is no longer limited to purely economic matters.[81] UNCLOS is an illustrative example. As a matter of fact, this has become a practical necessity for third States in order to ensure full European representation in the appropriate manner. This may sometimes be conditioned by a declaration

79 Report of the International Law Commission (Sixth-seventh session), UN Doc. A/70/10, 14 August 2015, paras 55–107, <http://legal.un.org/ilc/reports/2015/> (accessed 2016).

80 EU statement on customary international law, 4 November 2015, <https://papersmart.unmeetings.org/media2/7654697/european-union-cluster-2-.pdf> (accessed 24 October 2016).

81 See generally, e.g. Esa Paasivirta and Pieter Jan Kuijper, 'Does One Size Fit All? The European Community and the Responsibility of International Organizations' (2005) 36 NYIL 169, 204–212.

of its competences or other conditions such as arrangements regarding voting rules.[82]

The sense of practical necessity to treat the EU as a special case amongst international organisations is reflected in the second report of Sir Michael Wood, the ILC Special Rapporteur for its work on the identification of customary international law. Concluding his investigation of international organisations, he states the following:[83]

> The practice of those international organizations (such as the European Union) to which member States sometimes have transferred exclusive competences, may be equated with that of States, since in particular fields such organizations act in place of the member States [...] This applies to the actions of such organizations, whatever forms they take, whether executive, legislative or judicial. If one were not to equate the practice of such international organizations with that of States, it would in fact mean that, not only would the organization's practice not count for State practice, but its Member States would be deprived or reduced of their ability to contribute to State practice in cases where the Member States have conferred some of their public powers to the organization.

The Special Rapporteur's reflections indeed make practical and legal sense. It should be emphasised that international treaty practice, especially when occurring on a large scale, and the practice relevant to custom are not worlds apart. If multilateral treaties provide room for the participation of an organisation such as the EU it would make sense to consider customary international law along the same lines.

In this context one could also refer to the above mentioned ITLOS Advisory Opinion in case No 21[84] relating to IUU-fishing. The case is related to matters within the core competences of the EU and closely connected with customary international law as far as issues pertaining to international responsibility

---

82 See for instance articles 4–5 of UNCLOS and the accompanying declaration of competence: [1998] OJ L179/129.

83 The Special Rapporteur's Second Report on identification of customary international law, para. 44, UN Doc. A/CN.4/672 of 22 may 2014, <http://legal.un.org/docs/?symbol=A/CN.4/672> (accessed 24 October 2016).

84 Request for an Advisory Opinion Submitted by the Sub-Regional Fisheries Commission (2 April 2015), <https://www.itlos.org/en/cases/list-of-cases/case-no-21/> (accessed 24 October 2016).

are concerned. One of the four questions was clearly addressing the EU's responsibility. In essence, it concerned a situation where a fishing license is issued in the framework of a fishing access agreement between the EU and a coastal State and involving a violation of the fisheries legislation of a coastal State by a vessel flying the flag of a Member State of the organisation. The question was whether the organisation or its relevant Member State should be responsible/liable for the violation of due diligence obligations incumbent on the flag State over its vessels. Hence, the issue was related to the EU's exclusive competence in the field of fisheries and its implications in respect of international responsibility.

ITLOS pointed out that the liability of an international organisation is 'linked with its competence'.[85] It held that where the organisation, 'in the exercise of its exclusive competence in fisheries matters', concludes an access agreement with the relevant coastal States 'the obligations of the flag States become the obligations of the international organization'. 'Accordingly', it continued, 'only the international organization may be held liable for any breach of its obligations arising from the fisheries access agreement, and not its Member States'.[86]

While the ITLOS opinion was related to UNCLOS and the question raised issues regarding situations normally covered by an 'EU-only agreement' (as fisheries access agreements are concluded between a coastal State and the EU, without its Member States), it is nevertheless quite possible, and even likely, that the approach can be of relevance to legal developments more generally. Namely, in so far as the legal logic is the same (i.e. that liability is linked with competence) there does not seem to be a reason why the basic approach should be very different in other contexts, unless a particular treaty provision provides otherwise.

The ITLOS opinion could be put in the context of UN efforts aiming to codify relevant international rules relating to organisations' responsibility in the ILC Draft Articles on the Responsibility of International Organizations (2011).[87] One of the problems faced by the ILC was the limited practice involving international organizations, and that is why the *lex specialis* rule contained Article 64, foreseeing a possibility of special rules on issues of responsibility, was considered of particular importance. Here it suffices to note that the

85 Ibid, para 168.

86 Ibid, paras 172–173.

87 These draft articles are now contained and taken note of in UN General Assembly Resolution 56/83 (12 December 2011), UN Doc A/RES/56/63.

ITLOS advisory opinion seems to contribute to developments precisely in that direction.[88]

It is also of interest to note that in the ITLOS advisory opinion, the EU's treaty practice was alluded to, especially in the separate opinion of Judge Paik as he went on to examine post-UNCLOS developments more broadly. It entailed, amongst other treaty practice, the EU's bilateral fisheries access agreements. In this respect, he noted that 'this treaty practice has been widespread and consistent' and opined on the basis of his review that the flag State duty to ensure compliance of its fishing vessels with the laws and regulations of the coastal State constitute a customary rule of international law.[89]

6 Conclusion

This chapter has focused on four ways how the European Union can contribute to the law of the sea. It has outlined the potential of the EU legal system to contribute to the effective implementation of the law of the sea rules. It has discussed the public interest aspects related to the use of the oceans in the light of the practice of the EU judiciary. It has also reviewed the basic disposition of the EU to dispute settlement and its prospects to contribute to customary international law.

No doubt there are other avenues for EU contributions than these broad categories and processes, including in the areas of the environment, climate change, fisheries, security or shipping. And no doubt the EU continues to contribute to the law of the sea given the growing importance of the maritime environment.

At the beginning of this chapter, it was recalled that the EEC was present as a mere observer at the Third Conference on the Law of the Sea. In the negotiations, opened in April 2016, for developing a legally binding instrument under UNCLOS on the conservation and sustainable use of marine biodiversity of

88 From the EU viewpoint the particular difficulty with the ILC draft rules is that they do not foresee that an international organisation acts, as part of its normal practice, via the authorities of its Member States, rather than thorough its own 'organs' or 'agents' as in the case of a traditional international organisation. See Pieter-Jan Kuijper & Esa Paasivirta, 'EU International Responsibility and Its Attribution: From the Inside Looking Out' in Malcolm Evans and Panos Koutrakos (eds), *The International Responsibility of the European Union* (Hart Publishing 2013) 35, 54–55.

89 Separate opinion of judge Paik, paras 17 and 19.

areas beyond national jurisdiction, the EU is a full participant. The applicable UN procedures have been adjusted to reflect its position as a party to UNCLOS.[90] These adjustments are a reflection of important changes that have taken place over time. Such developments in procedure and international standing are also symptomatic of the potential contributions that the EU can make and what other participants in the international community can expect from it.

90 In the opaque UN language UN General Assembly Resolution 69/292 of 19 June 2015 provides that 'the participation rights of the international organization that is a party to the Convention shall be as in the Meeting of States Parties to the Convention and that this provision shall constitute no precedent …' (para 1(j)).

CHAPTER 12

The *Frente Polisario* Judgments: An Assessment in the Light of the Court of Justice's Case Law on Territorial Disputes

*Álvaro de Elera**

1 Introduction

Ricardo Gosalbo was Director of the External Relations directorate in the Council Legal Service from 1998 until 2015. Ever since my arrival in his team in 2013 I always found Ricardo readily available to share some of his extensive legal wisdom with me, just as he did with all the other members of the team and beyond. One of the pleasures of working with him is that he always displayed a very fine instinct for the political implications of each and every Court case.

During my time in the team with Ricardo, the Frente Polisario[1] brought two cases against the Council in 2013 and 2014, which are certainly to be counted among those of special political significance. And indeed, being agent in these cases, I remember discussing them with Ricardo at length and identifying them as having the potential for being extremely significant in the understanding and application of international law by the Court of Justice of the EU (CJEU), mainly because there is a territorial dispute underlying them.

At the time of writing the last revision of this contribution, the Court of Justice has issued on 21 December 2016 its judgment in Case C-104/16 P,[2] concerning the appeal brought by the Council against the General Court's ruling in Case T-512/12,[3] and the High Court of England has sent a request for preliminary ruling to the CJEU on the validity of the EU-Morocco agreements in the context of the Western Sahara dispute (Case C-266/16, currently ongoing).

* The views expressed here are solely those of the author and do not represent the views of the Council or its Legal Service. The author would like to thank Ana Palacio for her insightful comments. Any errors or inaccuracies are the author's sole responsibility.

1 *Frente Po*pular de *Lí*beración de *Sa*guía el-Hamra y *Río* de Oro, an entity striving for the self-determination of Western Sahara. The background concerning the territory is briefly sketched further below.

2 Case C-104/16 P *Frente Polisario v Council* EU:C:2016: 973.

3 Case T-512/12 *Frente Polisario v Council* EU:T:2015:953.

 | DOI 10.1163/9789004347175_013

This brings the series of Western Sahara-related cases up to a total of four for the time being.

Moreover, Ricardo has in the meantime himself published an excellent article on the judgment in Case T-512/12[4] which analyses much better than I could hope to do that judgment and its consequences.[5] I will therefore limit myself to try to complete the analysis started together with Ricardo on the Polisario saga, placing it in the context of other cases where the CJEU had to deal with territorial disputes.

2 Selected Jurisprudence of the CJEU Related to Territorial Disputes Prior to the *Polisario* Cases

Dealing with territorial disputes[6] is by no means unexplored territory for the CJEU. Indeed, during its more than 60 years of existence, the Court had to rule on a number of cases related to such disputes. All of them are linked to international agreements relating to different subject-matters and concluded between the Community/Union and other subjects of international law. The actions brought before the Court ranged from preliminary rulings to actions for damages. I will address below some of the most salient pre-Polisario cases, to provide some legal context for the analysis.

4 Ricardo Gosalbo, 'El Frente Polisario, las normas del derecho internacional y el derecho de la Unión Europea. Apuntes en torno a la sentencia del Tribunal General, de 10 de diciembre 2015, T-512/12, Frente Polisario/Consejo' (2016) 20 (No.53) Revista de Derecho Comunitario Europeo 21.

5 Other scholars have, unsurprisingly, found interest in the Polisario saga. See Denys Simon and Anne Rigaux, 'Le Tribunal et le droit international des traités: un arrêt déconcertant…' (2016) 26 No. 2 Europe 5; Sandra Hummelbrunner and Anne-Carlijn Prickartz, 'It's not the Fish that Stinks! EU Trade Relations with Morocco under the Scrutiny of the General Court of the European Union' (2016) 19 Utrecht Journal of International and European Law 19; Paula Mori, 'La sentenza T-512/12, Frente Polisario c. Consiglio: un'incerta qualificazione guiridica del rappresentante del popolo sahrawi' (2016) Il diritto dell'Unione Europea retrieved from <http://www.dirittounioneeuropea.eu/images/osservatorio_mori_2.pdf> (accessed 10 January 2017); Oliver Peiffert, 'Le recours d'un mouvement de libération nationale à l'encontre d'un acte d'approbation d'un accord international de l'Union: aspects contentieux', (2016) RTDEur 319; Juan Soroeta, 'La sentencia de 10 de diciembre de 2015 del Tribunal General de la UE (T-512/12)' (2016) 38 Revista General de Derecho Europeo 202.

6 For the purposes of this contribution, the concept of 'territorial disputes' refers to disputes of territorial nature concerning non-eu States or entities. Disputes happening exclusively between Member States, such as for instance those concerning Gibraltar or the maritime delimitation of Croatian-Slovenian waters, will not be treated here.

2.1 *Agreements with a Third State that Does Not Exercise Sovereignty over Part of Its Internationally Recognised Territory: Cases C-432/92* Anastasiou I, *C-219/98* Anastasiou II *and C-140/02* Anastasiou III

Before the accession of Cyprus to the Union in 2004, EU relations with the island were framed by the EC-Cyprus Association Agreement of 19 December 1972.[7] In the first of these preliminary rulings,[8] the Court was requested to interpret that agreement by deciding on the possibility to import agricultural products from Cyprus with certificates issued by the authorities of the self-proclaimed Turkish Republic of Northern Cyprus (TRNC).[9]

The United Kingdom and the Commission had argued before the Court that to do otherwise would implicitly discriminate against Cypriot nationals or companies not established in the part of the island under the control of the Government of the Republic of Cyprus, which would in their view be contrary to Article 5 of the EC-Cyprus agreement (an anti-discrimination clause)[10]

---

7 Agreement establishing an Association between the European Economic Community and the Republic of Cyprus [1973] OJ L 133/1. For the situation after Cyprus' accession to the EU, see especially Protocol No 10 on Cyprus to the Act concerning the conditions of accession of the Czech Republic, the Republic of Estonia, the Republic of Cyprus, the Republic of Latvia, the Republic of Lithuania, the Republic of Hungary, the Republic of Malta, the Republic of Poland, the Republic of Slovenia and the Slovak Republic and the adjustments to the Treaties on which the European Union is founded [2003] OJ L 236/955 and Council Regulation (EC) No 866/2004 of 29 April 2004 on a regime under Article 2 of Protocol No 10 of the 2003 Act of Accession [2004] OJ L 161/128. See also the cases cited below n 15.

8 Case C-432/92 *The Queen v Minister of Agriculture, Fisheries and Food, ex parte S.P. Anastasiou (Pissouri) Ltd and others* EU:C:1994:277 (*Anastasiou I*). The other two cases are Case C-219/98 *Regina v Minister of Agriculture, Fisheries and Food, ex parte S.P. Anastasiou (Pissouri) Ltd and Others* EU:C:2000:360 (*Anastasiou II*) and Case C-140/02 *Regina on the application of S.P. Anastasiou (Pissouri) Ltd and Others v Minister of Agriculture, Fisheries and Food* EU:C:2003:520 (*Anastasiou III*). For a detailed analysis of the different cases in the Anastasiou saga see Stefan Talmon, 'The Cyprus question before the European Court of Justice' (2001) 12 EJIL 727; Stéphanie Laulhé Shaelou, 'The European Court of Justice and the Anastasiou Saga: Principles of Europeanisation through Economic Governance' (2007) 18 European Business Law Review 619; Patrick Tani, 'The Turkish Republic of Northern Cyprus and International Trade Law', (2012) 12 Asper Review of International Business and Trade Law 115; Nikos Skoutaris, 'The application of the acquis communautaire in the areas not under the effective control of the republic of Cyprus: the Green Line Regulation' (2008) 45 CML Rev 727.

9 None of the EC Member States recognised the TRNC at the time. This is still the case today.

10 This provision reads as follows: 'The rules governing trade between the Contracting Parties may not give rise to any discrimination between the Member States, or between nationals or companies of these States, nor nationals or companies of Cyprus'.

and to the Advisory Opinion of the International Court of Justice (ICJ) in the *Namibia* case.[11]

The Court rejected these arguments. According to the Court, such an interpretation would basically amount to the imposition of unilateral measures by the Union (as the Republic of Cyprus would not agree to the recognition of certificates issued by the TRNC), incompatible with the general objectives of the Agreement, especially in view of Article 3(3) thereof.[12] It is to be noted that the Court did not reject the argument that refusing certificates issued by TRNC could amount to a discrimination between Cypriot companies or nationals and therefore to an infringement of Article 5 of the agreement. It held however that Article 5 could not 'lead to a departure from the fundamental rules of that Agreement which determine its operation in the manner intended by the Contracting Parties'.[13] It moreover rejected the argument by the Commission and the UK regarding the International Court of Justice's Advisory Opinion in the *Namibia* case, dismissing such argument by simply stating that 'the special situation of Namibia and that of Cyprus are not comparable from either the legal or the factual point of view'.[14]

The approach of the Court in this case turned on the avoidance of unilateral measures and the principle of non-interference. As explicitly stated by the Court, 'The problems resulting from the de facto partition of the island must be resolved exclusively by the Republic of Cyprus, which alone is internationally recognized'.[15]

2.2 *Agreements with Third States Covering an Area Disputed between Them: Cases T-572/93 and C-293/95 P* Odigitria

The General Court in the context of an action for damages, and subsequently the ECJ on appeal, had to deal here with an interesting case. The European Community had concluded fishing agreements and protocols with both

11 *Legal Consequences for States of the Continued Presence of South Africa in Namibia (South West Africa) notwithstanding Security Council Resolution 276 (1970)*, Advisory opinion of 21 June 1971 (1971) ICJ Reports 16.

12 *Anastasiou I* (n 8), para 46. Article 3(3) stated that: 'The Contracting Parties shall take all appropriate measures, whether general or particular, to ensure fulfilment of the obligations arising out of the Agreement. They shall refrain from any measure likely to jeopardize the achievement of the aims of the Agreement'.

13 *Anastasiou I* (n 8), para 44.

14 Ibid, para 49.

15 Ibid, para 47. The Cyprus issue has been other times before the Court, including after the accession of Cyprus to the Union. See, among others, Cases C-420/07 *Apostolides* EU:C:2009:271 and, more recently, T-41/16 *Northern Cyprus Chamber of Commerce v Commission* EU:T:2016:217.

Senegal[16] and Guinea-Bissau[17] respectively covering the waters of each of these States. Senegal and Guinea-Bissau had at the time an ongoing case before the ICJ concerning the exact delimitation of their marine areas, one specific area being in dispute between both.

In 1990 a fishing vessel flying a Greek flag was boarded by Guinea-Bissau authorities in the disputed waters; the vessel had a fishing licence issued by Senegal. The cargo was confiscated and the master was sentenced to pay a fine. After that, the master of the vessel lodged an action for damages against both the Council and the Commission.[18]

The arguments of the applicant were interesting from the viewpoint of the obligations incumbent on the Union institutions when dealing with territorial disputes. He claimed that the Council and the Commission should have excluded the disputed waters from the fisheries agreements and protocols with Senegal and Guinea-Bissau, pending the resolution of the matter by the ICJ, and that not having done so made them responsible for the damages suffered.

The territorial scope of the respective agreements was slightly different, the Senegal agreement making reference to the 'waters over which the Republic of Senegal has sovereignty or jurisdiction', whereas the agreement with Guinea-Bissau made reference to 'waters over which the Republic of Guinea-Bissau has jurisdiction'[19] without any reference to sovereignty. However, this difference had no bearing on the General Court's reasoning, which was summarised in paragraph 38 of its ruling. There, the General Court held that:

> As regards the content of that agreement, it must be observed that the Community institutions enjoy a wide discretion in the field of the Community's external economic relations, as in the corresponding internal field of the common agricultural policy. In concluding the agreements and protocols with the two States in question, the Council and the Commission did not go beyond the limits of the discretion which they have in this matter and did not in any case adopt a measure manifestly

16 Agreement between the Government of the Republic of Senegal and the European Economic Community on fishing off the coast of Senegal [1980] OJ L 226/16.

17 Agreement between the Government of the Republic of Guinea Bissau and the European Economic Community on fishing off the coast of Guinea Bissau [1980] OJ L 226/33.

18 For an analysis of the case before the General Court see Theodoros Katsoufros, 'Réflexions sur l'arrêt Odigitria du Tribunal de première instance des Communautés européennes' (1995) 41 Annuaire français de droit international 711.

19 Article 1 of the EC-Senegal Agreement (n 16) and of the EC-Guinea-Bissau Agreement (n 17) respectively.

inappropriate in relation to the objective which they were pursuing. *The Council and the Commission could not have asked for the zone in dispute to be excluded from those agreements without taking a position on matters forming part of the internal affairs of non-member States.* If the Community opposed the claims of the States concerning the zones over which they claim to have jurisdiction or opposed the exercise of that jurisdiction when a dispute exists, those non-member countries would very probably refuse to conclude such agreements with the Community. Moreover, if the Community asked for zones to which other States lay claim to be excluded, that move would certainly be interpreted as interference by the Community in those disputes. The exclusion of such zones at the Community's request would also have the effect of weakening the claim of the non-member State in question to have the right to exercise such jurisdiction. *The fact that such disputes are submitted to arbitration or are the subject of legal proceedings strengthens that argument, since, where proceedings are pending before the ICJ, it is not appropriate for the Community to take a position on disputes between non-member States.*[20]

The Court of Justice later on confirmed this ruling on appeal, without analysing the underlying territorial dispute.[21] When the Court had to rule on the appeal, Senegal and Guinea-Bissau had reached an out-of-court settlement in the form of an international agreement for the joint exploitation of the disputed maritime area.

The main point in this ruling was that the Community could not interfere in the internal affairs of non-Member States by excluding a disputed zone from the application of an agreement with them.

2.3 *Agreements with a Third State and with Another Subject of International Law: Case C-386/08* **Brita**

In this case the Court had to issue a preliminary ruling on whether the customs authorities of a Member State could refuse to grant preferential treatment under the EC-Israel Agreement[22] to goods originating in the West Bank (more specifically in Israeli settlements there), especially in view of the fact that there

20 Case T-572/93 *Odigitria AAE v Council and Commission* EU:T:1995:131 (emphasis added).

21 Case C-293/95 P *Odigitria v Council and Commission* EU:C:1996:457.

22 Euro-Mediterranean Agreement establishing an association between the European Communities and their Member States, of the one part, and the State of Israel, of the other part [2000] OJ L 147/3.

was an EC-PLO Agreement[23] covering the territories of the West Bank and the Gaza Strip.[24] The issue required therefore an interpretation of both the EC-Israel Agreement and the EC-PLO Agreement. The analysis by the Court here was original in its approach.[25]

It was clear that the application of the EC-Israel Agreement to products originating from the West Bank and the Gaza Strip would empty the EC-PLO Agreement of any meaningful purpose. But instead of going down the road of the EU legal principle of *effet utile*, the ECJ preferred to resort to a concept of public international law, the principle of '*pacta tertiis nec nocent nec prosunt*', to state that the EC-Israel Agreement could not be interpreted in a way that would imply its application to West Bank products as that would have the effect of creating 'an obligation for a third party without its consent', the obligation being for the Palestinian Authorities 'to refrain from exercising the competence conferred upon them by virtue of the (...) EC-PLO Protocol',[26] and

23 Euro-Mediterranean Interim Association Agreement on trade and cooperation between the European Community, of the one part, and the Palestine Liberation Organization (PLO) for the benefit of the Palestinian Authority of the West Bank and the Gaza Strip, of the other part [1997] OJ L 187/3.

24 Article 83 of the agreement with Israel states: '*This Agreement shall apply*, on the one hand, to the territories in which the Treaties establishing the European Community and the European Coal and Steel Community are applied' (emphasis added). At the same time, Article 73 of the EC-PLO Agreement established that '*This Agreement shall apply*, on the one hand, to the territories in which the Treaty establishing the European Community is applied and under the conditions laid down in that Treaty and, on the other hand, *to the territory of the West Bank and the Gaza Strip*' (emphasis added).

25 Case C-386/08 *Firma Brita GmbH v Hauptzollamt Hamburg-Hafen* EU:C:2010:91 (*Brita*). This case, for its legal peculiarities but probably also because of the equally peculiar political context within which it is set, has been treated extensively by scholars. See, among others, Paul James Cardwell, 'Adjudicating on the Origin of Products from Israel and the West Bank: Brita GmbH v. Hauptzollamt Hamburg-Hafen' (2011) 17 Eur Public L 37; Guy Harpaz and Eyal Rubinson, 'The interface between Trade, Law and Politics and the Erosion of Normative Power Europe: Comment on Brita' (2010) 35 EL Rev 551; Marc Maresceau, 'The Brita Ruling of the ECJ: a Few Comments' in Inge Govaere, Reinhard Quick and Marco Bronckers (eds), *Trade and Competition Law in the EU and Beyond* (Edward Elgar Publishing 2011) 276; Laura Puccio, 'Understanding EU Practice in Bilateral Free-Trade Agreements: Brita and Preferential Rules of Origin in International Law' (2011) 36 EL Rev 124; Rass Holdgard and Ole Spiermann, 'Review of Case C-386/08, Brita GmbH v. Hauptzollamt Hamburg-Hafen Judgment of the Court of Justice (Fourth Chamber) of 25 February 2010' (2011) 48 CML Rev 1667; and Pieter Jan Kuijper, 'Case C-386/08, Brita GmbH v. Hauptzollamt Hamburg-Hafen Judgment of the Court of Justice of 25 February 2010' (2010) 37 Legal Issues of European Integration 241.

26 *Brita* (n 25), para 52.

that it was moreover not possible for EU and Member States authorities to choose between both agreements for dealing with products originating from the West Bank and the Gaza Strip.

The reasoning of the Court was that: (1) the EC-PLO agreement conferred on Palestinian authorities certain competences; (2) the application of the EC-Israel agreement to West Bank products would impose on the Palestinian authorities an obligation, that of abstaining from exercising those competences; (3) this would be a violation of the principle of '*pacta tertiis nec nocent nec prosunt*' as that obligation would have been imposed on Palestinian authorities without their consent.

It is to be noted that, by following this line of reasoning, the Court decided to consider that the origin of the competences of Palestinian authorities was neither any kind of sovereignty or jurisdiction exercised by the Palestinian authorities over the Gaza and West Bank territories, nor very simply the territorial scope of the EC-PLO agreement, but rather the fact that *that agreement* conferred certain competences on the PLO authorities. This may be read *a contrario* as implying that without such conferral the PLO authorities would not be able to exercise control over the products originating from the West Bank and Gaza. The origin of the powers of the Palestinian authorities seems to be in this context the agreement of the PLO with the EC, in the reading of the Court.

Additionally, the possible conflict between two existing agreements was not solved by simply saying that the territorial scope of the agreements was different (without a conflict being therefore possible), that an application of the EC-Israel agreement to Gaza and the West Bank would deprive the EC-PLO Protocol of any *effet utile*, or by referring to the principle of non-interference as in *Odigitria*. Instead, the Court resorted in a rather eccentric way to a principle of public international law.

3 The *Frente Polisario* Saga before the CJEU

3.1 *The Western Sahara Dispute*

The territory of Western Sahara was formally claimed by Spain in 1884 with the Spanish presence progressively increasing during the first part of the 20th Century. After their respective independences in 1956 and 1960, both Morocco and Mauritania eventually claimed the territory, with which they had borders. Within the territory itself, autochthonous resistance against the Spanish presence crystallised in the *Frente Po*pular de *Li*beración de *Sa*guía el Hamra y *Río* de Oro (the Frente Polisario, henceforth '*Polisario*'), created in 1973, and whose ultimate objective was and remains the full independence of the territory.

In 1963 the territory was included in the United Nations' list of non-self-governing territories. In 1974 the General Assembly of the United Nations issued a resolution reaffirming the right of the population of Western Sahara to self-determination[27] and requested the International Court of Justice for an advisory opinion on the status of the territory and its links with Mauritania and Morocco. In its advisory opinion, the International Court of Justice concluded that the territory could not be considered as *terra nullius* before Spanish arrival and that the links between the territory and both Morocco and Mauritania, while existing, were not of such a nature as to render the right to self-determination of the population of the territory inapplicable.[28]

In November 1975, Spain, Morocco and Mauritania signed a tripartite agreement following which Spain ultimately left the territory in the hands of the latter two States. The Polisario opposed the agreement, declared independence in February 1976 when Spain left the territory to Mauritania and Morocco and started a guerrilla war against both of them. In 1979 Mauritania abandoned its portion of the territory, being replaced by Morocco in most of it. Ever since then, Morocco and the Polisario have been in dispute over the territory. In 1991, both parties agreed to the so-called Settlement Plan which led to a still effective cease-fire and to the establishment of the UN's peace force (MINURSO). The ultimate objective of the Plan was the holding of a referendum which, due to differences regarding the census of voters, has still not taken place.

As of today, the Western Sahara is still listed in the UN's list of non-self-governing territories, and the UN's General Assembly adopts every year a resolution on 'The Question of Western Sahara' recalling such status and the need to find a solution to the situation of the territory, most recently in December 2015.[29]

3.2 *The Action in Case T-512/12*

In Case T-512/12 the Polisario requested the annulment of Council Decision 2012/497/EU of 8 March 2012[30] concluding an Agreement on liberalisation measures concerning agricultural and fish products with Morocco.[31] In support

27 UN doc. A/RES/3292 (XXIX), adopted on 13 December 1974.

28 *Western Sahara*, Advisory Opinion of 16 October 1975 (1975) ICJ Reports 12.

29 UN Doc. A/RES/70/98, adopted on 9 December 2015.

30 [2012] OJ L 241/2.

31 Agreement in the form of an Exchange of Letters between the European Union and the Kingdom of Morocco concerning reciprocal liberalisation measures on agricultural products, processed agricultural products, fish and fishery products, the replacement of Protocols 1, 2 and 3 and their Annexes and amendments to the Euro-Mediterranean Agreement establishing an association between the European Communities and their

of its action, the Polisario set out a rather wide-ranging series of pleas based on both EU and international law.[32] The General Court issued its ruling on 10 December 2015 (*Polisario* judgment), annulling the Council Decision 'insofar as it approves the application of [the] agreement to the Western Sahara'.[33] The Commission had intervened in support of the Council. The Council brought an appeal against this judgment, which is discussed below.[34]

3.3 *The Judgment in Case T-512/12: Admissibility*

Before ruling on the eleven pleas raised by the Polisario, the first question that the General Court had to address was that of the admissibility of the action, which had been put into question by Council and Commission on two different counts: lack of standing and lack of direct and individual concern of the Polisario. This point is in itself one that distinguishes the Polisario case from all other previous cases concerning territorial disputes, and is by no means minor: does an entity such as the Polisario have capacity to act before the EU courts? And, in the affirmative, could the Polisario be directly and individually concerned by a Council decision concluding an international agreement between the Union and a third State?

Member States, of the one part, and the Kingdom of Morocco, of the other part [2012] OJ L 241/4.

32 The pleas were eleven, namely: lack of sufficient justification; failure to respect the principle of consultation; infringement of fundamental rights; infringement of the principle of coherence; infringement of the European Union's founding values and of the principles guiding the Union's external action; failure to comply with the objective of sustainable development; conflict with the principles and objectives of the Union's external action in the field of development cooperation; conflict with a number of agreements concluded by the Union (including the Association Agreement with Morocco and the United Nations Convention on the Law of the Sea); infringement of the origin criterion deriving from the United Nations Convention on the Law of the Sea; and conflict with general international law. Many of the possible pleas in a potential case had already been identified by scholars, see Armin Steinbach, 'The Western Sahara Dispute: A Case for the ECJ?' (2012) 18 Columbia J Eur L 415.

33 Case T-512/12 *Frente Polisario v Council* EU:T:2015:953 (*Polisario* judgment).

34 Case C-104/16 P. In his opinion of 13 September 2016 (EU:C:2016:677), AG Wathelet proposed that the Court set aside the judgment of the General Court in so far as it approves the application of that agreement to Western Sahara and dismiss the action for annulment brought by the Polisario as inadmissible. He added that in the alternative, in the event that the Court of Justice did not concur with his view that the Agreements are not applicable to Western Sahara and ruled that the contested decision was of direct and individual concern to the Polisario Front, the appeal should be dismissed.

Regarding the *capacity to act*, in paras 52 to 60 of the ruling, the General Court concluded that the Polisario could be considered a 'legal person' within the meaning of Article 263 TFEU even though it did not have legal personality under any national law. To reach that conclusion the General Court established that the Polisario had its own statutes and an internal structure which allowed it to have the autonomy necessary to act legally.[35] It went on to state that while no binding Union legal acts had been addressed to the Polisario,[36] both the fact that it was one of the parties to a conflict which the UN is striving to solve and the fact that the Union institutions support the efforts of the UN in that regard were reason enough to consider the Polisario as a 'legal person' in the sense of Article 263 TFEU.

It can be debated whether the reasoning by the General Court has some merit or not, but what is certain is that it departs from previous case law on the matter. Indeed, while the CJEU had in some limited cases accorded the status of 'legal person' within the meaning sense of Article 263 TFEU to entities not having legal personality, such entities were required to fulfil two cumulative conditions: (1) to have 'independence and responsibility even if limited';[37] and (2) to have been treated as an independent legal entity by the institutions, whether by being the addressee of an act of the institutions or by having been recognised by the institutions as their interlocutor.[38] The fact remains that, while the Polisario may be considered to fulfil the first of these conditions, it does not fall under any of the two situations of the second condition: it has not been the addressee of any act of the institutions and the institutions have not recognised it as their interlocutor.[39] Therefore, and while the General Court tried to seek support in existing case law to explain its position in this regard, that position amounts to relaxing the requirements established by previous case law and to potentially enlarging the number of entities that could be

35 *Polisario* judgment (n 33), para 54.

36 And that, contrary to the PLO case, the Community/Union has not concluded any kind of agreement with the Polisario.

37 See the order in Case C-15/63 *Lassalle v Parliament* EU:C:1964:9.

38 See in general Case T-161/94 *Sinochem Heilongjiang v Council* EU:T:1996:101, para 31. For the addressee situation see judgment in Case C-229/05 P *PKK and PNK v Council* EU:C:2007:32, para 112. For the interlocutor situation, see judgments in Cases C-175/73 *Union Syndicale v Council* EU:C:1974:95, para 12 and C-135/81 *Groupement des Agences de Voyages v Commission* EU:C:1982:371, paras 9 and 11.

39 While the institutions do not contest the status of the Polisario as one of the parties to the negotiations concerning the final status of Western Sahara, this is not the same as considering the Polisario as an interlocutor of the institutions.

considered as 'legal persons' within the meaning of Article 263 TFEU without having legal personality, with consequences to be ascertained.

Some *general considerations about Polisario's direct and individual concern* are pertinent here. After having attributed to the Polisario the status of 'legal person' in the sense of Article 263 TFEU, the General Court went on to analyze whether the Polisario is directly and individually concerned by the contested act. The General Court started by implying that it is only in the case where the agreement itself were to apply to the territory of Western Sahara (which the General Court considered to be the case[40]), the Polisario could be directly and individually concerned.[41] This premise seems of course necessary to any conclusion upholding the admissibility of the action: if the agreement were not to be applied in the territory of the Western Sahara it would seem impossible to imagine any possible direct and individual concern of the Polisario.[42]

Here too, this reasoning appears to be at odds with established case law. Indeed, the General Court had already established that 'an act of an institution adopted pursuant to the Treaty, as a unilateral act of the Community, cannot create rights and obligations outside the territory' of the Union and that 'Therefore, the scope of the contested decision is limited to that territory and it has no legal effect' beyond it.[43] Put differently, a Council decision concluding an international agreement cannot bring about a change in the legal position of any natural or legal person beyond the Union. Applying this case law to the Western Sahara situation it seems clear that the Decision annulled by the General Court in Case T-512/12 could only produce its effects (and therefore be liable to affect the legal situations of natural or legal persons) in the territory to which the Treaties apply so that, even if the agreement were to be found as applying to the Western Sahara, such application would in any event not derive from the Council decision. As a consequence, the Council decision could never concern the Polisario on the basis of the application of the agreement to

40 *Polisario* judgment (n 33), para 103.

41 Ibid, para 73.

42 However, by assuming that the application of the agreement to the territory of Western Sahara inevitably leads to the Polisario being directly and individually concerned by the decision concluding that agreement, the General Court *de facto* operates a full identification between the Polisario, the Western Sahara territory and its inhabitants. This in turn would amount to considering the Polisario as the sole party allowed to express the will of the territory and its inhabitants concerning possible international instruments affecting them.

43 Order in Case T-212/02 *Commune de Champagne and Others v Council and Commission* EU:T:2007:194, para 90.

Western Sahara. The reasoning of the General Court seems therefore based on an erroneous premise.

When passing to the issue of *direct concern*, the General Court's reasoning is rather surprising. After establishing that the agreement was indeed being applied to the territory,[44] the General Court continued to state that at least certain of the provisions of the EU-Morocco agreement have direct effect[45] and then also that such provisions 'produce effects on the legal situation of the totality of the territory to which the agreement applies'[46] and that in this case and because of the territorial dispute this meant that the Polisario (as well as the Kingdom of Morocco) was directly concerned.[47] This reasoning may be questioned.

First of all, the concept of direct effect does not relate to *territories* but to *individuals*: it means that individuals may directly rely before courts on rights conferred on them by provisions of international agreements; however, territories cannot rely on any rights, so the concept of direct effect would be of no relevance here. Second, and for the same reason, no provision of an international agreement considered to have direct effect may, merely for that reason, have effects on the 'legal situation of the totality of the territory to which the agreement applies'[48] as territories are not subjects of law having the capacity to enjoy or assume rights and legal duties and therefore do not have any 'legal situation' that can be affected in such way.[49] Third, the fact that some of the provisions of a given agreement may have direct effect does not mean in any way that the decision concluding that agreement directly concerns all the persons who could potentially rely on such provisions. The reasoning used by the General Court here would lead to the conclusion that anybody who could rely

44 *Polisario* judgment (n 33), para 103.

45 Ibid, para 108.

46 Ibid, para 109.

47 Ibid, para 110.

48 Ibid, para 109.

49 To say, as the General Court does, that the 'legal situation of the territory' is affected because the provisions establish how certain products may be exported to or imported from the Union to that territory, is mystifying: it is the companies and individuals in Morocco (including to these effects in Western Sahara) and in the Union that will see their legal situation affected by those provisions, but not any 'territory' as they do not have any 'legal situation' of that kind which can be affected. Additionally, if it were true that territories were to have such a 'legal situation' capable of being changed, the concept of direct effect would be irrelevant: all provisions of an agreement covering that territory would by definition change its 'legal situation' by the simple fact of applying in it, irrespective of their possible 'direct effect'.

on a single provision of an international agreement having direct effect should also be considered, for the very same reason, to be directly concerned within the meaning of Article 263 TFEU by the decision concluding the agreement.[50]

A more general point is whether non-privileged applicants may actually contest decisions concluding international agreements at all, for general lack of direct concern. In principle it is inconceivable that a decision concluding an agreement might affect the legal situation of a given person without the

50 And this, depending on how one looks at the legal nature of Council decisions concluding agreements, could be sufficient under Article 263 TFEU to give standing to seek the annulment of those decisions, since if such decisions were to be considered as 'regulatory acts', only direct concern (and not individual concern) would be required under Article 263 TFEU. In fact, the General Court may have been aware, at least to a certain extent, of the problems raised by the establishment of such an eccentric link between the concepts of direct effect and direct concern, and this could be the reason why it discarded considering Council decisions under Article 218 TFEU as 'regulatory acts' within the meaning of Article 263 TFEU (paras 68–72 of the ruling): since the General Court's reasoning regarding direct concern in this case rests on the existence of direct effect (thus without implementation measures) of the agreement, every person being able to rely on provisions of an agreement having direct effect would automatically have standing to challenge the decision concluding that agreement if this type of decision were to be considered as a 'regulatory act' within the meaning of Article 263 TFEU. An additional problem in this respect is that the General Court's assessment of the legal nature of Council decisions under Article 218 TFEU is not very solid: based on Article 289(2) TFEU, the General Court's reasoning amounts to affirming (paras 70–71) that the adoption of *all* regulations, directives or decisions by the Parliament with the participation of the Council or vice versa constitute a special legislative procedure so that those legal acts are therefore to be considered as legislative. However, the General Court seems to have forgotten that Article 289(2) TFEU starts by saying 'In the specific cases provided for by the Treaties (…)'; this could be interpreted, and has consistently been interpreted by the Council, as meaning that an act should be considered as adopted under a special legislative procedure (and therefore as a legislative act) only in the cases when an explicit reference to that procedure is made in the specific legal basis (this actually happens close to 40 times in the TFEU), which would leave out Article 218 TFEU decisions and transform them into 'regulatory acts' within the meaning of Article 263 TFEU, with the consequences mentioned above. This reading requiring an explicit mention of the procedure in the legal basis would be confirmed by the fact that the adoption of all measures under Articles 349 and 352 TFEU *always* requires the consent of the European Parliament; however, these Articles give the Council the choice to adopt measures under them by resorting to a special legislative procedure or not. This would show the possibility of having measures adopted with the participation of both Council and Parliament but without the procedure (and thus the measures) being legislative.

application of other intermediate rules, as required by the case law.[51] At the very least, it will be the agreement itself (or, more usually, its implementing measures) that will affect individual legal situations, but not the decision on conclusion as such. This seems clear unless one operates within the legal fiction of considering that for the purposes of assessing the direct concern of a decision concluding an agreement both the agreement and the decision are to be considered as being one single legal act.

In any event, and quite apart from these general considerations, the General Court failed to explain how the Decision concluding the agreement directly affected the legal situation of the Polisario. The agreement establishes preferential trade measures for certain agricultural and fish products, and therefore only economic operators active in the field – the Polisario not seemingly being one of them – could claim that their legal situation is directly affected. In summary, the reasoning of the General Court on direct concern is not in the very least convincing.

Finally, the issue of *individual concern* is disposed of by the General Court in three short paragraphs.[52] Based on the *Plaumann* test,[53] the General Court asserted that the Polisario indeed enjoys certain attributes which are peculiar to it and finds itself in circumstances in which it is differentiated from all other persons since it is 'the only other participant in the UN-led negotiations between it and the Kingdom of Morocco with a view to determining the definitive international status of Western Sahara',[54] something that would be difficult to question. However, what the General Court did not do is to address the first part of the *Plaumann* test, i.e., it did not explain how the Decision would affect the Polisario by reason of those differentiating circumstances. The legal situation of the Polisario in the 'UN-led negotiations' cannot be considered to be in the very least affected by the annulled decision, nor did the General Court claim this to be the case. Moreover, the General Court had already established that 'natural or legal persons acting under the fourth paragraph of Article 230 EC [the Polisario not being any other thing] may not, in order to show that they are individually concerned by a Community act, rely only on the consequences of the act at issue on the collectivity or the entirety of their members'.[55] In these circumstances, Polisario's individual concern is more than dubious.

51 *Polisario* judgment (n 33), para 105.

52 Ibid, paras 111–113.

53 See Case C-25/62 *Plaumann & Co v Commission* EU:C:1963:17.

54 *Polisario* judgment (n 33), para 113.

55 See Case T-37/04 *Região Autónoma dos Açores v Council* EU:T:2008:236, para. 53.

All in all, the reasoning of the General Court regarding admissibility is not very persuasive. It may have been motivated by a drive to ensure the judicial protection of the Polisario, the problem with this being that:

> According to settled case-law, the Courts of the European Union may not, without exceeding their jurisdiction, interpret the conditions under which an individual may institute proceedings against a regulation in a way which has the effect of setting aside those conditions, expressly laid down in the Treaty, even in the light of the principle of effective judicial protection.[56]

3.4 *The Judgment in Case T-512/12: Substance*

When coming to the substance, and as mentioned above, the Polisario had put forward a series of eleven pleas in law. The General Court first dismissed all of the eleven pleas to conclude that there was no absolute prohibition on the Union concluding international agreements that might apply to disputed territories.[57] After that, the General Court somehow magically extracts from the first plea (lack of motivation) an additional plea of manifest error of assessment.[58] On that basis, it considered that the Council must examine itself, before concluding an agreement that might cover a disputed territory, that the production of goods covered by that agreement does not entail an exploitation of natural resources detrimental to the population of the territory or violations of the fundamental rights of that same population,[59] without explaining the source of such an obligation. Since the Council did not carry out such an assessment prior to adopting the contested decision, the General Court considered that the Council had made a manifest error of assessment[60] and annulled the decision 'insofar as it approves the application of [the] agreement to the Western Sahara'.

Parts of the General Court's reasoning call for a critical assessment. One of those parts is precisely the *addition of a plea in law* not initially put forward by the Polisario. It is at the very least odd that the General Court rejects the

56 See Case T-18/10 *Inuit Tapiriit Kanatami and Others v Parliament and Council* EU:T:2011:419, para 51.

57 *Polisario* judgment (n 33), paras 215–222.

58 Ibid, paras 125 and 226.

59 Ibid, para 241.

60 Ibid, para 247.

11 pleas in law to then transform a plea of lack of motivation into an additional plea of manifest error of assessment. The question is first raised that the rights of the defence of the Council could have been breached by such operation since 'the principle of equality of arms – together with, among others, the principle of audi alteram partem – is no more than a corollary of the very concept of a fair hearing' which 'the EU institutions may also rely on'.[61]

Additionally, and perhaps more importantly, it is unclear what kind of consequences the General Court intended to derive from its reliance on such a plea in law. Indeed, the Council decision was annulled because the Council had allegedly failed to consider certain matters when conducting its policy assessment leading to the adoption of the decision. The plea in law relied on by the General Court seems thus to be procedural and formal. Does this mean that the mere performance of the analysis required by the General Court would 'cure' the decision? In other words, would it be sufficient for the Council to show that the consideration of the human rights situation in Western Sahara had been part of its assessment at the time of adopting the Decision for this decision to be fully legal? And, for the sake of argument, what would happen if the analysis had revealed a negative assessment of that situation? Could the Council still adopt the Decision, the requirement being only one of procedure and not one of substance? Or would the Council then be obliged not to adopt the Decision? In the latter case the reason for annulment would no longer be a formal one but one of substance, yet the General Court did not say that.

A criticism could also be made concerning the *margin of discretion of the Council* when adopting decisions on the conclusion of international agreements. In paragraph 225 of the judgment, the General Court made reference to the Council's alleged obligation to examine 'carefully and impartially all the relevant facts of the individual case', supposedly based on the case law of the Court in cases C-269/90 *Technische Universität München* and C-77/09 *Gowan*.[62] The context within which that case law was developed was fundamentally different, however, as such an obligation has been imposed on the EU legislature only when it adopts individual/administrative decisions or when decisions, not being individual/administrative in nature, must be based on technical expertise. In the context of external relations, the legal context of the Council's

61 Cases C-514/07 P *Sweden v Association de la presse internationale ASBL (API) and Commission* and C-528/07 P, *Association de la presse internationale ASBL (API) v Commission* and C-532/07 P *Commission v Association de la presse internationale ASBL (API)* EU:C:2010:541 paras 88–89.

62 Respectively EU:C:1991 :438 and EU:C:2010:803.

discretion is defined precisely by Case T-572/93 *Odigitria*, in which the Court established that

> ... the Community institutions enjoy a wide discretion in the field of the Community's external economic relations, as in the corresponding internal field of the common agricultural policy ... having regard to the discretionary power conferred on the Council in the implementation of the common agricultural policy, review by the Community Court must be limited to examining whether the measure in question is vitiated by a manifest error or misuse of powers, or whether the authority in question has manifestly exceeded the limits of its discretion.[63]

While theoretically one could try to reconcile the two factors (i.e. a wide margin of discretion coupled with a need to examine carefully and impartially all the relevant facts of the individual case), in practice such a requirement would do away with the supposedly margin of discretion of the Council. Indeed, in the context of external relations, the complexity and number of factors to be considered by the institutions would make it virtually impossible for them to be sure of having considered all the relevant facts of the individual case. The introduction by the General Court of this requirement could thus entail a considerable amount of political and legal uncertainty and potentially lead to obstructing the effective conduct of the Union's foreign policy.

Yet another problematic issue is the *partial annulment* decided by the General Court. The Council Decision was annulled 'insofar as it approves the application of [the] agreement to the Western Sahara', which means that the Decision remained valid for the remainder, the annulment therefore being partial. What this partial annulment means is in itself far from clear, but in any event it seems to be at odds with the case law of the Court of Justice since, as explained in the ruling in Case C-425/13:

> As regards the conditions for partial annulment of an EU act, it is clear from settled case-law that such annulment is possible only in so far as the elements whose annulment is sought may be severed from the remainder of the act. The Court has repeatedly ruled that that requirement of severability is not satisfied where the partial annulment of an act would have the effect of altering its substance. Review of whether the contested provisions are severable requires consideration of their scope, in order

63 Case T-572/93 *Odigitria* EU:T:1995:131, paras 38 and 36.

> to be able to assess whether their annulment would alter the spirit and substance of the decision challenged.[64]

Once again, many questions do arise concerning this point. Indeed, taking account of the fact that neither the decision nor the agreement which it concluded make any reference whatsoever to the Western Sahara, it remains a mystery how the decision could be annulled insofar as it approves the application of the agreement to that territory. It is also far from clear how the annulled elements, whatever they actually are, can be severed from the remainder of the act as established by the case law. Finally, it is also open to question whether such a unilateral modification of the scope of the agreement cannot be said to alter the 'spirit and substance' of the decision concluding it. In sum, the partial annulment concluded by the General Court does not seem to follow the criteria established in this respect by previous case law.

Turning to the obligations imposed by the General Court on the Council, the legal reasoning used by the General Court to establish an *obligation for the Council to carry out an analysis of the situation of human rights* is difficult to follow and even more difficult to share. The General Court established in paragraph 228 of the judgment an obligation for the Council to check whether the activities of production, outside the Union, of the products covered by the agreement could infringe a number of rights enshrined in the EU Charter of Fundamental Rights. It is relevant to note that what the General Court asked the Council was to verify the compatibility of the activities of production with human rights, and not of the agreement or the decision concluding it, as those were considered as not being incompatible with the human rights obligations incumbent on the Union. However, such an obligation would amount to an extra-territorial (and thus legally impossible) application of the EU Charter of Fundamental Rights. It would also amount to making the legality of Union acts dependent on acts of third States (or rather on their compatibility with human rights requirements), which would compromise the autonomy of the Union's legal order.

The General Court's reasoning in this respect seems to seek to ensure respect for the human rights of the population affected by the agreement. However, the General Court did not explain why, if that is the case, Article 2 of the Association Agreement between the Union and Morocco, which establishes that human rights are an essential part of that agreement,[65] is not better suited

64 Case C-425/13 *Commission v Council* EU:C:2015:483, para. 94.

65 The agreement concluded by the annulled decision does nothing other than to modify the Association Agreement and is in that sense not an autonomous agreement but an

for that purpose. It would seem that a dynamic clause such as that contained in Article 2 of the Association Agreement, which allows the continuous assessment of the human rights situation in the parties' respective territories, would be better suited for the purpose intended by the General Court than a single assessment at the time of concluding the agreement and performed on the basis of an hypothesis concerning the possible future impact of that agreement on the human rights situation.

Finally, the *obligation for the Council to carry out an analysis of the situation of natural resources*, established by the General Court in paragraph 241 of its judgment on the basis of Article 73 of the UN Charter, is also a contentious point. Article 73 UN Charter is addressed to, and establishes obligations for, the 'Members of the United Nations which have or assume responsibilities for the administration of territories whose peoples have not yet attained a full measure of self-government'. As a consequence, no obligations may be imposed on the Union or its institutions on the basis of that Article. It is to be additionally noted that Article 73 UN Charter does not comply with the requirements established by the Court of Justice for individuals to rely on international law provisions, as it 'does not establish rules intended to apply directly and immediately to individuals and to confer upon them rights or freedoms capable of being relied upon against States'.[66] Article 73 can then hardly form the basis for any rights of individuals or any obligations for the Union.

As just seen, the judgment of the General Court in Case T-512/12 seems to be too audacious in departing from established case law.

3.5 *The Judgment in Case C-104/16 P*

As mentioned above, the Court of Justice issued on 21 December 2016 its ruling in Case C-104/16 P after an expedited procedure; the Council had brought its appeal against the ruling of the General Court in Case T-512/12 on 19 February 2016. The Court of Justice ruled by upholding the Council's appeal and setting aside the judgment of the General Court in Case T-512/12. It did so after finding that the Polisario could not be directly and individually concerned as the agreement at stake could not be interpreted as applying to the Western Sahara. On the basis of that finding, it dismissed the action for lack of standing of Polisario and did not go into all the pleas in law put forward by the Council.

To come to that point, the Court of Justice considered that 'the conclusion of the General Court in paragraph 103 of that judgment that the Liberalisation

integral part of the Association Agreement. Therefore Article 2 of the Association Agreement is fully relevant in this context.

66 See Case C-308/06 *Intertanko* EU:C:2008:312, para 64.

Agreement "also applies to the territory of Western Sahara" is based, not on a finding of fact, but on a legal interpretation of that agreement made by the General Court on the basis of Article 31 of the Vienna Convention'.[67]

However, the Court of Justice considered that 'in order to be able to draw correct legal conclusions from the absence of a stipulation excluding Western Sahara from the territorial scope of the Association Agreement, in interpreting that agreement, the General Court was bound not only to observe the rules of good faith interpretation laid down in Article 31(1) of the Vienna Convention but also that laid down in Article 31(3)(c) of that convention, pursuant to which the interpretation of a treaty must be carried out by taking account of any relevant rules of international law applicable in the relations between the parties', and that those rules were the principle of self-determination, the rule codified in Article 29 of the Vienna Convention according to which a treaty is binding upon each party in respect of its entire 'territory' unless a different intention appears from the treaty or is otherwise established, and the principle of the relative effect of treaties.[68]

After analysing the three rules, the Court of Justice comes to the conclusion that all three prevent an interpretation of a Agreement with Morocco as covering Western Sahara when the Agreement does not explicitly cover the territory.[69] Indeed, *the principle of self-determination* implies, as specified by the UNGA and the ICJ, a distinct and separate status of non-self-governing territories, including thus the Western Sahara. As regards the *rule codified in Article 29 of the Vienna Convention*, the Court of Justice considers that if an agreement is supposed to apply beyond the 'geographical space over which that State exercises the fullness of the powers granted to sovereign entities by international law', that treaty must expressly provide for it in accordance with international practice – which was not the case in the Agreement at stake. Finally, the *principle of relative effects of the treaties* means that the people of Western Sahara must be regarded as a 'third party' within the meaning of the principle of the relative effect of treaties, and that an implementation covering the Western Sahara must receive the consent of such a third party, something which was not proven in this case.

On that basis, the Court of Justice established that it was wrong for the General Court to consider that the Agreement could have been interpreted as

67 See Case C-104/16 P, EU:C:2016:973, para 81.
68 Ibid, paras 86–87.
69 Ibid, paras 88–108.

covering the Western Sahara. The Court of Justice then went on to say that no subsequent practice could justify such an interpretation.[70]

Finally, the Court does not mention the need for any assessment to be performed by the Council concerning human rights or natural resources before concluding international agreements, and all its analysis is restricted to the very specific case of non-self-governing territories.

The legal analysis by the Court may seem, under international law, immaculate and is certainly much closer to the orthodoxy of international and Union law. It is questionable however that the first question to be addressed was the application of the Agreement to Western Sahara. Contrary to the Court of Justice's arguments in paragraph 82 of its judgment, it is not the case that 'the positions of the Council and the Commission before the Court on that point ultimately converge' and that therefore 'a preliminary examination of the merits of the conclusion reached by the General Court as to the application of the Agreement to the territory of Western Sahara' was needed. Indeed, as can be seen from paragraphs 78 and 79 of the appeals judgment, the positions of Council and the Commission do not in fact converge and, at least as far as the Council is concerned, do not need the analysis of such question. While the Commission position was that the agreement could not be interpreted as meaning that it was legally applicable to Western Sahara, *the Council position was that the interpretation of the Agreement to ascertain whether or not it covered Western Sahara was irrelevant and unnecessary*, since in any event the application to any territory outside the boundaries of the Union could not be the result of a Union act, including the Council decision that the Polisario had attacked, in accordance with the jurisprudence in *Commune de Champagne*. Therefore, neither the General Court nor the Court of Justice needed to assess whether or not an interpretation of the agreement to cover Western Sahara was legally possible or correct. The Council position was that legally possible or not, existing or not, such an application could anyway never stem from the Council decision and that therefore the Polisario (nor anybody else) could not derive from such an application any standing to attack the Council Decision concluding the agreement.

4 Other Pending Western Sahara Cases

At the time of writing this article, there are two other pending cases before the Union Courts concerning the Western Sahara. The first is Case T-180/14, where

70 Ibid, paras 117–125.

the Polisario has requested the annulment of a Council decision to conclude a Fisheries Protocol with Morocco.[71] The second is Case C-266/16, concerning the request for a preliminary ruling submitted to the ECJ by the High Court of Justice of England and Wales[72] on interpretation and compatibility with international law of the Association Agreement and the Fisheries Partnership Agreement between the Union and Morocco.[73] The question of admissibility, which is central to the first case, as it was equally important in Cases T-512/12 and C-104/16 P, will not be at issue here and, this being a preliminary ruling, the ECJ will in principle have to deal directly with the substance. The impact of the ruling in Case C-104/16 P in these other cases cannot be predicted as the factual and legal circumstances are not identical.

5 Assessing the Polisario Saga in the Context of Previous Case Law Relating to Territorial Disputes

Regarding the substance, and when comparing the rulings with the previous cases dealing with territorial disputes mentioned above, the results are mixed. Indeed, if the *Anastasiou* cases are taken as reference, it could be argued that the Western Sahara dispute is an internal affair of Morocco ('which alone is internationally recognized') and that therefore the Union should refrain from adopting unilateral measures concerning the application of the agreement to the territory, especially in view of the fact that Morocco's clear and explicit intention was for the agreement to apply to the Western Sahara, which it considers an integral part of its own territory.

When looking at *Odigitria*, the General Court seems to have gone much further in the *Polisario* case, probably due to the hybrid nature of the Western Sahara territory as both non-self-governing *and* disputed. On the one hand, the General Court asserts that the possibility to conclude an agreement which might apply to a disputed territory had already been established by *Odigitria*.[74] However, what the General Court has implicitly accepted in the *Polisario* case

71 Council Decision 2013/785/EU of 16 December 2013 on the conclusion, on behalf of the European Union, of the Protocol between the European Union and the Kingdom of Morocco setting out the fishing opportunities and financial contribution provided for in the Fisheries Partnership Agreement between the European Union and the Kingdom of Morocco [2013] OJ L 349/1.

72 *Western Sahara Campaign v HMRC and DEFRA*, [2015] EWHC 2898 (Admin).

73 Fisheries Partnership Agreement between the European Community and the Kingdom of Morocco [2006] OJ L 141/4.

74 Ibid, para 221.

is that the Union may conclude agreements with third States that might apply to non-self-governing territories (even if they are disputed as this one is). This is something altogether different from the application to a territory which is disputed between two sovereign States (as was the case in *Odigitria*). On the other hand, the General Court has established an obligation, of unknown legal origin, to assess the impact of any such agreements on the natural resources of the territory and on the fundamental rights of the population of that territory. This could potentially imply that, were such assessment to be negative, the Council could/should refuse to include the disputed territory in the agreement, thereby taking a position on the dispute, which the General Court did not consider as appropriate in *Odigitria*.[75] The Court of Justice has not mentioned any of this in its own judgment, but has established that the population of a non-self-governing territory must give its consent for any agreement to be implemented in that territory and this irrespectively of whether or not the agreement is for their benefit.

Finally, while the comparison between the *Polisario* cases and *Brita* is difficult as there were not two conflicting agreements at issue, the EU Courts also seem to have gone further in the *Polisario* case. Indeed, in *Brita* the question at stake was the joint interpretation of two agreements concluded by the Union, it then being irrelevant that one of them was concluded with a non-State. By contrast, in the *Polisario* cases the position of the non-State has been taken into consideration even in the absence of any legal instrument framing the relations of the Union with that non-State.

The General Court seems to have gone legally much further in the *Polisario* case than the EU Courts had done in their previous case law concerning territorial disputes. The Court of Justice, however, seems to have adopted a more orthodox approach and circumscribed its analysis to the specific situation of non-self-governing territories.

6 Conclusion

The CJEU has had to deal on a few occasions with cases stemming from territorial disputes of a different factual and legal nature. Yet before the first *Polisario* case, the EU Courts never had to deal with a direct action brought by one of the parties to the dispute, a party moreover which is not a State.

75 Of course, attention should be paid to the fact that, again, the dispute in *Odigitria* was between sovereign States, unlike the one concerning Western Sahara.

While the General Court's legal reasoning cannot be said to be completely inconsistent with the EU Courts' previous case law concerning territorial disputes, there are certain parts of its reasoning which are surprising. Concerning the admissibility of the action, the General Court seems to have favoured giving a possibility to the Polisario to have its views heard rather than being consistent with the previous case law on the matter. On the substance, the General Court juggled with the pleas in law put forward by the applicant in order to create a new one which then became the basis for annulment. Moreover, it imposed a duty on the institutions of the Union to assess the impact of a future agreement covering a territory on the human rights situation in and the natural resources of that territory before concluding the agreement, without a convincing explanation of the origins of such an obligation. And finally it decided a puzzling partial annulment of the contested decision, which also seems to be at odds with previous case law of the EU Courts.

The Court of Justice has taken a more cautious and orthodox approach, circumscribing its analysis to the case of non-self-governing territories and refraining from imposing of the Union institutions the performance of certain analyses before the adoption of decisions concluding international agreements.

Two cases concerning the Western Sahara are still open, and I am sure that Ricardo will follow them with great interest.

PART 4

Specific EU *External Policies*

The Common Foreign and Security Policy

CHAPTER 13

EU Common Foreign and Security Policy and Protection of Fundamental Rights

Christiaan Timmermans

1 Introductory Remark

In 2011 Ricardo Gosalbo Bono published a most impressive and stimulating essay on the genesis and evolution of the notion of the Rule of Law, *der Rechtsstaat, l'État de droit*, including the dimension of fundamental rights, comparing that evolution in various jurisdictions and in international law.[1] Reading this text one is struck by his open-mindedness, fundamentally optimistic without being naïve. I recognised the much-appreciated former colleague, amiable in his presentation but persistent and consistent in his legal argumentation. Arguing with him on a point of law was a challenge and a pleasure at the same time. To honour him I want to explore further one of the issues he discussed in his essay.

2 Common Foreign and Security Policy and Protection of Fundamental Rights after the Lisbon Treaty

The Lisbon Treaty has made explicit and clarified the relationship between the Common Foreign and Security Policy (CFSP) and the protection of fundamental rights. That protection, which has been recognised in the first place as one of the fundamental values of the Union (Article 2 TEU), must also be promoted and pursued as one of the objectives of the Union's external action (Article 3(5) TEU). This is reaffirmed in the opening article of the Chapter laying down general provisions on the Union's external action (Article 21(1) and (2)(b) TEU). To put the matter beyond all doubt, Article 23 TEU makes explicit that this equally applies to the CFSP. In his article Ricardo Gosalbo Bono amply

1 Ricardo Gosalbo Bono, 'État de droit et droit de l'Union européenne' (2011) Nos. 544, 545 and 546 Revue du Marché commun et de l'Union européenne (1st part, 13; 2nd part, 96; 3rd part, 156).

 DOI 10.1163/9789004347175_014

illustrates how this objective is actually pursued and made operational within the framework of the various policies developed by the Union with regard to third countries.

Apart from being an objective of the CFSP, the protection of fundamental rights is of course also a value to be respected by the Union itself when adopting CFSP measures. The EU Charter of Fundamental Rights (the Charter) (Article 6(1) TEU) and fundamental rights as general principles of the Union's law (Article 6(3) TEU) also apply to the CFSP. Nowhere in the Treaties is there any exception in that respect. Indeed, how could the Union be exempt from having to respect its own fundamental values?

In the same vein, the obligation imposed on the Union under Article 6(2) TEU to accede to the European Convention for the Protection of Human Rights and Fundamental Freedoms (ECHR or Convention) has been quite generally worded. It is the Union as such that should accede, covering all its policies and fields of activity. To carve out the CFSP from accession would be difficult to justify, even leaving aside that the Convention itself excludes general reservations by contracting parties (Article 57). It is true that Protocol No 8 to the Lisbon Treaty requires the accession agreement to preserve the specific characteristics of the Union and Union law. However, with regard to the general obligation for the Union to respect fundamental rights, also in the field of CFSP, it would be difficult to detect any specificity warranting special treatment, all the less so when taking into consideration Articles 6(3) TEU and 52(3) of the Charter.

Effective protection of fundamental rights can only be ensured if persons have access to a court in case of a violation or presumed violation of those rights. Under the previous Treaties the Court of Justice of the European Union (CJEU) did not have any jurisdiction with regard to CFSP acts or decisions, apart from ensuring that CFSP measures did not encroach upon Community competences (ex-Article 47 TEU). It could however claim jurisdiction with regard to measures enacted under the first pillar implementing a CFSP decision laying down restrictive measures against a third country (on the basis of ex-Articles 301 and 60 of the Treaty establishing the European Community (TEC)).

The Lisbon Treaty has enlarged the CJEU's jurisdiction. The CJEU continues to have full jurisdiction with regard to restrictive measures implementing a CFSP decision to interrupt or reduce, in part or completely, economic and financial relations with one or more third countries. Article 215(1) TFEU constitutes the legal basis for such measures. According to Article 215(2) TFEU restrictive measures implementing a CFSP decision may also be adopted against natural or legal persons and groups or non-State entities. In Case C-130/10, *European Parliament v Council*, the CJEU clarified that Article 215(1) TFEU mirrors ex-Articles 60 and 301 TEC.[2] Those articles, as the Court has decided in *Kadi I*, already allowed sanctions against natural or legal persons linked to a third country's regime.[3] Article 215(1) TFEU must therefore be considered to allow the same. Article 215(2) TFEU mirrors the legal bases used for the regulations concerned by the *Kadi* case (ex-Articles 60, 301 and 308 TEC).[4] This new legal basis concerns CFSP-related sanctions of a financial or economic nature, for instance to combat international terrorism concerning persons not linked to a third country regime. Such sanctions too fall within the scope of the CJEU's normal jurisdiction. The CJEU is also competent with regard to financial sanctions against terrorists or presumed terrorists imposed under policies to combat terrorism within the framework of the Area of Freedom, Security and Justice on the basis of Article 75 TFEU. Thus, these sanctions are not CFSP-related.[5] Finally, the CJEU has now obtained, by virtue of Article 275 (2) TFEU, a new limited jurisdiction with regard to restrictive measures against natural or legal persons adopted by the Council within the framework of the CFSP. This, apparently, concerns sanctions which cannot be adopted on the basis of Article 215(2) TFEU because they are not of a financial or economic nature, such as travel restrictions, visa bans, etc.[6]

We may conclude that since the Lisbon Treaty, and this means real progress, persons affected have at least access to legal protection at EU level with regard to sanctions of a financial or other nature (visa ban, travel restrictions). I shall not discuss here the question of whether the CJEU's jurisdiction under Article 275(2) TFEU remains limited to legal review within the framework of an action for annulment under Article 263 TFEU or is without prejudice, as has been argued in academic writing,[7] to a possible preliminary ruling jurisdiction under Article 267 TFEU or jurisdiction for damages actions under Article 340 TFEU.

---

2 EU:C:2012:472, para 52.

3 Joined Cases C-402/05 P and C-415/02 P *Yassin Abdullah Kadi and Al Barakaat International Foundation v Council and Commission* EU:C:2008:461, para 166.

4 Case C-130/10 *European Parliament v Council* EU:C:2012:472, para 53.

5 Ibid, para 59.

6 See for instance Joined Cases C-478/11 P to 482 /11 P *Laurent Gbagbo and Others v Council* EU:C:2013:258.

7 See more particularly, also with further references, Christophe Hillion, 'A Powerless Court? The European Court of Justice and the EU Common Foreign and Security Policy' in Marise Cremona and Anne Thies (eds), *The European Court of Justice and External Relations Law – Constitutional Challenges* (Hart Publishing 2014) 47. See however AG Kokott's View in Opinion 2/13 (EU:C:2014:2454, paras 85–95). The General Court has declined jurisdiction with regard to actions for damages in Case T-328/14 *Mahmoud Jannatian v Council* EU:T:2016:86, paras 30–31.

In any event, it is interesting to note that the CJEU, in its first judgments in cases raising the issue of the scope of its jurisdiction regarding the CFSP, has emphasized that the Treaty provisions restricting that jurisdiction (Articles 24(1) TEU and 275(1) TFEU) should be interpreted narrowly, because they derogate from the general rules on the CJEU's jurisdiction according to Article 19 TEU.[8]

In spite of these clarifications and innovations, there remain gaps in possible legal protection for natural and legal persons against CFSP measures. One example might be damages caused by Union missions of a civilian or military nature in third countries.[9] Normally, the Union will conclude an agreement with the third country concerned to regulate the status of these missions and their members (questions of immunity), and provide for dispute settlement procedures as well as arbitration procedures to decide on private party claims.[10] Whether these procedures ensure legal protection equivalent to normal judicial protection might be questionable. Another question is whether these arrangements would always provide for the exclusion of possible claims introduced before Member States' courts.

Indeed, where the Union courts lack jurisdiction, the national courts of the Member States must step in and ensure effective legal protection according to well-established principles of the CJEU case law,[11] now also codified by the TEU (Article 19(1)). It is important to note in that regard that the Treaty provisions on CFSP, including the Common Security and Defence Policy (CSDP), emphasize the role of the Member States in the execution and implementation of these policies (see Article 24(1) TEU with regard to the CFSP generally). CSDP missions outside the Union must be undertaken using capabilities provided

---

8 Case C-658/11 *European Parliament v Council* EU:C:2014:2025 (*Mauritius*), para 70 and Case C-439/13 P *Elitaliana SpA v Eulex Kosovo* EU:C:2015:753, para 42. The latter judgment is particularly interesting because the Court accepted jurisdiction with regard to a conflict about the procedure awarding a public contract launched by the CFSP mission Eulex Kosovo. In that regard see also Case C-455/14 P *H v Council and Commission* EU:C:2016:569.

9 For examples of such missions see Ricardo Gosalbo Bono (n 1) 3rd part, 158–166 (paras 135–152).

10 For an example of a military mission and a so called Status Agreement, see respectively Council Decision 2013/34/CFSP of 17 January 2013 on a European Union military mission to contribute to the training of the Malian Armed Forces (EUTM Mali) [2013] OJ L14/19 and Agreement between the European Union and the Republic of Mali on the status in the Republic of Mali of the European Union military mission to contribute to the training of the Malian Armed Forces (EUTM Mali) [2013] OJ L106/2.

11 Case C-97/91 *Oleificio Borelli SpA v Commission* EU:C:1992:491; Case C-50/00 P *Unión de Pequeños Agricultores v Council* EU:C:2002:462; Case C-583/11 P *Inuit Tapiriit Kanatami and Others v European Parliament and Council* EU:C:2013:625.

by the Member States (Article 42(1) and (3) TEU). This might be an argument for accepting the direct responsibility of a sending Member State for the actions carried out by its personnel, civilian or military, including for damage caused.[12] Were a case to be brought before a national court, it is that court which will decide on the admissibility of that claim, applying national law. It cannot be excluded that a national court, depending on the circumstances of a case, will hold the Union responsible, not the Member State, and dismiss the claim. In that scenario there will exist a clear lacuna in legal protection and thus a problem with Article 47 of the EU Charter of Fundamental Rights. A similar lacuna might become apparent with regard to actions causing damage carried out by members of CFSP missions in third countries belonging to the staff of the EU itself. Possible claims for compensation could be handled under arbitration procedures provided for by a so-called Status Agreement. In the absence of such procedures claims could be brought before a court of the third country concerned, immediately triggering questions of immunity. Quite probably, such actions could not be introduced before the EU General Court because of lack of jurisdiction.

Could the ECHR be invoked in such a situation? Would the European Court of Human Rights (ECtHR or Strasbourg Court) admit a complaint against the Member State concerned for violation of Articles 6 and 13 ECHR? In its *Behrami* decision regarding missions in Kosovo under the ultimate control of the United Nations (UN) the Strasbourg Court dismissed the complaints, holding that the actions concerned were attributable to the UN and not to the defendant States.[13] Would it be possible to bring a complaint against all Member States as the Contracting Parties of the EU Treaties on the grounds that they had failed to provide for sufficiently effective mechanisms of legal protection in the field

12 See on the question of responsibility for CSDP operations Gilles Marhic, 'Violations of Human Rights and International Humanitarian Law in the Context of Missions: Assessing the Responsibility of the European Union', in Mariano Aznar and Milena Costas (eds), *The Integration of the Human Rights Component and International Humanitarian Law in Peacekeeping Missions Led by the European Union* (CEDRI/ATLAS 2011) 111; Frederik Naert, 'The International Responsibility of the Union in the Context of Its CSDP Operations' in Panos Koutrakos and Malcolm Evans (eds), *The International Responsibility of the European Union* (Hart 2013) 313; Aurel Sari and Ramses Wessel, 'International Responsibility for EU Military Operations: Finding the EU's Place in the Global Accountability Regime' in Bart Van Vooren, Steven Blockmans and Jan Wouters (eds), *The EU's Role in Global Governance: The Legal Dimension* (OUP 2013) 126.

13 *Behrami v France* App no 71412/01 and *Saramati v Germany, France and Norway* App no 78166/01 (ECtHR, 2 May 2007). See also *Al-Jedda v United Kingdom* App no 27021/08 (ECtHR, 7 July 2011).

of CFSP, according to the *Matthews* scenario?[14] This cannot be excluded.[15] The situation would of course be entirely different once the Union has acceded to the Convention. Then, a complaint could be directly addressed to the Union. But that is precisely what the CJEU could not accept in its Opinion 2/13 concerning the draft agreement on the accession of the European Union to the Convention for the Protection of Human Rights and Fundamental Freedoms (draft Accession Agreement[16]).[17]

3 The Draft Accession Agreement

The drafters of the draft Accession Agreement have been attentive to the problem of a possible lacuna of legal protection in the field of the CFSP. Care has been taken to prevent a Member State from exonerating itself from its obligations under the Convention for actions carried out by persons falling within its jurisdiction, because of their action being attributable not to the Member State but to the EU. With this in mind, Article 1(3) of the draft Accession Agreement stipulates that the EU shall only be bound by the obligations imposed by the Convention for acts, measures or omissions of its institutions, bodies, offices or agencies, or of persons acting on their behalf. Conversely, acts, measures or omissions of organs of a Member State or of persons acting on its behalf shall be attributed to that State, even if such acts, measures or omissions have occurred when implementing EU law. The draft Explanatory Report[18] suggests that this formal criterion of attribution would prevent the *Behrami* case law of the Strasbourg Court from applying, so that a Member State could not deny its responsibility under the Convention by arguing that the Union was ultimately responsible because of the Union having caused it to act as it did.[19]

---

14 *Denise Matthews v United Kingdom* App no 24833/94 (ECtHR, 18 February 1999).

15 cf *Gasparini v Italy and Belgium* App no 10750/03 (ECtHR, 12 May 2009).

16 The draft Accession Agreement has been published as appendix I to the Final Report of the Negotiating Group to the Steering Committee for Human Rights (CDDH) of the Council of Europe (doc 47 + 1(2013)008rev2 <http://www.coe.int/t/dghl/standardsetting/hrpolicy/Accession/Meeting_reports/47_1(2013)008rev2_EN.pdf> accessed 20 November 2016 (Final Report to CDDH)).

17 EU:C:2014:2454. See below.

18 The draft Explanatory Report has been published as appendix V to the Final Report to CDDH.

19 Draft Explanatory Report (n 18), paras 22–25.

Indeed, the draft Accession Agreement makes a fundamental distinction between 'actorship' and responsibility. Actorship is the criterion determining against whom an application should be addressed. This is the actor itself, the initiator of the action, which is the object of the complaint. Even if a Member State's action has been entirely determined by EU law, the application should be brought against the Member State, not the Union. The co-respondent mechanism also allows the party responsible (either fully or partly) to be brought into the procedure before the Strasbourg Court.[20] The co-respondent mechanism enables the Strasbourg Court to condemn both a Member State and the Union for a violation without having to determine their respective shares of responsibility. Both will be held jointly responsible.

In this way, the drafters have sought to avoid that where an action by a Member State's nationals within the framework of a CFSP operation, for instance a mission in a third country, could be attributed to the Union according to the *Behrami* approach, the Union would be systematically condemned for violation of Articles 6 and 13 ECHR because of the absence of legal protection at EU level.[21] However, that possibility remains, as already observed, where EU personnel participate in such a mission. In the absence of a competent Union court to decide on possible claims against the Union for compensation of damages, an application could be made before the Strasbourg Court to condemn the Union for not providing the necessary legal protection. Or would the complainant have access to the national courts in application of Article 274 TFEU, as advocated by Advocate General (AG) Kokott in Opinion 2/13?[22]

To summarise, as I understand it, the functioning of the mechanism provided for by the draft Accession Agreement in cases concerning the CFSP for which the CJEU does not have jurisdiction:

– If the CFSP act is implemented by a Member State act, that act may be attacked before the national courts and may also eventually become the object of a complaint before the Strasbourg Court. The co-respondent mechanism will allow the EU to become a party to that procedure and the EU could be condemned together with the Member State. The EU may then be obliged under the Convention to abolish or amend the CFSP act. The CJEU

---

20 Draft Accession Agreement (n 16), art 3.

21 See Géraud de Bergues, Diégo Colas and Natacha Rouam, 'La France dans le cadre des négociations d'adhésion de l'Union européenne à la Convention européenne de sauvegarde des droits de l'homme' (2014) XV Annuaire Français de Relations Internationales 339, 345–348.

22 View of AG Kokott (EU:C:2014:2475), paras 96–103.

cannot be involved in this procedure because it lacks preliminary jurisdiction and the prior involvement procedure of Article 3(6) of the draft Accession Agreement cannot be applied. Indeed, the CJEU cannot acquire new competences simply as a result of the accession (Article 1(3) of the draft Accession Agreement, Article 6(2) TEU and Protocol No 8).

- In the absence of a national implementing act a complaint could be directly brought against the EU before the Strasbourg Court, the CJEU having no jurisdiction. If the EU were condemned, it would have to abolish or amend the CFSP act. If the EU were condemned for not providing adequate legal protection, the EU Treaties would have to be amended. If legal redress against CFSP acts for which the CJEU lacks jurisdiction were sought through the national courts, the first scenario would have to apply. The Member State concerned would be responsible for the decisions of its national courts and could ultimately be brought before the Strasbourg Court. The co-respondent mechanism would allow the involvement of and ultimately the condemnation of the EU as well as the Member State concerned.

4 Opinion 2/13

The CJEU has not been able to accept this mechanism.[23] In so far as it lacks competence on CFSP matters to ensure protection of fundamental rights, the Strasbourg Court would, through the EU's accession, acquire an exclusive jurisdiction in that regard.[24] For further explanation the Court refers to its Opinion 1/09 on the European Patents Court.[25] According to that Opinion, jurisdiction to carry out a judicial review of EU acts, including with regard to fundamental rights, cannot be conferred exclusively on an international court which is outside the institutional and judicial framework of the EU. That being so, the draft Accession Agreement fails to have regard to the specific characteristics of EU law with regard to the judicial review of CFSP acts.[26] In other words the lack of jurisdiction of the CJEU, and the impossibility to grant exclusive jurisdiction to an outside court following therefrom, must be regarded as a specific characteristic of EU law.

This reasoning is very terse and, in my view, not really convincing. Three short comments:

23 Opinion 2/13 (n 17).
24 Ibid, para 255.
25 EU:C:2011:123.
26 Opinion 2/13 (n 17), para 257.

- Would the Strasbourg Court indeed acquire an *exclusive* jurisdiction? What about the national courts? Nothing is said about their possible role. This is all the more astonishing since AG Kokott was able to arrive at a positive conclusion precisely because of the guarantees of judicial protection provided by the national courts.
- Is Opinion 1/09 on the European Patents Court really a relevant precedent? Is the case of the Patents Court (as it was then structured), really comparable with the position of the Strasbourg Court after accession? Could the compatibility control carried out by the Strasbourg Court be qualified as judicial review? Well, not in the traditional sense. The Strasbourg Court does not express itself on the legality of a contested measure of a contracting party; it cannot annul that measure or declare it invalid. The Patents Court would have acquired exclusive jurisdiction for litigation by private parties concerning Community patents (for instance on patent infringement, counterclaims for the revocation of patents and much more). The Patent Court would also have been granted competence to give a binding interpretation of EU rules, depriving national courts of that jurisdiction, and in so doing, of their competence to submit questions for a preliminary ruling to the CJEU. None of these aspects would apply to the Strasbourg Court after accession. The national courts would retain their jurisdiction and their lack of competence to request preliminary rulings under Article 267 TFEU would not be a consequence of EU accession to the ECHR. So, there exist important differences between the structure of the Patents Court and the mechanism of the draft Accession Agreement.
- It is something of a paradox to see the absence of jurisdiction qualified as a specific characteristic of EU law justifying the refusal to grant exclusive jurisdiction to the Strasbourg Court. I feel sympathy for the statement of AG Kokott that this 'can hardly be used as an argument against recognition of the jurisdiction of the judicial body of an international organisation' and that 'the effectiveness of legal protection for individuals is strengthened, rather than weakened, in such a situation by the recognition of an international jurisdiction'.[27]

My impression is that this reasoning does not really express the fundamental objections of the Court. To reveal those objections we have to read behind the reasoning; or better still, to read between the lines. Indeed, the Court was confronted with an almost impossible dilemma because of its (partial) lack

27 View of AG Kokott (n 22), para 193.

of jurisdiction to protect fundamental rights with regard to CFSP measures. To follow the view of AG Kokott and to accept full jurisdiction of the national courts to step in where the CJEU lacked competence, would have meant accepting as adequate a system of legal protection against Union acts lacking all the essential elements of the EU system of judicial protection and the safeguards for uniform interpretation following therefrom: the preliminary ruling procedure, the *Foto Frost* doctrine (the incompetence of national courts to rule on the invalidity of Union decisions),[28] the direct actions, the infringement procedure, the damages actions.

On the other hand, the Court could hardly have said that judicial protection by the national courts alone, in the absence of its own jurisdiction, would necessarily be inadequate and insufficient. Moreover, explicitly recognising lacunae in the Union's system of legal protection would have revealed the existence of a systemic deficiency in the EU system of access to justice and fundamental rights protection. That by itself would have constituted a bar to accession (and raised problems with regard to Article 47 of the EU Charter of Fundamental Rights).

I do not think that accepting the role of the national courts as guardians of the rule of law with regard to CFSP acts for which the CJEU lacks jurisdiction, would necessarily cause problems with Articles 6 and 13 ECHR. A possible solution could have been for the Court to leave some margin for future interpretation of the notion of restrictive measures for which the Court has competence (in fact this is what the Court has done) and to insist on the need for effective legal protection on the national level, building on Article 19(1) TEU and existing case law. Such a solution could easily have been devised on the basis of elements of the Commission's position and that of AG Kokott.

The Court has not been willing to do that.

Obviously, the Court cannot accept that in the autonomous and constitutionalised legal system of the EU with its own, albeit limited, powers, including its own fully-fledged judicial system, one of the essential responsibilities of the judiciary, which is to ensure respect for fundamental rights, could be outsourced to a foreign court or be entrusted to the national courts alone. That would cause an unacceptable rupture of the foundations of the EU constitutional system.

One may ask the question whether such an objection does not openly ignore the explicit will of the authors of the Treaties as expressed in Articles 6(2) and 24(1) TEU and 275 TFEU? Well, it may come close to that. Admittedly, the

28 Case 314/85 *Foto-Frost v Hauptzollamt Lübeck-Ost* EU:C:1987:452.

Court has not said that it considers the exclusion of its jurisdiction with regard to CFSP acts as contrary to the basic laws of the Union. But that day may still come.

5 Concluding Remarks – What Now?

If my reading of the Opinion 2/13 is correct, adapting the draft Accession Agreement to meet the objections of the Court is not a possible way out.[29] For instance, to clarify and insist on the role of the national courts as the guarantors of legal protection against CFSP acts would not help. That was the solution of AG Kokott, which the Court has not been willing to accept. As the ECHR does not allow for general reservations, amending the EU Treaties so as to grant the CJEU full jurisdiction on CFSP matters seems to be the only way to pass the hurdle to accession.

29 See on this question also Jean-Paul Jacqué's forthcoming contribution in the new book on the 60th Anniversary of the Rome Treaties edited by Antonio Tizzano (CJEU 2017).

The Common Commercial Policy

CHAPTER 14

Of Transferred Competence, Institutional Balance and Judicial Autonomy – Constitutional Developments in EU Trade Policy Seven Years after Lisbon

Frank Hoffmeister

1 Introduction

As Director of the external relations team in the Council Legal Service since 1998 and a law professor at the Institute for European Studies (Vrije Universiteit Brussels) Ricardo Gosalbo Bono always combined practice and theory in a remarkable fashion. His interests span from the classic subjects of war and peace and the law of the United Nations to the intricacies of EU foreign policy and the diversity of national legal systems, which he still teaches at the Institute. I had the pleasure to participate in some oral defences as a reader where he acted as promotor for LLM students from all parts of the world in that capacity. Needless to say that these examinations were also quite enlightening, not only for the future-to-be master of law, but also for the co-examiner!

Among Ricardo's academic credentials we also find the interesting entry that the University of Barcelona appointed him in 2002 as Honorary Professor of International Trade Law. As a core field in the EU's external policies, trade has thus not only crossed his desk regularly in the Council's *Justus Lipsius* building, but he also invested some of his large academic energy into it. An example thereof can be found in his excellent overview article 'The Organization of the External Relations of the European Union in the Treaty of Lisbon'[1] from 2011. In the section on the Common Commercial Policy (CCP), Ricardo identified no less than six important constitutional developments when comparing the new Article 207 TFEU to the ex-Article 133 of the Treaty establishing the

1 Ricardo Gosalbo Bono, 'The Organization of the External Relations of the European Union in the Treaty of Union' in Panos Koutrakos (ed), *The European Union's External Relations: A Year After Lisbon* (2011) CLEER Working Paper 2011/3 <http://www.asser.nl/upload/documents/772011_51358CLEER%20WP%202011-3%20-%20KOUTRAKOS.pdf> accessed 15 November 2016.

 | DOI 10.1163/9789004347175_015

European Community (TEC). Quite naturally, they relate to the scope of newly transferred competences and the institutional balance between the institutions.[2] As I remember vividly his oral presentation in Bristol on these matters, it came to my mind to revisit this topic roughly seven years later. So, in honour of Ricardo, I take his observations as a starting point, while adding my own thoughts on the matter to catch up with recent developments. To complete the picture, the topic of judicial autonomy is added. It has not been in our minds immediately after the entry into force of the Lisbon Treaty, but came to prominence in the public debate about the direction of the EU's investment policy. In particular, in respect to the investment chapter in the Transatlantic Trade and Investment Partnership (TTIP), under negotiation between the EU and the United States between 2015 and 2016, some critics made the point that establishing international investment tribunals could undermine the role of the Court of Justice of the European Union (CJEU). Since this also has a constitutional dimension, it seems to sit well with Ricardo's other topics.

2 The Scope of the Lisbon Transfer of Competence

2.1 *Trade in Services and Commercial Aspects of Intellectual Property*

Since Lisbon the Common Commercial Policy also comprises 'trade in services' and 'commercial aspects of intellectual property' under Article 207(1) TFEU. Farsighted, Ricardo has opined that 'This will include in principle all matters by the GATS [General Agreement on Trade in Services] and the TRIPS [Trade-Related Aspects of Intellectual Property Rights] agreements within the context of the WTO [World Trade Organisation]'[3] which had hitherto been considered of mixed competence under the previous treaty regime.[4] And indeed, the CJEU subsequently handed down two important judgments in which both points were affirmed.

2.1.1 Trade in Services

First, the CJEU clarified the scope of the new competences on services in the case relating to the Council of Europe Convention on audio-visual services.[5] The Council had changed the legal basis for the conclusion thereof from

2 Ibid, 16–19.

3 Ibid, 17.

4 Opinion 1/94 (*WTO Agreement*) EU:C:1994:384.

5 European Convention on the Legal Protection of Services based on, or consisting of, Conditional Access (24 January 2001) CETS no 178.

Article 207 TFEU to Article 114 TFEU (internal market). In the Council's view, the Convention had gone beyond the scope of Directive 98/84/EC on audio-visual services.[6] In particular, two Convention provisions (Articles 6 and 8) about confiscatory measures had no corollary in the Directive. For the Council, it was thus not possible to conclude this Convention on the basis of the EU's trade powers. The Court rejected the Council's position. It stressed that the main objective of the Convention was to extend the EU *acquis* on audio-visual services to Council of Europe States, which brings it within the scope of the Common Commercial Policy. Importantly, the Court also did not agree with the claim from Poland and Sweden that 'criminal law' provisions could never be based on Article 207 TFEU as such line of argument could not explain why Article 114 TFEU would be any better in this regard.[7] As a result, the Court held that the entire Convention should be based on Article 207 (4) TFEU.[8] This important finding made it clear that there are no particular limitations under Article 207 TFEU as regards the 'deepness' of a certain provision. As long as the subject matter deals with services under Article 207(4) TFEU, it is less relevant whether a trade provision prohibits, authorises or even requires civil, administrative or even criminal action from the parties to the agreement. Moreover, it confirmed earlier case law relating to 'ancillary' provisions, implying that the Common Commercial Policy can cover an act where its primary purpose is to regulate trade with third countries.[9]

In return, the Treaty of Lisbon has unfortunately not brought all forms of services within exclusive Union competence. Article 207 (5) TFEU keeps the lex specialis of Article 91 TFEU alive for the conclusion of chapters on transport services. As this provision falls within shared competence, it is hence important to find out whether specific transport provisions in a trade agreement mirror *internal acquis* or not. If the Union has covered a particular transport service field by internal legislation, this could create an exclusive competence under Article 3(2) TFEU. If, however, that is not the case, it remains within the political discretion of the Council whether to exercise shared transport competence through the conclusion of the trade agreement or to fall back into a mixed agreement.

6 Directive 98/84/EC of the European Parliament and the Council of 20 November 1998 on the legal protection of services based on, or consisting of, conditional access [1998] OJ L320/54.

7 Case C-137/12 *Commission v. Council* EU:C:2013:675, para 72.

8 Ibid, para 81.

9 Allan Rosas, 'EU External Relations: Exclusive Competence Revisited' (2015) 38 Fordham Int LJ 1073, 1083.

2.1.2 Commercial Aspects of Intellectual Property Rights

Second, the CJEU dealt with the scope of the new competence on commercial aspects of intellectual property rights in the *Daiichi Sankyo* case.[10] Showing in detail that previous exceptions under ex-Article 133(6), second subparagraph and ex-Article 133(7) TEC had become obsolete under the Lisbon Treaty, the Court came to the conclusion that the Union is now exclusively competent to conclude the WTO TRIPS Agreement.[11] This ruling clearly rejected the arguments put before the Court by a number of Member States that the question should be approached under the old case law relating to the mixed nature of the TRIPS Agreement, implying that the majority of TRIPS rules and in particular the ones on patentability are still outside the EU's competence.[12] Again, this judgment has an important significance for the EU's treaty-making practice. As it refers to the entire TRIPS Agreement, it also includes Article 61 thereof, according to which WTO members shall also take criminal sanctions in certain cases of intellectual property rights (IPR) infringements. Prior to the judgment, the Member States had always insisted on 'splitting' the negotiation of IPR chapters in EU trade agreements between the Presidency of the Council and the Commission. Giving the Presidency the lead on 'criminal sanctions' was still practiced with respect to the ACTA Agreement,[13] the ratification of which as a mixed agreement later on failed in some Member States and the European Parliament (EP)[14] alike. After *Daiichi* it should now be clear that the entire IPR chapter in a trade chapter falls within the EU's competence. Hence, it does neither trigger the need to have two negotiators nor does it turn an EU trade agreement into a mixed one. Nevertheless – and in the view of the present author erroneously – the Council still excluded criminal sanctions in the IPR chapter of the Deep and Comprehensive Free Trade Agreement (DCFTA)

---

10 Case C-414/11 *Daiichi Sankyo Co. Ltd and Sanofi-Aventis Deutschland GmbH v DEMO Anonimos Viomikhaniki kai Emporiki Etairia Farmakon* EU:C:2013:520.

11 Ibid, paras 53–62.

12 Rosas (n 9) 1082.

13 Anti-Counterfeiting Trade Agreement between the European Union and its Member States, Australia, Canada, Japan, the Republic of Korea, the United Mexican States, the Kingdom of Morocco, New Zealand, the Republic of Singapore, the Swiss Confederation and the United States of America (for the text, see Council doc 12196/11 of 23 August 2011).

14 European Parliament legislative resolution of 4 July 2012 on the draft Council decision on the conclusion of the Anti-Counterfeiting Trade Agreement between the European Union and its Member States, Australia, Canada, Japan, the Republic of Korea, the United Mexican States, the Kingdom of Morocco, New Zealand, the Republic of Singapore, the Swiss Confederation and the United States of America (12195/2011 – C7-0027/2012 – 2011/0167(NLE) [2013] OJ C349E/552).

with Ukraine (Chapter 4 of the Association Agreement) from provisional application in 2014.[15]

2.2 *Investment Protection*

The situation is less clear with respect to investment protection in Article 207(1) TFEU. In this regard, Ricardo took the position that 'the notion of "foreign direct investment" excludes portfolio investments and perhaps post-establishment investment protection'.[16]

The idea to exclude the whole range of investment protection from Article 207 TFEU probably had its roots in the traditional understanding that EU trade policy is foremost geared towards more liberalisation of trade, rather than protecting investment. However, Article 206 TFEU expressly mentions among the objectives of the CCP to work on the 'progressive abolition of the restrictions on (...) foreign direct investment'. Such restrictions may not only result from outright denial of market access (e.g. not granting a licence to a company which wishes to establish itself), but also from conditions governing the subsequent exercise of economic activity. Those conditions have a direct or indirect impact on trade and thus fall under the traditional scope of Common Commercial Policy.[17] Accordingly, it makes sense to include the entire corpus of standard bilateral investment agreement (BIT) clauses in the scope of Article 207 TFEU.[18] And indeed, the three institutions later on agreed in a number of legal acts to deal with such investment protection standards under Article 207 TFEU. We can refer in particular to the two regulations on the fate of Member State Bilateral Investment Treaties[19] and questions of liability under future EU

---

15 Council Decision 668/2014 (EU) of 23 June 2014 on the signing, on behalf of the European Union, and provisional application of the Association Agreement between the European Union and the European Atomic Energy Community and their Member States, of the one part, and Ukraine, of the other part, as regards Title III (with the exception of the provisions relating to the treatment of third-country nationals legally employed as workers in the territory of the other Party) and Titles IV, V, VI and VII thereof, as well as the related Annexes and Protocols [2014] OJ L278/1, art 4, 2nd indent.

16 Gosalbo Bono (n 1) 17.

17 *Daiichi Sankyo* (n 10), para 51.

18 See Jan Ceyssens, 'Towards a Common Foreign Investment Policy? – Foreign Investment in the European Constitution' (2005) 32 Legal Issues of Economic Integration 259, 276–278; August Reinisch, 'The Division of Powers Between the EU and Its Member States "After Lisbon"' in Marc Bungenberg, Joern Griebel and Steffen Hindelang (eds), *Internationaler Investitionsschutz und Europarecht* (Nomos 2010) 99, 109.

19 Regulation (EU) 1219/2012 of the European Parliament and of the Council of 12 December 2012 establishing transitional arrangements for bilateral investment agreements between Member States and third countries [2012] OJ L351/40.

investment protection standards.[20] The Council has also adopted a number of negotiation directives, in which it asked the Commission to negotiate such standards in EU free trade agreements (Canada, Singapore, India, USA, Japan) or in a stand-alone agreement (China, Myanmar). Hence, constitutional practice has made it clear that post-establishment investment protection is nowadays generally covered by Article 207(1) TFEU.

Having said this, one should add that the institutions have not been able to agree about the precise scope of this investment protection power. Echoing Ricardo's remark about portfolio investment, the Council laid down the following marker in the negotiation directives with the United States of 17 June 2013:

> The aim of negotiations on investment will be to negotiate investment liberalisation and protection provisions *including areas of mixed competence, such as portfolio investment, property and expropriation aspects*, on the basis of the highest levels of liberalisation and highest standards of protection that both Parties have negotiated to date.[21]

The underlying argument on the first point is pretty straightforward at first sight: as the Lisbon Treaty explicitly mentions foreign 'direct' investment, it deliberately omitted portfolio investment, which is thereby excluded. Admittedly, this line of reasoning is shared by the *Bundesverfassungsgericht*[22] and many academic authorities. However, at second sight, doubts can be shed on this proposition. First, there is nothing in the *travaux préparatoires* which hints at a deliberate exclusion. Nobody in the Working Group on External Relations[23] of the Convention on the Future of Europe (which established the first draft

---

20 Regulation (EU) 912/2014 of the European Parliament and of the Council of 23 July 2014 establishing a framework for managing financial responsibility linked to investor-to-state dispute settlement tribunals established by international agreements to which the European Union is party [2012] OJ L257/121.

21 'Directives for the negotiation on the Transatlantic Trade and Investment Partnership between the European Union and the United States of America', adopted on 14 June 2013 (Council doc 11103/13 DCL 1) <http://data.consilium.europa.eu/doc/document/ST-11103-2013-DCL-1/en/pdf> accessed 6 October 2016, para 22 (emphasis added).

22 German Federal Constitutional Court, Judgment of the Second Senate of 30 June 2009 – 2 BvE 2/08 <http://www.bundesverfassungsgericht.de/SharedDocs/Entscheidungen/EN/2009/06/es20090630_2bve000208en.html> accessed 20 November 2016 (English translation of the Decision on the Lisbon-Treaty).

23 Working Group VII – 'External Action', 'Final report of Working Group VII on External Action' (CONV 459/02 of 16 December 2002) (Final report of WG VII).

of the EU Constitution[24]) had proposed such exclusion. We also have no positive evidence to indicate how the notion of 'foreign direct investment' entered the Convention text of the *Praesidium*. Rather than detecting any will to limit EU external competences, the final report of the working group on external action speaks about the need to further maximise the EU's effective action on the international scene.[25] Second, the exclusion of portfolio investment from EU competence does not make much economic sense. Why should the EU be exclusively competent to regulate the (stronger) control of a company operating in Europe by an American national, when the (less strong) financial participation of an American in such a company would remain a national matter? Third, Article 63(1) TFEU already protects portfolio investment against restrictions under the free movement of capital. As the prohibition also covers capital movement between Member States and third countries, it can be argued that the Lisbon Treaty itself has harmonised the field on portfolio investment. In turn, at least Article 63 TFEU in conjunction with Article 3(2) TFEU create an exclusive competence also for that matter.[26]

The Council's second point on property is also subject to controversy. In Council working groups the argument was often made that the EU could not be competent to negotiate standard clauses on expropriation because the Treaty would carve out those matters anyway under Article 345 TFEU. That proposition is, however, not sustained by the CJEU. While the Treaties do not 'prejudice the rules in Member States governing the system of property ownership', the Court has always found that property issues are not exempted from the EU Treaties.[27] If a measure from a Member State interferes with the property of an established company from another Member State, such interferences can be scrutinised under Article 50(1) TFEU and the proportionality thereof is even subject to Article 17 of the EU Charter of Fundamental Rights on the protection of property. Moreover, even EU secondary law can affect property rights.[28] It follows that Article 345 TFEU does not contain a prohibition of harmonisation

---

24 European Convention Secretariat, 'Draft Treaty Establishing a Constitution for Europe' (CONV 850/03 of 18 July 2003).

25 Final report of WG VII, 16, para 19: 'Notwithstanding the varying delimitations of competencies between the Union/Community and Member States, the varying roles of the actors (institutions and Member States) and different decision-making procedures in different fields, it is essential to maximise the coherence and efficiency of EU external action'.

26 Commission, 'Towards a comprehensive European international investment policy' (Communication) COM (2010) 343 final, 8.

27 Case C-463/00 *Commission v Kingdom of Spain* EU:C:2003:272 (*Golden Shares*), para 67.

28 Case C-309/96 *Daniele Annibaldi v Sindaco del Comune di Guidonia and Presidente Regione Lazio* EU:C:1997:631, para 23.

within the meaning of Article 207(6) TFEU. Rather, the purpose of the latter provision is to exclude from the scope of the Union's CCP agreements which would lead to the harmonisation of national laws and regulations in areas such as social security, education, culture and public health, where the Lisbon Treaty contains outright prohibitions of harmonisation (e.g. Article 168(5) TFEU), as Ricardo has – in my view convincingly – emphasised.[29]

In sum, it can be concluded that the transfer of competence on investment matters to the EU has been complete. But as there is an open disagreement between the Council and the Commission on the issue, the only way forward is to receive clarification from the CJEU. Against that background the Commission decided in October 2014 – confirmed in May 2015 – to ask the CJEU for an opinion on the EU-Singapore Free Trade Agreement based on Article 218(11) TFEU.[30] That highly important case will hence provide the Court with an occasion to look into the scope of the EU's investment policy under Article 207 TFEU in great detail.

2.3 *Sustainable Development*

Finally, in some Member States the thesis has come up more recently that also the EU Chapters on sustainable development in free trade agreements would fall within mixed competence. For example, in an opinion written for the German Ministry of Economy on the Comprehensive Economic and Trade Agreement (CETA),[31] Prof. Mayer made the argument that the Union only enjoys supporting powers in the area of labour protection domestically. Hence, only Member States could take international commitments on labour issues.[32]

This line of thinking seems to overlook an important strain of CJEU jurisprudence and recent practice, though. Early on, the CJEU underlined that EU trade policy can also pursue development or foreign policy goals.[33] Accordingly, the Generalised System of Preferences (GSP) for developing countries was always based on Article 207 TFEU and its predecessors. The most recent GSP

29 Gosalbo Bono (n 1) 18.

30 Opinion 2/15 (pending).

31 Franz C Mayer, 'Stellt das geplante Freihandelsabkommen der EU mit Kanada (Comprehensive Economic and Trade Agreement, CETA) ein gemischtes Abkommen dar?' (28 August 2014) available through <http://www.bmwi.de/DE/Presse/pressemitteilungen,did=655700.html> accessed 6.October 2016.

32 Ibid, 20.

33 Case 45/86 *Commission v Council* EU:C:1987:163, paras 17–21; Case C-70/94, *Werner*, EU:C:1995:328, para 10.

Regulation[34] deals with sustainable development in so far as it conditions in Article 9(1)(b) the granting of extra-preferences to the compliance with certain core Conventions ('GSP plus'). In Annex VIII no less than eight International Labour Organization (ILO) Conventions are mentioned, which deal with issues such as forced or child labour, the freedom of association and coalition, equality of men and women as well as minimum age of workers. Apparently, the EU legislator found it possible to integrate such goals into the Union's Common Commercial Policy. If now Article 207 TFEU empowers the Union to adopt unilateral legal acts on such matters, nothing prevents the Union from fostering the same goals with provisions on sustainable development in a trade agreement.

In addition, the Treaty of Lisbon has strengthened that link even more. Under Article 207(1), second sentence TFEU, the Common Commercial Policy shall contribute to the Union's overall external objectives, among which sustainable development figures prominently in Article 21(2)(d) TFEU. Moreover, Article 3(5) TEU strengthens the link between trade and the socio-economic development of a country when referring to 'free and fair trade', adding another objective under primary law to the CCP.[35] Finally, the established practice of the institutions also points to that direction. Based on a proposal from the Commission, the Council neither excluded that chapter from provisional application in the EU-Korea[36] nor in the EU-Columbia/Peru[37] or in the EU-Central-America Agreements.[38] Hence, both institutions affirmed the position

34 Regulation (EU) 978/2012 of the European Parliament and of the Council of 25 October 2012 applying a scheme of generalised tariff preferences and repealing Council Regulation (EC) 732/2008 [2012] OJ L303/1.

35 See Angelos Dimopoulos, 'The Effects of the Lisbon Treaty on the Principles and Objectives of the Common Commercial Policy' (2010) 15 European Foreign Affairs Review 153, 162–163.

36 Art 3(1), 1st indent, of Council Decision 2011/265/EU of 16 September 2010 on the signing, on behalf of the European Union, and provisional application of the Free Trade Agreement between the European Union and its Member States, of the one part, and the Republic of Korea, of the other part ([2011] OJ L127/1), which covers also Chapter 13 on sustainable development.

37 Art 3(1) of Council Decision 2012/735/EU of 31 May 2012 on the signing, on behalf of the Union, and provisional application of the Trade Agreement between the European Union and its Member States, of the one part, and Colombia and Peru, of the other part ([2012] OJ L354/1), only excludes art 2 (weapons of mass destruction), art 202(1) (TRIPS) and arts 291–292 (geographical indications) of the agreement from provisional application, thus covers arts 267–286 on sustainable development.

38 Art 3(1) of Council Decision 2012/734/EU of 25 June 2012 on the signing, on behalf of the European Union, of the Agreement establishing an Association between the

that sustainable development chapters are covered by the Union competence under Article 207 TFEU.

3 The New Institutional Balance in Trade Policy

In addition to a substantial transfer of competence to the EU, the Lisbon Treaty also changed considerably the institutional balance in trade policy. Whereas that policy was mainly conducted by the Commission and the Council in the past, the European Parliament has become an important actor in the field. In order to grasp precisely the new role of this institutional triangle, a distinction between internal acts and international agreements should be made.

3.1 *Internal Acts*

Under Article 207(2) TFEU the Council and the Parliament define by means of regulations the 'framework' for implementing the Common Commercial Policy. Such regulations are to be adopted in accordance with the ordinary legislative procedure, giving much more power to the Parliament than before.

Legally, this begged the question how to draw the line between such framework legislation and the power of the Commission to adopt implementing acts under Article 291 TFEU, as Ricardo pointed out in his above-mentioned contribution.[39] In practice, this intricate issue was tackled early on in connection with the horizontal comitology regulation. Although there was considerable resistance on the part of some Member States during 2010, the Council finally agreed to give up its previous prerogative to adopt definitive trade-defence measures itself.[40] Rather, according to the comitology regulation published in

European Union and its Member States, on the one hand, and Central America on the other, and the provisional application of Part IV thereof concerning trade matters ([2012] OJ L 346/1), which declares the entire Part IV of the Association Agreement with Central-America applicable with the exception of art 271 (criminal enforcement of intellectual property rights). That includes title VIII on sustainable development (arts 284–302 of the Agreement).

39 Gosalbo Bono (n 1) 18.

40 See Council Regulation (EC) 1225/2009 of 30 November 2009 on protection against dumped imports from countries not members of the European Community (codified version) [2009] OJ L343/51, art 9(4). Under that provision (applicable as of 2004 – Council Regulation (EC) 461/2004 [2004] OJ L77/12) the Council adopted a Commission proposal for a definitive measure unless a simple majority of Member States would vote against the proposal. Before that, the Council needed a simple majority in favour of adopting a definitive measure.

2011,[41] implementing acts on the Common Commercial Policy nowadays also fall within the normal comitology rules (Article 2(b)(iv) of the Regulation). In particular, the Commission adopts provisional anti-dumping and countervailing duties as an 'immediately applicable implementing act' (Article 8(5) of the Regulation). For definitive measures, the examination procedure is used with some nuances (Article 4(5) of the Regulation). Importantly, the Commission is now also adopting those implementing acts, and only a negative opinion from the Member States in the Appeals Committee (with qualified majority) can stop it. Until now though, only one trade defence implementing act from the Commission has reached the Appeals Committee, and its revised version was not voted down there. This shows that, on trade defence issues, the institutional balance has shifted from the Council to the Commission.[42] Politically, this has the important implication that such measures can be taken more easily, which in turn makes it less attractive for companies or third States to lobby Member States against a draft measure for reasons which are not related to the file.

When it comes to the ordinary legislative procedure, there are no special rules in the area of the Common Commercial Policy. Accordingly, the Commission proposes the act upon which the Parliament and the Council act following the elaborate process set out in Article 294 TFEU. In practice, this gives considerable power to all the three institutions, which use to settle their differences in the so-called *informal trilogues*. In the first seven years of the Lisbon treaty, it seems that the institutional balance also delivered a number of important results. For example, the legislature revised the General System of Preferences[43] and adapted the Market Access Regulation[44] for certain African countries, which in turn brought new dynamics into the negotiation of some economic partnership agreements with that region. As already mentioned

41 Regulation (EU) 182/2011 of the European Parliament and of the Council of 16 February 2011 laying down the rules and general principles concerning mechanisms for control by Member States of the Commission's exercise of implementing powers [2011] OJ L55/13.

42 Tibor Scharf, 'Decision-Making in EU Trade Defence Cases after Lisbon: An Institutional Anomaly Addressed?' in Christoph Herrmann, Bruno Simma, Rudolf Streinz (eds), *Trade Policy between Law, Diplomacy and Scholarship – Liber Amicorum in Memoriam Horst G. Krenzler* (EYIEL special issue, Springer 2015) 403.

43 Regulation (EU) 978/2012 of the European Parliament and of the Council of 25 October 2012 applying a scheme of generalised tariff preferences and repealing Council Regulation (EC) 732/2008 [2012] OJ L303/1.

44 See the Regulation (EU) 527/2013 of the European Parliament and of the Council of 21 May 2013 amending Council Regulation (EC) 1528/2007 (Market Access Regulation) as regards the exclusion of a number of countries from the list of regions or states which have concluded negotiations [2013] OJ L165/59.

above, two important regulations in the field of investment were agreed as well. Moreover, we can find a number of safeguard regulations accompanying new free trade agreements,[45] specific WTO-related legislation[46] or instruments regulating trade in dual-use goods[47] or seal products.[48] In general, the system has thus worked well. While a legislative process usually takes at least a year, there can also be accelerated processes in cases of political urgency. Such situations can occur, in particular, when autonomous trade concessions are given for political reasons. We have thus seen considerable efforts to put into place just in time the trade regime for Moldova in mid-2011[49] and for the Balkans in the end of 2011.[50] Most importantly, in April 2014, the EU also quickly granted autonomous preferences to Ukraine,[51] which were extended in record-speed by the EP and the Council at the end of October 2014 to last until the end

45 See e.g. the Safeguard Regulation accompanying the EU-Korea Free Trade Agreement (Regulation (EU) 511/2011 of the European Parliament and of the Council of 11 May 2011 implementing the bilateral safeguard clause of the Free Trade Agreement between the European Union and its Member States and the Republic of Korea [2011] OJ L145/19).

46 Regulation (EU) 654/2014 of the European Parliament and of the Council of 15 May 2014 concerning the exercise of the Union's rights for the application and enforcement of international trade rules and amending Council Regulation (EC) 3286/94 laying down Community procedures in the field of the common commercial policy in order to ensure the exercise of the Community's rights under international trade rules, in particular those established under the auspices of the World Trade Organization [2014] OJ L189/50.

47 Council Regulation (EC) 428/2009 of 5 May 2009 setting up a Community regime for the control of exports, transfer, brokering and transit of dual-use items [2009] OJ L134/1, as last amended by Regulation (EU) 599/2014 ([2012] OJ L173/79).

48 Regulation (EC) 1007/2009 of the European Parliament and of the Council of 16 September 2009 on trade in seal products [2009] OJ L179/26, as amended by Regulation (EU) 2015/775 ([2015] OJ L262/1).

49 Regulation (EU) of the European Parliament and of the Council of 8 June 2011 amending Council Regulation (EC) 55/2008 introducing autonomous trade preferences for the Republic of Moldova [2011] OJ L165/5.

50 Regulation (EU) 1336/2011 of the European Parliament and of the Council of 13 December 2011 amending Council Regulation (EC) 1215/2009 introducing exceptional trade measures for countries and territories participating in or linked to the European Union's Stabilisation and Association process [2011] OJ L347/1.

51 Regulation (EU) 374/2014 of the European Parliament and of the Council of 16 April 2014 on the reduction or elimination of customs duties on goods originating in Ukraine [2014] OJ L118/1.

of 2016,[52] to provide political space for the tri-lateral negotiations with Russia on the effects of the EU-Ukraine Association Agreement.[53]

Exceptionally, though, an ordinary legislative procedure is not being finalised within good time. Like for acceleration, mainly political rather than legal reasons can be identified for that. For example, the Commission proposal of March 2012 to introduce a European system on how to deal with third-country bidders in the EU procurement market[54] was considered by a blocking minority in the Council as vesting too much power into the Commission and carrying too great risks of protectionism. Accordingly, the Council has not yet mandated the Presidency to enter into negotiations with the Parliament although the latter has adopted its position at first reading[55] and the Commission has revised its proposal in January 2016.[56] Similarly, the Commission proposal on the modernisation of trade defence instruments of 2013 got stuck in the Council for three years, where another blocking minority did not want to open discussions about the eventual narrowing down of the so-called lesser-duty rule in the fear of tougher duties in the future.[57]

In sum, the institutional balance for internal acts in EU trade policy can now be compared to other areas of internal EU policy-making. While the Commission is carrying a great responsibility in implementing the EU's trade defence policy, the Council and the Parliament usually live up to their joint task in defining the framework legislation in the field upon a Commission proposal.

52 Regulation (EU) 1150/2014 of the European Parliament and of the Council of 29 October 2014 amending Regulation (EU) 374/2014 on the reduction or elimination of customs duties on goods originating in Ukraine [2014] OJ L313/1.

53 On the background see Gunnar Wiegand and Evelina Schulz, 'The EU and Its Eastern Partnership: Political Association and Economic Integration in a Rough Neighbourhood' in Herrmann, Simma and Streinz (eds) (n 42) 321–326.

54 Commission, 'Proposal for a regulation of the European Parliament and of the Council on the access of third-country goods and services to the Union's internal market in public procurement and procedures supporting negotiations on access of Union goods and services to the public procurement markets of third countries' COM (2012) 124 final.

55 Frank Hoffmeister, 'The EU Public Procurement Regime on Third-Country Bidders – Setting the Cursor Between Openness and Reciprocity' in Harri Kalimo and Max S Jansson (eds), *EU Economic Law in a Time of Crisis* (Edward Elgar Publishing 2016) 84–86.

56 COM (2016) 34 final.

57 For details see Frank Hoffmeister, 'Modernising the EU's Trade Defence Instruments: Mission Impossible?' in Herrmann, Simma and Streinz (eds) (n 42) 365.

3.2 *Trade Agreements*

In view of the extensive practice of the European Union to engage bilaterally with third countries on free trade agreements since 2009 it is not surprising that a number of constitutional questions had to be solved on the way. It seems appropriate to track these down by following the usual 'life' of an agreement since its inception.

3.2.1 Negotiations

Under Article 218(2) TFEU, the first step is the authorisation to open negotiations by the Council, which regularly adopts negotiating directives as well to guide the Commission in the negotiations. For decades, such negotiations directives were kept confidential so as not to allow the negotiation partner to look at the EU's cards. Hence, the Commission and the Council classified them as restricted and 'access to document requests' from the public were regularly denied. However, when the EU started negotiating with the United States about a Transatlantic Trade and Investment Partnership (TTIP) in summer 2013, that practice came soon into public disregard. Many activists and social groups complained about the 'secrecy' of the negotiations, implying that the EU would negotiate away public interests behind closed doors. In order to counter-balance this widespread misconception the EU Trade Commissioner De Gucht asked the Council in 2013 and in 2014 twice to declassify the TTIP negotiation directives. Although the decision about classification of a document appears to be a procedural issue which the Council can decide upon by simple majority (Article 238(1) TFEU), Member States insisted on unanimity because they considered that the directives were mixed. Unable to find consensus on lifting confidentiality, the Council hence postponed any move towards more transparency. Only the Italian Presidency managed in October 2014 to overcome the conservative resistance in some capitals, so that the TTIP negotiation directives were finally released to the public.[58] This important precedent is now also cited by the current Commission in its new trade strategy of October 2015. The Commission will now invite the Council to publish the relevant negotiation directives at the launch of any negotiations for a new trade agreement.[59] If the Council were to follow this invitation, such new practice would

58 The TTIP negotiating guidelines are reprinted in Pieter Jan Kuijper and others, *The Law of EU External Relations – Cases, Materials, and Commentary on the EU as an International Legal Actor* (2nd edn, OUP 2015) 57–66.

59 Commission, 'Trade for all – Towards a more responsible trade and investment policy' (Communication, 14 October 2015) <http://trade.ec.europa.eu/doclib/docs/2015/october/tradoc_153846.pdf> accessed 20 November 2016, Ch. 3.2.

be a powerful contribution to more transparency and public communication with the citizens. At the same time, the institutions would have to make sure that no sensitive data on market access commitments would be contained therein so as to avoid that the negotiating partner has an easy access to the Union's red lines in negotiations.

During the negotiations, the Commission is supposed to regularly report to a special committee appointed by the Council under Article 207(3) TFEU and to the European Parliament,[60] another constitutional novelty of Lisbon.[61] Two points are worth mentioning here. First, in the area of trade, the consultations with the Member States are taking place in the Council's Trade Policy Committee (TPC) in a cooperative spirit. As the Court has recently clarified, the Council can require the Commission to regularly report on the progress in the negotiations to a Committee or even the Council itself.[62] However, at the same time the Council or the Committee cannot define EU negotiating positions and impose them on the Commission. Such attempts would jeopardise the institutional balance laid down in treaties and have thus been declared null and void in the negotiating directives for an international environmental agreement.[63] Second, the Commission can equally not receive any binding instructions from the European Parliament. In practice, it informs the so-called ad hoc groups in the International Trade (INTA) Committee[64] and takes into account majority views formulated there. If those are also echoed in resolutions of the entire Parliament, the Commission is well advised to consider them in the negotiations in order to increase the chance of getting the agreement accepted at approval stage. Such interaction can clearly be demonstrated on the substance of a couple of files, such as investment policy (where the Parliament pushed for reforms from investor-to-State settlement towards a Court system) or sustainable development (where the Parliament is in favour of stronger enforcement[65]). On the other hand, the differences on the modalities of how to protect intellectual property rights worldwide could not be bridged between

60 The EP has a right to be informed under Article 218(10) TFEU.

61 Gosalbo Bono (n 1) 18.

62 Case C-245/13 *Commission v Council* EU:C:483, paras 60–73.

63 Ibid, paras 74–97.

64 Under para 24 of the Framework Agreement on relations between the European Parliament and the European Commission ([2010] OJ L304/47), the Commission informs the responsible Committee of the Parliament or the plenary, as appropriate, about the negotiations of an international agreement.

65 For details see Frank Hoffmeister, 'The European Union as an International Trade Negotiator' in Joachim A Koops and Gjovalin Macaj (eds), *The European Union as a Diplomatic Actor* (Palgrave Macmillan 2014) 145–146.

the Commission and the Parliament with the effect that ACTA[66] was actually voted down in Strasbourg.

3.2.2 Signature, Provisional Application and Conclusion

Once the negotiations are completed, the Commission will propose to the Council to sign and provisionally apply the agreement. Under Article 218 (5) TFEU there is no role for the European Parliament at this stage. However, in practice, a distinction has been regularly made.

If, on the one hand, the agreement needs to be signed and provisionally applied very quickly, the Council can make use of its prerogatives without any political risk. An example was the 'Banana-Agreement' between the EU and a number of Latin-American States, which was put into early provisional application by the Council in May 2010[67] without involving the Parliament. The Parliament then ratified the text in February 2011, paving the way to its formal conclusion by the Council in March 2011.[68]

If, on the other hand, an important trade agreement is at stake which defines the long-standing relations with a third country, the Parliament gets the possibility to voice its opinion before provisional application. This practice started following a commitment of the former EU Trade Commissioner De Gucht during his hearing in February 2010, and repeated later on in public speeches.[69] Significantly, the Council added such a condition even formally into its first decision on provisional application of a new Free Trade Agreement (FTA). In the decision on the EU-Korea Free Trade Agreement, the entry into force of a safeguard regulation (decided in the ordinary legislative procedure by the Council and the Parliament) was set as a pre-condition for provisional

66 See n 13 and 14.

67 Council Decision 2010/314/EU of 10 May 2010 on the signing and provisional application of the Geneva Agreement on Trade in Bananas between the European Union and Brazil, Colombia, Costa Rica, Ecuador, Guatemala, Honduras, Mexico, Nicaragua, Panama, Peru and Venezuela and of the Agreement on Trade in Bananas between the European Union and the United States of America [2010] OJ L161/ 1.

68 Council Decision 2011/194/EU of 7 March 2011 on the conclusion of a Geneva Agreement on Trade in Bananas between the European Union and Brazil, Colombia, Costa Rica, Ecuador, Guatemala, Honduras, Mexico, Nicaragua, Panama, Peru and Venezuela and of an Agreement on Trade in Bananas between the European Union and the United States of America [2011] OJ L88/1. See also on this topic the chapter by Ricardo Passos in this book.

69 See e.g. Karel De Gucht, 'The Implications of the Lisbon Treaty for EU Trade Policy' (S&D seminar on EU Trade Policy, Oporto, 8 October 2010) <http://trade.ec.europa.eu/doclib/docs/2010/october/tradoc_146719.pdf> accessed 20 November 2016.

application to start as of 1 July 2011.[70] Politically, the safeguard regulation was voted in Parliament at the same time as the agreement as such, namely in February 2011. Hence, the Council effectively made the date of provisional application dependent on a positive vote of the Parliament on the agreement although such a condition does not exist in Article 218 (4) TFEU. Interestingly, such links were later on also created with respect to other trade agreements before the Parliament, most importantly on the one between the EU and Ukraine.[71] Here, the Council proceeded first with a provisional application of the preamble and the political chapters in March 2014[72] – interestingly, this included for the first time the provisional application of Common Foreign and Security Policy (CFSP) provisions as part of the Union's competence.[73] In June 2014, the Council then extended the provisional application to the remaining EU parts of the Association Agreement,[74] but following the trilateral talks with

70 Council Decision 2011/265/EU (n 36), art 3(2).

71 See generally on the EU-Ukraine Association Agreement Guillaume Van der Loo, *The EU-Ukraine Association Agreement and Deep and Comprehensive Free Trade Area* (Brill Nijhoff 2016).

72 Council Decision 2014/295/EU of 17 March 2014 on the signing, on behalf of the European Union, and provisional application of the Association Agreement between the European Union and the European Atomic Energy Community and their Member States, of the one part, and Ukraine, of the other part, as regards the Preamble, Article 1, and Titles I, II and VII thereof [2014] OJ L261/1.

73 The *chapeau* of art 4 of the Council Decision 2014/295/EU (n 72) contains the following new language: 'Pending its entry into force, and in accordance with Article 486 of the Agreement and subject to the notifications provided for therein, the following parts of the Agreement shall be applied on a provisional basis between the Union and Ukraine, but only to the extent that they cover matters falling within the Union's competence, including matters falling within the Union's competence to define and implement a common foreign and security policy: (...)'. See also the chapters by Frederik Naert and Ricardo Passos in this book.

74 Council Decision 2014/668/EU of 23 June 2014 on the signing, on behalf of the European Union, and provisional application of the Association Agreement between the European Union and the European Atomic Energy Community and their Member States, of the one part, and Ukraine, of the other part, as regards Title III (with the exception of the provisions relating to the treatment of third-country nationals legally employed as workers in the territory of the other Party) and Titles IV, V, VI and VII thereof, as well as the related Annexes and Protocols [2014] OJ L278/1; Council Decision 2014/669/EU of 23 June 2014 on the signing, on behalf of the European Union, of the Association Agreement between the European Union and the European Atomic Energy Community and their Member States, of the one part, and Ukraine, of the other part, as regards the provisions relating to the treatment of third-country nationals legally employed as workers in the territory of the other party [2014] OJ L278/6.

Russia, the provisional application of the trade parts were postponed to January 2016.[75] All this was done in the clear understanding that the European Parliament would give its positive vote to the conclusion of the agreement, which actually occurred in mid-September 2014 in a solemn act,[76] which was synchronised with the ratification of the agreement in the Ukrainian Parliament.

At the conclusion stage, the Council takes the decision after formal approval of the European Parliament under Article 218(6)(a)(v) TFEU. This power of the Council to conclude the international agreement also entails the power to add a reservation to it, if warranted.

3.2.3 Bilateral Dispute Settlement

Most modern trade agreements also contain bilateral State-to-State dispute settlement provisions. They are modelled alongside the WTO system. Hence, ad hoc panels can decide on a bilateral trade dispute between the EU and its trading partners if previous government consultations cannot resolve it. In practice, though, this possibility has not been used yet. Under the EU-Korea Free Trade Agreement, the Commission was close to triggering the more modest mediation mechanism under Chapter 14 in view of technical barriers for car parts, but finally decided against the proposition in view of the agreement found in the Trade Committee operating under that agreement to amend the relevant Annex 2-C of the Agreement.[77]

While this issue has thus not provided us with the first bilateral dispute settlement case, it nevertheless triggered interesting institutional questions. Could the Commission have decided to bring such a case against a third country on its own? What would have been the roles of the Council and the Parliament in that respect? Given that there is no major difference between a multilateral and a bilateral trade dispute the Commission would have

75 Council Decision 2014/691/EU of 29 September 2014 amending Decision 2014/668/EU on the signing, on behalf of the European Union, and provisional application of the Association Agreement between the European Union and the European Atomic Energy Community and their Member States, of the one part, and Ukraine, of the other part, as regards Title III (with the exception of the provisions relating to the treatment of third-country nationals legally employed as workers in the territory of the other Party) and Titles IV, V, VI and VII thereof, as well as the related Annexes and Protocols [2014] OJ L289/1.

76 European Parliament, 'European Parliament ratifies EU-Ukraine Association Agreement' (Press release, 16 September 2014) <http://www.europarl.europa.eu/pdfs/news/expert/infopress/20140915IPR62504/20140915IPR62504_en.pdf> accessed 20 November 2016.

77 Commission, 'Report from the Commission to the European Parliament and the Council – Annual Report on the Implementation of the EU-Korea Free Trade Agreement' COM (2015) 139 final, 9.

probably taken a decision to initiate the dispute and to present the legal arguments before the Panel after consulting the other two institutions. This longstanding WTO practice (where the Commission also represents the EU in all phases of litigation)[78] has in the meantime also been confirmed by the CJEU with respect to litigation under the United Nations Convention on the Law of the Sea (UNCLOS).[79] In that case, the CJEU held that Article 335 TFEU empowers the Commission to represent the EU before an international court.[80] Moreover, presenting a position *before* an international court cannot be conflated with taking a position *in* an international body set up by an agreement to which the EU is a party under Article 218(9) TFEU. Accordingly, no prior Council decision is necessary for submitting a Commission brief on behalf of the EU under this provision.[81] Finally, the policy-making role of the Council under Article 16 TEU does not mean that the Commission needs to ask for an authorisation of the Council for the content of its written submissions, since making legal arguments on the basis of established EU law and international law practice does not amount to taking policy choices.[82] Rather, this activity belongs to the foreign policy prerogatives which are typically vested in the executive institution, i.e. the Commission as the representative of the EU under Article 17(1) TEU in the trade policy context. In exercising this prerogative, the Commission is, though, under an obligation of sincere mutual cooperation in accordance with article 13(2) TEU, which means that it shall consult the Council before submitting a brief.[83]

3.2.4 Termination

Finally, questions of institutional balance may come up when a trade agreement or its provisional application has to be terminated. As the Lisbon Treaty is silent about the issue, two propositions can be made in light of the constitutional traditions of Member States.[84] A termination decision could be qualified as the '*actus contrarius*' of the conclusion decision. Under that

---

78 See Ullrich Wölker, 'Die Stellung der Europäischen Union in den Organen der Welthandelsorganisation' (2012) Europarecht Beiheft 2/2012 125, 134.

79 For details of the EU's litigation practice under UNCLOS see Esa Paasivirta, 'The European Union and the United Nations Convention on the Law of the Sea' (2015) 38 Fordham Int LJ 1045, 1056–1061.

80 Case C-73/14 *Council v Commission* EU:C:2015:663, paras 58–59.

81 Ibid, paras 63–67.

82 Ibid, paras 68–77.

83 Ibid, paras 84–89.

84 For an overview of the constitutional approaches in EU Member States on the termination of international agreements see Kuijper and others (n 58) 93–95.

approach, the Council would have to terminate upon proposal of the Commission and after approval of the European Parliament. Alternatively, termination could be seen as an executive act, often dictated by international urgencies to react quickly to changed circumstances, which make the continued application of an agreement politically unfeasible. In that scenario, the subsequent information of the Parliament or a fast-track consultation is defendable.

In pre-Lisbon practice, the Council terminated trade agreements without any involvement of the Parliament.[85] As the Parliament had to be consulted during conclusion, this was already an indicator that a pure *actus contrarius* theory had not been applied in the past (as otherwise the Parliament would have had to be consulted also for termination). After Lisbon, no termination of a trade agreement has yet occurred. However, an interesting parallel can be drawn to the termination of the provisional application in another field of EU exclusive external competence.

In the case of the EU-Guinea Fisheries Agreement, the Commission proposed to the Council to terminate provisional application because of serious human rights violations committed by Guinea. The Council took such decision under Article 218(5) TFEU[86] and the Council President designated the competent Commissioner to carry out the notification under Article 25(2) of the Vienna Convention by a letter to the Guinean authorities. The Parliament was not asked for approval or consulted although it had also become competent under Lisbon to approve international fisheries agreements under Article 218(6)(v) TFEU. This example not only reaffirms that the Council is the competent institution for termination decisions;[87] it also shows that the prior involvement of the European Parliament is not legally necessary in such situations.

---

85 Council Decision 2004/589/EC of 19 July 2004 concerning the notification to the Republic of Korea of the withdrawal of the European Community from the Agreement on telecommunications procurement between the European Community and the Republic of Korea [2004] OJ L260/8.

86 Council Decision 2009/1016/EU of 22 December 2009 repealing Decision 2009/473/EC concerning the conclusion of an Agreement in the form of an Exchange of Letters on the provisional application of the Fisheries Partnership Agreement between the European Community and the Republic of Guinea [2009] OJ L348/53.

87 Jenő Czuczai, 'The Autonomy of the EU Legal Order and the Law-Making Activities of International Organizations – Some Examples Regarding the Council's most Recent Practice' (2012) 31 YEL 452, 457 who also gives interesting details about the Guinea case.

4 Judicial Autonomy

Finally, important constitutional questions are also arising in the trade field vis-à-vis the role of the CJEU: what are the constitutional limits which need to be observed when creating a new international judicial body which can take decisions binding the European Union?

While there was relatively little room for controversy in the traditional State-to-State dispute settlement chapters of EU trade agreements, the issue has come to the forefront more recently in the investment field. Here, the first EU agreements containing investment protection chapters, such as the EU-Canada CETA and the EU-Singapore FTA, also contain a possibility for the investor to bring claims against the Union under the so-called 'investor-to-State dispute settlement' mechanism (ISDS). Those claims are to be decided by ad hoc Tribunals. In the alternative, the competence to decide investment cases would be vested into a standing Investment Court, if the Commission proposals of September 2015 in the TTIP negotiations[88] were acceptable to the US and ratified by both sides. In either case (ad hoc Tribunal or standing Investment Court) the legal question is how to reconcile the jurisdiction of such international judicial bodies with the judicial autonomy of the European Union.

The starting point is clear: the competence of the EU in the field of international relations and its capacity to conclude international agreements necessarily entails the power to submit issues for the decisions of a court which is created or designated by such agreements as regards the interpretation and application of their provisions.[89] However, such jurisdictional powers of an international body may not have an adverse effect on the autonomy of the EU legal order.[90] In Opinion 2/13 on EU accession to the European Convention

88 Commission, 'Chapter II – Investment' (TTIP draft text, September 2015). <http://trade.ec.europa.eu/doclib/docs/2015/september/tradoc_153807.pdf> accessed 20 November 2016. For a first discussion of the proposal see Stephan W Schill, 'The European Commission's Proposal of an "Investment Court System" for TTIP: Stepping Stone or Stumbling Block for Multilateralizing International Investment Law?' (2016) 20(9) ASIL Insights <https://www.asil.org/insights/volume/20/issue/9/european-commissions-proposal-investment-court-system-ttip-stepping> accessed 20 November 2016.

89 Opinion 1/91 (*Draft agreement relating to the creation of the European Economic Area*) EU:C:1991:490, para 40; Opinion 1/09 (*Draft agreement on the European and Community Patents Court*) EU:C:2011:123, para 74.

90 Opinion 1/00 (*Proposed agreement between the European Community and non-Member States on the establishment of a European Common Aviation Area*) EU:C.2002:231, paras 21–26.

for the protection of Human Rights and Fundamental Freedoms (ECHR)[91] the Court has identified at least five principles that need to be observed in this regard. Leaving aside the controversy whether those principles are well justified or not, they are certainly defining the kind of relationship the CJEU is willing to entertain with other courts and tribunals.[92]

First, the decisions of the international judicial body shall not bind the Union institutions to a particular interpretation of EU law.[93] Second, nothing should undermine the exclusive competence of the CJEU to interpret EU law under Article 344 TFEU, according to which Member States undertake not to submit a dispute concerning the interpretation and application of the Treaties to any method of settlement other than those provided in the Treaties themselves.[94] Third, the international body shall not take – even implicit – decisions about the division of competences between the EU and its Member States.[95] Fourth, nothing in an international agreement should affect the monopoly of the CJEU to render preliminary rulings on the interpretation of EU law.[96] Fifth, the external body may not control acts adopted under the CFSP for compliance with the international instrument in question as long as the CJEU itself is barred from doing so under EU law.[97]

Applying those principles to chapters on dispute settlement in the investment field, it becomes clear that a number of safeguards need to be put into an EU trade agreement to protect the judicial autonomy of the European legal order. First, whenever an international investment tribunal or court is deciding a case against the EU, it shall only apply and interpret the international agreement between the EU and the third State in line with the 1969 Vienna Convention on the Law of Treaties. In doing so, it will also have to look at the impugned EU act as a question of fact. But it will only be able to find whether such act has complied with the EU's obligations under the international investment standard contained in the EU agreement with the third State in question and not take a position about the compliance of the act with the EU Treaties. That judgment is reserved to the CJEU. Such system is currently successfully applied in the WTO, where Panels and the Appellate Body apply

---

91 EU:C:2014:2454.

92 For an excellent discussion of Opinion 2/13 see Piet Eeckhout, 'Opinion 2/13 on EU Accession to the ECHR and Judicial Dialogue: Autonomy or Autarky?' (2015) 38 Fordham Int LJ 955.

93 Opinion 2/13 (n 91), para 184.

94 Ibid, para 201.

95 Ibid, paras 223–225.

96 Ibid, para 241.

97 Ibid, paras 254–255.

and interpret the covered WTO agreement in line with customary rules of interpretation (Article 3.2 of the Dispute Settlement Understanding (DSU)[98]) but do not interfere with the interpretation of EU law even if an EU measure is at stake. Drawing inspiration from this division of tasks, EU investment chapters thus regularly contain a similar provision on the applicable law. For example, Article 8.31 CETA provides:

(1) When rendering its decision, the Tribunal established under this Section shall apply this Agreement as interpreted in accordance with the *Vienna Convention on the Law of Treaties*, and other rules and principles of international law applicable between the Parties.
(2) The Tribunal shall not have jurisdiction to determine the legality of a measure, alleged to constitute a breach of this Agreement, under the domestic law of a Party. For greater certainty, in determining the consistency of a measure with this Agreement, the Tribunal may consider, as appropriate, the domestic law of a Party as a matter of fact. In doing so, the Tribunal shall follow the prevailing interpretation given to the domestic law by the courts or authorities of that Party and any meaning given to domestic law by the Tribunal shall not be binding upon the courts or authorities of that Party.[99]

Such formulation makes it hence crystal-clear that no investment tribunal will have the power to take decisions with the effect of binding the EU to a particular interpretation of EU law, hereby respecting the Court's first principle referred to above. Rather, these courts enforce the partial legal order created by the agreement to which the EU contributed itself. If such courts find that a certain EU measure, e.g. a Commission State aid decision (even if upheld by the CJEU) would violate the international obligation, such an international ruling would create a conflict between the two legal orders, and may well put pressure on the EU to modify its act. However, such a ruling cannot be seen as an attack on the EU's judicial autonomy.[100] Rather, such an adverse ruling

98 Understanding on Rules and Procedures Governing the Settlement of Disputes, Marrakesh Agreement Establishing the World Trade Organization, Annex 2 <https://www.wto.org/english/docs_e/legal_e/28-dsu.pdf> accessed 1 December 2016.

99 CETA draft text <http://trade.ec.europa.eu/doclib/docs/2014/september/tradoc_152806.pdf> accessed 20 November 2016.

100 But see Steffen Hindelang, 'Repellent Forces: The CJEU and Investor-State Dispute Settlement' (2015) 53 Archiv des Völkerrechts 68, 75 who argues that an adverse investment ruling could create a 'significant spill-over effect' on the EU's legal order, which the CJEU might classify as violating the EU's legal autonomy.

would create a classical conflict between international law and EU law, which would have to be solved in line with the Treaty rules on the relationship between these two legal orders, as interpreted by the CJEU.[101] Otherwise, the EU could become incapable to take any international legal commitment with binding dispute settlement: the mere hypothetical loss of a case with its repercussion on the domestic institutions (including domestic courts) to adjust the impugned act cannot prevent the EU from becoming a party to such dispute settlement system.

Equally, ISDS provisions in EU investment agreements do not pose particular problems with respect to Article 344 TFEU, the second principle of the CJEU. There is no risk that one EU Member State brings a dispute on EU law against another Member State under an EU investment agreement, as the latter confers rights of action to investors from third States against the Union or to EU investors against the third State, but not to EU Member States. As a side remark, one may notice that the CJEU's requirement that intra-EU cases should be made legally impossible through a specific clause in the international agreement to which the EU becomes a party is a very far-reaching proposition. Today the WTO Dispute Settlement Understanding already allows in theory that one EU Member State brings a claim against another one, as all Member States are WTO members alongside the EU. However, that mere possibility is restrained by the EU obligation under Article 344 TFEU not to do so, as the subject matter of such a WTO dispute between EU Member States would necessarily involve a trade question falling within Union competence. Also in practice, such a scenario has so far not arisen.[102] Hence, asking for a specific exclusion of intra-EU disputes in the international agreement to mirror the EU-internal obligation under Article 344 TFEU seems unnecessary.

In return, the CJEU's third principle, according to which an international judicial body should not decide on the division of competence between the EU and its Member States, is very relevant in the investment context. In this respect, the ISDS clauses in CETA have further developed a system which was already introduced into the Energy-Charter Treaty, to which both the EU and

101 See e.g. Case 181/73 *R. & V. Haegeman v Belgian State* EU:C:1974:41.

102 The closest scenario of an intra-EU dispute before the WTO was a case brought by Denmark in respect of the Faroe Islands in 2013 against the EU on restrictive measures relating to Atlanto-Scandian herring (DS 469 <https://www.wto.org/english/tratop_e/dispu_e/cases_e/ds469_e.htm> accessed 1 December 2016). The case was discontinued because a friendly settlement was reached in summer 2014 when the fishing quota was reduced. DS 469 was not a proper intra-EU case, though, as the EU Treaty does not apply to the Faroe Islands. For purposes of international litigation, the Faroe Islands acted hence as a non-eu entity.

its Member States are a party. For such a mixed situation an investor should actually come first to the EU institutions and the Member State concerned, which will then define who is the appropriate defendant. Such requirement was laid down in a Declaration under the Energy Charter, and has now become a formal requirement under Article 8.21 CETA. The latter provision states:

> (1) If the dispute cannot be settled within 90 days of the submission of the request for consultations, the request concerns an alleged breach of the Agreement by the European Union or a Member State of the European Union and the investor intends to initiate a claim pursuant to Article 8.23, the investor shall deliver to the European Union a notice requesting a determination of the respondent.
> (2) The notice shall identify the measures in respect of which the investor intends to initiate arbitration proceedings.
> (3) The European Union shall, after having made a determination, inform the investor as to whether the European Union or a Member State of the European Union shall be the respondent.

Importantly, inside the EU, such determination is then made according to specific rules agreed to by the legislator in Regulation 912/2014,[103] whose final interpretation is vested in the CJEU. This mechanism should thus in principle satisfy the Court's principle.[104]

However, if the EU does not manage to make such an internal determination under paragraph 3, the agreement contains subsidiary rules under paragraph 4, reading:

> In the event that the investor has not been informed of the determination within 50 days of delivering its notice requiring such determination:
> (a) If the measures identified in the notice are exclusively measures of a Member State of the European Union, the Member State shall be the respondent;
> (b) If the measures identified in the notice include measures of the European Union, the European Union shall be the respondent.

103 Regulation (EU) 912/2014 of the European Parliament and of the Council of 23 July 2014 establishing a framework for managing financial responsibility linked to investor-to-state dispute settlement tribunals established by international agreements to which the European Union is party [2014] OJ L257/121.

104 Hindelang (n 100) 81–82 with further discussion.

In any case, either an EU determination under paragraph 3 or the application of the criteria under paragraph 4 will be binding on the investment tribunal (Article 8.21, paragraph 7 CETA). This prevents the investment tribunal from determining itself who is the proper respondent in a case. At the same time, a Canadian investor has the guarantee that either the Union or a Member State can always be brought before an investment tribunal. Accordingly, and unlike in the proposed co-respondent mechanism under the ECHR where the European Court of Human Rights could have taken a final decision on the proper co-respondent,[105] there is no implicit determination of an investment tribunal about the division of powers between the Union and its member States.

When looking at the fourth principle, there is currently no danger that an investment court could undermine the power of the CJEU to render preliminary rulings. Rather to the contrary: according to the CJEU's own jurisprudence in *Nordsee*[106] and *Eco Swiss*[107] arbitration tribunals are not considered national courts which can send preliminary questions to Luxembourg. Neither could a domestic court in an EU Member State ask the international investment body for a preliminary ruling on investment related matters, thereby shortcutting the CJEU if the matter also involves questions of EU law. Hence, the issue of the proper prior involvement of the CJEU does not arise in the investment context.

Finally, measures interfering with the rights of an investor are highly unlikely to fall within the ambit of CFSP as they are normally executive administrative action or, in a few cases, legislative regulatory interferences. I am not aware of a situation where a foreign policy act has given rise to investment litigation. And if an international sanction by the EU (such as a decision freezing funds of certain listed persons) under Article 215 TFEU affected a foreign investor, the general exclusion of the CJEU's jurisdiction over CFSP acts would not come into play. Rather, for such sanctions the CJEU would have jurisdiction to review it under Article 275(2) TFEU. Accordingly, the risk that international investment courts would scrutinize EU sanctions decisions which are beyond the CJEU's reach (the Court's fifth principle) does in practice not arise.

105 Under art 3(5) of the draft Accession Agreement to the ECHR, a Contracting Party is to become a co-respondent either by accepting an invitation form the European Court of Human Rights *or by decision of the European Court of Human Rights upon the request of that Contracting Party*. This latter part was not compatible with the judicial autonomy of the European Union.

106 Case 102/81 *Nordsee Deutsche Hochseefischerei GmbH v Reederei Mond Hochseefischerei Nordstern AG & Co. KG and Reederei Friedrich Busse Hochseefischerei Nordstern AG & Co. KG* EU:C:1982:107.

107 Case C-126/97 *Eco Swiss China Time Ltd v Benetton International NV* EU:C:1999:269.

It follows from the above analysis that nowadays even trade agreements raise important questions relating to the judicial autonomy of the European Union. However, with carefully calibrated provisions relating to the power of future international investment tribunals, such autonomy is safeguarded in the EU's negotiating and treaty-making practice on investment protection.

5 Conclusion

The EU's Common Commercial Policy has developed significantly after the entry into force of the Lisbon Treaty. Following Ricardo's helpful indications of 2011 about the main constitutional novelties in the field, this article has tried to trace down the 'state of the art' seven years later. In a nutshell, the main conclusions are the following ones.

The EU's trade powers are by now 'rounded up'. With the interpretative help of the CJEU, the EU has become competent on all issues relating to trade in goods, services, and commercial aspects of intellectual property rights, meaning that the whole area of TRIPS and GATS nowadays fall under exclusive competence.[108] The breadth of the investment title is currently pending in Luxembourg. As non-trade objectives should be integrated into the CCP under Article 207(1) second sentence TFEU, it can also be safely assumed today that EU trade agreements may contain a number of non-traditional chapters dealing with issues such as sustainable development. Accordingly, it should be possible to base modern EU trade agreements on Article 207 TFEU alone, unless there are separate transport provisions which merit special treatment according to paragraph 5 thereof.

The new post-Lisbon institutional balance between the Parliament, the Commission and the Council is broadly established as well. On the EU internal scene, the Council and Parliament adopt together framework legislation, whereas the Commission runs the executive trade defence measures. Occasionally, a draft legislative proposal gets stuck for political reasons, but the legal rules and procedures follow the mainstream of other policy areas. Moreover, a number of important constitutional questions with respect to the negotiation, conclusion and enforcement of trade agreements have been solved in the past seven years. We see an emerging trend towards more transparency, and the leading role of the Commission as trade negotiator and litigator has been confirmed. Moreover, the European Parliament has asserted an ever-important role during the final steps, including on provisional application. The Council

108 Rosas (n 9) 1095.

continues to have the last word in the conclusion of such legally binding international agreements.

On judicial autonomy, some uncertainty has been generated by Opinion 2/13 on the EU's accession to the European Convention on Human Rights. Assessing its significance for the EU's ability to set-up international judicial bodies specialised in investment protection, a careful scrutiny of the Court's principles has shown that a proper distinction between the conventional task of an international investment tribunal or court to apply and interpret the EU agreement in question and the constitutional role of the CJEU to safeguard the autonomy of the EU legal order can be made. By way of example, specific CETA clauses both with respect to the determination of the proper respondent in an investment context and with respect to the applicable law make sure that such distinction is respected. Accordingly, new enforcement chapters on investment matters in EU free trade agreements do not pose a threat to the EU's judicial autonomy.

Justice and Home Affairs

CHAPTER 15

Variable Geometry, Justice and Home Affairs and the Conduct of EU External Relations

*Ivan Smyth**

1 Introduction

Since the entry into force of the Treaty of Lisbon on 1 December 2009 EU external relations have proved a fruitful area for litigation in front of the Court of Justice of the European Union (CJEU). A significant subset of the cases to date have concerned questions relating to Title V (Area of Freedom, Security and Justice) of the TFEU and the possible application of Protocol No. 21 on the position of the United Kingdom (UK) and Ireland in respect of the Area of Freedom, Security and Justice (JHA Protocol).[1] The interaction of the EU's external relations and the JHA Protocol provides an excellent illustration of the operation of variable geometry in practice and the difficult questions that it may give rise to. This chapter examines the approach taken by the CJEU when addressing questions relating to the choice of legal base for EU external agreements where it has been argued that a JHA legal base should be included in the Council Decisions authorising the negotiations and adoption of negotiating directives, or on signature and/or conclusion of an agreement by the EU.

2 A Brief Overview of the Operation of the JHA Protocol to International Agreements

The JHA Protocol is relevant where it has been decided that it is the EU that will exercise competence in respect of the JHA elements of an international

* The views expressed in this article are personal to the author and do not reflect the position of the Government of the United Kingdom. The author wishes to acknowledge the helpful comments received on an earlier draft from Alistair Robinson, Iain MacLeod, and Adrian Roberts.

1 This article is limited to looking at the effect of the case law on Protocol no. 21 to the Treaties. It does not consider the consequences for Denmark under Protocol no. 22 on the position of Denmark nor the impact of Protocol no. 19 on the Schengen acquis integrated into the framework of the European Union and Protocol no. 20 on the application of certain aspects of art 26 TFEU to the United Kingdom and to Ireland.

 | DOI 10.1163/9789004347175_016

agreement. Where an international agreement contains content falling within the potential scope of Title V TFEU but which remains within the scope of the EU and Member States' shared competence, it is possible for the Member States to determine that they wish to continue to exercise their competence in this regard rather than the EU. In this event the JHA Protocol is not applicable as it is the Member States who assume responsibility for meeting the JHA obligations under the international agreement not the EU.

The JHA Protocol applies both to international agreements entered into by the EU and to EU internal legislation. In respect of international agreements the JHA Protocol attaches not to the international agreement itself but rather to the decisions adopted by the Council to authorise the opening of negotiations and/or to approve the signing and conclusion of the agreement. The effect of the JHA Protocol is, however, that provisions of an international agreement which fall within the scope of Title V and which have been concluded by the EU on that basis cannot apply to the UK and/or Ireland as a matter of EU law unless the UK and/or Ireland have exercised their opt-in under the JHA Protocol in relation to the relevant EU decisions.[2] Where the UK and/or Ireland have decided not to opt-in to the EU decisions covering the JHA provisions of an agreement, in case of mixed agreements, they will nevertheless be bound by those provisions in their own right and will have to respect their obligations to the non-EU parties to the agreement in respect of those provisions.

The citation of a Title V TFEU legal base in any of the above decisions will automatically trigger the application of the JHA Protocol which provides that, where a proposed measure is adopted pursuant to Title V TFEU, the UK and Ireland shall not take part in the adoption of such a decision (Article 1). However Articles 3 and 4 of the JHA Protocol provide the UK and Ireland with the possibility of notifying that they wish to take part in the adoption and application of any proposed decision or at a later stage that they wish to accept that decision after its adoption. If the UK and/or Ireland do wish to opt-in to a proposed decision before its adoption by the Council then they must do so within three months of its presentation to the Council.

Where the UK and/or Ireland decide to opt-in to a decision authorising the opening of negotiations for an international agreement the opt-in is limited to the negotiation of that agreement and does not create any rights or obligations in respect of the subsequent decisions authorising the signing or conclusion of that agreement. Separate opt-in decisions will need to be taken by the UK or Ireland, in accordance with Article 3 of the JHA Protocol if they wish to take

---

2 Art 2 of the JHA Protocol makes express reference to 'provision of any international agreement concluded by the Union pursuant to that Title'.

part both in the decision to sign the agreement (Article 218(5) TFEU) and in the decision concluding it (Article 218(6) TFEU). It should be noted that, if the UK or Ireland notifies that it wishes to take part in the authorising of negotiations for or signing of an international agreement, such notification should generally be followed by notification of the participation of that Member State in the decision concluding the agreement. However, if the UK or Ireland does not exercise its opt-in in relation to the decision on signature of an agreement it may still decide to opt-in to the subsequent decision on conclusion by the EU of an agreement within three months of its publication. It is normal practice for international agreements with JHA content to include language in a recital which allows for a possible future notification to the country concerned of a UK and/or Ireland opt-in and the consequences that arise therefrom.[3]

As Advocate General Kokott recognised in her Opinion in Case C-431/11 *United Kingdom v Council*:

> It is particularly clear in a case like the present one that the choice of the correct legal basis is of considerable practical and institutional, indeed constitutional importance. The choice of legal basis paves the way for determining whether the United Kingdom and Ireland are able to exercise the special rights conferred on them by the 'opt-in' under Protocol No. 21 to the TEU and to the TFEU.[4]

---

3 See e.g. the following recital text from the EU-Ukraine Association Agreement: 'CONFIRMING that the provisions of this Agreement that fall within the scope of Part III, Title V of the Treaty on the Functioning of the European Union bind the United Kingdom and Ireland as separate Contracting Parties, and not as part of the European Union, unless the European Union together with the United Kingdom and/or Ireland jointly notify Ukraine that the United Kingdom or Ireland is bound as part of the European Union in accordance with Protocol No. 21 on the position of the United Kingdom and Ireland in respect of the area of Freedom, Security and Justice annexed to the Treaty on the Functioning of the European Union. If the United Kingdom and/or Ireland ceases to be bound as part of the European Union in accordance with Article 4a of Protocol No. 21 or in accordance with Article 10 of Protocol No. 36 on transitional provisions annexed to the Treaties, the European Union together with the United Kingdom and/or Ireland shall immediately inform Ukraine of any change in their position, in which case they shall remain bound by the provisions of the Agreement in their own right. The same applies to Denmark, in accordance with Protocol No. 22 on the position of Denmark, annexed to the Treaties'. (Association Agreement between the European Union and the European Atomic Energy Community and their Member States, of the one part, and Ukraine, of the other part [2014] OJ L161/1).

4 Opinion of AG Kokott in Case C-431/11 *United Kingdom of Great Britain and Northern Ireland v Council* EU:C:2013:187, para 33.

Furthermore, since the entry into force of the Lisbon Treaty there has been a change of practice in relation to the decisions needed for adopting negotiating directives, signature and conclusion of agreements where the need for a Title V TFEU legal base has been identified. Previously the practice in the external field had been to combine both the Title V TFEU and non-Title V TFEU elements in a single Council decision. However, recently the practice is to separate out the Title V elements into a separate decision.[5]

The justification for the change of practice is that according to the JHA Protocol the UK and Ireland do not take part in JHA measures unless they exercise their option to do so. When the Council decides therefore on the signature and conclusion of international agreements which include provisions creating legal obligations for the Union falling within the scope of Title V TFEU the Council should adopt two separate decisions: one decision covering the JHA provisions and another decision covering the other non-JHA provisions of the agreement. This is necessary because the voting rights within the Council regarding the adoption of each of these decisions are different and because the provisions of the agreement falling within the scope of Title V TFEU are not binding on the UK and Ireland in their capacity as Member States of the Union (unless the UK and Ireland exercise their right to opt in).

The benefit of this approach is that it makes clear what elements of the agreement fall within the scope of Title V TFEU and therefore are within the scope of the JHA Protocol. However, the citation of substantive legal bases and splitting an agreement into its JHA and non-JHA elements does require a detailed analysis of the subject-matter of the agreement and can at times be a fraught exercise. This is particularly so at the negotiating directives stage where the precise scope of what is to be negotiated may be unclear.

3 Choice of Legal Base

Several of the recent external policy cases have given rise to questions around whether specific international agreements involving the EU contain provisions whose content falls within Title V and thus whether the legal base of

5 See e.g. the Council Decisions in relation to the EU's accession to the Protocol of 2002 to the Athens Convention relating to the Carriage of Passengers and Luggage by Sea, 1974 (Athens Protocol) where there are two separate Council Decisions: Council Decision 2012/22/EU in respect of the non-Title V elements (everything other than Articles 10 and 11 of the Athens Protocol) ([2012] OJ L8/1) and Council Decision 2012/23/EU in respect of the Title V elements of the Protocol (Articles 10 and 11 only of the Athens Protocol) ([2012] OJ L8/13).

the accompanying Council decisions should contain a Title V legal base and attract the operation of the JHA Protocol. Whilst the CJEU has followed its well rehearsed test for determining the appropriate legal base the implications of its judgments have important consequences for the UK and Ireland.

Before turning to examine the case law it is perhaps helpful to set-out briefly the CJEU's traditional approach to determining the choice of legal base for an EU external agreement. According to the CJEU the choice of legal base must be based on objective factors which are amenable to judicial review and which include, in particular, the aim and content of the agreement.[6] This is to be identified by conducting an examination of the actual provisions of the agreement. If an examination of the text reveals that there are in fact two (or more) aims or components, the general rule is to seek a single legal basis by identifying the essential nature of the system envisaged ('predominant purpose') and removing those aspects which are merely incidental. Thus if one aim can be clearly said to be the predominant purpose the EU decision must be based on a single legal basis, namely that required by the predominant purpose.[7] However, if it is established that the agreement simultaneously pursues several objectives which are inseparably linked without one being incidental or ancillary in relation to the other, the decision must be founded on the corresponding legal bases.[8] In addition, the CJEU has held that recourse to a dual legal basis is not

6 Opinion 2/00 (*Cartagena Protocol*) EU:C:2001:664, para. 22.

7 See e.g. Case C-36/98 *Kingdom of Spain v Council* EU:C:2001:64, paras 58–59 where the Court stated: '58. It follows from a consistent line of decisions that in the context of the organisation of the powers of the Community the choice of a legal basis for a measure must rest on objective factors which are amenable to judicial review. Those factors include in particular the aim and the content of the measure (see, in particular, Case C-269/97 *Commission* v *Council* [2000] ECR I-2257, paragraph 43). 59. If examination of a Community measure reveals that it pursues a twofold purpose or that it has a twofold component and if one of these is identifiable as the main or predominant purpose or component, whereas the other is merely incidental, the act must be based on a single legal basis, namely that required by the main or predominant purpose or component (see, to that effect, the judgment in Case C-42/97 *Parliament* v *Council* [1999] ECR I-869, paragraphs 39 and 40)'. The CJEU confirmed the continued veracity of this approach recently in its judgment in Case C-130/10 *Parliament v Council* EU:C:2012:472, paras 42–46.

8 Case C-336/00 *Republic of Austria v Martin Huber* EU:C:2002:509, para 31 where the Court noted: 'Exceptionally, if it is established that the act simultaneously pursues a number of objectives, indissociably linked, without one being secondary and indirect in relation to the other, such an act may be founded on the various corresponding legal bases (see, to that effect, the *Titanium dioxide* judgment, paragraphs 13 and 17, and *Parliament* v *Council,* cited above, paragraph 38, as well as Opinion 2/00 [2001] ECR I-9713, para. 23)'.

possible where the procedures laid down for each legal basis are incompatible with each other.[9]

In practice it will only be necessary to add a corresponding legal basis where there are specific substantial commitments or provisions relating to funding by the EU. By contrast individual legal bases have tended not to be required where commitments relate to non-binding forms of cooperation or dialogue[10] or where a commitment is clearly dependent on other provisions of the agreement.

The recent case law on choice of legal base involving Title V and the operation of the JHA Protocol can be loosely divided into two different strands:

- Cases requiring a determination to be made between a Title V and Non-Title V legal base for an EU agreement; and
- Cases where an international agreement contains subject matter capable of falling within Title V but the question arises as to whether such content is merely ancillary to another purpose.

3.1 *Title V TFEU or Non-Title V TFEU?*

The CJEU's approach to the first strand of cases is illustrated by three separate judgments involving challenges by the UK concerning the use of Article 48 TFEU to update provisions relating to social welfare in Protocols to the European Economic Area (EEA), EU-Switzerland and EU-Turkey Agreements respectively. These cases are relevant to the issue of variable geometry because, depending on which legal base applied to the three contested measures different procedures would apply having significant consequences for the UK and for Ireland. In all three cases the UK opposed the use of Article 48 TFEU and argued that the correct legal base should have been Article 79 TFEU, which would in turn have triggered the application of the JHA Protocol.

Unlike measures adopted under Article 48 TFEU, the measures adopted under Article 79 TFEU would apply to the UK and Ireland only if they exercised the option to be bound by those measures pursuant to the JHA Protocol. Thus if all the contested measures were adopted under Article 48 TFEU the UK and Ireland would be deprived of the option that they had, by virtue of the JHA Protocol, not to participate in the relevant EU decisions and not to be bound by them.

Briefly the facts in the three cases[11] were as follows:

---

9 Case C-130/10 (n 7), paras 45–49.

10 Case C-268/94 *Portugal v Council* EU:C:1996:461, para 75.

11 The UK was supported by Ireland in all three cases.

- Case C-431/11 (*EEA* case)[12] – The UK sought annulment of a Council Decision[13] adopted under Article 48 TFEU and in the context of the EEA Agreement[14] which had the effect of extending the EU's *acquis* to nationals of the three European Free Trade Association (EFTA) States[15] lawfully resident in the EU and to EU citizens lawfully resident in those States. The UK argued that the Council Decision in question was not concerned with the adoption of social security measures necessary to provide freedom of movement for workers. In the UK's view the subject matter concerned the free movement rights of legally resident third country nationals and as such fell within the EU's common immigration policy and ought to have been adopted under Article 79 TFEU to which the JHA Protocol attached.
  The Council disagreed. The subject Council Decision extended the EU's *acquis* on social security systems to the EFTA States which was 'indispensable' to the main objective in the EEA Agreement of guaranteeing EFTA nationals effective freedom of movement within the EU. As such Article 48 TFEU was the appropriate legal base. Furthermore to consider that the proposed amendment to the EEA Agreement formed part of the EU's immigration policy would not be in line with the EU's commitments under the EEA Agreement and would jeopardise the attainment of the main objective of providing for the fullest possible realisation of the internal market within the whole EEA.
- Case C-656/11 (*Swiss* case)[16] – The UK sought annulment of a Council Decision[17] coordinating the social security schemes of the EU and Switzerland under the EU-Switzerland Free Movement Agreement (FMOP Agreement).[18]

12 Case C-431/11 *United Kingdom of Great Britain and Northern Ireland v Council* EU:C:2013:589.

13 Council Decision 2011/407/EU of 6 June 2011 on the position to be taken by the European Union within the EEA Joint Committee concerning an amendment to Annex VI (Social Security) and Protocol 37 to the EEA Agreement [2012] OJ L182/12.

14 Agreement on the European Economic Area [1994] OJ L1/3.

15 Iceland, Norway and Lichtenstein.

16 Case C-656/11 *United Kingdom of Great Britain and Northern Ireland v Council* EU:C:2014:97.

17 Council Decision 2011/863/EU of 16 December 2011 on the position to be taken by the European Union in the Joint Committee established under the Agreement between the European Community and its Member States, of the one part, and the Swiss Confederation, of the other, on the free movement of persons as regards the replacement of Annex II to that Agreement on the coordination of social security schemes [2011] OJ L341/1.

18 Agreement between the European Community and its Member States, of the one part, and the Swiss Confederation, of the other, on the free movement of persons [2002] OJ L114/6.

Once again the UK argued that the legal base for the Decision should be Article 79 TFEU. The UK asserted that by not choosing the Title V legal base the Council had denied the UK its rights under the JHA Protocol. Furthermore, according to the UK Article 48 TFEU could not be extended to address third-country nationals or economically inactive persons.

By contrast the Council argued that the Council Decision was designed to implement the free movement of persons between the EU and the Swiss Confederation by extending the EU's *acquis* on the coordination of social security systems to both lawfully resident Swiss nationals in the EU and to EU nationals residing lawfully in the Swiss Confederation. Furthermore, the Council argued that the exclusion of the UK and Ireland from the scope of the Council Decision would jeopardise the aims of the FMOP Agreement and due to a lack of uniformity would undermine the EU's obligations to the Swiss Confederation.

- Case C-81/13 (*Turkey* case)[19] – The UK sought annulment of the Council Decision[20] on the position to be taken on behalf of the EU with regard to the coordination of social security systems between the EU and Turkey again arguing that Article 79 TFEU should be the legal base rather than Article 48 TFEU. The decision sought to repeal and replace an existing measure covering the application of Member State social security schemes to Turkish workers and their families which, in turn, gave effect to aspects of the 1963 EU-Turkey Association Agreement[21] dealing with the movement of workers. The UK distinguished this case by arguing that the aim of the challenged Council Decision was not to extend the provisions of the single market to Turkey; instead it was a measure 'limited to updating the limited rights presently enjoyed by Turkish workers' under Decision No.3/80.[22]

---

19 Case C-81/13 *United Kingdom of Great Britain and Northern Ireland v Council* EU:C:2014:2449.

20 Council Decision 2012/776/EU of 6 December 2012 on the position to be taken on behalf of the European Union within the Association Council set up by the Agreement establishing an association between the European Economic Community and Turkey, with regard to the adoption of provisions on the coordination of social security systems [2012] OJ L340/19.

21 Council Decision 64/732/EEC of 23 December 1963 on the conclusion of the Agreement establishing an Association between the European Economic Community and Turkey [1964] OJ P 217/3685.

22 Decision 3/80 of the Association Council of 19 September 1980 on the application of the social security schemes of the Member States of the European Communities to Turkish workers and members of their families [1983] OJ C110/60 (also commonly referred to as the 'Additional Protocol').

The Council argued that the aim of the Decision was securing freedom of movement for workers by providing for the partial coordination of social security systems between the EU and Turkey.

In all three cases the CJEU applied its classical test for determining the choice of legal base.[23]

In the *EEA* case the CJEU considered the purpose of the contested Council Decision in the context of the nature and purpose of the EEA Agreement. The EEA Agreement established a close association between the EU and the EFTA States based on special, privileged links with one of its principal aims being to provide for the fullest possible realisation of the free movement of, inter alia, persons within the whole EEA, so that the internal market established within the EU is extended to the EFTA States. The EEA Agreement enshrines the freedom of movement for workers among Member and EFTA States and recognises their rights in the field of social security. The association established covers closer cooperation in the field of social policy and requires the parties to facilitate cooperation and to abstain from any measure liable to jeopardise the attainment of the objectives pursued by the agreement. The contested decision regulated the social rights of nationals of the three EFTA States concerned and the social rights of EU citizens in those EFTA States making it possible to retain the extension of social rights to nationals of the States concerned. As such the CJEU held it was precisely one of the measures by which the law governing the EU internal market was to be extended as far as possible to the EEA, with the result that nationals of the EEA States concerned benefit from the free movement of persons under the same social conditions as EU citizens. In those circumstances the CJEU determined that it was possible for it to be legitimately adopted on the basis of Article 48 TFEU.

The CJEU went on to reject the UK argument that Article 79(2) TFEU could form the basis for the challenged Council Decision holding that this provision had to be interpreted in the context of which it forms part (policies on border checks, asylum and immigration) of Title V TFEU and in the light of Article 79(1) TFEU, under which the EU seeks to develop a common immigration policy. This was, taking account of the context of the development of the EEA Agreement, manifestly irreconcilable with the purpose of the Council Decision.

As regards the material scope of the JHA Protocol the CJEU noted that it was expressly limited to the area of freedom, security and justice and must be given a strict interpretation. It is not within the spirit and purpose of the JHA Protocol to give the UK and Ireland free discretion as regards participation in

23 See e.g. case C-431/11 (n 12), para 44.

measures adopted by the Union institutions and the binding effect on them in other areas of EU law, in particular in the context of the internal market or the association of third countries. Consequently, the opt-in could not be applicable to the adoption of measures like the decision at issue which concerned the extension of internal market rules to third countries.

At the hearing in the *Swiss* case the UK (at the CJEU's invitation) argued that the decision at issue was adopted in a different context to that at issue in the *EEA* case. The CJEU's conclusion in the *EEA* case had been founded on the finding that a close association existed between the EU and the EFTA States and that the EEA Agreement had the aim of providing for the fullest possible realisation of the free movement of inter alia, persons within the whole EEA, so that the internal market is extended to the EFTA States. The UK claimed that no similar instrument binding the EU and the Swiss Confederation exists. Second, the FMOP Agreement did not reflect those characteristics and in many respects fell short of the EEA Agreement in terms of ambitions, liberalisation and legal integration.

The CJEU rejected the UK's arguments. The Council Decision in question was intended to settle the position to be taken by the EU in the Joint Committee established by the FMOP Agreement as regards the amendment of Annex II on the coordination of social security schemes. The FMOP Agreement is one of a series of seven sectoral agreements, the objective of which is to strengthen the economic ties between the EU and the Swiss Confederation. Under the FMOP Agreement, the free movement of persons between the parties was to be based on the rules applying in the EU. By concluding in 2002 the FMOP Agreement, the EU extended to the Swiss Confederation the application of its legislation concerning coordination of social security systems. The main aim of the Decision was to update the legislation extended to the Swiss Confederation by the FMOP Agreement to take account of developments in the EU acquis and retaining the extension of social rights to citizens of the States concerned as intended by the FMOP Agreement since 2002. In the light of the context of the challenged Council Decision and its content and aim, it was properly adopted under Article 48 TFEU.

In the *Turkey* case, the CJEU followed a similar approach but recognised that the nature and purpose of the agreement between the EU and Turkey was different. The EEC-Turkey Agreement and the Additional Protocol did not mean that the right to freedom of movement within the EU enjoyed by nationals of the Member States was extended to Turkish nationals. Turkish workers do not have the right to enter the EU freely and do not have the right to move freely between the Member States. Similarly, the Council Decision was not aimed at extending to Turkey the new EU regime coordinating social security systems but was limited to updating the limited rights presently enjoyed by Turkish workers.

Nevertheless the CJEU rejected the UK assertion that Article 79 TFEU was the correct legal base. The EEC-Turkey Agreement provides that freedom of movement for workers between EU Member States and Turkey will be secured by progressive stages. The decision constituted a further stage in progressively securing freedom of movement for workers between the EU and Turkey and in developing the links created by their association agreement. However the CJEU went on to comment that in the absence of any extension of the internal market or of the free movement of persons to Turkey and given that Turkey had not been placed on the same footing as a Member State for the purposes of those rules, the Decision could not legitimately be adopted solely on the basis of Article 48 TFEU. The CJEU commented that as a rule, it is only in the sphere of the internal policies and actions of the EU or of the external actions relating to third countries which can be placed on the same footing as Member State of the EU that Article 48 TFEU empowers the EU to adopt measures in this area. However, Article 217 TFEU (the general association agreement clause) necessarily empowers the EU to guarantee commitments towards third countries in all the fields covered by the TFEU. Accordingly, in the view of the CJEU, the Council is entitled, on the basis of Article 217 TFEU, to adopt a measure in the framework of an association agreement on condition that that measure relates to a specific area of EU competence and is also founded, on the legal basis corresponding, in the light in particular of its aim and content, to that area. Therefore, although the decision could not legitimately be adopted solely on the basis of either Article 217 TFEU or Article 48 TFEU, it could be adopted where both articles were cited, since it had been adopted in the framework of an association agreement and was aimed at the adoption of measures coordinating social security systems.

In all three cases the UK had also argued that because Article 79 TFEU had previously been used for the purposes of adopting similar measures for other third countries[24] it should apply equally in these cases. The CJEU dispensed with this argument in cursory terms commenting in the *EEA* case:

> Lastly so far as concerns the argument put forward by the United Kingdom and Ireland that recourse to Article 79(2) TFEU is justified in the present case by reason of the fact that that provision has already been used by the EU legislature as the basis for the adoption of similar decisions

24 Such as the People's Democratic Republic of Algeria, the State of Israel, the Former Yugoslav Republic of Macedonia, the Kingdom of Morocco and the Republic of Tunisia.

> concerning other third countries, that argument cannot be upheld in the present case.
>
> In that regard, suffice it to note that in accordance with settled case-law, the legal basis for an act must be determined having regard to its own aim and content and not to the legal basis used for the adoption of other EU measures which might, in certain cases, display similar characteristics (…).[25]

Finally, it is perhaps worth noting that in all three of these cases the CJEU was asked to make a simple determination between a Title V and a non-Title V legal base. In no case to date has the CJEU been asked to address the potentially more vexed question of whether the JHA Protocol can apply to a situation where no Title V legal base has been or is proposed to be cited but nevertheless an international agreement arguably contains JHA content. It remains for the CJEU to be confronted with this conundrum.

3.2 *Ancillary to the Predominant Purpose?*

The second stream of legal base case law requires a more complex analysis of the terms of an agreement than was at issue in the cases referred to above. Although the approach followed by the CJEU is similar, the question is not whether one legal base trumps another legal base per se but rather revolves around the question of whether the proposed international agreement can be clearly said to pursue one predominant objective against which all the other possible purposes pursued by the agreement can be deemed to be ancillary, incidental or even incorporated. In many cases, it will be clear that the agreement does contain some provisions which may be substantive but yet remain incidental to an overriding policy objective and as such do not merit the citation of a separate legal base. A determination, however, that the predominant purpose of an agreement is not JHA related can have significant repercussions for the UK and Ireland in relation to the application of the JHA Protocol where the UK and Ireland consider that an EU agreement contains JHA content.

Until recently the traditional approach had been that the principle concerning incidental purposes or components was not applicable to international agreements establishing partnership and cooperation between the EU and third countries. This was premised on the fact that such agreements were geared to creating a comprehensive relationship covering many different areas

25 Case C-431/11 (n 12), paras 66–67. See also: Case C-656/11 (n 16), para 48; Case C-81/13 (n 19), para 36.

of cooperation. Unlike an internal EU measure, which generally covers a specific area or a specific international agreement, partnership and cooperation agreements cover almost all the areas of competence provided for in the Treaties and establish a comprehensive relationship between the EU and the third country or region concerned. The inherent aim of such agreements is to establish a full relationship or partnership by cooperating in as many different areas as possible. As a result it was not possible to identify a particular area as predominant compared to others. Practice therefore had been to cite multiple legal bases.

However, in Case C-377/12 *Commission v Council* (*Philippines* case)[26] the Commission sought the annulment of the Council Decision for the signing of a Framework Agreement on Partnership and Cooperation between the EU and the Philippines (Framework Agreement).[27] The Commission had initially proposed that the Decision be adopted under Article 207 TFEU (Common Commercial Policy) and Article 209 TFEU (development cooperation). The Council decided, when adopting the Decision on signature, that additional legal bases, including Article 79(3) TFEU, a Title V legal base, should be added.[28] The Commission challenged the inclusion of the additional legal bases arguing that they were unnecessary because, save for the trade provisions, all the provisions in the agreement were designed to pursue the development of the Philippines and did not impose extensive and distinct obligations.

The Council, supported by five Member States,[29] disagreed. According to the Council, EU agreements establishing partnership and cooperation with third countries (sometimes called framework agreements) sought to establish a comprehensive relationship covering many different areas of cooperation. The nature and content of such agreements had evolved in conjunction with the extension of the competences of the EU and no particular area could be identified as predominant compared to others. A specific or substantial commitment required the addition of a corresponding legal basis. As the most

26 Case C-377/12 *Commission v Council* EU:C:2014:1903.

27 Council Decision 2012/272/EU of 14 May 2012 on the signing, on behalf of the Union, of the Framework Agreement on the Partnership and Cooperation between the European Union and its Member States, of the one part, and the Republic of the Philippines, of the other part [2012] OJ L134/3.

28 Art 79(3) TFEU provides that 'The Union may conclude agreements with third countries for the readmission to their countries of origin or provenance of third-country nationals who do not or who no longer fulfil the conditions for entry, presence or residence in the territory of one of the Member States'.

29 France, Poland, Sweden, the Netherlands and the United Kingdom all intervened on the side of the Council. The European Parliament sided with the Commission.

limited specific obligation could lead to a wide development of the external relations with the third country party to the framework agreement in that specific area (for example transport or environment as in the case in point), the criterion proposed by the Commission that an obligation must be extensive in order to constitute an objective distinct from those of the development cooperation could not be accepted.

The Council argued that in accordance with CJEU's judgment in Case C-268/94 *Portugal v Council*[30] when a clause in an agreement prescribes in concrete terms the manner in which cooperation in a specific area is to be implemented, that agreement must be founded on the corresponding legal basis. Each specific area of an agreement of this kind must be considered separately, irrespective of any concurrent development aid programme in that area, while taking account of the legal, binding and self-standing nature of the obligations entered into. The Council submitted that the content of the Framework Agreement confirmed its approach and did not assign a predominant role to any particular area, such as development cooperation. Furthermore the Framework Agreement's structure confirmed that it related to the establishment of a comprehensive multi-dimensional relation.

The CJEU had not previously been called upon to issue an opinion on the question of the choice of legal basis in the case of an international agreement where one of its components fell within the scope of Title V of the TFEU and where there were other significant and self-standing purposes.[31] Indeed, it was

30 Case C-268/94 *Portuguese Republic v Council* EU:C:1996:461.

31 An earlier case had addressed in a peripheral manner the question of whether a Title V legal base was required. In Case C-137/12 *Commission v Council* EU:C:2013:675 (*Conditional Access* case), the Commission sought the annulment of the Council Decision 2011/853/EU on the signing on behalf of the Union of the European Convention on the legal protection of services based on or consisting of conditional access [2011] OJ L336/1. The Commission challenged the Council's assertion that the Convention should be signed as a mixed agreement by the Union and the Member States arguing that the EU enjoyed exclusive competence and that the choice of the legal base for the Decision (art 114 TFEU in combination with art 207 TFEU) was incorrect. Poland and Sweden in their interventions argued that the provisions of the Convention dealing with confiscation measures and related judicial cooperation were incompatible with the choice of an art 207 TFEU legal base. At the oral hearing stage the Council argued that justice and home affairs matters could never be incidental as this would deprive the UK and Ireland of their opt-in. Both the Advocate General and the Court rejected this line of argument holding that the focus of the Convention was the Common Commercial Policy. Neither the Council nor the Commission had raised any points on Title V or the JHA Protocol in their initial pleadings. The UK in its intervention did not raise any arguments relating to the need to cite a JHA legal base or the application of the JHA Protocol.

considered in certain quarters that Title V measures, whatever their position in an EU agreement, could not be regarded as incidental since they concerned matters which fell within the scope of Title V of the TFEU and were consequently covered by the JHA Protocol. The JHA Protocol constitutes part of the Union's primary law and binds all the EU Member States and Institutions. It was argued that applying case law concerning the incidental nature of components to provisions which, if adopted in isolation, would fall within the scope of the JHA Protocol would amount to circumventing the latter by depriving the UK and Ireland of the right to decide whether they wished to be bound to these provisions by the Union thereby divesting the JHA Protocol of any useful effect.

Addressing the arguments before it the CJEU first recalled that in accordance with its settled case law the choice of the legal basis of an EU measure must rest on objective factors amenable to judicial review including the aim and content of the measure.

The CJEU noted, having regard to its previous judgment in Case C-268/94 *Portugal v Council*, that the fact that a development cooperation agreement contains clauses concerning various specific matters could not alter the characterisation of the agreement. This must be determined having regard to its essential object and not in terms of individual clauses unless those clauses impose such extensive obligations that they can be said to constitute distinct objectives apart from development cooperation.[32]

The CJEU considered that the notion of development cooperation should be interpreted broadly, referring extensively to the European Consensus – a non legally binding statement of a political nature[33] and Regulation (EC) 1905/2006 of the European Parliament and of the Council establishing a financing instrument for development cooperation.[34] According to the CJEU, EU policy in the field of development cooperation is not limited to measures directly aimed at the eradication of poverty, but also pursues other objectives referred to in Article 21 TEU such as fostering the sustainable economic social and environmental development of developing countries with the primary aim of eradicating poverty.[35] In the view of the CJEU the Framework Agreement was focused on development:

32 Case C-377/12 (n 26), para 39.

33 Joint Statement by the Council and the representatives of the Governments of the Member States meeting within the Council, the European Parliament and the Commission on European Union Development Policy: 'The European Consensus' [2006] OJ C46/1.

34 [2006] OJ L378/41.

35 Case C-377/12 (n 26), para 37. See also Opinion of AG Mengozzi in the same case (EU:C:2014:29), paras 63–65.

> [I]t is apparent from the whole of the Framework Agreement that the cooperation and partnership provided for by it take account especially of the needs of a developing country and therefore contribute to furthering in particular pursuit of the objectives referred to in Articles 21(2) (d) TEU and 208 (1) TFEU.[36]

The CJEU then went on to consider whether the provisions of the Framework Agreement relating to readmission of nationals[37] to transport and to the environment whilst also contributing to the pursuit of the objectives of development cooperation nevertheless contained extensive obligations so as to constitute distinct objectives which were neither secondary nor incidental.[38]

As regards readmission the CJEU acknowledged that the provisions of the Framework Agreement contained specific obligations. Nevertheless these provisions did not prescribe in concrete terms the manner in which cooperation concerning readmission of nationals was to be implemented, a conclusion which, in the view of the CJEU, was reinforced by the commitment to conclude a readmission agreement.[39] The CJEU concluded therefore that the readmission provisions could not be considered to constitute distinct objectives which were neither secondary nor incidental from those of development cooperation. Consequently the CJEU ruled that the Council was wrong in selecting Article 79(3) TFEU as one of the legal bases for the contested decision.[40]

---

36 Case C-377/12 (n 26), para. 47.

37 Readmission was addressed in art 26 of the Framework Agreement, headed 'Cooperation on Migration and Development'. The Court recognised that there were two legal obligations concerning readmission in the agreement – first the legal obligation to readmit and secondly the obligation to enter into a future readmission agreement. The relevance of the second element was that the Court considered the first legal obligation was in and of itself not sufficient to warrant the citation of a Title V legal base because the parties anticipated a more detailed agreement to flesh out the practical modalities applicable to readmission. The second obligation is given expression in art 26(4) of the Agreement which provides: 'The Parties agree to conclude as soon as possible an agreement for the admission/readmission of their nationals, including a provision on the readmission of nationals of other countries and stateless persons'.

38 Case C-377/12 (n 26), para 48.

39 Ibid, paras 57–58.

40 AG Mengozzi in his Opinion (n 35) noted however at para 77 that 'If, as I believe, Article 79(3) TFEU was wrongly included as a legal basis in the PCA, equally it must be stated firmly and unequivocally that the anticipated international agreement, provided for in Article 26(4) of the PCA, cannot be concluded on the basis of development cooperation but must be concluded on the basis of Article 79 TFEU. It is indeed when that agreement is concluded – namely when the European Union is preparing to adopt a measure based

4 What Lessons Can Be Drawn from the Case-Law of the CJEU on Choice of Legal Base to Date?

Views differ on how significant the case-law referred to above is and whether it can be said that the CJEU has consistently undermined the JHA Protocol by restrictively interpreting the scope of Title V of the TFEU.[41] It is generally accepted, however, that the test applied by the CJEU is consistent with its approach over many years and was not especially crafted for the JHA Protocol. Nevertheless, some commentators consider that the CJEU's approach favours the choice of a single legal base where possible and this could in practice operate against the inclusion of a Title V TFEU legal base. Some believe that the approach taken by the CJEU in the *Philippines* case will have the effect of favouring broadly expressed legal bases such as trade and development over secondary legal bases. The effect of this may be that Title V TFEU will only be used as a legal basis for international agreements that are clearly sectoral in nature and not for agreements that cover a multitude of different clauses and different provisions.[42]

Some commentators have also expressed concern that the CJEU is now interpreting the EU's development cooperation competence so widely that it can subsume Title V TFEU to it.[43] Others have questioned the veracity of the CJEU's finding in the *Philippines* Case that readmission issues fell within the scope of development cooperation policy, even if they contained legally binding obligations as long as those obligations were not very specific. This failed to consider whether the provisions in question contributed to the development

on a provision falling under Title V TFEU – that the full effectiveness of Protocols Nos. 21 and 22 will be ensured, together with the rights of the Member States concerned'.

41 See e.g. European Union Committee, *The UK's Opt-in Protocol: Implications of the Government's Approach* (House of Lords Reports 2014–15, 136) 47–52, where at para 168 the Committee noted the view of Professor Marise Cremona that the CJEU's approach was one that had been adopted consistently by the Court over many years and was not especially crafted for the JHA Protocol whilst at para 172 the Committee noted that Professor Damian Chalmers was critical of the CJEU's reasoning and considered that there was the possibility that 'the safeguards for the British Government position that were negotiated under Protocol 21 have been largely eroded' and that this was 'a long way from what was anticipated'.

42 See comments by Professor Marise Cremona in her evidence to the House of Lords Scrutiny Committee (ibid, paras 169–170).

43 In this regard see e.g. the interesting commentary on the *Philippines* case by Morten Broberg and Rass Holdgaard entitled 'Demarcating the Union's Development Cooperation Policy after Lisbon: Commission v. Council (Philippines PCFA)' (2015) 52 CML Rev 547.

of the country concerned, which was the core of the legal base.[44] Others have commented that the CJEU's approach to determining legal base is defective because it requires a formal and restrictive approach to sensitive provisions in the Treaties.[45] Furthermore, the distinction between predominant and ancillary is very context-specific and requires the CJEU to conduct a complex analysis in every case.

The conclusions of the House of Lords European Union Committee in its report on 'The UK's Opt-in Protocol: Implications of the Government's Approach' perhaps most accurately reflect the collective academic view of the CJEU's approach and its implications. The House of Lords Committee commented:

> We conclude that the CJEU's approach to determining legal base in the (...) cases relating to Title V does not differ from its established case law.
>
> We agree with witnesses who have suggested that the CJEU's approach to determining the legal base of international agreements means that the complexity of an agreement is not always reflected in the resulting choice: it renders somewhat invisible the ancillary or secondary objective, including ancillary or secondary JHA objectives (...)
>
> Nevertheless, this does not, in our view, amount to a deliberate undermining of the safeguards in the opt-in Protocol.[46]

It is perhaps worth considering, however, some of the practical consequences which flow from the CJEU's findings in the cases referred to above.

The CJEU has been consistent in stating that it is not procedures such as the JHA Protocol that define the choice of legal basis of a measure but the legal

44 See comments by Professor Damian Chalmers reported in the House of Lords Report (n 41), para 179 where he is quoted as saying: 'I cannot quite see how readmission treaties help the development of the third country concerned. It has to take its own citizens – and, perhaps, citizens of neither the EU nor that country – back on to its territory if they have lived there in transit. I cannot see how that helps their development. The mere fact that there is some EU legislation – EU soft law – that refers to readmission as part of the development process is not convincing. As the Court of Justice says in most of its case law, the mere fact that the EU has taken one approach in the past to the legal scope of its powers does not create a precedent to bind the Court of Justice in the future'.

45 Professor Basilien-Gainche is also reported in the same report as commenting that she thought the CJEU's approach to determining legal base was 'defective', because it required it to take a 'formal and restrictive' approach to sensitive provisions in the EU Treaties, particularly JHA policies under Title V (ibid, para 180).

46 Ibid, paras 183–185.

basis of a measure that determines the procedures to be followed in adopting that measure.[47] This is not a contentious finding from a legal perspective.

Furthermore the CJEU, when determining the legal basis of a measure, applies the same test irrespective of whether the policy framework is that of development cooperation or another policy. The only nuance is that development cooperation is defined so broadly at EU level that it is perhaps more difficult to show that, alongside the large number of sectors it can encompass, there remains another objective or there is more than one objective both distinct from those pursued by the development cooperation and inseparably linked to the measure in question. Thus based on the CJEU's reasoning in the *Philippines* judgment, the likelihood is that the CJEU in considering an agreement with a significant development focus will find any JHA content therein is merely ancillary to the predominant development cooperation objective and therefore no Title V legal base is needed and the JHA Protocol is not engaged.[48]

Thus if an international agreement to be entered into either by the EU alone or together with the Member States as a mixed agreement includes provisions having JHA content and in the case of a mixed agreement it has not been made clear that Member States intend to exercise the JHA competence in their own right, is concluded by the EU on the basis of Article 209 TFEU alone (development cooperation) or both Articles 209 and 207 TFEU (Common Commercial Policy) on the grounds that those provisions are merely ancillary or secondary the consequence is that the provisions of the agreement falling within the scope of Title V TFEU, will be equally applicable to the UK and Ireland as Member States of the Union. According to the CJEU's judgment in the *Philippines* case, this is possible not only where the international agreement in question contains general non-binding provisions in that area but also where it contains

47 See e.g. Case C-130/10 (n 7), paras 79–80: 'While it is true that choosing between Articles 75 TFEU and 215 TFEU as the legal basis for the contested regulation has consequences for the Parliament's prerogatives, inasmuch as the former provides for recourse to the ordinary legislative procedure whereas, under the latter, the Parliament is merely informed, that fact cannot, however, determine the choice of legal base. As the Council argues, it is not procedures that define the legal basis of a measure but the legal basis of a measure that determines the procedures to be followed in adopting that measure'. See also Jeno Czuczai, 'The Powers of the Council Concerning the Emergency of International Terrorism after the Judgment in Case C-130/10 Parliament v. Council' in Inge Govaere and Dara Poli (eds), *EU Management of Global Emergencies-Legal Framework for Combating Threats and Crises* (Brill-Nijhoff 2014) 102ff.

48 Of course it might not only be JHA content that might be at issue bearing in mind that in the *Philippines* case the Court also dismissed the Council's attempts to include additional transport and environment legal bases.

specific obligations in that area insofar as they are not extensive enough to constitute a distinct objective.

In the *Philippines* case by relying on the secondary and incidental nature of the provisions on readmission the CJEU did not explicitly address the Council's argument that applying this approach to readmission or other provisions in the JHA field would undermine the rights of the UK and Ireland under the JHA Protocol and would deprive the JHA Protocol which, as part of the Union's primary law has the same value as the Treaties, of its useful effect. It is open to question how the CJEU would have ruled if the readmission provision in the Philippines Agreement had contained more developed hard obligations normally found in a readmission agreement rather than just being an aspiration. This leaves open the possibility for a future case where more detailed readmission provisions are incorporated into the agreement. The CJEU may then be faced with having to determine whether such detailed provisions can constitute a distinct and non-ancillary objective.

It is not clear whether the CJEU's reasoning in the *Philippines* case regarding the extent to which provisions in the latter area may be treated as secondary – in relation to or subsumed within – development cooperation is equally applicable in the case of association agreements (Article 217 TFEU) and agreements concerning economic, financial and technical cooperation with third countries other than developing ones (Article 212 TFEU). In the *Philippines* Case the CJEU relied heavily on the linkages in the actual agreement to the EU's wider development objectives as set down in the European Consensus to justify its findings. It is questionable, therefore, whether its analysis could be easily extrapolated per se to other areas of EU policy such as economic, financial and technical cooperation agreements with non-developing third countries. However, recent indications suggest that the Commission and Council may argue that in the absence of any clear and distinct JHA obligations of a non-ancillary nature both association and economic, financial and technical cooperation agreements can be entered into based on Articles 217 and 212 TFEU without the need for citation of a JHA legal base and thus without triggering the JHA Protocol. This may lead to further cases being taken to the CJEU.

In all the cases to date because the CJEU has established that either the legal base should not be JHA or that the JHA content is ancillary to or subsumed within a non-JHA predominant purpose it has not had to pronounce on how the duty of sincere cooperation would operate in respect of the UK and Ireland where they opt out of an EU decision but are nevertheless bound by the provisions of an agreement in their own right. However, the CJEU was clearly concerned about this issue in its judgments in the *EEA*, *Switzerland* and *Turkey* cases. Most tellingly it stated in the *EEA* case that:

> Next, the possibility cannot be discounted that recourse to Article 79(2) TFEU, entailing an opt-out clause for the United Kingdom and/or Ireland, would in practice be liable, in breach of Article 3 of the EEA Agreement (…) to undermine the realisation of the objectives pursued by that agreement. In particular, in the event that no agreement were to be concluded between those Member States and the EFTA States concerned, such recourse would give rise to two parallel regimes for the coordination of social security systems.[49]

It is difficult to say to what extent the CJEU's findings were influenced by this concern but its significance cannot be discounted. It remains to be seen how the CJEU might deal with the possible interface of the application of the duty of sincere cooperation and the JHA Protocol in a future case.

Furthermore, by finding in the *Philippines* case that no JHA legal base needed to be included the CJEU neatly side-stepped the question of whether split decisions covering the JHA and non-JHA aspects of the agreement would have been required. It remains to be seen in a future case whether the CJEU will uphold the practice of the Council to require split decisions for the JHA and non-JHA aspects of an agreement.

---

49 Case C-431/11 (n 12), para 65. AG Kokott was even more forceful in her Opinion in this regard noting: '74. It is not the spirit and purpose of Protocol No. 21 to give the United Kingdom and Ireland free discretion as regards participation in measures adopted by the Union institutions and the binding effect on them in other areas of EU law, in particular in the context of the internal market or the association of third countries. 75. Consequently, the opt-in cannot be applicable to the adoption of measures which – like the Council decision at issue – concern the extension of the rules applicable within the internal market to third countries. 76. It would significantly affect the functioning of an association agreement – especially the functioning of the EEA Agreement, which leads to a full association in the field of the internal market and free movement of persons – if individual European Union Member States applied, vis-a-vis the Associated States or their nationals, only some of the Union acquis and could thus insist on special treatment. 77. If it were also intended to apply the opt-in and thus ultimately the idea of an a la carte Europe for measures like the contested decision, not only would this jeopardise the internal market, as one of the central pillars of the European Union, but it would also fundamentally call into question the existence of the EEA. There would be a danger of fragmentation of this internal market, expanded to include the three EFTA States Norway, Iceland and Liechtenstein, with negative repercussions for the equal treatment of all persons and undertakings active in this internal market and for the uniformity of the conditions of competition applicable to them'. (Opinion of AG Kokott (n 4), paras 74–77).

5 Conclusion

The jurisprudence to date suggests that although the CJEU has applied its traditional analysis to determining the choice of legal base for international agreements it is nevertheless conscious of the implications for the coherence of the EU's external action where the JHA Protocol is engaged. On this basis, in the cases to date, arguably the CJEU has strived to find arguments to justify its rejection of JHA legal bases.

For the Member States relying on the JHA Protocol it is particularly important therefore clearly to demarcate the nature and purpose of any clauses in an international agreement with JHA content. Provisions which provide merely for cooperation in matters which fall within the scope of Title V TFEU will, as the case-law demonstrates, not be sufficient in and of themselves. Similarly, clauses in an agreement which provide for the possible future conclusion of an agreement in relation to Title V matters will not be sufficient to trigger the operation of the JHA Protocol. The JHA elements of any agreement need to be substantive, distinct and clear so as to avoid being classified as merely ancillary to or subsumed within a predominant non-JHA objective.

In light of the judgment in the *Philippines* case particular regard should be had to the possibility that the CJEU may take account of other instruments to find that an agreement pursues a non-JHA predominant purpose. This is particularly the case where agreements pursue a development cooperation objective. In practice, it will be increasingly important for the UK and Ireland, at the stage of formulating the negotiating directives, to insist that either an agreement should not include JHA content or where it does that such content must be substantive and fulfil a distinct purpose to ensure a JHA legal base is required and the JHA Protocol engaged. Even then they are not guaranteed that this will in fact be the case.

In the relatively few cases to date where the JHA Protocol Member States have successfully argued that an international agreement requires the citation of both JHA and non-JHA legal bases the Council has been confronted with the complex matter of defining the extent of the JHA content and adopting split JHA and non-JHA Council decisions for both the decisions on signature and conclusion. This is a less than ideal solution adding an unwelcome layer of complexity to what can already be difficult external and internal negotiations. It remains to be seen how the CJEU might react if and when it is asked to rule on the split decision practice adopted by the Council. It may serve as an additional reason for the CJEU to find that the JHA content is neither distinct nor non-incidental/ancillary.

A possible solution to address some of the difficulties that have arisen to date might be for the Council and Commission to agree that where it is considered desirous to have distinct Title V TFEU provisions in an umbrella agreement these are negotiated in the form of self-standing Protocols. This would avoid the need for split decisions in relation to the main body of the agreement and justify their treatment as a distinct objective. This might also be welcomed by negotiating partners as being more transparent. That said, however, it may not prevent arguments over what constitutes JHA substance and which precise JHA legal bases may be required to be cited in the Council decisions relating to the self-standing Protocol.

The difficult question of the extent to which the JHA Protocol Member States may in practice be compelled by the duty of sincere cooperation to follow an EU position even where they have exercised their right not to participate in the EU's exercise of competence for some provisions remains to be determined by the CJEU. To date it has not opined directly on the point although its obiter comments in the *EEA* case addressed above suggest an unfavourable direction of travel for the UK and Ireland.

Finally, the experience to date with the interface of the JHA Protocol and EU agreements also serves as an example for other areas of the Treaties where differential application of Treaty obligations to some Member States exist. With the desire for the EU to enhance the external dimension of the euro-area questions will no doubt arise as to how this can be accommodated within the existing framework of the Treaties in a way which does not prejudice the position of the non-participating Member States. As demonstrated by the experience with the interaction of EU external relations and the JHA Protocol the complexity and sensitivity of the legal issues that may arise should not be underestimated.

PART 5

EU International Agreements

CHAPTER 16

Recent Case Law of the European Court of Justice Relating to Article 218 TFEU

Allan Rosas

1 Introduction

During the last years, the European Court of Justice (ECJ)[1] has once again been confronted with issues relating to the external relations of the EU. This renewed interest in the law of EU external relations has no doubt been at least partly triggered by the entry into force of the Treaty of Lisbon (on 1 December 2009), which has introduced a number of new or newly drafted provisions of relevance in this regard. This fairly recent case law has, above all, addressed questions of exclusive versus shared competence, as well as the powers and procedures applicable to the conclusion of international agreements on behalf of the EU. In some judgments belonging to the first category, the Court of Justice has determined the existence of an EU exclusive competence, on the basis of either the Common Commercial Policy prescribed in Articles 3(1) and 207 TFEU or the so-called *AETR/ERTA* principle mentioned in Article 3(2) TFEU.[2] In other judgments, the Court has been faced with various questions relating to the interpretation of Article 218 TFEU, which concerns the negotiation and conclusion of international agreements.

The present contribution, devoted to a great European civil servant, scholar, friend, and former colleague, will focus on the last aspect, the case law relating to Article 218 TFEU. This provision provides a fair amount of rules which tell us how the EU may become bound by international agreements, including other acts having legal effects which are adopted by a body set up under an

1 The expression 'European Court of Justice', abbreviated as the 'ECJ', will be used here to denote what in art 19(1) TEU is referred to as the 'Court of Justice', as distinct from the General Court and specialised courts (the only example of a specialised court was the EU Civil Service Tribunal, which was merged with the General Court on 1 September 2016). The institution encompassing the two courts is in arts 13(1) and 19(1) TEU denominated 'Court of Justice of the European Union'.

2 See notably Allan Rosas, 'EU External Relations: Exclusive Competence Revisited' (2015) 38 Fordham Int LJ 1073.

 | DOI 10.1163/9789004347175_017

agreement which concerns matters falling within Union competence. The Article also includes a rule on the suspension of the operation of an agreement (Article 218(9) TFEU).[3] In addition to Article 218, the TFEU contains some provisions relating specifically to the conclusion of certain categories of agreements such as agreements concluded under the Common Commercial Policy (Article 207 TFEU). Moreover, Article 219 TFEU provides for special rules relating to monetary or foreign exchange matters which derogate from Article 218 TFEU. The following discussion will be limited to the case law concerning Article 218 TFEU. It will be assumed that the Union has competence to conclude a given agreement, whatever is the nature of such a competence (exclusive, shared, or other).[4]

2 The Scope of Article 218 TFEU: General Considerations

The primary object and purpose of Article 218 TFEU is to lay down rules on the negotiation and conclusion of international agreements between the Union and third States or international organisations which will, in principle, always be applicable, without prejudice to the derogatory rules contained in Article 219 TFEU. Subject to a caveat which will be mentioned below (Section 3), Article 218 TFEU does not concern the conclusion of international agreements by the EU Member States, which is regulated by the national law of each Member State.[5] The provision does cover, on the other hand, the conclusion by the EU of *mixed* agreements, in other words agreements also to be concluded by some or all Member States,[6] in which case both Article 218 TFEU (for the EU part)

3 On the suspension of the operation of treaties in general, see the Vienna Convention on the Law of Treaties (adopted 23 May 1969, entered into force 27 January 1980) 1155 UNTS 331, arts 57–60.

4 On the different categories of Union competence see e.g. Allan Rosas, 'Exclusive, Shared and National Competence in the Context of EU External Relations: Do Such Distinctions Matter?' in Inge Govaere and others (eds), *The European Union in the World: Essays in Honour of Marc Maresceau* (Martinus Nijhoff Publishers 2014) 17.

5 On the status in EU law of agreements concluded by the Member States see Allan Rosas, 'The Status in EU Law of International Agreements concluded by EU Member States' (2011) 34 Fordham Int LJ 1304. A certain reserve has to be made with respect to agreements concluded by the Member States where the substance of the agreement in question is considered as falling under an EU exclusive competence, see below, Section 3.

6 See e.g. Christophe Hillion and Panos Koutrakos (eds), *Mixed Agreements Revisited: The EU and its Member States in the World* (Hart Publishing, 2010), passim.

and the applicable national rules (for the conclusion of the agreement on behalf of a Member State) become relevant (see further below, Section 4).

The broad scope of Article 218 TFEU has been recognized by the ECJ in a judgment relating to an agreement concluded by the EU with Mauritius in application of Article 37 TEU relating to the Common Foreign and Security Policy (CFSP). In this judgment the Court pointed out that the objective of Article 218 TFEU, following the entry into force of the Treaty of Lisbon, is 'in order to satisfy the requirements of clarity, consistency and rationalisation', to lay down 'a single procedure of general application concerning the negotiation and conclusion of international agreements which the [EU] is competent to conclude in the fields of its activity, including the CFSP, except where the Treaties lay down special procedures'.[7] That Article 218 TFEU also covers CFSP agreements is already clear from the text of its paragraphs 3 and 6, which provide for special rules applicable to the initiative to open negotiations and the role of the European Parliament in the conclusion of a CFSP agreement, respectively.

These special rules are applicable where the agreement relates 'exclusively or principally' or 'exclusively' to the CFSP. If the agreement relates exclusively or principally to the CFSP, the recommendation to the Council should according to Article 218(3) TFEU be submitted by the High Representative of the Union for Foreign Affairs and Security Policy (High Representative)[8] instead of the Commission. If, again, the agreement relates 'exclusively' to the CFSP, the European Parliament is under Article 218(6) TFEU excluded from the consent and consultation procedures. According to the ECJ, this exclusion of the Parliament relates to agreements founded exclusively on a *substantive* CFSP legal basis.[9] As to the involvement of the Parliament in the conclusion of such CFSP-only agreements, the Court in the above-mentioned judgment confirmed that Article 218(10) TFEU, which requires that the Parliament be 'immediately and fully informed at all stages of the procedure', applies to CFSP agreements as well and concluded that there had been a violation of this requirement in the case at hand.[10]

In order to determine the scope of Article 218 TFEU, one also needs to know what is meant in this provision by 'agreement'. In this regard, the ECJ has long been following a broad approach. The Court has recently had occasion to refer

7 Case C-658/11 *Parliament v Council* EU:C:2014:2025, para 52.

8 See Gisela Müller-Brandeck-Bouquet and Carolin Rüger (eds), *The High Representative for the EU Foreign and Security Policy: Review and Prospects* (Nomos 2011), passim.

9 Case C-658/11 (n 7), paras 56–59.

10 Ibid, paras 69–87. In the same vein, Case C-263/14 *Parliament v Council* EU:C:2016:435, paras 68–85.

to, and confirm, this case law in stating that the expression 'agreement', in accordance with the case law, is to be understood 'in a general sense to indicate any undertaking entered into by entities subject to international law which has binding force, whatever its formal designation'.[11]

In this case, the Court was faced with a declaration made by the EU which was regarded by the Court as an offer to Venezuela, whereby the EU proposed to the latter that it could utilise, on certain conditions, part of the surplus of the allowable catch in the exclusive economic zone of French Guyana, in accordance with relevant provisions of the UN Convention on the Law of the Sea.[12] As the conduct of Venezuela was deemed to constitute acceptance of this offer, there was a concurrence of wills and the expression of this concurrence constituted an agreement 'given that, in international law, whether such an agreement is formally established in a single document or in two or more related written instruments is irrelevant'.[13] And as the declaration made by the EU was a constituent element of such an international agreement, that declaration, albeit being as such of a unilateral nature, fell within the scope of Article 218 TFEU.[14]

The Court had already come to a similar conclusion in an Opinion given shortly before the judgment referred to above. At issue in the Opinion was whether the competence to issue declarations accepting the accession of third States to the Hague Convention on the Civil Aspects of International Child Abduction of 1980 had passed from the EU Member States to the EU itself.[15] This Convention provides for a peculiar procedure of accession, entailing that

11 Joined Cases C-103/12 and C-165/12 *Parliament v Council* EU:C:2014:2400. The judgment here refers to Case C-327/91 *France v Commission* EU:C:1994:305, para 27, and earlier case law. See also Delano Verwey, *The European Community, the European Union and the International Law of Treaties* (TMC Asser Press 2004) 89–100.

12 See arts 61–62 of the Convention, which was concluded by the EU in 1998 (Council Decision 98/392/EC of 23 March 1998 concerning the conclusion by the European Community of the United Nations Convention of 10 December 1982 on the Law of the Sea and the Agreement of 28 July 1994 relating to the implementation of Part XI thereof [1998] OJ L179/1). See also Esa Paasivirta, 'The European Union and the United Nations Convention on the Law of the Sea' (2015) 38 Fordham Int LJ 1045 as well as the chapter by Esa Paasivirta in this book.

13 Joined Cases C-103/12 and C-165/12 (n 11), paras 61 and 73. The Court here refers to Opinion 1/13 (*Hague Convention on the Civil Aspects of Child Abduction*) EU:C:2014:2303, para 37, given shortly before the judgment (see below).

14 Joined Cases C-103/12 and C-165/12 (n 11), para 83; cf Opinion of AG Sharpston in the same case (EU:C:2014:334).

15 Opinion 1/13 (n 13).

accession will have effect only as regards the relations between the acceding State and a Contracting Party which has declared its acceptance of the accession.[16] A number of Member States argued that the request for an Opinion by the Commission should be declared inadmissible, inter alia, because the act of accession and the declaration of acceptance do not represent two corresponding expressions of intent since they do not form part of a reciprocal relationship and so the request did not concern the conclusion of an international agreement and was thus not covered by Article 218(11) TFEU concerning requests for opinions relating to 'agreements envisaged'.[17]

The Court declared the request admissible (and held ultimately that the acceptance of the accession of a third State to the Hague Convention had become an EU exclusive competence).[18] In doing so, the Court recalled that under Article 2(1)(a) of the Vienna Convention on the Law of Treaties, an international agreement may be embodied in a single instrument or in two or more instruments. The Hague Convention provides for two related instruments, namely the instrument of accession and the declaration of acceptance of accession. According to the Court, the expression of intent in these two instruments relate to the same objective, namely to establish obligations under the Convention in the bilateral relations between the two parties and the two instruments, taken together, produce this effect. Since the declaration of acceptance was a constituent part of an international agreement concluded with a third State, it was according to the Court encompassed by the concept of 'agreement' as referred to in Article 218 TFEU.[19]

In this context it can also be noted that in a recent judgment, the Commission was condemned for having signed on its own, without Council decision, an addition to a memorandum of understanding with Switzerland.[20] This case, however, which concerned a formally non-binding understanding, was not decided on the basis of Article 218 TFEU but by reference to Articles 13, 16 and 17 TEU, which relate to the respective powers of the Council and the Commission and the institutional balance in this respect.

---

16 See Hague Convention on the Civil Aspects of International Child Abduction (concluded 25 October 1980) Hague XXVIII (Hague Convention), art 38.

17 Opinion 1/13 (n 13), paras 29–32. On the procedure for requesting opinions of the ECJ as to whether an agreement envisaged is compatible with Union law see Stanislas Adam, *La procédure d'avis devant la Cour de justice de l'Union européenne* (Bruylant, 2011).

18 Rosas, 'EU External Relations: Exclusive Competence Revisited' (n 2) 1090–1091.

19 Opinion 1/13 (n 13), paras 38–42.

20 Case C-660/13 *Council v Commission* EU:C:2016:616.

3 Agreements Concluded by Member States and Article 218(9) TFEU

Article 218(9) TFEU establishes a somewhat simplified procedure for not only the suspension of international agreements but also establishing the positions to be adopted on the Union's behalf in a body set up by an agreement when that body is called upon to adopt acts having legal effects (with the exception of acts supplementing or amending the institutional framework of the agreement). This provision reflects the trend to give international organisations powers to adopt acts which may have legal effects even without ensuing national (or in this case, Union) acts of adherence.[21] In accordance with the idea that new international commitments should be entered into by the Council, just as a decision of the Council is also needed for the conclusion of agreements, it is, as a rule, for the Council, on a proposal of the Commission or the High Representative, to adopt a decision establishing the Union position to be advanced when the international body in question is about to adopt an act having legal effects.[22] This principle knows about one derogation: According to Article 218(7) TFEU, the Council, when concluding an agreement, may, by way of derogation from, inter alia, Article 218(9) TFEU, authorise the negotiator (normally the Commission) to approve on the Union's behalf modifications to the agreement where it provides for them to be adopted by a simplified procedure or by a body set up under the agreement.

In a case concerning an EU position to be adopted in the General Assembly of the International Organisation of Vine and Wine, the ECJ was faced with the question as to whether Article 218(9) TFEU could also be applied in a situation where the EU is not a Contracting Party to the agreement establishing the organisation but the act to be adopted by it falls within the competence of the EU.[23] The Court had already previously held that in such situations it is still

21 See e.g. Bernd Martenczuk, 'Decisions of Bodies Established by International Agreements and the Community Legal Order' in Vincent Kronenberger (ed), *The European Union and the International Legal Order: Discord or Harmony?* (TMC Asser Press 2001) 141.

22 This procedure, on the other hand, provides no guarantee that the Union may not be bound by a decision which it has itself opposed (since such decisions may sometimes be adopted by majority voting). See also Case C-246/07 *Commission v Kingdom of Sweden* EU:C:2010:203, paras 92–100, where Sweden was condemned for having put forward a national proposal within the framework of an international environmental convention and its institutional setting which provides for a system where a party, including the EU, could become bound by a decision not supported by it, unless it has explicitly opted out from the decision.

23 Case C-399/12 *Federal Republic of Germany v Council* EU:C:2014:2258. See also Inge Govaere, 'Novel Issues Pertaining to EU Member States Membership of Other International Organisations: The OIV Case' in Govaere and others (n 4) 225.

possible (and sometimes indeed necessary) to establish a Union position to be presented by the Member States which are Contracting Parties and which are then required to act in the Union's interest.[24]

The Court now found that Article 218(9) TFEU is applicable in such situations, despite the fact that the Union is not itself a Contracting Party and that the other provisions of this Article applies to agreements concluded by the Union only. While the wording of the provision did not exclude such a broad interpretation, the main argument in its favour was supposedly the interest of legal security and clarity as a non-applicability of Article 218(9) TFEU would have left the establishment of a Union position to be presented in such bodies in a legal limbo. As Article 218(9) TFEU only applies to acts 'having legal effects', the Court also had to analyse the nature of the recommendations of the international organisation at issue, concluding that these recommendations had a direct impact on the relevant Union *acquis* and thus produced legal effects.[25]

4 The Conclusion of Mixed Agreements

The existence of mixed agreements is a peculiar feature of the external relations of the EU which is not easily to be found with respect to other subjects of international law.[26] The duty of cooperation, as formulated by the ECJ, functions as a general obligation for the Union and the Member States to collaborate closely, in order, as the Court has said, to ensure 'unity in the international representation of the Union'. Making this principle operational in concrete situations is often fraught with considerable difficulties, however.[27]

---

24 Case C-45/07 *Commission v Hellenic Republic* EU:C:2009:81, paras 30–31; see also Opinion 2/91 (*Convention no 170 of the International Labour Organization concerning safety in the use of chemicals at work*) EU:C:1993:106, para 5; Rosas, 'The Status in EU Law of International Agreements concluded by EU Member States' (n 5) 1331–1335.

25 *Germany v Council* (n 23), para 64. See also Jeno Czuczai, 'The Autonomy of the EU Legal Order and the Law-Making Activities of International Organizations' (2012) 31 YEL 452, who provides examples of recent Council practice in this regard.

26 On the various problems which arise with respect to the negotiation, conclusion, application and implementation of mixed agreements see, in addition to Hillion and Koutrakos (n 6): Allan Rosas, 'The European Union and Mixed Agreements' in Alan Dashwood and Christophe Hillion (eds), *The General Law of E.C. External Relations* (Sweet & Maxwell 2000) 200; Joni Heliskoski, *Mixed Agreements as a Technique for Organizing the International Relations of the European Community and its Member States* (Kluwer Law International 2001).

27 On the duty of cooperation see notably *Commission v Sweden* (n 22), with references to earlier case law.

In the context of Article 218 TFEU, the problem of mixed agreements has arisen in regard to the procedures to be followed when such agreements are concluded. In a recent case, the Commission brought an action against the Council seeking the annulment of a 'hybrid' decision adopted both by the Council of the EU and by the Representatives of the Governments of the Member States, meeting within the Council, with respect to certain transport agreements of a mixed nature.[28] The ECJ observed that the decision in question merged two different acts, namely, an act relating to the signing and provisional application of the agreements on behalf of the EU and an act relating to the provisional application of those agreements by the Member States, 'without it being possible to discern which act reflects the will of the Council and which the will of the Member States'.[29]

It followed that the Member States participated in the adoption of an act which partly fell within the scope of Union law and thus should have been adopted by the Council whereas the Council's involvement covered aspects which fell within the scope of the national law of each of the Member States (as well as international law). Whilst the elements concerning the provisional application of the agreements by the Member States required their unanimous agreement, Article 218(8) TFEU provides that the Council must act, on behalf of the Union, by a qualified majority. According to the Court, the two acts, brought together in the contested decision, could not therefore be validly adopted under a single procedure and the decision was found to be incompatible with Article 218(2), (5) and (8) TFEU and accordingly, also Article 13(2) TEU (which requires that each institution shall act within the limits of the powers conferred on it in the Treaties and in conformity with the procedures, conditions and objectives set in them).[30]

This judgment clarifies an issue which has been the subject of disagreement and uncertainty in the past. It should be noted that the Court reached its verdict after having examined the Council's argument that the contested decision in fact reflected the *duty of cooperation* which is imposed on the EU and the Member States in the field of mixed agreements. It is true that in an earlier case relating to the duty of cooperation, the Court had taken into account an 'arrangement' concluded by the Council and the Commission setting up a coordination procedure between the Commission and the Member States to decide on the exercise of responsibilities or on statements on particular points within the context of an international organisation of which

28 Case C-28/12 *Commission v Council* EU:C:2015:282.

29 Ibid, para 49.

30 Ibid, paras 52–53.

both the Union and its Member States are members.[31] According to the Court, 'the arrangement', which according to the referred judgment was binding on the two parties, represented 'fulfilment of [the] duty of cooperation between the [Union] and its Member States'.[32] When concluding this 'arrangement', the Council seems to have acted, as it were, on behalf of the Member States while the Commission was acting in the Union interest. In the recent case of 2015 referred to above, on the other hand, the Council was not acting on behalf of the Member States but as the institution called upon, under Article 218(5) TFEU, to adopt decisions authorising the signing and, if necessary, provisional application of international agreements on behalf of the Union. Such a law-creating act, according to the Court, cannot be merged with an intergovernmental act adopted by the Member States and the Court concluded that the principle of duty of cooperation 'cannot justify the Council setting itself free from compliance with the procedural rules and voting arrangements laid down in Article 218 TFEU'.[33]

5 EU Involvement in International Dispute Settlement Procedures

Also the participation of the EU in international dispute settlement procedures has been a source of controversy between the Commission and the Council, the latter insisting that the EU position to be presented before dispute settlement bodies be approved by the Council, in a way comparable to the conclusion of international agreements.

The ECJ has in its earlier case law touched upon some aspects of this question without having had to face the problem head on. First of all, the Court, faced with a challenge to the Commission's right to commence legal proceedings in a third State, held that Article 335 TFEU (ex-Article 282 of the Treaty establishing the European Community (TEC)), which provides that in each of the Member States, the Union may, inter alia, be a party to legal proceedings and be 'To this end' represented by the Commission, is, despite being restricted to Member States on its wording, 'the expression of a general

31 Case C-25/94 *Commission v Council* EU:C:1996:114, paras 48–50. See also Joni Heliskoski, 'Internal Struggle for International Presence: The Exercise of Voting Rights in the FAO' in Dashwood and Hillion (n 26) 79. On the duty of cooperation, see also n 27 as well as the chapter by Marise Cremona in this book.

32 Case C-25/94 (n 31), para 49.

33 Case C-28/12 (n 28), para 55.

principle'.[34] Second, with respect to the Commission's duty to ensure the correct implementation of an international agreement (in the concrete case the Association Agreement with Turkey), concluded by the Union, the Court observed that:

> [I]t follows from Article [17 TEU] that the Commission, as guardian of the [TFEU] and the agreements concluded under it, must ensure the correct implementation by a third country of the obligations it has assumed under an agreement concluded with the [Union], using the means provided for by the agreement or by the decisions taken pursuant thereto.[35]

Against this backdrop, it is not surprising that the Court, in a recent judgment, has held that the Commission could, without obtaining the prior approval of the Council, submit a written statement on behalf of the EU to the International Tribunal for the Law of the Sea on the request for an advisory opinion made by a sub-regional fisheries commission.[36] Whilst the Council and the Member States argued that Article 335 TFEU concerns only proceedings before national courts, the Court repeated its earlier statement that this provision, despite its wording, expresses a general principle and that it provides a basis for the Commission to represent the Union before the International Tribunal for the Law of the Sea.

As to the argument that the matter was covered by Article 218(9) TFEU concerning positions to be adopted on the Union's behalf in bodies set up by international agreements (which, as noted above, requires a decision of the Council), the Court held that this procedure was not applicable for the determination of a position to be expressed on behalf of the Union before an international judicial body requested to give an advisory opinion, 'the adoption of which falls solely within the remit and responsibility of the members of that

---

34 Case C-131/03 *R.J. Reynolds Tobacco Holdings, Inc. and Others v Commission* EU:C:2006:541, para 94.

35 Case C-204/07 P *C.A.S. SpA v Commission* EU:C:2008:446, para 95. See also Allan Rosas, 'International Dispute Settlement Procedures: EU Practices and Procedures' (2003) 46 German Yearbook of International Law 284, 317–320, where reference is made (p. 319) to a judgment of the then Court of First Instance (now the General Court) holding that the Commission has a duty to ensure the correct implementation by a third country of the obligations it has contracted to fulfil under an agreement concluded by the Union, 'using the means provided for by the agreement or by the decisions taken pursuant to it' (Joined Cases T-186/97 and others *Kaufring AG and Others v Commission* EU:T:2001:133, paras 270–271).

36 Case C-73/14 *Council v Commission* EU:C:2015:663.

body, acting, to that end, wholly independently of the parties'.[37] As regards, finally, the argument that the Commission was prevented from doing what it did because of Article 16(1) TEU, which refers to the task of the Council to 'carry out policy-making (…) functions as laid down in the Treaties', the Court considered that the purpose of the statement submitted to the Tribunal 'was (…) not to formulate a policy' in relation to fishing, but, on the basis of an analysis of the relevant provisions of international and EU law, to present 'a set of legal observations' aimed at enabling the Tribunal to give an informed advisory opinion on the questions put to it.[38]

In the light of this judgment, and the earlier case law referred to above, it would seem that Article 218 TFEU is about *norm-creation*, be it in the form of concluding international agreements or establishing a Union position on decisions to be taken by international bodies, not about the 'interpretation and application' of existing norms.[39] The latter function belongs to the Commission's prerogatives, in the light of Article 17(1) TEU (the Commission 'shall ensure the application of the Treaties, and of measures adopted by the institutions pursuant to them' and 'shall oversee the application of Union law under the control of the Court of Justice') and Article 335 TFEU.

6 Negotiating Directives

Whilst the preceding discussion has mainly centered around issues relating in one way or another to the scope and general applicability of Article 218 TFEU, there is a recent case addressing more specific questions of procedure and the division of powers between the Council and the Commission when it comes to the negotiation phase of treaty-making. In this regard, Article 218(2), (3) and (4) TFEU provides for a Council decision to authorise, on a recommendation of the negotiator, the opening of negotiations, and, as the case may be, address 'directives' to the negotiator and designate a special committee 'in consultation with which the negotiations must be conducted'. The negotiator is normally the Commission, unless the agreement falls under the CFSP, in which

37 Ibid, para 66.

38 Ibid, para 71.

39 In Case C-73/14 (n 36), para 70, the Court observed that the Commission statement 'consisted in suggesting answers to the questions raised (…) by setting out the manner in which the [EU] envisaged the interpretation and application' of three agreements relating to fishing, including the UN Convention on the Law of the Sea.

case the High Representative may be appointed negotiator (sometimes the Commission and the High Representative are appointed as a team).

In the case mentioned, the Commission brought an action against the Council challenging the legality of the negotiating directives addressed to it by the Council, arguing that these directives went too far in expanding the powers conferred on the Council and the special committee designated by it and imposing obligations on the Commission which were not consistent with its role as the negotiator.[40] The Court partially dismissed the Commission's application for annulment of the contested decision, holding, inter alia, that Article 218(4) TFEU empowers the Council to set out 'procedural arrangements governing the process for the provision of information, for communication and for consultation between the special committee and the Commission'.[41]

On the other hand, the Court did find that two elements in the directives went too far and accordingly annulled that part of the challenged Council decision. This part of the decision authorised 'detailed negotiating positions of the Union' to be established within the special consultative committee or within the Council and also provided that the special committee, 'before each negotiating session', could 'establish negotiating positions'.[42] The Court observed that these stipulations constituted provisions seeking to bind the negotiator and that they went beyond the consultative function assigned to the special committee as well as the power of the Council to draw up negotiating directives, in authorising the Council to impose 'detailed negotiating positions' on the negotiator in the course of on-going negotiations (these findings are arguably without prejudice to the possible right of the Council to amend the negotiating directives themselves). These elements infringed the obligation laid down by Article 13(2) TEU to act within the limits of the powers conferred on the Council by Article 218(2) and (4) TFEU and also infringed the principle of institutional balance.[43]

7 Concluding Remarks

The case law discussed above has clarified a number of issues relating to the interpretation and application of Article 218 TFEU. Some elements have been

40 See Case C-425/13 *Commission v Council* EU:C:2015:483 as well as the chapters by Hubert Legal and Marise Cremona in this book.

41 Case C-425/13 (n 40), para 78.

42 Ibid, para 85.

43 Ibid, paras 91–92.

confirmed rather than clarified or developed. One example is the concept of 'agreement' as envisaged in this provision. The ECJ has confirmed an approach already discernible in earlier case law, in other words that the concept should be given a broad interpretation and that also two acts which, if taken by themselves, are of a unilateral character, may, if taken together, become a constituent part of an international agreement. It is also obvious from the wording of Article 218 TFEU that it applies to CFSP agreements as well (although the role of the European Parliament is limited to being immediately and fully informed at all stages of the procedure).

Most other judgments can be considered as clarifications or even developments, as compared with the earlier case law based on ex-Article 300 TEC. As pure clarification can be considered the very recent judgment in which the Court annulled those parts of negotiation directives which gave the Council, or a consultative committee appointed by it, the powers to establish 'detailed negotiation positions' in the course of on-going negotiations.[44] The very nature of treaty negotiations implies a certain margin of manoeuvre for the negotiator and Article 218 TFEU does not contain anything which would suggest that the Council may go beyond its powers to authorise the opening of negotiations, to issue general directives for the negotiator and to designate a special committee in consultation with which the negotiations must be conducted. Of course, the Commission must also take into account that the final product has to be approved by the Council and, as the case may be, by the European Parliament, and thus the consultation with the special committee and the provision of information to the European Parliament should normally induce the Commission to avoid accepting solutions which risk to become unacceptable for these two institutions.

A clarification which, at least on the face of it, may seem less obvious for some is the recent judgment taking a negative position on the conclusion of mixed agreements by a 'hybrid' decision of the Council and the Representatives of the Governments of the Member States meeting within the Council.[45] Many would argue that such a combined decision would constitute a pragmatic way of ensuring, in the light of the duty of cooperation, a common front with the Union and its Member States seen as one rather than many parties, in accordance with the idea of unity of international representation of the EU. It is nevertheless not very surprising that the ECJ here took a strict and formal approach, as we are in fact not dealing principally with a situation of external representation but with the internal decision-making procedure of a Union

44 Case C-425/13 (n 40).

45 Case C-28/12 (n 28).

institution, the question of legal bases and accordingly also of voting rules (qualified majority or unanimity). The outcome should probably be seen against the backdrop of the Court's case law relating to two or more legal bases which cannot be combined in the same act (incompatible legal bases) even if both legal bases are contained in the same Union Treaty. This case law is based on the idea that imposing one type of procedure on the decision-making process could compromise the procedures provided for under the other legal basis.[46] Such considerations seem to apply, a fortiori, to hybrid decisions combining a Union act with a bundle of national acts based on the national law of each Member State.

Another clarification which was preceded by quite some discussion was delivered by the ECJ in the case relating to the adoption of a Union position on a question which is on the agenda of an international organisation of which only the EU Member States but not the Union itself are members, in situations which fall within the competence of the Union.[47] There is no provision in Article 218 TFEU or elsewhere in the TFEU which would deal specifically and explicitly with such a situation. That the Court held that Article 218(9) TFEU is applicable is probably to be explained by the fact not only that the wording of that provision, if taken alone, does not exclude this interpretation but also that without the applicability of this provision these situations would have been in a legal limbo and caused legal uncertainty and disputes between the Commission and the Council/the Member States. The judgment makes it clear that under Article 218(9) TFEU, it is for the Council, on a proposal from the Commission or the High Representative on CFSP matters, to establish the relevant Union position.

This broad interpretation of Article 218(9) TFEU is not in contradiction with the Court's recent judgment ruling that this provision is *not* applicable to the decision to submit a statement on behalf of the EU to the International Tribunal for the Law of the Sea on the request for an advisory opinion made by a fishery commission.[48] This judgment can be said to be based, at least implicitly, on the idea that Article 218 TFEU, including Article 218(9) TFEU, is about establishing new legal rules (norm-creation), not about presenting legal interpretations before dispute settlement bodies which, when taking decisions, act independently of the parties and, in any case, are not empowered to modify the law, but only to interpret and apply it.

46 See e.g. Case C-130/10 *Parliament v Council* EU:C:2012:472, para 45 and case law cited.

47 *Germany v Council* (n 23).

48 Case C-73/14 (n 36).

The case law discussed above already covers many parts of Article 218 TFEU and clarifies many points which have been a matter of discussion and controversy in the past. This case law does not, on the other hand, exhaust all questions which may arise with respect to the interpretation and application of this Article. To mention but a few examples of questions which may still have to be clarified by the ECJ, one wonders about the precise delimitation of the powers of the Council and the Commission/the High Representative when it comes to the need to submit recommendations with a view to obtaining an authorization to negotiate and in this context also the question as to whether, and under what conditions, the Council may amend the negotiation directives which it may have addressed to the negotiator. And what about possible limits to the powers of the Commission/the High Representative to propose, or not to propose, the conclusion of an agreement which it has negotiated or to withdraw such a proposal before it has been adopted by the Council?[49]

To mention yet another example, it could be asked whether the above-mentioned judgment concerning Article 218(9) TFEU, holding that it is applicable also to the establishment of a Union position on a question to be decided by a body set up under an agreement to which the EU is not a party, could be of relevance for situations envisaged in Article 218(7) TFEU. The latter provision, by derogation from Article 218(9) TFEU, provides that the Council may authorise the negotiator to approve modifications to an agreement where it provides for such modifications to be adopted by simplified procedure or by a body set up under the agreement.

Whilst these are examples only, they should suffice to show that problems relating to the interpretation and application of Article 218 TFEU will most likely continue to arise in the work of the three main political EU institutions and that it is possible that some of them will in the future become issues also before the ECJ.

49 On the right of the Commission to withdraw legislative proposals see Case C-409/13 *Council v Commission* EU:C:2015:217 and the chapter by Marise Cremona in this book.

CHAPTER 17

Some Issues Related to the Provisional Application of International Agreements and the Institutional Balance

*Ricardo Passos**

1 Introduction

This article will focus mainly on the institutional balance in the context of the provisional application of the international agreements concluded by the European Union, and in particular whether the European Parliament should be more involved in this matter.

Several questions may be raised in this context, namely: how to evaluate the EU part of an agreement when a decision is taken by the Council on provisional application of a mixed agreement? Is this question linked to the consent of the Parliament? Should the provisional application only commence after consent has been given by the Parliament? Should the Parliament have a role in determining the provisions of the agreement to which provisional application applies? What procedures could be put in place with a view to enabling the Parliament to have a say before the Council decides on the provisional application?

This topic is a humble contribution for further reflection. If I chose it, it is also because I sometimes discussed subjects new to me with Ricardo Gosalbo Bono, and benefited from his experience in the field of EU external relations law. This is a way of paying tribute to him and thanking him for all the years in which we have worked together and had open discussions about EU law. His opinions were always extremely acute and useful, even if it happened that we sometimes defended different views when I was representing the European Parliament in past years as a Director in its Legal Service.

The purpose of provisional application is to give immediate effect to all or some of the substantive provisions of a treaty without awaiting the completion and effects of the formal requirements for entry into force contained therein. The Vienna Convention on the Law of the Treaties of 1969 foresees the

* This contribution was drafted when the author was Director in the European Parliament. The opinions expressed are purely personal.

 | DOI 10.1163/9789004347175_018

possibility that an agreement (or part of it) be applied provisionally, if that is provided for either in the agreement or is the will of the parties.[1] This is justified in cases where the ratification process is expected to take some time (e.g. the need to complete the constitutional procedures for the ratification of multilateral agreements) or for other reasons (urgency or as a matter of precaution to build trust in highly sensitive agreements).[2] In the case of the Association Agreement with Ukraine, the provisional application was foreseen with a view to advancing the early impact of reforms.[3]

2 The Provisional Application in the European Union until the Treaty of Lisbon

In the European Union, provisional application was often used, even before it was provided for in the Treaties.[4] This practice was criticised by the Parliament, which argued that the latter was placed before a *fait accompli* and obliged to take the provisional application into account as a budgetary authority.[5] The Treaty of Amsterdam inserted a specific provision stipulating that the Council decision on the signing of an agreement may be accompanied by a decision on provisional application, but in that case 'The European Parliament shall be immediately and fully informed of any decision under this paragraph

1 Vienna Convention on the Law of Treaties (adopted 23 May 1969, entered into force 27 January 1980) 1155 UNTS 331 (Vienna Convention), art 25(1).

2 International Law Commission, 'First report on the provisional application of treaties, Prepared by Mr. Juan Manuel Gómez-Robledo, Special Rapporteur' (3 June 2013) UN doc A/CN. 4/664; see also, Jenő Czuczai, 'Mixity in Practice: Some Problems and Their (Real or Possible) Solution' in Christophe Hillion and Panos Koutrakos (eds) *Mixed Agreements Revisited – The EU and its Member States in the World* (Hart Publishing 2010) 241ff.

3 Commission, 'Proposal for a Council Decision on the signing, on behalf of the European Union, and provisional application of the Association Agreement between the European Union and its Member States, of the one part, and Ukraine, of the other part' COM (2013) 289 final; this proposal was submitted before the crisis in Ukraine.

4 It was used 200 times between 1976 and 1990, see Gregorio Garzón Clariana, 'L'application provisoire des accords internationaux de la Communauté' in Paul Demaret, Inge Govaere and Dominik Hanf (eds), *30 Years of European Legal Studies at the College of Europe – Liber Professorum 1973–74 – 2003–04* (Cahiers du Collège d'Europe, Peter Lang 2005) 482. Between 2004 and 2009, provisional application was provided for 80 times. Since 2009 on average one third of the agreements concluded by the EU are applied provisionally.

5 Garzón Clariana (n 4) 482.

concerning the provisional application and suspension of agreements' (ex-Article 300(2), third subparagraph of the Treaty establishing the European Community (TEC)). However, only very exceptionally was the Parliament given the possibility to react to the provisional application in cases where its consent was required.[6]

The non-involvement of Parliament was explained by the fact that provisional application was generally used for the trade part of mixed agreements, on which Parliament had no say before the Treaty of Lisbon.[7] Yet in some EU-only agreements (e.g. fisheries agreements), provisional application had immediate budgetary consequences which the Parliament had to accept, although it had not been able to express any possible reservations, and in some cases the Parliament did have the power not to consent to the agreement in question (e.g. Fisheries Partnership Agreement with Morocco).[8]

3 The Impact of the Treaty of Lisbon

3.1 *The Enhancement of the Parliament's Powers*

It is true that under the Treaties as amended by the Treaty of Amsterdam, the role of the European Parliament was not very significant concerning the

6 See the Energy Charter Treaty in 1994, where the Commission decided to consult the Parliament on the provisional application because the Parliament would subsequently have to give its consent (see the reference to the opinion of the Parliament in the third ('having regard') recital of Council Decision 94/998/EC of 15 December 1994 on the provisional application of the Energy Charter Treaty by the European Community ([1994] OJ L380/1) and the 'Estevan Bolea report' of the Committee on Research, Technological Development and Energy (doc A4-0092/94)). This agreement is rather exceptional, since the decision on the conclusion was adopted by the Council and the Commission, because it related to the three Treaties (Council and Commission decision 98/181/EC, ECSC, Euratom of 23 September 1997 on the conclusion, by the European Communities, of the Energy Charter Treaty and the Energy Charter Protocol on energy efficiency and related environmental aspects [1998] OJ L69/1).

7 Catherine Flaesch-Mougin and Isabelle Bosse-Platière, 'L'application provisoire des accords de l'Union européenne' in Inge Govaere and others (eds) *The European Union in the World – Essays in Honour of Marc Maresceau* (Martinus Nijhoff Publishers 2014) 302ff.

8 Council Regulation (EC) 764/2006 of 22 May 2006 on the conclusion of the Fisheries Partnership Agreement between the European Community and the Kingdom of Morocco [2006] OJ L141/1 (EU-Morocco Fisheries Partnership Agreement). See the problems related to the Second Protocol to this Agreement eventually concluded (for a period of four years – 15 July 2014–2018) by Council Decision 2013/785/UE of 16 December 2013 ([2013] OJ L349/1), following a rejection by the European Parliament on 14 December 2011 (doc P7_TA(2011)0569).

negotiation and conclusion of international agreements.[9] It was only with the Treaty of Lisbon that its role changed substantially. As a consequence, the Parliament now has to give consent essentially to all trade agreements and mixed agreements concerning TFEU policies. Yet the Treaty of Lisbon did not explicitly extend the new powers of the Parliament to the provisional application of agreements, at least not specifically.

According to Article 218(5) TFEU 'The Council, on a proposal by the negotiator, shall adopt a decision authorising the signing of the agreement and, if necessary, its provisional application before entry into force'. The crucial provision in this regard is Article 218(10) TFEU, which holds that 'The Parliament shall be immediately and fully informed at all stages of the procedure', that is to say also concerning provisional application.

It can be argued that the *effet utile* of this requirement to inform is that Parliament must not be put before a *fait accompli,* but that it must be placed in a situation where it can express its views on provisional application before the latter is decided by the Council. This is particularly important because if an agreement is already provisionally applied, the non-consent of the Parliament should have as a consequence that the provisional application be terminated, once the Council has notified the third country concerned accordingly.[10] This happened with the SWIFT Agreement[11] and with the Second Protocol annexed to the Fisheries Partnership Agreement with Morocco. In both cases, the Council decided on provisional application without seeking the views of the Parliament in advance, and eventually the negative vote had the effect of terminating these agreements.[12]

---

9 Except association agreements or agreements modifying an act adopted under the co-decision procedure, or establishing an institutional framework, or with notable financial implications.

10 According to art 25(2) of the 1969 Vienna Convention, 'Unless the treaty otherwise provides or the negotiating States and negotiating organizations (…) have otherwise agreed, the provisional application of a treaty or a part of a treaty with respect to a State or an international organization shall be terminated if that State or that organization notifies the States and organizations with regard to which the treaty is being provisionally applied of its intention not to become a party to the treaty'.

11 Agreement between the European Union and the United States of America on the processing and transfer of Financial Messaging Data from the European Union to the United States for purposes of the Terrorist Finance Tracking Program [2010] OJ L8/11.

12 Concerning the SWIFT Agreement, Parliament refused to give consent on 11 February 2010 (doc P7_TA(2010)0029) and concerning the Second Protocol to the Fisheries Partnership Agreement with Morocco, Parliament refused to give consent on 14 December 2011 (doc P7_TA(2011)0569).

In these two instances, the Parliament criticised the fact that its consent was to a certain extent made more difficult because the agreements were already provisionally applied (particularly where several months have elapsed before the Parliament's consent is requested by the Council). Indeed, in some cases, the agreement in question is provisionally applied for several years. How can the Parliament then take the responsibility of rejecting the agreement years later and thus terminate its effects?[13] Even if the Parliament surely remains free to reject such an agreement, the impact of its vote risks frustrating considerably the legitimate expectations created by the European Union, and this raises an obvious political issue.

Indeed, this may have a very negative impact on the stability of international relations and on the legitimate expectations of the Member States, but also those of third countries, private companies and citizens benefiting from the envisaged agreement.[14] It is very important to avoid this kind of disruption and the principle of mutual sincere cooperation among institutions (Article 13(2) TEU) and the proper institutional balance should apply in full.

3.2 *The Scope of the Provisional Application*

Another criticism is about the scope of the provisional application concerning mixed agreements. This application concerns, in principle, only the part of the agreement falling within EU competence. The decision establishing the provisions of the agreement which can (or cannot) be provisionally applied raises political and legal issues because the boundary between EU and Member States' competences is often a complex task, and can end up creating legal uncertainty for the parties to the agreement and persons or economic operators.

---

13 For example, the Council adopted a decision on the signing, on behalf of the European Union, and provisional application of the Framework Agreement between the European Union and its Member States, on the one part, and the Republic of Korea, on the other part on 10 May 2010 (Council Decision 2012/40/EU [2013] OJ L20/1), but this Agreement was only transmitted to Parliament in order to obtain its consent on 12 February 2014. Parliament gave its consent on 16 April 2014 and the Council concluded the agreement on 12 May 2014. The Agreement eventually entered into force without any decision on its provisional application.

14 It is important to note that, under international law, the Union has to respect its obligations resulting from an agreement provisionally applied (see further Heike Krieger, 'Article 25 – Provisional Application' in Oliver Dörr and Kirsten Schmalenbach (eds), *Vienna Convention on the Law of the Treaties – A commentary* (Springer 2012) 420; also Garzón Clariana (n 4) 482).

Some examples demonstrate these difficulties.[15] The first concerns the use of a general and rather imprecise clause, reading as follows: 'as concerns elements falling within the competence of the Community, the Agreement shall be applied on a provisional basis'.[16] In other instances, the agreement itself empowers the Union to indicate the parts of the agreement to be applied provisionally, and the decision on signature and provisional application indicates these parts and provisions.[17] The decision concerning the Association Agreement with Chile indicates the articles to be applied provisionally.[18] By contrast, the decisions on the Trade Agreement with Colombia and Peru[19] and on the Free Trade Agreement with Korea[20] indicate the provisions which shall not

---

15 This problem does not exist in EU-only agreements, because for them the provisional application relates in principle to the whole agreement (e.g. the First Protocol annexed to the EU-Marocco Fisheries Partnership Agreement (n 8), and the provisional application of a series of EU Agreements with several third States concerning the points system applicable to heavy goods vehicles travelling through Austria during a certain period of time: see Council Decisions 2004/181/EC, 2004/182/EC, 2004/183/EC and 2004/184/EC, all 13 January 2004 [2004] OJ L57 respectively pp. 13, 16, 19 and 22).

16 Council Decision 2008/805/EC of 15 July 2008 on the signature and provisional application of the Economic Partnership Agreement between the CARIFORUM States, of the one part, and the European Community and its Member States, of the other part [2008] OJ L289/1, art 4. See also Partnership and Cooperation Agreement between the European Union and its Member States, of the one part, and the Republic of Iraq, of the other part [2012] OJ L204/20, art 117 and Council Decision 2012/418/EU of 21 December 2011 on the signing, on behalf of the European Union, and provisional application of certain provisions of this Partnership and Cooperation Agreement ([2012] OJ L204/18), art 3 ('Article 2, and Titles II, III, and V of the Agreement shall be applied provisionally, in accordance with Article 117 of the Agreement only in so far as it concerns matters falling within the Union's competence (...)').

17 Association Agreement between the European Union and its Member States, of the one part, and Ukraine, of the other part [2014] OJ L161/3 (EU-Ukraine Association Agreement), art 486(4).

18 Art 2 of the Council Decision ([2002] OJ L352/1) enumerates the articles to be applied provisionally. It reads as follows: 'The following provisions of the Association Agreement shall be applied on a provisional basis pending its entry into force: Articles 3 to 11, Article 18, Articles 24 to 27, Articles 48 to 54, Article 55(a), (b), (f), (h), (i), Articles 56 to 93, Articles 136 to 162, and Articles 172 to 206'.

19 Council Decision 2012/735/EU of 31 May 2012 on the signing, on behalf of the Union, and provisional application of the Trade Agreement between the European Union and its Member States, of the one part, and Colombia and Peru, of the other part [2012] OJ L354/1.

20 Council Decision 2011/265/EU of 16 September 2010 on the signing, on behalf of the European Union, and provisional application of the Free Trade Agreement between the

be applied provisionally. This may result in some difficulties of interpretation, or more importantly, in some inconsistencies: for example, in some cases the 'human rights clauses' – dear to the Parliament – are applied provisionally (e.g. Partnership and Cooperation Agreement with Iraq, Trade Agreement with Peru and Colombia), whereas in other agreements they are not (Association Agreement with Central America).[21] This obviously has a political impact on the EU relationship with these countries because if there is a violation of these clauses, it is possible to decide to suspend the agreement. The Parliament is simply not aware of the reasons for this divergence of approach.[22]

Therefore, in order to achieve the necessary institutional balance, a proper involvement of the Parliament seems to be justified. Now that its consent is generalised, the provisional application may be considered as closely linked with the very scope of the consent. The Court of Justice of the European Union (CJEU) acknowledges the enhanced role of the Parliament in the *Mauritius* judgment when it holds that the Parliament is entitled to exercise its right of scrutiny and to make known its views in the phase preceding the conclusion of an agreement.[23] The CJEU has explicitly extended the scope of the right of the Parliament to be informed of the provisional application of an international agreement. In its judgment in the *Tanzania* case, the Court emphasised that 'the procedure for negotiating and concluding international agreements laid down in Article 218(10) TFEU includes (...) the decision on the provisional application of the agreement before its entry into force and the conclusion of the agreement'.[24]

In its relations with the Commission, according to the existing Framework Agreement between the two institutions, the Commission must leave Parliament sufficient time for it to be able to express its point of view and for the Commission to take Parliament's views into account as far as possible.[25] In this regard, the Commission 'shall inform the Parliament as early as possible

European Union and its Member States, of the one part, and the Republic of Korea, of the other part and [2011] OJ L127/1.

21 Council Decision 2012/734/UE of 25 June 2012 on the signing, on behalf of the European Union, of the Agreement establishing an Association between the European Union and its Member States, on the one hand, and Central America on the other, and the provisional application of Part IV thereof concerning trade matters [2012] OJ L346/1.

22 Flaesch-Mougin and Bosse-Platière (n 7) in particular 311–312.

23 Case C-658/11 *Parliament v Council* EU:C:2014:2025, in particular para 86.

24 Case C-263/14 *Parliament v Council* EU:C:2016:435, para 76.

25 Framework Agreement of 20 October 2010 on relations between the European Parliament and the European Commission [2010] OJ L304/47, point 24.

when it intends to propose its provisional application to the Council and the reasons therefor, unless reasons of urgency preclude it from doing so'.[26] The Parliament is therefore not only informed, but is given an opportunity to issue its views in a timely manner on the provisional application of an agreement, before the Council takes its decision. This is particularly meaningful when a choice is made on the parts of the agreement to be applied provisionally in mixed agreements (see the complex problems on the provisional application of the Ukraine Association Agreement).

4 Some Ideas to Develop Cooperation Between Parliament, Council and Commission

In order to achieve this goal, cooperation is needed between the three institutions on the implementation of Article 218(5) TFEU. Two possibilities might be advanced to involve the Parliament:

(a) One possibility is that the Commission presents two separate proposals to the Council: one proposal for a Council decision on the signature of the agreement and another proposal for a Council decision on provisional application, after having given the opportunity to the Parliament (in practice, the responsible parliamentary committee) to express its position on this proposal. It is true that Article 218(5) TFEU may be interpreted as if the signature and provisional application were part of the same decision, but it can be argued that proceeding in two phases does not go against this provision. This procedure would have the advantage of involving the Parliament, at an early stage, in the decision applying an agreement provisionally. Indeed, if the Parliament adopts a resolution – on the basis of the proposal on signature transmitted to it by the Commission, in accordance with Article 218(10) TFEU – stating that it will decline to give consent, the Commission should in that case refrain from proposing the provisional application to the Council. It is assumed that the Council can only decide on provisional application if the Commission makes such a proposal, even though the Council may modify that proposal.

(b) Another possibility is that the Commission submits to the Council two proposals at the same time: one concerning signature and provisional application and a second one concerning the conclusion of the agreement.

26 Ibid, annex III, point 7.

> The first proposal does not indicate the exact date at which provisional application of the agreement would commence, with a view to enabling the Parliament to express its position on the question whether or not the agreement should be applied provisionally. The first proposal could stipulate that the notification indicating the date when provisional application would commence should be transmitted to the third country subsequently. It could be agreed that this notification would be transmitted at a certain date or after the Parliament has given its consent. This procedure has the advantage that provisional application does not commence if the Parliament refuses to give consent. It has the disadvantage that the Parliament cannot express its views on the question of the provisional application itself and its scope, but only on its consent (or not) to the agreement.

This latter procedure has already been applied by the Commission. For example, concerning the Association Agreement with Ukraine, the Commission made the following suggestion in its proposal of 15 May 2013 on the signing and provisional application of the Agreement:

> With a view to taking into account the enhanced role of the European Parliament, the Commission considers that the Council should send the notification referred to in Article 486(4) of the Agreement[27] only after a certain lapse of time so as to allow the European Parliament to express its views.[28]

However, on 17 March 2014 and 23 June 2014, the Council adopted its decisions on the signing and provisional application, modifying the scope of the latter, without making any reference to the Commission's suggestion.[29] In this

---

27 Article 486(4) of the EU-Ukraine Association Agreement (n 17) reads as follows: 'The provisional application shall be effective from the first day of the second month following the date of receipt by the Depositary of the following: – the Union's notification on the completion of the procedures necessary for this purpose, indicating the parts of the Agreement that shall be provisionally applied; and – Ukraine's deposit of the instrument of ratification in accordance with its procedures and applicable legislation'.

28 COM (2013) 289 final (n 3) 6.

29 Council Decision 2014/295/EU of 17 March 2014 on the signing, on behalf of the European Union, and provisional application of the Association Agreement between the European Union and the European Atomic Energy Community and their Member States, of the one part, and Ukraine, of the other part, as regards the Preamble, Article 1, and Titles I, II and VII thereof [2014] OJ L161/1; Council Decision 2014/668/EU of 23 June 2014 on the signing,

particular case, where the Council changed substantially the provisions of the agreement to be applied provisionally, Parliament was merely informed. It eventually supported the provisional application, essentially on political grounds.[30,31]

In the Free Trade Agreement with Korea,[32] in the Multipartite Trade Agreement with Colombia and Peru[33] and in the Association Agreement with Central America,[34] the Council made the notification triggering provisional application to the third countries in question only after the Parliament had given consent.[35] However, in the Partnership and Cooperation Agreement with Iraq,

---

on behalf of the European Union, and provisional application of the Association Agreement between the European Union and the European Atomic Energy Community and their Member States, of the one part, and Ukraine, of the other part, as regards Title III (with the exception of the provisions relating to the treatment of third-country nationals legally employed as workers in the territory of the other Party) and Titles IV, V, VI and VII thereof, as well as the related Annexes and Protocols [2014] OJ L278/1.

30 European Parliament resolution of 17 July 2014 on Ukraine (P8_TA-PROV (2014)0009), para 1.

31 As a matter of fact, in this case the provisional application took effect after Parliament's consent, because the latter was given on 16 September 2014 and the provisional application began on 1 November 2014.

32 Council Decision 2011/265/EU (n 20). In its proposal on the signature and provisional application (COM (2010) 136 final), the Commission used the same language as in the Association Agreement with Ukraine. The Council adopted its decision on 16 September 2010 and the Parliament gave its consent on 17 February 2011 (P7_TA (2011)0063). The notification to Korea was only transmitted on 1 July 2011 ([2011] OJ L168/1), after Parliament's consent.

33 The two Commission proposals (COM (2011) 570 final and COM (2011) 569 final) were submitted on 22 September 2011, the Council adopted its decision on 31 May 2012 (Council Decision 2012/735/EU (n 19)), and the Parliament gave its consent on 11 December 2012 (P7_TA-PROV(2012)0481). According to art 3(2) of the Council's Decision 'In order to determine the date of the provisional application of the agreement, the Council shall fix the date by which the notification referred to in Article 330(3) thereof is to be sent to Colombia and Peru'. This notification was transmitted after the Parliament had given consent.

34 Council Decision 2012/734/EU (n 21).

35 In relation to these agreements (see notes 32, 33 and 34) Parliament and Council had to adopt, under the ordinary legislative procedure, regulations aiming at implementing the safeguard clauses contained in the agreements. See Regulation (EU) 511/2011 of the European Parliament and of the Council of 11 May 2011 implementing the bilateral safeguard clause of the Free Trade Agreement between the European Union and its Member States and the Republic of Korea [2011] OJ L145/19; Regulation (EU) 19/2013 of the European Parliament and of the Council of 15 January 2013 implementing the bilateral safeguard clause and the stabilisation mechanism for bananas of the Trade Agreement between the

the Council made the notification triggering provisional application of the agreement with effect as of 1 August 2012, before the Parliament had given consent. In this case, moreover, the provisional application required the establishment of an institutional framework (Cooperation Council and a Cooperation Committee).[36]

Concerning the Comprehensive Economic and Trade Agreement (CETA), the Commission adopted three proposals on the same day. On 5 July 2016 it adopted a proposal for the decision on signature in one act,[37] a proposal for the decision on provisional application in a second act[38] and a proposal for a decision on the conclusion in a third act.[39]

In this context, it is worth referring to the statement made by Ms Malmström at the hearing before the Parliament as Commissioner candidate in 2014, in response to the question 'Does the Commissioner-designate formally commit himself/herself to not requesting provisional application of trade agreements including trade chapters of association agreements before the European Parliament gives its consent on those agreements?':

> During the last five years a practice has developed not to provisionally apply politically important trade agreements before the European Parliament has had the opportunity to give its consent. This was the case for the Free Trade Agreement with Korea, the multiparty trade agreement with Colombia and Peru and EU-Central America Association Agreement.

European Union and its Member States, of the one part, and Colombia and Peru, of the other part [2013] OJ L17/1; and Regulation (EU) 20/2013 of the European Parliament and of the Council of 15 January 2013 implementing the bilateral safeguard clause and the stabilisation mechanism for bananas of the Agreement establishing an Association between the European Union and its Member States, on the one hand, and Central America on the other [2013] OJ L17/13.

36 See Flaesch-Mougin and Bosse-Platière (n 7) in particular the references to these agreements at pp. 307–308.

37 Commission, 'Proposal for a Council Decision on the signing on behalf of the European Union of the Comprehensive Economic and Trade Agreement between Canada of the one part, and the European Union and its Member States, of the other part' COM (2016) 444 final.

38 Commission, 'Proposal for a Council Decision on the provisional application of the Comprehensive Economic and Trade Agreement between Canada of the one part, and the European Union and its Member States, of the other part' COM (2016) 470 final.

39 Commission, 'Proposal for a Council Decision on the conclusion of the Comprehensive Economic and Trade Agreement between Canada of the one part, and the European Union and its Member States, of the other part' COM (2016) 443 final.

> Even if the power to decide on provisional application lies with the Council rather than with the Commission, I agree that this practice should continue. I am ready, when proposing decisions to sign politically important trade agreements which fall under my responsibility, to ask Council to delay provisional application until the European Parliament has given its consent. However, we need certain flexibility in applying such a practice as there will always be occasions where the urgency of a particular file, or its technical character, mean that it is unwarranted to delay its application pending the EP's consent. This was the case for the provisional application of the Association Agreements with Georgia and Moldova, on the one hand, and of very technical measures such as the adaptation of our international agreements as a result of Croatia's accession to the EU. In any event, in such cases I undertake to inform the Chair of the INTA Committee and to seek his views on such course of action.[40]

5 Conclusions

Both procedures indicated in (a) and (b) above are legally possible but the first – which has not yet been used – allows a deeper involvement of the Parliament in the decision-making process relating to provisional application.

This matter may evolve with the modification of the Interinstitutional Agreement on Better Law-Making between the European Parliament, the Council and the Commission concerning international agreements.[41] Negotiations on the implementation thereof are still pending. Indeed, even if the Commission is currently obliged, on the basis of the existing Framework Agreement of 20 October 2010, to inform the Parliament and take its position into account when it intends to propose provisional application of an agreement (Annex III, point 7 mentioned before), there is no interinstitutional agreement creating this obligation on the Council. Yet it can be argued that the Council is under

40 Hearing of Cecilia Malmström, Commissioner-designate (Trade) (European Parliament, Brussels, 29 September 2014) <http://www.europarl.europa.eu/hearings-2014/en/schedule/29-09-2014/cecilia-malmstrom> accessed 15 November 2016.

41 [2016] OJ L123/1 (IIA on Better Law-making). The IIA on Better Law-making is without prejudice to the Framework Agreement of 20 October 2010 on relations between the European Parliament and the European Commission ([2010] OJ L304/47) (see IIA on Better Law-making, annex II).

this obligation on the basis of Article 218(10) TFEU, as the CJEU underlined in the *Mauritius* and in the *Tanzania* cases.[42]

The institutions, in particular the Council (and also the High Representative), are aware of this legal obligation. In the aforementioned Interinstitutional Agreement they have agreed that:

> The three institutions acknowledge the importance of ensuring that each institution can exercise its rights and fulfil its obligations enshrined in the Treaties as interpreted by the Court of Justice regarding the negotiation and conclusion of international agreements. The three institutions commit to meet within 6 months after the entry into force of the present agreement in order to negotiate improved practical arrangements for cooperation and information sharing within the framework of the Treaties, as interpreted by the Court of Justice.[43]

If none of the options (a) and (b) above is considered adequate or feasible, the institutions could at least envisage an informal mechanism for dialogue, as foreseen in paragraph 25 of the Interinstitutional Agreement concerning a modification of the legal basis of a legislative proposal.

According to this provision:

> The Commission shall provide, in relation to each proposal, an explanation and justification to the European Parliament and to the Council regarding its choice of legal basis and type of legal act in the explanatory memorandum accompanying the proposal. The Commission should take due account of the difference in nature and effects between regulations and directives. (…)
>
> If a modification of the legal basis entailing a change from the ordinary legislative procedure to a special legislative procedure or a non-legislative procedure is envisaged, the three Institutions will exchange views thereon.
>
> The three Institutions agree that the choice of legal basis is a legal determination that must be made on objective grounds which are amenable to judicial review.
>
> The Commission shall continue to fully play its institutional role to ensure that the Treaties and the case-law of the Court of Justice of the European Union are respected.[44]

---

42 See n 23 and 24.

43 IIA on Better Law-making, para 40.

44 Ibid, para 25.

It would indeed be possible to apply by analogy this mechanism concerning disputes relating to legal basis to the question of provisional application of international agreements, where the latter is proposed by the Commission.

A requirement to launch this dialogue before a decision is taken by the Council on provisional application would indeed oblige the institutions to exchange views, where necessary, which would perhaps prevent further legal disputes on this matter.

CHAPTER 18

The Use of the CFSP Legal Basis for EU International Agreements in Combination with Other Legal Bases

*Frederik Naert**

1 Introduction

In this contribution, I will address the use of Article 37 TEU as the substantive[1] Common Foreign and Security Policy (CFSP) legal basis for international agreements negotiated, signed and concluded by the Union (hereinafter, for the sake of convenience, I will refer to agreements concluded by the Union), and especially its combination with other substantive legal bases in such agreements.[2]

I will first provide a brief overview of the kinds of agreements that have been concluded only under the CFSP legal basis (2). These will not be discussed further, except for pirate transfer agreements relating to operation Atalanta, which have given rise to litigation in respect of their legal basis. Next, I will examine where a CFSP legal basis has been combined with a non-CFSP sectoral legal basis (3). This is followed by the recourse (or not) to the CFSP legal basis in horizontal / framework agreements with third States (4). I will then examine some general and procedural aspects of combining CFSP and non-CFSP legal bases for agreements (5), before offering some final remarks (6).

As Ricardo Gosalbo Bono spent considerable time working on legal aspects of the CFSP, both as a practitioner and as an academic,[3] I trust this topic will

* The views expressed are solely those of the author.

1 I will not address questions relating to the procedural legal basis, except in Section 5.

2 The legal basis/bases is/are identified in the Council decisions relating to these agreements (i.e. those authorising the opening of negotiations and appointing the negotiator as well as those on signature and conclusion, and, where relevant, provisional application) and generally not in the agreements themselves and legal challenges are brought against and through those decisions (as regards the latter, see the chapter by Álvaro de Elera in this book).

3 See e.g. Ricardo Gosalbo Bono, 'Some Reflections of the CFSP Legal Order' (2006) 43 CML rev 377.

 | DOI 10.1163/9789004347175_019

be of interest to him and I hope that the gradual but clear evolution in this field will be to his liking.

2 Types of Agreements Concluded Only on the CFSP Legal Basis

2.1 *Overview*

Several publications have described the use of agreements adopted solely relating to the CFSP and adopted on the basis of Article 37 TEU, or its pre-Lisbon equivalent (ex-Article 24 TEU).[4] These can be divided into the following kinds of agreements:

- Status of forces or status of mission agreements with States in which EU operations launched under its Common Security and Defence Policy (CSDP;[5] a specific sub-policy of the CFSP) take place;[6] as well as similar agreements with transit States;[7]

4 e.g. Piet Eeckhout, *External Relations of the European Union. Legal and Constitutional Foundations* (Oxford University Press 2004) 157–160 and 182–184 and, very extensively, Daniel Thym, 'Die Völkerrechtlichen Verträge der Europäischen Union' (2006) 66 Zeitschrift für ausländisches öffentliches Recht und Völkerrecht 863. See also the references below in n 5. I will not discuss agreements concluded between Member States in relation to the CFSP, such as the Agreement between the Member States of the European Union concerning the status of military and civilian staff seconded to the institutions of the European Union, of the headquarters and forces which may be made available to the European Union in the context of the preparation and execution of the tasks referred to in Article 17(2) of the Treaty on European Union, including exercises, and of the military and civilian staff of the Member States put at the disposal of the European Union to act in this context (EU SOFA) [2003] OJ C 321/6.

5 On international agreements concluded in the framework of this policy see generally Panos Koutrakos 'International Agreements in the Area of the EU's Common Security and Defence Policy', in Enzo Cannizzaro, Paolo Palchetti and Ramses Wessel (eds), *International Law as Law of the European Union* (Martinus Nijhoff 2011) 157 and Aurel Sari, 'The Conclusion of International Agreements by the European Union in the Context of the ESDP' (2007) 56 ICLQ 53.

6 For the model texts on which such agreements are based, see on the one hand Council documents 12616/07 of 6 September 2007 and 11894/07 of 20 July 2007 as well as COR 1 of 5 September 2007; and on the other hand Council doc. 17141/08 of 15 December 2008. It should be noted that in some 'non-executive' military missions (training and advisory missions), the title SOMA has been used for military missions but in such cases the content follows the model SOFA. For specific examples, see e.g. Council Decision 2008/266/CFSP of 28 January 2008 concerning the conclusion of the Agreement between the European Union and the Republic of Chad on the status of the European Union-led forces in the Republic of Chad,

- Agreements with third States participating in such operations (in *ad hoc* cases[8] or in the form of framework participation agreements covering participation by a given third State in any CSDP operation in which it participates[9]);
- Agreements on the transfer of persons detained by such operations to the State in which they operate or to other states in the region; such agreements have been concluded primarily in respect of operation Atalanta (see below, Section II.2) but also in relation to EUFOR RCA;[10]
- Other agreements on cooperation in crisis management;[11]

[2008] OJ L 83/39 (text of the agreement at p. 40); Council Decision 2013/178/CFSP of 25 February 2013 on the signing and conclusion of the Agreement between the European Union and the Republic of Mali on the status in the Republic of Mali of the European Union military mission to contribute to the training of the Malian Armed Forces (EUTM Mali) [2013] OJ L 106/1 (text of the agreement at p. 2); and Council Decision 2013/450/CFSP of 22 July 2013 on the signing and conclusion of the Agreement between the European Union and the Republic of Niger on the status of the European Union mission in Niger CSDP (EUCAP Sahel Niger) [2013] OJ L 242/1 (text of the agreement at p. 2). See also A. Sari, 'Status of Forces and Status of Mission Agreements under the ESDP: the EU's Evolving Practice' (2008) 19 EJIL 67.

7 e.g. Council Decision 2008/178/CFSP of 28 January 2008 concerning the conclusion of the Agreement between the European Union and the Republic of Cameroon on the status of the European Union-led forces in transit within the territory of the Republic of Cameroon [2008] OJ L 57/30 (text of the agreement at p. 31).

8 e.g. Council Decision 2009/597/CFSP of 27 July 2009 on the signing and provisional application of the Agreement between the European Union and the Republic of Croatia on the participation of the Republic of Croatia in the European Union military operation to contribute to the deterrence, prevention and repression of acts of piracy and armed robbery off the Somali coast (Operation Atalanta) [2009] OJ L 202/83 (text of the agreement at p. 84) (before Croatia's accession to the EU).

9 e.g. Council Decision 2011/318/CFSP of 31 March 2011 on the signing and conclusion of the Framework Agreement between the United States of America and the European Union on the participation of the United States of America in European Union crisis management operations [2011] OJ L 143/1 (text of the agreement at p. 2).

10 Council Decision 2014/537/CFSP of 3 July 2014 on the signing and conclusion, on behalf of the European Union, of the Agreement between the European Union and the Central African Republic concerning detailed arrangements for the transfer to the Central African Republic of persons detained by the European Union military operation (EUFOR RCA) in the course of carrying out its mandate, and concerning the guarantees applicable to such persons [2014] OJ L 251/1 (text of the agreement at p. 3).

11 On 6 December 2016, an EU-US Acquisition and Cross-Servicing Agreement for CSDP operations was signed. See EEAS, 'Joint Press Release: The European Union and the

- Agreements on the exchange of classified information with third States and international organisations;[12]
- Agreements on cooperation with other international organisations in the field of the CFSP. Only few of these have been concluded as legally binding agreements – there is one with the International Criminal Court[13] and there are negotiations for one with the United Nations.[14] Some recourse has been had to political arrangements,[15] such as the famous EU-NATO 'Berlin plus' arrangements.[16]

United States Sign Military Logistical Assistance Agreement', 6 December 2016 <https://eeas.europa.eu/node/16575_en> (accessed on 11 December 2016). See also below n 14 on negotiations for an agreement with the UN.

12 E.g. Council Decision 2012/486/CFSP of 23 July 2012 concerning the signing and conclusion of the Agreement between the Organisation for Joint Armament Cooperation and the European Union on the protection of classified information [2012] OJ L 229/1 (text of the agreement at p. 2) and Council Decision 2010/53/CFSP of 30 November 2009 concerning the conclusion of the Agreement between Australia and the European Union on the security of classified information [2010] OJ L 26/30 (text of the agreement at p. 31).

13 Council Decision of 10 April 2006 concerning the conclusion of the Agreement between the International Criminal Court and the European Union on Cooperation and Assistance [2006] OJ L 115/49 (text of the agreement at p. 50).

14 Council Decision authorising the opening of negotiations with a view to concluding a Framework Agreement on Cooperation between the United Nations and the European Union in the context of their respective crisis management operations, adopted on 16 March 2015 (see the outcome of the 16 March 2015 Council meeting, Council Doc. 7265/15, p. 16).

15 I will not touch here on the question to what extent relations with other international organisations can be based on Article 220 TFEU (covering both the CFSP and other Union policies). See Ricardo Gosalbo Bono and Frederik Naert, 'The Reluctant (Lisbon) Treaty and Its Implementation in the Practice of the Council', in Piet Eeckhout and Manuel Lopez-Escudero (eds.), *The European Union's External Action in Times of Crisis* (Hart 2016) 13, 49 and see the chapter by Stephan Marquardt in this book.

16 These Berlin plus arrangements (which are not in the public domain) set out in particular EU access to NATO planning, NATO European command options, and EU use of NATO assets and capabilities. See the summary entitled 'EU-NATO: The Framework for Permanent Relations and Berlin Plus', available at <http://www.consilium.europa.eu/uedocs/cmsUpload/03-11-11%20Berlin%20Plus%20press%20note%20BL.pdf> (accessed on 11 December 2016). On the nature of these arrangements, see Gosalbo Bono (n 3) 362–363. On EU-NATO relations, see Frederik Naert, 'EU Crisis Management Operations and Their Relations with NATO Operations', in Zoltan Hegedüs et al. (eds), *NATO Legal Deskbook* (NATO 2010, 2nd edn) 281.

I will not further address such agreements but would merely comment that, given the wide scope of the CFSP,[17] a wide variety of agreements could be concluded on the basis of Article 37 TEU and the above types are by no means the only possible ones, nor do they necessarily cover all agreements concluded or being negotiated in the field of the CFSP. Furthermore, some CFSP agencies may conclude administrative arrangements with (the competent authorities of) third States or international organisations. This is notably the case for the European Defence Agency and the EU Satellite Centre, where this is subject to approval by the Council.[18]

2.2 *Pirate Transfer Agreements and the Scope/Delimitation of the CFSP Legal Basis*

To my knowledge, there are only two cases in which an action was brought before the CJEU challenging (directly or indirectly) the legal basis of an agreement concluded solely under Article 37 TEU or ex-Article 24 TFEU. Both cases, in which I was an agent for the Council, concern agreements on the transfer of suspected pirates captured by the military CSDP operation Atalanta (EUNAVFOR Somalia) to States in the Horn of Africa, and more specifically Mauritius and Tanzania, and the way they are treated.[19]

---

17 Article 24(1) TEU states that 'The Union's competence in matters of common foreign and security policy shall cover all areas of foreign policy and all questions relating to the Union's security'. But see below on the delimitation with other external Union policies and/or external dimensions of internal policies.

18 See respectively Council Decision (CFSP) 2015/1835 of 12 October 2015 defining the statute, seat and operational rules of the European Defence Agency (recast) [2015] OJ L 266/55 (art 26) and Council Decision 2014/401/CFSP of 26 June 2014 on the European Union Satellite Centre and repealing Joint Action 2001/555/CFSP on the establishment of a European Union Satellite Centre [2014] OJ L 188/73 (art 20).

19 Similar agreements have been concluded with Kenya (pre-Lisbon: Council Decision 2009/293/CFSP of 26 February 2009 concerning the Exchange of Letters between the European Union and the Government of Kenya on the conditions and modalities for the transfer of persons suspected of having committed acts of piracy and detained by the European Union-led naval force (EUNAVFOR), and seized property in the possession of EUNAVFOR, from EUNAVFOR to Kenya and for their treatment after such transfer [2009] OJ L 79/47 (text of the agreement at p. 49); no longer in force) and the Seychelles (Council Decision 2009/877/CFSP of 23 October 2009 on the signing and provisional application of the Exchange of Letters between the European Union and the Republic of Seychelles on the conditions and modalities for the transfer of suspected pirates and armed robbers from EUNAVFOR to the Republic of Seychelles and for their treatment after such transfer [2009] OJ L 315/35 (text of the agreement at p. 37)).

In the first case, the European Parliament (EP) challenged the Decision on the signing and conclusion of the Agreement with Mauritius,[20] claiming that the Agreement and Decision did not relate exclusively to the CFSP but also related to police and judicial cooperation under the Area of Freedom, Security and Justice (AFSJ) as well as the Union's development cooperation policy and that, consequently, the EP's consent was necessary to conclude this agreement.[21] Oddly, the EP did not claim that the legal bases pertaining to the latter two policy areas were required (admitting that the CFSP aspect was predominant) but it argued that this was an agreement founded on the CFSP legal basis which nevertheless incidentally related to policies other than the CFSP and that such agreements require the EP's consent, since they would not exclusively relate to the CFSP for the purposes of Article 218(6) TFEU. The Court rejected this argument, ruling that 'it is the substantive legal basis of the decision concluding [an] agreement which determines the type of procedure applicable under paragraph 6 of [Article 218 TFEU]' and that 'where the decision concluding the agreement in question is legitimately founded exclusively on a substantive legal basis falling within the CFSP, it is the type of procedure provided for in the first part of the second subparagraph of Article 218(6) TFEU that is applicable' and therefore concluded that 'the contested decision could be adopted without the consent or consultation of the Parliament' (since the EP had accepted that the elements allegedly pertaining to the AFSJ and development policy were only ancillary).[22]

20 Council Decision 2011/640/CFSP of 12 July 2011 on the signing and conclusion of the Agreement between the European Union and the Republic of Mauritius on the conditions of transfer of suspected pirates and associated seized property from the European Union-led naval force to the Republic of Mauritius and on the conditions of suspected pirates after transfer [2011] OJ L 254/1 (for the Agreement itself, see ibid, p. 3).

21 Pursuant to Article 218(6) TFEU, the conclusion of international agreements requires the EP's consent or consultation except as regards agreements exclusively relating to the CFSP.

22 Case C-658/11 *Parliament v Council* EU:C:2014:2025, paras 43–63, especially paras 45, 58–59 and 62. The decision was however annulled – while maintaining its effects – because the Court ruled that the Council had not sufficiently informed the Parliament under Article 218(10) TFEU. See Claudio Matera and Ramses Wessel, 'Context or Content? A CFSP or AFSJ Legal Basis for EU International Agreements – Case C-658/11, European Parliament v Council (Mauritius Agreement)' (2014) Revista de Derecho Comunitario Europeo 1047; Andrea Ott, 'The Legal Basis for International Agreements post-Lisbon. Of Pirates and the Philippines' (2014) MAASTRICHT J EUR & COMP L 739; Annegret Engel, 'Delimiting Competences in the EU: CFSP versus AFSJ Legal Bases' (2015) 21 EUR PUBLIC L 47; P. Van Elsuwege, 'Securing the Institutional Balance in the Procedure for Concluding

The second case concerns the (decision on the signing and conclusion of the) agreement with Tanzania.[23] This time, the EP submitted that the aim and content of the Agreement directly relate to judicial cooperation in criminal matters and to police cooperation and that, consequently Articles 82 and 87 TFEU must be added to Article 37 TEU as the correct substantive legal basis and that the correct procedural legal basis was Article 218(6)(a)(v) TFEU, which requires the consent of the EP. In her Opinion delivered on 28 October 2015, Advocate General Kokott took the view that the decision was correctly based solely on Article 37 TEU:[24]

> 62. ... The rules concerning the area of freedom, security and justice are not necessarily the *sedes materiae* in every case where measures having some connection with the subjects of judicial cooperation in criminal matters or police cooperation are to be adopted.
>
> 63. ... the crucial factor is that the relevant rules in Articles 82 TFEU and 87 TFEU deal only with cooperation *within the Union.*
>
> ...
>
> 65. There may certainly be cases where cooperation with a third State is also capable of helping to achieve the objectives of the area of freedom, security and justice within the Union (see the second variant of Article 216(1) TFEU) and thus of giving that area a genuine 'external dimension'. Examples are the inclusion of Norway, Iceland, Liechtenstein and Switzerland in the Schengen area or the Lugano Convention, ... However, external action has no evident repercussions on the area within the Union in the case of cooperation like that with Tanzania, ...
>
> 66. That cooperation between the Union and Tanzania is intended solely to promote *international security* outside the territory of the Union. ...

International Agreements: *European Parliament* v. *Council* (*Pirate Transfer Agreement with Mauritius*)' (2015) 52 CML Rev. 1379 and Joris Larik, 'Democratic Scrutiny of EU Foreign Policy: from Pirates to the Power of the People (Case C-658/11 Parliament v. Council)', 14 August 2014, <http://europeanlawblog.eu/?p=2469> (accessed on 12 December 2016).

23 Council Decision 2014/198/CFSP of 10 March 2104 on the signing and conclusion of the Agreement between the European Union and the United Republic of Tanzania on the conditions of transfer of suspected pirates and associated seized property from the European Union-led naval force to the United Republic of Tanzania [2014] OJ L 108/1 (for the agreement itself see p. 3).

24 Case C-263/14 *Parliament v Council* EU:C:2015:729, see paras 50–73. AG General Bot also came to this conclusion in his Opinion of 30 January 2014 in Case C-658/11 *Parliament v Council* EU:C:2014:41, paras 86–130.

> 67. On the other hand, a specific connection with *security within the European Union* or with the national security of its Member States is not evident. It would be only very indirect if it did exist, ...
>
> 68. Nor can an internal Union dimension be inferred from the mere fact that suspected pirates who are to be transferred to the Tanzanian authorities by EU NAVFOR are temporarily on board EU Member States' warships and are detained there. Although the persons concerned are thus temporarily subject to the sovereignty of the Member States and are therefore also able to benefit from guarantees laid down by EU law (...) this does not mean that they come within the territory of the Union and thus within the geographical scope of the area of freedom, security and justice.

Advocate General Kokott also appears to endorse the possibility of having a dual CFSP-AFSJ legal basis in principle (see further sections 3 and 4 below).[25]

In its judgment, delivered on 14 June 2016, the Court followed Advocate General Kokott and ruled that the decision was correctly based solely on Article 37 TEU.[26] The Court held that:

> 54. Accordingly, an examination of the aim of the EU-Tanzania Agreement confirms that the procedure of transferring persons arrested or detained by EUNAVFOR established by the Agreement constitutes an instrument whereby the European Union pursues the objectives of Operation Atalanta, namely to preserve international peace and security, in particular by making it possible to ensure that the perpetrators of acts of piracy do not go unpunished.
>
> 55. Since the Agreement falls predominantly within the scope of the CFSP, and not within the scope of judicial cooperation in criminal matters or police cooperation, the contested decision could legitimately be based on Article 37 TEU alone. ...

---

25 EU:C:2015:729, paras 53 ('... the Court has certainly not thus far rejected the possibility of such a dual legal basis in a case like the present one') and 57 ('It is therefore perfectly conceivable, in principle, to have recourse, for the approval of an international agreement for the [EU], to competences in the area of freedom, security and justice or to have a dual substantive legal basis by exercising additional competences' [to the CFSP]).

26 EU:C:2016:435, paras 42–55. Here too the decision was however annulled – while maintaining its effects – because the Court ruled that the Council had not sufficiently informed the Parliament under Article 218(10) TFEU. On the latter topic, see the chapter by Ricardo Passos in this book.

The Court does not provide much guidance on the demarcation between the CFSP and the AFSJ more generally, except for the following:

> Admittedly, as stated by the Advocate General in point 60 of her Opinion, some of the obligations laid down by the EU-Tanzania Agreement appear, at first sight, to relate to the field of cross-border judicial cooperation in criminal matters and police cooperation, when they are considered individually. However, as also observed by the Advocate General, the fact that certain provisions of such an agreement, taken individually, have an affinity with rules that might be adopted within a European Union policy area is not, in itself, sufficient to determine the appropriate legal basis of the contested decision. As regards, in particular, provisions of the EU-Tanzania Agreement concerning compliance with the principles of the rule of law and human rights, as well as respect for human dignity, it must be stated that such compliance is required of all actions of the European Union, including those in the area of the CFSP, as is clear from the provisions, read together, set out in the first subparagraph of Article 21(1), Article 21(2)(b) and (3) TEU, and Article 23 TEU. That being the case, the Court must also assess that agreement in the light of its aim.[27]

These two cases clarify that the CJEU applies its traditional jurisprudence on the choice of legal bases also where the choice is between a CFSP and non-CFSP legal basis. Therefore, where an agreement (or other act or measure) has a predominant aim or component and any other aims or components which it may have are only ancillary, the corresponding single legal basis will apply.[28]

The next sections explore what happens when an agreement has both CFSP and non-CFSP objectives or components and neither of the two is ancillary. In such cases, according to the CJEU:

> With regard to a measure that simultaneously pursues a number of objectives, or that has several components, which are inseparably linked without one's being incidental to the other, the Court has held that, where various provisions of the Treaty are therefore applicable, such a measure will have to be founded, exceptionally, on the various corresponding legal bases (…). None the less, … recourse to a dual legal basis is not possible where the procedures laid down for each legal basis are incompatible with each other (…).[29]

---

27 See para 47 of the *Tanzania* judgment (n 24).

28 Ibid, para 44.

29 See e.g. Case C-130/10 *Parliament v Council* EU:C:2012:472, paras 44–45.

3 The Combination of a CFSP Legal Basis with Another Sectoral Legal Basis

In the pre-Lisbon era, agreements concluded by the Union under the then third pillar, i.e. based on ex-Article 38 TEU, were also concluded on the basis of ex-Article 24 TEU, which was the CFSP legal basis.[30] Ex-Article 38 TEU did not itself contain a procedure, and the procedure for concluding agreements under this provision was set out in ex-Article 24 TEU. Since the practice of the Council is to refer to both the substantive and the procedural legal basis for its acts, the inclusion of ex-Article 24 TEU does not necessarily mean that such agreements were based on a dual substantive legal basis. Rather, it would seem that in many cases ex-Article 24 TEU was included only as the procedural legal basis.[31] Nevertheless, in some cases there does seem to have been a dual substantive legal basis.[32] Pre-Lisbon, this combination did not raise too many challenges, as the procedural legal basis was the same and both were *Union* (as opposed to *Community*) legal bases.

Except for these cases, to my knowledge, the first time the Union concluded an agreement under a combined CFSP and non- CFSP substantive legal basis, was Council Decision 2012/308/CFSP of 26 April 2012 on the accession of the European Union to the Treaty of Amity and Cooperation in Southeast Asia.[33]

This decision was based on Article 37 TEU (as well as Article 31(1) TEU, which lays down the voting rule), in conjunction with Articles 209 and 212 TFEU, as

30 See the discussion by Ramses Wessel, 'Cross-Pillar Mixity: Combining Competences in the Conclusion of EU International Agreements' in Christophe Hillion and Panos Koutrakos (Eds.), *Mixed Agreements in EU Law Revisited* (Hart Publishing 2010) 30, 34–36.

31 e.g. this was presumably the case for Council Decision 2009/820/CFSP of 23 October 2009 on the conclusion on behalf of the European Union of the Agreement on extradition between the European Union and the United States of America and the Agreement on mutual legal assistance between the European Union and the United States of America [2009] OJ L 291/40.

32 This appears to have been the case for some security agreements concluded under this dual legal basis (e.g. Council Decision 2007/274/JHA of 23 April 2007 concerning the conclusion of the Agreement between the European Union and the Government of the United States of America on the security of classified information [2007] OJ L 115/20), as such agreements had also been concluded on a CFSP only legal basis (e.g. Council Decision 2003/211/CFSP of 24 February 2003 concerning the conclusion of the Agreement between the European Union and the North Atlantic Treaty Organisation on the Security of Information [2003] OJ L 80/35), and are concluded under a CFSP only legal basis in post-Lisbon practice (even if the information that may be exchanged under such agreements is not limited to the CFSP) – see above.

33 [2012] OJ L 154/1.

well as the procedural legal basis of Article 218, paragraphs (6)(a) and (8), second subparagraph TFEU. Thus it combines the CFSP legal basis with the legal bases for development cooperation policy as well as that for economic, financial and technical cooperation with countries other than developing countries. This is clearly explained in the second and third recitals to this decision, which provide that:

> (2) The Treaty aims to promote peace, stability and cooperation in the region. To this end, it calls for the settlement of disputes by peaceful means, the preservation of peace, the prevention of conflicts and the strengthening of security in Southeast Asia. Hence, the rules and principles set out in the Treaty correspond to the objectives of the Union's common foreign and security polity.
>
> (3) Furthermore, the Treaty provides for enhancing cooperation in economic, trade, social, technical and scientific fields as well as for the acceleration of economic growth in the region by promoting a greater utilisation of the agriculture and industries of the nations in Southeast Asia, the expansion of their trade and the improvement of their economic infrastructure. Therefore, the Treaty promotes cooperation with the developing countries of that region as well as economic, financial and technical cooperation with countries other than developing countries.

It is also worth noting that the decision was adopted on a joint proposal of the High Representative of the Union for Foreign Affairs and Security Policy (High Representative) and of the European Commission.[34] That proposal already contained these combined legal bases and the accompanying explanatory memorandum stated that:

> The accession to the TAC [Treaty of Amity and Cooperation in Southeast Asia] is based both on the development of relationships with regional organisations which share the principles referred to in article 21, paragraph 1 TEU in the framework of CFSP and on non-CFSP policies (development cooperation as well as economic, financial and technical cooperation (Articles 209 and 212 TFEU).

34 JOIN/2012/01 final, 16.2.2012, <http://eur-lex.europa.eu/legal-content/EN/TXT/PDF/?uri=CELEX:52012JC0001&rid=2> (accessed on 12 December 2016).

Thus not only the Council but also the Commission and the High Representative, and also the EP, which gave its consent,[35] took the view that it is possible to combine a CFSP and non-CFSP legal basis for the conclusion of international agreements.[36]

Indeed, there are indications in Article 218 TFEU that the Union can conclude international agreements relating to both the CFSP and one or more non-CFSP policies.[37] In particular, its third paragraph states that 'The Commission, or the High Representative [...] where the agreement envisaged relates exclusively *or principally* to the [CFSP], shall submit recommendations to the Council, which shall adopt a decision authorising the opening of negotiations and, depending on the subject of the agreement envisaged, nominating the Union negotiator *or the head of the Union's negotiating team*' (emphasis added). The mention of an envisaged agreement 'principally' relating to the CFSP suggests that it is possible to have combined CFSP and non-CFSP legal bases.[38] The possibility to nominate (the head of) a negotiating team also supports this possibility: it seems unlikely that the team was intended to cover anything other than a combined High Representative – Commission negotiating team and that would only make sense for such a CFSP and non-CFSP combination.[39]

---

35 European Parliament legislative resolution of 18 April 2012 on the draft Council decision on the accession of the European Union to the Treaty of Amity and Cooperation in South-east Asia (07434/2012 – C7-0085/2012 – 2012/0028(NLE)). The resolution does not question in any way the legal bases concerned.

36 It is interesting to note that the authorisation to negotiate this accession was given in 2006, i.e. pre-Lisbon, and that at that time, accession by the Union and Community under the CFSP and Community legal bases seems to have been regarded as possible. See JOIN/2012/01 final, explanatory memorandum, p. 2 ('The Council, in its 2768th meeting of 4–5 December 2006, authorised the Presidency and the Commission to negotiate the European Union's and the European Community's accessions to the TAC'). The Council Legal Service issued an opinion on this envisaged accession, which is partially in the public domain: see Council doc. 11511/06 (including an identification of TAC provisions relating to the CFSP and to Community policies). See also below on the pre-Lisbon situation.

37 See also Wessel (n 30), 51–52 and Alan Dashwood, 'Mixity in the Era of the Treaty of Lisbon', in Hillion and Koutrakos (eds) (n 30), 353–355 and 365.

38 At least on the assumption that the other policy/policies, while not being the main one(s), would nevertheless not be merely ancillary, for otherwise the corresponding legal basis/bases would not have to be added.

39 Since art 218 TFEU does not address aspects particular to mixed agreements, this wording presumably does not envisage a negotiating team comprising Union and Member State negotiators. Compare the analysis of Mauro Gatti and Pietro Manzini, 'External Representation of the European Union in the Conclusion of International Agreements' (2012)

This view would also be most in line with the evolution towards more coherent EU external relations with a single set of overarching external relations objectives, laid down in Article 21 TEU.[40] While the latter do not override or render irrelevant the distinct legal bases for the various specific policies within those external relations, it can hardly have been the objective to prohibit the conclusion of international agreements covering several of those policies.

The combination of CFSP and non-CFSP legal bases in agreements is also facilitated by the fact that Article 40 TEU now protects both the CFSP and the other Union policies from interference[41] and that both policies are now placed on an equal footing.[42] In fact, it was not uncontested whether before the Treaty of Lisbon mixed EC-EU agreements were possible.[43] To my knowledge, only two such agreements were concluded, and they concerned the former 'third Pillar' rather than the CFSP.[44]

---

49 CML Rev 1703, especially 1707–1710 and 1720–1723. See also the chapter by Stephan Marquardt in this book.

40 However, the introduction of these horizontal objectives was accompanied by the suppression of specific CFSP objectives. Article 23 TEU on the CFSP now merely refers back to Article 21 TEU. This does not make the delimitation between the CFSP and other Union policies easier. See e.g. Peter Van Elsuwege, 'EU External Action after the Collapse of the Pillar Structure. In Search of a New Balance between Delimitation and Consistency' (2010) 47 CML Rev 987 and Peter Van Elsuwege, 'The Interface between the Area of Freedom, Security and Justice and the Common Foreign and Security Policy of the European Union: Legal Constraints to Political Objectives' in Ronald Holzacker and Paul Luif (eds), *Freedom, Security and Justice in the European Union: Internal and External Dimensions of Increased Cooperation after the Lisbon Treaty* (Springer 2013) 119. The judgment in Case C-263/14 (see Section 2.2 above) has shed some – but not much – light on this.

41 Unlike ex-Article 47 TEU, which only protected Community policies against encroachment by the CFSP.

42 Pursuant to the third paragraph of Article 1 TFEU, the TEU and TFEU have the same legal value.

43 For voices in favour see e.g. M.-G. Garbagnati Ketvel,'The Jurisdiction of the European Court of Justice in Respect of the Common Foreign and Security Policy' (2006) 55 ICLQ 77, 92–94; L. Grard, 'La condition internationale de l'Union européenne après Nice' (2000) 10 Revue des affaires européennes 374, 377–378; Thym (n 4), 908–912; Delano Verwey, *The European Community, the European Union and the Law of Treaties* (TMC Asser Press 2004) 83 and 'Editorial Comments. The European Union – A New International Actor' (2001) 38 CML Rev 827–828. Compare the question and challenges identified by Frank Hoffmeister, 'Curse or blessing? Mixed Agreements in the Recent Practice of the European Union and its Member States', in Hillion and Koutrakos (eds) (n 30) 251–253.

44 Namely (i) the Agreement between the European Union, the European Community and the Swiss Confederation on the latter's association with the implementation, application and development of the Schengen acquis (Luxembourg, 26 October 2004; see EU Council

Finally, the differences in the procedures applicable under the CFSP and non-CFSP legal bases as regards agreements are not as profound as those between the procedures applicable to internal CFSP acts and non-CFSP acts and should be regarded as compatible.[45] In particular, a combination of voting by qualified majority and unanimity within the Council also occurs in cases where several non-CFSP legal bases apply for decisions relating to international agreements and some are subject to qualified majority while others are subject to unanimity. The CJEU has never cast doubt on the compatibility of this combination.[46] Likewise, differences in the role of the EP have not been held to be incompatible either in relation to international agreements with multiple legal bases.[47] By contrast, as regards internal acts, it is quite clear from

---

Doc. 13054/04 for the text; [2004] OJ L 368/26 for the EU signature decision and [2004] OJ L 370/78, for the EC signature decision, both providing for provisional application; [2008] OJ L 53/50 (corrig. [2008] OJ L 110/16) for the EU conclusion decision and [2008] OJ L 53/1 for the EC conclusion decision) and (ii) the Protocol between the European Union, the European Community, the Swiss Confederation and the Principality of Liechtenstein on the accession of the Principality of Liechtenstein to the Agreement between the European Union, the European Community and the Swiss Confederation on the Swiss Confederation's association with the implementation, application and development of the Schengen acquis (EC and EU signature decisions, in [2008] OJ respectively L 83/3 and L 83/5 (corrig. [2008] OJ L 110/16)). See also Gilles de Kerchove and Stephan Marquardt, 'Les accords internationaux conclus par l'Union européenne' (2004) 50 Annuaire français de droit international 820; Garbagnati Ketvel (n 43) 93–94 and Stephan Marquardt, 'La capacité de l'Union européenne de conclure des accords internationaux dans le domaine de la cooperation policière et judiciaire en matière pénale', in Gilles de Kerchove and Anne Weyembergh (eds.), *Securite et justice: enjeu de la politique extérieure de l'Union européenne* (Editions de l'ULB 2003) 189.

45 See also Van Elsuwege (n 22) 1393 and Piet Eeckhout, *EU External Relations Law* (OUP 2011, 2nd edn.) 184 (noting the possibility of recourse to two separate Council decisions on signature/conclusion if necessary).

46 The Court also accepted the combination of qualified majority and unanimity in the Council in Case C-166/07 *Parliament v Council* EU:C:2009:499, paras 66–69 (*International Fund for Ireland*) and in Joined Cases C-402/05 P and C-415/05 P *Yassin Abdullah Kadi and Al Barakaat International Foundation v Council and Commission* EU:C:2008:461, paras 212 and 235–236. See also the chapter by Marise Cremona in this book at 431 n 28 and accompanying text.

47 e.g., in Opinion 1/94 of 15 November 1994 (*Competence of the Community to conclude international agreements concerning services and the protection of intellectual property*), EU:C:1994:384, the Court held that the competence was mixed and that the Union competence was based not only on the common commercial policy under Article 113 TEC (as in force at the time). Following this opinion, no less than 11 substantive legal bases (Articles 43, 54, 57, 66, 75, 84(2), 99, 100, 100a, 113, and 235 TEC as in force at the time) were

the Court's case law that such procedures cannot be combined, in particular where that would combine the ordinary legislative procedure with CFSP decision-making.[48]

A second example of the combined use of the CSFP and a non-CSFP sectoral legal basis relates to the International Science and Technology Centre. The Agreement to continue this Centre was negotiated and signed under CSFP and Euratom legal bases, as well as a TFEU legal basis (at least for the signature): see Council Decision (EU) 2015/1989 of 26 October 2015 on the signing, on behalf of the European Union, of the Agreement continuing the International Science and Technology Center.[49] The substantive legal bases cited in this decision are Articles 31(1) and 37 TEU (i.e. CSFP) and Article 180 TFEU (i.e. research and technological development). The third recital clarifies that '[*t*]*he conclusion of the Agreement is subject to a separate procedure as regards*

included in Council Decision 94/800/EC of 22 December 1994 concerning the conclusion on behalf of the European Community, as regards matters within its competence, of the agreements reached in the Uruguay Round multilateral negotiations (1986–1994), OJ L 336, 23.12.1994, p. 1. Some of these required the assent of the Parliament (which is referred to in the decision), others only consultation and at least one (Article 113 TEC) neither assent nor consultation.

48 See especially Case C-130/10 *Parliament v Council* EU:C:2012:472, paras 44–45 and especially paras 47–49 ('while Article 75 TFEU provides for application of the ordinary legislative procedure, …, Article 215(2) TFEU, …, entails merely informing the Parliament. In addition, recourse to Article 215(2) TFEU, …, requires a previous decision in the sphere of the CFSP, …. As a general rule, adoption of such a decision calls for unanimous voting in the Council acting alone. … Differences of that kind are such as to render those procedures incompatible. … It follows from the foregoing that, even if the contested regulation does pursue several objectives at the same time or have several components indissociably linked, without one's being secondary to the other, the differences in the procedures applicable under Articles 75 TFEU and 215(2) TFEU mean that it is not possible for the two provisions to be cumulated, one with the other, in order to serve as a twofold legal basis for a measure such as the contested regulation'). Compare Eeckhout (n 45) 185–186.

49 [2015] OJ L 290/7. For the earlier steps in the procedure, see Joint Proposal for a Council Decision on the signature of the Agreement continuing the International Science and Technology Center between the European Union and EURATOM acting as one Party and Georgia, Japan, the Kingdom of Norway, the Kyrgyz Republic, the Republic of Armenia, the Republic of Kazakhstan, the Republic of Korea, the Republic of Tajikistan, and the United States of America, JOIN(2015) 29 final, also contained in Council doc. 11436/15 of 11 August 2015. This document proposed two parallel procedures: one for the signature of the Agreement under the TEU/TFEU legal base and a parallel procedure for the conclusion of the Agreement under the EURATOM Treaty, citing Articles 29 and 37 TEU and Article 218 TFEU as well as Article 101 of the EURATOM Treaty.

matters falling within the competence of Euratom'. Indeed, in parallel, the Council adopted Decision (EURATOM) 2015/1990 of 26 October 2015 approving the conclusion, by the European Commission, on behalf of the European Atomic Energy Community, of the Agreement continuing the International Science and Technology Center, citing Articles 4 and 101 of the Euratom Treaty.[50]

A third and most recent example concerns the Agreement establishing the EU-LAC International Foundation. The Council Decision on the signing of this agreement cites as legal bases Articles 37 TEU and Articles 209(2) and 212(1) TFEU.[51]

To my knowledge, to date these three cases remain the only examples of such a combined legal basis.

4 Recourse to the CFSP Legal Basis in Horizontal Agreements with Third States[52]

While the scarce recourse to agreements based on a combined CFSP and sectoral non-CFSP legal basis could be explained in part by the fact that it may often be possible to split such agreements and thereby avoid the complications of such a combined dual legal basis, it is, at first sight, more surprising that the CFSP legal basis has not been included very often in horizontal agreements with third countries, i.e. agreements covering a wide range of policy areas, including aspects of foreign policy and security.

In fact, before the Treaty of Lisbon, the consistent practice of the Council was that the foreign policy and external security issues were not included as competences exercised under the CFSP Treaty provisions but rather as part of Member States' competence. The same was true for the former third pillar. Hence, none of these agreements were concluded also by the Union (as opposed to the European Community/Communities).

A case which came close to including a CFSP legal basis in a horizontal agreement was a 2002 Agreement between the EU and Lebanon concerning Cooperation in the Fight against Terrorism.[53] It was closely connected to the

50 [2015] OJ L 290/8.

51 Council Decision (EU) 2016/1873 of 10 October 2016 on the signing, on behalf of the European Union, of the Agreement establishing the EU-LAC International Foundation [2016] OJ L 288/1.

52 This section draws on Gosalbo Bono and Naert (n 15).

53 Agreement in the Form of an Exchange of Letters between the European Union and the Republic of Lebanon concerning Cooperation in the Fight against Terrorism, Council

Euro-Mediterranean Agreement establishing an Association between the EC and its Member States, of the one part, and Lebanon, of the other.[54] Yet it does not constitute such a mixed agreement because it is formally separated from the latter. This practice was not followed in other cases.[55]

Initially, this general approach was maintained by the Council also after the Treaty of Lisbon.[56] In this respect, the Commission repeatedly proposed negotiating directives (and even negotiated agreement texts) for 'EU only' agreements, i.e. non-mixed agreements to which only the Union and not the Member States would be a party. However, this has been nearly systematically rejected by the Council, which has insisted on negotiating mixed agreements. In particular, Member States within the Council have repeatedly chosen not to exercise shared competences which had not already been exercised, have considered that some elements of envisaged agreements fell within exclusive Member State competence, and/or have chosen not to exercise the Union's CFSP competence. Indeed, while the Treaty of Lisbon's expansion of EU competences (albeit at the same time within very explicit limits) has reduced the number of cases in which mixed agreements are possible[57] or

---

doc. 7494/02 of 17 April 2002 (as corrected by Council doc. 10574/02 of 9 July 2002) (this agreement does not seem to have been published in the OJ; it entered into force on the same day as the Association Agreement with Lebanon). For other examples of early consideration of cross-pillar mixity which did not bear fruit, see Hoffmeister (n 43) 251–253.

54 The text of the agreement *inter alia* states that 'The European Union and Lebanon reaffirm the importance of the fight against terrorism and, *in the context of their Association Agreement*, and in accordance with international conventions, relevant UN resolutions and with their respective legislation and regulations, agree to cooperate in the prevention and suppression of acts of terrorism' (emphasis added).

55 See Thym (n 4) 898–899.

56 See e.g. the Council Decision 2012/272/EU of 14 May 2012 on the signing, on behalf of the Union, of the Framework Agreement on Partnership and Cooperation between the European Union and its Member States, of the one part, and the Republic of the Philippines, of the other part [2012] OJ L 134/3 (this decision was annulled in Case C-377/12 *Commission v Council* EU:C:2014:1903, on grounds not affecting this point). Decision 2012/272/EU did not include a CFSP legal basis although the agreement (for the text, see Council doc. 15616/10 of 21 January 2011) contains provisions on foreign policy and security cooperation. The situation was similar for the agreement with Mongolia, see Council Decision 2012/273/EU of 14 May 2012 on the signing, on behalf of the Union, of the Framework Agreement on Partnership and Cooperation between the European Union and its Member States, of the one part, and Mongolia, of the other part [2012] OJ L 134/4.

57 Since there will be more cases where matters fall entirely within exclusive Union competence. See e.g. Opinion 1/13 (*Convention on the civil aspects of international child abduction*) EU:C:2014:2303 and Case C-114/12 *Commission v Council* EU:C:2014:2151.

necessary,[58] there is nothing in that Treaty which precludes the continued conclusion of mixed agreements when both Union and Member State competences are involved.[59]

Nevertheless, on several occasions the Council has designated the High Representative as the negotiator for matters falling within the CFSP in the Council decision authorising the opening of negotiations for matters within *Union* competence.[60] In fact, this was not entirely new, and pre-Lisbon negotiating mandates for horizontal mixed agreements had sometimes designated the Presidency, assisted by the Secretary General of the Council / High Representative for the CFSP, to negotiate in respect of matters coming within Titles V and VI of the TEU.[61]

58 In cases where an agreement could be fully covered by Union competence but that competence is in part non-exercised shared competence and/or CFSP, the choice can be made to exercise this competence or not. See in this respect also Article 2(2) TFEU, Protocol 25 on the exercise of shared competence and Declaration No. 18 relating to the delimitation of competences.

59 See also Dashwood (n 37) 351 ('There is … nothing in the Treaty of Lisbon that can be seen as deliberately designed either to facilitate or to impede recourse to mixity') and Alan Rosas, 'The Future of Mixity', in Alan Dashwood, 'Mixity in the Era of the Treaty of Lisbon', in Hillion and Koutrakos (eds) (n 30) 367 ('Mixity is here to stay').

60 See e.g. Council Decision authorising the opening of negotiations with the Republic of Kazakhstan for an enhanced Partnership and Cooperation Agreement between the European Union and its Member States, of the one part, and the Republic of Kazakhstan, of the other part (Council doc. 8282/11 of 13 April 2011), art 2(2) ('The High Representative shall negotiate, in relation to matters within the common foreign and security policy as set out in the negotiating directives, the provisions of the Agreement concerning the general principles and essential elements of the Agreement and the provisions relating to political dialogue and cooperation'). This was the case even though the Council and the Member States envisaged a mixed agreement, see the accompanying Decision of the representatives of the governments of Member States, meeting within the Council, authorising the European Commission to negotiate, on behalf of the Member States, the provisions of an enhanced Partnership and Cooperation Agreement between the European Union and its Member States, of the one part, and the Republic of Kazakhstan, of the other part, that fall within the competences of the Member States (Council doc. 8283/11 of 13 April 2011). This approach of dual decisions authorising the opening of negotiations with the EU decision covering CFSP matters was also adopted *inter alia* in relation to the negotiations for horizontal agreements with Georgia, Armenia and Azerbaijan by the Council on 10 May 2010 (see e.g. Council doc. 9559/10 of, 8) and with Australia (for the latter, see Council doc. 14657/11 of 4 October 2011).

61 See e.g. the decision on Council Negotiating Directives for a new Agreement to provide a comprehensive framework for EU/Russia relations and related note to the Council (partially declassified in Council doc. 8829/08 EXT 2 of 22 December 2009), in which the

However, at the stages of signature and conclusion, the Council has generally opted for not accepting that the CFSP competence should be exercised by the Union, leaving it to be exercised by the Member States as part of national competences in mixed agreements. Yet there are some developments in this respect.

First, the fairly recent decisions on the signature and provisional application of the (mixed) association agreements with Ukraine,[62] Georgia[63] and Moldova[64] include a CFSP legal basis. This development was prompted by a strong political desire for a swift provisional application of these agreements not only in the field of trade (and other non-CFSP Union policies), but also in the area of political and foreign policy cooperation. This was especially the case for the association agreement with Ukraine. This swift provisional

---

Council authorised 'the Commission to negotiate a new EU-Russia Agreement to replace the Partnership and Cooperation Agreement; for matters coming within Titles V and VI of the EU Treaty (CFSP and police and judicial cooperation in criminal matters), the negotiations shall be conducted with the Presidency, assisted by the SG/HR, in full respect of their respective responsibilities set out in the relevant treaty provisions'. On the negotiator and negotiating directives pre-Lisbon, see also Jenő Czuczai, 'Mixity in Practice: Some Problems and Their (Real or Possible) Solutions', in Hillion and Koutrakos (eds.) (n 30) 234–238.

62 Council Decision 2014/295/EU of 17 March 2014 on the signing, on behalf of the European Union, and provisional application of the Association Agreement between the European Union and the European Atomic Energy Community and their Member States, of the one part, and Ukraine, of the other part, as regards the Preamble, Article 1, and Titles I, II and VII thereof [2014] OJ L 161/1 (citing articles 31(1) and 37 TEU as substantive legal bases, in addition to art 217 TFEU; furthermore, art 4 of Decision 2014/295/EU identifies the provisions to be provisionally applied and specifies that they are to be provisionally applied 'only to the extent that they cover matters falling within the Union's competence, including matters falling within the Union's competence to define and implement a common foreign and security policy'). For the text of the Agreement between the European Union and its Member States, of the one part, and Ukraine, of the other part, see ibid, p. 3.

63 Council Decision 2014/494/EU of 16 June 2014 on the signing, on behalf of the European Union, and provisional application of the Association Agreement between the European Union and the European Atomic Energy Community and their Member States, of the one part, and Georgia, of the other part [2014] OJ L 261/1 (citing art 37 TEU among the legal bases).

64 Council Decision 2014/492/EU of 16 June 2014 on the signing, on behalf of the European Union, and provisional application of the Association Agreement between the European Union and the European Atomic Energy Community and their Member States, of the one part, and the Republic of Moldova, of the other part [2014] OJ L 260/1 (citing art 37 TEU among the legal bases).

application was not considered practicable if the foreign policy provisions were to be exercised as part of Member State competence, since the domestic law of several Member States does not allow for provisional application and since it often takes several years before all Member States have concluded their ratification procedures for such agreements. This approach has also been followed in other cases.[65]

However, it is not envisaged that the CFSP legal basis will be included in the EU decision to conclude the agreement with Ukraine.[66] Thus there still appears to be a reluctance to include this legal basis when it comes to the conclusion of horizontal agreements.

Secondly, the position is different in relation to the stabilisation and association agreement with Kosovo. In this case, in order to avoid the difficulties resulting from the non-recognition of Kosovo as a State by some Member States, the agreement had to be a 'Union only' agreement. It was negotiated,[67] signed[68] and concluded[69] as such, with a CFSP legal basis.

---

65 See e.g. Council Decision of 26 October 2015 on the signing, on behalf of the European Union, and provisional application of the Enhanced Partnership and Cooperation Agreement between the European Union and its Member States, of the one part, and the Republic of Kazakhstan, of the other part, EU Council doc. 9445/15 (combining art 37 TEU with several TFEU legal bases).

66 See the draft Council Decision on the conclusion, on behalf of the European Union, of the Association Agreement between the European Union and the European Atomic Energy Community and their Member States, of the one part, and Ukraine, of the other part, with the exception of the provisions relating to the treatment of third-country nationals legally employed as workers in the territory of the other party (Council doc. 13613/3/13 of 20 June 2014), which contains no reference to art 37 TEU. Interestingly, Council Decision (EU) 2015/1420 of 16 March 2015 on the position to be taken on behalf of the European Union within the Association Council established by the Association Agreement between the European Union and the European Atomic Energy Community and their Member States, of the one part, and Ukraine, of the other part, with regard to the adoption of a Recommendation on the implementation of the EU-Ukraine Association Agenda [2015] OJ L 221/4, is based only on art 217 TFEU as substantive legal basis without mention of a CFSP legal basis. Yet the text of the draft Association Agenda as annexed to the Joint Proposal (contained in Council doc. 5910/15 ADD 1) includes a significant section on foreign and security policy (see point III.2.3).

67 See Commission, 'EU starts the Stabilisation and Association Agreement Negotiations with Kosovo', MEMO/13/938 of 28 October 2013, <http://europa.eu/rapid/press-release_MEMO-13-938_en.htm> (accessed on 12 December 2016) (inter alia stating that '... the ... Agreement will be concluded in the form of an EU-only agreement. The negotiations will be led by the Commission and the provisions on the political dialogue and the [CFSP] will be negotiated by the High Representative ...'). For the Commission's

The particular case of association agreements raises a further question in relation to the use of the CFSP legal basis.[70] In particular, given that the legal basis of Article 217 TFEU for such agreements is in principle of a horizontal nature, and has always been used without adding any sectoral legal basis, the question was whether it was necessary to add the CFSP legal basis. The specific nature of this policy justifies that the CFSP legal basis is added. Indeed, the fourth recital of the decision on the signing of the agreement with Kosovo explains that:

> The Agreement provides for the establishment of an association between the Union and Kosovo involving reciprocal rights and obligations, common actions and special procedure. It also contains provisions falling within the scope of Chapter 2 of Title v of the [TEU] concerning the Common Foreign and Security Policy of the Union. The decision to sign the Agreement should therefore be based on the legal basis providing for the establishment of an association allowing the Union to enter into commitments in all areas covered by the Treaties and on the legal basis for agreements in areas covered by Chapter 2 of Title V of the TEU.

---

recommendation, see doc. COM(2013) 200 final of 22 April 2013, <http://ec.europa.eu/enlargement/pdf/key_documents/2013/ks_recommendation_2013_en.pdf> (accessed on 12 December 2016) (the Commission's practice is to not include substantive legal bases in proposals for decisions authorising the opening of negotiations but the proposal includes the High Representative in the negotiating team and the explanatory memorandum states that 'the negotiations are likely to relate to both non-CFSP and CFSP matters' (p. 3)).

68 See Council Decision (EU) 2015/1988 of 22 October 2015 on the signing, on behalf of the Union, of the Stabilisation and Association Agreement between the European Union and the European Atomic Energy Community, of the one part, and Kosovo (*), of the other part ((*)This designation is without prejudice to positions on status, and is in line with UNSCR 1244/1999 and the ICJ Opinion on the Kosovo declaration of independence) [2015] OJ L 290/4 (including art 37 TEU among the legal bases).

69 Council Decision (EU) 2016/342 of 12 February 2016 on the conclusion, on behalf of the Union, of the Stabilisation and Association Agreement between the European Union and the European Atomic Energy Community, of the one part, and Kosovo*, of the other part (* This designation is without prejudice to positions on status, and is in line with UNSCR 1244/1999 and the ICJ Opinion on the Kosovo declaration of independence) [2016] OJ L 71/1 (including art 37 TEU and art 217 TFEU as the substantive legal bases).

70 I will not address the question of the different prerogatives of the European Parliament in relation to agreements concluded on the basis of art 37 TEU and art 217 TFEU here, as the impact of different roles of the Parliament is addressed above in n 46 and accompanying text.

This is repeated in the fourth recital of the decision on the conclusion of the agreement.

The persistent preference of (most) Member States for exercising the foreign and security policy provisions in horizontal agreements as Member State competence rather than Union competence under the CFSP is difficult to explain on legal grounds, taking into account the specific nature of the CFSP.[71] In particular, the decision-making rules in the CFSP ensure control by the Member States through unanimous decision-making in the Council.[72] Moreover, there is no 'occupied territory' in the field of the CFSP and when the CFSP is exercised, this does not in any way prevent Member States from continuing to exercise their foreign policies.[73] In this respect CFSP competence is similar to

71 On the distinct nature of the CFSP, see e.g. Panos Koutrakos, *EU International Relations Law* (Hart 2015, 2nd ed.) 416–421; Eeckhout (n 45) 167 and 171 and Geert De Baere, *Constitutional Principles of EU External Relations* (Oxford University Press 2008) 110–112.

72 See e.g. the UK's review of the balance of competences in this respect: UK Government, *Review of the Balance of Competences between the United Kingdom and the European Union. Foreign Policy*, 22 July 2013, <https://www.gov.uk/government/consultations/foreign-policy-report-review-of-the-balance-of-competences> (accessed on 12 December 2016). The executive summary says on p. 5 that 'The majority of the evidence affirmed that, in CFSP ..., the balance of competence lies squarely with the Member States. All significant decisions are made by unanimity, so each Member State has a power of veto, ...' and point 6.4 of the conclusions on p. 88 states that 'The majority of our evidence judged that Member States were firmly in charge of the [CFSP] ..., and could act unilaterally when they judged fit, ...'. See also Jan Wouters and Thomas Ramopoulos, *Revisiting the Lisbon Treaty's Constitutional Design of EU External Relations* (Leuven Centre for Global Governance Studies Working Paper No. 119, September 2013), <http://www.fp7-frame.eu/wp-content/materiale/w-papers/WP119-Wouters-Ramopoulos.pdf> (accessed on 12 December 2016), 9–10. The limited exceptions to unanimity voting in CFSP matters (see Article 31(2) TEU) have so far never been applied in practice.

73 See Declarations Nos 13 and 14 concerning the CFSP. The former inter alia states that:

'the provisions in the [TEU] covering the [CFSP], including the creation of the office of High Representative ... and the establishment of an External Action Service, do not affect the responsibilities of the Member States, as they currently exist, for the formulation and conduct of their foreign policy nor of their national representation in third countries and international organisations.'

The latter inter alia provides that:

'In addition to the specific rules and procedures referred to in paragraph 1 of Article 24 of the [TEU], ... the provisions covering the [CFSP] including in relation to the High Representative ... and the External Action Service will not affect the existing legal basis, responsibilities, and powers of each Member State in relation to the formulation and conduct of its foreign policy, its national diplomatic service, relations with third countries

the so-called 'parallel' Union competences[74] in the areas of research, technological development and space as well as development cooperation and humanitarian aid, for which 'the exercise of that competence shall not result in Member States being prevented from exercising theirs' (Article 4(3) and (4) TFEU).

Moreover, in practice, the implementation of the foreign policy parts of such agreements essentially concerns matters on which there is a Union CFSP position or action. Thus, it seems that the reluctance of the Member States to agree to the exercise by the EU of its CFSP competence in horizontal international agreements is mainly due to a preference by the Member States to emphasise their own presence in the framework of such agreements. It may also be one of the ways in which some Member States try to help ensure that horizontal agreements remain mixed.

The reluctance of the Council and the Member States to conclude Union only horizontal agreements has not discouraged the Commission and the High Representative from maintaining their efforts to strive towards such agreements.[75] It remains to be seen whether they will succeed in these efforts, including in the wake of the negative outcome of the Dutch referendum on the Association Agreement with Ukraine.[76] Yet even where they do not and such

---

and participation in international organisations, including a Member State's membership of the Security Council of the United Nations.'

74 See also Ramses Wessel, 'The EU As a Party to International Agreements: Shared Competences, Mixed Responsibilities' in Alan Dashwood and Marc Maresceau (eds), *Law and Practice of EU External Relations: Salient Features of a Changing Landscape* (Cambridge, Cambridge University Press, 2011) 157.

75 For recent examples, see JOIN(2015) 35 final, Joint Proposal for a Council Decision on the signing, on behalf of the European Union, of the Cooperation Agreement on Partnership and Development between the European Union and the Islamic Republic of Afghanistan, 17 December 2015; and JOIN(2016) 37 final, Joint Proposal for a Council Decision on the signing, on behalf of the European Union, of the Framework Agreement on Partnership and Cooperation between the European Union and the Government of Malaysia, 4 August 2016 (Council doc. 11644/16 of 5 August 2016).

76 On 6 April 2016, a majority of those who voted in this referendum (the level of participation was 32 %) voted against the agreement (61 %). It is first and foremost for the Dutch Government to decide what this will mean for its ratification of the agreement. Beyond that, this precedent comes on top of the often long periods which some Member States take to ratify horizontal mixed agreements. This could give rise to some reflection on whether the perceived advantages of mixity still outweigh its disadvantages. In that context, somewhat less expansive but Union only horizontal agreements could have some appeal.

agreements remain mixed, the CFSP legal basis could be included.[77] In fact, there are some very recent indications that this might happen in at least some cases, notably for Kazakhstan.[78]

5 Some General and Procedural Aspects of Combining CFSP and Non-CFSP Legal Bases for Agreements

When a CFSP legal basis and a non-CFSP legal basis are combined for concluding an international agreement, a number of questions arise. I will address some of these here, but this is not an exhaustive list of all the issues that may arise in this respect.

First, Article 218(3) TFEU mentions a recommendation from '[t]he Commission, or the High Representative [...] where the agreement envisaged relates exclusively or principally to the [CFSP],...'. This seems to suggest that recommendations can only be submitted by either the Commission or the High Representative but not by both together.[79] Yet such an interpretation would not be consistent with the respective prerogatives of both actors in the case of an agreement covering CFSP and non-CFSP aspects where neither is predominant. It is therefore not surprising that this provision has been interpreted and applied as permitting joint recommendations by the High Representative

77 e.g. JOIN(2016) 26 final, Joint Proposal for a Council Decision on the conclusion of the Enhanced Partnership and Cooperation Agreement between the European Union and its Member States, of the one part, and the Republic of Kazakhstan, of the other part, 7 June 2016 (Council doc. 10023/16 of 8 June 2016),which includes art 37 TEU among the legal bases. See also next note.

78 On 14–15 November 2016, the Council agreed in the principle on the (conclusion of the) Enhanced Partnership and Cooperation Agreement between the EU and Kazakhstan and requested the consent of the European Parliament for this (Council doc. 14418/16 of 14 November 2016, 11). The text of the draft Council Decision on the conclusion, on behalf of the Union, of the Enhanced Partnership and Cooperation Agreement between the European Union and its Member States, of the one part, and the Republic of Kazakhstan, of the other part, i.e. for a mixed agreement, does include the CFSP legal basis (Council doc. 12409/16 of 25 October 2016).

79 In this sense: Koutrakos (n 71) 138–140 and Dashwood(n 37) 354–355. See also art 218(9) TFEU in relation to proposals for a decision suspending application of an agreement and establishing the positions to be adopted on the Union's behalf in a body set up by an agreement, when that body is called upon to adopt acts having legal effects.

and the Commission.[80] Similarly, proposals for decisions on signature and conclusion have been presented by the Commission and the High Representative where the Council appointed both as negotiators.[81] Joint proposals have also been made in relation to Union positions in international bodies under Article 218(9) TFEU.[82]

Secondly, the designation of the negotiator or head of the negotiating team has also led to some discussion.[83] In addition to the question of mixity and the possible role of the Member State exercising the rotating Presidency of the Council in relation to negotiations for matters falling within Member State competences,[84] questions arise as to the respective roles of the Commission and High Representative/European External Action Service (EEAS). Article 218(3) TFEU provides for '…, depending on the subject of the agreement envisaged, nominating the Union negotiator or the head of the Union's negotiating team'. In cases where the Council has designated both the Commission and the High Representative, the Council has appointed one of them as head of the Union's negotiating team[85] and has left to the High Representative (and through her the EEAS) and the Commission the freedom to arrange their cooperation and coordination throughout the process of negotiation. In practice, in some cases, the Commission appears to have given the lead to the EEAS even where the Commission has been designated as head of the negotiating team,

80 e.g. Joint Recommendation for a Council Decision authorising the opening of negotiations for a Framework Agreement between the European Union and Japan. See also the chapter by Stephan Marquardt in this book.

81 See the example of the TAC cited above (the High Representative succeeded the Presidency which had been appointed as negotiator for the CFSP elements pre-Lisbon) and the examples above in n 76 and 77.

82 e.g. JOIN(2015) 4 final, Joint Proposal for a Council Decision on the Union position within the Association Council established by the Association Agreement between the European Union, the European Atomic Energy Community and its Member States, of the one part and Ukraine, of the other part with regard to the adoption of a Recommendation on the implementation of the EU-Ukraine Association Agenda, 18.2.2015.

83 Compare the analysis of Gatti and Manzini (n 39), 1703–1734, especially 1707–1710 and 1720–1723; Eeckhout (n 45), 196–197 and Koutrakos (n 71), 140–142. See also the chapter by Stephan Marquardt in this book.

84 See e.g. the Council decision on the negotiations with Kazakhstan (n 60) art 1(2): 'A representative of the Presidency of the Council will accompany the Commission in the negotiations for matters falling within the competences of the Member States' (adding that this is 'without prejudice to future decisions of the Member States relating to the designation of their representative on matters falling within their competences' (art 1(3)).

85 See e.g. the Council decision on the negotiations with Kazakhstan (n 60) art 2(1).

at least in terms of the actual negotiations.[86] This can probably be explained by the fact that the Commission no longer has geographical desks (these were all transferred to the EEAS upon the establishment of the latter and the Commission has designated the most relevant thematic Directorate General as its lead service for each geographical area).

Thirdly, the determination of which legal bases are required for the negotiation, signature and conclusion of an international agreement can be a difficult exercise.[87] This is by no means limited to agreements that have a CFSP legal basis. Nor is it a new issue. However, some of the amendments introduced by the Treaty of Lisbon have given rise to additional difficulties.[88]

In this respect, the Court has indicated that the centre of gravity test which it had already applied to sectoral agreements (e.g. in the choice between environment and trade legal bases[89]) also applies to horizontal international agreements. This follows in particular from its judgment of 11 June 2014 in the *Philippines* case.[90] In this judgment the Court rejected the addition of specific sectoral legal bases to the development – which it apparently considers to be of a more general nature – and trade legal bases in the Framework Agreement on Partnership and Cooperation with the Philippines, which is a horizontal agreement.

In this recent case law, the Court thereby appears to set aside its previous case law, in which the Court upheld that the conclusion of horizontal international agreements required the insertion of as many legal bases as competences were exercised.[91] However, the Court does not seem to apply its new approach consistently. In particular, in its judgment of 18 December 2014 in Case C-81/13, *United Kingdom v Council*, relating to the decision on the position

---

86 Compare the case study by Hrant Kostanyan in 'Examining the Discretion of the EEAS: What Power to Act in the EU-Moldova Association Agreement?' (2014) EUR FOREIGN AFFAIRS REV 373, 373–392.

87 See e.g. Geert De Baere, 'From "Don't Mention the Titanium Dioxide Judgment" to "I Mentioned it Once, But I Think I Got Away with It All Right": Reflections on the Choice of Legal Basis in EU External Relations after the Legal Basis for Restrictive Measures Judgment' (2012–2013) CAMBRIDGE Y EUR LEGAL STUDIES 537; Marcus Klamert, 'Conflicts of Legal Basis: No Legality and No Basis but a Bright Future under the Lisbon Treaty?' (2010) 35 EL REV 497 and Ott (n 22) 739–752.

88 This section draws on Gosalbo and Naert (n 15).

89 See e.g. *Opinion 2/00* of 6 December 2001 (Cartagena Protocol) EU:C:2001:664, paras 23 and 42. For an example of a dual legal basis, see e.g. Case C-94/03 *Commission v Council* EU:C:2006:2 (Rotterdam Convention).

90 Case C-377/12 *Commission v Council* EU:C:2014:1903.

91 See notably Opinion 1/94, discussed above n 47.

on the coordination of social security systems to be taken by the EU within the Association Council with Turkey, the Court held that the correct legal bases would have been a combination of Article 217 TFEU (the general legal basis for association agreements) and Article 48 TFEU (the specific legal basis for social security measures necessary to provide freedom of movement for workers).[92] As a result, choosing the correct legal basis or bases for international agreements and decisions on EU positions remains a significant challenge.[93]

The Court has also made it clear that the special position of some Member States under Protocols 21 and 22 does not affect at all its traditional case law (including the centre of gravity) on the choice of legal bases.[94] The same appears to apply to the choice of legal bases when a CFSP legal basis is involved together with non-CFSP legal bases.[95]

Fourthly, the combination of legal bases also raises questions concerning the decision-making process. Assuming that the decision-making procedures for CFSP and non-CFSP legal bases are compatible as regards agreements (see above), the question nevertheless arises whether the differences in procedure should be reflected in separate decisions on the signing and conclusion of agreements.

The Council has not adopted separate decisions under the CFSP legal basis, nor has this been proposed by the High Representative and Commission.

---

92 EU:C:2014:2449. See especially paras 62 ('the Council is entitled, on the basis of Article 217 TFEU, to adopt a measure in the framework of an association agreement on condition that that measure relates to a specific area of EU competence and is also founded ... on the legal basis corresponding, in the light in particular of its aim and content, to that area') and 63. See also the chapter by Ivan Smyth in this book.

93 Furthermore, in recent case law the Court seems to give more weight to the objective of a measure than to its content: see e.g. Case C-43/12 *Commission v Parliament and Council* EU:C:2014:298.

94 See notably Case C-656/11 *United Kingdom v Council* EU:C:2014:97, para 49 ('Nor is the legality of the choice of the legal basis for a European Union measure affected by the consequence that the choice may have as regards whether Protocol No 21, and Protocol No 22 on the position of Denmark ..., apply') and Case C-81/13 *United Kingdom v Council* EU:C:2014:2449, para 37 ('Protocol No 21 is not capable of having any effect whatsoever on the question of the correct legal basis') as well as Case C-377/12 *Commission v Council* (*Philippines case*) EU:C:2014:1903, paras 34–60, especially paras 57–60. For a further case on the delimitation between the FSJ and other Union policies, see Case C-431/11 *United Kingdom v Council* EU:C:2013:589, paras 45–68. See also the chapter by Ivan Smyth in this book.

95 Case C-658/11 *Parliament v Council* EU:C:2014:2025, para 45, discussed in Section 2.2 above.

However, there could be cases where this might have to be considered.[96] In particular, under the CFSP, when abstaining in a vote, a Member State may make a formal declaration and in that case it is not obliged to apply that decision but it has to accept that the decision commits the Union and it has to refrain from any action likely to conflict with or impede Union action based on that decision (Article 31(1), second subparagraph, TEU[97]). If this possibility applies also to decisions relating to agreements and were to be used,[98] a separate decision might be necessary.[99]

By contrast, where an AFSJ legal basis is required in combination with a non-AFSJ legal basis for Council decisions on the signing or conclusion of an agreement, the Council now generally splits such decisions.[100] The reason for this is that the Council is composed differently under the respective legal bases since Denmark and, depending on the case, the UK and Ireland, do not take part in the adoption of AFSJ measures. However, this is a fairly recent development and the past practice of the Council has not been uniform in this respect.[101]

---

96 Wessel (n 30) 51–52, even seems to regard two separate decisions as the correct way to proceed more generally for a combined CFSP and non-CFSP agreement.

97 This is usually referred to by the doctrine as 'constructive abstention' and sometimes (also) as 'qualified abstention'. See e.g. Marise Cremona, 'Enhanced Cooperation and the European Foreign and Security and Defence Policy' in José Maria Beneyto (ed.), *Unity and Flexibility in the Future of the European Union: the Challenge of Enhanced Cooperation* (CEU Ediciones 2009) (available at <http://www.ceuediciones.es/documents/ebookceuediciones1.pdf> (accessed on 12 December 2016)) 75, 87. The latter description best captures its less constructive nature in comparison with the normal abstention.

98 To my knowledge, it has only been used once in relation to an 'internal' CFSP decision.

99 This situation might also need to be reflected in the agreement concerned – compare the clauses reflecting the UK, Irish and Danish position in agreements in the AFSJ.

100 The practice on splitting has also arisen in other contexts, e.g. between the Community/Union and Euratom. To my knowledge, practice in that respect has not been consistent. See also the chapter by Ivan Smyth.

101 For an example of the UK position, see the Statement by the UK upon the adoption of Council Decision 2014/164/EU of 11 February 2014 on the conclusion, on behalf of the European Union, of the Protocol against the Illicit Manufacturing of and Trafficking in Firearms, Their Parts and Components and Ammunition, supplementing the United Nations Convention against Transnational Organized Crime [2014] OJ L 89/7, reproduced in Council doc. 10191/1/14 REV 1, p. 11: 'the UK considers that the Council Decision should have been split into two, to cover both the non-Title V, and the Title V, aspects of the Firearms Protocol'. Compare the Commission's statement reproduced in Council doc. 13375/13, p. 6: 'insofar as the splitting of the Decision intends to reflect the different voting requirements pursuant to the application of Protocol 21, the Commission notes that a Decision authorising negotiation of an international agreement is not a 'measure' in the sense of that Protocol. Accordingly, it is not appropriate to split the Decision authorising negotiations'.

In a number of cases such decisions have been 'split',[102] whereas in other cases they have not.[103]

102 e.g. in relation to the conclusion of the 2002 Protocol to the Athens Convention relating to the Carriage of Passengers and their Luggage by Sea (see Council Decisions 2012/22/EU and 2012/23/EU of 12 December 2011 concerning the accession of the European Union to the Protocol of 2002 to the Athens Convention relating to the Carriage of Passengers and their Luggage by Sea, 1974, respectively with the exception of Articles 10 and 11 thereof and as regards Articles 10 and 11 thereof [2012] OJ L 8, respectively 1 and 13) and of the Association Agreement with Ukraine (see the decisions cited *supra* n 62 and 66 as well as Council Decision 2014/669/EU of 23 June 2014 on the signing, on behalf of the European Union, of the Association Agreement between the European Union and the European Atomic Energy Community and their Member States, of the one part, and Ukraine, of the other part, as regards the provisions relating to the treatment of third-country nationals legally employed as workers in the territory of the other party [2014] OJ L 278/6 (based on art 79(2)(b) TFEU) and draft Council Decision on the conclusion, on behalf of the European Union, of the Association Agreement between the European Union and the European Atomic Energy Community and their Member States, of the one part, and Ukraine, of the other part, as regards provisions relating to the treatment of third-country nationals legally employed as workers in the territory of the other party, EU Council doc. 14011/3/15 of 20 June 2015 (ibid)). For a pre-Lisbon example of splitting, see, e.g. Council Decision 2006/616/EC of 24 July 2006 on the conclusion, on behalf of the European Community, of the Protocol Against the Smuggling of Migrants by Land, Sea and Air, supplementing the United Nations Convention Against Transnational Organised Crime concerning the provisions of the Protocol, in so far as the provisions of this Protocol fall within the scope of Articles 179 and 181a of the Treaty establishing the European Community and Council Decision 2006/617/EC of 24 July 2006 on the conclusion, on behalf of the European Community, of the Protocol Against the Smuggling of Migrants by Land, Sea and Air, supplementing the United Nations Convention Against Transnational Organised Crime concerning the provisions of the Protocol, in so far as the provisions of the Protocol fall within the scope of Part III, Title IV of the Treaty establishing the European Community [2006] OJ L 262, respectively 24 and 34, as well as two similar decisions concerning the Protocol to Prevent, Suppress and Punish Trafficking in Persons, Especially Women And Children, supplementing that same UN Convention (ibid, 44 and 51 respectively).

103 e.g. the decision on the signing of the Framework Agreement on Partnership and Cooperation with the Philippines included an AFSJ legal basis together with other legal bases (but the Court rejected the addition of the FSJ and other sectoral legal bases, holding that only the development and trade legal bases were correct; see *supra* n 90 for the judgment in that case). See also Council Decision 2012/418/EU of 21 December 2011 on the signing, on behalf of the European Union, and provisional application of certain provisions of the Partnership and Cooperation Agreement between the European Union and its Member States, of the one part, and the Republic of Iraq, of the other part [2012] OJ L 204/18.

6 Some Final Remarks

While there is ample practice of agreements concluded only under a substantive CFSP legal basis, there are rather few cases so far in which international agreements have been concluded under both a CFSP and one or more non-CFSP legal bases.

While that combination of legal bases poses a number of questions and challenges, it is possible, as increasingly frequent recent practice has shown.

The scarce recourse to such combined legal bases is perhaps not so surprising as regards the combination of TFEU sectoral legal bases with a CFSP legal basis, as it may be less common for these two policy fields to be combined. Nevertheless, one could expect it to occur more frequently in some areas, such as development and security, given the recognised nexus between both policies.

The very limited practice is more surprising in relation to horizontal agreements, which almost invariably contain a significant section on foreign policy and security. As long as these agreements are mixed, Member States and the Council appear to be very reluctant to agree to conclude such agreements under a CFSP legal basis. Their willingness to include the CFSP legal basis in decisions authorising the opening of negotiations and on the signing and provisional application of agreements nevertheless appears to be a step in an evolution towards accepting the CFSP legal basis also for the conclusion and the latest developments indicate that this may now be accepted in at least some cases. The latter is in any event unavoidable for any 'Union only' horizontal agreements.

CHAPTER 19

EU Treaty-Making after the Lisbon Treaty – A Test Case for Mutual Sincere Cooperation?

Marise Cremona

1 Introduction

This contribution on mutual sincere cooperation between the institutions is offered in appreciation and friendship to Ricardo Gosalbo Bono who as a Director in the Council Legal Service epitomised the virtues of cooperation, respect and courtesy. The fact that many of the cases discussed here involve inter-institutional disputes is not intended as an invitation to think in terms of institutional winners or losers. Nor are such disagreements incompatible with the duty of mutual sincere cooperation. On the contrary, institutional disagreements can be valuable opportunities to debate and clarify their respective roles in the EU's constitutional structure, and nowhere perhaps is this more apparent than in the field of external relations.

The Lisbon Treaty introduces for the first time an explicit reference to the duty of sincere cooperation applied to the institutions. It is included in Article 13(2) TEU:

> Each institution shall act within the limits of the powers conferred on it in the Treaties, and in conformity with the procedures, conditions and objectives set out in them. The institutions shall practice mutual sincere cooperation.

The Court of Justice of the European Union (CJEU) had already interpreted the general duty of sincere cooperation (which now appears in Article 4(3) TEU) as applying to the institutions as well as the Member States. In a case involving the need for the Parliament to give its opinion under the former consultation procedure, the Court said that 'inter-institutional dialogue, on which the consultation procedure in particular is based, is subject to the same mutual duties of sincere cooperation as those which govern relations between Member States and the Community institutions (…)'.[1]

1 Case C-65/93 *European Parliament v Council* EU:C:1995:91, para 23.

 DOI 10.1163/9789004347175_020

And in this case, although the essential procedural requirement of Parliamentary consultation was not complied with, this was the result of 'the Parliament's failure to discharge its obligation to cooperate sincerely with the Council' and did not justify annulment of the act.[2] Thus a failure to observe the duty of cooperation had a substantive legal effect. In Article 13(2) TEU, also, mutual sincere cooperation is presented as an obligation.

Although the 'mutual duty of sincere cooperation' between institutions has been recognised for some time, its explicit inclusion in the Treaties, together with some changes to the institutional participation in decision-making introduced by the Lisbon Treaty, has led to an increased reliance on the principle. It is increasingly referred to in inter-institutional litigation, and especially in cases concerning the exercise of external powers. The CJEU is starting to give some substance to the principle, as it has done over many years in dealing with Member State-EU relations. This seems a good moment, therefore, to consider the nature of the duty of mutual sincere cooperation as expressed in Article 13(2), and how it relates to other principles which govern the structure of EU external relations, such as the principles of conferral and institutional balance. The focus will be mainly, though not exclusively, on treaty-making – in other words the operation of the principle of mutual sincere cooperation in the context of Article 218 TFEU. This provision has not only acquired considerable detail, and additional length, over the years. It now brings together all the procedural rules governing the different stages of treaty-making:

> Article 218 TFEU constitutes, as regards the conclusion of international treaties, an autonomous and general provision of constitutional scope, in that it confers specific powers on the EU institutions. With a view to establishing a balance between those institutions, it provides, in particular, that agreements between the European Union and one or more third States are to be negotiated by the Commission, in compliance with the negotiating directives drawn up by the Council, and then concluded by the Council, either after obtaining the consent of the European Parliament or after consulting it.[3]

As Alan Dashwood has said, 'The special constitutional significance of Article 218 TFEU lies in the fact that international agreements provide one of the

2 Ibid, para 28.

3 Case C-425/13 *Commission v Council* EU:C:2015:483, para 62.

sources of the EU's positive law'.[4] Article 218 TFEU articulates the roles and the powers of the different actors involved in treaty negotiation and conclusion and in the ongoing management of treaty-based relations: the Council, the Commission, the High Representative (of the Union for Foreign Affairs and Security Policy), the European Parliament and even the CJEU itself. It therefore provides a testing-ground for what the duty of inter-institutional cooperation might entail. The procedure is of course very different from the EU's ordinary legislative procedure, but nonetheless 'must take account of the specific features which the Treaties lay down in respect of each field of EU activity, particularly as regards the powers of the institutions'.[5] The relationship between those respective powers and mutual sincere cooperation in applying Article 218 TFEU is at the heart of this chapter.

2 To Whom is the Duty Owed?

First let us consider to whom the duty of cooperation is owed. Article 13(2) refers to 'mutual' sincere cooperation, and the idea of mutuality also appeared in the 1995 judgment cited earlier.[6] This refers to mutuality between the institutions, a duty owed to each other, albeit in the interests of the Union. Article 4(3) TEU refers to the principle of sincere cooperation in relations between the Union and the Member States. Although the original wording of this provision created a duty that was apparently unidirectional (owed by the Member States to the Community),[7] it was in practice interpreted as mutual,[8] and Article 4(3) TEU now makes that explicit: the Union and the Member States 'in full mutual respect' are to assist each other in carrying out the tasks which flow from the Treaties. Here the mutuality is between Member States and Union. In Article 13(2) it is between the institutions. Could it be argued that the institutions also owe a duty of cooperation to the Union as such?

---

4 Alan Dashwood, 'EU Acts and Member State Acts in the Negotiation, Conclusion and Implementation of International Agreements' in Claire Kilpatrick and Marise Cremona (eds), *EU Legal Acts – Challenges and Transformations* (OUP) (forthcoming).

5 Case C-658/11 *European Parliament v Council* EU:C:2014:2025, para 53.

6 Case C-65/93 (n 1), para 23.

7 In its pre-Lisbon version, art 10 EC provided that 'Member States shall take all appropriate measures, whether general or particular, to ensure fulfilment of the obligations arising out of this Treaty or resulting from action taken by the institutions of the Community. They shall facilitate the achievement of the Community's tasks. They shall abstain from any measure which could jeopardise the attainment of the objectives of this Treaty'.

8 See e.g. Case C-45/07 *Commission v Hellenic Republic* EU:C:2009:81, paras 25–26.

The Commission has argued this point in a pair of recent cases in the context of challenges to a Council act. Both cases involved so-called 'hybrid' decisions, that is, a decision adopted by both the Council and by the Representatives of the Member States meeting within the Council. In Case C-114/12 the decision authorised participation in the negotiation of a Council of Europe Convention on the protection of broadcasting organisations.[9] The decision was based on an assumption of shared competence and the negotiation of a mixed agreement, the Commission negotiating on behalf of the Union and the Presidency on behalf of the Member States, and it included provision for cooperation in the course of the negotiations. The Commission contested both the categorization of the Convention as falling under shared competence and the adoption of the hybrid decision. Case C-28/12 concerned the decision on signature and provisional application of two linked mixed agreements on air transport.[10] The agreements provided for the accession of Iceland and Norway to the EU-USA agreement on air transport that had been concluded in 2007. In this case, it was accepted on all sides that the agreements in question would be mixed; however again the Commission contested the use of a hybrid decision. The Commission's plea as regards the duty of sincere cooperation in Article 13(2) was clearly a subsidiary one,[11] but it is worth mentioning here since it was based on an argument that the duty of inter-institutional cooperation is linked to a duty to the Union:

> By allowing the Member States to intervene in EU procedures, the Council (…) failed to act in conformity with the principle of sincere cooperation, in that it should have exercised its powers so as not to circumvent the EU procedures set out in Article 218 TFEU. The Council breached that principle both in terms of inter-institutional relations and with regard to the EU as a whole.[12]

Thus although the Council's action was concerned with the relations (and cooperation) between the Union and Member States, the Commission sought to link this to a duty on the part of the institutions towards 'the EU as a whole',

9 Case C-114/12 *Commission v Council* EU:C:2014:2151.

10 Case C-28/12 *Commission v Council* EU:C:2015:282.

11 See below for further discussion of Case C-28/12.

12 Opinion of AG Mengozzi in Case C-28/12 *Commission v Council* EU:C:2015:43, para 35 (summarising the Commission's argument). Very similar wording was used in the Commission's plea in Case C-114/12 (n 9) (see the summary in the Opinion of AG Sharpston, EU:C:2014:224, para 191).

which would then form part of the mutual cooperation required by Article 13(2).

In neither case did the Court address this argument directly. In Case C-114/12, AG Sharpston took the view that no separate finding on this plea was necessary since the hybrid decision was in any event unlawful, either on the ground that the EU's competence is exclusive, or on the ground that such a hybrid decision contravened the Council's powers under Article 218 TFEU.[13] In Case C-28/12, AG Mengozzi expressed doubts about the existence of an institutional duty of cooperation towards the Union as such; he argued that 'the EU institutions are part of the EU, and therefore they constitute the EU itself. The configuration of such a duty of cooperation would seem to me to amount to confirmation of a duty to cooperate with oneself'.[14] This duty could in fact be expressed, the Advocate General (AG) argued, in terms of the duty of inter-institutional cooperation together with the obligation to act in the interests of the EU and in conformity with its objectives (an obligation also expressed in Article 13 TEU).

It is better, then, to see the Article 13(2) TEU-based duty of cooperation as owed mutually by the institutions to each other. Cooperation is something to be *practiced*, which suggests day-to-day practical relations. Nevertheless, this duty – like the duty to cooperate with the Member States under Article 4(3) TEU – is clearly intended to serve the interests of the Union; it is a practical way in which the institutions, within the Union's institutional framework, may carry out their obligation to 'promote its values, advance its objectives, serve its interests (…) and ensure the consistency, effectiveness and continuity of its policies and actions'.[15]

3 Cooperation and Conferral of Powers

Inter-institutional cooperation is closely linked to the respective powers of the institutions concerned, as evidenced by the fact that the principle of conferral and the duty of cooperation are placed together in Article 13(2). This relationship operates in two ways.

First, and most obvious, the duty of cooperation does not itself delimit the institutions' powers but gives guidance as to how they are to be used. It therefore operates on the institutions when acting *within* their respective spheres

13 Opinion of AG Scharpston (n 12), paras 193–195. The Court annulled the decision on the ground of exclusive competence.

14 Opinion of AG Mengozzi (n 12), fn 56.

15 Art 13(1) TEU.

of competence and cannot justify acting outside their conferred powers, or sanction a departure from the allocation of competences to the different institutions:

> Under Article 13(2) TEU, the European Union's institutions are to practice mutual sincere cooperation. That sincere cooperation, however, is exercised within the limits of the powers conferred by the Treaties on each institution. The obligation resulting from Article 13(2) TEU is therefore not such as to change those powers.[16]

There is no doubt, for example, that the 2010 inter-institutional agreement between the Commission and the European Parliament, including its provisions on the negotiation of international agreements, is intended to provide a framework for 'sincere cooperation' as well as the effective and transparent exercise of the institutions' respective powers. According to its preamble 'this Framework Agreement does not affect the powers and prerogatives of Parliament, the Commission or any other institution or organ of the Union, but seeks to ensure that those powers and prerogatives are exercised as effectively and transparently as possible'.[17] The Council nevertheless expressed the view that the agreement threatens the institutional balance established in the Treaties, although the possibility of legal action threatened in 2010 has not materialized.[18]

This principle – that the obligation of sincere cooperation cannot alter the institutions' powers – is well illustrated by Case C-28/12, in which the Court held that the adoption by the Council of a 'hybrid' decision on the signature and provisional application of a mixed agreement was an infringement of Article 218(2), (5) and (8) TFEU and Article 13(2) TEU.[19] The Commission argued first that the Council had altered the decision-making procedures for international

16 Case C-73/14 *Council v Commission* EU:C:2015:663, para 84; similar phrasing has been used in many other cases.

17 Framework Agreement on relations between the European Parliament and the European Commission [2010] OJ L304/47.

18 According to the Council statement on Relations between the European Parliament and the Commission, 21 October 2010, 'The Council notes that several provisions of the Framework Agreement have the effect of modifying the institutional balance set out in the Treaties in force, according the European Parliament prerogatives that are not provided for in the Treaties and limiting the autonomy of the Commission and its President. The Council is particularly concerned by the provisions on international agreements, infringement proceedings against Member States and transmission of classified information to the European Parliament'. (Council doc 15172/10).

19 Case C-28/12 (n 10).

agreements set out in Article 218 TFEU by adopting a joint decision with the Member States; and second that the consensus-based procedure implied by Member State participation infringed the voting rules of Article 218(8) TFEU, which prescribed qualified majority voting (QMV) for this agreement.

The Council based its argument on the fact that the Treaties do not establish a procedure for the negotiation and conclusion of mixed agreements, and that that absence left room for the Council to exercise its autonomy to establish such procedures, in a form which would not prejudice Article 218 TFEU. In fact, the Council argued with some justification, the hybrid decision represented the hybrid nature of a mixed agreement, where both Union and Member State competences are exercised, and the hybrid decision was in fact an expression of the duty of sincere cooperation. Since it was common ground that the agreement should be mixed, the Council argued:

> [I]t is incumbent upon the Member States and the European Union to cooperate closely with regard to mixed agreements and to adopt a common approach in order to ensure unified representation of the European Union in international relations. The adoption of a joint decision is the expression of the cooperation thereby imposed.[20]

In an earlier case involving a hybrid decision,[21] AG Sharpston had accepted that cooperation is an 'essential condition' for the exercise of shared competence and that 'a joint decision is an expression of perhaps the closest form of cooperation'; nevertheless she argued both that 'procedural rules cannot be set aside in the name of the principle of sincere cooperation',[22] and that the principle of sincere cooperation 'can be relied upon only by an institution acting within the limits of its competences'.[23] In Case C-28/12 the Court agreed: 'that principle [the duty of cooperation] cannot justify the Council setting itself free from compliance with the procedural rules and voting arrangements laid down in Article 218 TFEU'.[24] The principle of conferral, here applied to the Council's decision-making powers under Article 218 TFEU, established a precondition for the application of other principles, even one as important as the duty of cooperation.

---

20 Ibid, para 28.

21 Case C-114/12 (n 9).

22 Opinion of AG Sharpston (n 12), para 195.

23 Ibid, para 175. On that occasion the Court did not decide the issue, since it took the view that competence was in any case exclusive.

24 Case C-28/12 (n 10), para 55.

So how were the procedures laid down in Article 218 TFEU compromised by the hybrid decision? The Court characterised the decision as indivisible:

> [T]he Member States participated in the adoption of the act relating to the signing of the agreements at issue on behalf of the European Union and their provisional application by it although, under Article 218(5) TFEU, such an act must be adopted by the Council alone. Moreover, the Council was involved, as an EU institution, in the adoption of the act concerning the provisional application of those agreements by the Member States although such an act falls within the scope of, first of all, the internal law of each of those States and, then, international law.[25]

AG Mengozzi analysed this point in terms of the autonomy of the institutions. In his view the merger of the EU and intergovernmental decisions into an 'indissociable whole' could 'constitute a dangerous precedent of contamination of the autonomous decision-making process of the EU institutions that is liable, therefore, to cause damage to the autonomy of the EU as a specific legal system'.[26]

In the second place, the Court found, bringing together the consensus-based intergovernmental procedure and the Article 218 TFEU procedure deprived of any real substance the QMV voting required under Article 218 (5) and (8) TFEU: 'The two different acts, brought together in the contested decision, cannot therefore be validly adopted under a single procedure (…)'.[27] This is not a simple incompatibility of legal bases. There are judgments where the Court has taken the position that it is impossible to combine legal bases which require unanimity and QMV respectively, but the *Kadi* judgment shows that this is in fact possible at least in some circumstances.[28] The problem here was that, as the Court says, there were *two different acts*, one a Union act under Article 218 TFEU and one intergovernmental. The unanimous decision was not based on Article 218(8) TFEU, which allows for unanimity in some cases; to the extent that Article 218(8) TFEU was applied to the decision, it specified QMV.

---

25 Ibid, para 50.

26 Opinion of AG Mengozzi (n 12), para 80.

27 Case C-28/12 (n 10), para 52.

28 Joined Cases C-402/05 P and C-415/05 P *Yassin Abdullah Kadi and Al Barakaat International Foundation v Council and Commission* EU:C:2008:461. See also Case C-166/07 *European Parliament v Council* EU:C:2009:499 (*International Fund for Ireland*), a case where the Court held that a Regulation should have combined the co-decision procedure required by a cohesion policy legal basis with the unanimity in Council required by the flexibility clause.

Thus insofar as the Council may wish to establish procedures for mixed agreements, these must not alter the rules set out in Article 218 TFEU for the negotiation and conclusion of agreements by the EU. These decision-making rules 'are laid down in the Treaties and are not at the disposal of the Member States or of the institutions themselves'.[29] However these rules are 'blind' to mixed agreements and proceed as if every agreement was concluded by the EU alone. Although the Court has not set itself against mixed agreements, it is here insisting that they must not impact on the Union's procedures or the autonomy of the Union as a treaty-maker.[30]

Before we leave this aspect of sincere cooperation, let us consider the question: sincere cooperation may not be used to extend the institutions' powers, but might it influence the choice of which of those powers should be used? In Case C-48/14,[31] the European Parliament argued, inter alia, that in choosing to use legislative powers under the Euratom Treaty instead of the TFEU, the Council had infringed the duty of sincere cooperation since it thereby excluded the Parliament as co-legislator. The Court did not agree. Having decided that the choice of the Euratom Treaty as a legal basis could be justified, it simply says that the resulting reduced role for the Parliament was a natural consequence of the choice of the drafters of the Treaties. This is unexceptional reasoning, but the CJEU, in this case as in others,[32] pays little attention to the dynamic of its approach to choice of legal basis and its consequences. The CJEU does not, when a legal basis is challenged, assess whether an alternative proposed legal basis would be appropriate or even preferable. It simply assesses whether the legal basis actually chosen is defensible. This is in line with its constitutional role, but it tends to favour the original choice made and precludes discussion of whether other factors might support a different choice. As a result, it is difficult to see sincere cooperation playing much of a role in encouraging the legislature, or the EU treaty-maker,[33] to act under one power rather than another.

In summary, then, sincere cooperation operates within the bounds of the institutions' powers, and can neither increase them, nor operate as some kind of 'flexibility clause'. What, then, are its effects?

---

29 Case C-28/12 (n 10), para 42.

30 On the other hand, participation of the Member States in a mixed agreement, certainly does impact on the *Member States'* autonomy as treaty-makers (see e.g. Case C-246/07 *Commission v Kingdom of Sweden* EU:C:2010:203).

31 Case C-48/14 *European Parliament v Council* EU:C:2015:91.

32 See e.g. Case C-130/10 *European Parliament v Council* EU:C:2012:472, as regards the role of the Parliament in the adoption of Common Foreign and Security Policy (CFSP)-related acts.

33 See Case C-658/11 (n 5).

Mutual sincere cooperation expresses the idea that each institution should respect and allow full expression to the powers of the other institutions: 'each of the institutions must exercise its powers with due regard for the powers of the other institutions (…)'.[34] This is not just a question of respecting institutional balance and the other institutions' prerogatives, although it does encompass this. It also means that the institutions in their mutual relations should seek to maximize the degree to which each can fulfil its functions in the EU system. Each institution has an autonomy, which is represented by its particular role, but that autonomy should not be exercised at the expense of the autonomy of the other institutions. Here perhaps we can see the meaning of mutuality and the sense in which mutual cooperation is needed to preserve, or to achieve, institutional balance.

This aspect of mutual sincere cooperation requires an understanding, not only of the formal legal powers of each institution, but also the purpose of those powers: what function it serves, and the role it plays in a particular process or specific procedural context. In the process of treaty-making, for example, we need to understand the part played by the Council, the Commission, and the European Parliament, as well as that of the CJEU. As expressed by the CJEU itself, the mutual sincere cooperation required by Article 13(2) TEU 'is of particular importance for EU action at international level, as such action triggers a closely circumscribed process of concerted action and consultation between the EU institutions'.[35] From this perspective, mutual sincere cooperation may contribute to the interpretation of the scope of the institutions' powers, as well as to how they are exercised.

For example, in Opinion 1/13 the Court addressed the question of whether the opinion procedure of Article 218(11) TFEU was being appropriately used.[36] A Commission proposal to establish a Union position on the acceptance of third State accessions to an international convention had not been accepted by the Council, the Council taking the view that the matter should be dealt with under Member State, not EU, competence. In response to an argument that there was no 'envisaged' agreement within the terms of Article 218(11) TFEU, and that the Commission was using the opinion procedure to raise issues which should instead have been raised in infringement proceedings against the Member States, the Court took a broad view of the applicability of the prior opinion procedure. The request for an opinion, the Court held, 'is not conditional upon

34 Case C-425/13 (n 3), para 69.

35 Ibid, para 64.

36 Opinion 1/13 (*Convention on the civil aspects of international child abduction*) EU:C:2014:2303.

the EU institutions having reached final agreement on whether the exercise of the EU's external competence is possible or appropriate'.[37] An agreement is envisaged by the Union, it argued, when it is envisaged by any one of the institutions that plays a part in the procedure under Article 218 TFEU, and the Commission is certainly one of those institutions. Here we see the Court giving weight to the individual part played by the different institutions in the treaty-making process, interpreting its own jurisdiction and the right to request an opinion in such a way as to ensure that an institutional disagreement does not prevent the expression of 'a legitimate concern on the part of the institutions concerned to know the extent of the respective powers of the EU and the Member States (…)'.[38]

This aspect of the duty of sincere cooperation is very evident in Case C-425/13, which concerned the negotiation of an agreement with Australia on greenhouse gas emissions trading schemes.[39] At issue was the balance between the Commission's prerogatives as negotiator on behalf of the Union and the Council's right to address negotiating directives to the negotiator and appoint a special committee 'in consultation with which the negotiations must be conducted' (Article 218(4) TFEU). In negotiating the balance, the Court has regard to the roles of the different players: the Council, as the institution which authorises the negotiations and sets the basic parameters (the 'directives'); the Commission which as negotiator is not simply a mouthpiece of the Council; the special committee, which is there in a consultative role and to liaise between the Commission and the Council, but which should not be directing the Commission's negotiation. To what extent does the Commission's role as treaty negotiator give it the right to order the 'negotiating space', the arrangements and conditions under which the negotiations take place? Does not the Council's power to adopt negotiating directives encompass the right to establish such arrangements? Indeed the Council argued that the 'arrangements are nothing more than a specific expression of how the institutions should translate the principle of sincere cooperation in the context of international negotiations'.[40] The Court's judgment is revealing. It first dismisses the Commission's claim that the Council's decision infringed Article 218(2) and (4) TFEU by requiring the Commission to report regularly on the negotiations to the special committee and the Council itself. The reporting requirement was examined by the Court in the light of the specific role played by each institution, and was

37 Ibid, para 49.

38 Ibid, para 46.

39 Case C-425/13 (n 3).

40 Ibid, para 50.

judged necessary: it enabled the committee to play its consultative role, and in its view it was 'expedient' for the Council to have regular information about an agreement that it would eventually be asked to approve. This means that the Council, in designating a special committee, must be able to determine the arrangements by which it is to be consulted:

> Article 218(4) TFEU must be interpreted as empowering the Council to set out, in the negotiating directives, procedural arrangements governing the process for the provision of information, for communication, and for consultation between the special committee and the Commission, as such rules meet the objective of ensuring proper cooperation at the internal level.[41]

Why is it the Council – rather than the Commission – that has the right to establish these rules of cooperation? Since the Lisbon Treaty allows for the designation of a special committee *by the Council*, this gives it the power to establish the procedural arrangements for cooperation in the framework of that committee.[42]

However the Court also established limits to the Council's ability to direct the negotiation. The elements of the Council's decision and its Annex which envisaged that the special committee may establish detailed negotiating positions of the Union were held to go beyond the consultative function given to the committee by Article 218(4) TFEU and to be an infringement of the Commission's prerogatives as negotiator. In addition to these limits on the powers of the committee, the Court draws a distinction between the Treaty-given right of the Council itself to address directives to the negotiator and the imposition of 'detailed negotiating positions'.[43] In exercising its right to adopt directives, which are intended to have legal effect on the negotiator to whom they are addressed, the Council must respect the autonomy of the Commission as (in this case) the negotiator.

---

41 Ibid, para 78.

42 AG Wathelet took the view, on the contrary, that the Council's power was simply to authorise the opening of negotiations and to appoint, if it wished, an advisory committee; in his view the adoption of procedural provisions governing the operation of relations between the committee and the Commission would impinge on the Commission's negotiating discretion (Opinion of AG Wathelet in Case C-425/13 *Commission v Council* EU:C:2015:174, paras 156–163).

43 Case C-425/13 (n 3), paras 88–92.

A similar approach was taken by the Court in Case C-409/13, which although concerned with a legislative procedure rather than with treaty-making, demonstrates that similar principles will apply to the procedural rules governing the exercise of the legislative function. Does the Commission, as the institution with the prerogative to initiate legislative proposals, have complete freedom to withdraw a proposal during the legislative process? Does the Commission's role as initiator imply a right simply to start the process going, and then to hand over to the co-legislators without any subsequent control over the end result? Or does the Commission retain an interest and a role in the legislative process which entitles it to decide that its original proposal has (in its view) lost its purpose?

The proposal in this case was for a Regulation governing the grant of macro-financial assistance (MFA) to third countries in balance of payments difficulties. Previously taking the form of ad hoc measures adopted on the basis of the flexibility clause (now Article 352 TFEU), the new framework Regulation was to be based on Articles 209 and 212 TFEU. The difference of opinion between the Commission on the one hand and the Council and European Parliament on the other concerned the procedure for taking individual decisions on granting MFA. The Commission took the view that to insist on the ordinary legislative procedure for each grant of MFA under the Regulation deprived the framework Regulation of its purpose, and eventually it withdrew the proposal. As in Case C-425/13, each institution clearly had powers relative to the procedure at issue: the Commission has a power of initiative and a power to amend or withdraw a proposal; the question here is whether and to what extent the discretion to withdraw a proposal is subject to constraints based on regard for the undoubted powers of the Council and Parliament as co-legislators to amend the original proposal. As we have seen, what is required by the duty of mutual sincere cooperation requires an understanding of the rationale for the powers granted to each institution in a particular process. AG Jääskinen argued that the Commission's power to withdraw a proposal was 'the ultimate manifestation of the Commission's monopoly on initiating legislation taken as an expression of its role as guardian of the interest of the European Union', its 'constitutional prerogative' to assess whether a legislative proposal is in the interest of the Union.[44] However this power is subject to limits, based on the link between the power of initiative and the power of withdrawal,[45] and on the duty of cooperation: 'the power of withdrawal is subject to a fundamental limit

44 Opinion of AG Jääskinen in Case C-409/13 *Council v Commission* EU:C:2014:2470, para 48.

45 In particular, the AG suggests that the power to withdraw a proposal is subject to time-limits, based on the stages of the legislative process (ibid, paras 57–63).

resulting from the need to comply with the principle of sincere cooperation referred to in Article 13(2) TEU'.[46]

The Court defines the constraints on the Commission's power to withdraw in terms of respect for the functions of the other actors in the process: the Commission does not have 'a right of veto in the conduct of the legislative process'.[47] However this entails a constraint on how the power to withdraw the proposal is exercised, not a constraint on the power itself. The Court does not say that the Commission may only withdraw a proposal under certain substantive conditions (e.g. a significant change of circumstances). Instead it subjects the Commission's power to a procedural constraint: 'it must state to the Parliament and the Council the grounds for the withdrawal, which, in the event of challenge, have to be supported by cogent evidence or arguments'.[48] And the Court is prepared to examine those grounds in the light of the obligation on the Commission – based on the duty of sincere cooperation – to take full account of the concerns underlying the amendments proposed by the Council and Parliament. After a reasonably detailed analysis of the debate the Court accepts that the Commission 'was entitled' to consider that the proposed Regulation, as amended, had lost its *raison d'etre*.[49] It is not so much that the Court shared this view (though it appears that it did), rather that the view was one the Commission was 'entitled' to take, that it was based on a reasonable assessment of the position. The procedural obligations on the Commission in satisfying the duty of sincere cooperation do not stop here: the Court then turns to consider the steps taken by the Commission to reach a solution acceptable to all, and concludes that it had fulfilled that duty.

Here we can clearly see the duty of sincere cooperation shaping the exercise of institutional powers, by requiring respect for the role of the other institutional players, and as we might expect this duty has a strong procedural dimension. Indeed what we find in practice is an emphasis on a particular aspect of the inter-institutional relationship, the need to exchange information, to communicate reasons, to consult. In some cases this obligation is written into the Treaties, as for example the Parliament's right to be informed of the process of treaty negotiation under Article 218(10) TFEU. Significantly, in interpreting this provision as an essential procedural requirement, even (perhaps especially) in the case of a CFSP agreement, the Court relies on the purpose behind the Parliament's role in the treaty-making process:

---

46 Ibid, para 65.

47 Case C-409/13 *Council v Commission* EU:C:2015:217, para 75.

48 Ibid, para 76.

49 Ibid, para 94.

> That rule is an expression of the democratic principles on which the European Union is founded. (…) [T]he Parliament's involvement in the decision-making process is the reflection, at EU level, of the fundamental democratic principle that the people should participate in the exercise of power through the intermediary of a representative assembly.[50]

The need for communication and information-sharing between institutions, even where not explicit in the Treaties, is implemented inter alia via inter-institutional agreements, enabling each institution to play its part in the process and serving the aim of sincere cooperation. As we have seen, it may also be articulated in Council decisions authorising the opening of negotiations and adopting negotiating directives, but it also operates outside the treaty-making context. For example, in the recent *ITLOS* judgment the Court held that 'the principle of sincere cooperation requires the Commission to consult the Council beforehand if it intends to express positions on behalf of the European Union before an international court'.[51] Sincere cooperation certainly cannot be reduced to an obligation to inform and consult, but this sharing of information is an inescapable part of cooperation, enabling the institutions both to fulfil their individual function in the system and to operate together.

4 Conclusion

In this short meditation on the obligation to practice mutual sincere cooperation, I have postulated a close link between sincere cooperation and the principle of conferral. This does not mean that they are the same thing. Sincere cooperation cannot define the boundaries of power; instead it establishes the principle on which that power is to be exercised. In doing so we need to pay attention to the purposes for which the specific powers were given, what the function of the institution in question is in the particular process under consideration, and how that function relates to the other institutions. As a principle, sincere cooperation can help to ensure that each institution, while ensuring that its own prerogatives are respected, respects the role and function of other institutions in the process. Inevitably its emphasis is on the operation

---

50 Case C-658/11 (n 5), para 81. This idea is not new: in Case C-65/93 (n 1), the obligation (as it then was) to consult the Parliament was said to be based on the principle of institutional balance and on the 'fundamental democratic principle' of consultation of people through their representatives.

51 Case C-73/14 (n 16), para 86.

of procedures, such as treaty-making, and at its heart lies the concept of cooperation facilitated by communication, consultation and information-sharing.

The CJEU is certainly not the only institution that helps to shape the content of sincere cooperation in practical terms.[52] The Council, Commission and European Parliament may also do this through inter-institutional agreements, both general and ad hoc.[53] But as the cases we have discussed here show, the CJEU is contributing to the process. In doing so it is engaged in establishing and protecting an institutional space within which policy may be formed, in which the different actors understand and work within their respective roles. For this reason I would argue that the duty of sincere cooperation is one of the structural principles which shape and construct this institutional space, creating a legal structure which is protective of the powers of the different actors in the system, and supported by the principles which govern their relations.[54]

52 The application of the duty of sincere cooperation to the CJEU itself is a further question, which there is no space here to consider further. As with the other institutions it is closely connected to the principle of conferral, the need for the CJEU to operate within its own jurisdictional boundaries while enabling the other institutions to fulfil their functions.

53 C-25/94 *Commission v Council* EU:C:1996:114.

54 Marise Cremona (ed), *Structural Principles in EU External Relations Law* (Hart Publishing) (forthcoming).

Epilogue

CHAPTER 20

La liberté du négociateur de l'Union – raison d'être et limites

*Hubert Legal**

Depuis mon arrivée au Conseil en 2008 jusqu'en 2015, j'ai connu Ricardo Gosalbo Bono comme le patron du droit des relations internationales de l'Union au sein du Secrétariat général du Conseil. Un patron respecté et apprécié pour sa science et son expérience du droit international public, pour sa disposition affable et accommodante qui a permis de sortir de moult impasses par des arrangements ingénieux et pour sa capacité à s'entourer d'équipes soudées, expertes et infatigables. Il a fait de sa direction une micro-société qui, sans se prendre pour une élite, a souvent été perçue comme telle par les collègues la fréquentant sans en être, et aussi parfois traitée comme telle – ce qui a de bons côtés, ainsi que de moins plaisants, la vie institutionnelle ne privant pas les frustrations insidieuses d'occasions de s'exprimer.

Ce professionnalisme au service du compromis a, de plus, été lourdement mis à contribution pendant notre période de coexistence administrative, qui n'a pas été celle du pain et des roses pour trouver la place du Conseil dans le système de relations internationales résultant du traité de Lisbonne. Un Conseil qui a dû apprendre à laisser au haut représentant de l'Union pour les affaires étrangères et la politique de sécurité, au Service européen d'action extérieure et à la Commission, ainsi – à son niveau – qu'au Président du Conseil européen, le rôle de représenter l'Union tout en faisant comprendre auxdits représentants que leur liberté de parole n'était pas sans limites et qu'il revenait au Conseil de fixer la ligne; qui a dû apprendre également qu'il lui appartenait de tenir tête à des interlocuteurs institutionnels jouant parfois la carte de la désinvolture, de l'exaspération ou de la véhémence et de ne pas se laisser dicter sa conduite pour définir la marche à suivre, sans pour autant verser dans la dérive de pratiques purement nationales ignorant les procédures établies – manière de fuir la difficulté dont la tentation n'est pas mince pour les États membres dotés d'une présence internationale significative, lorsqu'ils se sentent le cuir agacé par un excès de mesquinerie bureaucratique.

---

* Les opinions exprimées ici sont purement personnelles et n'engagent en aucune manière le Service juridique du Conseil ou le Conseil de l'Union européenne.

 | DOI 10.1163/9789004347175_021

Les talents de pédagogue de Ricardo Gosalbo Bono ont trouvé leur emploi dans ce contexte où la variabilité des pratiques selon les secteurs, l'inachèvement des clarifications jurisprudentielles et la lassitude occasionnée chez les représentants des États membres par des problématiques institutionnelles répétitives, mal comprises et toujours laissées en suspens ne font pas du travail de juriste une sinécure. Il est bien plus facile de dire ce que le droit impose – du moins lorsque c'est le cas … – qu'aménager dans un cadre imparfait les formules qui permettent aux intérêts légitimes de concourir paisiblement à la composition et à la défense de positions communes. La radicalité du censeur est une pose confortable, quand chercher l'harmonie est une tâche ingrate. Mon éminent collègue n'a pas choisi l'aisance.

Et ce rocher sans cesse remonté sur la pente (ou ce foie sans cesse régénéré pour mieux qu'un vautour le dévore…), il n'en est pas de meilleur exemple que la négociation des accords internationaux impliquant l'Union, qui devrait être affaire, entre institutions et États membres, de doigté et non de conflit puisqu'elle vient à la confluence de préoccupations également dignes: l'unité de représentation, la cohérence des politiques de l'Union, la sauvegarde des prérogatives nationales.

Pourtant la querelle, voire la provocation, jettent trop souvent notre bel équipage à la verse et livrent nos systèmes aussi pensés que justes à une risée honteuse. J'ai toujours vu Ricardo attelé à remonter, sans répit et sans lassitude visible – intime, je ne sais pas –, notre train sur les rails, ce qui est œuvre d'abnégation quand d'infiniment moins capables péroraient sur le tarmac en blâmant l'univers des effets de leur propre imprudence.

Il faut pour une négociation complexe un bon dosage entre une ferme direction quant à la ligne à tenir et une aptitude du porte-parole à établir avec ses homologues les conditions propices à un accord. Un corset ne laisse pas le jeu suffisant dans les entournures; la bride laissée sur le cou livre l'animal à son *ego* dont l'insignifiance n'échappe qu'à lui-même. Etre tenu pour être libre, savoir jusqu'où l'on peut aller trop loin. Bien sûr qui sait se tenir n'a pas besoin qu'on l'y force. Qui a parfaitement intégré à son être individuel les enjeux des politiques de l'Union, les priorités et les nuances, l'intégration et la mixité, et bien sûr tous les détails des matières techniques, n'a nul besoin de directives précises. Qu'il se livre à son penchant spontané et ce qui viendra à lui plaire sera naturellement le mieux pour tous. Mais ce bel oiseau, ce prodige en qui l'Europe vient fleurir et s'incarner, cette pelote de tant de fils que le commun confond, où le trouve-t-on? Ne traiterait-on pas à bon droit de mégalomane et de charlatan celui qui prétendrait en être?

Pourtant, il en est. Il en est que le feu des accords grandit, au point qu'ils incarnent et personnifient dans une certaine mesure la partie qu'ils représentent;

de grands négociateurs. Eux ne sont ni véhéments ni agressifs, juste un peu impatients mais avec bienveillance de retour devant des mandants qui sont un peu d'eux-mêmes mais capables chacun de ne percevoir qu'une partie du tout dont eux seuls portent l'intégralité infiniment complexe. D'ailleurs leur exaltation, vêtue d'atours modestes et bonhommes, impressionne ceux à qui, ayant posé le casque sur le scooter, ils font rapport de leurs campagnes ébouriffantes. Il y a du surhomme en eux, ainsi naturellement qu'en elles, un feu qui brûle et qu'on respecte.

Mais il ne découle de leur grandeur fonctionnelle et temporaire, de leur aura fugace, ni que les compétences qui les portent sont exclusives ni que la camaraderie qu'ils établissent avec leurs adversaires en forgeant ensemble un objet de cœur autant que de droit doive affecter jamais la prévalence des intérêts de l'Union et des États membres tels que ceux-ci les comprennent, avec leurs vues étroites et leurs soucis pédestres, avec leurs limites mais avec leur autorité de propriétaires, réalité brutale qui revient avec d'autant moins de finesse qu'on a voulu l'ignorer.

On conviendra néanmoins que négocier est sans doute un art mais certainement un métier et que, comme tout métier, celui qui l'exerce ne peut s'en acquitter convenablement que si des amateurs ne s'emploient pas à lui tenir la main en plein cœur de l'action. Monsieur Matisse, vous devriez mettre plus de rouge sur la droite de mon tableau. Merci mon bon ami, j'y songerai mais – dans l'intérêt de votre investissement – laissez-moi peindre. C'est ce qu'a exprimé la Cour, en des termes moins imagés, dans l'affaire C-425/13 introduite par la Commission (*ETS Australie*), en jugeant le 15 juillet 2015 que le Conseil ne pouvait pas, sans méconnaître l'étendue de ses attributions, charger un comité spécial d'arrêter avant chaque session de négociation des positions détaillées comportant obligation pour le négociateur de s'y soumettre lors de cette session.[1] Cependant, la censure de la Cour a une portée extrêmement restreinte, puisqu'elle estime parfaitement conforme au partage des rôles entre Conseil et négociateur, élément de l'équilibre institutionnel, qu'il soit fait obligation à ce dernier de faire rapport après chaque session au comité spécial désigné par le Conseil, de lui permettre de suivre et guider son action, en fournissant notamment toute la documentation utile, et de demander son autorisation pour accomplir certaines démarches. La Cour permet même au comité d'établir des positions détaillées avant chaque session, pour autant qu'elles se présentent comme des recommandations ne revêtant pas un caractère contraignant. Monsieur Matisse doit entendre les suggestions mais il ne lui est pas interdit de s'en écarter, étant entendu qu'il supporte seul la responsabilité du produit

1 Affaire C-425/13 *Commission c. Conseil* EU:C:2015:483.

final, que le client ne sera pas tenu de lui acheter bien qu'il l'ait poursuivi de ses commentaires tout au long des séances… Il est peu probable qu'un artiste même quelconque trouve à s'accommoder d'une telle procédure.

Mais cela n'est pas la même chose. Ce n'est pas son seul renom qu'engage le négociateur en apposant son paraphe à l'œuvre collective. C'est celui de l'Union comme acteur international, lequel affecte, bien qu'à des degrés variables, celui des États membres. Ainsi, dire au Conseil qu'il n'a qu'à attendre passivement le produit fini pour se prononcer sans contrainte sur l'opportunité d'autoriser la signature et la conclusion d'un accord, c'est faire peu de cas soit de l'Union, en prenant le risque qu'elle acquière la réputation d'un partenaire peu fiable, soit – plus vraisemblablement – du Conseil, en comptant que, même en désaccord, il n'osera pas se rendre responsable d'une crise diplomatique. Ce qui est d'ailleurs plutôt une reconnaissance du réalisme et du bon sens des États membres, dont il faut se réjouir même si dogmatisme et obstination serviraient mieux les intérêts institutionnels du Conseil…

Mais réduire le maître des accords de l'Union qu'est le Conseil, aux termes de l'Article 218, paragraphe 2, TFUE, au silence et à l'impuissance d'une chambre d'enregistrement ne peut être une option permise par les traités. Dès lors, une définition effective du cadre, procédural et matériel, dans lequel s'inscrit la participation des représentants de l'Union à un exercice international de négociation est une nécessité impérieuse d'intérêt général. Elle exige, ex ante et à tout moment où des tournants de la négociation le requièrent à nouveau, un mandat de substance définissant les objectifs que l'Union poursuit, les contraintes qu'elle s'impose où qui s'imposent à elle et les lignes rouges, offensives et défensives, qui conditionnent la participation à l'accord – selon l'appréciation du Conseil au moment où il délivre l'autorisation de négocier. Elle suppose aussi qu'une organisation procédurale adéquate permette au Conseil de réagir en connaissance de cause et en temps utile s'il en est besoin, sans imposer un carcan au négociateur dans ses choix tactiques et son traitement du détail, mais sans dépendre entièrement de son bon vouloir quant à la nécessité de faire remonter les choix majeurs de nature à affecter l'équilibre de l'instrument final.

Des divergences de vues ont existé quant au caractère obligatoire ou non pour le négociateur des directives, de fond et de procédure, qui peuvent accompagner l'autorisation – et l'accompagnent en règle générale – et constituent avec lui ce que l'on appelle le mandat. En estimant recevable le recours formé, dans l'affaire C-425/13 précitée, en vue de l'annulation de certaines dispositions des directives de négociation annexées à une autorisation de négocier un accord, la Cour a tranché la question en relevant explicitement que de telles directives étaient destinées à produire des effets de droit. En effet, si elles n'étaient qu'une indication purement illustrative, elles ne constitueraient pas un acte susceptible de recours puisqu'elles ne 'feraient pas grief'. Au contraire, elles sont ici comprises comme étant une partie intégrante de l'autorisation de négocier, comme une pièce d'encadrement dont le respect s'impose au titre des deux principes de l'équilibre institutionnel et de la coopération sincère (dont l'arrêt *Conseil c. Commission*, C-73/14, du 6 Octobre 2015 (*ITLOS*),[2] a souligné la pertinence en l'espèce), et non comme un colifichet, un billet d'humeur, une simple annotation portée sur l'enveloppe du mandat qu'il conviendrait de déchirer avec elle.

Ce dont il est par-dessus tout besoin pour donner à l'Union, en complément du statut juridique que nul ne lui conteste, une stature de partenaire de plein exercice sur la scène du droit international, c'est de confiance de la part des États membres envers ceux qui agissent au nom de l'Union, c'est-à-dire, par le truchement des compétences transférées, en leur nom collectif. Cette confiance ne peut s'obtenir sans tourner le dos aux travers infantiles qui aujourd'hui inhibent toute expression majeure de l'Union dans le domaine de l'action internationale. Le périmètre de l'Union ne peut se constituer durablement dans le droit des traités si sa conquête est acquise par le harcèlement des États membres et l'irrespect du Conseil. En effet, aucune considération procédurière ne peut obliger le Conseil à donner suite aux recommandations que lui présente la Commission ou le Haut Représentant en vue de l'ouverture de négociations ni aux propositions de signature ou de conclusion d'accords que lui soumet le négociateur qu'il a désigné. Quand bien même la Cour donnerait raison aux auteurs d'actions dirigées contre le Conseil, pour quelque motif que ce soit, l'annulation contentieuse d'une décision du Conseil fondée sur l'Article 218 du TFUE ne ferait pas naître une décision contraire, elle priverait de base légale toute action internationale entreprise par l'Union à partir de la décision contestée en remettant les cartes entre les mains du Conseil pour toute action future. La Cour rappelle régulièrement que l'annulation partielle d'un acte de l'Union n'est pas possible lorsque cette annulation partielle aurait pour effet de modifier cet acte, dans sa substance ou dans son esprit.[3] Le juge peut en effet censurer un acte mais il ne peut modifier son contenu (ce qu'il ferait en annulant une disposition particulière non séparable du reste de l'acte) sans se substituer à une institution dans l'exercice de ses prérogatives, comportement dont le caractère ultra vires sauterait aux yeux.

Il en résulte qu'un effort de mise en confiance des membres du Conseil devrait aller de soi. Au lieu de quoi, communication tardive des actes de négociation,

2 EU:C:2015:663.

3 Affaire C-425/13 (n 1), para 94.

insistance délibérée sur le fait que certaines transmissions ne sont pas aux fins de la fixation d'une position, mais aux seules fins d'information (pour ne pas traiter le Conseil différemment du Parlement européen, peut-on supposer), revendication systématique d'une compétence exclusive de l'Union, offensive victorieuse contre les actes hybrides ne sont que quelques exemples d'une orientation institutionnelle souvent perçue comme vexatoire. Il est impossible de généraliser, naturellement. Les exemples contraires existent également. Mais, sur un fond interinstitutionnel aussi grinçant, les négociateurs avisés ne s'aventurent pas dans les méandres de tractations complexes sans s'assurer discrètement du soutien de quelques acteurs clés parmi les États membres.

Les acteurs clés!... Ceux qui ont (ou ont encore) la capacité d'exister dans le concert des nations indépendamment de leur représentation par l'Union. Ceux qui, par leur seul désintérêt, peuvent amener l'étiolement, l'obsolescence des structures construites sur les traités. Certes leur autonomie réelle s'est un peu émoussée au fil des ans mais ils continuent à rendre inévitable une *realpolitik* fort éloignée de la méthode communautaire. Cette dérive résulte de plusieurs facteurs, mais on peut penser que l'un d'entre eux a quelque chose à voir avec les mauvaises pratiques institutionnelles décrites plus haut. Quand la délibération régulière est polluée par des querelles dénuées d'intérêt, la consultation réelle et la coopération effective prennent d'autres voies, moins légitimes, mais beaucoup plus efficaces... Ainsi, les négociateurs, si réticents à se voir imposer des structures de suivi contraignantes par le Conseil, ne sont pas avares de contacts aussi informels qu'intenses avec les '*major stakeholders*' dont certains ne sont rien d'autre que des administrations d'État. Preuve, s'il en fallait une, que les États membres et le Conseil ne sont pas deux expressions du même principe.

Les États membres n'ont vocation à s'exprimer que sur les accords relevant pour tout ou partie de leur compétence nationale, tandis que le Conseil, en tant qu'institution de l'Union, n'a vocation à agir que dans le cadre des compétences de celle-ci. Ce qui ne lui interdit pas – à condition de ne pas mélanger les genres, nous a dit la Cour dans l'arrêt du 28 avril 2015 dans l'affaire C-28/12 *Commission c. Conseil* (*actes hybrides*)[4] – de fournir un cadre de réunion aux représentants des gouvernements et de veiller à assurer l'unité la plus large possible quant à la façon dont sont présentées au monde extérieur les positions relevant du volet national et celles relevant du volet de l'Union. Il va de soi que les directives de négociation devraient concourir à cet effort de convergence.

La recherche de l'unité la plus large possible, et en tout cas de la complémentarité d'approche entre l'Union et les États membres, dans le respect de

4 EU:C:2015:282.

leurs compétences respectives, ne se décrète pas en fixant d'emblée la position de l'Union, puis en déduisant du devoir de coopération sincère (en l'espèce mal interprété) une obligation pour les États de s'y rallier dans le champ, devenu périphérique, de leurs compétences; elle suppose un effort systématique, dont seul le Conseil peut être le lieu, pour faire précéder toute décision relative à une négociation d'accord de l'Union d'un examen des positions auxquelles chaque Etat membre est en mesure de se rallier au titre de ses compétences propres – et ce quelle que soit la règle de vote que la matière de l'accord prescrit.

C'est en outre au Conseil qu'il revient, dans le large domaine des compétences partagées, de décider s'il y a lieu d'exercer, d'étendre, voire de restreindre les compétences exercées de l'Union. Il vaut mieux qu'il en décide, ouvertement et dans la transparence, et sans préjudice des compétences du Parlement européen, plutôt que d'être forcé à vivre dans une alternance insignifiante d'embuscades, d'anicroches et de menaces de contentieux, alors qu'en parallèle d'autres institutions politiques – dont ce n'est pas le rôle selon les traités – mènent en sous-main un jeu d'essence rigoureusement intergouvernementale.

L'étendue des compétences exercées de l'Union, dans la sphère de la mixité, est un choix politique qui s'exerce par la voie de la conclusion d'accords internationaux, acte du Conseil, et se prépare par la délivrance des autorisations de négocier correspondantes. Aucune règle de droit ne crée d'obligation au Conseil d'agir s'il n'en reconnait pas l'opportunité politique. Il est dès lors entièrement maître du jeu – y compris vis-à-vis de la Cour – et, s'il n'exerce pas toujours cette prérogative pleinement, c'est qu'il ne peut ou ne veut pas s'en soucier aussi systématiquement que ses interlocuteurs institutionnels. C'est aussi, naturellement, que les membres du Conseil sont également les représentants des États membres et qu'entre la part de l'Union et la part nationale, il peut arriver que la seconde l'emporte dans leurs affections sinon dans leurs votes.

On peut le regretter car le rôle institutionnel du Conseil est juridiquement indépendant du caractère exclusif ou partagé de la compétence de l'Union dans la matière où se situe un accord. Hormis la recherche de convergence entre les positions nationales et de l'Union évoquée plus haut, ce rôle ne devrait pas être plus minime lorsque la compétence appartient exclusivement à l'Union. Il est pourtant de notoriété publique qu'une telle circonstance de droit modifie fondamentalement les paramètres de la négociation en ce qui concerne la définition et l'exécution du mandat, et jusqu'au style des rapports entre institutions. Donc, bien que le Conseil doive être radicalement distingué des États membres dont les représentants le composent, l'intérêt accru de ceux-ci pour les sujets sur lesquels leur gouvernement conserve une compétence propre est de nature à mieux garantir en pratique l'effectivité de l'action du Conseil en la matière. En toute hypothèse, il n'est rien que l'on puisse y faire, puisque nul n'envisagerait de faire dépendre de pareilles considérations le choix de l'étendue des compétences confiées à l'Union. Ce serait l'effet pervers de mauvaises pratiques.

Mais n'entrons pas dans le domaine des récriminations sordides et des sous-entendus mesquins. Nous pensons ici à Ricardo, et ce ne serait pas rendre hommage à sa haute figure de conciliateur de jeter de l'huile sur le feu. En même temps, rappeler les principes contre vents et marées est une tâche (et parfois une corvée) à laquelle nul ne l'a jamais vu se dérober. Qu'il me pardonne dès lors ces quelques considérations mal construites et balbutiantes par lesquelles je m'efforce de m'inscrire dans son sillage en chérissant les heures où nous avons, ensemble, plongé la charrue dans le même sillon à la gauche du bout de la table du comité des représentants permanents (deuxième partie), tel un attelage de laboureurs harassés mais complices.

Mes amitiés, Monsieur le Directeur!

Et concluons ensemble que, si l'Union dispose de la personnalité juridique en droit international, elle jouira pleinement de l'autorité politique qui donne vie à ce principe lorsque ses négociateurs auront la tranquille assurance qui succède aux maladies infantiles de la revendication institutionnelle et vient de la reconnaissance confiante de ses bases. Il appartient au négociateur de l'Union d'être alerté des intérêts collectifs des 28 États membres comme des soucis primordiaux de chacun d'entre eux. Il lui appartient de ne pas confondre les États membres avec le Conseil et de ne pas donner à penser que, si la compétence de l'Union est exclusive, alors il est son seul maître. Alors il fera vivre une Union respectée de tous, du dedans comme du dehors, et qui n'a pas besoin de songer à s'ffirmer de manière autonome, tant son autorité ira de soi.

Index

Studies in EU External Relations: Titles in Series (http://brill.com/seur)

Hans Merket, *The EU and the Security-Development Nexus: Bridging the Legal Divide* (2016), ISBN: 9789004315020

Mauro Gatti, *European External Action Service* (2016), ISBN: 9789004322769

Guillaume Van der Loo, *The EU-Ukraine Association Agreement and Deep and Comprehensive Free Trade Area* (2016), ISBN: 9789004298644

Dimitry Kochenov & Elena Basheska (Eds.), *Good Neighbourliness in the European Legal Context* (2015), ISBN: 9789004299771

Inge Govaere & Sara Poli (Eds.), *EU Management of Global Emergencies* (2014), ISBN: 9789004268326

Martina Spernbauer, *EU Peacebuilding in Kosovo and Afghanistan* (2014), ISBN: 97890042657070

Henri de Waele & Jan-Jaap Kuipers (Eds.), *The European Union's Emerging International Identity* (2013), ISBN: 9789004230989

Enzo Cannizzaro, Paolo Palchetti, and Ramses A. Wessel (Eds.), *International Law as Law of the European Union* (2011), ISBN: 9789004188570

Kirstyn Inglis, *Evolving Practice In EU Enlargement With Case Studies In Agri-Food And Environment Law* (2010), ISBN: 9789004181663

Stéphanie Laulhé Shaelou, *The EU and Cyprus* (2009), ISBN: 9789004176195

Peter Van Elsuwege, *From Soviet Republics to EU Member States* (2 *Vols*) (2008), ISBN: 9789004169456

Maximilian B. Rasch, *The European Union at the United Nations* (2008), ISBN: 9789004167148